Frontiers in Economic History

Economic historians have contributed to the development of economics in a variety of ways, combining theory with quantitative methods, constructing new databases, promoting interdisciplinary approaches to historical topics, and using history as a lens to examine the long-term development of the economy. Frontiers in Economic History publishes manuscripts that push the frontiers of research in economic history in order to better explain past economic experiences and to understand how, why and when economic change occurs. Books in this series will highlight the value of economic history in shedding light on the ways in which economic factors influence growth as well as social and political developments. This series aims to establish a new standard of quality in the field while offering a global discussion forum toward a unified approach in the social sciences.

Bas Van Leeuwen • Dmitry Didenko
Matteo Calabrese • Meimei Wang

Innovation and Economic Development in Eurasia, 500 BCE-Present

The Roots of Divergence

Springer

Bas Van Leeuwen
International Institute of Social History
Amsterdam, The Netherlands

Matteo Calabrese
Bocconi University
Milan, Italy

Dmitry Didenko
Russian Presidential Academy of National Economy and Public Administration
Moscow, Russia

Meimei Wang
Chinese Academy of Social Sciences
Institute of Economics
Beijing, China

ISSN 2662-9771 ISSN 2662-978X (electronic)
Frontiers in Economic History
ISBN 978-3-031-97042-9 ISBN 978-3-031-97043-6 (eBook)
https://doi.org/10.1007/978-3-031-97043-6

This Springer imprint is published by the registered company Springer Nature Switzerland AG
The registered company address is: Gewerbestrasse 11, 6330 Cham, Switzerland

Preface

This book examines the economic history of Eurasia from the mid-first millennium BCE to the present day—a vast expanse of land stretching from China to Western Europe and encompassing diverse climatic zones and cultural traditions. Over the centuries, this macro-region witnessed profound transformations, from the rise and fall of nomadic empires to the integration of the region into global economic networks.

Focusing on Northern Eurasia, in this book we aim to understand why some areas experienced faster, and more sustained growth than others. We explored how new ideas were created (invention/innovation), how different countries used these ideas (adoption), and how these factors influenced long-term economic differences and similarities (divergence/convergence). These key drivers are examined over time and across a wide variety of regions, considering factors such as state involvement, urbanization, the development of specific resources (e.g. fertile land), labour relations, and prices and wages.

The book adopts a dual approach, namely examining long-run economic growth and technological development while going beyond traditional GDP metrics to address broader concepts, such as well-being, happiness, and environmental sustainability. Through comparisons of Northern Eurasia's subregions, it highlights the importance of situating economic growth theories within the specific historical and regional contexts that shaped them.

This study draws on a wide range of primary and secondary sources, including ancient Chinese, English, and Russian chronicles, early modern government publications, and contemporary economic data. Several datasets have also been used and some novel approaches have been applied to newly collected statistics. While the availability and reliability of these sources vary over time and across space, we have sought to integrate diverse perspectives to provide a nuanced and balanced account.

Amsterdam, The Netherlands — Bas Van Leeuwen
Moscow, Russia — Dmitry Didenko
Milan, Italy — Matteo Calabrese
Beijing, China — Meimei Wang

The Authors

* Dr. Bas van Leeuwen (International Institute of Social History, Amsterdam)
* Dr. Dmitry Didenko (Russian Presidential Academy of National Economy and Public Administration, Moscow)
* Dr. Matteo Calabrese (Bocconi University, Milan).
* Dr. Meimei Wang (Institute of Economics, Chinese Academy of Social Sciences, Beijing)

The four authors have a long history of writing papers together on quantitative economic history related to China, Central Asia and Russia, and Western Europe stretching back from the present day to ancient times. Realizing the focus of this body of work had not been on long run and regional trends, the initial aim of this book was to place the various papers in a proper chronology and derive conclusions from them.

In the process of writing, however, we encountered many unanswered questions, and were confronted with a lack of data, all of which needed to be addressed. This led to much new text, analyses, and internal and intra-country comparisons. Nevertheless, some papers have been, to some extent, used in this book after editorial approval:

- Földvári P. Van Leeuwen B (2012) Comparing per capita income in the hellenistic world: the case of Mesopotamia. Rev Income Wealth 58(3):55–568
- Didenko DV (2023) How demographic shocks affected the production-factor income and the institutional path of the Russian pre-industrial economy. Russ Peasant Stud 8(2):6–20
- Van Leeuwen B, Didenko D, Földvári P (2015) Inspiration vs. perspiration in economic development of the former Soviet Union and China (ca. 1920–2010). Econ Transit 23(1):213–246
- Van Leeuwen B, Philips RCM, Buyst E (eds) (2020) An economic history of regional industrialization. (Routledge explorations in economic history). Routledge, Oxford and New York

- Van Leeuwen B, Wang M, Bosma U (2023) 'Industrial revolutions' in a globalizing world, 1760–present. In: Labory S, Thomlinson P (eds) Handbook of industrial development. Edward Elgar, Cheltenham, pp 18–36
- Xu Y, Van Leeuwen B, Van Zanden JL (2018) Urbanization in China, ca. 1100–1900. Front Econ China 13(3):322–368

Specification of Contribution to the Book by Dr. Dmitry Didenko

The evidence and analysis on the Central Eurasia (Russia/USSR/NIS) were contributed mainly by Dmitry Didenko as a leading researcher employed by the Russian Presidential Academy of National Economy and Public Administration (RANEPA) under the following projects.

"Challenges and conditions for economic development in the regions of European Russia, the Siberia, and the Far East in the nineteenth to early twentieth centuries: natural environment, technology and resources" *(7.8)*:

5.4 Geography
10.3.4 The development of intranational inequality

"Stages of industrial development and intensification of agriculture: quality of economic growth in the regions of the Russian Empire, early nineteenth to early twentieth centuries" *(10.13)*:

4.4 Timing of the fertility transition and human capital rise
5.3 Institutions and culture
10.3.1 Anthropometric measures: The importance of being tall

"Factors of socio-economic development of the regions of the Russian Empire in the nineteenth to early twentieth centuries" *(10.20-2023-2)*:

3.2 Agricultural technology and labour productivity before the Agricultural Revolution
4.1 Unified growth theories
4.3 The divergence of modes of production
5.2 (The weight of) TFP growth as an indicator of long-run growth
5.5 Direction of technical change: Land rent to wage ratio
6.5 Government, c. 1860–present
8.3.3 A case of Central Eurasia (Sect. 8.3 GDP per capita growth and fiscal policy)
10.5.2 Awareness of pollution
10.6 Measuring happiness as a perception-based indicator

"Urbanization in the post-reform Russia in the modernization processes perspective: the role of industrial development, transportation network, migration flows" *(10.21-2023-1)*:

4.2 Urbanization
4.5 Government extraction and taxation
4.6 Trade and empire
6.6 Transport, c. 1860–present
9.3 External factors: divergence and convergence

"Russia's military modernization in the second half of the nineteenth to first half of the twentieth century" *(10.8-2024-1)*:

4.7 Conclusion: Smithian and Northian growth
6.2 From cottage to factory, c. 1760–1840
6.4 Institutions, c. 1860–present
7.2 Modes of production and labour relations
8.4 Monetary command-administration economy in the USSR versus China
8.5 Conclusion (to Chap. 8 "The Effect of Government Expenditure and Monetary Expansion on Economic Growth")

"Economic statistics and the Russian state: historical experience of interaction (mid-nineteenth to first third of the twentieth century)" *(10.9-2025-1)*:

10.2 Composite well-being: Human Development Index (HDI)
10.3.2 Housing

"Studying Formation and Development of Human Capital in Russia in the Global Context: Long-term Tendencies, Factors, Structural Dynamics (from the nineteenth century to the beginning of the twenty-first century)", within the programme to facilitate the establishment and development of world-class research centres "Human Capital Multidisciplinary Research Centre" funded by the Ministry of Science and Higher Education of the Russian Federation (075-15-2020-908, 075-15-2022-326):

3.3 A case study of a big external shock: the Black Death
9.4.2 Human factors (labour and human capital)
9.4.3 Inequality
9.5.3 Future growth predictions: Russia
10.3.3 Income inequality
10.3.5 Social spending and social transfers
10.4 Immaterial components of well-being

Some of the material included in the parts of the book indicated above may arise from other projects.

Acknowledgements

Dr. Bas van Leeuwen

This book is inspired by the support and guidance of various individuals and institutions. I am greatly indebted to Professor Jan Luiten van Zanden who, since my Masters study at Utrecht University, set me on the path of economic history and global economic growth. This continued when he was my PhD supervisor at the International Institute of Social History (IISH) and continued after that time when we crossed paths on various projects. I also extend my gratitude to Dr. Peter Földvári, with whom I wrote various related papers that greatly inspired this book, as well as Prof Yi Xu. I would like to extend my gratitude to my colleagues at the IISH and Utrecht University for providing a friendly and stimulating intellectual environment.

I am also grateful to the European Research Council as the research leading to these results received funding from the ERC under the European Union's Horizon 2020 Programme/ERC-StG 637695—HinDI, as part of the project "The Historical Dynamics of Industrialization in North-Western Europe and China ca. 1800–2010: A Regional Interpretation". This funding allowed us to get access to sometimes difficult to access data.

Finally, I wish to express my appreciation to my family and friends for their support and encouragement during the writing of this book. In particular, my cousin Caroline van Leeuwen was frequently open to listen to yet another story on available data or updating a chapter. Last but not least, I would like to warmly thank my wife, Jieli Li, and our children, Alex van Leeuwen, Lucas van Leeuwen, and Jason van Leeuwen, for their patience and understanding.

I naturally accept responsibility for the contents of my contributions, including possible errors and omissions.

Dr. Dmitry Didenko

I am grateful for the kind assistance by my colleagues from the RANEPA and other research institutions. Special thanks are due to Roman Konchakov for his encouragement and overall support of the research. Gratitude is expressed to Maria Karpenko for the data collection based on her professional work with the primary sources. Much inspiration and general research skills were provided by Leonid

Borodkin during the many years of our academic cooperation. Much of the work on transportation, technological development, and human capital was done at the RANEPA-based Centre for Russian Studies directed by Carol Leonard. I am grateful to her for the long-lasting participation in extensive discussions, which expanded my research perspectives. Also, I thank other colleagues for interesting discussions and topical advice: Igor Kuznetsov and Vladislav Afanasenkov on agriculture, Irina Shilnikova on industry, Vladimir Popov and Girsh Khanin on national accounts and social indicators, Sofia Salomatina and Anna Dmitrieva on financial indicators, Elena Korchmina and Timur Valetov on trade, government services measurement, and price indices, Evgenii Grishin on GIS (Fig. 6.7 "Railway transport versus traditional routes in European Russia, early twentieth century"). I naturally accept full responsibility for the contents of my contributions, including possible errors and omissions.

All Authors We are grateful to Simon Fletcher at Bourchier for his meticulous language check. No doubt, this has greatly improved the readability of the book.

Disclaimer The findings, interpretations, and conclusions are the authors' own views, which may not be shared by the institutions of their affiliation.

Competing Interests The authors have no competing interests to declare that are relevant to the content of this manuscript.

Contents

List of Figures

List of Tables

Chapter 1
Introduction

Abstract Long-run economic growth is essentially driven by technology and institutions. Various studies aim to identify this relationship either by comparing growth over time or across countries. Here, we try to combine both types of studies in a single approach for Northern Eurasia (i.e. the region broadly covering China, the former Soviet Union (FSU) area, and Western Europe). This allows us, rather than relying on one theory, to analyse the origin and weight of different factors of growth, such as human capital and institutions (including state capacity).

1.1 Ancient and Medieval Times: The Great Crossing

When looking at the last two millennia of global economic growth, the First Industrial Revolution in eighteenth-century Great Britain appears as a striking watershed. Within a century, the country's per capita GDP surged by a factor of 2.8, marking an unprecedented transformation. But how did industrialization begin? Why did its development vary so significantly across regions?

We can argue that the determinants of economic growth (or the lack thereof) lie in the complex interplay of several factors—most notably, the diffusion of technological knowledge and the readiness of institutions to adopt and adapt to these innovations—igniting progress in some places while bypassing others.[1] In past scholarship, GDP (Gross Domestic Income) growth between *c.* 1 CE and 1000 CE was considered to be non-existent or even declining. Recently, with a revived interest in historical national accounting, the medieval figures (*c.* 1000 CE) have been revised upward, largely because higher shares for manufacturing and pasture have been found in the economies of the time. Leaving GDP per capita of the previous period unaltered would thus imply increased economic growth in the first millennium. However, some of the estimates for *c.* 500 BCE–200 CE have also been revised upwards, thus once more reducing first millennium CE growth rates.

[1] This potentially involves what is sometimes referred to as synchronized cycle growth.

B. Van Leeuwen et al., *Innovation and Economic Development in Eurasia, 500 BCE-Present*, Frontiers in Economic History,
https://doi.org/10.1007/978-3-031-97043-6_1

Two main conclusions follow from these new insights. First, it seems that per capita income in both 1 CE and 1000 CE was significantly higher than the *c.* Intl'$ 500 in 1990 purchasing power.[2] Lo Cascio and Malanima (2009) revised Maddison's estimates for the Roman Empire to find that the per capita income was around Intl'$ 1000 (again in 1990 purchasing power); Maddison estimated Intl'$ 570. For Italy, they arrived at an even higher per capita income of Intl'$ 1400. Second, as both per capita income in medieval and ancient times are revised upwards, the economic position of ancient economies as relative to medieval economies remained roughly stable or even improved over the first millennium CE. For an example of the increasing economic prosperity of ancient economies, we might refer again to Italy, where per capita GDP during the first millennium CE seems to have declined (Maddison 2007; Lo Cascio and Malanima 2009). This is backed up by anthropometric evidence. Angel (1984) claims that people in the Eastern Mediterranean reached their maximum stature between *c.* 200 BCE and 120 CE, this height only being seen again after 1500 (Table 2.1). Both Japan and China also provide examples of, at most, low growth (Broadberry et al. 2018, 2021; Bassino et al. 2019).

Can the process (or absence) of growth divergence that began in the first millennium CE be explained if technology was the long-run factor affecting growth? Was growth also affected by the presence of other factors that affected the efficient adoption of technology, including the institutional environment, geographical features, and exogenous shocks such as wars, epidemics, and climate cycles?

In the context of divergent growth patterns, the ultimate factors mentioned here have been frequently considered in the literature as playing a role in ancient, medieval, and modern economies. First, declining marital fertility might lead to fewer children, and hence more investment in the remaining children. However, before the nineteenth and twentieth centuries, we find limited evidence that this occurred. Second, countries that had been isolated in ancient and medieval times appear to become more entrepreneurial. Third, the existence of institutional practices aimed at blocking the implementation of new inventions varied between countries. In this respect, political fragmentation, which occurred in Europe from the fall of the Roman Empire until the aftermath of the Second World War, resulted in a higher chance that in any given country there would be an institutional environment that was more favourable to technological improvement (even in the presence of long-run blocks to innovation in the majority of European countries, it is still likely that there would be a country without such blocks). Fourth, it made a difference who created and implemented these new technologies. In China, the introduction of new technologies, that is, new agricultural methods and new crop varieties, was often supported by the government. Yet these Chinese inventions focused on the bigger landlords, while in Europe, peasants and sub-urban classes dominated. The implementation of these new technologies also depended on their direction, that is, whether they were labour saving or capital saving. In China, government, landlords,

[2] International dollar is a currency with the same purchasing power as the United States dollar at a given year.

and lineage (i.e. clan)-managed institutions encouraged fewer, and capital-saving, technologies. This implied an initially rising, and later declining, land rent to wage ratio. On the contrary, there was a labour-saving path on the other side of the Eurasian continent, with the land rent to wage ratio declining. Fifth, the different settings for production, either more capital or labour intensive, also implied that the fertility transition happened later in China than in the West, and consequently that the average skills, experience, and well-being of the population (constituting so-called human capital) improved more slowly than in the former.

So far, we have briefly explored temporal and regional aspects. In order to analyse regional interactions, we rely on four non-overlapping major cases that together stretch across the entire Eurasian continent: Southern Europe, North-Western Europe, Central Eurasia, and China. Whereas China has been China for almost all history, a different representative country could be used for the other regions. For example, Southern Europe could be represented by the Roman Republic and Empire, the Renaissance Italian states, or the unified Italian Kingdom and Republic of the last 150 years. North-Western Europe could be represented by the Netherlands, Sweden (covering all of Scandinavia at its greatest extent), and the United Kingdom. We may geographically designate Russia and the area of the FSU as "Central Eurasia" while indicating the statistical area (European Russia, FSU) or larger (Russian Empire, Russian Federation) or smaller (Russia, USSR) areas, using historical country names where necessary. Indeed, Central Eurasia includes the geographic and cultural region encompassing the landmass between Central Europe, East, and South Asia, with such polities as the Tsardom of Russia (1547–1721), the Russian Empire (1721–1917), the Soviet Union (1922–1991), and the Newly Independent (post-Soviet) States in Eastern Europe, the Caucasus, and Central Asia.

However, owing to data limitations, we frequently analyse other representative parts of the four major regions (e.g. Holland or England in North-Western Europe, similar to European Russia or Central Asia in Central Eurasia, and Inner Mongolia or Xinjiang in China). It is worth noting here that Russia is frequently attributed to Eastern Europe on the grounds that its statehood originally emerged there and that most of its population (as well as that of the USSR) always lived in the European part of the country, although most of its territory lies in Asia. These territories (Siberia and the Far East) were absorbed in the sixteenth and the seventeenth centuries. Russia interacted with various states in Central Asia for most of its history, but it was not until the eighteenth century that the Russian Empire began to absorb their territory (today's independent states of Kazakhstan, Kyrgyzstan, Uzbekistan, Turkmenistan, and Tajikistan). The Russian Federation was the core part of the USSR (dissolved in 1991), comprising about half of its population and gross domestic product (GDP). From 2015, Russia and some other post-Soviet states (Armenia, Belarus, Kazakhstan, Kyrgyzstan) have participated in the Eurasian Economic Union with free movement of goods, services, capital, and labour.[3] This is one of the reasons why "Eurasia" has a narrow sense in these countries, meaning all the

[3] https://eaeunion.org/?lang=eng

post-Soviet area, sometimes with minor extensions into former socialist countries such as Mongolia.

1.2 Late Medieval and Early Modern Period: Agricultural and Industrial Growth

Shocks, as mentioned in Sect. 1.1, while inevitably changing the balance of production factors, might also trigger subsequent patterns of (sustained) growth. The most obvious example of this type of shock is the Black Death of the fourteenth century, the most striking effect of which was a stark population drop. However, this triggered different effects in Europe, Russia, and China. In Europe, wages rose, hence decreasing the land rent to wage ratio. On the contrary, in China, where sufficient labour was available and the Black Death was less influential, land rents declined somewhat, but wages were hardly affected, thus leading to just a marginal decline in the land rent to wage ratio. This led to labour-saving technologies in England and just a minor change in this respect in China, thus exacerbating the differences that already existed. However, there are four reasons why this pressure for labour-saving technology did not trigger sustained growth.

First, the state might exert pressure by means of taxation on farming populations, thus repressing incentives towards capital-intensive investments. Second, as pointed out earlier, wages hardly affected estates, so in those regions where landlords were leading technology innovation (as in China), no incentives for capital-saving technologies emerged. Third, farm size increased in England, while in China there was more labour-intensive land use. Fourth, even if there was a tendency towards more intensive land use, as in China, it might play out differently. Many technologies, after all, save both capital and labour. In addition, labour might be so expensive that it becomes profitable to invest in capital schemes that bring that cost down. In this specific set of conditions, the government might even push towards the use of more capital-intensive investments.

Even though these factors might have reduced the effect of the shock caused by, for example, the Black Death, they did not completely nullify it. Indeed, the interaction of all the factors mentioned here led to different growth patterns in Western Europe and China—but until the technological changes in late eighteenth-century England, differences remained relatively small. Indeed, there was a limited amount of technology available in both areas until the outbreak of the Agricultural Revolution of the eighteenth century, when in England existing farming knowledge was paired with the demand for technological solutions, while in China this occurred only at the beginning of the twentieth century. This early advance in England was driven by, inter alia, the replacement of fallow land by turnips and clover, which strongly increased agricultural productivity. In addition, although this is far from unanimous in the literature, another argument goes that farm sizes increased in England and decreased in China, thus, more demand for technology is being generated in the former. A fourth argument that has been put forward focuses on the selective breeding that took place in both China and England at this time. Finally, the rise of human capital, especially in England, caused a rise in technological innovation.

In sum, although England had some advantages, most notably in the early availability of technology, replacement of the fallow system, and an increase in human capital, between the Black Death and the eighteenth century, the real jump in agricultural growth only occurred in the eighteenth century. This affected industry and services (notably, the trade and transport sector, state-financed bureaucracy, and the military). Since the income elasticity of demand was much higher in industry and services, rising per capita income strongly increased demand in those areas. This was intimately linked with urbanization, as in Europe, manufacturing occurred in cities. Hence, technology in industry and services increased faster than it did in agriculture from the eighteenth century onwards. This was to some extent counterbalanced by outward migration from the cities by workers who were employed in proto-industrial activities in the countryside, where real wages were higher.

In China, however, this urban structure did not develop: rich areas such as the Yangtze faced de-urbanization, and wages were structurally lower in developed regions than in those that were less developed. This might have been caused by the different political environment in Chinese cities together with labour and manufacturing being located in the countryside. Indeed, between 1400 and 1800, China moved away from an urban structure that was dominated by just a few large consumer cities towards a more dispersed system. A large number of small towns boomed, becoming even more prosperous than the cities to which they were linked.

The growing importance of the periphery in China undermines the analysis put forward by Acemoglu and Robinson (2012) that "extractive institutions" put in place by the state hindered its economic development. The data suggest that such extractive institutions (as measured by urban primacy) appear to have been more effective for the period of economic prosperity during the Song dynasty (960–1279) than during the Qing dynasty (1644–1912).

1.3 Start of Modern Growth and the Great Divergence

We have dealt so far predominantly with agricultural technology. Yet, notwithstanding its importance, a further question arises: what drove industrial technology ahead of agricultural technology in England from *c.* 1750, Russia from *c.* 1880, and China from *c.* 1900?

To take China first, in the Song dynasty (960–1279), industry was driven by handicraft supply and demand, and improved transport. However, this picture remained static, not changing that much until the beginning of the twentieth century. So, what drove the differences in manufacturing and services technology expressed in England, Russia, and China? First, Pomeranz (2000) has argued that there was limited technological improvement in the Yangtze delta because of a lack of both colonial expansion and accessible coal reserves. Other influential incentives have since been suggested, such as institutions (e.g. Acemoglu and Robinson 2012), a higher European receptiveness to technology (e.g. Mokyr 2012), and a favourable factor price combination such as low coal prices and high wages (Allen 2011).

Second, it was mostly regions with high market potential that held the highest shares of secondary sector employment in Asia around 1900. From this perspective, as in the European case, changes in transport networks and the spatial distribution of economic activities to a large extent explain the location of industry (e.g. Krugman, 1991; Bogart, 2010; Bogart and Chaudhary, 2013; see also Kingsmill, 1898). In Russia, as in Europe and the United States in the nineteenth century, the building of railways fuelled the price of land, a classic benefit of transportation investment in largely agrarian countries. The development of a railway network preceded the launch of modern growth in agriculture (Leonard et al., 2021).

Third, at the same time, from Gerschenkron's (1962) point of view, one would expect that later industrializers in Asia relied more upon capital and energy-intensive production than their European counterparts (e.g. Allen 2003; Földvari et al. 2015). Furthermore, Gerschenkron (1962) and Amsden (1989) argue that in late industrializers, the government took a more active role in the industrialization process, in particular by supplying capital and promoting entrepreneurship. Capital intensity and government involvement were thus characteristics of lagging countries. Whereas the original division was initially between capital-saving technologies in China and labour-saving technologies in England, over time technology became more labour saving also in China. Indeed, when technologies decrease in price or demand for capital-intensive goods in developing economies increases, developed countries outsource production of less capital-intensive goods (from a developed country's perspective, but more capital intensive from a developing country's perspective), and therefore the whole system can benefit from the introduction of new technologies. This explains why countries such as Japan and China began with capital-saving technologies but over time moved to labour-saving technologies. A trace of Japan's capital-saving past can still be seen in its remarkably high labour share in GDP. But another reason for the high share of labour in the GDP of former latecomers to industrialization is that even though labour-saving technologies have a positive effect on labour productivity, they have a negative effect on household consumption, private sector investment, net exports, and government consumption (Wolf 2014; Fukao et al. 2019). For developed countries, these negative effects also exist, but since they took place in the past, they no longer hinder these economies. Hence, even newly developing economies might be hesitant to replace all capital-saving technologies. In this respect, government intervention can be a balancing act between various positive and negative societal factors, and this balancing act becomes increasingly difficult once more government intervention is required. For two extreme cases of government control, such as China and the FSU countries, it appears that, until the reforms that moved away from socialist models were launched, both experienced a more rapid accumulation of physical capital than human capital, as well as less rapid economic growth in terms of per capita GDP. In hindsight, one might argue that in the post-reform period, both China and the FSU had to change their methods of production, increasing their human capital relative to their physical capital. China did this by increasing human capital, while FSU did it by lowering physical capital. Hence, it should come as no surprise that, with a decline in physical and, to a lesser extent, human capital, the technical frontier (how efficient human and physical capital were used) regressed in the FSU during the first few years following reforms, a trend that only changed in the late 1990s and early 2000s. This offers a stark contrast with China, where the general technology frontier expanded considerably shortly after reforms took place.

1.4 Recent Growth, *c*. 1900–Present

In the eighteenth and nineteenth centuries, a combination of factors contributed to the economic take-off that took place, mostly in Great Britain. This changed somewhat from 1900 onwards, when some factors gained importance and others lost it. Furthermore, whereas the first Industrial Revolution relied heavily on inventions, subsequent revolutions (such as electricity, ICT, and Artificial Intelligence) emphasized innovation (building upon existing knowledge). This section discusses the factors that contributed to the spread of industries across different countries, with a focus on the contrasting cases of East and West Eurasia. These factors included cottage industries, factors of production, institutions, government, and transport.

First, both England and China saw a rise in cottage industries (e.g. textiles, paper in China) owing to improved market access, knowledge transfer, and increased income. However, China's cottage industries remained stable, or growing, until the mid-twentieth century, and there was less emphasis on innovations and capital-intensive production. England, instead, began the process of transition to larger factories already in the eighteenth and nineteenth centuries. Second, at the same time, commodified labour increased more in Western countries than in Eastern Europe and Asia, contributing to higher total factor productivity (TFP) growth and technological advancements in the subsequent Industrial Revolutions. Third, in China, state-led policies and institutional constraints played a greater role in shaping economic outcomes. Fourth, similarly, with regard to transport, government intervention played a more significant role in Central and East Asia than in Western Europe (see also Gerschenkron 1962). In China and the USSR, the state controlled major infrastructure projects, including railways and highways, in an effort to accelerate industrialization. This stands in contrast to the more market-driven approach in Europe, where private investment played a key role in infrastructure development.

Government intervention also extended to fiscal and monetary policy. Fiscal policies in Western Europe during the early twentieth century were characterized by increasing government taxation, which helped fund industrial expansion and public infrastructure. By contrast, countries such as China and the Soviet Union relied on centralized state planning, which led to high levels of investment but also created inefficiencies in resource allocation. Monetary expansion and financial deepening were critical to long-run economic growth. Already by 1890, countries with deeper levels of monetization, such as the Netherlands and the UK, had already set themselves on a path towards stronger economic growth compared with economies with limited access to credit, such as Russia and Eastern Europe.

The role of institutions in economic growth became increasingly prominent throughout the twentieth century. European institutions evolved in ways that inherently promoted market competition and innovation, whereas China and Russia maintained strong state control over economic activity. Institutional borrowing played a significant role in shaping economic growth, with some countries adopting Western administrative and economic frameworks, while others remained largely reliant on indigenous institutions until the late twentieth century. The role of social actors also evolved as the middle class expanded and corporations and entrepreneurs became more involved in economic decision-making. This shift further paved the way for human capital to establish itself as a central driver of economic growth, a trend that became particularly evident in the post-World War II period.

In a more general perspective, economic growth in the late twentieth and early twenty-first centuries has been shaped by global divergence and convergence dynamics. Some theories suggest that core regions (such as Western Europe and the United States) have continued to dominate global innovation, while peripheral economies have focused on replication and low-cost production. However, recent evidence suggests a gradual convergence, driven by technological spillovers, human capital accumulation, and global trade. In particular, China's rise as a global economic power can be attributed to its ability to integrate external knowledge while maintaining state-led growth strategies. Likewise, Russia's lack of human capital at the end of the twentieth century was one of the reasons for it to experience economic stagnation.

1.5 Beyond GDP: Inequality, Well-being, Pollution, and Happiness

So far, our measures of economic growth and convergence have mainly dealt with per capita GDP. Yet well-being consists of more than just income. It should also include measures of education, life expectancy, and so on. Over time, various alternative indicators have emerged to better capture the multidimensional nature of human development, moving beyond GDP as the sole measure of progress.

One example is the Human Development Index (HDI), which results in an index consisting of income, education, and life expectancy. It has been further refined into inequality-adjusted versions that better reflect disparities within societies. Other measures, such as the Historical Index of Human Development (HIHD), provide long-term perspectives on human development, showing how well-being has evolved over centuries. While these indices offer a broader picture, they also reveal stark regional differences in well-being.

Beyond composite indices, material indicators of well-being, such as anthropometric measures and housing quality, can be used to further shed light on long-run regional living standards. Average height, for example, has been used as a proxy for nutritional status and health conditions, revealing how economic growth has not always translated into better physical well-being. During periods of rapid industrialization, some populations experienced declines in height due to worsening living conditions, increased inequality, and urban overcrowding. Similarly, housing conditions reflect broader economic and social trends. In many countries, urbanization has led to improvements in housing quality over time, but disparities remain, particularly in access to basic services such as clean water and sanitation.

Perception-based measures add another dimension to well-being, capturing aspects such as corruption, pollution, and social trust. Studies on historical perceptions of governance (e.g. Helliwell and Huang 2008; Olarewaju et al. 2024) indicate that societies with lower levels of corruption tend to experience higher levels of well-being, as trust in institutions fosters economic stability and social cohesion. Environmental quality is also crucial to well-being. Industrialization has often come at the cost of increased pollution, affecting both health and quality of life. Over time, growing awareness of environmental issues has led to efforts to mitigate pollution through regulation and technological innovation.

Happiness and subjective well-being should therefore find their way into macroeconomic indicators of economic growth. Surveys measuring life satisfaction show that while economic growth generally correlates with higher happiness levels, the relationship is not linear. A society's progress should not be measured solely by its economic output but also by its ability to foster a life in which individuals feel fulfilled, secure, and free to pursue their aspirations. This becomes even more relevant in a world where rapid technological advancements, particularly the AI revolution, are reshaping the foundations of human progress. While AI holds the promise of being a powerful catalyst for exponential economic growth, it also represents a roll of the dice on utopias, carrying the risk that technology may ultimately dictate rather than empower.

References

Acemoglu D, Robinson J (2012) Why nations fail: Origins of power, poverty, and prosperity. Crown, New York, NY

Allen RC (2003) Farm to factory: A reinterpretation of the Soviet industrial revolution. Princeton University Press, Princeton

Allen RC (2011) Why the industrial revolution was British: Commerce, induced invention, and the scientific revolution. Econ Hist Rev 64(2):357–384

Amsden A (1989) Asia's next giant: South Korea and late industrialization. Oxford University Press, New York

Angel LJ (1984) Health as a crucial factor in the changes from hunting to developed farming in the Eastern Mediterranean. In: Cohen MN, Armelagos GJ (eds) Paleopathology at the origins of agriculture. Academic Press, Orlando, pp 51–73

Bassino J-P, Broadberry SN, Fukao K, Gupta B, Takashima M (2019) Japan and the great divergence, 730-1874. Explor Econ Hist 72:1–22. https://doi.org/10.1016/j.eeh.2018.09.002

Bogart D (2010) A global perspective on railway inefficiency and the rise of state ownership, 1880–1912. Explor Econ Hist 47(2):158–178

Bogart D, Chaudhary L (2013) Engines of growth: The productivity advance of Indian Railways, 1874–1912. J Econ His 73(2):339–370. https://doi.org/10.1017/S0022050713000291

Broadberry S, Guan H, Li D (2018) China, Europe, and the great divergence: a study in historical national accounting, 980–1850. J Econ Hist 78(4):955–1000. https://doi.org/10.1017/S0022050718000403

Broadberry S, Guan H, Li D (2021) China, Europe, and the great divergence: a restatement. J Econ Hist 81(1):1–17. https://doi.org/10.1017/S0022050721000292

Földvári P, Van Leeuwen B, Didenko D (2015) Capital formation and economic growth under central planning and transition: a theoretical and empirical analysis, ca. 1920–2008. Acta Oeconomica 65(1):27–50

Fukao K, Ito K, Perugini C (2019) A microeconomic analysis of the declining labor share in Japan. ADBI Working Paper 925. Asian Development Bank Institute, Tokyo

Gerschenkron A (1962) Economic backwardness in historical perspective: a book of essays. Harvard University Press, Cambridge

Helliwell JF, Huang H (2008) How's your government? International evidence linking good government and well-being. Br J Polit Sci 38(4):595–619

Kingsmill TW (1898) Inland communications in China. Kelley & Walsh, Shanghai

Krugman P (1991) Increasing returns and economic geography. J Polit Econ 99(3):483–499. https://doi.org/10.1086/261763

Leonard CS, Nazarov Z, Borodkin LI, Karpenko MA, Konchakov RB (2021) Land prices and railroad building in European Russia, 1860s to the early 1900s. Russ J Econ 7(2):93–104

Lo Cascio E, Malanima P (2009) GDP in pre-modern agrarian economies (1-1820 AD): a revision of the estimates. Rivista di Storia Economica XXV(3):387–415

Maddison A (2007) Contours of the world economy, 1-2030 AD. Essays in macro-economic history. Oxford University Press, Oxford

Mokyr J (2012) The enlightened economy: an economic history of Britain 1700–1850. Yale University Press, New Haven

Olarewaju T, Tamvada JP, McDowall-Emefiele S, Swaray R (2024) Perception of corruption as a business obstacle, generalized trust and relation centrism in low- and middle-income nations: The moderating influence of governance. Rev Manag Sci. Online publication. https://doi.org/10.1007/s11846-024-00802-9

Pomeranz K (2000) The great divergence: China, Europe, and the making of the modern world economy. Princeton University Press, Princeton and Oxford

Wolf M (2014) The shifts and the shocks: What we've learned –and have still to learn –from the financial crisis. Penguin, London

Chapter 2
Income and Growth in the Ancient and Early Medieval World

Abstract Even though many changes have been applied to estimates of income in ancient and medieval times, the growth patterns between *c*. 500 BCE and 1000 CE have essentially remained unaltered. This changed around the tenth and fourteenth century CE, when the urbanized parts of Italy were the first to overtake China's per capita gross domestic product (GDP), a development referred to as the "Great Crossing". In this chapter, we disentangle the various reasons, divided into seven groups. First, we look at the Palaeolithic period until 500 BCE to distinguish long-run patterns. Second, given the predominantly Malthusian nature of general economies in this phase, drastic reductions or increases of population could result in increases or decreases of GDP per capita. Third, social relations and class structure varied strongly among regions, thus influencing commercialization and technological change. Fourth, the share of manufacturing in the economy, which has, in general, a higher per capita productivity than agriculture, might also cause differences in income. Fifth, the structure of agriculture could also affect income. For example, a higher share in pasture might reduce income expressed in calories but increase it in monetary values. Calculations for Italy, Byzantium, and Mesopotamia find that the difference in per capita income is about 45%, explained by agriculture and manufacturing. Sixth, climate might affect productivity. Seventh, technological development played an important role in economic growth, where Europe took over from East Asia in the early modern period.

We would like to acknowledge that some parts from this chapter are obtained from Földvári and Van Leeuwen (2012).

B. Van Leeuwen et al., *Innovation and Economic Development in Eurasia, 500 BCE-Present*, Frontiers in Economic History,
https://doi.org/10.1007/978-3-031-97043-6_2

2.1 Importance of Economic Structure

As seen in Chap. 1, growth patterns between ancient and medieval times have essentially withstood the test of time. Yet as we see in Chap. 3, in around the tenth and fourteenth centuries CE, the urbanized parts of Italy were the first to overtake China's per capita gross domestic product (GDP), a development referred to as the "Great Crossing". This has attracted much academic interest.

Indeed, academic interest in comparative research on the standards of living and income per capita of pre-industrial societies has grown significantly in recent times. This is partly owing to increased use of cliometrics in historical research, which allows researchers to build long-run income series, and partly owing to a revived interest in global and temporal income comparison. Global comparisons hinge on modernization theory, which basically states that when less-developed countries come into contact with more developed countries, they start moving on the path to development.[1] This paradigm rests on the same historically optimistic progressivist thinking as Liberalism and Marxism, with an emphasis on active and proactive policies (a developmental state) as well as on the elimination of destructive forms of class struggle. This discourse of linear modernization as Westernization theory, however, has been largely refuted, notwithstanding a minor comeback in the 1990s. The rejection of modernization theory can be linked to the end of Cold War literature, instigated by Fukuyama 1992, and by the earlier wave of decolonization in the 1960s that, contrary to modernization theory's predictions, did not lead to modern growth in the former colonized countries. This shift saw the emergence of dependency theory, especially popular in the 1960s and 1970s, arguing that developed countries force developing countries into the production of low-value-added goods such as raw materials. Hence, no convergence in terms of per capita income occurs. An extension of dependency theory, and in many ways similar, is world-systems theory.[2] This places the relationship between countries in a capitalist framework, claiming that the switch from the feudal to the capitalist system is crucial. World-systems theory relied on a broader concept of capitalism in which free markets are an exception and socialism becomes a kind of peripheral state capitalism (Sect. 2.3). Unsurprisingly, it thus focuses on the division of labour (between skilled and

[1] Modernization Theory is the paradigm that considers traditional societies develop by employing a mixture of domestic and borrowed institutions. As a result of this development, their social and economic structure and their cultural patterns tend to converge with those of modern Western societies. Originally, a linear version of the theory argued the importance of institutional imports, whereas revised versions stress the essential importance of domestic conditions driving change (see also Calabrese and Van Leeuwen 2023). One of the streams of literature within this paradigm is Development Economics, in which the focus is placed on improving well-being in developing countries.

[2] World-Systems Theory is a framework that views the historical development of a global capitalist economy as a highly hierarchical system with unequal flows of goods, capital, and labour between a core/semi-periphery/periphery. This theory explains the factors behind both divergence and convergence. For an author developing his writing from dependency theory to world-systems theory, see Frank (1998) as an example.

unskilled, for example), based on the power and capital intensity of core countries. World-systems theory has been criticized on various grounds, a major one being that it focuses on the nation state, which is seen as being either too small or too large a unit. For example, Robinson (2011) argues that bigger global regions have their own dynamics which have to be taken into account. Likewise, in assemblage theory (Hamilakis and Jones 2017), which is especially important in archaeology, smaller units are studied through the analysis of a certain number of artefacts from a regional, topical, or temporal perspective.

The importance given to various factors driving long-run growth, such as social classes and population pressure, thus depends on the academic tradition. Nevertheless, irrespective of academic heritage, most scholars agree that, where previously no surprises were thought to be found, mostly because of an overly simplified view of the Malthusian trap,[3] significant differences and previously unbelievably high income levels are now estimated for historical societies.[4] This shift also affects other branches of the literature: where people in ancient societies were once thought to have had completely different ideas from today concerning economics and society (see the primitivist–modernist debate), working market frameworks (where certain goods are subjected to market prices) have now been found in ancient societies (e.g. Finley 1973; Temin 2002; Van der Spek et al. 2018).

Yet what we know about the income in ancient economies is based mainly on estimates for Rome, while medieval economies, besides Italy, are represented by Holland, Spain, and England, with the recent addition of China (Broadberry et al. 2018) and Japan (Bassino et al. 2019). Bearing in mind the assumptions about temporal and regional links, for example, from world-systems theory and assemblage theory, various growth theories have been applied to explain both historical and regional differences. Obviously, these regions and time periods are significantly different in terms of economic structure, institutional history, and geographical features (e.g. Acemoglu et al. 2005), and this may influence the observed evolution of income. The importance of these growth factors is frequently established by economic historians using the non-sustainable growth theories that were developed in the late nineteenth and early twentieth centuries (e.g. Thomas Malthus, Johann Heinrich Von Thunen, Karl Marx, and Adam Smith). Hatcher and Bailey (2011) divide these types of growth theory for medieval England into three groups, namely population and resources; class, power, and property relations; and commercialization. It is important to note that not only do theoretical models often overlap, but economic historians also often adopt an eclectic approach that uses evidence outside the formal boundaries of the models.

[3] Namely, not considering the role of several variables including production in non-agricultural sectors or productivity fluctuations. See, for example, Malthus (1999).

[4] Several studies have been carried out for medieval Europe, including Holland, Italy, and Spain, between about 1000 CE and 1800 (Malanima 2011; Van Zanden and Van Leeuwen 2012; Broadberry et al. 2013; Álvarez-Nogal and Prados de la Escosura 2013), while studies on the ancient period include the Roman Empire (e.g. Scheidel 2010; Lo Cascio and Malanima 2009), Athens (Amemiya 2007), and Mesopotamia (Bedford 2007).

First, population and resources are based on a supply and demand model of land and labour. It moves between land abundance (thus increasing the wage to land rent ratio) and labour abundance (thus reducing the wage to land rent ratio). A second theory to be placed in this group is marginal product theory: the existence of higher land rents leads to the use of less productive land. Since increasingly low-quality land is being used for production, the land that is newly cultivated eventually becomes so unproductive that productivity per head actually declines. A third theory applied in this context is Malthusianism in its strict form, with population rises causing a reduction in per capita output. One might compare this with Boserup (1965), who instead claimed that population pressure might generate more technology and output.

These theories on population and resources may, either directly or via the second group of theories (class, power, and property relations), affect economic development. Indeed, social classes may be affected by population changes: an increase in population might strengthen the position of landlords and create serfdom as well as urban and commercial centres (Hatcher and Bailey 2011). This causality (from population size to social class) is predominantly supported by scholars adhering to population and resources theories. Yet the opposite causality (from social class to population size) applies to the second group of theories, relating to class, power, and property relations, where social factors such as lord–peasant relations and culture all change the land to labour ratio (Hatcher and Bailey 2011, 68). Indeed, Brenner (1976) claims that social relations were unaffected by demographic or commercial effects. Hence, as also pointed out by Marx, social structure affected economic forces such as labour and technology.

Contrary to Malthusians, who essentially believe in a stagnant per capita income, Marxist scholars, much like Smithian scholars (proponents of the third group, commercialization), believe there is some upward trend in development and technology. As Marxist political economy rested on a Smithian and Ricardian methodological basis, as early as the Communist Manifesto division of labour, specialization, exchange, and commodification were stressed as the forces driving progressive development.[5] But the novel Marxist idea was that of the compliance between productive forces and the relations of production. The former includes both human capacities to produce, the basis for the subsequent neoclassical construction of the concept of human capital, and the means (instruments) of production, the level of which is determined by the underlying level of technology. The latter concept of relations of production grounded the subsequent key institutionalist concept. Yet for Marxists, owing to their idea of the unfair distribution of value added between the classes, the increased use of technology brought about essentially constant (or even diminishing) per capita welfare for most of the population. For them, class struggles limited the increase in technology use, resulting in an essentially constant per capita output. For commercialization scholars, this does not hold true. Their basic underlying idea is that a rise in population density enhances transport, specialization, and labour division, which causes a rise in output per capita. Obviously, market access, specialization, and labour division only allow economic growth up to a certain point, after which stagnation may set in again.

[5] http://www.marx2mao.com/M&E/CM47.html

None of these three groups of theories therefore puts technology front and centre. This is logical since we are largely discussing agricultural societies here, which, rather than using division of labour, had limited access to transport and markets and limited capital to be invested. As agriculture specialized (in cattle, rice, etc.), limited agricultural capital investment during fast population growth thus increased the land rent to wage ratio. This implies that redundant labour was still being placed in agriculture, thus leading to involution (Geertz 1963).

In order to analyse growth, it is therefore important to look at the drivers of growth within the agricultural sector. First, before turning to the theories summarized here, we first have to assess how much growth and technology in the ancient period affected technology and growth in subsequent periods (Sect. 2.2). Second, besides local differences in technology, local modes of labour production also played a role in growth patterns (Sect. 2.3). Third, social structure (class power and property relations), such as lords and labourers, serfdom, and so on, may lead to reduced growth (Sect. 2.4). Fourth, economic decline or stagnation in per capita GDP can be caused, in a Malthusian framework, by rapid population growth that is not matched by output growth. The rise in population thus causes downward pressure on per capita income (Sect. 2.5). Fifth, decreasing or stagnating per capita income may be a result of the economic structure; it may be caused, for example, by a decline in the manufacturing sector, partly as a result of the loss of export markets and partly because of a contraction in the local market (Sect. 2.6). Sixth, differences in per capita income may also be caused by structural variances in the agricultural sector itself. For example, in around 1300, England had a far lower share of manufacturing than Italy, but the pastoral sector was significant enough to help bring its per capita income closer to the Italian level, at a time when Italy was the leading economy in the European context (Malanima 2018). One underlying reason may simply be that more pasture is required than arable land for the same amount of nutritional value (Broadberry and Campbell 2009) (Sect. 2.7). Seventh, climate may affect production (Sect. 2.8). Eighth, long-run development may be caused by technological development, which increases output per labourer (Sect. 2.9). Finally, any new technology needs to be implemented for it to have an effect (Sect. 2.10).

2.2 Development of Technology since the Lower Palaeolithic

Technological development started in the Upper Palaeolithic period (*c.* 3 million years ago) with the introduction of the Oldowan technology (also called MOD 1—a simple tool made by chipping parts of a stone to give it sharp edges) about 3 million years ago. This began when *Homo erectus* (2 million–100,000 years ago) did not yet exist, and there is the possibility that even earlier tools existed that have not been recognized as such, made out of, for example, bones and stone.

Homo erectus took over the MOD 1 tools and refined them into Acheulean stone tools (MOD 2; more complicated pear-shaped hand axes, for example, to hunt animals and woodworking) from about 2 million years ago. Around 250,000 years ago, among the Neanderthals and *Homo sapiens*, a new technology emerged: Mousterian (MOD 3; stones were prepared to a desired size before being chipped and polished in the desired tool). This developed in Africa, around 100,000 years ago, into MOD 4 (long, thin stones shaped into spearheads, etc.). Around the same time, but especially from 40,000 years ago, the MOD 5 technique was developed by *Homo sapiens*; this featured thin, sharp blades, the inclusion of other raw materials such as ivory, and, especially, composite tools for hunting, needleworking, and so on. This, therefore, led to a diversification of industry. Contrary to MODs 1–4, MOD 5 was also characterized by regional specialization and was hence crucial for regional economic differences (Blaxland and Dorey 2018).

To discuss technical transfer, we start with Oldowan technology that was evenly spread across Eurasia along with the migration of the *Homo erectus* and *Homo heidelbergensis* who took the technologies from Africa.[6] Yet, looking at the so-called Movius line (e.g. Lycett and Norton 2010) in Fig. 2.1, the adoption of MOD 2

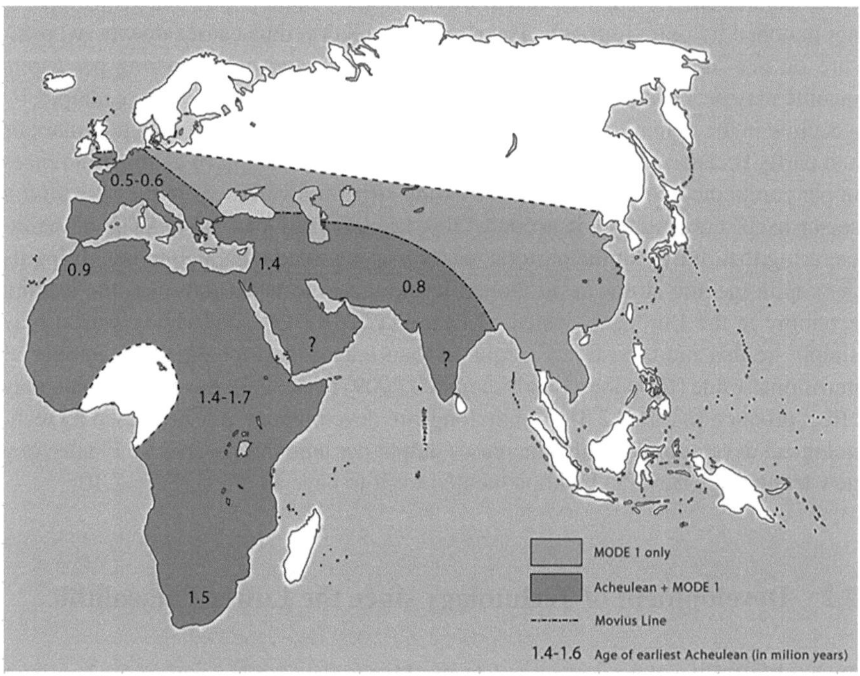

Fig. 2.1 Movius line, distinguishing the spread out of Africa of less-advanced Oldowan (MOD 1) and slightly more advanced Acheulean (MOD 2) technology. *Source:* Langbroek (2004)

[6] *Homo erectus* developed, via *Homo heidelbergensis* (*c.* 700,000–200,000 years ago) into the Neanderthals (400,000–40,000 years ago) and modern man (*Homo sapiens*; *c.* 300,000 years ago). *Homo erectus* spread across Eurasia from about 2 million years ago, thus offering the first possibility to spread manufacturing technology. This was followed by the migration of *Homo heidelbergensis* (*c.* 500,000 years ago) and eventually the Neanderthals (who evolved outside Africa about 500,000 years ago) and *Homo sapiens* (*c.* 70,000–50,000 years ago).

technology in Eastern Europe, Central Asia, and China ran behind the adoption of MOD 2 in Western Europe. Why was this the case?

One reason for this, more limited spread of MOD 2 technology, could be that MOD 1 technologies in China and Central Asia were so advanced that new MOD 2 tools were not needed to replace the old technology. After all, in Africa, both technologies were found side by side (Semaw et al. 2020). A second reason may be that migration to Asia occurred before the hand axe, characteristic of MOD 2 technology, had been invented. Third, it is possible that migration to Asia passed through regions where appropriate materials were unavailable and particular skills were thus forgotten. These two technologies were the same wherever they appeared, so both were likely available everywhere. The same applies to the subsequent MOD 3 and MOD 4 technologies, as *Homo sapiens* arrived at roughly the same time in Asia and Europe. Hence, it is not particularly useful to discuss the differences between these technologies.

More significant is whether MOD 5 technology was different in China, Central Asia, and Europe about 20,000 years ago (*c.* Upper Palaeolithic to Early Mesolithic), and which economic sector (e.g. agriculture, industry, or services) was dominant. First, was the technological level different? Figure 2.2 shows that in this period, more innovations occurred outside Africa (mostly in the Middle East), followed by East Asia and Europe. From the Bronze Age to Antiquity (*c.* 3000–500 BCE), East

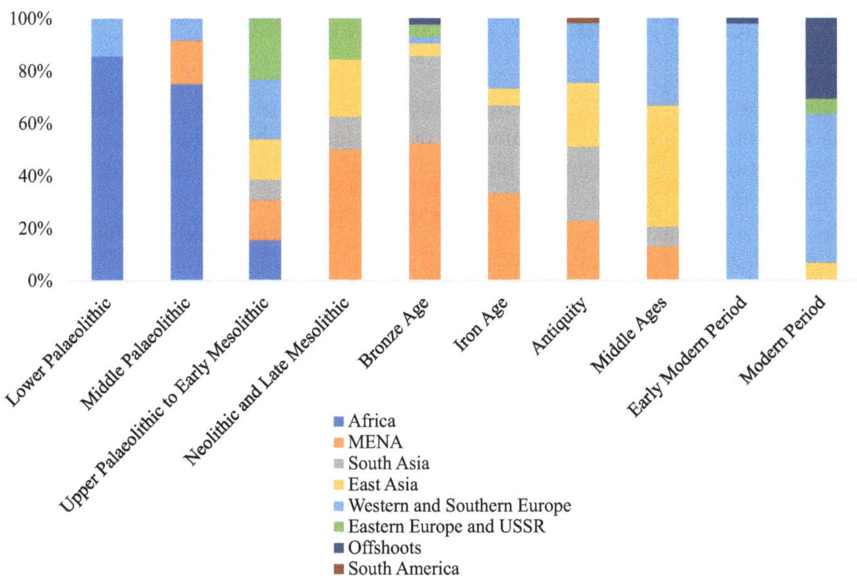

Fig. 2.2 Inventions from the Lower Palaeolithic (3 million years ago) to the present and by region. *Source:* https://en.wikipedia.org/wiki/Timeline_of_historic_inventions (accessed 2021).

Asia and Europe's share of inventions began to grow. Only in the early modern period (*c.* 1500–1800) did Europe overtake China (Chap. 1).

Second, what sector was dominant in technology? Most commentators claim it was agriculture. By means of the new technology, agricultural productivity went up, leading to a move from hunting and gathering to sedentary agriculture. Yet most scholars place the start of the First Agricultural Revolution in 10,000 BCE (e.g. Wu et al. 2019), that is, 10,000 years after the main introduction of MOD 5 technology in 20,000 BCE. However, as pointed out by Hibbs and Olsson (2004), as the agricultural transformation could take thousands of years, it is possible that the first steps towards an agricultural revolution were already being taken in 20,000 BCE. Indeed, even if it began in 10,000 BCE, there might have been regional differences in technological development. For example, Hibbs and Olsson (2004) argue that Eurasia changed rapidly, while other regions with less suitable conditions developed more slowly. Likewise, as is argued by Wu et al. (2019), technical development in China occurred mostly in the Yellow River region. This links to our findings in subsequent sections that there were both more inventions and more cattle in the Yellow River area than in the southern Yangtze region, which expanded economically later. Something similar might be observed in Europe, where Southern Europe was ahead of Western Europe in technology up to the ancient period but stagnated afterwards (Baten and Koepke 2005); this was expressed in human stature.

2.3 Modes of Production, c. 40,000 BCE–1000 CE

Technology development is often linked today to modes of production. But how did this work in ancient times? The mode of production combines the available factors of production (physical capital, human capital, and unskilled and skilled human labour) with labour relations (e.g. ownership or control of means of production, rules and mechanisms governing the interaction of owners and employees with political and social actors) (see Chap. 4). Labour relations thus affect how efficiently the existing factors of production can be used. This efficiency is referred to as the mode of production. Yet since the efficiency of the factors of production is, in modern theories, captured by total factor productivity (TFP), this implies that the mode of production is part of the more encompassing TFP.

While modes of production vary by region and time, any historical economic system consists of several of them, and the key issue becomes which new mode is appearing (or expanding) and which old one is disappearing (or shrinking).[7] Different modes of production have been described and labelled in the literature. Two antithetical modes of production can, at least in certain periods, coexist side by side in one area, rather than one immediately replacing the previous one. This is true

[7] The whole structure of a society is defined by the mode of production. After it has become the core of an economic and social system, it begins to affect other spheres of human life.

in market economies, with their capitalist mode of production, but is even more evident in the Asiatic mode of production and in Soviet-style socialism. In the first, the role of the state as the sole actor in the overall system of labour market relations has been heavily debated. In the second (Soviet style socialism), the presence of large market-based economic segments has been described in the literature.

One mode of production can thus crowd another out or, in certain cases, they can exist side by side. This varies over time and across regions. Finding such changes in the mode of production is no easy task. In this book, we take the International Institute of Social History (IISH) taxonomy of labour relations (2015) (see Hofmeester et al. 2016) as our main theoretical basis.[8] This refers to commodified labour,[9] tributary labour, reciprocal labour,[10] and non-working as modes of production. These modes are involved in both market and non-market institutions. There is therefore no place for capitalist and socialist modes of production in this taxonomy when referring to commodified labour for the market (or non-market). After all, from a Marxian point of view, the mode of production is labelled "capitalism" (as opposed to "commodified labour"), with free markets and private ownership of the means of production prevailing. This ownership of production is ultimately mirrored in the political sphere, thus becoming a source of unfair income distribution.[11]

Since the IISH taxonomy contains a wide-ranging set of labour relations that together make up the mode of production, this implies we must identify labour relations in historical periods in order to determine the dominant mode of production. For example, the self-employed, wage earners, indentured labourers, and slaves all belong to commodified labour. Following Lucassen (2021), who also used the IISH taxonomy, it could be argued that *Homo sapiens,* long before the Neolithic Revolution (Agricultural Revolution, *c.* 10,000 bce), had already formed into households with kin producers, being largely part of the reciprocal mode of labour production. Over time, this changed slightly. First, as highlighted in Sect. 2.2, it is noteworthy that MOD 5 technology exhibited signs of incorporating non-food consumption goods over 20,000 years ago. This evidence suggests the emergence of practices of wealth accumulation before the Neolithic Revolution. Second, the Neolithic Revolution of about 10,000 bce offered the opportunity to hoard food, and thus led to further enrichment of households (Lucassen 2021, 10). Third, in about

[8] Marx, for example, distinguished for Europe primitive society, slave society, feudal society, capitalist society, and socialist society. The IISH taxonomy of labour relations refers, inter alia, to reciprocal labour within the household, tributary labour, and commodified labour.

[9] Commodified labor encompasses labour treated as a marketable commodity, including wage work and slavery.

[10] Reciprocal Mode of Production refers to a labour system based on family or kin-based income extraction.

[11] Normally, the capitalist mode of production implies production based on industrial technologies (machines as the means of production). The socialist mode of production also hinged on the use of industrial technologies, which were nevertheless accompanied by a change in the political dimension in terms of the predominance of public property and a tendency towards curtailing markets.

7000 BCE, the emergence of the first cities led to an increased demand for non-kin labour, thus allowing a switch to commodified labour.

These three factors in turn triggered the rise of several new modes of labour relations, which can be defined, as argued by Lucassen (2021, 11), as "free wage labour, slavery, self-employment (including by tenants), and [...] employership". These can be considered a move away from the reciprocal mode of production to the tributary mode of labour production and the commodified labour mode. Indeed, while the reciprocal mode of labour production was based on one or multiple families/households/groups extracting income from others, the tributary mode of production heavily relied on forced labour, tributary serfdom, and so on. Although the tributary mode was important, it was progressively outshone by the expansion of forms of commodified labour, with the mode of production consisting of both market and non-market labour relationships. Indeed, the little data available on the share of modes of labour in 1500 (IISH Global Collab of Labour Relations 2015) show small shares of tributary production, with about 20–30% commodified labour. This implies that reciprocal labour, even though declining, remained high even until the sixteenth century.

2.4 Social Classes

As MOD 5 technology advanced and the consumption of non-food goods increased, there were concurrent shifts in social structures. In the literature on social structure, it is noted that classes affect the land to labour ratio, and especially the adoption of technology.[12] Indeed, Marxist literature shows that there was a large demesne sector in England in the fourteenth century, in which lords consumed more but farming did not use more land. This led to a lower land to labour ratio and, according to the literature, an artificial agrarian crisis was created. Malthusian literature opposes this theory, claiming that the stagnation in per capita income was entirely due to rising population numbers (and growth was due to a decline in population numbers). This claim is, in turn, attacked by Kominsky (1956), who suggests that population development was inconsistent with Malthusian interpretation.

We can test these hypotheses by looking at English data from Broadberry et al. (2015) (Fig. 2.3). First, we find that 25% of the arable acreage belonged to the demesne sector in the thirteenth century. This declined to 16% in the fourteenth century and dropped to 0% around the year 1500. So the story of a rise in the demesnes sector does not apply after 1300. Second, looking at population development, we find that the population drop during the Black Death led to a rise in land productivity (wheat yield per acre) in the short run but a decline in the long run. Hence, in the short run, Malthus dominated, but in the long run, either classes or

[12] Classes were institutionalized in the same way estates were in traditional, or pre-capitalist, societies.

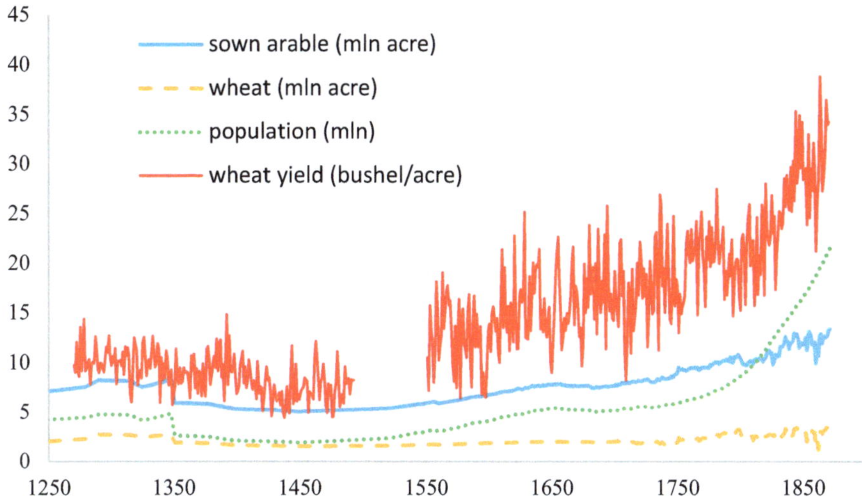

Fig. 2.3 Sown arable land area under wheat, population, and wheat yield in England, c. 1250–1870. *Source:* Broadberry et al. (2015)

trade played a role. This is not consistent with the Marxist literature, as it has to be combined with the reduced share of demesnes in agriculture we just observed. Third, sown arable decreased, but sown wheat did not. This implies not more land productivity, but higher consumption of wheat in the fourteenth century, suggesting the importance of either population or trade theories. Fourth, the population went up from about 1500, but so did land productivity (wheat yield). Fifth, in the late nineteenth century, population increased strongly and land use stagnated, but this was compensated for by both higher productivity and more imports.

It therefore seems that both population and resources and commercialization theories played a role. Social structure undoubtedly changed, but this was mostly a result of changes in population (e.g. the fall of serfdom). So the direct effect of social class was limited.

In China, just as in England, there was a significant expansion in cash crop cultivation, the commercialization of agriculture, and the development of the rural handicraft industry during the period between Tang and Qing (*c*. 700–1800) (Li 2003). In the Lower Yangtze region, a large number of agricultural labourers transferred to other sectors such as the handicraft industry or services. Women in particular were increasingly involved in mulberry growing and silkworm breeding instead of farming. As a result, labour shortages became widespread in the agricultural sector (Li 2000). The average size of farmland owned by individual households declined, but the output of each labourer and each unit of farmland increased (Li 2007). Along with the accumulation of wealth, a social class consisting of rich merchants, workshop owners, and landlords gradually developed.

However, this did not mean that in China fundamental social changes that affected technology either directly or via trade and population actually took place as they partly did in England. First, with relatively high labour quality, including professional capability, general commercial knowledge, and reading, writing, and calculation skills, many people were sufficiently capable of running small workshops independently, so they did not rely on bigger production organizations for their employment. Given that mechanical equipment was still unavailable and the construction of large workplaces cost too much, small family workshops remained dominant (Li 2000). In other words, development in terms of scale and modes of production stagnated.

Second, there were not many possibilities for commercial and industrial capital to grow into a force that could challenge the traditional economic system, which remained closely tied to landed capital. The large number of workshop owners as well as rich merchants had very close relationships with local rural clans in their home regions, meaning that the limited mobility of many production factors (i.e. labour, capital, and land) caused by the clan structure was a major obstacle to rural industrialization (Lai 2002). Generally speaking, in those regions with better developed commercial or industrial capital, traditional clan power was also stronger (Fu 1982). The financial success of these workshop owners and rich merchants was usually reflected in the purchase of real estate, such as land, houses, and gardens. Important merchants were usually important landlords. From a political perspective, they pursued official appointments or honours that might facilitate their business (Shang 1999). This gave the government the opportunity to control leading merchants in vital sectors such as grain, monetary metals, and salt, for example. As a result, a large proportion of social wealth was controlled by political power (Zhao 2021).

In sum, we can conclude that in China, not only did small-scale traders and shopkeepers block scale increases in demesnes and trade, but also, to a large extent, social wealth was used by the government for daily luxuries rather than to expand production. This limited development of production scale meant fewer opportunities for landless peasants to become employed industrial labourers (Department of Chinese History, Renmin University of China 1958). The situation was similar in medieval England, where both population and trade, rather than the government, primarily influenced the existing social classes—and hence the production environment.

2.5 Malthusian Population Pressure

Population rise and decline may affect per capita income. For example, the decline in per capita income in Mesopotamia during the Hellenistic period, as shown in Table 2.2, was caused by population loss owing to internal struggle. While the Achaemenid phase of the Persian Empire (550–331 BCE) was characterized by stability, the subsequent Hellenistic period was characterized by internal conflicts, which eventually culminated in a takeover by the Parthians in 141 BCE. The Hellenistic period was most likely also characterized by population growth. Population increases should, however, not be considered as indicative of the presence of economic growth during this period, as changes in population numbers need to be primarily interpreted from the standpoint of a Malthusian society and by no means from a modern perspective. While today's growth of income per capita usually simply means a more prosperous period, rising per capita income in a Malthusian regime is typically caused by a large-scale loss of population, mostly owing to some catastrophic event. In a society caught in a Malthusian trap, a larger population is indeed typically paired with lower per capita income. As such, the per capita income decline in the third century BCE may very well have been caused by population pressure. This period ended when Babylon was conquered by the Parthian kings in 141 BCE. Initially, this led to an improvement in economic indicators during the reign of Mithridates II (the Great) between 124 and 88 BCE, before another decline took place.

2.6 Manufacturing Industry

It is estimated that Mesopotamian GDP per capita between about 500 and 50 BCE increased from about 600 to 700, expressed in GK$ (1990) (Table 2.1). Even though these levels are significantly more than the generally accepted subsistence minimum of $400, they seem to be lower than the GDP per capita estimations for Rome or Athens. Differences in the land to population ratio cannot fully explain this measured divergence, which most likely reflects the role of other additional factors that should be considered as primary determinants of real economic growth. Mesopotamia was an overwhelmingly agricultural society with an abundance of low-cost foodstuffs and a relatively low GDP per capita. Even though we have no data on occupational distribution in Mesopotamia, we can turn to a census of rural regions in Ptolemaic Egypt that showed about 71% of people in agriculture versus 6.1% in industry (Clarysse and Thompson 2006, 1989–1191).[13] Athens, on the other hand,

Table 2.1 Per capita product in Western Europe from 1 CE to 1870 according to the Maddison and Lo Cascio and Malanima revision (in Intl'$ (in 1990 purchasing power parity) and index 1500 = 1)

Year	Maddison per capita GDP	Revision per capita GDP
1	576	1000
1000	427	900
1500	771	1350
1600	889	1250
1700	997	1400
1820	1202	1350
1870	1960	1960

Source: Maddison (2007) and Lo Cascio and Malanima (2009)

[13] Any omitted persons were assumed to have been employed in agriculture.

had a total GDP of 4430 silver talents for the fourth century BCE, according to the estimation by Amemiya (2007). This latter can be converted to a GDP per capita of GK$967 (1990), which is significantly (30–40%) higher than the estimate for Mesopotamia at about the same time.[14] This discrepancy should be attributed in part to the presence of a different underlying economic structure. Athens' food supply depended on large-scale imports that were traded through maritime commerce. It has also been calculated that around 56% of Athens' economy consisted of manufacturing, and that therefore it was able to offer a wide range of diversified goods, which at any point in their life cycle could be exchanged with imported food stocks (Amemiya 2007).

The Roman Empire is the next available economy for comparison. Maddison (2007) and Goldsmith (1984) estimated GDP per capita in Rome at around GK$570. However, recent revisions by Milanovic (2006) and the previously mentioned revision by Lo Cascio and Malanima (2009) instead set it at around GK$1000 in around 1 CE (Table 2.1). Of course, Rome was at this point a superpower compared with Mesopotamia, which was politically in decline. Indeed, Table 2.2 shows that per capita GDP in Mesopotamia around 100 BCE, when that region was in a phase of greater economic power, was GK$784, and therefore inferior to that of the Roman Empire one century later. The difference becomes larger when we look at the Italian part of the Roman Empire, for which Lo Cascio and Malanima (2009) estimate GDP per capita to be as high as GK$1400. This is about twice the GK$600–700 we find for Mesopotamia. This relationship also seems to hold once we compare real wages, measured in litres of wheat: Scheidel reports 7 litres per person per day in Rome, while an unskilled labourer's wages did not buy more than 2.5 litres in Babylon. Higher wages in Rome imply more value added per person, so either Rome was much more productive in terms of agriculture (which is possible, but Roman agriculture was certainly not three times as productive as Mesopotamia's) or

Table 2.2 Comparison of unskilled male labourers' subsistence ratios in south-eastern Han China, Babylonia, and the Eastern Roman Empire (Syria and Egypt)

	Southern China	Babylonia	Egypt	Syria
500 BCE		0.71		
100 BCE	0.87	0.51		
100 CE			0.55	
230 CE			0.56	
300 CE				0.65–0.78

Source: Van Leeuwen et al. (2013)

[14] With the estimated population of 220,000, we arrive at 0.020136 talents per capita, or 523.5 g of silver (using an Attic talent of 26 kg). Von Reden (2008) reports a barley price of 37 g of silver per 100 l, which means that this per capita income would have been enough to buy 1415 l of barley (equivalent to 1132 l of wheat in calorific value). Using the 1.17 l wheat to GK$ ratio, we arrive at 967 Int'$ (at 1990 purchasing power parity) as an estimate for Athenian GDP per capita in the fourth century BCE.

we should look at Roman manufacturing as the primary cause of this bonus in labour productivity. Athens should than be regarded as a centre of production for commodities that could be traded with imported food stocks. If we look at urbanization, an often-used indicator for manufacturing (e.g. Álvarez-Nogal and Prados de la Escosura 2013), we see that urbanization in around 1 CE in the Italian part of the Roman Empire was around 27% (Geraghty 2007, 1044, fn. 39, and 1048).[15] This is much higher than the 10% estimated for Mesopotamia. Hence, if we assume that labour productivity in manufacturing was about twice as high as in agriculture, the difference in economic structure alone would explain the 20% income gap between Rome and Mesopotamia.[16]

Comparing Mesopotamia and the Roman world with China is complicated. While some authors (e.g. Maddison 2007) claim that China during Han times was close to subsistence, others (e.g. Needham 1954, 1986; Elvin 1973) see it as relatively developed. To develop a broad idea about the differences between Europe and China, in Table 2.2 we report on ca. 100 BCE. With a subsistence ratio of 0.87, China was relatively developed, which is also shown by the per capita GDP of 710–813 (Intl'$ in 1990 purchasing power parity) in 980 CE (Broadberry et al. 2021; Solar 2021). But we should be careful not to exaggerate its wealth. First, a higher subsistence ratio could be caused by low food costs. Because pasture (e.g. meat) is much more expensive than arable farming (e.g. rice, wheat), pastoral economies, as in Europe, have lower subsistence ratios but higher GDP per capita. Second, per capita GDP, as we mentioned earlier, was likely higher in the Italian part of the Roman Empire, while Holland and England overtook China in per capita terms during the Black Death in the mid-fourteenth century. Hence, Chinese per capita income probably had little room for a high share in manufacturing, as is also found if we look at occupational distribution (Guo et al. 2019).

The debate on Malthusian dynamics in the Roman Empire is even less uniform than that for Mesopotamia. A traditional view arguing that the Roman world overall was basically unable to escape a Malthusian low equilibrium trap throughout its existence (Erdkamp 2016) has increasingly given space to more nuanced perspectives. While conclusive answers on the level of per capita income and population size (e.g. Saller 2002; Ward-Perkins 2005) in the Roman Empire are still far from being reached, a more complex system of interacting variables should be considered when applying the Malthusian framework to the Imperial phase. These include climatic stability, labour supply, productivity, level of urbanization, and the presence of market economy frameworks (Erdkamp 2016).

---

[15] For the whole of the Roman Empire, Goldsmith (1984, 272–273) estimated urbanization between 9% and 13%.

[16] A third of the Roman population was urban and two-thirds was rural. If we assume labour productivity to be twice as high in urban areas as in the countryside, we arrive at a total labour productivity of $(1/3) \times 2 + (2/3) \times 1 = 1.3$. For Babylon, the same numbers are: $(1/10) \times 2 + (9/10) \times 1 = 1.1$. Hence, labour productivity is about 20% higher in Rome purely because of the more extensive manufacturing sector.

However, two main observations can be made when approaching the analysis of the relationship between Malthusian dynamics and their effect on GDP per capita series in the context of ancient societies. The first obvious one is that high levels of income do not provide conclusive evidence of the absence of a Malthusian equilibrium, since rising per capita incomes can still exist when population growth outpaces per capita income growth (Temin 2013; Erdkamp 2016). Second, even with high levels of income, inequality might obstruct or alter Malthusian dynamics—for example, if the production of luxury goods rises (and consequently the GDP level increases) but food remains stable, this will not affect fertility and will therefore not produce rising Malthusian pressure on existing resources (Tisdell and Svizzero 2015; Wu et al. 2018). Such a framework can be considered as a form of class-integrated economic model, according to the Brenner debate (Brenner 1976; Kitsikopoulos 2000b).[17] Even though Brenner focused on the industrial and agricultural revolutions, this pattern of growth in ancient societies is based on increasing class differences in which the rich get richer without producing a downward Malthusian effect on income. This type of explanation is also invoked for China, where per capita income in the Han dynasty (around 1 CE) was sufficiently high, before moving to a downward trajectory of per capita income in the second millennium CE (Broadberry et al. 2018), suggesting higher class inequality in this latter phase.

2.7 Agricultural Structure

Mesopotamian GDP per capita in the fifth century BCE is thought to have been Intl'$ 700–750 (Földvari and Van Leeuwen 2012). This changed in around 100 BCE when, although the estimate for Mesopotamia remained higher than the subsistence level of GK$400 (Table 2.3), it was lower than the estimate for later periods of Antiquity in the Roman Empire (Lo Cascio and Malanima 2009) and Byzantium (Milanovic 2006). This contradiction is less serious than it seems, though. First, as mentioned earlier, it is possible that a weaker form of Malthusian growth occurred in which rising per capita incomes were paired with increasingly rapid population growth. Second, it might be that, whereas food production was bounded by Malthusian constraints, this did not apply to other sectors, thus allowing for economic growth in non-food sectors (as seen in the case of the manufacturing sector in Sect. 2.6).

Third, it might be that the average wage was similar in these countries in terms of calorific equivalent, but the price of calories differed. Indeed, since a unit of calories from meat is about ten times as expensive as from grain products, and even accepting a primitivist logic dictating that in ancient economies most people must

[17] The Brenner debate is a historical debate on the causes of the agricultural revolution in Europe, emphasizing the role of capitalism. According to this theory, in certain regions peasants were able to withstand their landlords and hence halt capitalist development, such as enclosure. In other regions, where landlords were more powerful, the landlords were able to extract a larger surplus.

Table 2.3 Per capita income in Mesopotamia, c. 384–60 BCE

Period (BCE)	Average income per capita (Intl' intl'$ in 1990 prices)
500 BCE	700–750
Persian empire (384–331 BCE)	722
Hellenistic empire (330–141 BCE)	617
New Persian empire (140–60 BCE)	784

Source: Földvari and Van Leeuwen (2012)

have been at subsistence levels (in terms of calories at least), a higher share of pasture must be paired with a higher GDP per capita in both monetary units and grain equivalents. That is why the production structure of an economy plays a prominent role. Countries with predominantly arable agriculture such as Mesopotamia or China could produce a unit calorie considerably more cheaply than countries with higher measured amounts of pasture such as Spain or England.

That Mesopotamians ate fewer animal products is supported by anthropometric evidence: even though the height of Mesopotamian skeletons seems not to deviate much from that of Greek skeletons (Jursa 2010, 797, using the data of Wittwer-Backofen 1983), this was not caused by extensive pasture. It may be attributable to a large intake of dates, which corresponds to a higher consumption of proteins, increasing human stature. Indeed, Jursa notes that the higher incidence of caries in Babylonian corpses from the third millennium BCE indicates a higher intake of carbohydrates and sugar: in dried form, dates have a high sugar content. The suggestion is therefore that the intake of pastoral products was probably low. Indeed, Sołtysiak (2010) shows that the Hellenistic Near East was characterized by an increase in nutrient deficiency diseases and infections.

In China the consumption of proteins was lower, mostly because of a reliance on rice for protein. As Anderson (1988) states, the intake of vegetables, fruit, and grains was predominant, while dairy products were only consumed in areas that were mostly inhabited by people of nomadic origin.[18] Pomeranz (2000) notes that, together with rice, bean products were the main supplier of protein and amino acids in China, whereas in most European countries, people depended on meat. This resulted in a height difference: while in China average height was around 167–169 centimetres (Table 3.1), in Europe it was slightly higher. In the Mediterranean, where, as Koepke and Baten (2008) show, there was a lower share of cattle than in North and Eastern Europe, it was 168 centimetres, while in more pasture-rich northwest Europe it was 169 centimetres (Baten and Koepke 2005).

It is important, though, to stress the existence of regional differences. In northern China large holdings existed; irrigation was seldom present; grains grown included

[18] Indeed, China has a long history of focusing on grain production while pasture is very limited. Even in 1930, only 1% of total farmland was dedicated to pasture, while in Europe animal husbandry is integrated with farming (Buck 1937).

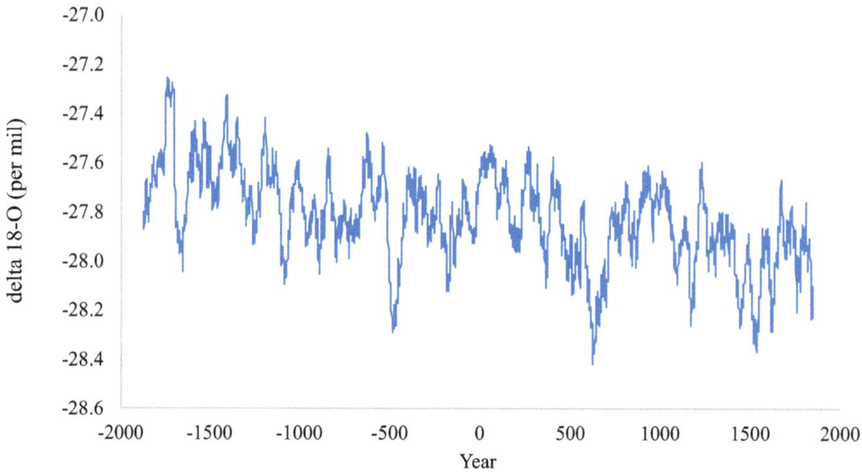

Fig. 2.4 Greenland ice core data, c. 1900 BCE–1900 CE (50-year moving average). *Note:* Lower values imply cooler weather. *Source:* Langway et al. (1985)

millet, wheat, barley, and sorghum; capital existed in the forms of ploughs and draught animals (oxen, donkeys, mules); and there was more pasture for productive animals (pigs and sheep). In southern China, however, small holdings existed; irrigation was common; rice was the dominant crop, with winter wheat and barley as secondary crops; and there were fewer draught animals (oxen) used (Bray 1984, 28). This might explain why in the first millennium around the Yangtze River human stature was considerably lower than around the more northerly Yellow River (Table 3.1).

One might also draw a comparison with Byzantium, where, around 1000 CE, GDP per capita was considerably higher than that of Mesopotamia (Milanovic 2006), even though there is little evidence of the presence of an extensive manufacturing sector. However, there is plenty of evidence that pasture increased between about 200 BCE and 1000 CE. For example, Wick, Lemcke, and Sturm (2003, 671) show a decrease in Quercus (oak) pollen percentages and a rise in *Artemisia* in Lake Van in Southeastern Turkey. Since *Artemisia* has a strong aroma and bitter taste that discourages herbivory, the increase in its pollen is indicative of an increase in pasture. The same evidence exists for Roman provinces around the Danube River, which show a considerable increase in Roman cattle and pig breeding (Bokonyi, 1988). Indeed, if we look at Byzantium in about 1000 CE, we again find a considerable amount of meat in food consumption. Meat rations in the army were around 60 kg per annum (Milanovic, 2006, Table 1), and the average per head of the population was close to 30 kg. Indeed, as pointed out by Milanovic, current meat consumption in Turkey is around 40 kg per year, so this estimate is not unlikely. With 30 kg a year of meat consumption, meat must have made up 17.5% of the food budget, twice the share of pasture in Mesopotamian agriculture. If we add other animal products such as wool, cheese, and milk, and assume that 80% of total consumption was food (in this case the share of meat in total consumption is 14%), we can safely set the share of pasturage in GDP in Byzantium at 28%.

2.8 Climate

Besides the factors already mentioned, climate played a role in the existence of growth spikes. We can assess long-run patterns in the northern hemisphere by looking at Greenland ice core data (Fig. 2.4), with lower data implying cooler weather in the northern hemisphere. The data show strong cold periods in about 500 CE and again in about 1500. It is unclear exactly why this happened, but it occurred on a global scale. Indeed, it matches with Huijs et al. (2014), who find a strong correlation between temperature, water, and agricultural output in 2nd–first century BCE Babylonia. It is also in line with the research by Büntgen et al. (2011), who, based on dendrochronological (tree ring growth) data, find that the cooling period of about 500 CE coincided with the fall of the Western Roman Empire and migration streams. Similarly, the Zheng et al. (2014) study on the Ming dynasty around 1500 found a cooler period. Similar evidence can also be found in Europe, where the medieval cooling period is often referred to as the Little Ice Age.

How does climate affect production? Most studies find that rising temperatures lead to increased production and trade, while declining temperatures cause famine and migration. For example, McCormick (2002) finds that increased temperatures around 1100 led to faster economic development in Europe. Likewise, Zheng et al. (2014) show that worsening of the climate ultimately led to lower agricultural output and to the fall of the Chinese Ming dynasty. It is important, though, to stress that the effect of climate varies by crop. For example, in Mesopotamia, the cooling period around 150 BCE led to lower date production but increased the production of barley, the latter benefiting from colder and wetter weather conditions (Huijs et al. 2014).

These shocks can also enhance the effects of the three groups of mechanisms mentioned in Sect. 2.1 (population, class structure, and commercialization), for example, via manufacturing shares in the economy, pasture, demand for technology, and social organization. One link with population theories concerns the working of climate via a Malthusian mechanism (a downward shock in output leads to famine and, ultimately, a decrease in population) or a Boserupian (1965) mechanism (an increasing population density forces farmers to adopt more technological and agricultural innovation, causing economic growth). Likewise, Blom (2019) argues for the importance of social and class factors by claiming that climate change contributed to a shift from feudalism, in which farmers had to surrender part of their harvests previously sent to the lord to the free market, thus increasing transport costs. This process was strengthened by the diminishing influence of family relations and guilds, which in turn strengthened market-based cities. All these factors enhanced market-led growth. Indeed, Van Leeuwen and Philips (2021) find that in around 1500, transportation costs in Western Europe started to decline, removing the negative effect of city clustering on markets.

2.9 Technological Development

Malthusian development, social classes, the share of manufacturing, agrarian structure, and climate may explain (temporary) economic differences, but long-run development still depends on differences in labour productivity owing to technology and labour organization. According to Wu et al. (2019), such changes in technology started to accumulate in China in about 2000 BCE. Even though Europe and the Middle East lagged behind China in many respects (e.g. the power-driven spinning machine was invented in China about 500 years before its introduction in England), they also had their fair share of inventions.

The reasons behind the emergence of innovations in technology are highly contested. One reason might be the existence of cattle farming (see also Sect. 2.5), which existed in Europe but was imported to China only around the second millennium BCE and never reached the European level (Lv et al. 2017). Indeed, in Europe, somewhere around the first millennium BCE, pasture had probably spread relatively evenly over the countries. These cattle shares seem to have remained fairly constant since the first millennium BCE (Koepke and Baten 2008). For example, in north-west Iberia, mixed arable/pastoral farming existed during the Metal Ages (*c.* 750 BCE) and extended during the Roman period. Obviously, this varied by region. For example, owing to rising income and population, pasture increased in Scotland in 735 CE (Dumayne-Peaty 1999). A further increase in pasture occurred in the sixteenth century (Millman 1975).

Contrary to the situation in Europe, in China the levels of pasture remained low and collapsed even further around 1000 CE. The downward trend in pasture lasted from the point at which Emperor Qinshihuang (rule 221–210 BCE) conquered the six kingdoms and united them as one empire until the late East Han. During this period, around 220 BCE–900 CE, pasture experienced an obvious boom and gradually expanded from north-west to south-east. From the tenth century, compared with farming, the share of pasture in agriculture declined again (Wang 2001), and pastoral production mainly relied on north and south-west China (Han 1999; Wu 1997; Cheng 1992).

Second, just looking at the pasture is insufficient, as technologies might also enhance arable output. One way of dealing with this is by looking at pollen data. This method, though it can be used to generate an overview of rises and declines of agriculture over time, varies significantly by region, country, and underlying geography. Hence, while a long-run view is possible, a cross-section of levels is difficult to establish (e.g. Li et al. 2015; Deza-Araujo et al. 2020). Indeed, up to 750–900 CE, in all regions of Europe, the Middle East, and China, we witness a rise in arable farming combined with relatively prosperous pastureland. Only after about 750 CE do we witness a divergence between regions, with a stagnating and declining arable sector in Europe and the Middle East and a slowly rising one in China. This all changed in around 1100 with a decline in arable farming in the Middle East and China, with Europe moving into an upward trajectory (Mighall et al. 2006). This is arguably best indicated for Eastern Europe by Izdebski et al. (2016). Depending on the region, we witness stagnation in the periods 400–700 CE and 1000–1100, with a strong rise afterwards, mostly in rye and wheat production. Clearly, agricultural change must have had an effect, but so must climate (Sadori et al. 2016).

Third, irrespective of external factors such as climate, human and technological factors must have played a role in agricultural output as well. For example, without necessarily arguing for a connection, the introduction of cattle to China in the second millennium BCE occurred at exactly the same time as Wu et al. (2019) witness a rise in technology from its previous, rather stagnating, Neolithic phase. Yet other authors have claimed that technology was broadly available (Kremer 1993), and that there was a back and forth between China and Europe, with the two alternating in taking the lead. Consequently, taking this concept to its logical conclusion, it was just luck if Europe was leading at the time of the Industrial Revolution (Goody 1996). Similarly, other scholars have considered Europe as somehow just lucky to conquer much of the world, thus gaining a small but enduring advantage. Yet others have claimed that Europe had deeper advantages related to, for example, culture (Khan 1998), religion (Weber 1951), or warfare/external pressure owing to its fragmentation (Diamond 1997; Chan and Laffargue 2012).

2.10 Implementation of Technological Development

Directly or indirectly, most studies agree that the number of inventions depends on population size (Kremer 1993). Therefore, the isolation, population size, and population density of countries affect their number of inventions. But basically, with some delay, ideas were broadly available for European, Central Asian, and East Asian civilizations, a point made in much of the literature up to the twentieth century (e.g. Clark and Feenstra 2003).

The question of technological development is thus simplified to focus on why certain countries implemented technologies more than others. Various explanations, mostly institution-based, have been proposed. First, before the advent of fast travel, countries that were more isolated—defined by Ashraf et al. (2010) as the mean time it takes to travel from the capital of a country to each square kilometre of land on Earth—tended to lay greater emphasis on entrepreneurship, which would subsequently propel them to an economic lead (Ashraf et al. 2010). Using this model, Georgia was the least isolated country, with an average distance of 5.5 weeks from any capital, and Malaysia was the most isolated, at 12.1 weeks. The model was expanded for the post-1500 period by Özak (2018), who argues that countries far from the pre-industrial (e.g. 1000 CE) technological frontier have today developed the best systems of technological development and entrepreneurship. Indeed, entrepreneurship, the practical application of new innovations, increased in Europe from at least the twelfth century onwards. For example, Ten Raa et al. (2009) find that for sixteenth- and seventeenth-centuries Holland, alongside technology, it was entrepreneurship (which encouraged innovation via openness and new modes of trade) that contributed to economic growth and innovation. In China, however, it appears that regions with low entrepreneurship today also had low entrepreneurship in the past (Opper and Andersson 2019, 1184), thus suggesting that simply adding more investment is insufficient for creating economic growth (e.g. McCloskey 2010).

A second branch of the literature about technical implementation argues that this implementation depends on political fragmentation (see Appendix A, B, and C). As a basic assumption, one could argue that neither China nor the Roman Empire was immune to Cardwell's Law, that is, the view that a single economy will inevitably move towards technological stagnation because of the resistance of interest groups in that country (Mokyr 1994). In this context, it is argued that European political fragmentation after 900 CE led to more competition, and consequently to a context in which countries were always vying to take the lead in terms of inventions. Conversely, the involvement of government as an alternative to state competition, as witnessed in China over the long term, proved less successful in reaching the same levels of innovation (Mokyr 1990). This theory was echoed by Chan and Laffargue (2012), who claim that Chinese state involvement was driven by external (military) pressure. When this pressure eased after the Yuan dynasty, the number of innovations reduced swiftly. A similar argument is made by Rosenthal and Wong (2011), who argue that China's lack of military conflict reduced the amount of manufacturing that occurred in cities (see also Van der Wee 1988).

A third branch of literature looks at the inventors themselves, as this affects both the speed and level of implementation. Various groups have been claimed to stimulate the adoption of inventions. First, as pointed out by Terpstra (2020) in line with the previously mentioned literature, technological inventions in ancient China occurred mostly as a result of government implementation, while in the Roman Empire, technology stagnated. For example, in China, the inventor of the use of mulberry tree bark for paper was a government official (Mokyr 2002). Ge (2018) notes that 71.9% of classic monographs on agronomy in the Song dynasty were written by officials or retired officials. In comparison, the Roman Empire was characterized by a disdain for non-agricultural activities by the landed elite, something that was also true in China. Yet other arguments, such as emperors repressing inventions or the opposition of labourers whose skills became obsolete, seem exaggerated (Terpstra 2020). A second debate about inventors involves landowners versus small-scale peasants, with the first group argued to be dominant in China and the latter in England, at least in terms of the way in which innovations spread to family-owned farms (Kitsikopoulos 2000a). This debate can be linked to a third one about the presence of risk-sharing institutions (e.g. redistributive institutions, such as England's Poor Relief Act of 1601) in the two geographical contexts and their effect on individual-level risk behaviour (Greif et al. 2011). The main risk-sharing institutions were mainly lineage-based in pre-modern China and state-based in England.

Typically, lineage-based institutions were governed by the elders of the community, whose behaviour was risk-averse. As the process of creating new knowledge and productivity often involves risk-taking, the presence of this type of institution in China should be considered as a reactionary bastion against productivity-enhancing activities (Greif et al. 2011).

Irrespective of these three groups of theories (on isolation, political fragmentation, and inventors), what is almost universally accepted is that a thriving process of technology accumulation in China lasted until around the Yuan dynasty in the fourteenth century (Elvin 1973; Chan and Laffargue 2012), after which it stagnated. This was contrary to Europe, where the number of inventions began to grow in the early modern period (e.g. Fig. 2.2). Elvin (1973), in his high-level equilibrium trap thesis, argues that Chinese stagnation was caused first by what could be called the law of the handicap of a head start, which came into play once early economic developers accumulated so much investment in reasonably efficient technologies that it became unprofitable to spend significant amounts of money on replacing them with expensive but only slightly more efficient tools. Second, because of high production efficiency, consumption demand did not encourage newer technology either. Doubt may be cast on this argument, though, as various authors, admittedly for the period after the first millennium, have argued that increased consumption was related to growth. For example, Wang and Van Leeuwen (2021) find that consumption increased in Anhui, Shanxi, and Zhejiang from the 1730s to the 1850s, based on their analysis of household division inventories. Fang (1996) and Huang (2009) also describe an upward trend of consumption, especially in food, housing, garments, and luxury goods. Third, a shift from Taoism to Confucianism shifted the intellectual environment away from natural sciences and towards the social sciences. The most obvious example of this concerns the predominantly social content of the civil examination programme, in which talented people aimed to pass various exams in predominantly Confucian texts to gain access to a government position.

However, as pointed out by Landes (2006), and in general in models evaluating the "appropriateness" of a technology based on countries' unique characteristics (e.g. Atkinson and Stiglitz 1969; Basu and Weil 1998), the problem was not in generating inventions but in the failure to implement them, mainly outside agriculture. Since technology in agriculture continued to develop past the first millennium, it does not offer a sufficient explanation for declining growth rates. We return to this issue in Chap. 3.

2.11 Conclusion

In this chapter, we have witnessed that ancient economies differed little in per capita GDP from those in the early medieval world. Developments occurred for six reasons, however. First, given the predominantly Malthusian nature of ancient economies, drastic reductions or increases in population numbers could result in increases or decreases in GDP per capita. Second, social relations and class structure varied strongly among regions, thus influencing commercialization and technological change. Third, manufacturing, which in general has a higher per capita productivity than agriculture, might also cause differences in income. Fourth, the structure of agriculture may also affect income. For example, a higher share of pasture might reduce income expressed in calories but increase income in terms of monetary value. One might calculate for Italy, Byzantium, and Mesopotamia that the difference in per capita income is 45–47%, explained by agriculture and manufacturing.[19] Fifth, climate might affect productivity. Sixth, technological development and implementation played important roles in economic growth when Europe took over from East Asia in the early modern period and from Eastern Europe in Antiquity (see also Chap. 5).

References

Acemoglu D, Johnson S, Robinson JA (2005) The rise of Europe: Atlantic trade, institutional change, and economic growth. Am Econ Rev 95(3):546–579
Amemiya T (2007) Economy and economics of ancient Greece. Routledge, London and New York
Álvarez-Nogal C, Prados de la Escosura L (2013) The rise and fall of Spain (1270–1850). Econ Hist Rev 66(1):1–37
Anderson E (1988) The food of China. Yale University Press, New Haven
Ashraf Q, Galor O, Özak Ö (2010) Isolation and development. J Eur Econ Assoc 8(2/3):401–412
Atkinson AB, Stiglitz JE (1969) A new view of technological change. Econ J 79(315):573–578
Bassino J-P, Broadberry SN, Fukao K, Gupta B, Takashima M (2019) Japan and the great divergence, 730–1874. Explor Econ Hist 72:1–22. https://doi.org/10.1016/j.eeh.2018.09.002
Basu S, Weil DN (1998) Appropriate technology and growth. Quart J Econ 113(4):1025–1054. https://doi.org/10.1162/003355398555829
Baten J, Koepke N (2005) The biological standard of living in Europe during the last two millennia. Eur Rev Econ Hist 9(1):61–95. https://doi.org/10.1017/S1361491604001388
Bedford P (2007) The Persian near east. In: Scheidel W, Morris I, Saller RP (eds) The Cambridge economic history of the Greco-Roman world. Cambridge University Press, Cambridge, pp 302–330
Blaxland, B., & Dorey, F. (2018). Complex technology. Australian Museum. Retrieved from https://australian.museum/learn/science/human-evolution/complex-technology/
Blom P (2019) Nature's mutiny: how the Little Ice Age of the long seventeenth century transformed the West and shaped the present. Liveright.
Bokonyi S (1988) Animal breeding on the Danube. In: Whittaker CR (ed) Pastoral economies in classical antiquity. Cambridge University Press, Cambridge, pp 171–176
Boserup E (1965) The conditions of agricultural growth: The economics of agrarian change under population pressure. G. Allen and Unwin, London
Bray F (1984) Agriculture. In: Needham J (ed) Science and civilisation in China, Biology and biological technology, Part II, vol 6. Cambridge University Press, Cambridge

[19] For the sake of simplicity, let us assume that meat consumption in Italy was the same as in Byzantium. In that case, in the scenario that all agricultural output was grain, agricultural value added would have been 0.28 × 0.1 + (1–0.28) = 74.8%, hence 25.2% lower in Rome. Altogether, differences in manufacturing and pasturage can explain a 45% difference in per capita incomes. Taking $1400 for Italy and $736 for Babylon, the observed income differential, 47%, is very close to this.

Brenner R (1976) Agrarian class structure and economic development in pre-industrial Europe. Past & Present 70:30–75. http://www.jstor.org/stable/650345
Broadberry, S., & Campbell, B. (2009). GDP per capita in Europe, 1300–1850. Paper presented at the World Economic History Congress, Utrecht.
Broadberry S, Campbell B, Van Leeuwen B (2013) When did Britain industrialise? The sectoral distribution of the labour force and labour productivity in Britain, 1381–1851. Explor Econ Hist 50(1):16–27. https://doi.org/10.1016/j.eeh.2012.09.003
Broadberry S, Guan H, Li D (2021) China, Europe, and the great divergence: a restatement. J Econ Hist 81(1):1–17. https://doi.org/10.1017/S0022050721000292
Broadberry S, Campbell B, Klein A, Overton M, Van Leeuwen B (2015) British economic growth 1270–1870. Cambridge University Press, Cambridge. (it is not specified in the text which of the two is the right one).
Broadberry S, Guan H, Li D (2018) China, Europe, and the Great Divergence: A study in historical national accounting, 980–1850. J Econ Hist 78(4):955–1000. https://doi.org/10.1017/S0022050718000403
Buck JL (1937) Land utilization in China. Commercial Press, Shanghai
Büntgen U, Tegel W, Nicolussi K, McCormick M, Frank D, Trouet V, Kaplan JO, Herzig F, Heussner K-U, Wanner H, Luterbacher J, Esper J (2011) 2500 years of European climate variability and human susceptibility. Science 331(6017):578–582. https://doi.org/10.1126/science.1197175
Calabrese, M., & Van Leeuwen, B. (2023). Socio-economic characteristics as determinants in the job market: the case of Piedmont in Italy (1867–2005). Munich Personal RePEc Archive https://mpra.ub.uni-muenchen.de/119299/
Chan KS, Laffargue J-P (2012) Foreign threats, technological progress and the rise and decline of Imperial China. Pac Econ Rev 17(2):280–303. https://doi.org/10.1111/j.1468-0106.2012.00582.x
Cheng M (1992) 宋代地域经济 [Regional Economy of the Song Dynasty]. Henan University Press, Kaifeng
Clark G, Feenstra RC (2003) Technology in the great divergence. In: Bordo MD, Taylor AM, Williamson JG (eds) Globalization in historical perspective. University of Chicago Press, Chicago, pp 277–321. https://doi.org/10.7208/chicago/9780226066910.003.0009
Clarysse W, Thompson DJ (2006) Counting the people in Hellenistic Egypt. Cambridge University Press, Cambridge
Department of Chinese History, Renmin University of China (1958) 评尚钺同志关于明清社会经济结构的若干观点 (A review on some of Shangyue's opinions about the social and economic structure in Ming China). 历史研究 (Hist Res) 12:21–35
Deza-Araujo M, Morales-Molino C, Tinner W, Henne PD, Heitz C, Pezzatti GB, Hafner A, Conedera M (2020) A critical assessment of human-impact indices based on anthropogenic pollen indicators. Quat Sci Rev 236(106):291. https://doi.org/10.1016/j.quascirev.2020.106291
Diamond J (1997) Guns, germs, and steel: The fates of human societies. W.W. Norton, New York, NY
Dumayne-Peaty L (1999) Late Holocene impact on the vegetation of southeastern Scotland: a pollen diagram from Dogden Moss, Berwickshire. Rev Paleobot Palynol 105:121–141. https://doi.org/10.1016/S0034-6667(98)00053-0
Elvin M (1973) The pattern of the Chinese past: a social and economic interpretation. Stanford University Press, Stanford
Erdkamp P (2016) Economic growth in the Roman Mediterranean world: An early good-bye to Malthus? Explor Econ Hist 60:1–20. https://doi.org/10.1016/j.eeh.2015.11.002
Fang X (1996) 清代江南农民的消费 (Consumption of peasants in Lower Yangtze Region in the Qing Dynasty). 中国经济史研究 (Res Chin Econ Hist) 3:91–98
Finley MI (1973) *The ancient economy*. University of California Press, Berkeley
Földvári P, Van Leeuwen B (2012) Comparing per capita income in the Hellenistic world: The case of Mesopotamia. Rev Income Wealth 58(3):555–568

Frank AG (1998) ReORIENT: Global economy in the Asian age. University of California Press, Berkeley
Fukuyama F (1992) The end of history and the last man. The Free Press, New York
Fu YL (1982) 明清封建各阶级的社会构成 (The Structure of Social Classes in Ming and Qing China). 中国社会经济史研究 (J Chin Soc Econ Hist) 1:7–20
Ge XH (2018) (葛小寒) A study of ancient agricultural book in Ming Dynasty: text and knowledge (明代农书研究) (Doctoral thesis). Nanjing Agricultural University, Nanjing
Geertz C (1963) Agricultural involution: the processes of ecological change in Indonesia. University of California Press, Berkeley and Los Angeles, CA
Geraghty R (2007) The impact of globalization on the Roman Empire, 200 BC – AD 100. J Econ Hist 67(4):1036–1061
Goldsmith RW (1984) An estimate of the size and structure of the national product of the early Roman Empire. Rev Income Wealth 30(3):263–288
Goody J (1996) The east in the west. Cambridge University Press, New York
Greif, A., Iyigun, M., & Sasson, D. (2011). Risk, institutions and growth: why England and not China? IZA Discussion Papers (No. 5598). Institute for the Study of Labor (IZA), Bonn. https://nbn-resolving.de/urn:nbn:de:101:1-201104134225
Guo Y, Zhang Z, Van Leeuwen B, Xu Y (2019) A view of the occupational structure in Imperial and Republican China (1640–1952). Aust Econ Hist Rev 59(2):134–158
Hamilakis Y, Jones AM (2017) Archaeology and assemblage. Cambridge Archaeol J 27(1):77–84
Han M (1999) 辽金农业地理 [Agricultural Geography of the Liao and Jin Dynasties]. Shehuikexue Wenxian Press, Beijing
Hatcher J, Bailey M (2011) Modelling the middle ages: the history and theory of England's economic development. Oxford University Press. Online edition. Oxford Academic, Oxford. https://doi.org/10.1093/acprof:oso/9780199244126.001.0001
Hibbs DA, Olsson O (2004) Geography, biogeography, and why some countries are rich and others are poor. Proc Natl Acad Sci USA 101(10):3715–3720. https://doi.org/10.1073/pnas.0305531101
Hofmeester, K., Lucassen, J., Lucassen, L., Stapel, R., & Zijdeman, R. (2016). The Global Collaboratory on the History of Labour Relations, 1500–2000: Background, set-up, taxonomy, and applications [Data set]. IISH Data Collection. https://hdl.handle.net/10622/4OGRAD, IISH Data Collection, V1.
Huang JB (2009) 民生与家计:清初至民国时期江南居民的消费 [People's Living Standard and Livelihood: Consumption of Residents in Lower Yangtze Region from Early Qing to Republican China]. Fudan University Press, Shanghai
Huijs J, Van Leeuwen B, Pirngruber R (2014) Climate, war and economic development: The case of second-century BC Babylon. In: van Leeuwen B, van der Spek R, van Zanden JL (eds) A history of market performance: from ancient Babylonia to the modern world. Routledge, pp 128–148
IISH Global Collab of Labour Relations (2015) https://datasets.iisg.amsterdam/dataverse/labour-relations-doc;jsessionid=6ce1dc0c65676b0ec98add490f5a?q=&types=datasets%3Afiles&page=1&sort=dateSort&order=asc
Izdebski A, Koloch G, Słoczyński T, Tycner M (2016) On the use of palynological data in economic history: New methods and an application to agricultural output in Central Europe, 0–2000 AD. Explor Econ Hist 59:17–39. https://doi.org/10.1016/j.eeh.2015.09.003
Jursa, M. (2010). Aspects of the economic history of Babylonia in the first millennium BC: economic geography, economic mentalities, agriculture, the use of money and the problem of economic growth. AOAT series.
Khan G (1998) Indian muslim perceptions of the West during the eighteenth century. Oxford University Press, Karachi
Kitsikopoulos H (2000a) Standards of living and capital formation in pre-plague England: a peasant budget model. Econ Hist Rev 53(2):237–261. http://www.jstor.org/stable/2598697

Kitsikopoulos H (2000b) Technological change in medieval England: a critique of the Neo-Malthusian argument. Proc Am Philos Soc 144(4):397–449. http://www.jstor.org/stable/1515619

Koepke N, Baten J (2005) The biological standard of living in Europe during the last two millennia. Eur Rev Econ Hist 9(1): 61–95. http://www.jstor.org/stable/41378413

Koepke N, Baten J (2008) Agricultural specialization and height in ancient and medieval Europe. Explor Econ Hist 45(2):127–146. https://doi.org/10.1016/j.eeh.2007.11.002

Kominsky. (1956). Evolution of feudal rent and Peut-on considerer le XIVth et le XVth siècles comme l'époque de l'écadence de l'économie européene. In *Studi in onore di Armando Sapori, i* (Milan, 1957).

Kremer M (1993) Population growth and technological change: One million B.C. to 1990. Quart J Econ 108(4):681–716. https://doi.org/10.2307/2118405

Lai YE (2002) The structure of traditional clan society and the route selection of rural industrialization (传统宗族社会结构与农村工业化道路抉择). Southeast Acad Res (东南学术) 4:100–106

Landes DS (2006) Why Europe and the West? Why not China? J Econ Perspect 20(2):3–22. https://doi.org/10.1257/jep.20.2.3

Langbroek, M. (2004). Out of Africa: An investigation into the earliest occupation of the Old World. https://doi.org/10.30861/9781841716046. Accessed from https://www.researchgate.net/figure/map-of-the-Movius-line-showing-the-geographic-dichotomy-between-exclusively-mode-1_fig5_257943701

Langway CC Jr, Oeschger H, Dansgaard W (eds) (1985) Greenland ice core: Geophysics, geochemistry and environment (Geophysical Monographs), vol 33. American Geophysical Union

Li BZ (2000) Early industrialization in the Yangzi Delta, 1550–1850 (江南的早期工业化1550-1850年). Social Sciences Academic Press (China), Beijing

Li BZ (2003) Economic history of Jiangnan from multiple perspectives, 1250–1850 (多视角看江南经济史1250-1850). SDX Joint Publishing Company, Beijing

Li BZ (2007) Agricultural development in the Yangtze Delta, 1620–1850 (江南农业的发展1620-1850). Shanghai Guji Press, Shanghai

Li M, Xu Q, Zhang S, Li Y, Dind W, Li J (2015) Indicator pollen taxa of human-induced and natural vegetation in Northern China. The Holocene 25(4):686–701. https://doi.org/10.1177/0959683614565955

Lo Cascio E, Malanima P (2009) GDP in pre-modern agrarian economies (1–1820 AD): a revision of the estimates. *Rivista di Storia Economica* XXV(3):387–415

Lucassen J (2021) The story of work: A new history of humankind. Yale University Press, New Haven and London

Lv P, Brunson K, Yuan J, Li Z (2017) Zooarchaeological and genetic evidence for the origins of domestic cattle in ancient China. Asian Perspect 56:92–120. https://doi.org/10.1353/asi.2017.0003

Lycett SJ, Norton CJ (2010) A demographic model for Palaeolithic technological evolution: the case of East Asia and the Movius Line. Quat Int 211(1–2):55–65

Malthus TR (1999) An Essay on the Principle of Population. Edited with an introduction by Geoffrey Gilbert. Oxford: Oxford University Press

Maddison A (2007) Contours of the world economy, 1-2030 AD. Essays in macro-economic history. Oxford University Press, Oxford

Malanima P (2011) The long decline of a leading economy: GDP in central and northern Italy, 1300–1913. Eur Rev Econ Hist 15(2):169–219

Malanima P (2018) Italy in the Renaissance: a leading economy in the European context, 1350–1550. Econ Hist Rev 71:3–30

McCloskey D (2010) Bourgeois dignity: why economics can't explain the modern world. University of Chicago Press, Chicago. Malthus, An Essay on the Principle of Population, in Oxford Worlds Classics reprint

McCormick M (2002) Origins of the European economy: Communications and commerce, AD 300-900. Cambridge University Press, Cambridge
Mighall TM, Martinez Cortizas A, Biester H, Turner SE (2006) Proxy climate and vegetation changes during the last five millennia in NW Iberia: Pollen and non-pollen palynomorph data from two ombrotrophic peat bogs in the northwestern Iberian Peninsula. Rev Paleobot Palynol 141:203–223
Milanovic B (2006) An estimate of average income and inequality in Byzantium around year 1000. Rev Income Wealth 52(3):449–470
Millman RN (1975) The making of the Scottish landscape. Batsford, London
Mokyr J (1990) The lever of riches: Technological creativity and economic progress. Oxford University Press, Oxford
Mokyr J (1994) Cardwell's law and the political economy of technological progress. Res Policy 23(5):561–574
Mokyr J (2002) The gifts of Athena: Historical origins of the knowledge economy. Princeton University Press, Princeton
Needham J (1954) Science and civilization in China, vol 1. Cambridge University Press, Cambridge
Needham J (1986) Introduction. In: Temple R (ed) China: land of discovery and invention. Wellingborough, Patrick-Stephens
Opper S, Andersson FNG (2019) Are entrepreneurial cultures stable over time? Historical evidence from China. Asia Pac J Manag 36(4):1165–1192
Özak Ö (2018) Distance to the pre-industrial technological frontier and economic development. J Econ Growth 23:175–221
Pomeranz K (2000) The great divergence: China, Europe, and the making of the modern world economy. Princeton University Press, Princeton and Oxford
Robinson WI (2011) Globalization and the sociology of Immanuel Wallerstein: a critical appraisal. Int Sociol 26(6):723–745
Rosenthal JL, Wong RB (2011) Before and beyond divergence: the politics of economic change in China and Europe. Harvard University Press, Cambridge, MA
Sadori L, Giraudi C, Masi A, Magny M, Ortu E, Zanchetta G, Izdebski A (2016) Climate, environment and society in southern Italy during the last 2000 years. A review of the environmental, historical and archaeological evidence. Quat Sci Rev 136:173–188
Saller RP (2002) Framing the debate over growth in the ancient economy. In: Scheidel W, Von Reden S (eds) The ancient economy. Routledge, New York, pp 251–269
Semaw S, Rogers MJ, Simpson SW, Levin NE, Quade J, Dunbar N, McIntosh WC, Cáceres I, Stinchcomb GE, Holloway RL, Brown FH, Butler RF, Stout D, Everett M (2020) Co-occurrence of Acheulian and Oldowan artifacts with Homo erectus cranial fossils from Gona, Afar, Ethiopia. Sci Adv 6(10):eaaw4694. https://doi.org/10.1126/sciadv.aaw4694
Scheidel W (2010) Real wages in early economies: Evidence for living standards from 1800 BCE to 1300 CE. J Econ Soc Hist Orient 53:425–462. Data downloaded from http://www.stanford.edu/~scheidel/NumKey.htm
Shang C (1999) The structure of social classes in Ming China (试论明代的社会阶级结构). Qingming Luncong (清明论丛) 1:317–333
Solar, P. (2021). China, Europe, and the Great Divergence: Further concerns about the historical GDP estimates for China. Working Papers 0217. European Historical Economics Society (EHES).
Sołtysiak, A. (2010). Paleopathology in ancient Mesopotamia: a short overview. British Association for Near Eastern Archaeology Annual Conference, Birmingham, 2007.
Temin P (2002) Price behavior in ancient Babylon. Explor Econ Hist 39(1):46–60
Temin P (2013) The Roman market economy. Princeton University Press, Princeton
Ten Raa, T., Mohnen, P., Van Zanden, J. L., & Van Leeuwen, B. (2009). Invention, entrepreneurship and prosperity: the Dutch Golden Age. Unpublished paper. Available at SSRN: https://ssrn.com/abstract=1528208 or https://doi.org/10.2139/ssrn.1528208

Terpstra T (2020) Roman technological progress in comparative context: The Roman Empire, Medieval Europe and Imperial China. Explor Econ Hist 75(101):300
Tisdell, C. A., & Svizzero, S. (2015). The Malthusian trap and development in pre-industrial societies: a view differing from the standard one. Social Economics, Policy and Development Working Papers 197551, University of Queensland, School of Economics.
Van der Wee H (1988) Industry dynamics and the process of urbanization-deurbanization in the Low Countries from the late Middle Ages to the eighteenth century. In: van der Wee H (ed) The rise and decline of cities in Italy and the Netherlands. University of Leuven Press, Leuven, pp 307–381
Van der Spek RJ, Van Leeuwen B, Van Zanden JL (eds) (2018) Money, currency and crisis: In search of trust, 2000 BC to AD 2000. Routledge, Oxon and New York
Van Leeuwen, R. Pirngruber, and J. Li (2013). The standard of living in ancient societies: a comparison between the Han Empire, the Roman Empire and Babylonia, No 45, Working Papers from Utrecht University, Centre for Global Economic History.
Van Leeuwen B, Philips R (2021) Market performance in the grain market of late medieval Western Europe (ca. 1300–1650). In: Moreno Garcia JC (ed) Markets and exchanges in pre-modern and traditional societies. Oxbow Books, pp 155–169
Van Zanden JL, Van Leeuwen B (2012) Persistent but not consistent: The growth of national income in Holland 1347–1807. Explor Econ Hist 49(2):119–130
Von Reden S (2008) Price fluctuations in Babylonia, Egypt and the Mediterranean world, third to first centuries BC. Paper presented at: Too much data? Generalizations and model-building in ancient economic history on the basis of large corpora of documentary evidence. Vienna 17–19 July 2008
Wang L (2001) Changes in animal husbandry in northern China during the medieval period (中古时期北方畜牧业的变动). Lishi Yanjiu (历史研究) 2001(1):33–47
Wang M, Van Leeuwen B (2021) Fenjiashu: economic development in the Chinese countryside based on household division inventories, ca. 1750–1910. Aust Econ Hist Rev 61(3):252–272
Ward-Perkins B (2005) The fall of Rome and the end of civilization. Oxford University Press, Oxford
Weber M (1951) In: Gerth HH (ed) The religion of China., Trans. , New York, Macmillan
Wick L, Lemcke G, Sturm M (2003) Evidence of late glacial and holocene climatic change and human impact in eastern Anatolia: high-resolution pollen, charcoal, isotopic and geochemical records from the laminated sediments of Lake Van, Turkey. The Holocene 13(5):665–675
Wittwer-Backofen U (1983) Einige neubabylonische Skelette aus Uruk. Baghdader Mitteilungen 14:71–94
Wu H (1997) Agricultural geography of the Yuan Dynasty (元代农业地理). Xi'an Ditu Press, Xi'an
Wu L, Dutta R, Levin DK, Papageorge NW (2018) Entertaining malthus: bread, circuses and economic growth. Econ Inq 56(1):358–380
Wu S, Wei Y, Head B, Zhao Y, Hanna S (2019) The development of ancient Chinese agricultural and water technology from 8000 BC to 1911 AD. Palgrave Commun 5:77. https://doi.org/10.1057/s41599-019-0282-1
Zhao YF (2021) Power and wealth: An observation of the social structural changes during the Ming and Qing era (权力与财富——对明清社会结构变化的一种侧面观察). Res Chin Econ Hist (中国经济史研究) 1:6–17
Zheng JL, Xia X, Fang X, Hao Q, Ge Q, Li B (2014) How climate change impacted the collapse of the Ming dynasty. Clim Change 127(2):169–182

Chapter 3
Further Medieval Economic Divergence: Technology Adoption in a Predominantly Agricultural World

Abstract In this chapter, we move on from the relative stability of the period between the ancient world and the medieval and early modern world. As Chap. 2 indicates, even though this period witnessed several factors that caused both positive and negative growth in income per capita, none of these led to sustained economic growth (the Malthusian pattern dominated). Yet there are many factors that could enhance the unsustainable growth shocks. Initially, an important role was played mostly by agriculture, although this did not lead to sustained growth. We examine in this chapter how technological inventions emerged and how they were implemented. This relates to, for example, cheaper capital and a higher demand for labour-saving technologies in Western Europe than in China. Even though pressure for labour-saving technologies was therefore clearly higher in England, the economic sectors in which technological change occurred prior to 1900, water control, planting methods, draught animals, seed selection, and human capital, were of roughly equal importance in China and England.

3.1 Introduction

As noted in Chap. 2, Malthusian growth, the share of manufacturing in income, social systems, agricultural structure, climate, and the increasing use of technologies all had the potential to (temporarily) affect the level of ancient and medieval per capita income. But how did this lead to long-run—or even sustained—growth, if at all?

Before turning to growth theories, a first answer to this question can be provided by taking a closer look at how China, Russia, and Europe grew economically over time. This can be done either by looking at local growth or alternatively by comparing regions, such as China, Central Eurasia, and Western Europe. Looking at gross domestic product (GDP) per capita, as mentioned in Chap. 2, ancient income differed little before 1000 CE. In China, per capita income stagnated between 1000 and 1500 (e.g. Solar 2021a). In medieval Europe, while a rise in per capita income has

B. Van Leeuwen et al., *Innovation and Economic Development in Eurasia, 500 BCE-Present*, Frontiers in Economic History,
https://doi.org/10.1007/978-3-031-97043-6_3

been estimated between 1000 and 1500 (e.g. Van Zanden 2005), Western Europe was by and large stagnant from the fifteenth century until the end of the seventeenth century, with the exclusion of Italy between the fourteenth and fifteenth centuries (Malanima 2018). So even though there was a slight divergence in the fourteenth century between Europe and China, it was only around 1600–1700 that the "Great Divergence" between Western Europe and China took place. To some extent this can be considered as consistent with the findings of Solar (2021b, forthcoming; see also Maddison 1998), who, using revised estimates from Broadberry et al. (2018), identified a "Great Crossing" somewhere between the tenth and the fourteenth centuries, when the most urbanized areas of what is now northern Italy overtook China in GDP per capita. Until about 1600–1700, figures stagnated for both Europe and China, before the former moved further ahead during the Great Divergence.

We can use estimates of human stature as a testing ground for these theories. In Table 3.1, we indeed see a decline in human height for China somewhere between 800 and 1150, followed by stagnation, and a further decline around 1700–1800, suggesting reduced well-being. Compared with a roughly stable height development over time in Europe (Baten and Koepke 2005), stature, like GDP per capita, seems to indicate a divergence in the Middle Ages, followed by stagnation, and a Great Divergence somewhere around 1700–1800.

Answering the question of how divergence was able to occur during the Great Crossing, some of the factors mentioned in Chap. 2 must have directly or indirectly boosted the supply (number of inventions) and direction (whether labour- or capital-intensive) of new technologies. There are various theories that explain non-sustained growth (see also Chap. 2). Yet for a long period, such as the Great Crossing, there must be another interaction that extended the duration of what was otherwise short-term growth. Unified growth theories (Chap. 4) are the best-known explanation for the transition from one-off growth spikes in historical times to sustained growth

Table 3.1 Height development in China, 100 BCE–1900 CE

	China		Yellow river	Yangtze		
Year	Men	Women	Men	Women	Men	Women
−100			167.0	151.0	161.0	150.0
0	169.5	159.1	165.3	159.2		
800	167.0	158.4				
1050			163.8	163.0		
1150	164.5	156.2				
1750			165.3	159.6		
1800			165.7	151.3		
1850	165.0					
1900	163.3					

Source: Baten et al. (2010), Hou (2013), Peng (2015), Sun and Hong (2015), and Zhou (2017)

today. Yet these are often dependent on threshold levels, as they are applied to income, production factors (such as human capital), and exogenous technology growth. These levels of production and technology may increase, even before the threshold level for modern growth is reached. This increase in growth factors in the grey area between traditional growth (Chap. 2) and modern economic growth (Chap. 4) is what we explore further here.

We begin by looking at an example of how technological inventions emerged and how they were implemented (Sect. 3.2). Initially, this mainly had an effect on population and agriculture for the simple reason that most people were engaged in agricultural work. Therefore, we compare this development with a case study of a population loss shock, the Black Death in the fourteenth century (Sect. 3.3) and end with a brief conclusion (Sect. 3.4).

3.2 Agricultural Technology and Labour Productivity before the Agricultural Revolution

In the same way as the rise in demand for capital-saving technologies did not preclude labour-saving technologies in China, an increased demand for labour-saving technologies did not necessarily lead to mechanization in England. Yet as Clark (2016) finds, in England land rents dropped significantly in the fourteenth century, with real wages going up (Fig. 3.4)—a trend that occurred in north-western Europe more generally (Pamuk 2007), thus suggesting the development of labour-saving technologies, including increases in farm size, which in turn required more technology for effective cultivation of the land. But even though there was a demand for labour-saving technologies in England,[1] we agree with Clark that labour productivity in agriculture only increased to a limited extent between 1200 and 1500 (see also Kitsikopoulos 2000a).

This limited increase took place mainly because of a lack of or under-utilization of technology. Indeed, as Bray (1994, 201) points out:

> [e]ver since the beginning of the "Agricultural Revolution" in the seventeenth century, farmers in Northwest Europe had cherished the hope of substituting machines for at least part of their labour force, which, as we mentioned earlier, was relatively expensive during this period of conflicting claims for labour. Many unsuccessful attempts were made to produce agricultural machines in the seventeenth and eighteenth centuries, and the need for such machines was felt more acutely as time passed.

Only by the eighteenth century had knowledge developed enough to create labour-saving technology and bring the Agricultural Revolution to its peak. While temporal and regional variations in ecological, institutional, and commercial features resulted in differences in technological diffusion and applicability, and

[1] We nevertheless reject Postan's view of static technology for the Middle Ages (Postan 1973; Kitsikopoulos 2000b).

therefore productivity levels (Kitsikopoulos 2000b), this does not mean that no development occurred before the eighteenth century (Chambers and Mingay 1966). Indeed, we might distinguish five main forms of early agricultural technical development.

First, the replacement of fallow land with turnips and clover increased intensive agricultural production as it fertilized the land. As pointed out by Broadberry et al. (2015a, b), in England in 1250, 42% of tilled land was fallow, declining to 38% in 1500. But the real decline occurred after 1500, with fallow land making up 11% by 1800. Similar developments occurred in China, with inventions in irrigation and new varieties that allowed double crop systems.

Second, there is a debate over the role of farm size. Although it has been argued that farm sizes increased in England, in China, it is generally claimed that they decreased. It is intuitively attractive to argue that the increase in England led to more wealth accumulation and hence to a higher demand for technology, while the reverse is true for China: decreases in farm size coincided with a decreasing demand for technology. This was partly because of the agricultural structure (less labour-intensive dry wheat/pasture versus more labour-intensive wet rice) and partly because of the inheritance system (single inheritance in north-western Europe, where one person inherited the complete farm versus equal inheritance in China, where each child inherited a part of the farm). Nonetheless, in the case of England, the importance of rising size seems to be refuted by Allen (1992), while the negative effect of the decline in farm size on economic growth in China is questioned by Wang and Van Leeuwen (2021).

Third, there was the development of infrastructure and a national market: while in England in around 1600 a market radius was on average 10 miles, by 1800 the market had become by and large national (Overton 1996). Indeed, Clark (2015) finds few trends towards market integration before 1500, but from then on, development occurred. Yet this does not imply that markets in Britain were much more developed than those in other countries. Shiue and Keller (2007) find that while market performance in Britain was higher than in Yangtze China, this difference was limited.

Fourth, selective breeding was relatively important in England (Walton 1986): even though it mostly developed from the eighteenth century onward, as shown in Table 3.2, growth also occurred between the fourteenth and sixteenth centuries. It is important to stress that this was not confined to animals; new grain varieties also increased yields. The situation was similar in China, where one well-known example is the selective breeding of goldfish; this started in the Song dynasty and was refined during the Ming and Qing dynasties (Barnes 2020). This example indicates the lack of focus on working animals, although the introduction of new, early ripening rice varieties occurred (Barker 2011), sometimes stimulated by the emperor (Ho 1956).

Fifth, as pointed out by Bray (1994), it was not until the eighteenth century that there was sufficient knowledge to develop the machines required for capital-intensive agriculture in England. In China, by contrast, agricultural technologies accelerated slowly between 2000 BCE and about 1400 CE but decelerated during the

Table 3.2 Yield of pork per pig in England (lb), 1300–1870

	Pork per pig (lb.)
1300–1309	64.1
1400–1409	66.6
1500–1509	69.3
1600–1609	72.0
1700–1709	86.6
1800–1809	112.7
1861–1870	132.4

Note: 1500–1509 is the mean of 1450–59 and 1550–59

Source: Broadberry et al. (2015a, b)

Ming and Qing dynasties (Wu et al. 2019). This may have been caused by a series of downward population shocks, which enhanced the agricultural technologies used by big landlords while simultaneously reducing the number of those landlords. Only in New China (1948–present) have we witnessed a significant increase in capital-intensive agricultural technology, although this has been partly brought about by a forced policy, given that these new technologies initially reduced output per worker.

The main finding of the comparison given here is that medieval and early modern technological development was broadly similar in China, Russia, and Western Europe. Just as in England, water control, planting methods, draught animals, seed selection, and human capital were important in, for example, China (Chang 2000). Yet capital pressure remained stronger in England than in China. In terms of the final outcome, this is comparable with the findings of Allen (2009) and Goldstone (2003), who essentially claim that technological progress in China rose until the eighteenth and nineteenth centuries, leading to an increase in farm labourer incomes but a decline in household income.

Yet although pressure for new capital in the West was already relatively higher than in China from the fourteenth century, relatively fast agricultural change in terms of increased mechanization only happened from the eighteenth century in England, when knowledge had developed sufficiently to meet the demand for new technology. In China, these new technologies were only introduced in the twentieth century, partly under pressure from the government and partly since specialization in the West was increasingly in capital-intensive sectors, thereby leaving less capital-intensive agriculture—albeit more capital-intensive than the previous rice growing—to developing economies. Consequently, labour productivity gain in China was initially small (Fig. 3.1), although land productivity increased to some extent (Fig. 3.2). In Central Eurasia (mostly European Russia), the long-term trend suggested by Strumilin (1966) was rising, although his guesstimate prior to the nineteenth century was based on rather scarce evidence. Our estimate based on the findings from the recent literature show that from the eighteenth to the early twentieth centuries productivity in agriculture took the form of an inverted U-shaped curve: it increased in the first half of the eighteenth century, following cultivation of

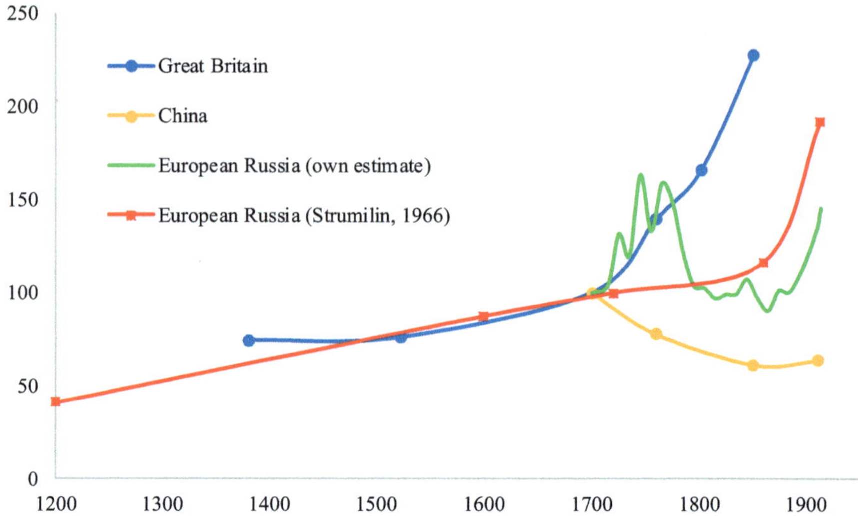

Fig. 3.1 Output per labourer in agriculture in Great Britain, China, and European Russia (1700 = 100), 1381–1914. *Note:* To estimate employment in Russian agriculture per total population of households, we use the evidence from MSP (1858, 2), which gives a coefficient equal to 0.64. *Source:* Great Britain: Broadberry et al. (2013); China: Guo et al. (2019); European Russia: Strumilin (1966, 170); (own estimate): Agricultural output and population: 1690s–1880s: Broadberry and Korchmina (2024), 1885–1913: Cheremukhin et al. (2017); Population (self)-employed in agriculture in rural and urban areas: Mironov (2018, vol. 1. 822, 826); Share of urban population: Vodarsky (1977, 152, 192) and Mironov (2018, vol. 1, 839, vol. 3, 752)

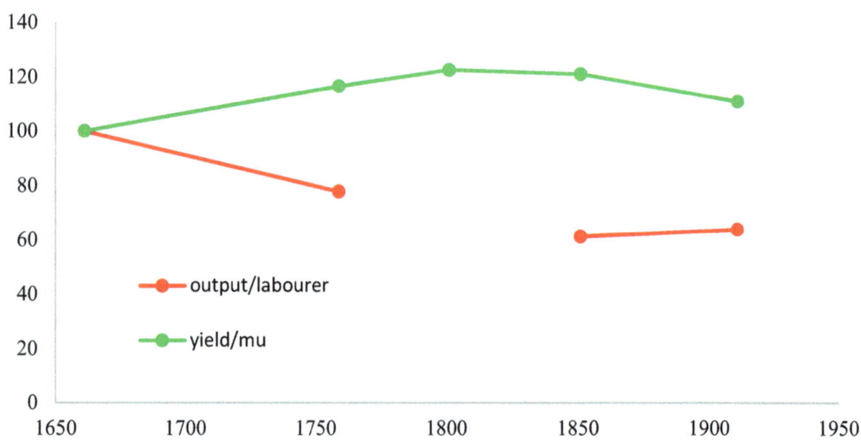

Fig. 3.2 Output per labourer in agriculture (1661 = 100) versus land productivity in jin/mu (1661 = 100) in China. *Source:* Xu et al. (2017) and Guo et al. (2019)

fertile black soils in the southern regions (Broadberry and Korchmina 2024, 1004–1006), then went down, similar to China and contrary to England. However, from the mid-1860s, productivity growth resumed modestly in Russia until the First World War, after land productivity started to increase from the 1840s (Fig. 3.3) and serfdom was abolished in 1861. However, although land productivity reached its previous peak of the mid-eighteenth century by the end of the Imperial period, labour productivity failed to do so.

Before the start of modern growth in European Russia (1880s), yield to seed ratio fluctuated within the range of 3.1–4.6. European Russia can be placed roughly between China and England, as land productivity based on grain harvests (Fig. 3.3) started to increase from the 1840s,[2] although it remained under serfdom—and modern economic growth did not begin for another 40–45 years.[3] Increases in land productivity coincided with periods of reform aimed at improving state-owned peasants' conditions and activities, implemented under the supervision of Pavel Dmitrievich Kiselyov (Andreeva, 2019, 27–45, 85–102).[4] Arguably, the reforms could therefore be said to have contributed to the emerging trend of rising land productivity. This became steeper in the late nineteenth and early twentieth centuries, at the start of the period of modern economic growth (Fig. 3.3). However, agricultural employment declined slowly before the 1917 Revolution. Only after the Second World War did land productivity increase rapidly—despite the failure to catch up with Western levels, as shown in Leonard (2011, 258)—while agricultural employment had been exhibiting the opposite trend since the 1920s.

So, although land productivity rose, this does not necessarily imply that new technology led to savings in capital, land, or labour. To look at these questions, in Table 3.3 we present the cost shares in agricultural production of land, labour, and capital at current prices, with decadal averages from serf emancipation to the development of the Stolypin reforms,[5] as estimated by Leonard (2011). We see that Russian agriculture was and remained labour-intensive, as was not uncommon for the developing world, while the cost share of labour somewhat decreased. As such, it was more comparable with China than England.

---

[2] This picture is clearest in the series by Ibragimova and Leonard presented in Leonard (2011, 289).

[3] The data were presented as a chart but not as a table.

[4] Pavel Dmitrievich Kiselyov (https://en.wikipedia.org/wiki/Pavel_Kiselyov), a staunch opponent of serfdom, headed the Ministry of State Properties, with multiple local branches, for 18 years (1837–1854). The organization of the ministry largely reflected his initiative to improve the administration of state-owned peasants, which accounted for about a third of the total population. He and his proponents introduced reforms involving the establishment of new mechanisms for the government administration of private serfs after their gradual emancipation. There is historiographical debate, however, over the extent to which these bureaucratic activities paved the way for the subsequent emancipation of the serfs in 1861.

[5] Started in 1906 by the then prime minister, Pyotr Arkadyevich Stolypin (https://en.wikipedia.org/wiki/Pyotr_Stolypin). He claimed that the transition period should be about 20 years. These reforms were aimed at abolishing institutional constraints to labour mobility, namely the peasant commune, stimulating private land ownership and encouraging migration from the overpopulated west to eastern provinces (Shelokhaev 2014).

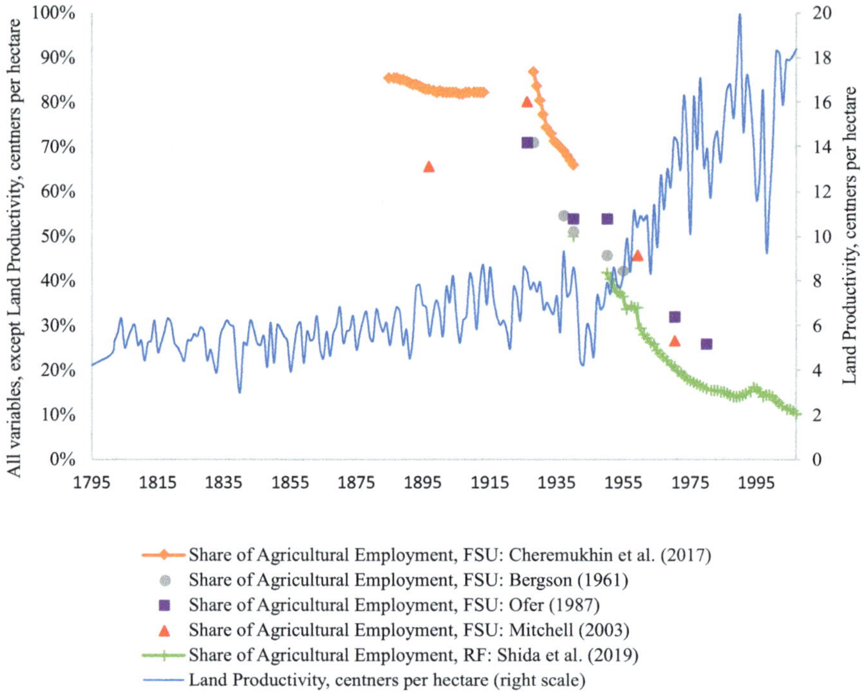

Fig. 3.3 Land productivity and share of employment in agriculture in Central Eurasia, c. 1795–2010. *Note:* Land productivity: 1795–1912: Russian Empire; 1913–1990: FSU; 1991–2007: Russian Federation. *Source:* Land productivity, yield to seed ratio: 1655–1795: Indova (1970, 146–148, 151–152); 1795–1912: Rastyannikov and Deryugina (2009, 67–68); Land productivity, centners per hectare: Rastyannikov and Deryugina (2009, 124–125); Share of employment in agriculture: Cheremukhin et al. (2017); Bergson (1961); Ofer (1987); Mitchell (2003) based on Bairoch et al. (1968), ILO (n.d.); Shida et al. (2019)

Table 3.3 Input cost shares in agriculture for 50 provinces of European Russia, 1861–1911 (%)

Decade/year	Capital share	Land share	Labour share	
1860s	13	5	82	100
1870s	11	5	83	100
1880s	11	6	83	100
1890s	11	10	78	100
1900s	13	13	73	100
1911	12	18	70	100

Source: Leonard (2011, 240–241)

3.3 A Case Study of a Large External Shock: The Black Death

As pointed out in Chap. 2, various factors can be seen as leading to one-off rises in per capita GDP, although none seems to have led to sustained growth. In addition, as pointed out in this chapter, any technological developments that did occur in

China were not just capital saving; they also occurred mostly through large clan-managed farms, while in Western Europe, tenants used labour-saving technologies. But how did this limited technological development hold up under GDP per capita increases caused by large drops in population, such as during the Black Death?

The importance of the Black Death varied by region; there was extremely high mortality in England and much lower mortality in Russia and China. Indeed, the following text from the Chronicles of the priory of the English town of Rochester, which dates back to 1348, the year in which the Great Plague broke out, gives a vivid description of events in England:

> [...]A great mortality [...] destroyed more than a third of the men, women and children. As a result, there was such a shortage of servants, craftsmen, and workmen, and of agricultural workers and labourers, that a great many of lords and people, although well-endowed with goods and possessions, were yet without service and attendance. [...] As remarked above, such a shortage of workers ensued that the humble turned up their noses at employment, and could scarcely be persuaded to serve the eminent unless for triple wages. Instead, because of the doles handed out at funerals, those who once had to work now began to have time for idleness, thieving and other outrages, and thus the poor and servile have been enriched and the rich impoverished. As a result, churchmen, knights and other worthies have been forced to thresh their corn, plough the land and perform every other unskilled task if they are to make their own bread.

(from *Historia Roffensis*, chronicle of the cathedral priory of Rochester, 1348, British Library (n.d.))[6]

Similar evidence, albeit with somewhat lower mortality, can be found for Russia.[7] Indeed, there is some evidence of several waves of a "Black Death" in Russia (including the areas under the Golden Horde and Lithuania) from the mid-fourteenth to the late fifteenth centuries (e.g. Urlanis 1941; Langer 1975). Frequent cases of high mortality in Russia caused by diseases and natural calamities (drought, floods, storms, frost) are also summarized in Kahan (1968). His catalogue contains 19 cases of epidemics in the fourteenth century—more than in any other century (Kahan 1968, 365).

The population losses in Russia caused by the Black Death (which mainly affected densely populated areas from Russia and Eastern Europe) are assessed to have been somewhat moderate in scale compared with Britain, while being roughly equivalent to that of non-British Western Europe. Langer (1975, 62) claims that Russia lost at least 25% of its population, without specifying whether this occurred as a result of a one-off event or was the cumulative effect of multiple smaller shocks. The latter is more likely, as he recognized that pre-plague levels (i.e. those of the mid-fourteenth century) were only restored by 1500. However, the negative effects of the plague were exacerbated by Russia's slow recovery from the Mongol invasions.

---

[6] British Library Online, http://www.bl.uk/learning/timeline/item126557.html (accessed 2023). See also Horrox (1994, p. 70).

[7] Much of the evidence on Russia in this section is from Didenko (2023).

Nefedov (2002) citing Urlanis (1941, 347) concludes that in Russia, given that its population density was lower than that of Europe, the first wave of the Black Death in the mid-fourteenth century did not lead to mortality exceeding 5% of the population, which could be restored within three or 4 years. Urlanis also argues that in rural areas mortality was much lower than in urban areas, for the same reason.

However, for a subsequent wave of the Black Death, Nefedov (2002) and Turchin and Nefedov (2009, 240–241) assess the drop in population more pessimistically, by a factor of two, based on archaeological findings of leather shoe remnants and birch scrolls in Novgorod from the first half of the fifteenth century. In north-western Russia (Novgorod and Pskov, which were highly developed trade centres with Western Europe), the drop in population was caused by famines and epidemics, while in the central region (Moscow, the Upper Volga basin), the main causes were civil war and external invasions, with famine and disease as secondary consequences of sociopolitical instability (Nefedov 2002).

The Chronicle of Novgorod reported two outbreaks of plague in 1352–1360, three outbreaks in 1389–1406, and four outbreaks in 1417–1424. The most disastrous was probably the one in 1417:

> […] The same summer and winter there was a fearful plague among the people in Novgorod, and in Ladoga, in Russa, Porkhov, Pskov, Tver, Dmitrov, and in Torzhok, and throughout their districts and villages. And how can I relate the fearful and terrible misery that there was during the whole plague? What grief the living had for the dead, for the deaths increased so in towns and villages that the living had barely time to make the dead tidy for burial; so many died every day, that they had not time to bury them; and many houses were closed unoccupied. First of all it would hit one as if with a lance, choking, and then a swelling would appear, or spitting of blood with shivering, and fire would burn one in all the joints of the body; and then the illness would overwhelm one; and many after lying in that illness died.

(from *The Chronicle of Novgorod*, 1417, Michell et al. 1914).[8]

The Pskov 3rd Chronicle reported somewhat more frequent outbreaks of plague (three in 1352–1370, four in 1390–1407, two in 1425–1426, and six in 1442–1487). Some of the outbreaks were the same as those reported in *The Chronicle of Novgorod* and related either to Pskov or Novgorod. *The Pskov 3rd Chronicle* provided more evidence than Novgorod's on the scale of the fatalities, especially during the first outbreak (1352), for which it gave the most detailed report:

> […] And so it was in those days: because of the great numbers of the dying, priests could not bring the dead from homes one at a time, so they gave orders that each person bring his dead to the churchyard. In one night thirty or more corpses might accumulate to be buried from a single church. They all received a communal funeral service with hymns, but each man, woman, or child was given individual absolution, and then three to five bodies were buried in a single grave. That is how it was at every church. There was nowhere to bury the

[8] The Chronicle of Novgorod, 1016–1471. Translated from the Russian by R. Michell and N. Forbes, with an introduction by C.R. Beazley, and an account of the text by A.A. Shakhmatov/ Camden Third Series. Vol. XXV. London: Offices of the Royal Historical Society, 1914, p. 186, http://faculty.washington.edu/dwaugh/rus/texts/MF1914.pdf.

> dead, for all the graveyards were filled, so large tracts outside of the churches and graveyards were dug up and the dead were buried in them.
>
> [...]
>
> No matter what class of people the sickness affected, be it rulers, the rich, common people, or even the poor, it was terribly deadly: over half died quickly, very few survived, and the rest perished.

(from *The Pskov 3rd Chronicle*, 1417, Savignac (2016)).[9]

These chronicles provide insufficient information on wages to draw conclusions on their dynamics. So we turn to the research literature, which offers other evidence.

Skilled labour was in short supply even before the plague, owing to slow recovery after the Mongol invasion, and much of the scarcity was increasingly addressed by the forced labour of peasants and a rise in urban slavery (Langer 1975, 62–63). The plague facilitated the expansion of monasteries, most of which were founded not in towns and cities but in forest hinterlands. But the growth in rural monastic estates was accompanied by an expansion of their urban branches. These were generally exempt from princely administration and taxation. The monasteries virtually dominated local labour markets for craftsmen and traders by attracting them to their tax-exempt urban enclaves, and they could also purchase slaves. Other non-ecclesiastical craftsmen were therefore placed in a disadvantageous position.

Turchin and Nefedov (2009, 242, 246) find that during the 1520s an unskilled worker in Moscow received a relatively high level of wages (11 kg of rye and oats per day, versus 3.6 kg in 1568), approximately the same in calories as that earned by unskilled workers in Germany in 1490–1510. As to land rents, in Central Russia during the beginning of the sixteenth century, a peasant family had to pay the lord with one-sixth of the crops from the total cultivated land.

This demographic cycle concluded in the 1560s with the wars in the west (Livonia, Poland-Lithuania, Sweden) and in the south (Crimean Khanate), intra-elite terror by Ivan IV the Terrible, and excessive extraction from households. A series of famines and plague outbreaks resulted in population decline in the 1570s, which was not assessed nationwide but was locally in the order of a third, 40%, or even half or more. Nefedov (2003, 68–70) finds that thereafter real wages increased by a factor of 2.5 for unskilled and 2 for skilled workers (carpenters, tailors). Land rents declined by a factor of three on gentry estate lands and a factor of two on state-owned lands, and state extraction from peasant households declined three- or fourfold.

A drop in population proportionally to England occurred in Russia in the early seventeenth century after the "great famine" of 1601–1603, subsequent violent revolts, external military conflicts, and state failure (the "Time of Troubles"). Unfortunately, the quality of Russia's population statistics is very poor prior to 1700; therefore, only indirect expert assessments are available. Turchin and Nefedov

[9] The Pskov 3rd Chronicle. Edited, translated, and annotated by D. Savignac. second ed. Crofton: Beowulf & Sons, 2016, https://sites.google.com/site/pskovrelease3/

(2009, p. 256) estimate that the famine of 1601–1603, caused by major natural calamities and a lack of food reserves, killed almost a third of the population.

As an overall result of these two demographic catastrophes over a 100-year period from the mid-sixteenth to the mid-seventeenth centuries, the Russian population is estimated to have fallen by approximately half, with the region around the capital Moscow experiencing the worst devastation, declining by a factor of 8 or 10 (Turchin and Nefedov 2009, 261). Such heavy losses were mostly due not to the famines and diseases themselves but to the subsequent violence of the civil war and external interference.

Some quantitative evidence on the consequences of the "great famine" and other "troubles" for the Russian labour market are presented in Turchin and Nefedov (2009, 258). They find that servant wages in monasteries increased by 50% compared with pre-famine years. Indirectly, Strumilin (1966, 36–39, 50–53, 56, 62) assesses the level of wages of artisans and hired manufacturing workers as historically high compared with both Kievan Rus' and the second half of the nineteenth century. Representing the official Marxist historiography that presumed the trend of worsening living conditions and increasing extraction, he notes that in the seventeenth century even rural labour was paid relatively highly, primarily because it was scarce.

The scholars cited here support the argument that it was pandemics, famines, or invasions, resulting in a substantial drop in population, that led to an increase in relative wages (also through grain price deflation), narrowing of skills, and a reduction in land rents in fifteenth-, sixteenth-, and seventeenth-century Russia. These findings were based on published monastery records and the conclusions of earlier scholars in the 1920s and 1930s (notably Boris Grekov and Mikhail Tikhomirov).

Somewhat similar evidence can be found in Hellie (1999, 413–473) on early seventeenth-century Russia just after the Time of Troubles. He expresses wages in silver rubles and does not apply any price index to the slightly rising (in most cases) nominal wages, although he is aware of inflation during the seventeenth century. Yet even without the reduction in the silver weight of coins by a third in 1636 and the failed attempt to issue copper coinage in the 1660s, prices were subject to inflation as the relative value of silver decreased during the seventeenth century. If the price index from Strumilin (1966, 76, 168–169) is applied, we clearly observe that wages were significantly higher after the Time of Troubles than they had become by the mid-seventeenth century, let alone closer to the end of the century. Skill premia (carpenters and smiths versus labourers and peasants) somewhat narrowed throughout the period.

Some data on wages are compared with grain prices and converted to grain in Nefedov (2011, vol. 2, 26–29). They are also compared with the prices in Western Europe at the start of the demographic cycle (early sixteenth century). He finds that wages in Russia were relatively high after the Time of Troubles. Furthermore, real wages increased from the 1640s to the 1690s. This was not unexpected because of colonization processes, which extended the resource frontier. These processes developed both in a southerly direction, opening access to fertile black soils, and towards Siberia—with its frigid climate but low indigenous population density and abundant natural resources. This increased labour scarcity in the centre of the country and stimulated the elite to impose restrictions on labour force mobility. Serfdom in Russia was finally instituted in the *Muscovite Law Code* (*Sobornoe Ulozhenie*) of 1649.[10]

Turchin and Nefedov (2009, 254–255) claim that the root cause of the continuing instability, which eventually led to state collapse and civil war, was an acute shortage of labour, economic distress among the elites, and the financial crisis of the state. This led the nobility to employ coercive methods to maintain their revenues. While in England and France these attempts failed, in Poland, Prussia, and Russia, the elites were successful in enserfing peasants. This supports Goldstone's neo-Malthusian demographic-structural theory (1991).[11]

As this theory claims, the state capacity cycle is caused by the impact of population movements on the economic, political, and social structures of traditional agrarian societies. Such movements represent centuries-long cyclical oscillations. The key driver here is that the population normally tends to grow faster than the resource carrying capacity. The latter is basically a function of technological level. Population growth in excess of land productivity gains has a fundamental effect on society's structures. The typical changes accompanying population growth are higher rents and land prices, increasing fragmentation of peasant holdings or high numbers of landless peasants, and increased migration of landless peasants to cities, that is, urbanization (Turchin and Nefedov 2009, 7).

Russian medieval history shows that demographic shocks may either alleviate intra-elite warfare (first half of the fifteenth century) or contribute to intra-elite competition and state failure (late sixteenth–early seventeenth centuries). In turn, socio-political instability negatively affected population dynamics by diminishing birth rates and increasing death rates, and by undermining productive institutions.

Even though in our third region, China, outbreaks of the Black Death occurred frequently during the fourteenth century, mortality remained even lower than in Russia. As calculated by Cao (1995), there were 31 records of outbreaks in 21 different years from 1297 to 1362 noted in *The History of the Yuan*, around 60% of these occurring in northern China. During 1344–1362, outbreaks occurred in 13 of the 19 years. Based on an analysis of the start of the epidemic, the environment, and the medical description of symptoms, Cao believed the epidemic was what would later be called the Black Death. During the same period, there were also frequent famines. The combined effect of famines and the Black Death made it very difficult for ordinary people to earn a living, leading to frequent rebellions and finally to the

---

[10] The Muscovite Law Code (Ulozhenie) of 1649. Translated and edited by R. Hellie. Irvine, CA: Charles Schlacks, 1988, chap. 11, http://individual.utoronto.ca/aksmith/resources/ulozh.html.

[11] Demographic-Structural Theory seeks to explain the underlying causes of political and social unrest by using a dynamic framework. Under the Malthusian regime of economic growth (a nearly constant resource carrying capacity), it is mainly demographic factors (such as population growth) and structural factors (such as social and economic inequality) that can create conditions that increase the likelihood of instability, such as revolutions, civil wars, and social unrest. This theory was revitalized by the Cliodynamics school of quantitative history (e.g. Turchin 2003).

end of Mongol rule over China in 1368. It was estimated that during the Yuan dynasty, the population peaked at approximately 80–90 million around 1340–1350. After that, a sharp decline followed. It is not easy to separate all the factors that resulted in population decrease, but scholars who have tried to estimate population statistics, such as Wu (2000) and Zhao and Xie (1988), believe that famines and wars had much more impact than the Black Death. First, despite the occurrence of the Black Death, the decline in population did not occur until the last years of the Yuan dynasty. Second, as argued by Han (2015), the Black Death was not a new epidemic for the region, and therefore China had experience dealing with it. In addition, the centralized governance system was very helpful in containing the epidemic's spread. As a result, the Black Death was less widespread than in Europe. There are records that note high population losses caused by the Black Death, but each time these happened in one or just a handful of provinces, or even in a smaller region. For example, in 1331, the Black Death outbreak in Hengzhou 衡州 Prefecture (Hunan province) led to the loss of 90% of the local population. In 1358, there were around 200,000 refugees from Shandong, Henan, and Hebei who died from the Black Death in Beijing (Cao 1995).

The negative population shock was thus higher in England than in Russia or China. Nevertheless, it affected the market rate of both land and labour. In China, it reduced income from land rents, but, given the abundant population, it hardly affected wages. The effect was therefore at most a small decline in the land rent to wage ratio. In Russia wages rose, just as they did in England. However, landowners retained power and limited the influence of labourers in the second serfdom. This limited the decline in the land rent to wage ratio. In England, falling land rents and rising wages reduced the land rent to wage ratio considerably, resulting in more labour-saving technologies.

This explains why small-scale farming became increasingly capital-intensive in Western Europe after the Black Death, while this did not occur in China or Russia. Indeed, in England, wages remained high (Fig. 3.4). But this did not apply in all

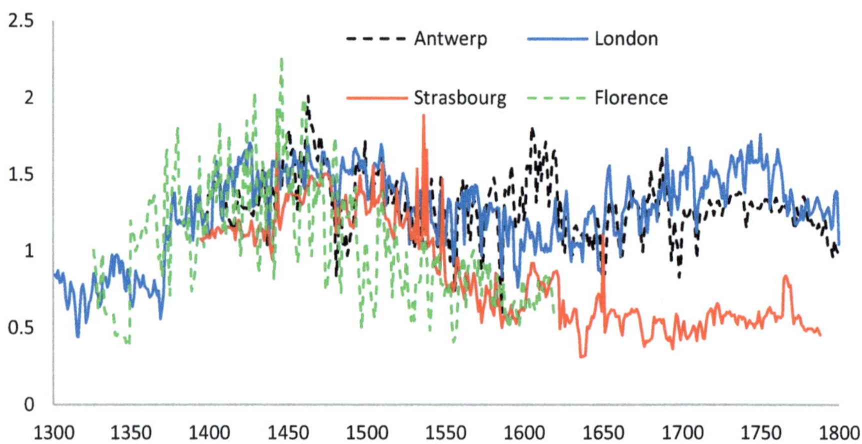

Fig. 3.4 Subsistence ratio in Europe, 1300–1800. *Source:* Allen (2001)

Western countries, an example being Italy, since there were also five counter-effects to wage growth.

First, if the state (and the nobility) were strong enough to increase taxation, as in Eastern Europe, it could reduce the benefits accruing from higher wages for peasants. In England, attempts in this direction were also made. For example, in 1351, the Statute of Labourers was adopted, forcing labourers to work for pre-Black Death wages. Furthermore, at the end of the fourteenth century, three consecutive poll taxes were levied. This led to peasant revolts, which, although suppressed, resulted in the Statute being withdrawn and the poll tax abolished. Taxation was increased in China in the same way, but here it was relatively successful. For example, the Yuan and late Ming dynasties increased taxation massively for the purpose of raising armies (Wang 1936). In addition, taxation led to a reduction in the profitability of new technologies, for example, a reduction in the profits of Chinese watermills. This shows how taxation can erode the effect of a loss in population and prevent tenants from adopting new technologies (e.g. Bray 1994, 55; Campbell 2009).

Second, since in China technology was mainly introduced by demesnes, and since technologies stemming from demesnes were not influenced by the Black Death, there were few additional incentives to increase technologies. Indeed, with high prices for land and draught animals, the cost of holding this type of livestock might have been even bigger than the benefits they brought in tilling the land. This might explain the rapid drop in GDP per capita in China after the Black Death to its pre-Black Death level, contrary to north-western Europe (Fig. 3.5).

Third, on average, the population drop led to an increase in farm size in Western Europe (Bray 1994, 200), while in China, land size became smaller and labour intensity became higher (Bray 1994, 170).

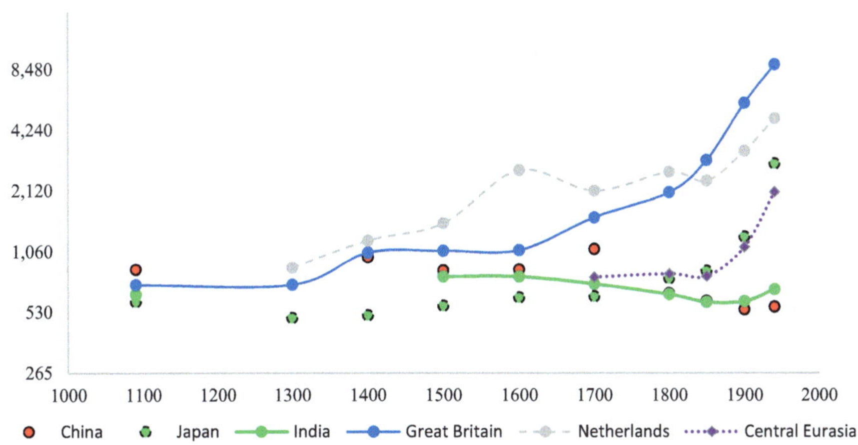

Fig. 3.5 GDP per capita in Intl' $ (in 1990 prices) in selected countries, c. 1100–1940. *Source:* Maddison (2007); Broadberry et al. (2018); Bolt and Van Zanden (2020); for Central Eurasia within the borders of the Russian (Muscovite) Tsardom, Russian Empire, and USSR: 1690s–1880s: Broadberry and Korchmina (2024); 1890s–1920s: Bolt and Van Zanden (2020); 1930s–1940s: Didenko et al. (2013); 1950s–2010s: Bolt and Van Zanden (2020)

3.4 Conclusion

In this chapter, we have moved on from the relative stability of the ancient world to the changing growth dynamics in the medieval world. As pointed out in Chap. 2, even though the ancient world had several possibilities for positive and negative growth in income per capita, none of these, by definition, led to sustained economic growth. Yet there were many factors that were able to enhance existing non-sustained growth shocks. One such approach was human capital accumulation, which most theories suggest leads to economic growth. Unified growth theories offer an explanation for such growth in human capital via reduced fertility rates owing to positive economic shocks, which in turn can lead to an extension in existing short-run growth periods (Chap. 4). Yet other mostly agricultural factors that increased output, albeit without leading to sustained growth, also played a role.

We find that it was primarily the incentive to create new technologies that drove what was mainly agricultural development. This was enhanced by a considerable number of labour-saving technologies in England. Obviously, these were initially mostly focused on agricultural technology. Yet the main conclusion is that available technological development was broadly similar in China and Western Europe. Just as in England, water control, planting methods, draught animals, seed selection, and human capital were important (Chang 2000). Yet capital pressure remained stronger in England than in China (Fig. 3.5).

Fourth, as mentioned earlier, in England, this combination of factors led to increased pressure for capital-saving inventions, which were introduced in the eighteenth and nineteenth centuries when knowledge had increased to sufficient levels to respond to this demand for labour-saving technology. For China, the pressure was more for land-saving technologies. Yet this does not necessarily imply that only land-saving technologies were possible: some technologies were both land- and labour-saving at the same time. Furthermore, the cost of capital-saving technologies might have decreased over time, making them accessible to China or Russia. In cases where capital costs were high compared with human costs, more capital-intensive invention was implemented in China. One such example concerns water-raising equipment (Bray 1994, 54).

In a fifth and final case, government pressure might stimulate capital investment. For example, Huang (1990, 129) points out that in "the first three decades of post-revolutionary rural China, [...] income per farm person stagnated side by side with vigorous agricultural modernization (tractor plowing, electrified pumping, chemical fertilizers, scientific seed selection, and the like) and urban development [...]".

References

Allen R (1992) Enclosure and the yeoman: The agricultural development of the South Midlands, 1450–1850. Clarendon Press, Oxford

Allen R (2001) The Great Divergence in European wages and prices from the middle ages tot he First World War. Explor Econ Hist 38:411–447

Allen R (2009) Agricultural productivity and rural incomes in England and the Yangtze Delta, c. 1620-c. 1820. Econ Hist Rev 62(3):525–550. http://www.jstor.org/stable/20542958. Accessed 28 Aug 2021

Andreeva TV (2019) На дальних подступах к Великой реформе: Крестьянские вопрос в России в царствование Николая I [The distant approaches to the Great Reform: The peasant question in Russia in the reign of Nicholas I]. Историческая иллюстрация [Historical Demonstration], St. Petersburg

Bairoch, P., Deldycke, T., Gelders, H., & Limbor, J. M. (1968). The working population and its structure. L'Institut de Sociologie, Université de Bruxelles.

Barker R (2011) The origin and spread of early-ripening Champa rice: its impact on Song Dynasty China. Rice 4:184–186. https://doi.org/10.1007/s12284-011-9071-7

Barnes S (2020) Inventory of the world in 100 animals. Simon & Schuster, London

Baten J, Koepke N (2005) The biological standard of living in Europe during the last two millennia. Eur Rev Econ Hist 9(1):61–95. https://doi.org/10.1017/S1361491604001388

Baten J, Ma D, Morgan S, Wang Q (2010) Evolution of living standards and human capital in China in the 18–20th centuries: Evidence from real wages, age-heaping, and anthropometrics. Explor Econ Hist 47(1):82–97. https://doi.org/10.1016/j.eeh.2009.05.002

Bergson A (1961) Real national income of Soviet Russia since 1928. Harvard University Press, Cambridge, MA

Bolt, J., & Van Zanden, J. L. (2020). Maddison Project Database, version 2020. Maddison style estimates of the evolution of the world economy: a new 2020 update.

Bray F (1994) The rice economies: Technology and development in Asian societies. University of California Press, Berkeley, Los Angeles, London

British Library (n.d.) Historia roffensis. British Library Online, http://www.bl.uk/learning/timeline/item126557.html.

Broadberry S, Korchmina E (2024) Catching-up and falling behind: Russian economic growth, 1960s–1880s. J Econ Hist 84(4):997–1028. https://doi.org/10.1017/s0022050724000287

Broadberry S, Campbell B, Van Leeuwen B (2013) When did Britain industrialise? The sectoral distribution of the labour force and labour productivity in Britain, 1381–1851. Explor Econ Hist 50(1):16–27. https://doi.org/10.1016/j.eeh.2012.09.003

Broadberry S, Campbell B, Klein A, Overton M, Van Leeuwen B (2015a) British economic growth 1270–1870. Cambridge University Press, Cambridge. (it is not specified in the text which of the two is the right one)

Broadberry S, Custodis J, Gupta B (2015b) India and the great divergence: an Anglo-Indian comparison of GDP per capita, 1600–1871. Explor Econ Hist 55:58–75. https://doi.org/10.1016/j.eeh.2014.04.003

Broadberry S, Guan H, Li D (2018) China, Europe, and the Great Divergence: A study in historical national accounting, 980–1850. J Econ Hist 78(4):955–1000

Campbell B (2009) Factor markets in England before the Black Death. Cont Change 24(1):79–106. https://doi.org/10.1017/S0268416008007058

Cao S (1995) Geographical environment and infectious diseases during the Song and Yuan dynasties (地理环境与宋元时代的传染病). Lishi Dili (历史地理), vol 12. Shanghai Renmin, Shanghai, pp 183–192

Chambers JD, Mingay GE (1966) The agricultural revolution, 1750–1880. Batsford, London

Chang T-T (2000) Rice, economic and biological importance. In: Kiple KF, Ornelas KC (eds) The Cambridge world history of food. Cambridge University Press, Cambridge, pp 132–133

Cheremukhin A, Golosov M, Guriev S, Tsyvinski A (2017) The industrialization and economic development of Russia through the lens of a neoclassical growth model. Rev Econ Stud 84(2):613–649. https://doi.org/10.1093/restud/rdw026

Clark G (2015) Markets before economic growth: The grain market of medieval England. Cliometrica 9(3):265–287. https://doi.org/10.1007/s11698-014-0118-x

Clark G (2016) Microbes and markets: Was the Black Death an economic revolution? J Demogr Econ 82(2):139–165. https://doi.org/10.1017/dem.2016.5

Didenko DV (2023) How demographic shocks affected the production-factor income and the institutional path of the Russian pre-industrial economy. Russ Peasant Stud 8(2):6–20. https://doi.org/10.22394/2500-1809-2023-8-2-6-20
Didenko D, Földvári P, Van Leeuwen B (2013) The spread of human capital in the former Soviet Union area in a comparative perspective: Exploring a new dataset. J Eurasian Stud 4(2):123–135. https://doi.org/10.1016/j.euras.2013.03.002. (Supplementary data retrieved from https://ars.els-cdn.com/content/image/1-s2.0-S1879366513000122-mmc1.zip, accessed via https://www.sciencedirect.com/science/article/pii/S1879366513000122)
Goldstone JA (1991) Revolution and rebellion in the early modern world. University of California Press, Berkeley and Los Angeles
Goldstone, J. A. (2003). Feeding the people, starving the state: China's agricultural revolution of the 17th/18th centuries. Paper prepared for a conference in London, September 2003.
Guo Y, Zhang Z, Van Leeuwen B, Xu Y (2019) A view of the occupational structure in Imperial and Republican China (1640–1952). Aust Econ Hist Rev 59(2):134–158
Han Y (2015) The spread and prevention of plagues in the Song Dynasty (宋代瘟疫的流行与防治). Commercial Press, Beijing
Hellie R (ed) (1988) The Muscovite Law Code (Ulozhenie) of 1649. Charles Schlacks, Irvine. Transl., ed. by R. Hellie. http://individual.utoronto.ca/aksmith/resources/ulozh.html.
Hellie R (1999) The Economy and Material Culture of Russia, 1600–1725. University of Chicago Press, Chicago. Dataset by Peter Lindert, 15 February 2006. https://gpih.ucdavis.edu/Datafilelist.htm
Ho P-T (1956) Early-ripening rice in Chinese history. Econ Hist Rev 9(2):200–218. https://doi.org/10.2307/2592433
Horrox R (ed) (1994) The Black death. Manchester University Press. Horrox, R. (Ed. & Trans.)
Hou, K. (2013). The research on the human skeletons from the Ming and Qing Dynasties tombs excavated in the new campuses of universities in Yuci, Shanxi. Doctoral dissertation, Jilin University.
Huang PCC (1990) The peasant family and rural development in the Yangzi Delta, 1350–1988. Stanford University Press, Stanford
ILO (n.d.). International Labour Organization. Yearbook of Labour Statistics. Geneva.
Indova EI (1970) Урожаи в центральной России за 150 лет (вторая половина XVII-XVIII в.) [Harvest in Central Russia for 150 years (second half of the 17th to the eighteenth century)]. In: Ежегодник по аграрной истории Восточной Европы за 1965 [Yearbook on agrarian history of Eastern Europe 1965]. Academy of Sciences of the USSR, Moscow, pp 141–155
Kahan A (1968) Natural calamities and their effect upon the food supply in Russia (an introduction to a catalogue). Jahrbücher für Geschichte Osteuropas, Neue Folge 16(3):353–377
Kitsikopoulos H (2000a) Standards of living and capital formation in pre-plague England: a peasant budget model. Econ Hist Rev 53(2):237–261. http://www.jstor.org/stable/2598697
Kitsikopoulos H (2000b) Technological change in medieval England: a critique of the Neo-Malthusian argument. Proc Am Phil Soc USA 144(4):397–449. http://www.jstor.org/stable/1515619
Langer LN (1975) The Black Death in Russia: its effects upon urban labor. Russ Hist 2(1):53–67
Leonard CS (2011) Agrarian Reform in Russia: The Road from Serfdom. Cambridge University Press
Maddison A (1998) Chinese economic performance in the long run. Organization for Economic Cooperation and Development (OECD), Paris
Maddison A (2007) Contours of the world economy, 1–2030 AD. Essays in macro-economic history. Oxford University Press, Oxford
Malanima P (2018) Italy in the renaissance: a leading economy in the European context, 1350–1550. Econ Hist Rev 71:3–30
Michell R, Forbes N, Beazley CR, Shakhmatov AA (eds) (1914) The Chronicle of Novgorod, 1016–1471, vol XXV. Offices of the Royal Historical Society, London. Transl. by R. Michell

and N. Forbes, with an introduction by C. R. Beazley, and an account by A. A. Shakhmatov. Camden Third Series. http://faculty.washington.edu/dwaugh/rus/texts/MF1914.pdf.
Mironov BN (2018) Российская империя: от традиции к модерну. [The Russian Empire: From Tradition to Modernity], vol 1–3), 2nd edn. Dmitrii Bulanin, St. Petersburg
Mitchell B (2003) International historical statistics: Europe. Palgrave Macmillan, Basingstoke
MSP (1858) Материалы для статистики России, собираемые по ведомству государственных имуществ [The data for Russia's statistics collected by the Ministry of the State Properties], vol 1, St. Petersburg
Nefedov SA (2002) О демографических циклах в истории средневековой России [On the demographic cycles in the history of medieval Russia]. Klio 3:193–203
Nefedov SA (2003) О возможности и применении структурно-демографическоы теории при изучении истории России XVI века [On the feasibility of applying the demographic-structural theory to the study of Russian history during the sixteenth century]. Otechestvennaya Istoriya 5:63–72
Nefedov, S. A. (2010–2011). История России. Факторныи анализ [Russia's History. Factor Analysis] (Vols. 1–2). Moscow: Territoriia Budushchego Publ. House.
Ofer G (1987) Soviet economic growth: 1928–1985. Journal of Economic Literature 25(4):1767–1833
Overton M (1996) Agricultural revolution in England: The transformation of the agrarian economy 1500–1850. Cambridge University Press, Cambridge
Pamuk Ş (2007) The Black Death and the origins of the 'Great Divergence' across Europe, 1300–1600. Eur Rev Econ Hist 11(3):289–317
Peng W (2015) A textual research of the height of Chinese people in the Qin-Han period (秦汉人身高考察). J Chin Hum 2015(6):20–44
Postan MM (1973) The medieval economy and society. University of California Press, Berkeley
Rastyannikov VG, Deryugina IV (2009) Урожайность хлебов в России, 1795–2007 [Grain crop productivity in Russia, 1795–2007]. Институт востоковедения РАН [Institute of Oriental Studies of the Russian Academy of Sciences], Moscow
Savignac D (ed) (2016) The Pskov 3rd Chronicle, 2nd edn. Beowulf & Sons, Crofton. Ed., transl., annot. by D. Savignac. https://www.academia.edu/28622167/
Shelokhaev VV (2014) The Stolypin variant of Russian modernization. Russ Stud Hist 53(2):29–55. https://doi.org/10.1080/10611428.2016.1229962
Shida Y, Kumo K, Nakamura Y (2019) Labor. In: Kuboniwa M et al (eds) Russian economic development over three centuries: new data and inferences. Palgrave Macmillan, Singapore, pp 105–132
Shiue C, Keller W (2007) Markets in China and Europe on the eve of the Industrial Revolution. Am Econ Rev 97(4):1189–1216
Solar P (2021a) China's GDP: Some corrections and the way forward. J Econ Hist:1–15. https://doi.org/10.1017/S0022050721000309
Solar, P. (2021b). China, Europe, and the Great Divergence: further concerns about the historical GDP estimates for China. Working Papers 0217. European Historical Economics Society (EHES).
Strumilin SG (1966) Очерки экономической истории России и СССР [Essays on Economic History of Russia and the USSR]. Наука [The Science], Moscow
Sun L, Hong Z (2015) A study of human statures of skeletons found in Han, Tang and Song dynasty tombs, Zhengzhou area. Acta Anthropologica Sinica 34(3):377–389
Turchin P (2003) Historical dynamics: why states rise and fall. Princeton University Press, Princeton, NJ
Turchin P, Nefedov S (2009) Secular cycles. Princeton University Press, Princeton, NJ
Urlanis BT (1941) Rost naseleniia v Evrope: Opyt ischisleniia [Growth of Population in Europe: An Estimation]. OGIZ—GOSPOLITIZDAT, Moscow

Van Zanden JL (2005) De timmerman, de boekdrukker en het ontstaan van de Europese kenniseconomie. Over de prijs en het aanbod van kennis voor de Industriële Revolutie. Tijdschrift voor Sociale en Economische Geschiedenis/Low Countr J Soc Econ Hist 2(1):105–120
Vodarsky IE (1977) Население России в конце XVII—начале XVIII века [Russia's population in the late 17th—early 18th centuries]. Наука [The Science], Moscow
Walton JR (1986) Pedigree and the national cattle herd circa 1750–1950. Agric Hist Rev 1986:149–170
Wang Y-C (1936) The rise of land tax and the fall of dynasties in Chinese history. Pac Aff 9(2):201–220. https://doi.org/10.2307/2751407
Wang M, Van Leeuwen B (2021) Fenjiashu: Economic development in the Chinese countryside based on household division inventories, ca. 1750–1910. Aust Econ Hist Rev 61(3):252–272
Wu S (2000) History of China's population: Liao, Song, Jin, and Yuan dynasties (中国人口史: 辽宋金元时期). Fudan University Press, Shanghai
Wu S, Wei Y, Head B, Zhao Y, Hanna S (2019) The development of ancient Chinese agricultural and water technology from 8000 BC to 1911 AD. Palgrave Commun 5:77. https://doi.org/10.1057/s41599-019-0282-1
Xu Y, Shi Z, Van Leeuwen B, Ni Y, Zhang Z, Ma Y (2017) Chinese National Income, ca. 1661–1933. Aust Econ Hist Rev 57(3):368–393
Zhao W, Xie S (1988) History of China's population (中国人口史). Renmin, Beijing
Zhou Y (2017) Research on stature of ancient groups in Beijing district. J Tianjin Norm Univ (Natural Science Edition) 2017(3):62–64

Chapter 4
The Change Towards Modern Growth: Proximate Causes

Abstract In this chapter, we consider which causes of growth (e.g. human capital, taxation, colonies) were the main factors in moving to modern (sustained) economic growth. The proximate factors are of a Smithian (commercialization) and Northian (institutional change) nature. Unsurprisingly, the importance of each factor varies by country.

However, trade/empire, urbanization, forced and free labour, and government power were important in both positive and negative ways, depending on the economic and political structure of the country in question. Noticeable are institutions, which played an interaction role, especially when the institutional framework of a country relied on the coexistence of both "Eastern" and "Western" institutions. Further, we discuss the effect of the demographic transition on human capital formation. After some time, human capital growth began to depend on technology (i.e. increasing income) rather than on fertility, thus obscuring the role of the latter in economic growth.

4.1 Unified Growth Theories

The patterns of growth tell us a lot about what proximate factors of growth (e.g. human capital, taxation, colonies) are important drivers of growth. We analyse these factors in this chapter, while we deal with long-run drivers, also called ultimate causes of growth, which are econometrically captured by total factor productivity (TFP, i.e. technology, institutions/culture and, in some scholars' views, geography) in Chap. 5.

This chapter partly depends on: Xu, Y., Van Leeuwen, B., and Van Zanden, J. L. (2018). "Urbanization in China, ca. 1100–1900." Frontiers of Economics in China. 13(3): 322–368.

B. Van Leeuwen et al., *Innovation and Economic Development in Eurasia, 500 BCE-Present*, Frontiers in Economic History,
https://doi.org/10.1007/978-3-031-97043-6_4

The slow rise (England), or stagnation (China and, to a large extent, Russia), in output per capita in agriculture mentioned in Chap. 3 lasted until the Industrial Revolution, when total output grew faster in England, thus leading to the "Great Divergence". Economic growth in China and Western Europe, after an initial stagnation/decline up to about 1000 CE, slowly rose afterwards. Italy,[1] in around 1400, passed China in per capita terms.[2] However, between the fifteenth century and the end of the seventeenth century, Western Europe and China were by and large stagnant once again (e.g. Malanima 2018). It was therefore only after the seventeenth century that England manifested a clear divergent (i.e. increasing) trend in per capita gross domestic product (GDP) growth. This can also be found in real wages: Italian real wages became lower than in England from the beginning of the eighteenth century, whereas they had been higher, or equal, in the previous two centuries (Malanima 2013, 2018; cf. Allen 2001, 2009, 2011). Indeed, contrary to Italy, England had entered in around 1700 an ascension phase that was destined to culminate in the First Industrial Revolution. The country's output started to grow, while Italy continued to be stagnant (e.g. Broadberry et al. 2018). A similar picture of stagnation, and even decline, can be found at the beginning of the eighteenth century in China, when the Great Divergence with rising industrial England occurred (Solar 2021), concurrently with the permanent freeing of the latter from the old Malthusian or involutionary relationship.

According to Clark (2015), it was indeed around the same period (*c.* 1700) that in England output started to grow faster than the population (Fig. 4.1), thus ending the Malthusian phase.[3] For China (Fig. 4.1b) and Russia (Fig. 4.1c), this break occurred around 1900.

These breaks caused the negative relation between income and population size (higher per capita GDP coincides with lower population) to turn positive (higher per capita GDP coincides with higher population). Yet this phase of a positive relation broke down in around 1990 in Russia (Fig. 4.1c) and 1910 in England (Fig. 4.1a). In this new phase, per capita income might strongly vary under the same size of population. In China, this last transition has yet to occur. However, with GDP per capita fluctuations under a constant population, one might expect to witness the same picture as in England and Russia.

[1] Italy here refers to the area that has been defined the cradle of the Renaissance, namely, between the southern borders of Tuscany, Umbria, and Marche, as far as the Alps (Malanima 2018, 5). Moreover, Tuscany's economic indicators are taken as a proxy for central and northern Italy, given the similarity of trends for these areas (Malanima 2018). In the same way, for China, the Yangtze delta is taken as the reference region (Solar 2021).

[2] Differently from what had been previously suggested (Broadberry et al. 2018), more recent studies have placed this "Great Crossing" of Europe over China around this date (Solar 2021).

[3] Again, according to some reconstructions (Broadberry et al. 2015), a first overcoming of the Malthusian trap, for England, should rather be situated immediately after the macro-economic upheaval that was sparked by the outbreak of the Black Death, although real output growth only started in the seventeenth century.

Late twentieth-century Central Eurasia is a major example of where GDP per capita (Fig. 4.1c for Russia, after 1990) varies irrespective of population size.[4] Two important factors leading to an acceleration in the process of escape from Malthusianism (so either an escape from a negative relation between population size and GDP per capita or from a positive relation during phases of modern growth)

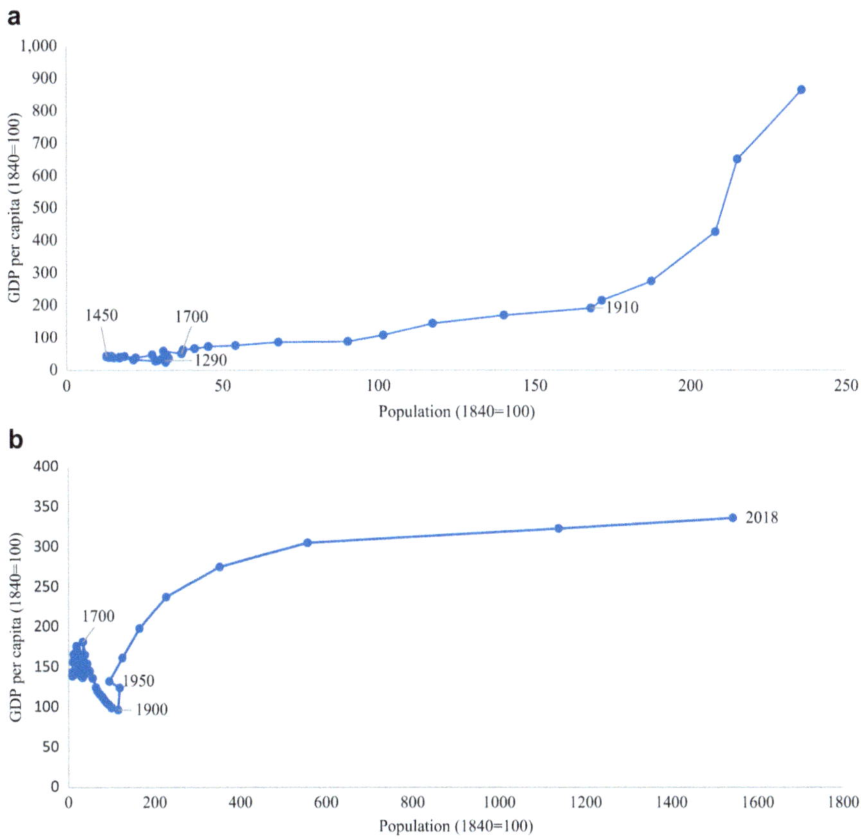

Fig. 4.1 (**a**) GDP per capita in Intl'$ (in 1990 prices) (1840 = 100) versus population (1840 = 100) in the United Kingdom, 1270–2018. *Source:* Broadberry et al. (2015); Bolt and Van Zanden (2020). (**b**) GDP per capita in Intl'$ (in 1990 prices) (1840 = 100) versus population (1840 = 100) in China, 980–2018. *Source:* Maddison (2007); Broadberry et al. (2018, 2021); Bolt and Van Zanden (2020). (**c**) GDP per capita in Intl'$ (in 1990 prices) (1840 = 100) versus population (1840 = 100) in Russia, 1690–2018. *Source:* GDP p.c. and population indices are calculated based on: 1690–1880: Broadberry and Korchmina (2024); 1890–1920: Bolt and Van Zanden (2020); 1930–1940: Didenko et al. (2013); 1950–2010: Bolt and Van Zanden (2020)

[4] In 1990–2018, population decreased in Russia and all of the European republics of the FSU. Only in Azerbaijan, a transcontinental country with a predominantly Muslim population, was it on the rise. The same is true for the countries in Central Asia.

c

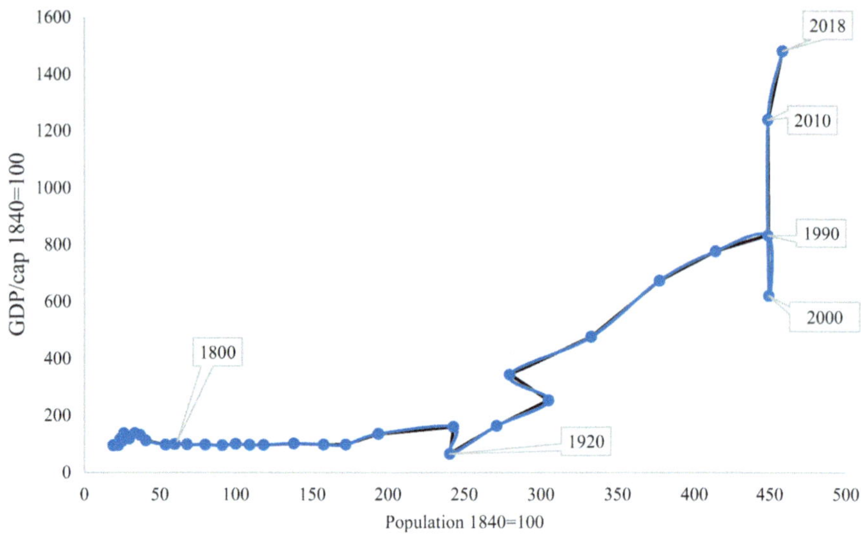

Fig. 4.1 (continued)

are the two world wars. Indeed, the negative (Malthusian) relationship for Central Eurasia lasted until the interwar period. Yet some signs of the escape can even be found in the late nineteenth century. However, growth rates of population at that time were still very high, while those from just before 1914 appeared to be relatively modest (see also Sect. 4.3), thus making the switch to modern growth more likely.

In sum, even though there have been earlier phases of per capita growth in England, the Malthusian phase made way for modern growth in around 1600–1700, resulting in increased productivity per labourer (see also Ang et al. 2013). Something similar occurred in Russia and China, but only around 1900 and even later (Maddison 2007; Broadberry et al. 2018, 2021). After the transition to "modern" growth in the late nineteenth century, the shape of the growth curve in Central Eurasia took on muted forms of exponential growth; that is, GDP per capita tended to grow somewhat faster than population. In the same way, the form of the curve in England fits an exponential trend. In China, it turns out to be logarithmic; that is, population tended to grow faster than GDP per capita before the pro-market reforms had strong positive effects. Afterwards, population growth seemed to be increasingly unconnected with income in China. In other words, both England and Central Asia/Russia witnessed a complete breakdown in the relationship between population size and GDP per capita, whereas in China the positive relation of income and population size remained, even though the population's decline occurring since the 2020s might also cause China to completely cut the (negative and positive) ties between population size and per capita GDP.

This shift from a traditional Malthusian system to modern economic growth (*c.* 1700 in England and *c.* 1900 or later in Russia and China) is obviously based on various factors, besides agricultural growth (Chap. 3). There are various theories connecting modern and pre-modern time periods. The most well known is Galor's (2011a) unified growth theory. Simply stated, this theory deals with the phase between Malthusian growth and modern growth, where the latter is human capital-driven. In this phase, technology and physical capital accumulation increase, thus temporarily raising output per person. Moreover, fertility declines and human capital per child increases, thus potentially creating permanent gains in per capita income and setting the stage for modern economic growth. This theory has met with some criticism. For example, Nielsen (2015) has argued that there was a gradual rise of GDP per capita in the long run, thus suggesting a lack of episodic take-off towards post-Malthusian growth. Yet, as pointed out in Chap. 3, even though "hard" Malthusian theory claims that the effect of any (slow) technical progress on per capita income was offset by population growth, this does not by definition imply that rising income might not affect population growth. In addition, the share of manufacturing and pasture in GDP might also increase per capita GDP, even without bringing it back to subsistence level, owing to population growth.

A second theory is from Hansen and Prescott (2002). They developed a model in which the changing relation between output and population (as we saw in Fig 4.1a–c) plays a main role and, contrary to various other unified growth theories, treats technology predominantly as exogenous.

A third, mainly empirical, model concerns a regression of growth rates on a set of explanatory variables (e.g. Barro 1991). After a lengthy debate about the significance of explanatory variables (e.g. Levine and Renelt 1991), Sala-i-Martin (1997) arrived at the conclusion that it was religion, region, politics, investment, and trade openness that were mostly significant, in other words mostly ultimate factors (Sect. 5.4) (Campante et al. 2021). This was expanded by including endogeneity: Allen (2003) identifies, besides agriculture (Sect. 3.2), also technology, representative government, population, and controlling an empire as determinant variables. Fundamentally, the main question is what maintained a high level of wages during the Malthusian phase. Allen's simulation shows that this was mostly high manufacturing productivity and trade, and empire benefits. As well as keeping up real wages, these factors eventually caused output to start growing faster than population.

In the subsequent sections, we identify the main proximate variables within these unified theories: urbanization (Sect. 4.2), forced and free labour (Sect. 4.3), fertility and human capital (Sect. 4.4), extraction and taxation (Sect. 4.5), and trade and empire (Sect. 4.6). In a growth accounting exercise, these are the proximate causes for growth. The remaining ultimate causes (i.e. technology, institutions/culture, and geography) are the topic of Chap. 5.

4.2 Urbanization

4.2.1 Link Between Urbanization and Manufacturing

Urbanization is an indicator of the shift in labour from countryside agriculture to urban manufacturing. Indeed, increasing levels of technology in agriculture lead to higher output per labourer (Chap. 3) and subsequently—also thanks to the low-income elasticity of agricultural products' demand—to surplus workforce, which is able to move from the periphery to urban areas to seek new sources of income. This occurred in Britain up to about 1750, concurrently with the progressive reduction of capital invested by the mainly landed nobility in traditional sectors—increasingly addressed towards state military campaigns in the previous years (Ventura and Voth 2015). This lack of rural capital, on the one hand, brought industrial/services entrepreneurs, who had traditionally been borrowers of the nobility, to finance themselves by means of investment in riskier industrial activities. On the other hand, this reduction in rural capital contributed to the lowering of wages in agriculture, and therefore created increased rural–urban migration flows; this kept urban industrial wages low and therefore suppressed the cost of labour for entrepreneurs in the cities. After about 1750, in England, this process triggered new investment in manufacturing technology (rather than in agriculture) during the Industrial Revolution, leading eventually to higher income per capita in urban areas, together with increasing rural–urban migration flows (Figs. 4.2, 4.3 and 4.4).

This shift from agriculture to manufacturing would be enhanced if a further shift in technologies from industry to agriculture took place (that is, if agricultural technology is developing more slowly than industrial technology, the former might

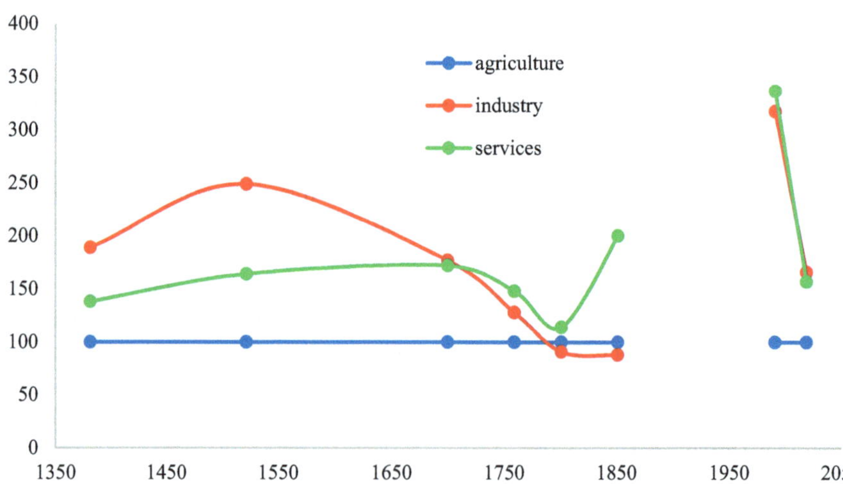

Fig. 4.2 Trend in labour productivity relative to agriculture (set at 100) by sector in Britain (1381–2019). *Source:* Broadberry et al. (2013); World Development Indicators (2021)

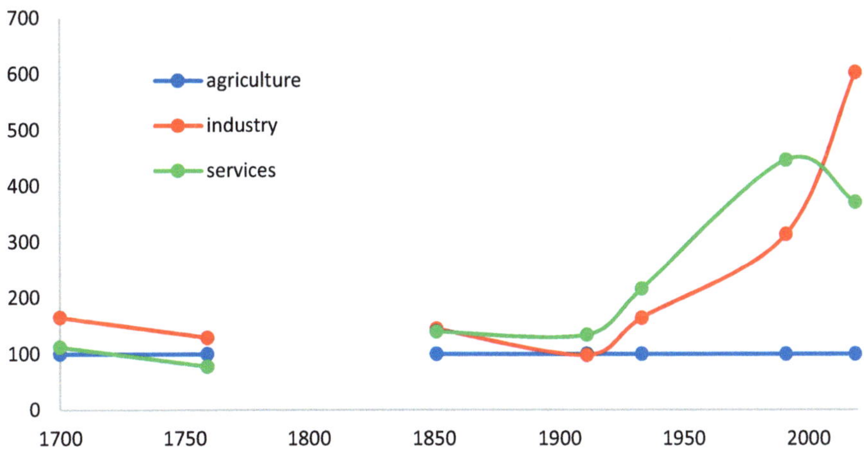

Fig. 4.3 Trend in labour productivity relative to agriculture by sector in China (1700–2019). *Source:* Guo et al. (2019); World Development Indicators (2021)

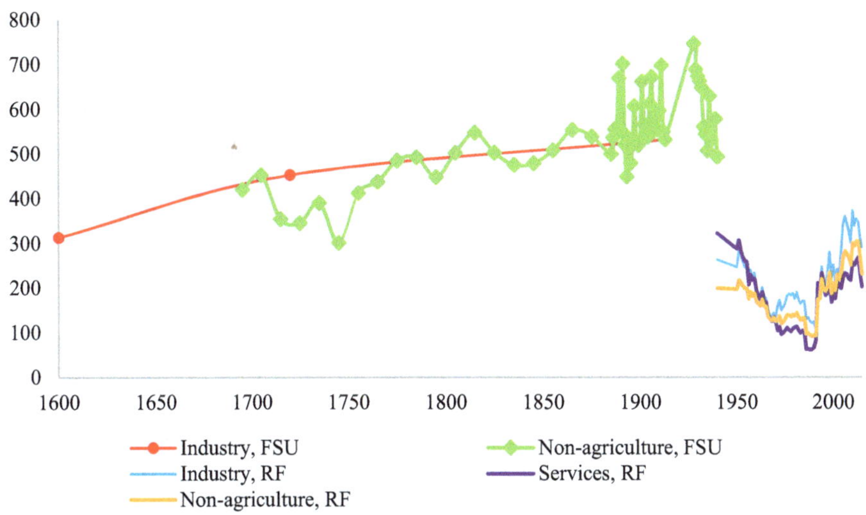

Fig. 4.4 Trend in labour productivity relative to agriculture in Central Eurasia (1600–2015) *Note:* FSU: Russian Tsardom (1600–1721), Russian Empire (1721–1913), Soviet Union (1928–1940); RF: Russian Federation (1940–2015, independent since 1992). *Source:* Industry, FSU: Strumilin (1966, 169–170); Non-agriculture, FSU: Broadberry and Korchmina (2024); Cheremukhin et al. (2017); Mironov (2018, vol. 1, 822, 826, 839, vol. 3, 752); Vodarsky (1977, 152, 192), Mironov (2018, vol. 1); Non-agriculture, RF, Industry, RF, Services, RF: Kuboniwa et al. (2019), Shida et al. (2019)

adapt some technologies from the latter). Consequently, even though it was slower than in industry, output per labourer continued to increase in agriculture. But owing to the low-income elasticity of agricultural products (rising wages do not imply higher per capita consumption of agricultural products), even more people moved to urban areas (Malanima 2010, 251–252).

Both in England and Central Eurasia, the pattern of relative change in productivity was somewhat similar, namely, it demonstrated the existence of waves. In Britain, the relative growth of productivity in manufacturing occurred after the "Black Death" in the fourteenth to sixteenth centuries, long before the Industrial Revolution. In the meantime, convergence with agriculture was in place as the latter increasingly relied on labour-saving technologies. In the nineteenth to twentieth centuries, a new phase of relative growth in productivity of the urban sectors was evidently related to various stages of the Industrial Revolution, which was followed by a new wave of convergence from the late twentieth century. In Central Eurasia, the growth in non-agricultural sectors also occurred both before and during industrialization. This was followed by their convergence with agriculture before industrial maturity had been reached (in the 1930s in the FSU, with Russia as its core part). Another wave of relative growth in productivity of the industrial sectors is related to the pro-market reforms of the 1990s–2000s, as we will discuss in the forthcoming chapters.

The pattern was very different in China. Capital (rather than labour) saving technology resulted in more people remaining in the countryside, leading to lower urbanization rates. Indeed, Fig. 4.3 shows that labour productivity in all sectors was more or less equal until 1911. This figure, therefore, has a correspondence with the stable or declining urbanization reported in Table 4.1. Moreover, as pointed out by Wang and Van Leeuwen (2021), most people introduced cottage and handicraft industries in rural rather than in urban areas in the eighteenth and nineteenth centuries, leading to a very different role of urbanization in China before modernization (*c.* 1930), in which manufacturing drew much more labour out of urban centres. Likewise, Buggle and Nafziger (2021) find that the experience of Russian serfdom generated persistent constraints on urbanization and structural change, resulting in slower city growth, lower industrial development, weaker infrastructure development, and, eventually, lower educational attainment and income levels. This long-lasting effect persisted through the late Imperial and Soviet periods to post-Soviet Russia (e.g. Galor et al. 2009). Indeed, contrary to England, in Russia, serfdom was maintained. Indeed, Markevich and Zhuravskaya (2018) suggest the strongly negative effects of serfdom by looking at differential economic changes up to 1897.

These fundamental differences in migration show up in what we know about migration patterns in Western Europe and China. In Western Europe, large migration streams were focused on urban cores: The Netherlands drew migrants from Germany and Scandinavia, in particular during its Golden Age in the seventeenth century. Similarly, England attracted large numbers of migrants from Ireland. So the dominant flow of migrants was from periphery to core, feeding urban agglomerations, and thus core regions such as the Low Countries and England grew more

Table 4.1 Urbanization ratios (%) by region and benchmark year (cities with more than 2000 inhabitants) in China, 1102–1918

	1102	1205	1290	1391	1630	1644	1776	1851	1893	1918
Hebei (including Rehe, Beijing, Tianjin, and Baoding)				10	18	16	13		8	
Shaanxi				8	9	7	5		7	
Shanxi				6	6	3	10	10	9	
Shandong				6	8	7	5	5	3	
Henan				7	7	6	5	4	5	
Jiangsu (including Shanghai)				14	18	16	14		14	
Zhejiang				14	18	16	10		14	
Fujian				14	10	10	6		7	
Jiangxi				6	8	8	8		7	
Huguang (including Hunan and Hubei)				9	12	10	6		6	
Guangdong				7	7	7	8		8	
Sichuan				10	10	4	7		7	
Anhui							5		5	
Gansu					9		3		5	
Guangxi				8	9	9	5		5	
Guizou					9	9	5	4	5	
Yunan					9	9	4		4	
Inner China	**11**	**12**	**12**	**10**	**12**	**11**	**7**	**7**	**7**	**13**
Yangtze Delta		**25**	**18**	**19**	**23**	**20**	**19**	**20**	**17**	**15**
Xinjiang							**7**		**8**	

Source: Xu et al. (2018)

rapidly than the periphery. The share of the North Sea region in the total population of Western Europe grew from 11% in 1500 to 20% in 1820 (and to 23% in 1900) (Van Zanden 2000), whereas, in the same period, the Chinese core (the Yangtze Delta) shrank in relative size. Indeed, in China, migration was focused on the periphery. Taiwan was peopled in various waves with migrants from Fujian in the eighteenth and nineteenth centuries, and during the final years of the Republican period (1945–1949), the population of Sichuan received migrants from the middle Yangtze area, the west, and north probably being the most popular destinations. These peripheral areas with a relatively low rate of urbanization saw their share of population increasing during the Chinese population explosion: Sichuan's share, for example, increased from 2.2% in 1393 to 3.9% in 1630, and further to 10.6% in 1893; Yunnan, another province with relatively high wage levels, saw its share increase from 1.3% in 1630 to 3.3% in 1893. The decline in the rate of urbanization during the Qing was therefore part of a much wider process of structural change. In Western Europe, cities were engines of technological and economic change; in post-Song China, they apparently did not play such a role, at least before 1900; see also the discussion in Rosenthal and Wong (2011) and Li and Van Zanden (2012).

In sum, three factors played a role in European urbanization during the eighteenth and nineteenth centuries (and, likewise, the Chinese and Russian urban decline and stagnation up to the nineteenth century). The first factor, as pointed out earlier, was that income growth resulted in disproportionate growth in demand for manufactured products and services, which were (mainly) produced in cities in Europe. Second, in Europe, contrary to China, technological change in the industry and services sectors was, from the eighteenth century onwards, more rapid than in agriculture, resulting in the long-term decline in prices of manufactured goods and certain services, such as transport. Likewise, since handicraft manufacturing remained located mostly in the countryside, income declined, and it was agricultural prices that were on the rise in England.

Indeed, it is remarkable that, notwithstanding the differences in manufacturing growth and urbanization in China, Russia, and England, the relative price of manufacturing goods versus agricultural products (Fig. 4.5) was comparable. For example, from about 1200 to 1500, England witnessed both urbanization and the rising prices of manufacturing products in relation to agricultural products. From 1500 to 1750, a convergence of manufacturing and agricultural prices occurred, with divergence after 1800, owing to fast technological change. Likewise, China shows a relative stability of prices for manufacturing and agricultural products up to 1900, with divergence afterwards. These price trends for both countries closely match the relative labour productivity seen in Figs. 4.2, 4.3, and 4.4. The same can be said about Russia, even with the shorter price history that lacks the upward part of the eleventh to fourteenth centuries. The two index ratios (starting from 1600 and 1800 and both terminating in 1913) demonstrate clear downward trends.

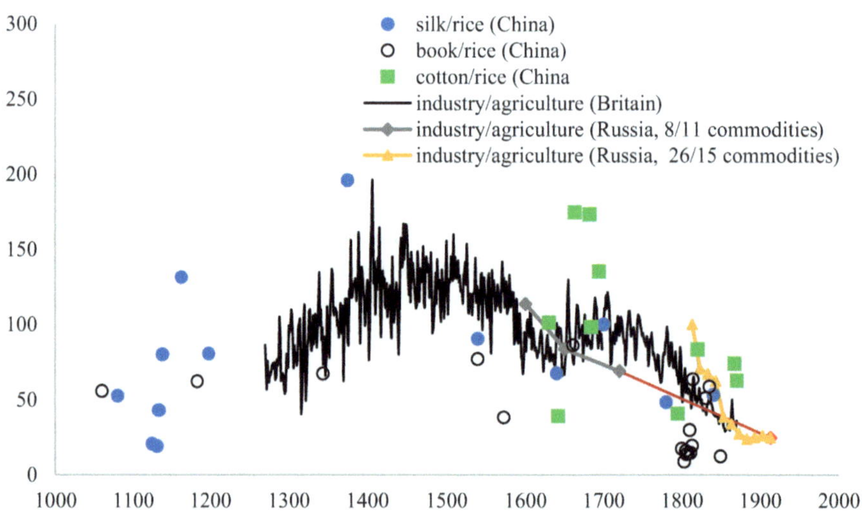

Fig. 4.5 Industrial price–agricultural price ratio in England, China, and Russia, c. 1000–1913. *Source:* Broadberry et al. (2015) for Britain; Peng (1957); Yi (1993) for China; Strumilin (1966) for Russia

This decrease in relative prices of manufacturing in England resulted in consumers buying on average more books, textiles, and kitchen utensils, and imported colonial goods such as coffee, tea, and sugar, while having a reduced purchasing power for foodstuffs (e.g. the per capita consumption of meat declined in absolute terms). The combination of rapid technological change and a "consumer revolution" boosted the share of manufacturing and services in employment and led to a rise in the urbanization ratio in Europe.

The third and final trends to some extent counterbalanced the others, with the ongoing reallocation of production processes between urban places and countryside; in particular, the rise of proto-industry (which occurred in waves) led to a parallel reallocation of manufacturing from cities to the countryside, where wages were lower. Eventually, the rapid growth of proto-industrial areas resulted in the formation of new urban agglomerations.

Urbanization in Europe is thus a clear indicator of the growth of manufacturing productivity. It is important to stress that this growth of urbanization in Western and Southern Europe can be traced back to the twelfth century, with the exception of the Netherlands and England, which only experienced urban growth from about 1400 onwards, with an acceleration after about 1750 (Malanima 2010, 239), thus pointing at industrialization. Yet this was much less the case in China and Central Eurasia. As urbanization in Europe (in towns with populations of 10,000 or higher) was much greater than in China (*c.* 8% versus 4%), this suggests that urbanization played less of a role in urban manufacturing in China. This implies no move from agriculture to urban industry, while the handicraft industry remained in rural areas, and both urbanization and wages both declined more quickly in poorer regions. One might argue that, in terms of the low levels of urbanization, Russia and Central Asia resemble China.

Indeed, in Eurasia outside Western Europe,[5] urban settlements appeared to be primarily, as was the case in China and Central Eurasia, military, administrative, and religious centres. From the early eighteenth century to the present time, settlements are officially recognized as cities or towns by the state. In the last quarter of the eighteenth and the first half of the nineteenth century, in the *Russian Code of Laws* (Полное собрание законов Российской империи, 1830–1916),[6] there was an article stating that if industry and trade developed in a rural settlement to such an extent that the population received its livelihood to a greater extent from these crafts than from agriculture, then the government should give an order that would define it as an urban area.[7] This is comparable to the situation in China, where urbanization began to grow from the start of the twentieth century.

---

[5] Where Russian statehood emerged, which subsequently transformed into the Russian Empire.

[6] This encompassed all of the tsars' and emperors' edicts on various topics since 1649, retrospectively systematized and published in 1830—with annual updates after that until 1916.

[7] On Russia see Mironov (2018, vol. 1, 791–792). Only in 1775 did the Russian government establish the position of *gradonachal'nik* as the only representative of the crown in most towns and cities. From that time, an urban settlement emerged as an independent administrative unit with specific state governing bodies, which contributed to delineation between townspeople and peas-

Yet, Chinese urban development grew faster than in Russia from the beginning of the twentieth century. So, how did Russia keep up with the growth in manufacturing? The answer is that official data on urban population underestimated the true scale of Russian urbanization from the 1860s. To give a fairer comparison, the scale of hidden urbanization, which was quicker than officially recorded statistics indicate, should be taken into account (Mironov 2018, vol. 1, 841–846).

4.2.2 Regional Developments

Arguably, a clearer picture of this process can be obtained by looking at regional developments in manufacturing and urbanization. Two trends are visible: during the Song era (960–1279), the share of the south, and in particular the share of the Yangtze Delta (Jiangsu and Zhejiang provinces), in total Chinese population increased: in the south, it climbed from 67% in 1205 to 81% in 1391, an increase partly driven by the rise from 6% to 13% of the two provinces that made up part of the Yangtze Delta. Thereafter, the trend reversed, and the share of Jiangsu and Zhejiang in the total population declined to 8% in 1776 and 4% in 1893. Since this was, from the Song period onwards, the most urbanized region—its urbanization ratio was about twice the national average—the relative decline of the Yangtze Delta in terms of total population contributed to the overall decline in the urbanization ratio. Indeed, the Lower Yangtze Delta started out with very high levels of urbanization, then, after a temporary decline during the Yuan dynasty (1279–1368) followed by a minor recovery in the early Ming (*c.* 1368–1450), slid into permanent decline until the first several years of the Republican period (the 1910s), thus suggesting an element of deindustrialization.

Although the figures on urbanization rates for Central Eurasia have a somewhat different methodological background, we can derive from the data noted here and from Fig. 4.6 that urbanization there in the late seventeenth to mid-eighteenth centuries was far below that of Western Europe and China. The level of concentration, which affects economies of scale, was low too. In 1678, only 77 of 200 Russian urban settlements had more than 2000 inhabitants (all of them in the European part), and in 1910 (before the Revolution), 489 of 700 (Mironov 2018, vol. 1, 791–792).[8]

ants in administrative terms. The Charter on the Rights and Benefits for the Towns of the Russian Empire (1785) completed the differentiation between urban areas and the countryside, urban and rural communities, in legal terms. However, throughout the eighteenth century, more than 50% of people who did not belong to the urban estate lived in towns and cities, and about 30% of all urban people (including merchants) lived in the countryside (Mironov 2018, vol. 1, 806–810).

[8] The actual urbanization level in eighteenth-century Russia was lower because agriculture was the core activity for a significant proportion of permanent urban inhabitants. Thus, in the 1760s no fewer than 58.9% of all Russian towns recognized by the state specialized in agriculture. This share had diminished to 22.0 by the 1850s and to 8.5 by 1897, when diversified urban settlements already prevailed. However, an agrarian town differed from a village since it performed at least one typically urban function. This could include being an administrative centre for a county or prov-

As in China, in Russia, there was also only a weak relationship between urbanization and manufacturing development. As can be seen from Fig. 4.6, Russia experienced a decline in urbanization for more than a century (from the mid-eighteenth century to the mid-nineteenth century). The factors behind this were threefold. First, there was the higher urban mortality rate. This was explained by overcrowding, which contributed to the spread of infectious diseases, poor sanitation, and unhygienic living conditions. Second, a small proportion of the peasantry migrated to urban areas. In addition to restrictions caused by serfdom, agriculture was more profitable than trade and manufacturing owing to the higher prices for agricultural commodities in the eighteenth century and the first quarter of the nineteenth. Third, Russian government policy restrained urban growth until the mid-nineteenth century (Mironov 2018, vol. 1, 838–841). Although the decrease in the share of urban population halted after the Emancipation and other reforms of the 1860s, urbanization remained sluggish: from 1856 to 1914, before the outbreak of the First World War, the share of the urban population only increased from 9% to 15.3%.[9]

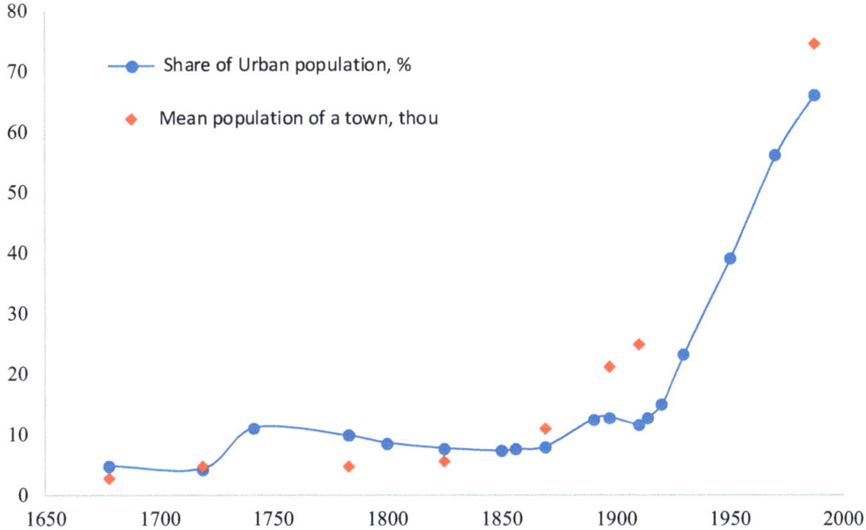

Fig. 4.6 Urban population in Central Eurasia, 1678–1987. *Source*: Vodarsky (1977, 152, 192), Mironov (2018, vol. 1, 839, vol. 3, 752, 799)

ince) or a trade and/or industry centre. It could also relate to human capital formation: a third of agrarian towns had some kind of educational establishment. Even the agricultural activities of the townspeople differed from those in villages; they were mainly engaged in gardening and growing technical crops, and were closely connected with markets (Mironov 2018, vol. 1, 811–815).

[9] Slow urbanization, even after the Emancipation of 1861, in which serfdom was de facto abolished, is explained by a number of factors. First, the peasants retained a significant fund of allotted land; naturally, they sought to retain it. Even those who permanently resided in urban areas refrained from breaking ties with the village where their families remained. The second factor was

This difference in urbanization rates is reflected in wage structures; rising urban manufacturing is associated with higher wages (Sect. 4.2.1). Indeed, in the seventeenth and eighteenth centuries, nominal wages (expressed as grams of silver) in the urban core of Western Europe (the Low Countries, England) were about three times the levels found in the periphery (e.g. Poland) (Van Zanden 1999). At the same time, international trade between the Baltic region and Western Europe was substantial: Western Europe imported grains, timber, and other primary commodities, in return for which it supplied international services and manufactured goods. This implies that, on balance, labour productivity in the North Sea area urban regions was such that it compensated for the much higher wages that had to be paid there. In real terms, the gap in wage levels was much smaller, but nevertheless persistent.

It was different in China (Table 4.2). Based on qualitative information from gazetteers regarding population, consumption, land use, industrial structure, trade, and taxation, Gao (1999) divides eighteenth-century China into different geo-economic areas ranging from "most advanced" to "less developed". Combined with research by Allen et al. (2011) on the spatial structure of Chinese nominal wages in the eighteenth century,[10] we find that in China, nominal wages were lowest in the most advanced provinces and highest in the less developed periphery. Until the early twentieth century, this pattern did not change much.[11] Apparently, the concentration of economic activities in the Yangtze Delta (or other urban areas of China) did not give rise to the scale and agglomeration economies that would have made possible higher levels of nominal and real incomes. The highest nominal wages were earned

that industrialization almost equally covered urban and rural areas. However, administrative urban status was not acquired by a settlement automatically after achieving a certain level of industrial and trade development, as was the case in many European countries, but according to government order. Third, if Russian rural settlements had become urban automatically upon reaching 2000 residents, as in some Western European countries (e.g. France), then the share of urban population would have reached 24% in 1857 and 32.3% in 1897. Fourth, although government policy regarding the growth in the number of cities underwent changes after the Emancipation of 1861, peasants' unwillingness to move into the urban estate impeded urbanization. The peasants had their own economic and social rationale. Obtaining urban status inevitably led to a hike in local taxes for self-government and the creation of new institutions that towns were obliged to have. In addition, the lands belonging to peasants changed their legal status so they were at the disposal of the town's government. Finally, since 1812, and especially after 1861, there were broad legal opportunities for peasants to engage in entrepreneurial activities by buying patents.

[10] Allen et al. took the best survey of nominal wage level in the construction industry, the *Wuliao jiazhi zeli of 1769* (《乾隆物料价值则例》), which is a very detailed and systematic government report on the nominal wages paid at construction projects in different regions across China. On this basis, Allen et al. constructed the regional pattern of nominal wage level in 24 districts covering provinces and big cities. By calculating the unweighted average of wage norms for labourers in all districts, we combined 24 districts into 19 provinces.

[11] As Allen et al. did in their paper, we also took the complete census of nominal wage levels in the construction industry in 1918 from *The Seventh Statistics of Agriculture and Commerce in Republican China* (《中华民国第7次农商统计》), which reported the nominal wages paid at construction projects in different regions across China at the same level of detail as the *Wuliao jiazhi zeli of 1769*. On this basis, we constructed the regional pattern of nominal wage level in 14 provinces across China in 1918.

Table 4.2 Nominal wages in tael per day in construction in core and peripheral regions of China, 1769 and 1918

Area	Province	1769		1918	
		Unskilled workers	Skilled workers	Unskilled workers	Skilled workers
Most advanced	Zhejiang	0.04	0.06	0.14	0.29
	Jiangsu (including Shanghai)	0.04	0.05	0.12	0.25
	Unweighted average	**0.04**	**0.06**	**0.13**	**0.27**
Advanced	Guangdong (including Canton)	0.04	0.05		
	Sichuan	0.05	0.06		
	Fujian	0.03	0.05	0.21	0.32
	Henan	0.04	0.04	0.16	0.22
	Hebei (including Beijing)	0.05	0.08	0.12	0.28
	Rehe	0.07	0.12	0.19	0.35
	Shandong	0.05	0.06	0.12	0.18
	Unweighted average	**0.04**	**0.06**	**0.16**	**0.27**
Less developed	Hunan	0.04	0.05		
	Hubei			0.11	0.22
	Shanxi	0.05	0.07	0.11	0.2
	Shaanxi	0.04	0.05		
	Heilongjiang	0.10	0.19	0.56	0.76
	Jilin	0.10	0.16	0.33	0.53
	Liaoning	0.06	0.10	0.28	0.43
	Xinjiang	0.10		0.63	0.81
	Gansu	0.04	0.05	0.18	0.26
	Yunnan	0.05	0.07		
	Taiwan	0.03	0.05		
	Unweighted average	**0.06**	**0.09**	**0.31**	**0.46**

Source: Subdivision of macro-regions according to their level of development, from Gao (1999); nominal wage in 1769 from Allen et al. (2011); and nominal wage in 1918 from *The Seventh Statistics of Agriculture and Commerce in Republican China* (中华民国第7次农商统计)

in the poorest areas of the country—almost empty regions, which attracted large numbers of migrants and grew much more rapidly than the Yangtze Delta. Indeed, Lee shows that immigrants in general lived better in peripheral areas than they did in the core areas from which they originated. The main reason for this was that they were able to rent more fertile land from local landlords and to monopolize both industry and service sectors in these regions.

A similar pattern of quasi-urbanization, combined with a spread of handicraft industries both in urban and in rural areas, can be identified in Russia. In Strumilin

(1966),[12] it is noted that both in the early eleventh century and early twentieth century, a skilled hired construction worker (e.g. carpenter) was paid almost the same consumer basket.[13] Hence, as in China, labour productivity in construction in Russia is implied to be roughly constant vis-à-vis agriculture before 1900, or somewhat above agriculture if the extraction rate had increased over time.[14] Yet, Strumilin (1966) acknowledges that in the seventeenth century, each kind of labour was paid its proper rate owing to the scarcity of supply (see Sect. 4.1). Likewise, in the eighteenth century, hired labour in manufacturing was still paid relatively high wages,[15] despite declining labour market dynamics (both for hired and forced labour).[16] After this period of income stability in Russia, Shipilov (2008) finds, as was the case in China, that the real level of workers' wages at the end of the nineteenth century decreased significantly compared with the first half of the eighteenth century, with the main decrease occurring in the period from the middle of the eighteenth century to the early nineteenth century.[17]

After 1900, Volkov (2016, vol. 2, 227) shows that the average share of wages in Russian industry output was 23.57% in 1900 and 12.67% in 1908. This evidence of low wage shares suggests that the distribution of value added in Russia was more in favour of human capital of free labourers in the seventeenth and eighteenth centuries and more in favour of physical capital in the early twentieth century (at the early stage of modern growth).[18] In other words, just as in England after about 1750, and

[12] In Strumilin (1966, 23–99), which uses both silver and consumer basket measures for comparing wages in pre-Revolutionary Russia over time, we can find the longest period of wage dynamics in Russia, from the early eleventh to the early twentieth century; to the best of our knowledge, no scholar has undertaken a similar effort. It covers basically European Russia and the Urals (since the eighteenth century).

[13] This consumer basket is corrected for some improvement in living conditions owing to the introduction of a number of new products, despite multiple devaluation of the silver currency and several times growth in labour productivity.

[14] Strumilin supported just this hypothesis, applying Marxist ideas to economic history analysis.

[15] The proportion of forced labour of serfs in Russian manufacturing increased significantly during the Petrine reforms in the early eighteenth century, when a strong boost was given to the sector by government efforts. The trend remained in force throughout the eighteenth century. In the first half of the nineteenth century, the opposite trend prevailed, and by 1861 (Emancipation) the serfs' share had already been reduced to 12.6% (Strumilin 1966, 52, 80).

[16] Serfdom basically meant the limitation of labour mobility and attachment to the lord, whether agricultural or manufacturing. Serfdom's practices varied depending on the area. In some areas (with fertile soils where grain production was profitable or for servants in large estates), it was closer to slavery, but in many areas, serfs could engage in entrepreneurial activities (sharing incomes with their lords). In the proto-industry, it meant forced (versus hired) labour, generally with dual remuneration (monetary and in-kind), normally smaller than hired wages. Wages for forced labour were a matter of incentives.

[17] The data in Shipilov (2008) fit into the pattern indicated in both Mironov (2012) and Nefedov (2011): some improvement in well-being in the late nineteenth–early twentieth centuries was accompanied by its significant fluctuations, initially appearing to be a correction to a downward trend in manufacturing wages from the mid-eighteenth to the early twentieth century.

[18] See also Mironov (2012) and Nefedov (2011).

in China after about 1900, Russia started to focus on capital-intensive technology after 1900, even though the development of the latter two might be less capital-intensive than in England. Indeed, the labour share in English income (rather than in industrial output) in about 1720 was about 60%, declining to 50% at the peak of industrialization in 1850 (Allen 2009; Piketty and Zucman 2014). This suggests that England was more capital-intensive.

4.3 Divergence of Modes of Production

4.3.1 Co-Existing Modes

High levels of manufacturing productivity, of which urbanization is a long-term indicator, can also explain the presence of high real wages during Malthusian phases. We can further build on this finding by arguing that long-run analysis of manufacturing productivity cannot fail to consider that the forces of production and the relations of production are inherently related (this originally Marxist idea was revitalized in, e.g. Klein 1985), ultimately influencing productivity trends in the context of social relationships. Forces and relations of production represent a sort of anthropological synthetic unity that can be defined as a mode of production (see also Wolf 1982), as pointed out in Sect. 2.3.

As seen in Sect. 2.3, for our analysis of the modes of production, we use the International Institute of Social History (IISH) taxonomy of labour relations. In this taxonomy, the four modes are reciprocal labour, tributary labour, commodified labour, and a residual group of non-working. The reciprocal mode can be described as small-scale and kin-ordered, typically emerging in socially embedded economic systems. The tributary production mode is instead class-based, and is often characterized by political control of production rather than of the means of production, in the hands of a class of rulers that extract tributes from the producer class. The commodified labour mode occurs when independent producers transition to wage labour, even if they are forced to sell their labour, and not necessarily for a monetary wage.

As mentioned in Sect. 2.3, labour relations on the basis of different modes of production can coexist, earlier ones even re-emerging among new modes if circumstances change. Slavery, for example, despite being widely condemned in contemporary society, persists to varying extents in numerous countries, often taking illegal or restricted legal forms, such as penal labour in the United States or Russia.[19] So what really changes in the transition from one mode of production to another? We opt for a quantitative answer to this question. What changes is the proportion of the various kinds of labour relations in a certain society. From this perspective, wage labour expanded its share until probably the 1970s and 1980s in industrialized econ-

[19] Much of the evidence on Russia in this Section is from Didenko (2024).

omies, but recently self-employment has begun to partially regain its share. This affects the dominant mode of production.

Besides co-existing modes of labour production, another way to look at existing blends is to regard changes in modes of production as shifting in a sequence of trials, successes, and errors. For example, slavery progressively diminished its share in labour relations in post-feudal Europe, while also becoming a less-effective mode of production (irrespective of moral condemnation), and therefore giving way to less onerous forms of dependency. Yet, under a different set of conditions, we might find the persistence and at times even predominance of slavery among populations and social systems that had already replaced slavery with subsequent modes of production in their home countries.[20] Markets developed in Mesopotamia faded with the fall of ancient societies, but revived later in the Hellenistic Mediterranean and Roman worlds. Again, after the expansion of tributary exchange in the Middle Ages, commodified relations took the lead during the Modern Era. We can observe something similar as regards the role of government in the production process. Massive state involvement in tributary relations in the early Asian civilizations was revitalized in Central Eurasia (USSR) with the application of industrial technologies and much more sophisticated institutions. The relics of the institutions of slavery (even though affecting only a modest share of the working population) and serfdom were suppressed or faded for the time being. But they were revived on a smaller scale when it appeared they were in demand again. Alternatively, the capitalist mode of production, with private property and markets, expanded in Central Eurasia from the mid-eighteenth to the early twentieth centuries, and has done so again from the late twentieth century.[21] Therefore, there are grounds to recognize cyclical patterns of modes of production (and, hence, labour relations). But these are not mere replications of the past. For example, today we have much more complicated markets (e.g. academic markets) than existed in Antiquity and early modern times, while other, more traditional markets have survived (e.g. markets for barber services). Should the emergence of new markets, again from a purely economic efficiency perspective, always be considered to be an improvement? For example, the Artificial Intelligence revolution may also cause rises in unemployment and income inequality.[22] Likewise, the illegal market for drugs may be very efficient, but not necessarily be very socially beneficial. Indeed, taking the distribution of commodified labour in market and non-market activities, we find that there is no linear relation. Rather, after an assumed minor increase in free market behaviour in the centuries up to

[20] The cases of slavery in the colonial periphery of the major West European nations (inherited by the US antebellum South) during early modern capitalism and mass use of penal labour during the Soviet industrialization effort.

[21] We can trace shorter fluctuations within these long-term oscillations.

[22] A similar argument can also be made for grain markets. As pointed out by Van der Spek et al. (2015), "despite all information coming to us via modern communication technology such as the Internet, people are just as unable nowadays to outsmart the market of primary products as they were in Babylonian times 600 BC". Indeed, they found the highest level of grain market efficiency in the early modern period.

1500–1800, from a peak of 95% of all labourers in commodified labour working in free labour markets in 1800, from about 1800 onwards, we witness a decrease in free market behaviour to about 90% in 2000 (IISH n.d.).

This has affected economic growth. As pointed out before, the mode of labour production works via TFP growth. Hence, the more efficient the mode of labour production, the higher the TFP growth, and hence the higher per capita GDP growth. Thus, we ran a brief regression between TFP growth and commodified labour and found it to be positive (see Table 4.3), while reciprocal labour was, at best, insignificant. This implies that, after removing outliers, the share of the commodified mode of labour productivity in TFP growth is somewhere between 10% and 50%. This partly explains why Western Europe had a higher share of commodified labour in 1700–1900 with, at the same time, higher TFP growth and higher growth of GDP per capita. Given the small number of observations in our dataset, not too much value should be attached to this, though.

4.3.2 Divergent Modes over Time in Pre-Industrial Northern Eurasia

Besides co-existing, modes of production have changed over time. Modes of production are affected by labour relations (whether slave, serf, and wage labourer). This is made visible in the IISH taxonomy of labour relations, which shows, for example, that slaves can be classified as tributary or as market slaves, with the former producing for the lord and the latter for the market. Slave labour can be found in Han China, the Roman Empire, and Ancient Russia (*kholopy* in Kievan Rus' and the Muscovy Tsardom up to the early eighteenth century). Whether this production type, under tributary mode, was suitable for increased labour productivity is doubtful. Indeed, a lack of population in the third-century CE Roman Empire caused landowners to turn increasingly to free labourers acting as tenant farmers (Mackay 2004). Yet, a rising population, combined with a strong government, led to increasing pressure for the use of serfs. But slavery remained small and declined slowly over time in Europe since it was inefficient in agriculture. However, commodified labour in the American and Caribbean colonies, on cotton and sugar plantations, seemed profitable owing to monopolies (Smith 1776).

In Russia, slaves (*kholopy*) attracted much attention in the first law code of Kievan Rus' in the eleventh century CE, which was known as "Russian Justice"

Table 4.3 Random effect regression of compound annual growth rate of TFP on share of commodified labour, c. 1500–2000

	Coefficient	Z
Constant	0.001	0.93
Commodified labour share	0.001	1.65
No. observations	11	

Source: See Table 4.4 and Table 5.1–5.2

(*Russkaia Pravda*).[23] Despite the existence of various forms of labour dependency, it is acknowledged in the literature that most of Russia's rural population consisted of free peasants who could change to another lord or who paid tribute to their local prince. This explains why, even before the sixteenth century, free markets were dominant (Sect. 4.3.1). It is also evident that slavery (*kholopstvo*) survived into the time of the centralized Tsardom of Russia (Muscovy), 1547–1721; it had several legal varieties and was regulated by a central government office (the Slavery Chancellery—*Kholopii Prikaz*). Most of the Russian *kholopy* cannot be identified as chattel slaves, as their master had some legal obligations, they lacked hereditary status, and they still had limited legal rights (Stanziani 2014, 88). Yet, slaves normally did not possess any personal property, unlike serfs, who did. Not surprisingly, household service was the main occupation of the former. In agriculture, slaves were more engaged in the cultivation of the lord's demesne than serfs were. Slaves are still estimated as having been 10–15% of Russia's population in the late sixteenth and early seventeenth centuries (Hellie 1982, 688–689). This percentage was much lower in Western Europe, even though many slaves continued to be transported from Africa to the Americas. But the spread of serfdom in Eastern Europe and Russia hampered slavery, which converged with the former and was eventually replaced by it. The central government's interest in tax extraction also played a role, as slaves were not subject to taxation while serfs were.[24]

Similarly to slaves, serfs witness different levels of productivity. A tributary exchange system may lead to, inter alia, tributary serfs as a labour relation, while commodified labour for the market can also lead to serfs, albeit with different characteristics. In Western Europe, serfdom rose again during the tenth century with the breakup of the Carolingian Empire, after a period of weak serfdom and strong government in the fourth-century Roman Empire. Hence, a tributary mode accompanied by the weak government led to serfdom. Over time, this weakened in Western Europe owing to powerful kings, towns, a growing economy, and a labour shortage owing to the Black Death, until it disappeared by around 1500 (Blum 1957), being replaced by a rise in wage earners.

In Eastern Europe, serfdom emerged around 1300–1500. A low population supplied the need to stimulate migration. After the Black Death, migration halted, causing a high land-to-labour ratio. This forced the lords to tie the peasants to the land by increasing labour dues. This was reinforced by increasing grain exports to Western Europe owing to the region's economic growth and increasing urbanization, while in Eastern Europe, the power of cities declined, and lords obtained more political power. In most countries, except Russia, serfdom was abolished during the Napoleonic period, from the start of the nineteenth century.

In China, the population was divided into the "four categories of the people" (四民), scholars, farmers, craftsmen, and merchants. Serfs were mostly engaged in

[23] Mentioned explicitly in 6 of 43 articles in the Short version of the eleventh century and 27 of 121 articles in the Expanded version of the twelfth century (Kaiser, tr. and ed., 1992, p. 15–34).

[24] Farming slaves were converted into serfs in 1679 while household ones were somewhat later, in 1723 (Hellie, 1982, p. 50, 666–667, 697, 716).

agriculture, which also occupied the vast majority of the population. Yet, as in Europe, China experienced roughly similar trends in serfdom. Under the tributary relations of ancient times, as in the fourth-century Roman Empire, serfdom emerged to prevent peasants from shirking by tying them to the land (Huang and He 2006); serfdom was more efficient than free labour. In combination with a centralized government, this led to increasing serfdom in about 1000 BCE (He 2013). One might consider that the second period of serfdom in China (as in medieval Western Europe) had different characteristics, such as a decentralized government and strong lords (as in the mid-Qing dynasty with serfdom being formally abolished late in the first half of the twentieth century. This is similar to Russia, where serfdom was officially abolished late (in 1959).

Did this abolition take place because of inefficiency in the serfs' labour productivity? Whereas Acemoglu and Robinson (2012) argue that this was the case, Stanziani (2014), for example, argues that serfdom created considerable economic development. Likewise, it is argued that the lords were the only political power that generated stability, and as such serfdom in Eastern Europe and Russia was simply the best option, even though it was not economically perfect. However, more recent research from Zhuravskaya and Markevich (2015) shows that per capita income in Russia in the nineteenth century would have been double its actual value had serfdom been abolished earlier. Wage labour is often seen as the most productive form of labour.

It should be noted that slavery greatly influenced private serfdom in Russia, which borrowed many norms from slavery in its various practices. Serfs could be bought and sold, or rented out or leased with the lord's land to which they were attached. These activities intensified after the nobles were exempted from military service in 1762, thus launching the emancipation of the estates. An effect of easing constraints on labour mobility was a worsening in serfs' conditions, as many lords chose to extract more from their estates. That this would not apply to a tributary mode of production is obvious. After all, paying money to a lord of a different social class is very likely inefficient. But also in a market mode of production, wages very often do not match labour productivity, and are hence inefficient. This was already true for the fourth-century Roman Empire, when free tenants slowly gave way to serfs.

These trends in mode of production (from kinship, via tributary, to commodified labour), combined with government (fragmentary or unified), urbanization, and economic growth, were affected by labour relations such as slavery, serfdom and wage labour. For example, Tilly (1990) argued, in the face of government structure and economic growth, that military modernization made development much more expensive, so only rich countries with a large population were able to generate a modern military. This means those in power needed to extract revenue (Sect. 4.5). Yet, how this extraction was done depended on the economic structure. In countries with independent landlords, absolutism arose (as in Russia).[25] Indeed, before the abolition of serfdom, it was mostly associated with the European part of Russia,[26] whereas in sparsely populated Siberia and the Far East, serfdom rarely existed if at all. The latter regions were at the frontier of colonization.

Dominated by merchants, city states came to existence (as in Venice or the Netherlands), while, if both landlords and merchants existed, some in-between form existed (as in China).

In Russia, the serfs were of private,[27] state, clerical,[28] and the Crown family possession. From the sixteenth to the eighteenth centuries, the Russian central government transferred state lands with peasants attached to the gentry in return for the latter's military service. The mobility of peasants on private estates was considerably restricted; however, these restrictions were never definitive and changed according to the estate and the economic situation (Stanziani 2014, 118). Taken together, the experiences of Russia, Prussia, Lithuania, and some parts of Poland lead to the conclusion that, on the whole, "second serfdom" was not so much a form of slavery but rather a set of legal constraints on labour mobility. These rules were dictated much less by a scarcity of population than by increasing demand for agricultural labour (Stanziani 2014, 137).

Just as in Europe, tributary serfdom was eventually replaced in Russia by commodified labour. Indeed, the proto-industrial and military effort by Peter I is associated with the expansion of serfdom into the mining and manufacturing sector. Earlier, in the seventeenth century, the recruitment of casual day labourers by hire from urban or semi-urban elements was the predominant form of employment in pre-industrial manufactories and other non-agricultural activities. Some payment in cash was involved, but the main form of remuneration remained in kind. This was an intermediary form of commodified labour, in which workers heavily relied on other sources of income, with implicit land rent being the most important. For example, in the early eighteenth century, Russian entrepreneurs had whole villages and even districts settled by Crown peasants who were "ascribed" to them, with the

---

[25] Which experienced strong intra-elite conflicts in the sixteenth–eighteenth centuries with the subordination of hereditary landed elite to the state in the early eighteenth century under Peter I, with the opposite trend in the second half of the eighteenth century and the signs of state capture by the landed elite under the reign of Peter III and Catherine II.

[26] In Imperial Russia's agricultural development, three major periods were defined in Leonard (2011, 254) as servile Russia (pre-1861), post-Emancipation Russia (1860s–1870s), and early industrialization (1880s–1910s).

[27] With certain exceptions, only the nobility had the right to possess serfs.

[28] Before the eighteenth century, it was the Russian Orthodox Church that possessed much land and many serfs besides the state. This served as an economic basis for Church autonomy. But under the reform implemented in 1764 by Catherine II, Church ownership was substantially curtailed in favour of state ownership in the core Russian provinces, later expanded to the provinces of modern Ukraine and Belarus. The Church was compensated by subventions from the state budget. Such policies were in line with those pursued by Peter I (early eighteenth century), who did not allow the election of a new patriarch and created the ministerial Holy Synod, which began the integration of the Church into the government's system of administration.

obligation to provide ancillary services in lieu of tax payments for which the employer had become responsible. Such practices soon expanded substantially. The other source of labour was "possessional peasants", a category that was created in 1721 to give non-nobles the temporary right to purchase villages with serfs to provide workforces for their factories. Skilled labour was in particular demand at that time, and this move was primarily targeted at restricting labour's mobility (Crisp 1978, 313–316).[29] From the early eighteenth until the late nineteenth century, Russian urban workers (artisans, craftsmen, apprentices, both self-employed and at manufactories) were members of guilds, which were primarily the instrument of state taxation (Crisp 1978, 316–317). They were bound to their places as taxpayers and could not leave without the local authorities' consent. This was generally given when there was need, although not without a charge; thus, mobility had certain transaction costs.

Under serfdom, two major types of activity evolved in the Russian secondary sector. The first of these involved the peasants, predominantly in densely populated central regions with a cold climate and less fertile soils. The supply of labour for hire grew both among Crown peasants and among privately owned serfs. These were off-farm workers (*otkhodniki*), who were allowed to pay rent from their off-farm earnings (*promysly*). The successful rise of serf entrepreneurs, founders of industrial dynasties that survived until the Revolution of 1917, began in the late eighteenth century and was a distinctive feature of industrial development in the first half of the nineteenth century. There were many instances of peasants being handed over to factories by their landlords or by the communes to work off arrears in rents or taxes, or debts in general. In such cases, the element of free hire was absent, the workers being no better than bonded labour.

The second type of activity involved the nobles, predominantly in the southern regions where agriculture was relatively productive. Large factories were founded by estate owners (*votchinnaia manufaktura*) as adjuncts to their lands, as supplementary sources of cash income that used their existing labour forces. Subsequently, though, there was a great variety in employment patterns. As factories operated all year round, a hereditary working class formed, divorced from other sources of income and trained in a particular craft.

Hired labour in manufacturing began to be increasingly important from the last third of the eighteenth century. Yet, there was a widening of the labour market that reduced the need to resort to such labour, especially in enterprises located near cities. Thus, during the first half of the nineteenth century, hired labour (even though

[29] Indeed, the creation of the Ural metallurgical complex at an appreciable distance from existing population centres and transportation routes made it almost impossible to attract a labour force of the size required by way of the market. In general, it can be said that in the eighteenth century, Russia succeeded in developing proto-industry for which there was large demand either from the state or from abroad over a fairly short time. It is unlikely that anything approaching the scale of output actually achieved would have proved possible without compulsion and without concentrated efforts being made by the state (Crisp 1978, 310–312, 317).

not completely free, if serfs were hired following the decision of their lords) outpaced forced labour in the Russian secondary sector.[30]

Domar and Machina (1989) use information relating to the price of land with and without resident peasants to argue that serfdom was profitable to the nobility up to 1861. Their findings support the argument that the reasons behind serfdom's abolition were principally ideological and cultural rather than just economic,[31] similar to Fogel and Engerman's (1974) thesis on slavery in the US South of the time.

After private serfs were emancipated in 1861, a transitional period was stipulated during which they were obliged to work for their landlords as they had before. This arrangement was to last for two years, during which redemption fees for land would be paid by the government to the lords, and peasant communes would become owners of the households' plots, after which they were obliged to pay annuities to the government. The basic problem for labour mobility was that this allotted land (which was normally allocated for each household) could be used only for their own production, or possibly for rent to other peasant commune members. This meant that peasants were still bound to their allotted lands economically, and that restrictions on mobility were lifted only very slowly.

Following the preparations that had been made from the late 1830s, a separate Emancipation Act that dealt with state serfs was adopted in 1863, without a lengthy transitional period, but also with communal land being allotted to commune members.[32]

The conventional view is that limited access by individual rural dwellers (as opposed to communes or households) to the ownership of land—enabling them to sell it or leave it in inheritance—was a conspicuous constraint on economic growth in the late nineteenth century (Leonard 2011, 140). Recent research (Cheremukhin et al. 2017) has cast doubt on the view that this was the major obstacle to the modernization of the Russian economy. As Crisp (1978, 323–325) argues, communal restrictions on rural–urban migration were not a binding constraint for industrialization. At that early stage, this limitation was offset by partial employment both in industry and in agriculture. Time sharing could be on a seasonal basis (in summer agriculture, in winter manufacturing). Peasants could therefore migrate from rural to urban areas for several months at a time. Furthermore, Russian manufacturing developed in rural areas, close to the workers' settlements. In both cases, Russian factory workers continued to be small landowners.

The commune was viewed both by the government and many of its critics as a viable institution that would allow the easing of social tensions and be a stabilizing influence. As modern economic growth began, government policies, while not

[30] See also Sect. 4.2.2. Looked at from the Marxist point of view, the workers employed in Russian factories of the proto-industrialization period were not proletarians whose labour capabilities were a commodity on the production factor markets. In many cases they remained potential agriculturalists and small landowners who had at their disposal alternative means of earning or supplementing their living (Crisp 1978, 318–323).

[31] In recent literature, this thesis is strongly voiced in Mironov (2018, vol. 2, 62–80).

[32] Russian Emancipation and the institutions of the transition period are documented in classic studies by Field (1976) and Zaionchkovsky (1978).

discouraging labour mobility, did not stimulate it either.[33] However, the destruction of landlords' estates during the first Russian Revolution (1905–1907) challenged this view. Legal constraints on rural labour mobility were therefore finally lifted in 1906 and 1907, and emigration to Siberia and the Far East was stimulated. These measures, initiated by the Prime Minister P. A. Stolypin,[34] allowed peasants to leave the commune, separate and unify their strips of allotted land, and turn the plot into private property that could be sold. Implementation of the Stolypin reforms was projected to take place over about two decades. Dismantling rural communal institutions was underway, but not rapidly. Only 10% of households in European Russia lived on farms independent from communes by the end of 1914 (Davies et al. 1994, 107).

Much evidence suggests that the vast majority of the economically active population was not enrolled in an organized wage economy even by the Revolution of 1917. The majority of farms were family units that relied almost entirely on family labour. Most workers in the secondary sector were also engaged in self-employed small-scale rural family units, manufacturing for a market (*kustari*) that dominated traditional urban craftsmanship (*remeslo*). The former industries developed most intensively in areas where the seasonal nature of agriculture was most pronounced, where land quality was relatively poor, and most importantly, where there was good access to markets. Only in a few areas, such as the western Baltic and some Polish regions, and in the south of European Russia, was all-year-round agricultural labour employed. In Central Russia, even large estates employed a small nucleus of permanent labourers, more in the nature of servants, and hired local peasants for seasonal work either for a daily wage or for an agreed payment for a particular job, or on the basis of crop-sharing or working to cover rents. Industries of this nature were most successful in areas that were not significantly ethnically Russian, such as the western and southern provinces and the Volga basin. Yet the rates of growth for numbers of wage earners well exceeded those for other labourers, both in agriculture and in industry. Moreover, the rise in the number of passports for "going-away" work (*otkhod*) was much steeper than the rise in wage-earning occupations as a whole, and steeper still than the growth in factory employment (Crisp 1978, 330–341).

In sum, the pattern that the more society is modernized, the more a market economy exists, and the more labour is free, appears to be a trend; however, slavery in the southern United States was a major exception, with minor exceptions occurring in British, Dutch, and French colonies in the seventeenth and eighteenth centuries. The timing of the abolition of serfdom in Russia and slavery in the United States also poses questions about the widespread usage of forced labour on the path to modern economy and society (Kolchin 1987). The common feature in these two societies was a high land-to-population ratio,[35] which contributed to a high demand

[33] A sophisticated internal passport system involved permits from the local authorities for long-distance migration, but requirements for these were not too strict.

[34] See Sect. 3.2.

[35] We highlight the dynamics of this key explanatory variable employed by Domar (1989) in Sect. 5.4.3 as the land rent to wage ratio.

for labour amid territorial expansion and frontier colonization in both countries.[36] The difference was that Russian serfdom emerged and developed in a less commodified economy,[37] while the rise and flourishing of southern United States slavery occurred within the industrializing economies of the northern United States and Europe (primarily England). Evidently, slave labour in America was more capital-intensive and used better agricultural techniques than serf labour did in Russia (Domar 1989, 229).

These parallels are also useful in explaining why resorting to forced labour may resume when a path to modernity is being pursued in an industrialized economy, examples being the USSR in the 1930s–mid-1950s and China in the 1960s–mid-1970s. In these cases, the strong ideology of those who are affecting coercion appears to be one of the crucial factors. And in both examples, the state was intervening to distribute commodities between rural and urban sectors and between civilian and military spheres (Sect. 6.2).

Indeed, as shown in Table 4.4, although commodified labour has a long history, it was mainly around 1700 that its growth started, from about 10%, continuing until the present 50% was reached. This process was not the same in all countries. In Western countries, from 1700 to 1900, commodified labour as a percentage of total labour was about 10 percentage points higher than in other countries. Yet, after 1900, the patterns in all countries were roughly the same.

4.4 Timing of the Fertility Transition and Human Capital Rise

4.4.1 Economic Growth and Declining Fertility

Fertility and human capital are widely discussed in the literature. It is especially important in Galor's unified growth theory, with a rise in income leading to a reduction in fertility, followed by a rise in human capital. After some time, this negative relation between fertility and human capital breaks down, and modern economic growth continues.

The question is whether a temporary income rise (from the factors mentioned in Chap. 2) decreases fertility. This is pointed out by Hu (2020), who finds for China that upper classes traditionally had more children than commoners, this being mostly driven by more marriages and occurring more strongly after 1600. No decline in fertility is detected in his analysis. Indeed, the focus on quantity rather than quality of children is also found by Shiue (2017), who, in a long-run study of Chinese clans, finds that before the seventeenth century, a negative relation between

[36] See Sect. 4.6.5.

[37] Yet, as shown in Sect. 4.6.3, money and trade penetration were on the rise in the second half of the eighteenth century, when private serfdom reached its peak in Russia.

Table 4.4 Share of commodified and reciprocal labour by country, 1500–2000 (%)

		Commodified labour	Reciprocal labour	Other
1500	China	9.5	72.3	18.2
	Taiwan	1.0	79.2	19.8
	Russia	0.1	75.3	24.6
	Italy/Venice	8.8	64.4	26.8
1650	Taiwan	1.0	79.2	19.8
	Indonesia	52.7	32.9	14.5
	Russia	1.5	74.6	23.9
	Italy/Venice	2.1	73.8	24.1
	Brazil	58.1	30.2	11.8
1800	China	9.8	47.9	42.4
	Russia	2.0	72.8	25.2
	Japan	11.0	60.2	28.9
	India	46.3	30.7	23.0
	Indonesia	38.2	46.8	15.0
	Spain	27.4	44.8	27.8
2000	China	57.2	24.1	18.6
	Russia	42.3	27.1	30.5
	Japan	48.0	12.2	39.9
	Spain	36.8	15.7	47.5
	the Netherlands	46.3	13.0	40.8
	United Kingdom	44.8	30.3	24.9

Source: IISH (n.d.)

fertility and human capital existed (lower fertility thus corresponding to higher human capital). Yet this negative relation disappeared in the eighteenth–nineteenth centuries, when the lower chance of passing the civil service examination (the exam necessary to obtain a highly desirable government position) meant that lower fertility had less use, as the chance of getting a government position was small anyway. Hence, the previously negative relationship between fertility and human capital became insignificant not because of modern growth, but because of less efficient human capital development. This can also be concluded by studying the development of human capital in Sect. 4.4.4.

This pattern was exactly reversed for Russia. It was the rich merchants who, in the early eighteenth century, were so reluctant to educate their offspring that they asked the Senate to make an exclusion for them when implementing the emperor's edict on conscription to numerical schools (*tsifirnye shkoly*), which were planned for every province but ultimately failed to appear. The merchants' first argument was one of high opportunity costs (they would be worse off without their children's assistance). So, even though the level of education in Russia was not slowing down growth, as was the case in China, it was removing labour from the labour market.

Indeed, it was argued that their offspring were learning by doing anyway.[38] However, fragmentary evidence indicates that literacy was relatively high among Russian merchants (comparable with that of the gentry) and increased over half a century (Kozlova 1999, 340). Later, in the nineteenth century, merchant capital was employed as a prominent source of charity funding for the construction and operation of schools. Although these funds were supplementary to public and household financing, donations from traders and entrepreneurs were relatively important during the early spread of education in Russia. Thus, trade development and human capital formation were interrelated processes, complementary to modern growth initiation.

4.4.2 European Marriage Pattern

A second reason (other than economic growth) for lower marital fertility (and hence increased human capital investment by households) is the so-called European Marriage Pattern. De Moor and Van Zanden (2010) claim this arose in the late Middle Ages in Western Europe owing to a combination of the Catholic Church's preaching of consensual marriage, the rise of labour markets, and inheritance rights. Before the late Middle Ages, family relations had been impersonal (organized between families) and dominated by the household heads. From the late medieval period onwards, more women worked outside the household in Europe, and the marriage age increased. Hence, according to De Moor and Van Zanden, fertility began to decline and more income was left for increasing human capital for the smaller number of children. There is evidence that this pattern also existed in Eastern Europe (Baten et al. 2017). Yet others (e.g. Dennison and Ogilvy 2014) claim that such a relationship did not exist. In China, even though scholars investigating the effect of the European Marriage Pattern looked there for evidence, the indications are less reliable. For example, at first sight, China did not make a transition, at least not formally, towards consensual marriage (see Table 4.5) until the

Table 4.5 Legal marriage age by men and women in China, 574 CE–c. 1910

	Legal marriage age	
	Men	Women
574	15	13
627	20	15
734	15	13
960–1127	16	14
1127–1279	16	14
Ming dynasty	16	14
Qing dynasty	16	14

Source: Zheng Huiyan (郑惠雁) (2001)

[38] This anecdotal evidence based on archival source is borrowed from Kozlova (1999, 334).

1930s. Although formal requirements changed little over time, there is only slight evidence that women's position in marriage differed much in practice from the situation in Europe. Indeed, as shown in Table 4.6, age at first marriage also increased in China. Hence, even though the European Marriage Pattern is important, in terms of affecting human capital, its effect seems limited in both China and Eastern Europe.

4.4.3 A Case Study: Fertility and Human Capital in Central Eurasia

Central Eurasia faced a similar pattern to China and Europe, with fertility remaining high until the nineteenth and twentieth centuries[39]; but human capital nonetheless started to rise from the nineteenth century. This matches the timing of the demographic transition that, for central Asia, is dated either from the 1860s (commencement in urban areas) (Mironov 2022), from the very late nineteenth century (Vishneskii 2006, 24), or from the first decade of the twentieth century (when a clear trend of fertility decline emerged) to the 1960s (when fertility decline had halted) (Zakharov et al. 2006, 157–158).[40]

The relation between income and fertility in Russia, though, is not entirely negative. As can be seen from Figs. 4.7 and 4.8, at the start of the transition (late nineteenth–early twentieth centuries), fertility was even modestly rising as an increase in incomes allowed people to increase natality.[41] Therefore, at that stage, the peoples of Central Eurasia could have remained within the same Malthusian trap as many developing nations, with fast-growing incomes and a population with steady

Table 4.6 Female age at first marriage in China, c. 581–1947

Period	Female age at first marriage	Source
581–619	16.83	Shen (2008)
618–907	16.2	Zheng (2001)
Song dynasty	19.04	Zheng (2010)
Qing	17.44	Zheng (2010)
1947	21	Van Leeuwen and Li (2022)

[39] Estimates based on documented evidence related to the European part of Russia in 1738–1748 are presented in Mironov (1991, 259, table 2).

[40] Coinciding with the time when urban population outnumbered rural on average in the USSR.

[41] These values of TFR (Total Fertility Rates) were derived from crude birth rates estimated in Kumo (2007), the same as in Kumo (2019), from where we borrowed IMR (Infant Mortality Rate), and from Zakharov (2008). The earlier estimates of TFR in Zakharov et al. (2006, 157) suggest that the decline in fertility had started already in 1896–1900. The estimates by Mironov (2022) also suggest that from 1859 to 1897 a similar indicator of fertility decreased in European Russia from 7.11 to 7.07, owing to the drop in urban areas from 6.34 to 5.29. Such a significant decrease in actual fertility may indicate commencement of its control (Mironov 2022, 5).

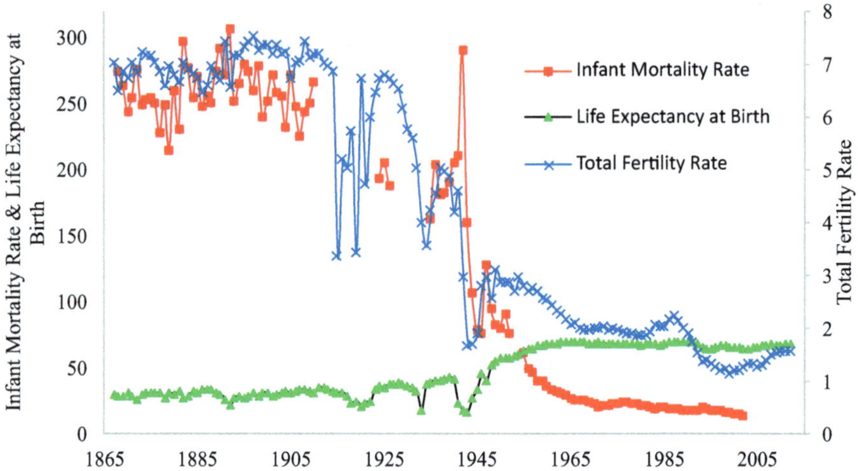

Fig. 4.7 Demographic transition indicators in Central Eurasia, 1867–2012. *Source:* Total fertility rate: Ajus and Lindgren (2015) based on Kumo et al. (2007), Zakharov (2008), HFD (2015); infant mortality rate: Kumo (2019); life expectancy at birth: Johansson, Lindgren (2014) based on Kumo et al. (2007), Andreev et al. (1992), and Andreev (1994), HMD (2009)

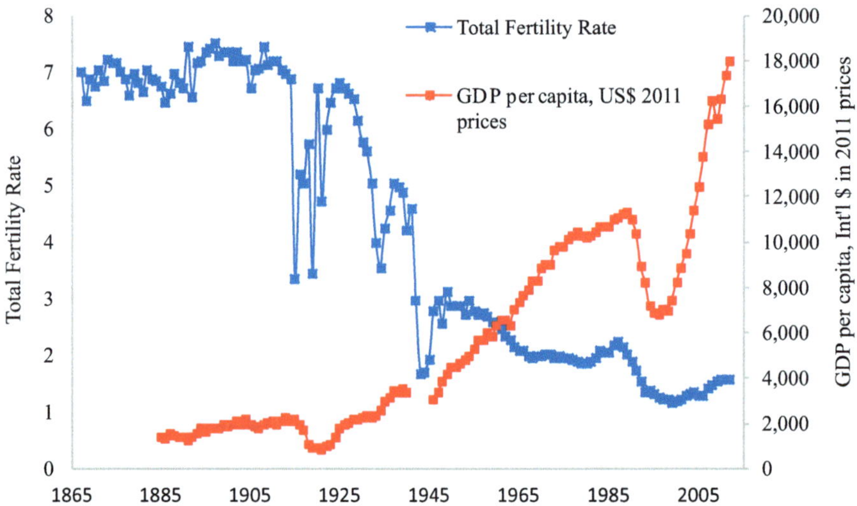

Fig. 4.8 Total fertility rate in Central Eurasia versus GDP per capita, 1867–2012. *Source:* Total fertility rate: Ajus and Lindgren (2015) based on Kumo et al. (2007), Zakharov (2008), HFD (2015); GDP per capita: Bolt and Van Zanden (2020)

long-term GDP per capita. But after the wartime (1914–1922) shock, recovery in total fertility rate (TFR) was not so complete as GDP per capita; then the TFR usually declined in times of peace with GDP per capita on the rise. However, the reverse correlation appeared to happen during wartime: TFR declined strongly with incomes. The same pattern was observed during the severe recession that accompanied the transition from a command[42] to a market economy, during the second demographic transition. The relationship between GDP per capita and TFR for the overall period 1867–2012 is shown in Fig. 4.9.[43] Likewise, we observe a rather high correlation of literacy and TFR (Fig. 4.10).

So, even though fertility might, at times and by region, affect literacy in Central Eurasia, the relationship is not always self-evident.

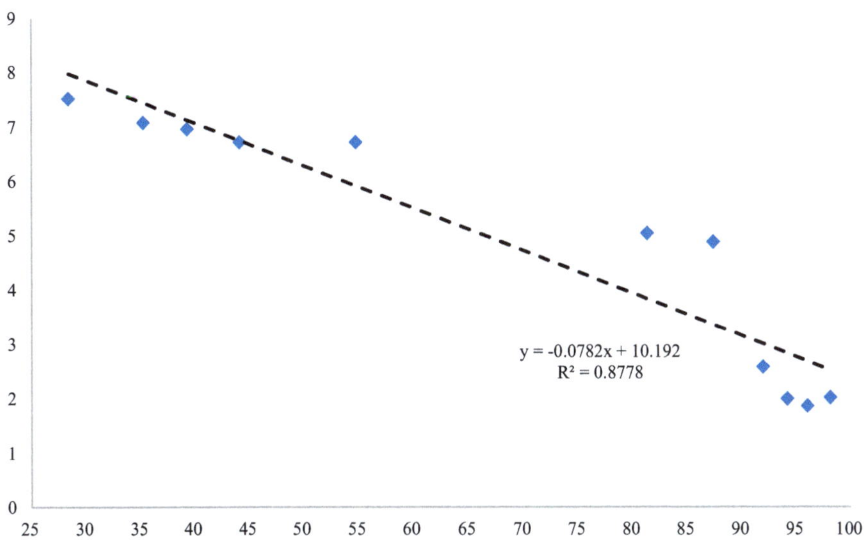

Fig. 4.9 Total fertility rate versus literacy in Central Eurasia, 1897–1989. *Source:* Total fertility rate: Ajus and Lindgren (2015) based on Kumo et al. (2007), Zakharov (2008), HFD (2015); literacy: Didenko et al. (2013) based on GKS (1989), GKS RF (1992), HSE IDEM (2011), Mironov (1985a, 1991, 2003), Poliakov (1992, 2007), TsSU (1929), TsUNKhU (1940). *Note:* 1670–1837: European part of Russia; 1897: Russian Empire; 1920–1989: the FSU, within its borders after 1945

[42] Command (or command-administration) economy is an economic system where the government controls and directs economic activity. The government enact its influence by central planning and state ownership in major industries; this leads to dominance of government investments and non-market price setting.

[43] As the data for demographic indicators for the most part of the nineteenth century do not match the territories for literacy, we were limited to the period from the first all-Russia census of 1897.

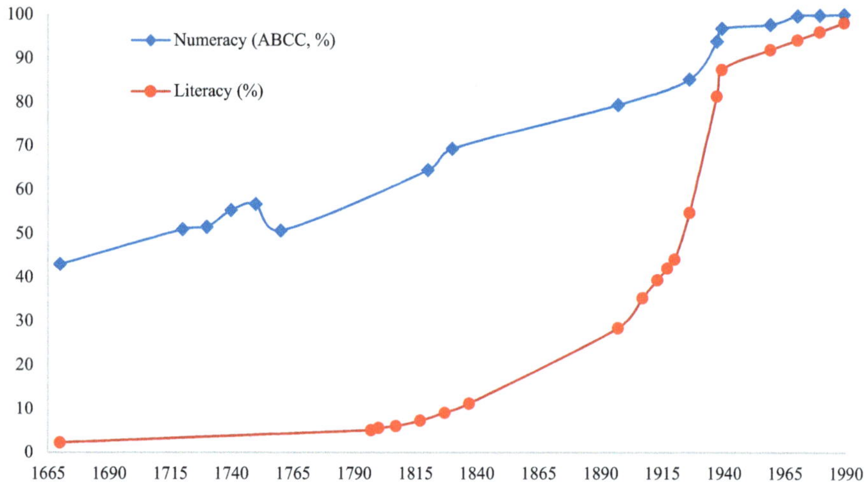

Fig. 4.10 Numeracy and literacy in Central Eurasia, 1670–1989. *Source:* Numeracy: Clio Infra (Baten and Blum 2015); literacy: Didenko et al. (2013) based on GKS (1989), GKS RF (1992), HSE IDEM (2011), Mironov (1985a, 1991, 2003), Poliakov (1992, 2007), TsSU (1929), TsUNKhU (1940). *Note:* 1670–1837: European part of Russia; 1897: Russian Empire; 1920–1989 the FSU, within its borders after 1945

4.4.4 Human Capital

Out of three important long-run indicators of human capital, the number of book imprints ran about parallel in Europe and China between the fourteenth and eighteenth centuries (McDermott 2005; Xu et al. 2021). Education after the seventeenth century was more dependent on income, rather than on the cost of books (Xu et al. 2021).

Likewise, there is human capital evidence based on the frequency of age heaping—the tendency to respond to a question about one's age with "more attractive" numbers, typically multiples of 5. Such data can be used as a proxy for the level of numeracy and therefore of the human capital level of a population in the absence of better sources (A'Hearn et al. 2009). It has been calculated that for Imperial Rome accurate reporting of age (also called the ABCC index) is roughly 55–67% of the total (Duncan-Jones 1977) and for China, between 500 BCE and 600 CE—by using data retrieved from the biographies of Chinese scientists throughout this period (see Du 1992)—a ABCC index of 66.67% can be found. The two results for Imperial Rome and China are therefore roughly similar.[44] This diverges somewhat in the following centuries. Evidence on age heaping, for example, suggests that correct reporting of age in Italy in 1520 was 55% and in 1720 around 76%. In China in 1670, it was 94%, while in 1720, it was 99%. In 1870, a level of around 100% of

[44] Once again with the caveat that these two macro-areas used different age calculation systems over time and regions, and that these results are based only on reports from the upper classes.

correct age reporting was reached in both areas (see A'Hearn et al. 2009; ClioInfra database). These estimates provide the first evidence that during the early modern period (see Fig. 4.10), China seemingly reached higher human capital levels than Southern Europe. Yet, since China has a different system of calculating age, the values for China are upward biased.

For Russia, numeracy is documented from the late seventeenth century and literacy from the late nineteenth century,[45] that is, long before the demographic transition and the launch of modern economic growth. Numeracy increased steadily,[46] while literacy skyrocketed during the educational revolution of the 1920s–1930s. Presumably, this was primarily because the eradication of illiteracy was one of the top priorities on the socialist political agenda. (The poster reproduced as Fig. 4.11, with the slogan "Illiterate is the blind person who is expected to be caught by bad luck and misfortune" was created at the start of the campaign.) Thereafter, the measurement of literacy in Russia was sensitive to gradual easing of the criteria, owing to its high political sensitivity.[47]

A third indicator of human capital is the skill premium. In Europe, this was, at about 50%, relatively low (Van Zanden 2005). Further, it was constant from about 1300 to 1900. As with book imprints, we find that the skill premium in Asia was constant and high before about 1750–1850, with a decline afterwards, followed by an increase again from about 1825 in Japan and about 1880 in India. For Russia, the evidence presented in Strumilin (1966, 55–56) shows that skill premiums in the ironworks near Moscow and in the Urals tightened over the two centuries—from 8.5 in the mid-seventeenth century to 2–2.33 in the mid-eighteenth century.

As for Russia, at the initial stage of modern growth, before the First World War and the Revolution of 1917, there is evidence that indicates some widening of the skill premium in the textile industry, and also among construction workers[48] (Borodkin 2001; Borodkin and Valetov 2001; Borodkin et al. 2008), much the same

[45] Although some guesstimates exist for the middle of the thirteenth century (1–1.5%) and the late seventeenth century (2–2.5%), and there is historical reconstruction by age cohorts backwards-shifting to the late eighteenth century in Mironov (1985a, 1991). Sample surveys conducted in the second half of the nineteenth century and documented in Rashin (1956, 284–306) generally support this reconstruction.

[46] As regards age heaping, the available evidence (CLIO-INFRA dataset) goes back to 1670, based on A'Hearn et al. (2009) and Hippe and Baten (2012). The latter goes back to 1640 for a couple of districts, and provides practically complete coverage for about 50 provinces of European Russia as of the 1897 census (by decadal birth cohorts). However, for 1897, their ABCC estimate for European Russia is significantly higher than the estimate for all the Russian Empire in Didenko, Van Leeuwen, and Foldvari (2013), namely 98% versus 79.4%. The level close to 100% is hardly consistent with a literacy rate of 30.1% for European Russia. In Didenko, Van Leeuwen, and Foldvari (2013), the ABCC for the USSR became 96.8%, with a reported literacy rate of 81.2% (very likely upward biased) as late as 1939.

[47] It is worth noting that writing skills were never taken into account in Russia and the USSR, as literacy was detected by straightforward questions regarding the respondents' ability to read at least one language in the censuses.

[48] For the textile industry these figures relate to Serpukhov, Moscow region, 1898–1914; for construction workers, they relate to the capital city of St. Petersburg, 1853–1910.

Fig. 4.11 Soviet propaganda poster from an early campaign for the eradication of illiteracy. *Source*: Wikimedia: https://commons.wikimedia.org/wiki/File:Likbez.JPG. *Note*: by Alexei Radakov. 1920 (https://commons.wikimedia.org/wiki/Category:Aleksey_Radakov)

as in Japan in 1825. Indeed, the observations in Strumilin (1966, 88) confirm that the skill premium widened at the early stage of modern growth. In St. Petersburg, skilled labour earned wages about 95% higher than the unskilled on average. This is a figure roughly equivalent to the gap observed in developing countries and in other countries that were experiencing industrialization in the nineteenth century, and much higher than the gap in the United States in the 1890s (Borodkin et al. 2008, 75, 76, 88).

For Russia in the early twentieth century, Cheremukhin et al. (2017) estimate returns to literacy in manufacturing (i.e. increased wages for literate people compared to illiterates) at 13%, while they are assumed to be around zero in agriculture. This is basically consistent with the finding of Didenko (2022, 78) of an 18% wage premium for each additional year of schooling based on the white- versus blue-collar workers industry wage differential in 1913.

It is important to observe that we are now, following Mokyr (2002), mostly considering prescriptive (practical) versus propositional (higher, theoretical) knowledge. One would expect that both types of human capital would be combined during an industrial revolution. Yet, on the contrary, human capital development in the Industrial Revolution is mostly found to be limited. This was true for China as well. For example, Bai (2013) finds that regions with more traditional learning (based on the civil examination) established fewer new factories. Some authors claim that in England it was mostly higher (propositional) human capital that focused on economic growth (Squicciarini and Voigtländer 2015). Yet, little evidence has been found by us, so we basically agree with the absence of technology–skill complementarity in the First Industrial Revolution (e.g. Philips 2020).

It is difficult to argue why human capital started to play a direct role in economic growth. Studies on the late nineteenth to the twentieth centuries (e.g. Prados de la Escosura and Rosés 2010; Felice 2012; Godo 2018; Godo and Hayami 2002; Kokkinen 2012; Ljungberg and Nilsson 2009; Turner et al. 2013), even though differentiated by regression forms and estimates of human capital, seem to agree on its importance. The best way to disentangle this is by looking at studies on developing economies, as they provide most information on the shift to human capital-driven economies. Van Leeuwen and Földvári (2008a, b), for example, show that Japan in the first half of the twentieth century showed a Lucasian pattern of growth, in which human capital is purely used to implement technology in production processes. Only once it came close to the production frontier (i.e. the maximum productivity based on new technologies) in the mid-twentieth century was human capital increasingly used to generate new technologies (Romerian growth). India and Indonesia only applied human capital to implement new technologies. So, Romerian growth is the successor of Lucasian growth.

For the twentieth and twenty-first centuries, there are many studies that show, for several reasons, why human capital does not affect growth; examples are the phase of deskilling during the First Industrial Revolution and the reduced growth of human capital at the end of the twentieth century and the beginning of the twenty-first century (Chap. 9 on twentieth and twenty-first centuries). As we see in Chap. 7, a focus on physical capital, rather than human capital-intensive goods, in socialist countries is one explanation. Another is institutions. A low level of human capital technologies is an additional one. Indeed, as pointed out by Pritchett, there were various reasons for human capital not creating higher productivity, that is, a perverse institutional governance environment, a fast-decreasing marginal return to education, as supply rose faster than demand for education, and educational quality that was so low it did not create additional skills.

4.4.5 Fertility and Human Capital

In many ways, the relation between fertility and human capital in China and Eurasia seems to deviate little from England, where fertility remained high until the nineteenth century (Wilson and Woods 1991), after which it was accompanied by a rise in human capital (Galor 2011b). Again, similar to China and Eurasia, Klemp and Weisdorf (2019), although confirming the relationship between literacy and fertility, find that human capital accumulation had already begun before the significant decline in fertility occurred.

What is thus quite interesting is that the rise in human capital in England, Eurasia, and China seems to occur a bit before the decline in fertility (Hippe and Baten 2012). In China and England, this was mostly because the upper classes led in literacy. In Russia, however, with the start of mass literacy campaigns during state socialism, inequality mainly occurred between the city and the countryside.

This suggests that, contrary to Central Eurasia and Europe, inequality in physical capital was initially enhanced in China, with the upper classes having low fertility, excess physical capital, and excess human capital. Only after human capital in China had lowered its expected returns by reducing access to schooling, thus making the acquisition of human capital less profitable (because both the achieved level of education and access to education determined education's potential profitability), did inequality decline, which occurred during the nineteenth century.

4.5 Government Extraction and Taxation

As pointed out by Davis and Henderson (2003), extraction and taxation can modify the inputs of any existing production system based on a certain amount of labour and physical capital—for example, by increasing prices of manufacturing products. Yet, they do not, by themselves, create factors of production such as labour, education (human capital), or (physical) capital that drive economic growth.

Extraction and taxation are thus important for manufacturing via urbanization (shifting labour to high productivity urban manufacturing and, hence, creating economic growth) as well as for labour relations, fertility, and human capital (creating human capital and, hence, causing economic growth). Government extraction and taxation can be captured, for regions and time periods with few data, by looking at urban primacy (the share of the largest capital city in total population). Bosker et al. (2013) demonstrate that this "primate city effect" (basically the effect of concentration of urban economic and political activities) is related to the political economy of states. In the Arab world, the urban system was dominated by a few large capital cities (Baghdad, Damascus, Cairo, Istanbul), which had the features of typical "consumer cities". European cities were on average much smaller and less dependent on the states they were part of—in particular during the Middle Ages, when "producer cities" dominated the urban landscape. This has also been demonstrated by recent research into historically contemporary urban systems (e.g. Ades and Glaeser 1995; Davis and Henderson 2003), which has shown that high levels of urban concentration are linked to a higher degree of political instability and a lack of democracy: "Urban giants ultimately stem from the concentration of power in the hands of a small cadre of agents living in the capital. This power allows the leaders to extract wealth out of the hinterland and distribute it in the capital" (Ades and Glaeser 1995, 224). When a few large cities dominate the urban landscape, this tends to be indicative of an urban system that is much more oriented towards serving the need of the political elites in these major cities (see also Bosker et al. 2013).

Table 4.6 allows us to identify the largest cities in China. In 1100, Kaifeng, the capital of the Northern Song, was the largest city, with probably about one million inhabitants; in 1200, this was Hangzhou, the capital of the Southern Song, with an estimated population of 1.1 million. The largest city in Europe in 1100 was Cordoba (80,000 inhabitants), and in 1200 Paris (110,000), only a fraction of the Chinese capitals. But in the nineteenth century, the largest city in China, Beijing, with about one million inhabitants, was probably smaller than Hangzhou in 1200, and in 1900, the commercial metropolis Shanghai counted only 900,000 people and had almost overtaken Beijing. In 1918, it was surpassed by another commercial metropolis, Guangzhou, with 1.6 million inhabitants. As Table 4.7 shows, the share of the primate city in the total population of China fluctuated throughout the period: it rose slightly from 1% in 1100 to 1.4% in 1400, only to be followed by a significant decline, before starting to recover early in the twentieth century. Over the same period, the tiny capital cities of Europe had grown considerably. Around 1800, London, which emerged as the largest city (surpassing Paris), was about the same size as Beijing, but after 1800 London underwent unparalleled growth. Around 1900, it had more than six million inhabitants, approximately 2.3% of the population of Western Europe. In the Arab world, this percentage fluctuated around 1.5%, with a tendency to rise to more than 2% after the consolidation of the Ottoman Empire: the share of the population living in Istanbul increased from 1.8% in 1500 to 2.2% in 1800 (Bosker et al. 2013).

As seen from Table 4.7, in terms of urban primacy, Russia (Rus') and Western Europe were stable and low (compared with China) between 1100 and 1400, with Russia lagging behind the West. The size of the primate city of the historical Russian states in the European part of Central Eurasia dropped from about 1500 until the twentieth century. In this, it mirrored China, even though it was ahead of China over

Table 4.7 Urban primacy in China, Western Europe, and Central Eurasia compared, 1100–1900

	Primate city (in 1000 inhabitants)			Primate city/Total population (in %)		
	China	Western Europe	European Russia/ Central Eurasia**	China	Western Europe	European Russia/ Central Eurasia
1100	1000	80	10/100–500	1.0	0.2	0.1/n.d.
1200	1100	110	35/100–500	0.8	0.2	0.2/n.d.
1300	1090	120	n.d./25–125	1.5	0.2	n.d./n.d.
1400/1391*	950	100	40/130–150	1.4	0.2	n.d./n.d.
1500		250	100/60		0.4	4.0
1600/30	1240	300	100/100	0.7	0.4	1.9
1700/1644	650	575	160/80	0.4	0.6	1.2
1800	987	948	270	0.3	0.7	0.6
1850	1063	2236	487.3	0.3	1.1	0.7
1900	1104	6226	1418	0.2	2.3	1.1
1918	1600		1469	0.4		0.8

Note: *1400 = Europe and 1391 = China; ** in the European part (Kyiv in 1100 and 1200, Moscow in 1400–1800) on the left and in the Asian part (Samarkand in 1100–1500; Bokhara in 1600–1700) on the right; wide magnitude of estimates for Samarkand

Source: Bosker et al. (2013), Xu et al. (2018), for Central Eurasia: Primate city: Wikipedia (Kyiv in 1000 and 1200 (https://ru.wikipedia.org/wiki/%D0%9D%D0%B0%D1%81%D0%B5%D0%BB%D0%B5%D0%BD%D0%B8%D0%B5_%D0%9A%D0%B8%D0%B5%D0%B2%D0%B0), Samarkand in *c.* 1400 (https://en.wikipedia.org/wiki/Timeline_of_Samarkand), Moscow from 1400 to 1800 (https://ru.wikipedia.org/wiki/%D0%9D%D0%B0%D1%81%D0%B5%D0%BB%D0%B5%D0%BD%D0%B8%D0%B5_%D0%9C%D0%BE%D1%81%D0%BA%D0%B2%D1%8B), St. Petersburg from 1850 to 1918 (https://ru.wikipedia.org/wiki/%D0%9D%D0%B0%D1%81%D0%B5%D0%BB%D0%B5%D0%BD%D0%B8%D0%B5_%D0%A1%D0%B0%D0%BD%D0%BA%D1%82-%D0%9F%D0%B5%D1%82%D0%B5%D1%80%D0%B1%D1%83%D1%80%D0%B3%D0%B0)), Suhareva (1958) for Samarkand in 1100 and 1200 (lower estimate), Bartol'd (1963) for Samarkand in 1100 and 1200 (upper estimate), Trever et al. (1950) for Samarkand in 1300; Chandler (1987) for Samarkand in 1400–1500 and Bukhara (Bokhara) in 1600; Population: Vernadsky (1973) for 1100 (=1000), Kuchkin (2013) for 1200, Mironov (2018) for 1500 (=1480), 1600 (=1580), 1700 (=1680), Broadberry and Korchmina (2024) for 1800 (=1815), 1850 (=1858), 1900 (=1897), 1918 (=1914)

the entire period. On the contrary, urban primacy in Western Europe increased over time and overtook both China and Russia around 1800.

In the Asian part of Central Eurasia, the high urbanization of Khwarazm and Transoxiana (Central Asia) brought it close to the Arab world at the turn of the first millennium. The size of the primate city was between China and the West before 1500, and the opposite since then. In terms of share of the primate city in terms of total population, Central Eurasia was closer to the West before the thirteenth century[49] and in the nineteenth century.

---

[49] This was when the Mongol invasion had devastating effects on both Asian and European parts of the supraregion. Nevertheless, the Asian part remained superior over the European Russian principalities in relative terms of primate city size. Recovery and unification occurred in both parts, in the European one under the Principality of Moscow (early fourteenth–fifteenth centuries) and in the Asian one under the Empire created by Tamerlane with the successor Timuride rulers (late

During the Song (960–1279), China had an urban system dominated by two capital cities, one in the Northern Song and one in the Southern Song, which together were responsible for around 2% of the total population. In terms of primacy, this was comparable to the Arab world, where similar huge cities were to be found. But this changed dramatically between 1100 and 1900. It can be argued that the size of a capital city in the first place reflects the capacity of the state to mobilize resources. From this perspective, the relative decline of the Chinese capital cities points to changes in the political economy of the country (see e.g. Ma 2011), ultimately leading to the declining capacity of the state to extract resources from the economy, and to maintain an efficient bureaucracy and supply public services. By contrast, Europe went through a process of state formation that greatly enhanced the capabilities of its states: In Western Europe, the share of taxation in GDP rose to 8%–12% in the first half of the nineteenth century, whereas the estimates for nineteenth-century China were as low as 2% of GDP (Ma 2011).

The contrasting paths of formation of the Chinese and European states also help to explain contrasts in the urbanization process. The changing position of the primate city in the economy and in the urban structure was part of a much broader change in the structure of urbanization. Both Skinner (1977) and Rozman (1973) point out that the Chinese urban system of the nineteenth century had a rather unbalanced structure, with its "peak" being quite flat. Rozman compares this with Japan, where Edo with its million inhabitants was huge; there, more than 3% of the total population lived in the capital, testifying to the ability of the Japanese state to tax its population. China moved away from such an urban structure dominated by one (or a few) large, extractive consumer cities, which undermines the analysis put forward by Acemoglu and Robinson (2012) that extractive institutions put in place by the state hindered economic development. The data suggest that such extractive institutions (as measured by urban primacy) appear to be more effective for the period of economic prosperity during the Song dynasty than for the Qing dynasty. This downward spiral also existed in central Asia.

4.6 Trade and Empire

4.6.1 Rising Trade

One argument for the beginning of industrialization, other than urbanization, labour structure, fertility and human capital, and extraction and taxation, concerns trade and empire. In the first centuries CE, it was the Silk Road. From 900 to 1300, trade in Southeast Asia is argued to have boomed owing to financial, political, and

---

fourteenth—fifteenth centuries). Yet the reversal of these trends occurred in the sixteenth–seventeenth centuries. The European part, with the Russian (Muscovy) Tsardom (sixteenth and seventeenth centuries), consolidated and developed, despite the waves of deep crises, while the Asian parts generally declined, with the Khanates and Emirates being engaged in warfare. Therefore, since the seventeenth century, the primate city was located in the European part of Central Eurasia.

technical/marine improvements in China (Wade 2009). From 1492 to 1800, during early modern times, continents became increasingly connected, and exchanges of products (and infectious diseases) began (see e.g. Reid 1988–1993). One might question who the winners of this exchange were. According to Maddison (2007), Western Europe made up 18% of world income in 1500, rising to 27% in 1820 in GDP. Likewise, China declined to about 29% in 1820. During the second phase of globalization after 1820,[50] dominated by trade liberalization and cheaper transport, this process continued, with a share of 32% for Western Europe and 11% for China. Hence, Western Europe overtook China in national income sometime before 1900.

How much was this change in economic structure due to the existence of (colonial) Empires? Gokmen et al. (2020) provide a database on "imperial capital", related to enhancing trade. They find that the more empires were present in a territory, the more trade—that is, a 10% increase in the time they shared an imperial capital increases bilateral trade by at least 1.15%. The highest relative effects of imperial capital on trade took place in the Belgian, Italian, and French colonial empires, while in China, the Wei, Jin, and Mongol empires were important in terms of trade, but the subsequent Ming and Qing were not (Gokmen et al. 2020, 126).

4.6.2 *Types of Trade*

The fundamental question here, therefore, is not just how much was being traded, but how it was done. We can look at three forms of exchange: (1) reciprocity (gift or barter), (2) redistribution (collection of goods and later distribution based on custom), and (3) exchange (goods and services are exchanged based on negotiated prices) (for modes of exchange also see Sect. 4.3 on labour relations). One might argue that China was a trade as gift exchange society as opposed to, for example, Babylonia and the Roman Empire, and the medieval Mongol rule over Russia, which received tribute from bordering states. Indeed, the Chinese tribute system was developed so that a given foreign country was arguably regarded as culturally inferior to the Chinese state, but, in exchange, could benefit from gift-based trade. One might question whether this was such a sharp divide. On the one hand, scholars such as Polanyi (1957) claim that for Babylonia, culture-based gift exchanges occurred in other regions such as Mesopotamia. On the other hand, Gerraty et al. and Van der Spek et al. (2015) claim that markets were much more extensive than one might expect.

The situation was no different in China. Indeed, looking at its trade, this was mostly gift-based tribute trade. The tributary system, just as the market system, had to fulfil a goal. The market economy dealt with the optimum allocation of labour, capital, and demand and supply factors by means of the "invisible hand". Yet the

[50] The first phase of globalization is often thought to cover the first interactions between continents and the resulting colonization, *c.* 1492–1800.

tributary system emerged in China in a system where non-Chinese had to come into contact with Chinese society. Thus, it touched on various aspects such as (1) culture, (2) political self-defence of Chinese rulers, (3) Chinese international relations, and (4) commercial activities (Fairbank and Teng 1941; Huang 2019). This mix of different aims, as instituted in the Ming (1368–1644) and Qing (1636–1912) dynasties, had much to do with the idea of Chinese cultural superiority that had been prevalent in previous dynasties. Obviously, these aims were from a Chinese perspective; other countries might view them differently. For example, whereas China witnessed trade with Siam (present-day Thailand) predominantly as tributary, the people in Siam witnessed it instead more as trade (Viraphol 1977). This does not mean that China ignored direct trade relations altogether. Especially in periods of tranquillity, seaborne trade was often approved by the emperor. Moreover, during the late eighteenth century and early nineteenth century, policies about the frequency of tributary activity became flexible, so embassies from tribute states such as Annam, Burma, Siam, and Liu-ch'iu increased in frequency. Fairbank and Teng (1941) note a marked increase in the average number of embassies per year from 1.16 during 1662–1761 to 1.68 during 1801–1860, when leaving Korea out as a constant factor. During 1796–1839, the average growth rate of tributary activity from Siam was around 30%. It therefore appears that embassies increased as the dynasty grew older; that the height of Ch'ing power in the eighteenth century saw less tributary activity than the period of decline in the first half of the nineteenth century. Since the second half of the nineteenth century, the establishment of more and more exchange markets along the border, open treaty ports, and customs that managed international trade made this trade more and more convenient. The development of international trade made tributary trade less attractive to those tribute states, and led to the gradual decline of tributary trade.

Non-tributary trade increasingly gained a foothold, especially in Western Europe, after the Roman tributary system went into decline. This can possibly be attributed to state fragmentation, implying that no state was powerful enough to exact tribute. Obviously, some forms of tribute remained, an example being the Vikings' exaction of tribute in exchange for non-plundering, but they were more limited than in China. Likewise, in the colonial period, tribute from the colonies existed, such as the nineteenth-century Dutch culture system, in which the indigenous population was forced to set aside part of its land to grow cash crops, in Indonesia, and the unequal trade of Great Britain with India.

In China, during the Qing dynasty, foreign embassies were increasingly organized for purely economic reasons. Even though some have blamed the Western powers that occupied China in the mid-nineteenth century for this focus on the economics of trade, it can also be found in earlier times. For example, economic decline in the late Sung dynasty led to diminishing importance of the tributary function, which was costly and had a strong trade function (Go 2018). Indeed, as pointed out by Fairbank (1942, 144), the total number of missions increased from 216 in 1662–1761 to 260 in 1762–1861, thus suggesting an increased demand for trade. Western European missions also arrived, but these were very direct in their effects and their numbers were quite limited.

4.6.3 Trade-Induced Growth in Non-Agricultural Society

Trade, therefore, follows from agricultural (and industrial) specialization via increasing population income. China was, as we have seen, more agricultural than Western Europe. But how to encompass differences between agricultural and urban areas in a model? We can begin with Smithian-type growth by stating that the division of labour depends on the number of people and, more specifically, those who interact. There is also a relationship with the socio-economic framework, including factors such as social status or the level of inequality, and of course technical change. Ortman and Lobo (2020) overcome the difficulties of identifying the variables of a Smithian-type model by distinguishing between Smithian and "modern" growth. They show that rising population, even in countries with low technological development, lead to more people interacting, which in turn leads to more labour specialization and more welfare.

Hence, it is also agricultural societies that may experience growing trade when populations rise. Indeed, Smithian-type growth is based on the division of labour, with the exchange of goods by means of trade being a clear candidate for driving pre-modern growth. But Smithian growth (even when adapted for a large agricultural sector) is not always dominant in early agricultural societies. Contrary to it, there is the involutionary growth model of Geertz (1963). This is basically the reverse of Smithian growth; it "refers to the growth mode of economic forms with underdeveloped markets, insignificant labour division and self-sufficient, not-for-market production". Whether China is dominated by Smithian or involutionary growth remains an unresolved issue.[51]

Most of Russia's foreign trade was with Europe owing to the latter's geographical proximity to the main centres of economic activities in Russia and its transportation network, with exports normally exceeding imports—especially with the launch of modern growth (Fig. 4.12a). Western European exports to the Central Asia region, for example, always represented a smaller share of its total exports in comparison with exports to other European regions (including the south, north, and east of Europe). Yet throughout the period between 1827 and the First World War, exports of Western Europe to Central Asia exceeded those to China (Fig. 4.12b).

[51] On the one hand, there are those studies that explain whether the economy was Smithian or not. First, Huang (1990) claimed that Western incursions in the nineteenth century increased involution. This worked via commercialization, which reduced handicrafts, and the cost of finance increased, essentially locking people up in the countryside. In addition, commercial crops had the same effect. Second, Elvin (1973) claimed it was high population and an equilibrium trap, rather than commercialization, in the nineteenth century that caused impoverishment in the countryside. Third, (Myers 1970; Brandt 1987) claim that commercialization did lead to growth, notwithstanding population pressure, owing to a move from handicrafts to a labour market (not towards agriculture) and commercial crops. On the other hand, there are those who claim it was in part Smithian (i.e. silk weaving and spinning), but this was insufficient for later modern growth. Rather, it was a combination of government regulation and markets that, after 1949, led to growth (Guan and Zhang 2017).

Russia specialized in agricultural exports and imports of manufactured goods. However, cross-border and distant trade with China through Central Asia was also practised. In the nineteenth and early twentieth centuries, the share of this was much less than that of Europe (Fig. 4.12c). Although the borders between the two countries were no shorter than Russia's with Europe, low population density in the

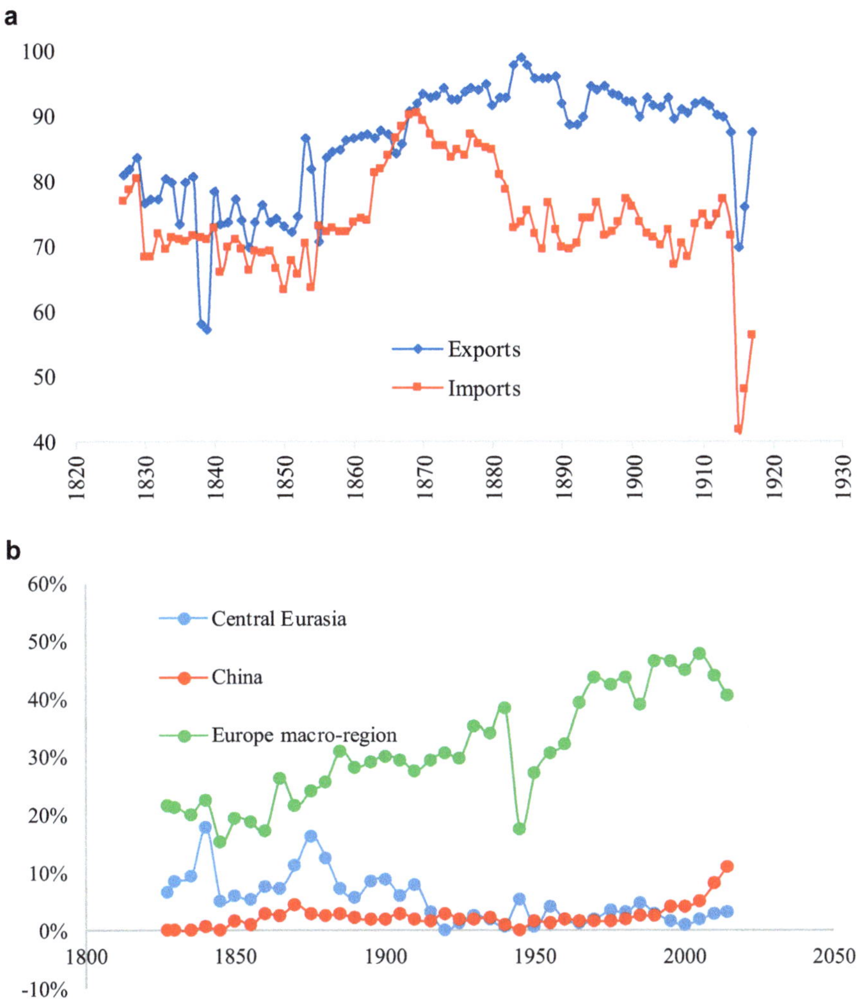

Fig. 4.12 (**a**) Share of European countries in Russia's foreign trade, 1827–1917 (in per cent). *Source:* Valetov (2017a) cross-checked with Mitchell (2003). (**b**) Share of total exports of Western Europe towards Central Eurasia, China, and Europe macro-region (south, east, north), 1827–2014. *Source:* Tradhist dataset, retrieved on 1 June 2023 from http://www.cepii.fr/CEPII/en/bdd_modele/bdd_modele_item.asp?id=32. See also Fouquin, M. and Hugot, J. (2016) Two Centuries of Bilateral Trade and Gravity Data: 1827–2014. CEPII Working Paper, N°2016-14. Authors' calculations. (**c**) Share of China in Russia's foreign trade, 1827–1917 (in per cent). *Source:* Valetov (2017a) cross-checked with Mitchell (2003)

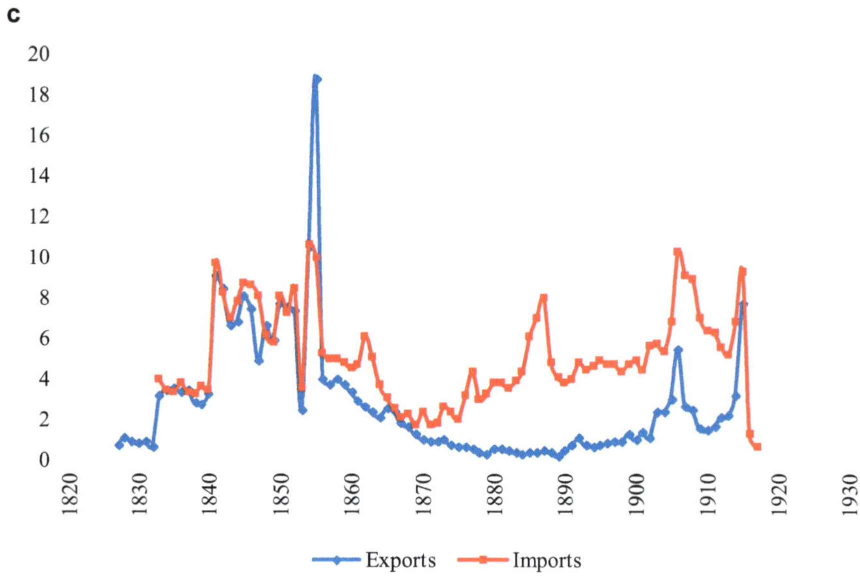

Fig. 4.12 (continued)

bordering regions plus weak market development, combined with a poor transportation network, played a role. In certain periods of warfare and internal unrest (the Opium Wars and the Taiping Rebellion, the Crimean War, the Russo-Japanese War, the First Russian Revolution, and the First World War), China's share in Russia's exports and imports tended to grow significantly, reaching 7–10%. What is interesting is that after the mid-1850s, Russia's imports exceeded exports, and this trend reinforced over time.

Even though the assessment of Russia's economic openness, also referred to as Smithian-type growth, in the late seventeenth century (trade being estimated as *c.* 20% of GDP) was exaggerated in Kotilaine (2005, 513), his estimate of total exports is basically in line with the trend in Fig. 4.13. The available evidence shows that from the mid-eighteenth to the mid-nineteenth centuries, the Russian Empire steadily increased its openness to the world economy.[52] The ratio of foreign trade to GDP was close to 15% at the time when modern economic growth was launched (late nineteenth–early twentieth centuries), having increased by about a factor of 4–5 in the course of the previous two centuries. This gave a substantial drive to commodification and external openness, taking into account that GDP per capita was only slightly above the level of the previous two centuries. Net exports were

[52] Some of its autonomous parts (Kingdom of Poland in 1815–1850, the Grand Duchy of Finland throughout the period of personal union with Russia, 1809–1917, Bessarabia (current Moldova) in 1812–1830, areas of the Caucasus and Transcaucasus in the first half of the nineteenth century, Emirate of Bukhara and Khanate of Khiva from the end of the 1860s to the mid-1890s) were not integrated into a single customs area, and trade with them was considered as trading with abroad (Valetov 2017b).

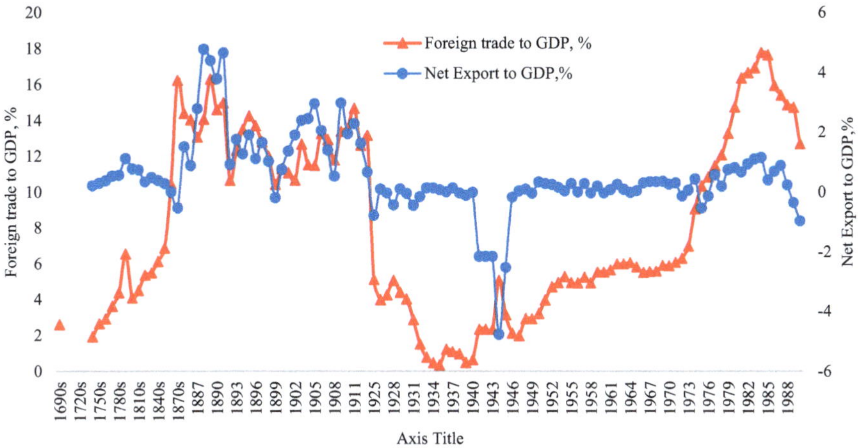

Fig. 4.13 Foreign trade in Russia's economy, 1740s–1990 (in per cent). *Note:* The estimate of openness tends to be the lower bound. The evidence in Thompstone (2008, 45–47) sheds light on the fact of about 1.5 times under-reporting of exports in the Russian official statistics of the late nineteenth to early twentieth centuries if compared with the statistics of her main trading partners; the size of smuggling imports in certain places several times exceeded imports through the customs in the 1860s. *Source:* GDP: 1690s–1880s: Broadberry and Korchmina (2024); 1885–1913: Cheremukhin et al. (2017). Exports: 1690s: Kotilaine (2005, p. 513); 1742–1799: Kahan (1985, p. 164). Imports: 1742–1759: Troitskii (1966, 185); 1760–1799: Kahan (1985, 193). Exports and imports: 1802–1913: Valetov (2017a) cross-checked with Mitchell (2003); 1925–1940: MVT (1960, 14); 1941–1945: Rosstat (2020, 186); 1946–1990: Mitchell (2003) based on the official statistics (MVT, n.d.)

predominantly positive, in line with mainstream mercantilist economic thinking of the time, although it appeared to be more volatile than the ratio of foreign trade to GDP.

So far, we have only talked about foreign trade. However, China and Russia, being much bigger in land area than Europe, are likely to have had significant internal (domestic) trade. However, Europe had a large share of intra-European trade compared with extra-European trade with Russia and China. The data on the size of domestic trade flows are difficult to obtain for Russia and China prior to the twentieth century. For China, we can proxy domestic trade (by using the taxed amount) as a share of total trade at roughly 66% in around 1800 (Ni 2016, Table 7.1). For Russia,[53] Soviet Marxist historiography stressed the trends to intensified exchange, commodification, and monetary penetration into the national economy. Koval'chenko and Milov (1974), based on an increasing correlation of price fluctuation in the provinces of European Russia, consider the processes of integration of local markets into the All-Russian single market.[54] However, they have much less to say about the quantitative dynamics of turnover, which should have been on a firm positive

[53] The available data basically cover the European part of the Russian Empire. Therefore, much of the story is based on the available fragmentary or indirect evidence, which we still find significant.

[54] See also Sect. 4.6.4.

track to allow prices to move in such coherent ways over time. Mironov (1981) reports much evidence for the growing intensity of trade, which contains information on the number of shops and other places of sale, commodity fairs in both urban and rural areas, their turnover,[55] and also on strengthening business links between merchants from various provinces. The development of trade routes by improving transport infrastructure (Kahan 1985, 283–310; Guangxiang 2016) and the near-constant long-term GDP per capita from the 1690s to the 1880s (Broadberry and Korchmina 2024) also support the argument. Recent research based on regional evidence has provided support for this suggestion.[56] The Western literature also basically supports the pattern, even if it is somewhat less optimistic about the social consequences of these trends.[57]

There are some other arguments supporting our view of Russia's domestic trade, in terms of rates of change, as quantitatively similar to its foreign trade. First, as internal customs were lifted and duties were eliminated in 1753–1754, following multiple merchants' requests, transaction costs diminished, thus allowing freer trade development. At the same time, the indirect taxation of trade (turnover taxes on alcohol, salt, and sugar) was one of the main sources of the state budget. The growth of the Russian fiscal state (Fig. 4.13) may be considered as indirect evidence of growth in trade turnover, as otherwise the tax burden would have been unlikely to rise fourfold under declining GDP per capita (by about 30% from the 1740s to the 1880s). Second, in the first half of the eighteenth century, the Russian merchant class was the most open to both urban and rural lower classes (Kahan 1985, 276). Moreover, this class lacked substantive features such as hereditary status: amount of capital and taxation status were the main criteria for entry into merchant guilds. Following the period when barriers were put in the way of upward mobility, these were eased during the "Great Reforms" of the 1860s–1870s. Third, from the early eighteenth century, crown peasants were allowed to trade in urban areas. Although their activities were restricted,[58] their role in trade increased rapidly after the mid-century (Kahan 1985, 275). With further reforms of the state-owned (1837–1841) and privately owned (1861) peasantry, opportunities for their trading activities were extending.

As for Central Eurasia, there is evidence that, until the third wave of globalization from the 1970s, as was also the case for Western Europe,[59] domestic and for-

[55] They provided most of the wholesale and a substantial portion of retail trade.

[56] E.g. Mizis (2006), starting from the mid-seventeenth century in the Central black-soil region, and Boiko (1996), in the Tomsk province of Siberia.

[57] E.g. Kahan (1985, 267–282).

[58] E.g. certain categories of peasants had the right for a long time to sell only the production either of themselves or of their lord.

[59] Western Europe includes the following countries and historical regions (alphabetical order): Alsace-Lorraine, Belgium, Bremen, Switzerland, Channel Islands, Germany, German Democratic Republic, Federal Republic (West Germany) France, Hamburg, Hanover, Hanseatic cities, Isle of Man, Eire, Liechtenstein, Lübeck, Luxembourg, Monaco, Mecklenburg, Netherlands, Oldemburg, Prussia, Sarre, Schleswig, Ulster, United Kingdom, Zollverein (see Tradhist dataset, retrieved on 1 June 2023 from *http://www.cepii.fr/CEPII/en/bdd_modele/bdd_modele_item.asp?id=32)*

eign trade had essentially been equal in size.[60] From the end of the nineteenth century, concurrently with the climax of the first wave of globalization, foreign exports to Russia (i.e. imports by Russia) constantly exceeded domestic trade. This trend remained stable during the interwar years and during the Second World War for the USSR. From the post-war period until the late 1970s, domestic and foreign exports were once again on average equivalent. Furthermore, Western Europe's foreign exports show a long-run tendency towards an average increase in the shares of total exports to other European macro-regions and to China, while there was a decrease towards North America and Central Eurasia (Fig. 4.14).

However, during the same time frame (1827–2014), the level of trade openness, calculated as the ratio of the sum of total imports plus exports to GDP, increased on average for all the regions of interest. The growth was particularly enhanced at the end of the first wave of globalization, before the First World War shock, and then

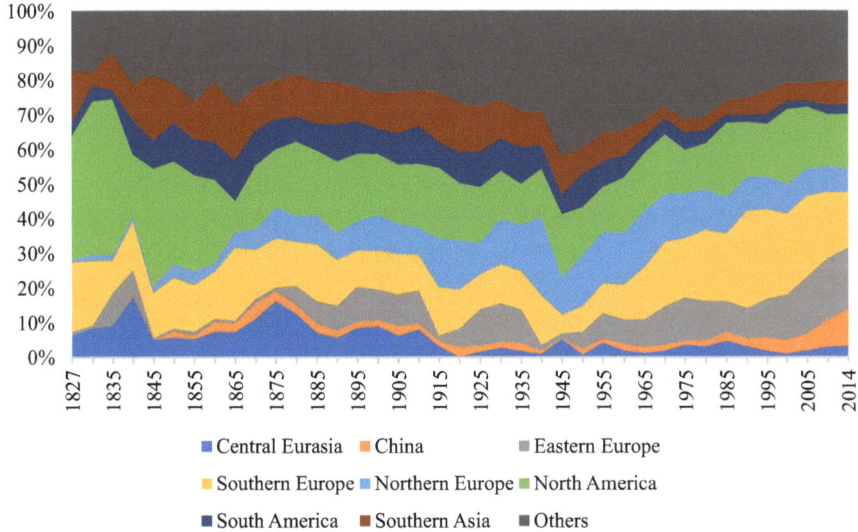

Fig. 4.14 Share of total exports from Western Europe to other regions, 1827–2014. *Source:* Tradhist dataset, retrieved on 1 June 2023 from http://www.cepii.fr/CEPII/en/bdd_modele/bdd_modele_item.asp?id=32. See also Fouquin, M. and Hugot, J. (2016) Two Centuries of Bilateral Trade and Gravity Data: 1827-2014. CEPII Working Paper, N°2016-14. Authors' calculations

[60] In the USSR, domestic trade (retail+wholesale) accounted for 80–100% GDP, retail only—about a half of that. While foreign trade (exports+imports)—amounted to just around 5% GDP in the 1950s–1960s, 10–15% GDP in the mid-1970s-1980s. For West Europe, which consisted of various countries, domestic trade = trade among Western European countries. This was roughly the same in China (by taxed amount, i.e. approximately by province). So, in both Western Europe and China, we define domestic trade as trade within countries (Western Europe) or provinces (China). For both regions, domestic trade is by and large 66%.

Russia has defined domestic trade much more widely, however. That is fine, but it cannot be directly compared to Western Europe and China.

most clearly from the 1990s, owing to the second wave of globalization and the openness reforms in China and Russia (Fig. 4.15). Russia's national statistics basically conform to these trends, with openness at about 15% at the end of the first wave of globalization and about 18% at the take-off of the second one.

Development in the share of domestic trade and total trade over time varied by region, however. In China, before 1850, the domestic trade/total was about 66% (Ni 2016).[61] The share of domestic trade in total trade declined over time arguably because of an increased openness to foreign trade.

For Russia, what is somewhat striking is that, contrary to China, there was an approximately constant ratio of both foreign and domestic trade to GDP under growing GDP per capita during the early stages of modern growth (1880s–1913).[62] Yet the evidence reported in Davydov (2016, 413–414) showing a 3.7 times increase of traders' savings in their bank accounts from 1897 to 1913 does not fit the conservative estimates.[63] This discrepancy may arise from increased under-reporting of turnover by domestic traders with tax evasion motives, or by the growing share of

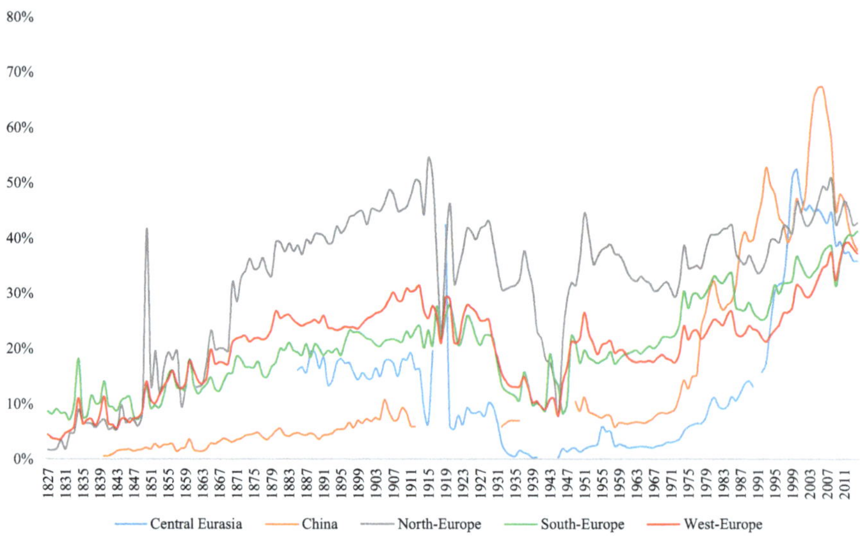

Fig. 4.15 Trade openness per region, 1827–2014. *Source:* Tradhist dataset, retrieved on June 1, 2023, from http://www.cepii.fr/CEPII/en/bdd_modele/bdd_modele_item.asp?id=32. See also Fouquin, M. and Hugot, J. (2016) Two Centuries of Bilateral Trade and Gravity Data: 1827-2014. CEPII Working Paper, N°2016-14. Authors' calculations

[61] After 1850, we have used Likin and Yangguan's biased domestic customs taxes

[62] Which follows from the data reported on volume of wholesale and retail internal trade both in Strumilin (1958, 680, 688. http://www.hist.msu.ru/Dynamics/data/11_012.xls, http://www.hist.msu.ru/Dynamics/data/11_017.xls) for 1885–1913 and Dikhtyar (1960, 73, 101, http://www.hist.msu.ru/Dynamics/data/11_006.xls, http://www.hist.msu.ru/Dynamics/data/11_016.xls) for 1899–1913. We have not found any updated series in the later literature.

[63] For the same period, turnover increased merely 2.1 times (Strumilin 1958).

direct procurements by businesses and government bodies, without traders' intermediation.[64] Nevertheless, in the absence of alternative estimates, we abstain from revising the figures for domestic trade turnover from Strumilin (1958, 680, 688) and Dikhtyar (1960, 73, 101). As it follows from these estimates, Russia's domestic trade to foreign trade ratio demonstrates a realistic pattern. It was equal to 3.6 in 1885 and 4.1 in 1913 (4.3 as the average over the period). We assume it somewhat diminished earlier (exponentially, to 2.3 in the 1690s).

Elevated values (Fig. 4.16) for the domestic trade to GDP ratio in the 1930s–1940s are primarily due to the increased tax burden, which was extracted primarily through retail trade turnover; after the Second World War, taxation appeared to be somewhat more equally distributed between economic agents. The decreasing ratio since 1940 is puzzling, despite there being much evidence that Soviet consumer services (including retail trade) became more and more underdeveloped. The share of private consumption in GDP decreased owing to the expansion of government consumption and fixed capital accumulation. Only partially can this be explained by the expansion of retail sales on semi-legal ("grey") and illegal ("black") markets, which were missed by the official statistics, and also the increasing share of concealed turnover on the legal markets.[65] However, a rise in urban workers' share in employment should have created demand for foodstuffs and consumer goods, which had previously been produced by rural workers who were self-employed in their households and had been sold in legal stores and markets. But the official data do not capture this effect. Moreover, the increase in household savings (from about 6% of GDP in the early 1960s to over 30% in the late 1980s), along with that of cash in circulation (from 3.8% of GDP in the early 1960s to 9.5% in the late 1980s),[66] captures the commodities shortage caused by the underdevelopment of retail trade. As of 1987, excessive savings and cash in hand caused by a shortage of retail trade were estimated at 70 billion rubles (close to 10% of GDP) inside the State Bank.[67] Later estimates of excessive savings confirm the level was close to this (Shida 2015, 55; Kim 1999, 662), with a rapid increase to 20% of GDP by the end of 1990 (Cottarelli and Blejer 1992, 280).

---

[64] Explicitly claimed in the research by Boiko (1996, 47–50) based on micro-level evidence.

[65] For example, Kim (2003) estimates the average share of informal expenditure in total expenditure amounted to 22.9% from 1969 to 1990, which would contribute an additional 6.8% to GDP. In Russia, where the share of the informal economy was among the lowest in the USSR, it was, excluding self-consumption, on average 6.5% GDP for the period 1960–1990 (Kuboniwa et al. 2019, 398). Likewise, Bokarev (1994, 139–140) shows that from 1955 to 1975 the share of household illegal incomes fluctuated between 5% and 12%, with the mean at 8% of total incomes. A theoretical construction of consumer markets hierarchy in the USSR, with assessment of the level of their relative (il)legality, was implemented by Katsenelinboigen (1977), who had inside knowledge of Soviet economic practices.

[66] As it follows from the data in Nakamura (2019).

[67] Kashin, ed. (2012, 190) https://www.cbr.ru/Content/Document/File?48221/ArchivalFonds_0.13.pdf)

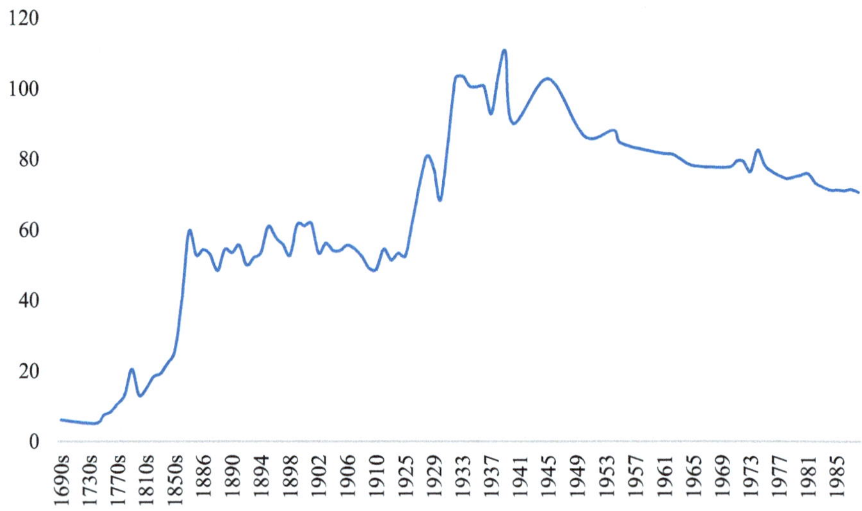

Fig. 4.16 Domestic trade in Russia's economy, 1690s–1988 (in per cent GDP). *Note:* 1. The estimate is based on the dynamics of domestic trade as a function of foreign trade, as in the sources to Table 4.16. The model assumes that the ratio of domestic to foreign trade changed exponentially in the 1690s–1860s to the same ratio as in 1885–1913 (for these years, we have estimates for both). The ratio in the 1870s–1880s is assumed to be the same as in 1885–1890. The resulting estimate for the 1790s to the 1860s is more conservative than the evidence in Mironov (1981, 162–163) on the growth of trade in fairs. We follow Broadberry and Korchmina (2024) that real GDP p.c. was approximately constant at the time. 2. The figures for the period of 1925–1955 are estimated on the assumption that the ratio between wholesale and retail trade was the same as in the early 1960s. The retail sales included those in state trade (at the prices established by the state) and cooperative trade (at semi-free prices with ceilings), agricultural markets (at free prices), also catering (mostly for employees at their workplaces). Private shops were nationalized in the late 1920s–early 1930s, but were soon replaced by agricultural (*kolkhoznye*) and second-hand commodities (*veshchevye*) markets. The latter were not covered by the official statistics. *Source:* 1690s–1880s: own estimate based on the sources from Table 4.16 on foreign trade dynamics; 1885–1913: domestic trade: Strumilin (1958, 680); GDP: Cheremukhin et al. (2017); 1925–1988: domestic trade: Lifits, ed. (1947); Prokopovich (1952); TsUNKhU (n.d.), TsSU (n.d.), Rosstat (2020); GDP: Didenko et al. (2013)

4.6.4 Economic Complexity and Trade

Economic complexity is another factor that drives trade (as well as income). It is expressed in the composition of a country's productive output and reflects the structures that emerge to hold and combine knowledge (Hausmann et al. 2014, 18). It basically refers to knowledge and factors of production in a country or a region: if these are greater, more diverse and networked, trade and growth occur. This therefore captures both the level of technological sophistication ("quality of countries' export baskets" in Hausmann et al. 2007), network effect, and diversification of exports in terms of the revealed comparative advantage of a national or sub-national economy (based on Balassa 1965). The basic idea rests on David Ricardo's example of trade between England and Portugal, where both countries benefited from it if Portugal specialized in wine (which required less labour per unit than cloth) and England specialized in cloth (which required less labour per unit than wine). In a way related to the variety of products and diversification, and aimed at enhancing the economic system's capacity to withstand risks and address challenges, un counter to Ricardo's example, as well as to Adam Smith's pin factory example, where each of many tasks was outsourced to another worker. So, an analysis of economic complexity raises three different questions. (1) Do countries have economic complexity? (2) Does economic complexity have a stronger effect than specialization? (3) If economic complexity exists, does this imply path dependency?

Present-day indices of economic complexity are quite straightforward. According to the Observatory of Economic Complexity,[68] the index for China went from 59 on trade in 1998 to 25 in 2012, Russia's level decreased from 21 in 1998 to 45 in 2021, while the UK remained essentially constant from 6 in 1998 to 11 in 2021. Yet, getting long-run data is complicated. It requires not only worldwide data on volume of trade broken down by country and commodity group,[69] but it also requires each commodity group to be assigned to a specific level of technological sophistication (historical product complexity).[70]

Thus, facing a lack of historical data for estimating economic complexity following the method in Hausmann et al. (2014), we need some proxy measures for the early modern period. One of these, market integration, can be used (for an overview see, e.g. Van Leeuwen and Philips 2021), as it connects regions and the number of products being produced in them. An obvious example is the Baltic Sea trade in grain from Poland to Western Europe (e.g. the Netherlands). Although strongly integrated, this only tells us that cheap Polish grain was sent to a much richer country, low in grain but high in industry, trade, and pasture.

For China, Kelly shows that, below a threshold of (level of) transportation, market integration does not occur, and, hence specialization as in north-western Europe does not occur either, owing to the lack of increased scale (Smithian-type growth). Above this threshold, market integration does occur. He argues that this was the case already during the Sung dynasty between the eighth and twelfth centuries CE. The idea is that some economic take-off occurs once new trade networks emerge—Adam Smith argued for the importance of inland waterways in China. The take-off of transport-driven economic development must have taken place in around 1000 CE (Broadberry et al. 2021). In the late Sung and Ming dynasties, stagnation occurred. It is claimed that the government played a role in this.

The late Sung and Ming phase of stagnation is not settled in the literature. For example, Xu et al. (2018), find that commercialization occurred in the mid-Ming dynasty with the rise of market towns. But more importantly, this mostly occurred

---

[68] https://oec.world/en/rankings/eci/hs6/hs96

[69] They have been available approximately since the early nineteenth century in Fouquin and Hugot (2016).

[70] They are not available in a structured form, to the best of our knowledge, yet the database on technology adoption (Comin and Hobijn 2009) has paved the way to constructing such a data set.

in the Yangtze area. A move away from richer urban areas to underdeveloped ones also occurred. For both these reasons, one may doubt the existence of rising commercialization in the Ming dynasty, and one might therefore expect lower economic complexity.

In this regard, we have another tool to explain the development of high wages in underdeveloped regions, as presented in Sect. 4.2 for China. Indeed, "[w]ithout a correspondence between urban intensity and the character of the rural sector within a macroregion, it is difficult to view a macroregion as a systematically integrated socioeconomic whole" (Sands and Myers 1986, 727). Sands and Meyers (1986) argue, therefore, that, except for the rich coastal provinces dominated by irrigation agriculture, other regions did not differ fundamentally from one another. Neither did the core and peripheral areas within macro-regions. Their conclusion is thus that "[m]arket systems (such as they were) for factor services (labour, land, capital, and entrepreneurship) and commodities existed outside and apart from China's urban Area" (Sands and Myers 1986, 738). This suggests another reason why wages were likely higher in the poorer regions of China—because of less dominance in factors of production in the developed regions.[71]

For European Russia, Koval'chenko and Milov (1974) examine fluctuations in prices for agricultural commodities in the provinces from the early eighteenth century to the early twentieth century. They argue that the processes of integration of local markets into the All-Russian single market were based on increasing correlation of price movements. These processes were underway as early as the eighteenth century, passed the threshold by the mid-nineteenth century, and were basically completed as regards the market for agricultural commodities by the 1880s, well ahead of the markets for factors of production. Mironov (1985b) also finds growing concurrence in price movement in local markets for cereals in the provinces of European Russia, but shifts the timing of the threshold in market integration over European Russia backwards to the second half of the eighteenth century. Yet the process was still underway until the early twentieth century.

Looking at economic complexity in foreign trade (Hausmann et al. 2014) from the early nineteenth to the early twentieth century, Russia's commodity exports (Valetov 2017a, 2017b) manifest sideways movement at best, with some tendency to deteriorate. The share of manufacturing products in exports never exceeded 21%; typically, it was below 5%. The share of agricultural products in exports increased from 20–30% to 60–70%, while the share of raw materials (and semi-finished products from mining) did the opposite. While in the early nineteenth century Russia continued to specialize in iron exports, it had lost its comparative advantage in the second half of the century, as the works constructed in the Urals in the early eighteenth century were becoming obsolete given the lack of substantial renovation; ironworks with state-of-the-art technologies, newly constructed in the Southern European provinces, were still not running at their full capacity. At the same time, a

[71] This rising commercialization is questioned. For example, Li (2000) claims to find disintegration at a regional level.

window of opportunity opened to increase the European market share for grain exports. Russia expanded this significantly in the late nineteenth century. Raw wood remained a prominent export item in which Russia retained its comparative advantage.

4.6.5 Rising Empires and Economic Growth

One might ask, if Smithian-type (or any other) trade-based growth actually existed, how this was influenced by the rise of empires. Allen (2003) claims that international trade was an important determinant for driving economic growth in northwestern Europe (see also Acemoglu et al. 2005). Other authors reject trade as a main driver (e.g. De Pleijt and Van Zanden 2016).

Yet, besides these empirical studies, the phenomena of globalizing trade and the rise of empires, which appeared alongside each other, were explained within the framework of world-system theory (WST). This considers the long-term trends of capitalist society as a world-system that is unified by flows of commodities, labour, and capital, divided into geographically defined structural subsystems: the core, semi-periphery, and periphery.[72] The key concepts of WST are world economy, world empires, and capitalism (see also Sections 2.1, 4.2, and 6.2).

Taking this perspective, the world economy is defined as the system in which powers and control are affected through a single unit of labour but multiple polities and cultures. In contrast, in world empires, there is a single political system over the area under control. In this environment, capitalism was from the beginning an affair of the world economy and not of nation-states (Wallerstein 2011 [1974], 63, 347–349). This idea can be traced back to the Communist Manifesto by Marx and Engels,[73] despite it not appearing to be the consensus among their followers. WST relies on a broader concept of capitalism than Marxism. The former can be summarized as a set of commodified economic activities that are aimed at profit maximization and infinite capital accumulation (Wallerstein 2004, 23–25; Arrighi 2010, 8–11). Therefore, in socialist countries, an extreme form of state capitalism (not merely a state-induced or state-led but a state-owned economy) appears to be the case (see also Chap. 7). A narrower Marxist concept is based on such essential characteristics as domination of private (versus public) property for the means of commodified production, aimed at the maximum private extraction of surplus value

[72] The concept of "longue durée" coined by Braudel (1973 [1967]; 1992 [1979]) became one of the key concepts in economic history.

[73] The basic idea was that the rapid development of modern industry had established the world market, for which the discovery and colonization of America as well as trade with the colonies paved the way. The concept of "world market" is frequently used in the founding work of 1848 (http://www.marx2mao.com/M&E/CM47.html)

from wage labour,[74] which is realized through the respective distribution of political powers, ideological, cultural, and other means of social control.

The state is conceptualized in Arrighi (2010, 28–37) based on a territorialist versus capitalist approach in which enterprises, their networks, and the whole world system operate. As opposed to Marxism,[75] in the WST framework, a state has a certain degree of autonomy and its own rational strategy, aimed at territorial expansion and a controlled population. Arrighi (2010, 34) clearly distinguishes political and economic logic: territorialist rulers identify power with the extent and populousness of their domains, and conceive of wealth or capital as a means towards and a by-product of the pursuit of territorial expansion; capitalist rulers, in contrast, identify power with the extent of their command over scarce resources and consider territorial acquisitions as a means towards and a by-product of the accumulation of capital. Thus, capitalism developed through the ambivalent interaction between economic and political interests and rationality, as well as through competition between various economic and political institutions.

The concept of "world" is also related to empires as large supra-state units. These are conceptualized as large power platforms, derived from the strategy of control over expanded territories, with ethically and culturally diverse populations; this results in the coercive redistribution of resources (Derluguian 2007). Economic flows from the periphery to the centre by force (tribute and taxation) and by monopolistic advantages in trade are therefore ensured. Political empires are a primitive means of economic domination.[76] The world economies that existed before capitalism always transformed into empires: China, Persia, and Rome. In contrast, capitalism is associated with the development of the world economy without the emergence of a unified political structure (Wallerstein, 2011 [1974], 15–16; 2004, 57–59).

It follows from the logic of WST that empires are not a necessary precondition for the world capitalist economic system, even though they made substantial contributions. Historically, the core of the world economy could be represented by city-states (such as Venice,[77] Genoa, Florence at the dawn of capitalism, Luxembourg, or Singapore today), small or medium-sized confederate states (such as the United Provinces of the Netherlands in the seventeenth–eighteenth centuries,[78] or Switzerland), large nation-states with huge colonial appendages (Britain and France in the eighteenth–mid-twentieth centuries), and federal states (primarily the United

[74] In national accounting, surplus value may be operationalized as entrepreneurial income.

[75] As the Communist Manifesto claims, "The bourgeoisie has at last, since the establishment of Modern Industry and of the world market, conquered for itself, in the modern representative State, exclusive political sway … The executive of the modern State is but a committee for managing the common affairs of the whole bourgeoisie" (http://www.marx2mao.com/M&E/CM47.html). This view does not presume any specific interest on the part of a state.

[76] In terms of neo-institutional economics, empires tend to have more transaction costs per capita than smaller states; this is caused by larger expenditures for operation and contract enforcement. But empires tend to produce large-scale effects and have a greater capacity for diversification.

[77] The state that most met the standards of the capitalist logic (Arrighi 2010, 38).

[78] Braudel (1992 [1979], 193–195).

States and the UK today). The polity was flexible, without a clear trend towards centralization or decentralization.

Taking a WST perspective, the traditional agrarian-coercive empires are separated from the later modern colonial empires, whose governing logic was capitalist. Thus, Russia, like Turkey or Portugal, emerged as a pre-capitalist, agrarian-coercive empire. Subsequently, these have long existed alongside capitalism while being increasingly penetrated by and incorporated into global capitalist networks. At the opposite end of the spectrum, the Netherlands, England, and France were capitalist nation-states in Europe—while at the same time operating overseas as territorialist empires (Derluguian 2007).

Indeed, it was the state that assisted "national" capitalists, absorbed their losses, and thus promoted world capitalism. Among typical instruments of state involvement in international commerce, the main ones were monopolies, the protectionist system, and mercantilist policies. Among monopolies, there were joint-stock chartered companies, which were part-governmental, part-business organizations that specialized territorially in the exclusion of other similar organizations. Furthermore, in the process of capitalist development, a large number of states created national economic barriers as a defensive mechanism for capitalists who were located in those states that were at a level below the strongest in the system (Arrighi 2010, 250).

Cases where the state assisted merchants in their trade can be found in Russian history as well. In the second half of the sixteenth century, the privileges issued by Ivan IV (the Terrible) to the Muscovy Company, incorporated in England, were of great importance for further development of Russia's commerce: this was a milestone in the history of Anglo-Russian relations.[79] In another example, the Russian-American company for the colonization of Alaska was chartered by Emperor Paul I (in 1799) and sponsored by the Russian state.[80]

As regards the role of trade in the Great Divergence, among the questions that arise from Fig. 4.20, the first is what inspired the development of long-distance trade on the part of European countries in the fifteenth to seventeenth centuries (and not on the part of China).[81] Indeed, the fact remains that those fast-growing countries in the sixteenth century, such as Holland and England, had the highest per capita merchant fleet. France only developed in this regard during the seventeenth century. This suggests a relationship with the rise of maritime empires. Indeed, Costa et al. (2015) show that empire trade for Portugal worked well and that the later eighteenth-century Portuguese decline was due to domestic reasons. Likewise, Broadberry and Gupta (2009) find that wages in England in the textile industry were much higher than in India, which spurred technological change and, in the nineteenth century, shifted the comparative advantage to England.

---

[79] See, e.g. Kotilaine (2005, 93–95).

[80] See, e.g. Lightfoot (2003).

[81] As Arrighi (2010, 35–37) puts it, why didn't China discover Portugal and take control over the Inner Asian trade several decades before the latter started the same movement eastwards?

By using the Climatological Database for the World's Oceans (CLIWOC),[82] based on data from ship logbooks from 1662 to 1850, we can follow the emergence of these maritime empires. Figure 4.20, depicting the travels of 1770, uses logbook reports from Dutch, French, English, and Spanish travellers. We add to the map an estimation of Chinese sea routes in the same period, based on an extrapolation from the sea routes depicted in the Qing Dynasty's "Selden Map" (Fig. 4.17).

As Arrighi (2010, 35–37) suggests, by the mid-fifteenth century, Asia was a purveyor of valued goods for the tribute-taking classes of Europe, and thereby exercised a powerful pull on Europe's precious metals. This structural imbalance in European trade with the East created strong incentives for European governments and businesses to seek ways and means, through trade or conquest, to retrieve the purchasing power that was relentlessly draining from West to East.

Therefore, the benefits to Portugal and other European states of discovering and controlling a direct route to the East were incomparably greater than the benefits of discovering and controlling a direct route to the West were for the Chinese state, whose agents weighed carefully the prospective benefits, costs, and risks. This can also be seen in local land routes. In Fig. 4.18, we plot the Ming dynasty courier routes and the main transport routes in 1933 in China. We find that road transport routes hardly changed in this period. In Fig. 4.19, actual travel times (so not driving without taking a break) are plotted, as this proxies transport better than mere

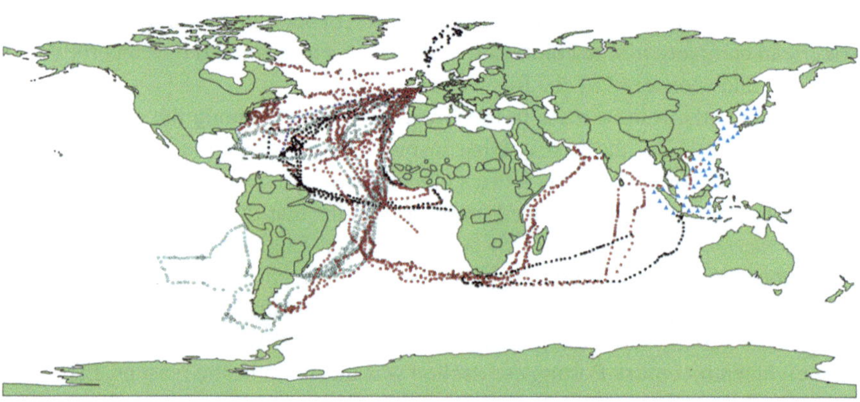

Fig. 4.17 Sea trade routes, c. 1770. *Legend:* Black is Dutch, red is English, blue is France, celeste is Spain; blue triangles are China. *Note:* Visualization of the authors based on CLIWOC dataset and shapefile of used shapefile 1715, retrieved at http://web.archive.org/web/20080328104539/http://library.thinkquest.org:80/C006628/download.html; China's sea routes are extrapolated from the "Selden Map" retrieved at Batchelor, R. (2013): The Selden Map Rediscovered: A Chinese Map of East Asian Shipping Routes, *c.* 1619, Imago Mundi: The International Journal for the History of Cartography, 65:1, 37–63, p. 3

[82] https://www.historicalclimatology.com/cliwoc.html

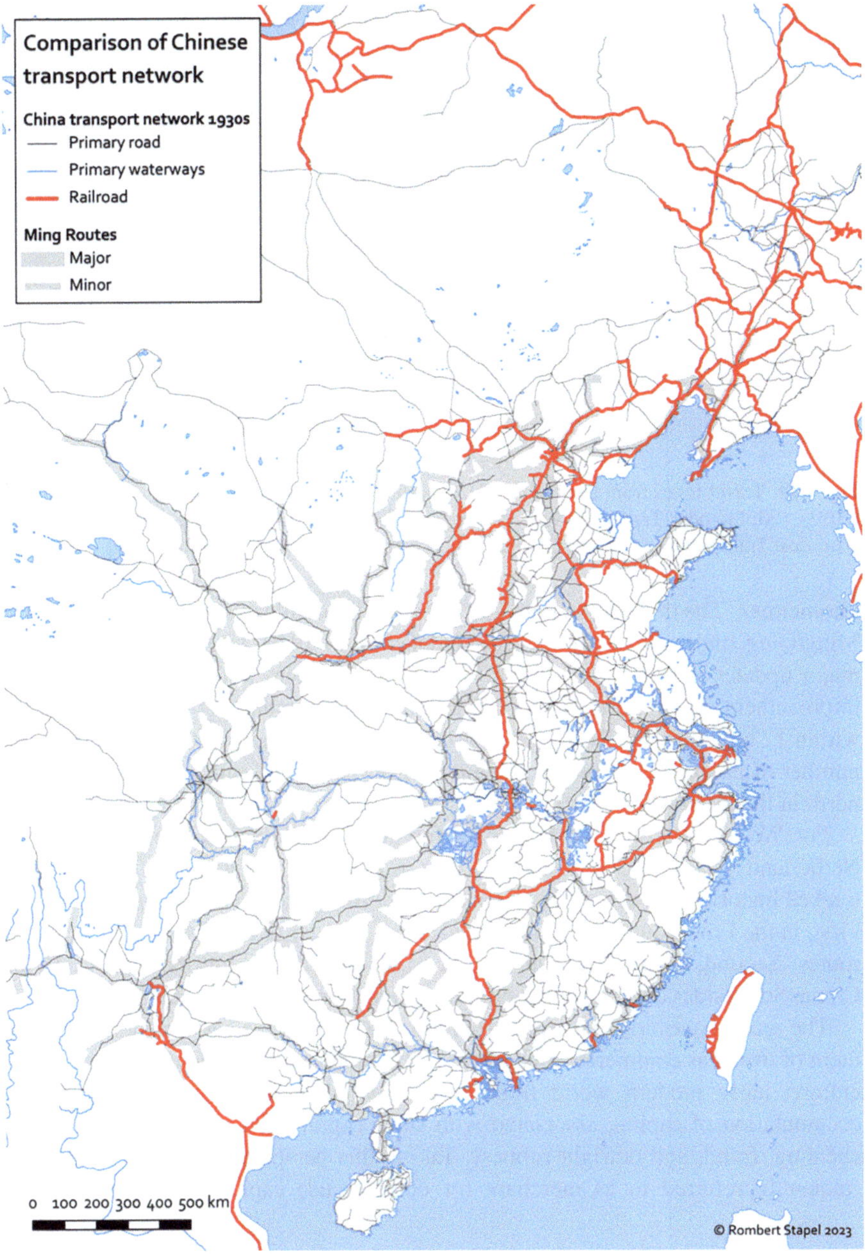

Fig. 4.18 Ming land-based courier routes compared with the main roads, railways, and waterways in 1933. *Source:* Stapel and Yuan (2023), "Multimodal Transport Networks in East Asia (Early Twentieth Century). Modelling Historical Transport Times Using GIS and Chinese Travel Documents" (forthcoming).

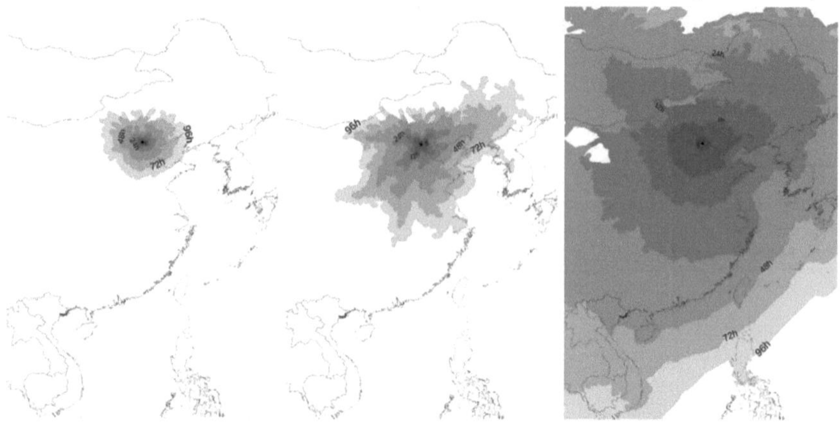

Fig. 4.19 Travel times from the capital of China (hours from Beijing). *Source:* Stapel and Yuan (2023), "Multimodal Transport Networks in East Asia (Early Twentieth Century). Modelling Historical Transport Times Using GIS and Chinese Travel Documents" (forthcoming)

kilometres.[83] The first map in Fig. 4.19 (1930 without railways) serves as a proxy for Ming/Qing trade routes; we can see updates up to 1930. In 2000, one might see major updates in travel times.[84] For ten coastal provinces in China, gives a further improvement, as it reports for the 1930s and 2010s the number of people reachable within 12 hours' travel. This proxy for domestic market access shows a shift in the number of people reachable in 12 hours' travel from the south in the 1930s to the north in the 2010s (Fig. 4.20).

For Western Europe, we have data for the Low Countries (Belgium and the Netherlands) in the 1930s (Fig. 4.21). Just as in China, it was mostly railways that tracked historical (in this case, Roman) roads. Yet, there are two main differences. First, in the Low Countries, Roman roads were less dense than Ming China courier routes. Second, there were many more roads in Western Europe than in 1930s China. So, besides colonial trade, domestic trade was quite important in Europe too.

The second question that arises from Fig. 4.21 is how the early modern development of overseas commerce affected further capitalist development. In Marxian literature, early modern world trade is considered an element of the primitive accumulation of capital, associated with slave capture and unequal exchange via cheating, fraud, and outright robbery. Taking this perspective, early capitalism is frequently referred to as merchant (or commercial) capitalism, the idea being

[83] It should be noted that modern navigation systems are much more accurate than they were in 1930. Furthermore, 2010 is set up so it matches 1930: no account is taken of obstacles such as borders.

[84] Available only for the ten coastal provinces.

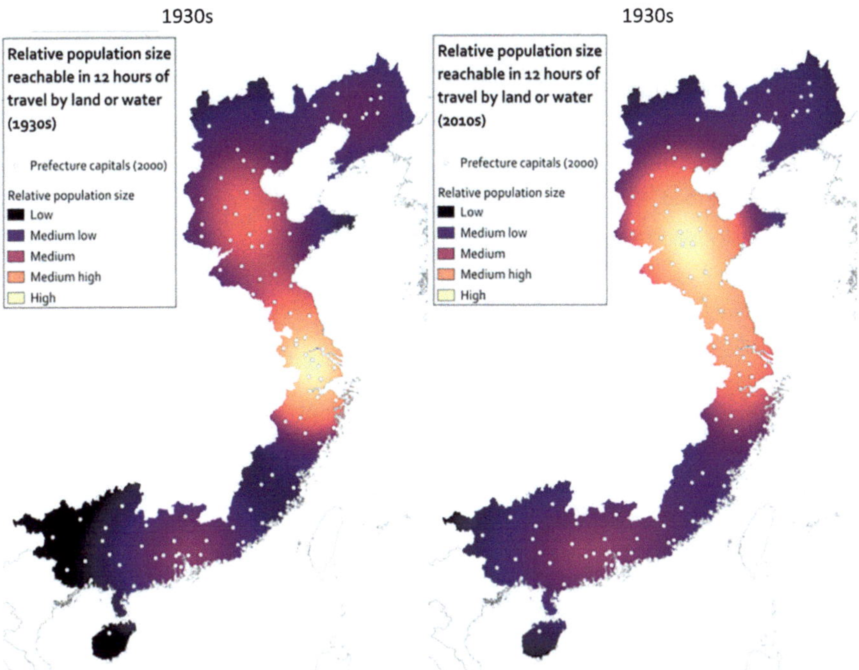

Fig. 4.20 The number of people in China reachable in 12 hours for the ten coastal provinces, 1930s and 2010s. *Source:* Stapel and Yuan (2023), "Multimodal Transport Networks in East Asia (Early Twentieth Century). Modelling Historical Transport Times Using GIS and Chinese Travel Documents" (forthcoming)

borrowed by other schools of thought (e.g. by the German historical school of economics).[85]

The WST explains that the secular change of world-economy hegemons is at the core of the system. Being associated with major fluctuations in international flows of trade (goods and services) and capital, they are determined by systemic cycles of capital accumulation and competition between the historical institutions of capitalism. Each cycle consists of a phase of material expansion followed by a phase of financial expansion. Financial expansion began when the leading business agencies of the preceding trade expansion switched their energies and resources from the commodity to the money trades (Braudel 1992, 242–248; Arrighi 2010, 88). Historically, these were a Genoese cycle, from the fifteenth to the early seventeenth centuries; a Dutch cycle, from the late sixteenth century through most of the eighteenth century; a British cycle, from the latter half of the eighteenth century through the early twentieth century; and a US cycle, which began in the late nineteenth

[85] Wallerstein opposed the separation "merchant versus industrial" and argued for "agricultural versus industrial" capitalism, based on defining the type of commodity (largely agricultural) that was produced for sale and profit in the world market.

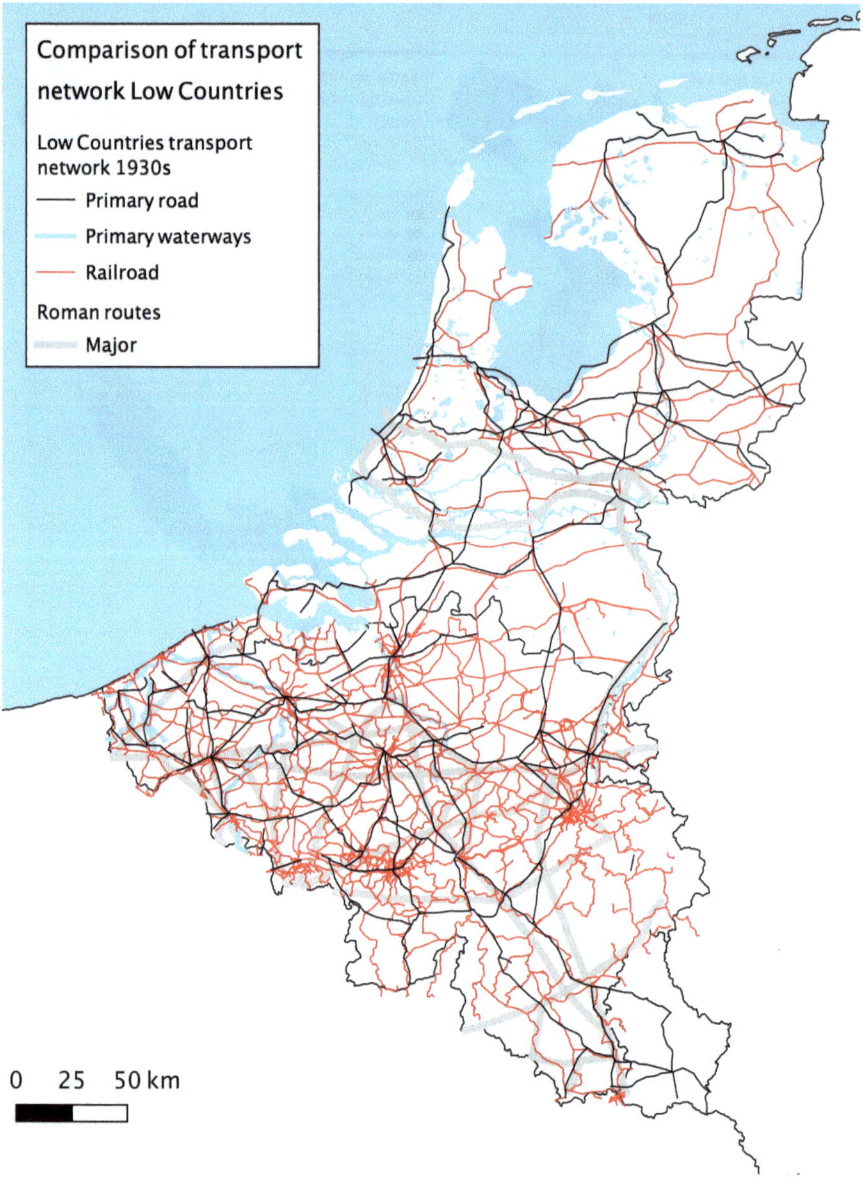

Fig. 4.21 Roman roads compared with main roads, railways, and waterways, in the Netherlands and Belgium, 1930s. *Note:* Some Belgian roads that were likely not main roads (as they ran parallel to actual main roads) have been removed. *Source:* Philips, Robin; Van Leeuwen, Bas; Stapel andYuan (2023), "Historical GIS for Belgium and the Netherlands (around 1890-1930-2010). Multimodal transport network and administrative boundaries", https://hdl.handle.net/10622/TF7HC2, IISH Data Collection, DRAFT VERSION.

century. The crises of over-accumulation that marked the transition from one organizational structure to another also created the conditions for the emergence of ever more powerful governmental and business agencies, which were capable of solving crises through the reconstitution of the capitalist world economy on larger and more comprehensive foundations (Arrighi 2010, 6–7, 341).

The quantitative evidence we have for the commodity structure of exports and imports begins in the nineteenth century, or in some cases from the eighteenth century; it covers the British and American cycles of accumulation, according to the timeline in Arrighi (2010, 5–7, 219–220).

Wallerstein (2011 [1974], 301–325) and Braudel (1992 [1979], 441–465) consider Russia as either a separate world economy (sixteenth–seventeenth centuries) or a periphery of the European capitalist world economy (since the eighteenth century). Besides low commodification of the economy, one of their arguments is that Russia's trade with the East, where colonization moved ahead, was of more importance than trade with the West before the eighteenth century. The quantitative and descriptive evidence presented in Kotilaine (2005) strongly questions (or rather refutes) this argument, even without overall estimates on the geographical composition of Russia's foreign trade.[86] This view was challenged by the scholars within the same school who argued that Russia from the sixteenth century was as much part of the world system as were Poland or Turkey.[87] Remarkably, Kotilaine (2005, 2–5, 510–514) emphasizes Russia's dependency on commerce in both directions. He points out the predominance of foreign merchants and the concentration of raw materials in exports and manufactured products in imports.

We should pay attention to trade's ambiguous role in the development of the Russian Empire, given the borderland colonization and open frontier (Khodarkovsky 2002; Sunderland 2004, 11–53).[88] In the process of territorial expansion, the fertile black soil region was brought under cultivation in the eighteenth century (Broadberry and Korchmina 2024, 1004–1005). But the population in vast areas of Siberia and the Far East remained very low relative to the Russian European core, and the region was poorly explored. Trade links between European Russia and the peripheral provinces in the Caucasus and Central Asia were of much less importance than the overseas possessions of Britain and France.[89] Territorial expansion of the Russian Empire in Central Asia was driven primarily by geopolitical competition with the British Empire and much less by economic factors.

---

[86] The products obtained from the colonized East (furs above all) were exported mainly to the West. Transportation networks westwards were much better developed than eastwards by the seventeenth century.

[87] Cited in Wallerstein (2011 [1974], xxv).

[88] The concept was coined in the late nineteenth–early twentieth centuries by F. J. Turner (1920, 11–38) with reference to the Northern American type of colonization.

[89] Many of these provinces were included in the Russian interior customs territory, and the statistics reported trade flows with them as domestic. However, some remained outside the interior customs territory, even though they were parts of the Russian Empire.

Taking a WST perspective, Russia changed its status from either an outsider or a periphery in the sixteenth and seventeenth centuries to a semi-periphery in the middle of the eighteenth century, and then back to a periphery until the late nineteenth century. In the eighteenth century, trade openness and a positive trade balance were on the rise. For example, goods produced by Russian iron works were exported to the West alongside agricultural commodities. Later, as the Industrial Revolution proceeded in the West, the composition of Russia's exports and imports more and more resembled that of a periphery. Despite the USSR becoming one of the two military superpowers in the second half of the twentieth century and gaining some features that indicated it should be included in the core, the commodity structure of Russian/Soviet foreign trade hardly supports this notion. Before the 1950s, exports primarily consisted of agricultural commodities, wood, fishery, and furs, while imports were manufactured consumer and producer goods. Only within a short period of time (1950s–end 1960s), at the height of its success in catching up with the West, did the exports of machinery increase. But even at the best of times,[90] the structure was characteristic for the semi-periphery, not the core. In the 1970s–1990s, agricultural exports was replaced by oil and gas; while imports of machinery were rising, as were agricultural products (Uegaki 2019, 306–309).

4.7 Conclusion: Smithian and Northian Growth

The factors underlying economic growth away from the Malthusian mechanism can be subdivided into Smithian (commercialization) and Northian (institutional) growth. In this chapter, we have looked at Smithian growth factors: urbanization, forced and free labour, fertility and human capital, extraction and taxation, and trade and empire. Northian factors are discussed in Chap. 5.

Unsurprisingly, some scholars attach more value to particular factors. As pointed out in Sect. 4.1, for example, Allen (2003) identifies,[91] besides agriculture (as mentioned in Chap. 3), technology, representative government, labour force, and empire as factors that prevented wages from returning to the low levels of the previous semi-Malthusian phase. Yet, Allen (2003) only looks at Western Europe. Other stud-

[90] At the turn of the 1960s to the 1970s, when the share of manufactured products was largest, that of primary products was the least in exports, while the share of machinery was the least in imports.

[91] Allen's model is based on a dozen countries' data with intervals of 50–100 years, which is hardly enough for statistically significant results. This partly explains why human capital, for example, appears to be insignificant. Moreover, urbanization levels are highly correlated with agricultural productivity. The latter naturally allows more people to engage in manufacturing and services. Another important issue is whether income surpluses, resulting from increased agricultural productivity, are channelled into capital accumulation or into demonstrative consumption (be this private or government). Allen (2003) omits a very important variable, namely the savings/investment rate. Its increase is necessary not only for the replacement of capital consumed, but also to allow stock to grow along with the population. Increasing the capital to output ratio is one of the crucial routes out of the Malthusian trap.

ies, inter alia, some endogenous growth studies, point to the importance of other factors such as human capital. However, the weight of inventions might also have had an effect.

Unsurprisingly, the importance of each factor varied by country. However, trade/empire, urbanization, forced and free labour (the mode of labour production), and government power were all important in both positive and negative ways, depending on the economic and political structure of the country in question. Further, we find that the demographic transition had a limited effect on human capital formation. Indeed, after some time, human capital growth depends on technology (that is, increasing income), rather than on fertility, thus obscuring its role in economic growth. Clearer is the role of government, which was more prevalent in East Asia than in Western Europe.

Trade and empire is one of various facets that are often claimed to be important when economic growth begins. Unsurprisingly, we have found that trade and empire had an important effect on breaking weak Malthusian bonds. There are many ways in which this could happen, but three examples will suffice. First, trade has multiple production modes, ranging from tribute trade to markets. In ancient times, most major countries had tributary states for trade, although there were also political reasons. Smaller countries clearly saw tributary trade as a market opportunity. In the West, the tributary system changed to market exchange most quickly owing to national fragmentation and a lack of economic growth. Indeed, in the late Song dynasty, economic stagnation and regional fragmentation also led to more embassies visiting the Chinese emperor (equalling more trade). Second, as opposed to the situation in China, capital accumulated in Russia by merchants through their trading activities could be invested in industrial enterprises once they emerged as profitable. Several waves of business start-ups in the second half of the nineteenth century (Russians borrowed the term "griunderstvo" from German) in mining and manufacturing occurred in Russia in the aftermath of the "Great Reforms" that were implemented in the 1860s–1870s (Moshenskii 2016, 20, 24, 56). Third, foreign trade enhanced technological borrowing from the West (mostly Europe) by importing machinery (a significant share of Russian imports) and fertilizers. This upgraded the consumer practices of the upper strata so they converged with Western standards. However, further diffusion by import substitution was limited owing to the low demand from a relatively poor population at this early stage of modern growth.

Human capital is a second indicator of the importance of economic growth. For example, merchants in Russia initially did not want to invest in human capital for their offspring. In China, though, despite merchants being lower class, they did want to. Yet, whereas the education system drove lower literacy rates in China, it was the changing role of merchants, combined with increasing economic growth, that lifted Russian human capital.

The mode of labour productivity is a third factor. We found a rapid increase in commodified labour between about 1700 and 1900 in Europe. Given that commodified labour leads to higher TFP growth, this implies that the mode of labour productivity had a higher effect on long-run growth in Western Europe after 1700. After 1900, this converged again among Western and non-Western countries.

The role of these factors (trade and empire, human capital, the mode of labour productivity, etc) could thus be different for the pioneers (the Netherlands and England) and the latecomers to industrialization. For a country with a catch-up strategy for development, with its economy oriented towards large-scale technological and institutional borrowing and adoption, it is vital that the population is educated enough to rapidly and successfully adopt new technologies. In this regard, the classic model by Nelson and Phelps (1966) points to the decisive importance of a critical mass of human capital in recipient countries in order to successfully borrow innovations from elsewhere. Furthermore, as Lau et al. (1993) claim, a critical mass of human capital stock is needed to promote growth. They discovered this to be three or four years of schooling after analysing cross-sectional evidence from Brazilian states. Neither early modern Europe nor pre-Revolutionary Russia had such a critical mass. In addition, besides human capital, a sufficient share of commodified labour is necessary to increase technological borrowing, as proxied by TFP.

The case of the Russian Empire highlights the important role of trade, which increased its penetration into the economy despite it being weak in comparison with other countries. Rapid development of trade, as a consequence of division of labour, provided evidence of Russia's position to reap the benefits of Smithian growth. However, this potential could not be realized in a sustained way before railways led to the integration of the economy from the late nineteenth century (Broadberry and Korchmina 2024, 1024).[92]

In sum, it was mainly trade and empire that strengthened the modern phase of economic growth. This was mainly true for lagging economies, which generally continued to lag in labour relations, human capital, urban modes of labour productivity, and population development well into the twentieth century. This was later combined with active government policies. Contrary to this finding, there were other factors besides trade in leading countries. For example, they had enough human capital to make the appropriate twists and turns during the Industrial Revolution, and were well ahead of developing economies in terms of the commodified labour mode of productivity.

References

A'Hearn B, Baten J, Crayen D (2009) Quantifying quantitative literacy: Age heaping and the history of human capital. J Econ Hist 69:783–808

Acemoglu D, Robinson J (2012) Why nations fail: Origins of power, poverty, and prosperity. Crown, New York, NY

Acemoglu D, Johnson S, Robinson JA (2005) Institutions as a fundamental cause of long-run growth. In: Aghion P, Durlauf SN (eds) Handbook of economic growth, vol 1A. Elsevier, Amsterdam, pp 385–472

Ades A, Glaeser E (1995) Trade and circuses: Explaining urban giants. Q J Econ 110(1):195–227

[92] The story of railway construction as a grand public–private investment project in Russia at the start of modern growth is discussed in Sect. 6.6.

Ajus, F., & Lindgren, M. (2015). Children per woman (Version 6). The Gapminder Foundation. Accessed from http://www.gapminder.org/downloads/documentation/gd008.

Allen RC (2001) The great divergence in European wages and prices from the Middle Ages to the First World War. Explor Econ Hist 38:411–447

Allen RC (2003) Progress and poverty in early modern Europe. Econ Hist Rev 56(3):403–443

Allen RC (2009) The British industrial revolution in global perspective. Cambridge University Press, Cambridge and New York

Allen RC (2011) Why the industrial revolution was British: Commerce, induced invention, and the scientific revolution. Econ Hist Rev 64(2):357–384

Allen R, Bassino JP, Ma DB, Moll-Murata C, Van Zanden JL (2011) Wages, prices, and living standards in China, 1738–1925: in comparison with Europe, Japan, and India. Econ Hist Rev 64(s1):8–38

Andreev EM (1994) Life expectancy and causes of death in the USSR. In: Lutz W, Scherbov S, Volkov A (eds) Demographic Trends and Patterns in the Soviet Union before 1991. New York, pp 279–293

Andreev EM, Darskij L, Kharkova T (1992) L'histoire de la population de l'URSS 1920–1959. Ann Démogr Hist:61–150. Accessed from https://www.persee.fr/doc/adh_0066-2062_1992_num_1992_1_1816

Ang J, Banerjee R, Madsen J (2013) Innovation and productivity advances in British agriculture: 1620–1850. South Econ J 80(1):162–186

Arrighi G (2010) The long twentieth century: Money, power, and the origins of our times, second edn. Verso Books, London and New York

Bai, Y. (2013). The effect of abolishing China's Imperial Examination on the adoption of western technology: a regression discontinuity design. Paper of Hong Kong University of Science and Technology.

Balassa B (1965) Trade liberalisation and "revealed" comparative advantage. Manch Sch 33(2):99–123

Barro RJ (1991) Economic growth in a cross section of countries. Q J Econ 106(2):407–443. https://doi.org/10.2307/2937943

Bartol'd VV (1963) *Туркестан в эпоху монгольского нашествия [Turkestan during the epoch of the Mongol invasion]*, vol 1. Издательство Восточной литературы [Oriental Literature Publishing House], Moscow

Batchelor R (2013) The Selden Map rediscovered: a Chinese map of East Asian shipping routes, c.1619. Imago Mundi 65(1):37–63. https://doi.org/10.1080/03085694.2013.733893

Baten, J., & Blum, M. (2015). Height [Data set]. https://hdl.handle.net/10622/IAEKLA. IISH Data Collection, V1.

Blum J (1957) The rise of serfdom in Eastern Europe. Am Hist Rev 62(4):807–836. https://doi.org/10.2307/1847310

Boiko VP (1996) Томское купечество в конце XVIII–XIX вв. Из истории формирования сибирской буржуазии [Tomsk merchants at the end of the 18th–20th centuries. From the history of the formation of the Siberian bourgeoisie]. Водолей [Aquarius], Tomsk

Bokarev Y (1994) Власть и преступность в России в период хрущевской оттепели и реформ 60-х - 70-х годов [Power and criminality in Russia in the period of Khrushchov's thaw and the reforms of the 1960s–70s]. Россия XXI [Russia XXI] 4–5:136–153

Bolt, J., & Van Zanden, J. L. (2020). Maddison Project Database, version 2020. Maddison style estimates of the evolution of the world economy: A new 2020 update.

Borodkin LI (2001) Неравенство доходов в период индустриальной революции. Универсальна ли гипотеза о кривой Кузнеца? [Income inequality in the period of industrial revolution. How universal is the Kuznets curve hypothesis?]. In: *Россия и мир. Памяти профессора Валерия Ивановича Бовыкина: сборник статей [Russia and the world. For the memory of Professor Valery Ivanovich Bovykin: Collection of essays]*, Moscow, pp 331–355. Российская политическая энциклопедия (РОССПЭН) [Russian Political Encyclopedia (ROSSPEN)]. http://www.hist.msu.ru/Labour/Article/borodkin.htm

Borodkin LI, Valetov TI (2001) Микроанализ данных о квалификации и динамике заработной платы рабочих-текстильщиков Товарищества мануфактур Н. Н. Коншина (конец XIX — начало XX вв) [Microanalysis of data on the qualifications and dynamics of wages of textile workers of the Association of Manufactories owned by N. N. Konshin (late 19th - early 20th centuries)]. In: Экономическая история. Ежегодник [Economic History. Yearbook]. 2000. Российская политическая энциклопедия (РОССПЭН) [Russian Political Encyclopedia (ROSSPEN)], Moscow, pp 351–388. http://www.hist.msu.ru/Labour/Article/borodkin2000/borodkin.htm

Borodkin LI, Granville B, Leonard CS (2008) The rural/urban wage gap in the industrialization of Russia, 1884–1910. Eur Rev Econ Hist 12(1):67–95

Bosker M, Buringh E, van Zanden JL (2013) From Baghdad to London, unraveling urban development in Europe, North Africa and the Middle East, 800–1800. Rev Econ Stat 95(4):1418–1437. https://doi.org/10.1162/REST_a_00362

Brandt L (1987) Farm household behavior, factor markets, and the distributive consequences of commercialization in early twentieth-century China. J Econ Hist 47(3):1–27. https://doi.org/10.1017/S0022050700048411

Braudel F (1973) Capitalism and material life, 1400–1800. HarperCollins Publishers, New York. (Original work published 1967)

Braudel F (1992) Civilization and capitalism (Vol. 3). The perspective of the world. University of California Press, Berkeley. (Original work published 1979)

Broadberry S, Gupta B (2009) Lancashire, India, and shifting competitive advantage in cotton textiles, 1700–1850: the neglected role of factor prices. Econ Hist Rev 62(2):279–305. https://doi.org/10.1111/j.1468-0289.2009.00482.x

Broadberry S, Korchmina E (2024) Catching-up and falling behind: Russian economic growth, 1960s–1880s. J Econ Hist 84(4):997–1028. https://doi.org/10.1017/s0022050724000287

Broadberry S, Campbell B, Van Leeuwen B (2013) When did Britain industrialise? The sectoral distribution of the labour force and labour productivity in Britain, 1381–1851. Explor Econ Hist 50(1):16–27. https://doi.org/10.1016/j.eeh.2012.09.003

Broadberry S, Campbell B, Klein A, Overton M, Van Leeuwen B (2015) British economic growth 1270–1870. Cambridge University Press, Cambridge

Broadberry S, Guan H, Li D (2018) China, Europe, and the Great Divergence: a study in historical national accounting, 980–1850. J Econ Hist 78(4):955–1000. https://doi.org/10.1017/S0022050718000403

Broadberry S, Guan H, Li D (2021) China, Europe, and the Great Divergence: a restatement. J Econ Hist 81(1):1–17. https://doi.org/10.1017/S0022050721000292

Buggle JC, Nafziger S (2021) The Slow Road from Serfdom: labor coercion and long-run development in the former Russian empire. Rev Econ Stat 103(1):1–17. https://doi.org/10.1162/rest_a_00857

Campante F, Sturzenegger F, Velasco A (2021) Proximate and fundamental causes of growth. In: Campante F, Sturzenegger F, Velasco A (eds) Advanced macroeconomics: an easy guide (Chap. 7). LSE Press, London. https://doi.org/10.31389/lsepress.ame.g

Chandler T (1987) Four thousand years of urban growth: an historical census. Edwin Mellon Press, Lewiston, NY

Cheremukhin A, Golosov M, Guriev S, Tsyvinski A (2017) The industrialization and economic development of Russia through the lens of a neoclassical growth model. Rev Econ Stud 84(2):613–649. https://doi.org/10.1093/restud/rdw026

Clark G (2015) Markets before economic growth: the grain market of medieval England. Cliometrica 9(3):265–287. https://doi.org/10.1007/s11698-014-0118-x

Comin, D. A., & Hobijn, B. (2009). The CHAT Dataset. NBER Working Paper No. 15319. September. https://www.nber.org/papers/w15319, https://data.nber.org/data-appendix/w15319/

Costa LF, Palma N, Reis J (2015) The great escape? The contribution of the empire to Portugal's economic growth, 1500–1800. Eur Rev Econ Hist 19(1):1–22

Cottarelli C, Blejer MI (1992) Forced savings and repressed inflation in the Soviet Union: some empirical results. IMF Staff Pap 39(2):256–286. https://www.elibrary.imf.org/downloadpdf/journals/024/1992/002/article-A002-en.xml

Crisp O (1978) Labour and industrialization in Russia. In: Mathias P, Postan MM (eds) The Cambridge economic history of Europe. Vol. VII. The industrial economies capital, labour, and enterprise. Part 2. The United States, Japan, and Russia. Cambridge University Press, pp 308–415

Davies RW, Harrison M, Wheatcroft SG (1994) The economic transformation of the Soviet Union, 1913–1945. Cambridge University Press

Davis J, Henderson V (2003) Evidence on the political economy of the urbanization process. J Urban Econ 53(1):98–125. https://doi.org/10.1016/S0094-1190(02)00504-1

Davydov MA (2016) Двадцать лет до Великой войны: российская модернизация Витте-Столыпина [Twenty years before the Great War: Russian modernization from Witte & Stolypin], second edn. Алетея [Alethea], St. Petersburg

De Pleijt AM, Van Zanden JL (2016) Accounting for the "Little Divergence": What drove economic growth in pre-industrial Europe, 1300–1800? Eur Rev Econ Hist 20(4):387–409

Derluguian GM (2007) Some ideas about empires on Europe's periphery (The worlds the Portuguese, the Russians, and the Turks created). Soc Evol Hist 6(1):145–154

Didenko DV (2022) Неравенство доходов в современной России на фоне долгосрочной исторической ретроспективы [Income inequality in contemporary Russia in the long-run historical perspective]. Terra Econ 20(2):72–85. https://doi.org/10.18522/2073-6606-2022-20-2-72-85

Didenko DV (2024) Трудовые отношения и способы производства в институциональном развитии России [Labour relations and modes of production under Russia's institutional development]. J Inst Stud 16(3):68–79. https://doi.org/10.17835/2076-6297.2024.16.3.068-079

Didenko, D., Földvári, P., and Van Leeuwen, B. (2013). The spread of human capital in the former Soviet Union area in a comparative perspective: exploring a new dataset. J Eurasian Stud, 4(2): 123–135. https://doi.org/10.1016/j.euras.2013.03.002. (Supplementary data retrieved from https://ars.els-cdn.com/content/image/1-s2.0-S1879366513000122-mmc1.zip, accessed via https://www.sciencedirect.com/science/article/pii/S1879366513000122)

Dikhtyar GA (1960) Внутренняя торговля в дореволюционной России [Domestic trade in pre-revolutionary Russia]. Издательство Академии наук СССР [The USSR Academy of Sciences Publishing House], Moscow

Domar ED (1989) The causes of slavery or serfdom: a hypothesis. In: Domar ED (ed) Capitalism, socialism, and serfdom. Cambridge University Press, pp 225–238

Domar ED, Machina MJ (1989) On the profitability of Russian serfdom. In: Domar ED (ed) Capitalism, socialism, and serfdom. Cambridge University Press, pp 239–279

Duncan-Jones RP (1977) Age-rounding, illiteracy and social differentiation in the Roman Empire. Chiron 7:333–354

Elvin M (1973) The pattern of the Chinese past: a social and economic interpretation. Stanford University Press, Stanford

Fairbank JK (1942) Trade and China's relations with the West. Far East Q 1(2):129–149. https://doi.org/10.2307/2049225

Fairbank JK, Teng S-y (1941) On the Ch'ing's tributary system. Harv J Asiat Stud 6(2):135–246. https://doi.org/10.2307/2718005

Felice E (2012) Regional convergence in Italy (1891–2001): testing human and social capital. Cliometrica 6(3):267–306

Field D (1976) The end of serfdom: Nobility and bureaucracy in Russia, 1855–1861. Harvard University Press, Cambridge, MA

Fogel RW, Engerman SL (1974) Time on the cross: the economics of American Negro Slavery. W.W. Norton and Company

Galor O (2011a) Unified growth theory. Princeton University Press, Princeton, NJ

Galor O (2011b) The demographic transition: causes and consequences. Cliometrica 6:1–28

Galor O, Moav O, Vollrath D (2009) Land inequality and the emergence of human capital promoting institutions. Rev Econ Stud 76(1):143–179
Gao WL (1999) 经济发展与地区开发：中国传统经济的发展序列(Economic growth and regional development: Development sequence of China's traditional economy). Ocean Press, Beijing, China
Geertz C (1963) Agricultural involution: The processes of ecological change in Indonesia. University of California Press, Berkeley and Los Angeles, CA
Godo Y (2018) Catch-up sustainable economic growth and education stock in East Asia. In: Yülek M (ed) Industrial policy and sustainable growth. Sustainable development. Springer, Singapore, pp 401–412
Godo Y, Hayami Y (2002) Catching-up in education in the economic catch-up of Japan with the United States, 1890–1990. Econ Dev Cult Change 50(4):961–978
Gokmen G, Vermeulen WN, Vezina PL (2020) The imperial roots of global trade. J Econ Growth 25:87–145
Gosudarstvennyi komitet RF po statistike (GKS RF) (1992) Сборник аналитических докладов по материалам переписи населения 1989 года [A Collection of Analytical Reports Based on the Population Census of 1989]. Республиканский информационно-издательский центр [The Republican Information and Publishing Center], Moscow
Gosudarstvennyi komitet SSSR po statistike (GKS). (1989). Итоги Всесоюзной переписи населения 1979 года. Пол, возраст и состояние в браке населения СССР. Том II. Часть1. Статистический сборник [The results of the All-Union Population Census of 1979. Gender, age and marital status of the population of the USSR. Volume II. Part 1. Statistical abstract]. Moscow.
Guan Y, Zhang D (2017) 斯密型增长——基于近代中国乡村工业的再评析("Smithian growth": Revaluating rural industry based on the modern Chinese rural industries). 历史研究 (Hist Res) 2:153–167
Guangxiang Z (2016) Transportation and economic development of Russia in 19th — beginning of 20th century. Istoriko-ekonomicheskie issledovaniya = J Econ Hist Hist Econ 17(4):645–696. https://doi.org/10.17150/2308-2588.2016.17
Guo Y, Zhang Z, Van Leeuwen B, Xu Y (2019) A view of the occupational structure in Imperial and Republican China (1640–1952). Aust Econ Hist Rev 59(2):134–158
Hansen GD, Prescott EC (2002) Malthus to Solow. Am Econ Rev 92(4):1205–1217
Hausmann R, Hwang J, Rodrik D (2007) What you export matters. J Econ Growth 12(1):1–25. https://doi.org/10.1007/s10887-006-9009-4
Hausmann R, Hidalgo CA, Bustos S, Coscia M, Simoes A, Yildirim MA (2014) The atlas of economic complexity: mapping paths to prosperity. MIT Press, Cambridge, MA. https://doi.org/10.7551/mitpress/9647.001.0001
He G (2013) The rise and fall of serfdom in China: a theory of institutional change. Econ Hist Dev Reg 28(1):69–86. https://doi.org/10.1080/20780389.2013.764677
Hellie R (1982) Slavery in Russia, 1450–1725. University of Chicago Press, Chicago
Hippe R, Baten J (2012) Regional inequality in human capital formation in Europe, 1790–1880. Scand Econ Hist Rev 60(3):254–289. https://doi.org/10.1080/03585522.2012.722677
Hu, S. (2020). Survival of the confucians: social status and fertility in China, 1400–1900. LSE Economic History Working Papers, No. 307. https://www.lse.ac.uk/Economic-History/Working-Papers
Huang PCC (1990) The peasant family and rural development in the Yangzi Delta, 1350–1988. Stanford University Press, Stanford
Huang C (2019) China's tributary system and national security in the Song Dynasty. J Chin Human 5:149–170. https://doi.org/10.1163/23521341-12340055
Huang T, He L (2006) 井田制研究——对先秦土地制度变迁的经济学解释(Research on the nine-square field system: Economic explanation to transformation of earth system in pre-Qin dynasty). 河南师范大学学报哲学社会科学版 (J Henan Norm Univ (Social Sciences Edition)) 33(5):99–103

Human Fertility Database (HFD). (2015). Max Planck Institute for Demographic Research (Germany) and Vienna Institute of Demography (Austria). https://www.humanfertility.org/cgi-bin/main.php.

Human Mortality Database (HMD). (2009). Joint project of the Department of Demography at the University of California, Berkeley (USA) and the Max Planck Institute for Demographic Research in Rostock (Germany). https://www.mortality.org/Home/Index.

IISH (n.d.) IISH, labour relations. Accessed from https://datasets.iisg.amsterdam/dataverse/labour-relations. The data are extracted from the treemap: https://treemap.iisg.amsterdam/treemap/.

Institute of Demography at the State Research University Higher School of Economics (HSE IDEM). (2011). Переписи населения Российской империи, СССР, 15 новых независимых государств [Population Censuses in the Russian Empire, the USSR, 15 Newly Independent States]. https://www.demoscope.ru/weekly/ssp/census.php.

Johansson, K., & Lindgren, M. (2014). Life expectancy at birth. Version 7. The Gapminder Foundation. http://www.gapminder.org/gapminder-world/documentation/gd004.

Kahan A (1985) The Plow, the Hammer and the Knout: an economic history of Eighteenth-Century Russia. University of Chicago Press, Chicago

Kaiser D (ed) (1992) The laws of Rus'—Tenth to fifteenth centuries (The laws of Russia, Series I), vol 1. Charles Schlacks, Jr., Salt Lake City, UT. Kaiser, D. (Trans) Accessed from http://faculty.washington.edu/dwaugh/rus/lexintro.html, https://web.archive.org/web/20220217084901/http://web.grinnell.edu/individuals/kaiser/shrp.html, https://web.archive.org/web/20220217103027/http://web.grinnell.edu/individuals/kaiser/exrp.html.

Kashin, Yu. I. (Ed.). (2012). По страницам архивных фондов Центрального банка Российской Федерации [Through the pages of the archival funds of the Central Bank of the Russian Federation]. Issue 13. Госбанк СССР и Минфин СССР в процессе мобилизации и использования сбережений населения (ведомственные материалы) [The State Bank of the USSR and the Ministry of Finance of the USSR in the process of mobilizing and using the savings of the population (departmental materials)]. Moscow: Bank of Russia. Accessed from https://www.cbr.ru/Content/Document/File/48221/ArchivalFonds_013.pdf.

Katsenelinboigen A (1977) Coloured markets in the Soviet Union. Sov Stud 29(1):62–85

Khodarkovsky M (2002) Russia's steppe frontier: The making of a colonial empire, 1500–1800. Indiana University Press, Bloomington—Indianapolis

Kim B-Y (1999) The income, savings, and monetary overhang of Soviet households. J Comp Econ 27(4):644–668

Kim B-Y (2003) Informal economic activities of Soviet households: size and dynamics. J Comp Econ 31(3):532–551

Klein MA (1985) The use of mode of production in historical analysis. Can J Afr Stud/Revue Canadienne Des Études Africaines 19(1):9–12. https://doi.org/10.2307/484645

Klemp M, Weisdorf J (2019) Fecundity, fertility, and the formation of human capital. Econ J 129(618):925–960. https://doi.org/10.1111/ecoj.12615

Kokkinen, A. (2012). On Finland's economic growth and convergence with Sweden and the EU15 in the 20th century. Statistics Finland. Research Reports. 258. https://www.stat.fi/tup/julkaisut/tiedostot/978-952-244-334-2.pdf.

Kolchin P (1987) Unfree labor: American slavery and Russian serfdom. Harvard University Press, Cambridge, MA

Kotilaine JT (2005) Russia's foreign trade and economic expansion in the seventeenth century: Windows on the World. Brill, Leiden—Boston

Koval'chenko ID, Milov LV (1974) Всероссиискии аграрныи рынок (XVIII—начало XX вв.): опыт количественного анализа [All-Russian agrarian market in the 18th and beginning of the nineteenth century: A quantitative analysis]. Наука [The Science], Moscow

Kozlova NV (1999) Российский абсолютизм и купечество в XVIII веке (20-е - начало 60-х годов) [Russian absolutism and merchants in the eighteenth century (20 s - early 60 s)]. Археологический центр [The Archaeological Center], Moscow

Kuboniwa M, Shida Y, Tabata S (2019) Gross domestic products. In: Kuboniwa M et al (eds) Russian economic development over three centuries: new data and inferences. Palgrave Macmillan, Singapore, pp 335–419

Kuchkin VA (2013) Население Руси в канун Батыева нашествия [The population of Rus' before Batyi's invasion]. In: Obrazy agrarnoi Rossii, IX—XVIII vv. [The images of agrarian Russia, 18th—19th centuries]. Индрик [Indrik], Moscow, pp 67–88

Kumo K (2019) Population. In: Kuboniwa M et al (eds) Russian economic development over three centuries: new data and inferences. Palgrave Macmillan, Singapore, pp 59–103

Kumo, K., Morinaga, T., & Shida, Y. (2007). Long-term population statistics for Russia, 1867–2002. RRC Working Paper Series No. 2. https://www.ier.hit-u.ac.jp/rrc/English/pdf/RRC_WP_No2.pdf.

Lau LJ, Jamison DT, Liu S-C, Rivkin S (1993) Education and economic growth: Some cross-sectional evidence from Brazil. J Dev Econ 41(1):45–70

Leonard CS (2011) Agrarian Reform in Russia: the road from Serfdom. Cambridge University Press, New York

Levine R, Renelt D (1991) Cross-country studies of growth and policy: methodological, conceptual, and statistical problems, vol 608. World Bank Publications

Li L (2000) Integration and disintegration in North China's grain markets, 1738–1911. J Econ Hist 60(3):665–699. https://doi.org/10.1017/S0022050700025761

Li BZ, Van Zanden JL (2012) Before the great divergence? Comparing the Yangzi Delta and the Netherlands at the beginning of the nineteenth century. J Econ Hist 72(4):956–989. https://doi.org/10.1017/S0022050712000754

Lifits MM (ed) (1947) Советская торговля за 30 лет [The Soviet trade over 30 years]. Gostorgizdat, Moscow

Lightfoot KG (2003) Russian colonization: The implications of mercantile colonial practices in the North Pacific. Hist Archaeol 37(4):14–28

Ljungberg J, Nilsson A (2009) Human capital and economic growth: Sweden 1870–2000. Cliometrica 3(1):71–95. https://doi.org/10.1007/s11698-008-0027-7

Lucas R Jr (1988) On the mechanics of economic development. J Monetary Econ 22(1):3–42

Ma, D. B. (2011). Rock, scissors, paper: The problem of incentives and information in traditional Chinese state and the origin of Great Divergence. LSE Working Paper, 152/11.

Mackay C (2004) Ancient Rome: A military and political history. Cambridge University Press, New York. Maddison Project Database, version 2020

Maddison A (2007) Contours of the world economy, 1–2030 AD. Essays in macro-economic history. Oxford University Press, Oxford

Malanima P (2010) Urbanization. In: Broadberry S, O'Rourke K (eds) The Cambridge economic history of modern Europe. Cambridge University Press, Cambridge, pp 235–263

Malanima P (2013) When did England overtake Italy? Medieval and early modern divergence in prices and wages. Eur Rev Econ Hist 17(1):45–70

Malanima P (2018) Italy in the renaissance: a leading economy in the European context, 1350–1550. Econ Hist Rev 71:3–30

Markevich A, Zhuravskaya E (2018) Economic effects of the abolition of serfdom: evidence from the Russian Empire. Am Econ Rev 108:1074–1117

McDermott J (2005) The ascendancy of the imprint in China. In: Brokaw CJ, Chow KW (eds) Printing and book culture in late imperial China. University of California Press, California, pp 55–107

Mironov BN (1981) Внутренний рынок России во второй половине XVIII– первой половине XIX века [Russian domestic market in the second half of the eighteenth century—first half of the nineteenth century]. Наука [The Science], Leningrad

Mironov BN (1985a) Грамотность в России 1797–1917 годов [Literacy in Russia in 1797–1917]. *История СССР [Istoria SSSR] 4*:137–153

Mironov BN (1985b) Хлебные цены в России за два столетия (XVIII—XIX вв.) [Bread prices in Russia for two centuries (XVIII—XIX centuries)]. Наука [The Science], Leningrad

Mironov BN (1991) The development of literacy in Russia and the USSR from the tenth to the twentieth centuries. Hist Educat Q 31(2):229–252
Mironov, B. N. (2003). Социальная история России периода империи (XVIII—начало XX в.): Генезис личности, демократической семьи, гражданского общества и правового государства [Gosudarstva Social History of Russia during the Empire period (XVIII—early XX century): The genesis of personality, democratic family, civil society and the rule of law] (third Vol. 2). St. Petersburg: Dmitrii Bulanin.
Mironov BN (2012) The Standard of Living and Revolutions in Russia, 1700–1917. Routledge, Abingdon, UK
Mironov BN (2018) Российская империя: от традиции к модерну. [The Russian Empire: From Tradition to Modernity], vol 1–3), second edn. Dmitrii Bulanin, St. Petersburg
Mironov BN (2022) Urban fertility in Russia in 1859–1913: On commencement of demographic transition. Popul Econ 6(2):1–13. https://doi.org/10.3897/popecon.6.e83642
Mitchell B (2003) International historical statistics: Europe. Palgrave Macmillan, Basingstoke
Mizis IA (2006) Формирование рынка Центрального Черноземья во второй половине XVII—первои половине XVIII вв. [Formation of the market of the Central Black-soil region in the second half of the 17th century - the first half of the 18th centuries]. Iulis, Tambov
Mokyr J (2002) The gifts of Athena: historical origins of the knowledge economy. Princeton University Press, Princeton
Moshenskii SZ (2016) Рынок ценных бумаг Российской империи [The securities market of the Russian Empire]. Moscow: Экономика [Economy]
MVT (Ministry of Foreign Trade of the USSR) (1960) Внешняя торговля СССР за 1918–1940 гг. Статистический обзор [Foreign trade of the USSR over 1918–1940. Statistical abstract]. Vneshtorgizdat, Moscow
MVT (Ministry of Foreign Trade of the USSR) (n.d.) Внешняя торговля СССР… Статистический сборник / обзор [Foreign trade of the USSR... Statistical abstract]. Vneshtorgizdat, Moscow
Myers R (1970) The Chinese peasant economy: agricultural development in Hopei and Shantung, 1890–1949. Harvard University Press, Cambridge, Mass.
Nakamura Y (2019) Money and finance. In: Kuboniwa M et al (eds) Russian economic development over three centuries: New data and inferences. Palgrave Macmillan, Singapore, pp 221–249
Nefedov, S. A. (2010–2011). История России. Факторный анализ. [Russia's History. Factor Analysis] (Vols. 1–2). Moscow: Territoriia Budushchego Publ. House.
Nelson RR, Phelps ES (1966) Investment in humans, technological diffusion, and economic growth. Am Econ Rev 56(2):69–75
Ni Y (2016) Customs duties in the Qing Dynasty, ca. 1644–1911. Brill, Leiden and Boston
Nielsen, R. W. (2015). Unified growth theory contradicted by the GDP/cap data. Accessed from http://arxiv.org/ftp/arxiv/papers/1511/1511.09323.pdf
Ortman S, Lobo J (2020) Smithian growth in a nonindustrial society. Sci Adv 6(25):eaba5694. https://doi.org/10.1126/sciadv.aba5694
Peng ZY (1957) 中国近代手工业史资料(1840–1949)[Archives on the history of modern Chinese handicraft industry, 1840–1949]. SDX Joint Publishing Company, Beijing
Piketty T, Zucman G (2014) Capital is back: wealth-income ratios in rich countries 1700–2010. Q J Econ 129(3):1255–1310
Polanyi K (1957) The great transformation: the political and economic origin of our time. Beacon Press, Boston
Poliakov IA (ed) (1992) Всесоюзная перепись населения 1939 г. Основные итоги [The All-Union Population Census of 1939 Main results]. Наука [The Science], Moscow
Poliakov IA (ed) (2007) Всесоюзная перепись населения 1937 г. Общие итоги. Сборник документов и материалов [The All-Union population census of 1937. General results. Collection of documents and materials]. Российская политическая энциклопедия (РОССПЭН) [Russian Political Encyclopedia (ROSSPEN)], Moscow
Prados de la Escosura L, Rosés JR (2010) Human capital and economic growth in Spain, 1850–2000. Explor Econ Hist 47(4):520–532

Pritchett L (2001) Where has all the education gone? World Bank, Washington, DC. https://openknowledge.worldbank.org/handle/10986/17434
Prokopovich SN (1952) Народное хозяйство СССР [The national economy of the USSR], vol 2. Chekhov Publishing House, New York
Rashin AG (1956) Население России за 100 лет (1811–1913). Статистические очерки [Russia's Population over 100 Years (1811–1913). Statistical Essays]. Gosstatizdat, Moscow
Reid, A. (1988–1993). Southeast Asia in the age of commerce (2 vols.). New Haven: Yale University Press.
Rosenthal JL, Wong RB (2011) Before and beyond divergence: the politics of economic change in China and Europe. Harvard University Press, Cambridge, MA
Rosstat. (2020). The Great Patriotic War: The anniversary statistical handbook. Moscow. https://eng.rosstat.gov.ru/storage/mediabank/aFUPCqQP/VOV_75_ENGLISH.pdf.
Rozman G (1973) Urban networks in Ching China and Tokugawa Japan. Princeton University Press, Princeton, NJ
Russian Code of Laws (1830–1916). [Полное собрание законов Российской империи]. https://nlr.ru/e-res/law_r/content.html.
Sala-i-Martin, X. X. (1997). I just ran four million regressions (Tech. Rep.). National Bureau of Economic Research.
Sands B, Myers RH (1986) The spatial approach to Chinese history: A test. J Asian Stud 45(4):721–743
Shida, Y. (2015). Forced savings in the Soviet republics: Re-examination. Institute of Economic Research, Hitotsubashi University. RRC Working Paper No. 54. http://hermes-ir.lib.hitu.ac.jp/hermes/ir/re/27497/RRC_WP_No54.pdf.
Shida Y, Kumo K, Nakamura Y (2019) Labor. In: Kuboniwa M et al (eds) Russian economic development over three centuries: new data and inferences. Palgrave Macmillan, Singapore, pp 105–132
Shipilov AV (2008) Уровень жизни рабочих в России в первой половине 18 в. [The standard of living of workers in Russia in the first half of the eighteenth century]. Voprosy istorii [Issues of History] 11:110–118
Shiue CH (2017) Human capital and fertility in Chinese clans before modern growth. J Econ Growth 22(4):351–396
Skinner W (1977) The city in late imperial China. Stanford University Press, Stanford, CA
Smith A (1776) In: Campbell RH, Skinner AS (eds) An inquiry into the nature and causes of the wealth of nations. Indianapolis, Liberty Fund, 1984
Solar P (2021) China's GDP: Some corrections and the way forward. J Econ Hist:1–15. https://doi.org/10.1017/S0022050721000309
Squicciarini MP, Voigtländer N (2015) Human capital and industrialization: evidence from the age of enlightenment. Q J Econ 130(4):1825–1883
Stanziani A (2014) Bondage: labor and rights in Eurasia from the sixteenth to the early twentieth centuries. Berghahn Books, New York
Stapel, R., & Yuan, W. (2023). Multimodal transport networks in East Asia (early twentieth century): modelling historical transport times using GIS and Chinese travel documents (forthcoming).
Strumilin SG (1958) Статистико-экономические очерки [Essays on statistics and economics]. Gosstatizdat, Moscow
Strumilin SG (1966) Очерки экономической истории России и СССР [Essays on Economic History of Russia and the USSR]. Наука [The Science], Moscow
Suhareva OA (1958) К истории городов Бухарского ханства (историко-этнографические очерки) [On the Urban History of the Bukhara Khanate (Historical and Ethnographic Essays)]. Uzbek SSR Academy of Sciences Publishing House, Tashkent
Sunderland W (2004) Taming the wild field: Colonization and empire on the Russian steppe. Cornell University Press, Ithaca; London
The Russian Code of Laws (1830–1916). The Russian Code of Laws [Полное собрание законов Российской империи]. https://nlr.ru/e-res/law_r/content.html.

Thompstone SR (2008) Российская внешняя торговля XIX — начала XX в.: организация и финансирование [Russian foreign trade in the 19th—early 20th centuries: organization and financing], Moscow. Российская политическая энциклопедия (РОССПЭН) [Russian Political Encyclopedia (ROSSPEN)]
Tilly C (1990) Coercion, Capital, and European States, AD 990–1990. B. Blackwell, Cambridge
Trever KV, Yakubovskii AY, Voronets ME (1950) Раннефеодальное общество в Мавераннахре XI-XII вв. [Early feudal society in Transoxiana]. In: Tolstov SP, Zakhidov VY, Guliamov YG, Nabiev RN (eds) История народов Узбекистана. Том 1. С древнейших времен до начала XVI века [History of the Nations of Uzbekistan. Vol. 1. From the Ancient Times to the Early sixteenth century]. Uzbek SSR Academy of Sciences Publishing House, Tashkent, pp 267–342
Troitskii SM (1966) Финансовая политика русского абсолютизма в XVIII веке [The Financial Policy of Russian Absolutism in the eighteenth Century]. Наука [The Science], Moscow
Tsentral'noe statisticheskoe upravlenie (TsSU SSSR) (1929) Всесоюзная перепись населения 1926 года [The All-Union Population Census of 1926], vol XVII. Izdanie TsSU Soiuza SSR, Moscow
Tsentral'noe statisticheskoe upravlenie (TsSU SSSR) (n.d.) Народное хозяйство СССР [National Economy of the USSR]. Финансы и статисктика [Finance and statistics], Moscow
Tsentral'noe upravlenie narodnokhoziaistvennogo uchota (TsUNKhU) (1940) Культурное строительство СССР: статистический сборник [Cultural construction of the USSR: a statistical collection]. Gosplanizdat, Moscow—Leningrad
TsUNKhU (n.d.) Tsentral'noe upravlenie narodnokhoziaistvennogo uchota [Central Board for National Economic Accounting]. Социалистическое строительство Союза ССР: статистическии сборник [Socialist construction of the USSR: Statistical Abstract]. Soiuzorguchot, Moscow
Turner FJ (1920) The frontier in American history. Henry Holt and Company, New York
Turner C, Tamura R, Mulholland S, Baier S (2013) How important are human capital, physical capital and total factor productivity for determining state economic growth in the United States, 1840–2000? J Econ Growth 18(4):319–371
Uegaki A (2019) Foreign trade. In: Kuboniwa M et al (eds) Russian economic development over three centuries: new data and inferences. Palgrave Macmillan, Singapore, pp 291–315
Valetov, T. I. (2017a). Проект "Статистика внешней торговли Российской империи": характеристика источника и цифрового ресурса [Project "The Russian Empire Foreign Trade Statistics": Source and Digital Resource Description]. Historical Informatics, 1, 5–14. https://doi.org/10.7256/2306-0891.2017.1.22195 (Data: http://www.hist.msu.ru/Dynamics/foreign_trade_en.htm).
Valetov TI (2017b) Структура экспорта Российской империи по ежегодникам внешней торговли 1802—1915 гг. [Structure of the Russian Empire Export in the Official Statistics Yearbooks of Foreign Trade 1802—1915]. Istoriya 8(7/61) http://history.jes.su/s207987840001954-8-1. http://www.hist.msu.ru/Dynamics/data/Valetov_ENOJ2017.pdf
Van der Spek RJ, Van Leeuwen B, Van Zanden JL (2015) Markets from Babylon to Belfast: some concluding remarks. In: van der Spek R, van Leeuwen B, van Zanden JL (eds) A history of market performance. Routledge, pp 529–544
Van Leeuwen B, Földvári P (2008a) Human capital and economic growth in Asia 1890–2000: a time-series analysis. Asian Econ J 22(3):225–240
Van Leeuwen B, Földvári P (2008b) How much human capital does Eastern Europe have? Measurement methods and results. Postcommunist Econ 20(2):189–201
Van Leeuwen B, Philips R (2021) Market performance in the grain market of late medieval Western Europe (ca. 1300–1650). In: Moreno Garcia JC (ed) Markets and exchanges in pre-modern and traditional societies. Oxbow Books, pp 155–169
Van Zanden JL (1999) Wages and the standard of living in Europe, 1500–1800. Eur Rev Econ Hist 3(2):175–198
Van Zanden JL (2000) Early modern economic growth: a survey of the European economy, 1500–1800. In: Prak M (ed) Early modern capitalism. Taylor & Francis, London, UK, pp 69–87

Van Zanden JL (2005) De timmerman, de boekdrukker en het ontstaan van de Europese kenniseconomie. Over de prijs en het aanbod van kennis voor de Industriële Revolutie. Tijdschrift voor Sociale en Economische Geschiedenis/Low Countr J Soc Econ Hist 2(1):105–120
Ventura J, Voth H-J (2015) Debt into growth: How sovereign debt accelerated the first industrial revolution. Mimeo
Vernadsky G (1973) Kievan Russia, Revised edn. Yale University Press, New Haven
Viraphol S (1977) Tribute and profit: Sino-Siamese trade, 1652–1853 (朝贡与利润: 1652—1853 年 的中暹贸易). Harvard University Press, Cambridge, Massachusetts and London, England
Vishnevskii A (2006) От какого берега мы отчалили [From which bank we departed]. In: Vishnevskii A (ed) Demographic modernisation of Russia: 1900–2000, Moscow, pp 13–64. Новое издательство [New publishinghouse]
Vodarsky IE (1977) Население России в конце XVII—начале XVIII века [Russia's population in the late 17th—early 18th centuries]. Наука [The Science], Moscow
Volkov VV (2016) "Дешево и сердито". Рынок труда в Европеиской России в конце XIX—начале XX в. [Cheaply and well done. Labour market in European Russia in the late 19th—early 20th centuries]. In 2 parts. Politekhnika-print, St. Petersburg
Wade G (2009) An early age of commerce in Southeast Asia, 900–1300 CE. J Southeast Asian Stud 40(2):221–265
Wallerstein I (2004) World-systems analysis: an introduction. Duke University Press, Durham, NC
Wallerstein I (2011) The modern world-system. Vol. I. Capitalist agriculture and the origins of the European world-economy in the sixteenth century (Original work published 1974). University of California Press, Berkeley
Wang M, Van Leeuwen B (2021) Fenjiashu: economic development in the Chinese countryside based on household division inventories, ca. 1750–1910. Aust Econ Hist Rev 61(3):252–272
Wilson C, Woods R (1991) Fertility in England: a long-term perspective. Popul Stud 45(3):399–415
Wolf E (1982) Europe and the people without history. University of California Press, Berkeley
Xu Y, Van Leeuwen B, Van Zanden JL (2018) Urbanization in China, ca. 1100–1900. Front Econ China 13(3):322–368
Xu, Y., Li, J., & Van Leeuwen, B. (2021) The printing industry in China, ca. 1368–1912: an international comparison. Unpublished paper.
Yi, Y. (1993). The study of book price in Tang, Song and Yuan Dynasty—the first study of Chinese book price in different dynasty. Editor's Friend, 2.
Zaionchkovsky PA (1978) The abolition of serfdom in Russia. Academic International Press, Gulf Breeze, FL
Zakharov SV (2008) Russian Federation: From the first to second demographic transition. Demogr Res 19(24):907–972. https://doi.org/10.4054/DemRes.2008.19.24
Zakharov SV, Vishnevskii AG, Sakevich VI (2006) Модернизация рождаемости [Modernization in births]. In: Vishnevskii A (ed) Демографичесчая модернизация России [Demographic modernisation of Russia: 1900–2000]. Новое издательство [The New Publishing House], Moscow, pp 149–254
Zheng HY (2001) 唐代和清代妇女婚姻家庭关系的比较研究 [A comparative study of women's marriage and family relationships in the Tang and Qing dynasties]. China University of Political Science and Law, Beijing
Zhuravskaya E, Markevich A (2015) Serfdom and Russian economic development. VoxEU. https://cepr-org.proxy.library.uu.nl/voxeu/columns/serfdom-and-russian-economic-development

Chapter 5
The Change to Modern Growth: Ultimate Causes (Technology, Institutions/Culture, and Geography)

Abstract In this chapter, we focus on the ultimate causes of economic growth. We find that the switch from Malthusian-type growth to modern growth occurred in around 1700 in the UK and 1900 in China. After introducing new estimates of total factor productivity as a measure of ultimate causes of growth, we detect a positive effect from the Black Death on technology that rapidly ebbed away. Yet while for England, productivity growth regained momentum somewhat after about a century, for both China and Italy, it remained low until the nineteenth century. We critically examine these dynamics. First, inventions in Western (and Eastern) Europe switched more from services and agriculture to industrial uses. As the latter had a bigger impact on growth in a proto-industrial world, this placed Europe in an advantageous situation compared with China, where inventions commonly occurred in services. Second, institutions played an important role. This includes both those that blocked convergence (for which we introduce variable time in office for mayors as a new indicator of the effect of local government on regional economies) and institutions that work as a factor of production (i.e. reduce the efficiency of newly implemented institutions). Third, over an extensive historical timeframe and across macro-areas such as continents, geography emerges as a significant explanatory factor: it plays a role in the three regions under consideration. One example of this is the influence of the black soil areas in northern Eurasia. The latter aspect operates through the demand for labour or capital-saving technology, with capital-saving technology being more prevalent in China, especially in the black soil area in the north of the country.

B. Van Leeuwen et al., *Innovation and Economic Development in Eurasia, 500 BCE-Present*, Frontiers in Economic History,
https://doi.org/10.1007/978-3-031-97043-6_5

5.1 The Drivers of Long-Run Economic Growth

In Chap. 4, we deal with various potential drivers of long-run growth. In this chapter we consider technological knowledge, as well as a country's capability to adopt and implement technology, even if it is initially introduced somewhere else. This latter factor has much to do with the institutional/cultural environment of a country and a varied group of geographical endowments, which together can be defined as "geography". The total factor productivity (TFP) of a country, as used in this chapter,[1] assesses the combined role of technology and institutions/culture while omitting geography for now. We discuss long-run TFP in Sect. 5.2.

Section 5.3 focuses on disentangling technology and institutions in TFP. The decomposition of TFP into technology and institutions is not straightforward. Even though technological growth is part of TFP, institutions/culture can either have a direct effect on productivity (i.e. be a factor of production) or be directly included in TFP (the latter we will refer to here as "institutional environment"). A standard equation to test the direct effect of institutions/culture on growth is presented by, for example Mankiw et al. (1992) and Hall and Jones (1999). They find that there is both a strong direct effect (institution/culture as a factor of production) and a strong correlation of growth with the residual, including institutional environment: The demonstration that institutions can be a factor of production is corroborated by significant cliometric evidence, but it may be questioned as it is not immediately evident how institutions have a direct effect on growth. In other words: you cannot increase production by simply adding more institutions. This seems to be confirmed by Eicher et al. (2006), who show that once institutions work indirectly via human and physical capital, their direct effect on growth becomes insignificant.[2] Hence, we limit our study to institutional environment, which is part of TFP.

In Sect. 5.4, we re-introduce geography, which seems to have had only a limited effect on economic growth. This leaves us with the direction of technical change in Sect. 5.5: Institutions and technology might increase TFP, but this still does not tell us if it is labour-saving or capital-saving.

[1] The definition of TFP is heavily debated, but it essentially represents an overarching indicator of the level of appropriateness of technology adoption, assessed in its interaction with the basic factors describing the general economic structure of a country (based on agriculture, industry, or services) ranging from the institutional background to the level of investments and the state of the labour market (e.g. wages, hours worked). For the debate around TFP definition and methodologies see Nadiri (1970); Hulten (2001); Van Beveren (2012); and Sickles and Zelenyuk (2019).

[2] In addition, the residual is no longer correlated with growth, thus implying no significant TFP and, hence, since institutional environment is part of TFP, no significant effect of institutional environment.

5.2 (The Weight of) TFP Growth as an Indicator of Long-Run Growth

Several studies calculate TFP growth as a measure of long-run growth, in contexts that range from East Asia (see Felipe 1999) to Europe (e.g. Gehringer et al. 2016; Beugelsdijk et al. 2018), and world-level (Baier et al. 2006). Even though various ways to calculate TFP growth are used, because of lack of data (see e.g. Antras and Voth 2003), very few studies on long-run TFP exist. Among those, for Holland, Van Zanden, and Van Leeuwen (2012, 126) show periods of rising TFP between 1540 and 1620 and then once more between 1665 and 1800. For England, some similar figures can be found in Broadberry (2021), with peaks after the Black Death around the second half of the fourteenth century, then in 1640–1690, and between 1830 and 1860. These results are in line with the findings of other authors. According to Crafts and Harley (2000) and Antras and Voth (2003), TFP in England increased mainly in the nineteenth century. Before that time, it was slow and largely driven by agriculture. Yet even in the late nineteenth century, TFP growth was slow. This implied that there were few technological benefits, or that they benefited the economy only at a later stage (e.g. Feinstein 1981; Crafts and Harley 1992; Antras and Voth 2003). Van Leeuwen et al. (2024) found, for Italy, peaks of TFP growth first, around the fifteenth century, and then starting from the second half of the nineteenth century. Between the sixteenth and the eighteenth century, however, they found negative TFP values, which indicate the presence of a quasi-stagnating productivity environment (Tables 5.1, 5.2, 5.3).

Table 5.1 TFP growth by country, c. 1340–1950 (Great Britain and the Netherlands)

	Great Britain				The Netherlands	
	Harley (1999)	Antras and Voth (2003)	Broadberry (2021)	Bergeaud et al. (2016)	Van Zanden and Van Leeuwen (2012)	Bergeaud et al. (2016)
1340–1400			0.39			
1400–1450			−0.35			
1450–1640			−0.26			
1540–1620					0.65	
1620–1665					−1	
1640–1690			0.4			
1665–1720					0.08	
1690–1830			0.16			
1720–1800					0.09	
1760–1800	0.19					
1770–1800		0.27				
1800–1830	0.5	0.54				
1830–1860	1	0.33	0.55			
1893–1913				0.74		1.1

(continued)

Table 5.1 (continued)

	Great Britain				The Netherlands	
1913–1936				1.14		2.41
1914–1919				−0.11		4.4
1920–1929				1.82		3.2
1930–1939				0.3		−0.29
1936–1951				1.12		2.92
1940–1953				1.95		3.58
1946–1973				1.95		5.74
1974–1992				1.26		0.94
1993–2010				1.26		0.84
2011–2020				1.27		0.3

Note: When necessary, Great Britain and the Netherlands are proxied by England and Holland

Table 5.2 TFP growth by country, c. 1340–1950 (Italy and Spain)

	Italy				Spain
	Malanima and Zamagni (2010)	Broadberry et al. (2011)	Antonelli and Feder (2020)	Van Leeuwen et al. (2024)	Prados de la Escosura and Roses (2021)
1360–1460				0.15	
1460–1580				−0.29	
1580–1770				−0.24	
1770–1860				−0.21	
1850–1872					0.4
1861–1913	1.11				
1873–1892		−0.41	−0.12		0.2
1893–1913		0.68	−0.54		−0.1
1913–1936	0.61	1.95	0.46		
1914–1919					−0.5
1920–1929					1.9
1930–1939					−4
1936–1951	1.52	2.05			
1940–1953					1.65
1946–1973		3.49	2.46		2.60
1974–1992		1.4	−0.01		1.8
1993–2010		0.26	0.2		−0.3
2011–2020					0.05

Note: Italy based on Malanima (2003, 2004) and Schmelzing (2019), lira to silver conversions based on Arroyo Abad (2006) and Malanima (2002)

Table 5.3 TFP Growth by Country, c. 1885–1940 (Russia)

		Russian Empire/Former Soviet Union				
		Cheremukhin et al. (2017)			Voskoboynikov (2021)	
	This text	Agriculture	Manufacturing	Ofer (1987)	Total	Industry
1885–1900		1.51	0.72			
1901–1913		1.35	0.67			
1914–1928		−0.85	1.92			
1929–1934	2.74	−0.14	−4.78	1.7		
1935–1940	−2.49	4.84	1.65			
1941–1950	1.04			1.6		
1951–1960	3.22			1.6		
1961–1973	0.69				2.38	1.28
1974–1985	−0.88				1.17	−0.79
1986–1990	−0.12				−0.60	0.77
1991–1998	−7.68				−5.20	−6.03
1999–2008	6.47				5.65	4.19
2009–2012					2.38	1.94

Note: Average annual change, percent

For Central Eurasia, we have series on conventional capital per labourer (K/L) data only from 1885. In their absence, we can proxy it by evidence of number of inventors, telegraph diffusion, and railway construction (see this section and Sect. 6.3). Yet the series starts from relatively high levels by cross-country comparisons at the time.

Source: Cheremukhin et al. (2017), Ofer (1987), and Voskoboynikov (2021) relate to the territory in historical borders; this text (based on Didenko et al. 2013) relates to all the countries of the former USSR

Somewhat surprisingly, TFP growth increased in agriculture more significantly than in manufacturing in the pre-revolutionary market economy in the Russian and Central Asian contexts.[3] The agricultural TFP growth decrease in 1929–1934 under the drive for collectivization and large-scale famine, moreover, looks rather modest. Additionally, manufacturing productivity decreased under mobilization-driven industrialization efforts in 1929–1934, primarily thanks to large inflows of capital. Our estimates of capital per labourer (K/L), based on Didenko et al. (2013),[4] provide us with a more acute pattern for Russia as regards an increase in general productivity in 1951–1960, its deceleration and decrease in 1961–1998, and the recovery in 1999–2008. Overall, the pattern of TFP growth is more optimistic for the period 1929–1960 than in Ofer (1987) and more pessimistic for the period 1961–2012 than in Voskoboynikov (2021).

We can extend the literature-based TFP growth rates mentioned earlier by using an alternative methodology. For China and Italy, we use an income-based approach

[3] If we compare the data from Table 5.3 and Table 3.3.

[4] Our estimates of the TFP for the former Soviet Union area with application of Cobb-Douglas production function augmented with human capital and based on the same source are discussed in Chap. 7.

(e.g. Antras and Voth 2003). A second method is based on a Cobb-Douglas production function: By regressing ln (GDP/capita) on ln (capital [K]/labour), the residual is argued to capture technological change. Unfortunately, the length of the series of historical TFP calculated by the Cobb-Douglas function is limited by capital, since GDP/capita series (Bolt and Van Zanden 2020) stretches back to about 600 CE and inventions even further, but capital does not. Yet we can look at the number of inventors by year and country to proxy technology (see Fig. 5.1). In that case, K/L is instead picked up by region and time dummies and we can project TFP further back in time.

We find for about 1900, a share of technology in growth of 0.6% in China versus 12% in the UK. Looking back further in time, the effect of technology becomes the same for China, with about 1.1% versus a low 0.8% for the UK. Additional countries are added in Fig. 5.2 (Table 5.4, 5.5).

Table 5.1 and Fig. 5.1 show that the weigh of innovations (at least in England) increased during the Industrial Revolution and until the 1950s. This was caused by three factors. First, even though the number of inventions was higher in China than in Western Europe until the thirteenth century, it decreased sharply afterwards. Second, in the long run, China showed a tendency to introduce more inventions in the service and agriculture sectors rather than in the secondary industrial sector. In Central Eurasia and Western Europe, the long-run focus was mostly on industry (see Fig. 5.2). Third, the impact of these inventions on growth and development was much higher when directed towards industry, thus creating a benefit for Europe (see Figs. 5.3 and 5.4).[5]

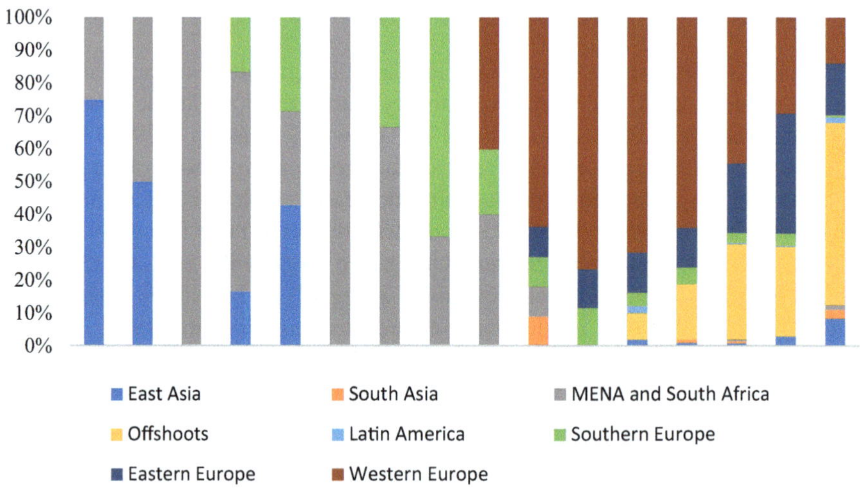

Fig. 5.1 Share of inventors by region and period, 1–2000 CE. *Source:* Wikipedia, https://en.wikipedia.org/wiki/List_of_inventors (accessed 2021)

[5]The fact that the Middle Ages and early modern period were characterized by a bigger share of service inventions globally does not mean no variances existed over time. First, as the absolute number of inventions in the Middle Ages and early modern period were about half that of the modern periods 1800–1900 and 1900–2000, this means that even though before 1800 the share of

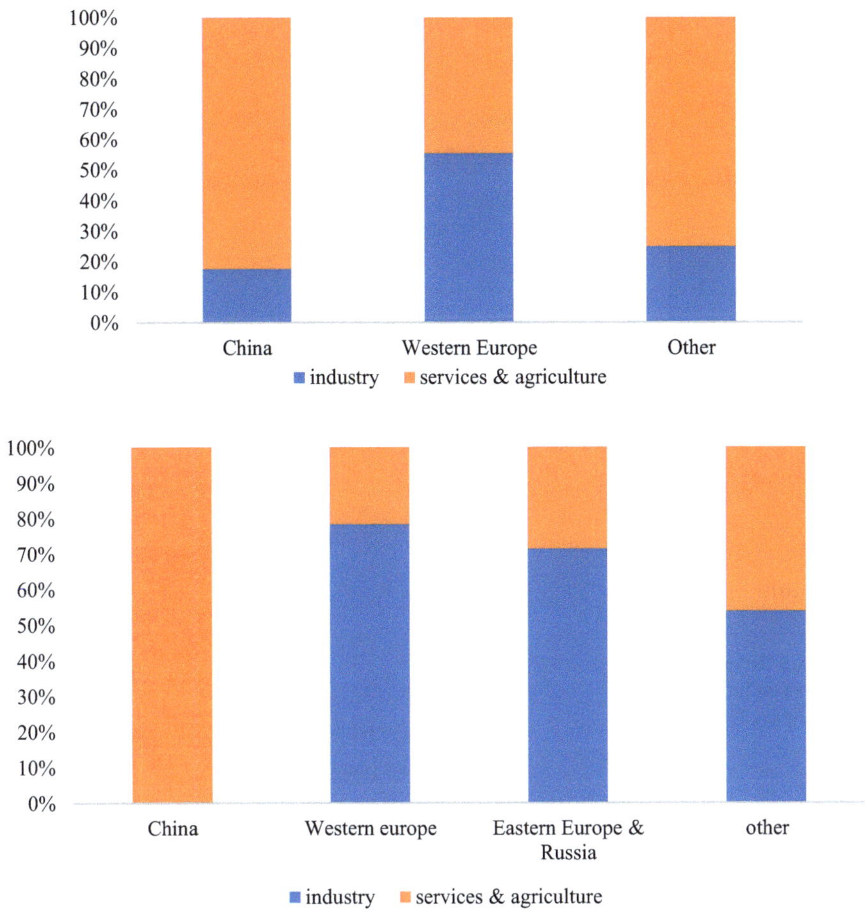

Fig. 5.2 (**a**) Number of inventions by sector in the medieval period (500–1500) by region. *Note:* Service inventions are (1) inventions in trade and transport and (2) final products. For example, a transistor is industry and a radio is service. *Source:* Wikipedia, https://en.wikipedia.org/wiki/Timeline_of_historic_inventions (accessed 2022). (**b**) Number of inventions by sector in the modern period (1900–2010) by region. *Source:* see below Fig. 5.2a.

The series on TFP growth give us a clear indication of productivity trends in the countries under examination. Yet, as mentioned in Sect. 5.1, knowing the value of TFP does not tell us how technology spread within and between countries—that is, the institutional environment). This brings us back to our initial question: To what extent do institutions and culture drive TFP growth?

service inventions was higher, the absolute number of service inventions was still higher after 1800, even in England. Second, there may be considerable differences by country/region. For example, in medieval China, the number of inventions dropped after about 1350, while the share of service inventions remained roughly constant. Given the rise in productivity of industry inventions, this implies even a larger fall-back for China in comparison with Western Europe.

Table 5.4 TFP growth by country, c. 1340–1950 (China)

	China	
	This text (income-based approach)	Feenstra et al. (2015)
1540–1620	−0.2	
1620–1665	−0.7	
1665–1720	1.0	
1700–1730	−0.06	
1730–1755	−0.2	
1755–1780	0.80	
1780–1805	−0.60	
1805–1830	0.20	
1861–1913	−0.10	
1913–1936	0.10	
1950–1966		−1.29
1966–1977		−1.27
1978–1993		0.52
1994–2006		1.16
2007–2019		0.45

Table 5.5 Regression of inventors on ln(GDP/L), c. 1000–2000 CE

	Coefficient	*t*-Value
Inventors	0.005	3.68
Inventors (lag 200 year)	0.027	2.57
Global regions (minus country)	0.004	1.76
Constant	8.445	42.87
Year fixed effects	Yes	
Country fixed effects	Yes	
Obs	65	
Adj. R2	0.875	

Note: If we estimate these data, we include a lag of 200 years (being the only significant lag) and whether nearby countries with technology had a positive effect (they do)

5.3 Institutions and Culture

5.3.1 The Role of Institutions and Culture in the Last Millennium

As pointed out in Sect. 5.1, TFP growth can consist of, on the one hand, technology and, on the other hand, institutions, with the latter indicating a wide array of determinants including culture and the accessibility of technology (i.e. institutional environment). In addition, institutions/culture can be a factor of production rather than

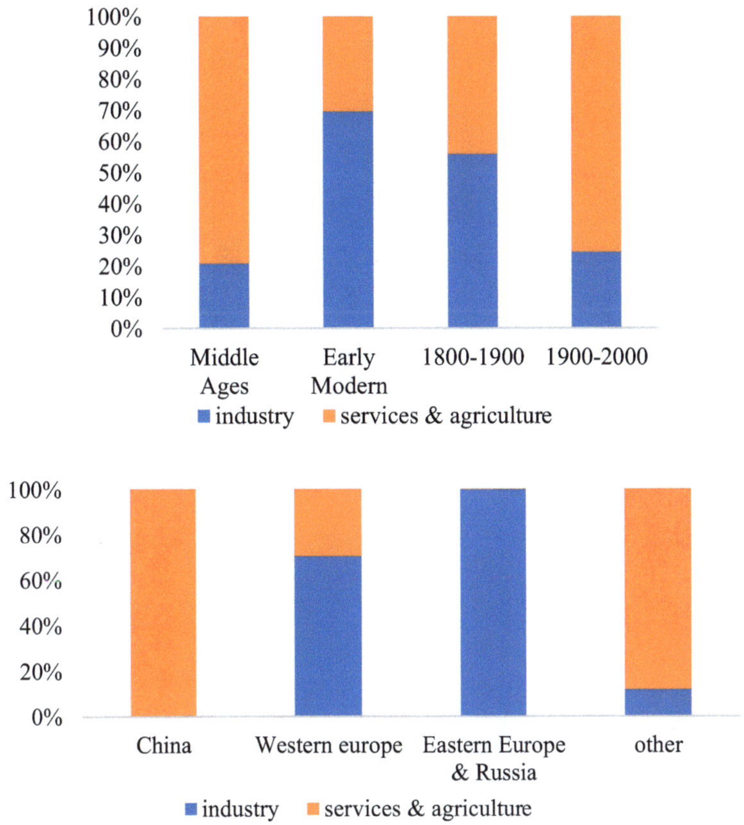

Fig. 5.3 (**a**) Global share of services and industry in total productivity increase of inventions between the Middle Ages (500 CE) and 2010. *Source:* see Fig. 5.2a. (**b**) Share of services and industry in total productivity increase of inventions in the modern period (1900–2000) by region. *Source:* see Fig. 5.2a.

part of TFP. As seen in Sect. 5.1, though, the assessment of institutions as a factor of production can lead to inconsistencies; for this reason, we focus in this section on the institutional environment.

Economic historiography has proved in many ways that the global institutional infrastructure of a country is a crucial element in long-run growth, resulting in less technical inefficiency and, in turn, economic convergence. Yet, there is, at the same time, evidence that institutions cannot be considered the secret ingredient for an always successful recipe. For example: why do certain countries with a good institutional environment sometimes face economic divergence while, vice versa, some countries with unfit institutions face convergence? To answer this question, various scholars have pointed at the different effect on the general economy of the presence of indigenous, as opposed to Western institutions, in colonial-type settings.

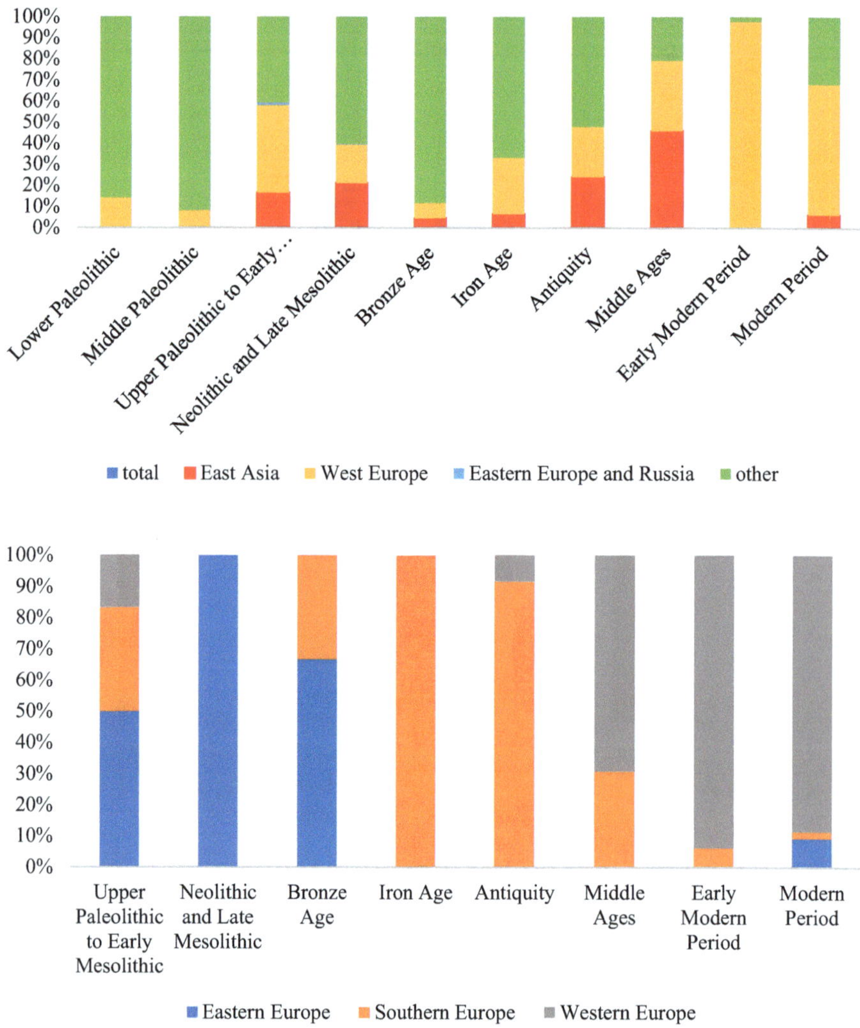

Fig. 5.4 (**a**) Inventions by period (from Upper Palaeolithic to the Modern period) and region globally. *Source:* https://en.wikipedia.org/wiki/Timeline_of_historic_inventions (accessed 2021). (**b**) Inventions by period (from Upper Palaeolithic to the Modern period) and region within Europe. *Source:* https://en.wikipedia.org/wiki/Timeline_of_historic_inventions (accessed 2021)

First, as mentioned in Chap. 3, a strong state can lead to less growth. This apparently paradoxical idea—which can be shortly summarized by Cardwell's Law: "a single economy will inevitably move towards technological stagnation due to resistance of interest groups in that country", see Mokyr (1994)—can be used here as a theoretical basis to explain the fact that European political fragmentation after 900

CE led to more competition between countries, specifically in terms of inventions. Second, as Popov (2014) argues, in Western Europe collectivist institutions, that is economic distribution within families, friendship groups, and guilds,[6] were dismantled, leading to more inequality and more capital investment at the expense of household consumption. In other regions this was not, or was only partially, the case.[7]

In sum, the weakening of the state and the breakdown of collectivist institutions led to the improved adoption and efficient use of technology as convergence in Western Europe's economic development took place. Between 1500 and 1950, a wide array of countries at different stages of proto-industrialization, and later industrialization—including colonial and former colonial countries, for example not only in Latin America but also Russia and, more broadly, the FSU—were copying Western institutions, which led to faster growth while nevertheless still maintaining an economic lag behind Western Europe.[8]

We can test this copying of foreign institutions, as opposed by sticking to indigenous institutions, by looking at technology in the three regions depicted in Figs. 5.4a and b (Europe, Russia, and China). Looking at the period up to the Bronze Age, Eastern Europe and Russia's European area had, together with East Asia, a dominant position in inventions. This changed from the Iron Age, when Russia's European area lost its position in relation to Southern Europe, that is the Roman Empire. The same occurred in East Asia in the Middle Ages. For Russia's European area, this decline corresponds with a period of increasing migrations, and invasions in their areas from Greece and the Roman period since the Iron Age. For China, this decline in technology coincides with the Tang (618–907), Song (960–1279), and Ming (1368–1644) dynasties. As also pointed out by Van Zanden and Van Leeuwen (2019), strong statehood at the start of the early Qing was weakened in the late Qing. These developments were to the benefit of Western Europe. Only from 1500 do we witness a return from Russia again in the number of inventors (Sect. 5.4). Technological growth thus suggests that Russia started to copy Western technology and institutions at that time. China's development, however, remained stagnant until the mid-twentieth century. This implies Chinese growth was based on indigenous institutions.

[6] The formation of guilds in the Russian Empire was caused by state fiscal needs, and was affected by the reforms of Peter I and his successors in the eighteenth century. The merchants ("*kuptsy*") were categorized according to the extent of their economic activities, in terms of their rights, privileges, dues, and obligations (Hittle 1979, 77–236; Kozlova 1999, 7–11, 367–372).

[7] A third factor might be random industrialization (i.e. luck) that could drive industry convergence (Lucas 2000).

[8] This copying occurred for various reasons, and is often mentioned as a reason for the failed growth of developing economies prior to 1960 as they supposedly broke down indigenous institutions. For example, colonial trade theory, colonialism, "sprouts of capitalism", commodity frontiers, and globalization (see e.g. Chap. 6) are all mentioned in the context of the failed growth of developing economies. Yet countries such as China, which did not copy much and kept their own collectivist, state powered institutions largely intact, started to grow much later (around 1950), even though the post-1950 type of growth might have been different and even more efficient than in, for example, Argentina.

5.3.2 *State Power and Collectivistic Institutions: The Long-Run Cases of China and Central Eurasia as Opposed to the Western European Model*

As we have seen in Sect. 5.3.1, there are two types of institutions that can be summarized as government and collectivist. First, in China, state institutions can be traced back to the Qin dynasty (221–206 BCE), which was united under a strong government and had a formalistic/legalist education system. The state was thus placed before society. Owing to a lack of external challenges, the ruler focused on avoiding internal political threats; economic growth was not prioritized. By over-emphasizing political stability, the government placed obstacles in the way of economic growth. Moreover, when the expansion of commerce and the market economy reached a certain level, the government tended to adopt various restraints. But when there were fewer limits placed on growth owing to insufficient state capacity, there was usually a good chance that economic development would take place. Indeed, it is possible to detect a long-run pattern, with each dynasty beginning with strong government and low growth and ending with a weak government, strong markets, and a significant growth increase (Fig. 5.5; see also Van Leeuwen and Van Zanden 2019). Similarly, after 1950, economic growth occurred in China notwithstanding the lack of connections with the Western liberal system. It is also possible to affirm that there has been a sort of consensus in the long run among state institutions and the population. Even today, people cling to the traditional institutions of government control: even in 2022, Chinese trust their national (and to a lesser extent local) government more than is the case in Russia, Japan, Italy, and the Netherlands (Fig. 5.6).

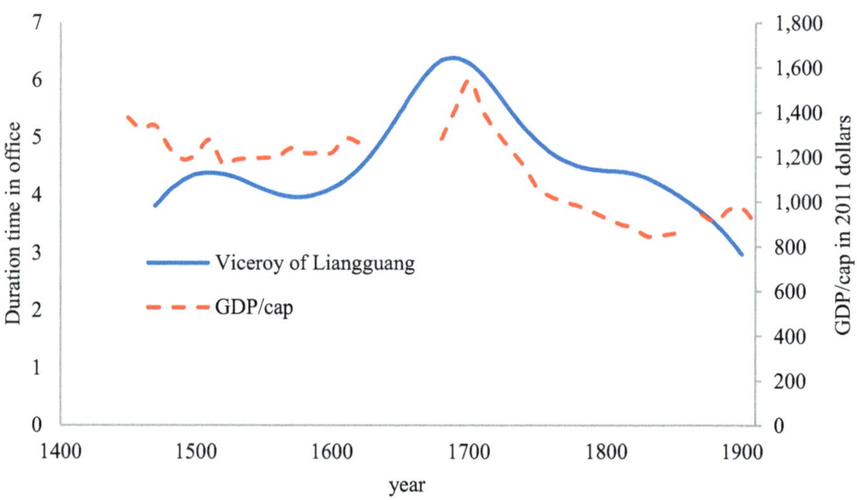

Fig. 5.5 Comparison of institutional development and GDP/cap in China, c. 1450–1910. *Source:* Wikipedia https://en.wikipedia.org/wiki/Viceroy_of_Liangjiang; Broadberry et al. (2018). *Note:* Obviously, strictly defined, mayors did not exist in China before the nineteenth century. However, we can look at the viceroys, and more specifically the Viceroy of Lianguang (i.e. Guangdong and Guangxi)

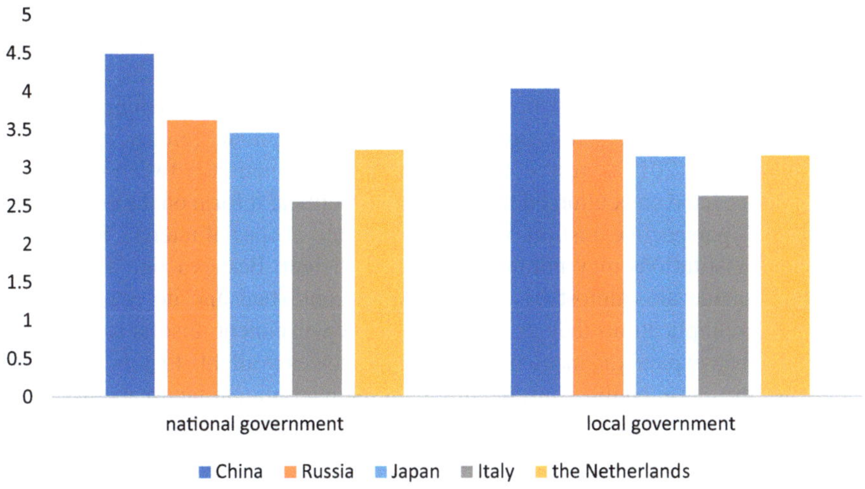

Fig. 5.6 How much trust do you have in national and local (municipal) government? Higher = more trust. *Source:* Private survey, April/June 2022

Contrary to the situation in China (see also Acemoglu and Robinson 2012), in Russia, the form of government did not lead to a closed economy, from the Iron Age steppe nomads to early political unity (Kievan Rus', nineth to twelfth centuries) to the contemporary post-Soviet space. In this respect, it resembled Western Europe. Its weak state meant it was affected by many technological and institutional influences—from the Byzantine Empire (i.e. of Roman descent) in the tenth century, from the medieval West in the eleventh and twelfth centuries (in the early phase of political fragmentation), from Mongols and Turks in the thirteenth to sixteenth centuries, in the fifteenth century from Byzantium again (although it was already declining), and since the fifteenth century again from the West (with political centralization). From the eighteenth century, the stream of borrowings strongly accelerated, with the primary sources for institutional changes being the Netherlands, Prussia, and other German states in the eighteenth century and France and Germany in the nineteenth century. The outcome was the Europeanization of the Russian nobility. English influence, however, seems to have been relatively weak. As regards Central Asia, since this came under Russian protection in the eighteenth and nineteenth centuries, from that time onwards, it experienced Western influences with Russian intermediation.

There were many attempts to catch up, and there was competition between the basic institutions of power and property and the European institutions of private property.[9] This competition has appeared to be a key factor in the institutional development of Russia over the past millennium (Nureev and Latov 2010). In the late

[9] The concept of power and property, popular from the post-Soviet Marxist perspective, originated in the studies of power in oriental societies by K. A. Wittfogel (1957) and L. S. Vasiliev (1982, 2011) and in the Russian studies by the American conservative historian R. Pipes (1995) (in the 1970s he coined the term "patrimonial state").

Imperial period, this competition resulted in mixed outcomes. While capitalism was in its medium to weak development phase, the point of no return to the "power" of capitalism had not been passed.

In discussing the characteristics of Russian modernization by catching up, from the early eighteenth century up to the early twenty-first century, Mau and Drobyshevskaya (2013) stressed the key role of coordination between economic reform on one hand and cultural development and political reform on the other hand.

From this perspective, institutional borrowings are of special interest. Replacing indigenous institutions may not necessarily be efficient. Best-practice institutions from the outside are, almost by definition, non-contextual and do not take into account the complications they may face in a new environment. Insofar as they narrow rather than expand the menu of institutional choices available to policy makers, they serve the cause badly. Thus, dealing with the institutional landscape in developing economies requires a second-best mindset; namely, economic growth-enhancing goals can be achieved through a number of different institutional designs in an unorthodox way if this serves to relax constraints elsewhere in the system. This leaves space for removing constraints in the future from a best-practice perspective (Rodrik 2008).

Institutional lending, by neglecting the recipient system, results in imposed institutions getting a bad name. This normally leads to passive resistance and an inefficient mix of new and old institutions. In particular, attempts to import market economy institutions and democracy, with weakened state capacity to ensure law and order, lead to an environment that is detrimental to growth (Popov 2013). Thus, second-best, or intermediary, institutions are needed to avoid an "institutional trap" (Polterovich 2005).

At the start of this cycle, borrowed technologies and institutions gave new impetus to convergence with the West; but after some time, Russia's economy stagnated. Serfdom is pointed out in the literature as the crucial factor that led to this slowdown and Russia's divergence from Western Europe.[10] The same basically holds for Poland (Malinowski and Van Zanden, 2017).

Since there was a lack of infrastructure and centralized taxation, Russia/FSU needed another way to strengthen the state through the promotion of growth. This was done by generating a common "Eurasian" identity for the Russian and Turkic people. The latter densely inhabit Central Asia (the Uzbeks are the most numerous; there are also Kazakh, Kyrgyz, and Turkmen nations) and also the European (Tatars,[11] Bashkir, Chuvash people) and Asian (Yakut, Tyvan people) parts of the Russian Federation. Political philosophers and public intellectuals who shared and proliferated this identity generally believed,[12] and continue to believe, that Eurasians are inherently comfortable with a strong state that rejects liberalism.[13] This stream

[10] See also Subheading 3.4.

[11] Tatars are the second ethnic group in the Russian Federation after ethnic Russians.

[12] As in the European typology, they can be labelled far-right ultranationalists.

[13] The most well-known contemporary neo-Eurasianist is Aleksandr Dugin (2012, 2021).

of thought emerged in the 1920s in those émigré circles that were tolerant towards Russian communists (Bolsheviks), appreciating their restoration of the state and associated national revival. Eurasianism, a political and cultural ideology with an anti-Western bias, asserts that Russia does not belong in either the European or Asian category, but is a distinct civilization, more characteristic of Asian (basically Turkic) than European features.[14] The founders of Eurasianism tried to understand why Marxist socialist ideas found so fertile a soil in Russian society, which appeared to be responsive to them and was to transform them into extreme government interference in economic and social life.[15]

It follows from this Eurasianist view that oriental collectivist institutions were more historically rooted in Russia than the institutions based on private property initially found in Catholic and Protestant Europe, which had been a potential threat to the integrity of the "Great Russian" way of life throughout the centuries. This idea conforms with the view that Russia's history was a competition either between the basic institutions of power and property (Nureev and Latov 2010) or between the collectivist institutions of the East and the individualist institutions of the West (Popov 2013, 2014).

In his revisionist book,[16] Allen (2003) finds positive effects of the forced Soviet industrialization that was based on heterodox institutional design. Tsarist Russia lacked many of the social, legal, and economic prerequisites of capitalist development as modernizers such as Sergei Yulyevich Witte and Pyotr Arkadyevich Stolypin failed to promote them. Substitutes for these missing prerequisites were mostly created by state direction (central planning, soft budget constraints), and coercion combined with stimulation (Allen 2003). In sum, institutions worked if they were either rooted in the past or systemically linked to it, while many Soviet innovations failed. What is striking is that those institutions that worked well at the early stage of industrialization proved inimical to technological progress, and in later stages contributed to the economy's stagnation (Allen 2003). This led to an "institutional trap" (Polterovich 2005), and the USSR failed to find a way out of it (see also Chap. 7).

[14] The origins of Eurasianism and other oriental-centred discourse in Russian socio-political thought of the eighteenth to early twentieth centuries are investigated in Schimmelpenninck van der Oye (2010).

[15] As one of the academic proponents of Eurasianism, the late Soviet historian Lev Nikolaevic Gumilev (1988, 1990) claimed some years before the dissolution of the USSR that close links between the Slavic and Turkic ethnic groups of the Eurasian steppe resulted in the formation of a Russian "super-ethnos" under the rule of the Mongols. In regarding Russian history through the lens of his "Passionate Theory of Ethnogenes", he applied the legacy of the major spokesmen of the cultural-historical school of the nineteenth century, such as Friedrich. Ratzel, Nikolay Yakovlevich Danilevsky, and Konstantin Leontiev, and of the twentieth century, O. Spengler and A. Toynbee. The latter's opposition to the world-historical school is based on the postulate that every cultural region has its own path of development, so that one cannot speak of the backwardness or stagnation of non-European people but can only note their special features (Gumilev 1990).

[16] It was a revisionist view, first of all, of the Bergsonian tradition of economic Sovietology, as well as the mainstream of historiography that focused on the Soviet era and is expressed in, for example, Davies et al. (1994) and Gregory (2003a, b).

So far, we have dealt with government. Collectivist institutions are the second type of local institutions, as mentioned earlier. In China, collectivism was rooted in individualism, that is, self-approval or self-fulfilment demand, so individualism had a different meaning than in Western Europe. Making as great a contribution as possible to one's individual family/clan was usually considered to be the primary life goal. Family centred values were extended to state/nation. This collectivism gradually came to be supported by the government, as it was an important positive force in keeping the state united.

In other words, collectivism/individualism was rooted in the family and the state. The roots applied to a lesser extent, to the middle classes. It was accepted that individualism was a crucial driving force for innovation and wealth creation. The efforts made by all individuals to satisfy their own demands led to the development of society and the economy. Therefore, the collectivist tradition, which has been kept alive until today, is usually criticized as one of the main reasons why China has lagged behind owing to its foundational role. However, collectivism is not necessarily "wrong". Domestic institutions (collectivism is not per se domestic) can work well, even if collectivist. Of course, some authors would disagree, but in 1950–1970, collectivism seemed to lead to less famine and more growth.

Collectivism was therefore an inherent element of the Chinese economy. The process of institutional copying from Europe resulted in a different outcome for Russia. Indeed, over the last three centuries Russia has interacted in various ways more with Europe than with China, and even with the Turkish world, which is an integral part not only of Central Asia but also of the contemporary Russian Federation. If we look at other East European countries (e.g. Poland-Lithuania), Russia has had more in common with them in terms of the timing of state formation, GDP/cap, late serfdom, and subsequent catching up. The striking differences with Western Europe (both Southern Europe and North-Western Europe) have persisted.

5.3.3 A Quantitative Measure of Institutional Environment

As we have seen, TFP can capture everything that contributes to growth, including both technology and institutional environment. Whereas geography is discussed in Sect. 5.4, here our focus is on the institutional environment.

In Fig. 5.7a, we show the decomposition of TFP by creating production frontiers for 1890 and 1930 for a group of selected countries. In this production frontier model, three factors can change the output per labourer. First, countries that are below the technical frontier can rise to this frontier (institutional environment). This implies that the efficiency of the used factors of labour and capital rises. Yet in Fig. 5.7a, it looks as if this is not the case: in both 1890 and 1930, China stays at the same distance from the production frontier. The USSR in 1930 appears to be more distant from the frontier than its predecessor, the Russian Empire, in 1890. Second, countries can move along the frontier to the right by adding more capital (capital accumulation), as Italy did from 1890 to 1930, remaining near the frontier. Third,

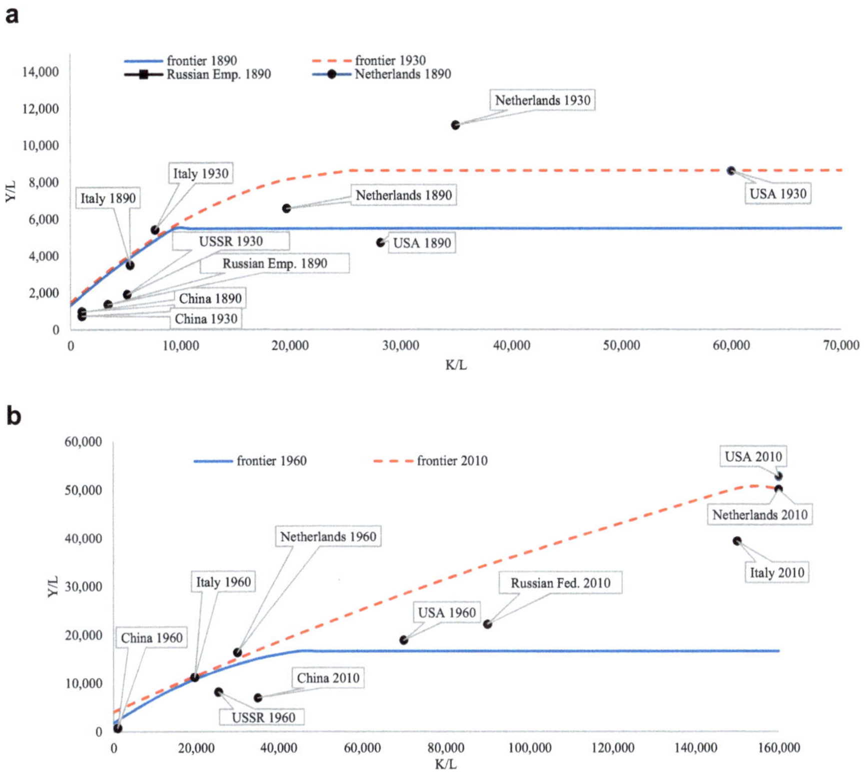

Fig. 5.7 (**a**) Production frontier, 1890 and 1930 *Source:* See Fig. 5.7b. (**b**) Production frontier, 1960 and 2010. *Note:* monetary indicators are in constant 2010 national prices (in million US$, 2010); 2. Gross fixed capital is in K/L; the latter may be overestimated for Russian Empire 1890 and underestimated for USSR 1930 and USSR 1960. *Source:* Bergeaud, A., Cette, G. & Lecat R. (2016) for the OECD countries; Cheremukhin, A., Golosov, M., Guriev, S., Tsyvinski, A. (2017) for Russian Emp. 1890; Didenko, D., Van Leeuwen, B. & Foldvari, P. (2013), Moorsteen and Powell (1966) for USSR 1930; Didenko, D., Van Leeuwen, B. & Foldvari, P. (2013), Van Leeuwen, B., Didenko, D., & Foldvari, P. (2015) for USSR 1960; Penn World Tables 9.0 (Feenstra et al., 2015), Rosstat for Russian Federation 2010 (https://rosstat.gov.ru/storage/mediabank/st_izn_of.xlsx); Maddison Project Database (2018) (Bolt and Van Zanden 2020) for conversion rates

countries can jump to a higher frontier, which implies general technical progress (Kumar and Russell 2002). In Fig. 5.4a, this is the case for the US.

Even though all three factors end up in growth, only options 1 (institutional environment) and 3 (general technical progress) are part of TFP and can hence create long-run growth. As many scholars are only interested in technology, various authors have tried to remove option 1 (institutional environment = technical efficiency) from TFP (e.g. Van Leeuwen et al. 2017). We have already mentioned that technical efficiency in our period of study must have been limited, but we can also test it by taking two countries that are at the technical frontier, that is, with no technical inefficiency (at the highest level of institutional environment). In such a case we can compare the UK in 1890 with the US in 2010 since both countries were at the technical frontier, we can calculate that 5.5% contribution of technology and 94% of capital accumulation made up for the difference in national income in 1890 and 2010.[17] In the case of China, it is 5.1% technology, 46.9% capital, and 48% (institutional environment) technical efficiency.[18]

It is clear that, if full catch-up were to occur, growth between 1890 and 2010 would consist of by and large 5% technology, 48% technical efficiency and 47% capital accumulation. As also found by Allen (2012, 5), there was no increase in output per head in countries with lower capital intensity; that is, the lower part of both the 1890 and 1930 frontier overlap. This implies that there is no technological progress by jumping to a higher production frontier. This changed at around a capital to labour ratio of 10,000, that is, around the year 1980.

As can be seen in Fig. 5.7b, China had very little option in 2010 to increase productivity by jumping to higher production frontiers. Yet inefficiency was substantial. So technical inefficiency (i.e. institutional environment) varied strongly by country and time. This leaves the effect of institutional environment as a factor affecting the growth rate in convergence.

5.3.4 Institutional Environment and Economic Convergence

We can visually represent the presence or absence of convergence by observing that the farther countries deviate from the mean per capita income, the faster (in general) their growth tends to be (Eichengreen et al. 2012; also, Musacchio and Werker 2016). This is illustrated in Fig. 5.8a and b, with the x-axis representing the log of GDP per capita in 2010 and the y-axis depicting compound annual growth rates between 2010 and 2018. Figure 5.8b demonstrates convergence, indicating that higher GDP per capita correlates with lower growth rates. In 1700 (Fig. 5.8a), the upward trend suggests a lack of convergence, implying that only a few low-income countries could benefit from new technologies.

Even though other factors may play a role in economic convergence (e.g. proximate factors such as amount of labour, and local demand), we can try to look at the

---

[17] We can compare the UK in 1890 with a GDP per capita of Intl'$ 5885 and a physical capital per capita of Intl'$11,651 with the US in 2010 with GDP per capita of Intl'$52,751, both of which were at the technical frontier. Inserting Intl'$ 11,651 in the frontier for 2010 results in a theoretical GDP per capita of Intl'$ 8481 for the UK in 2010. This results in a contribution of technology of Intl'$8481- Intl'$5885 = Intl'$2596. Or, in other words, Intl'$2595/(Intl'$ 52,751- Intl'$ 5885) = 5.5% contribution of technology and 94% of capital accumulation.

[18] In the case of China, in 1890, it was Intl'$964 with K/L of Intl'$1075. Again, the US in 2010 has a GDP per capita of Intl'$52,761. If we use the Chinese 1890 K/L ratio in 2010, this results in a GDP/cap of Intl'$2022. Hence, we obtain a growth of technology in China of Intl'$2022-Intl'$964*2 = Intl'$2572. The factor "2″ corrects for technical inefficiency for 1890. This boils down to Intl'$2572/(Intl'$52761- Intl'$964*2) = 5.1% and a technical efficiency of 48%, with the residual being capital accumulation.

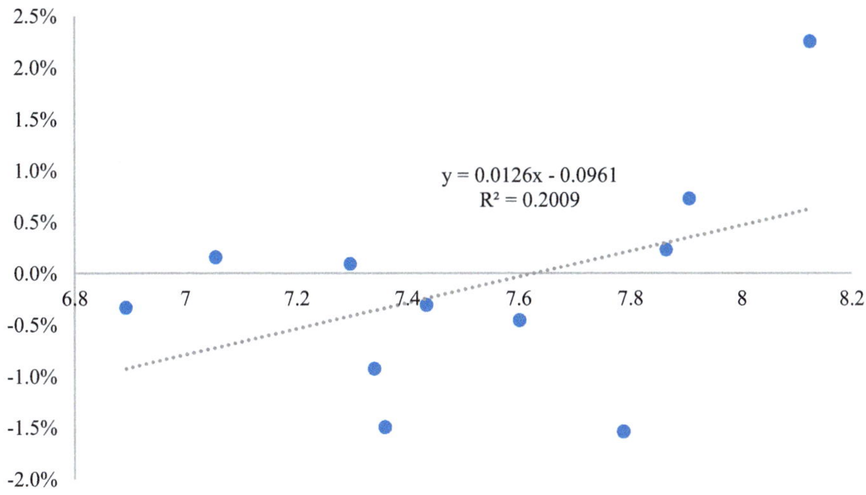

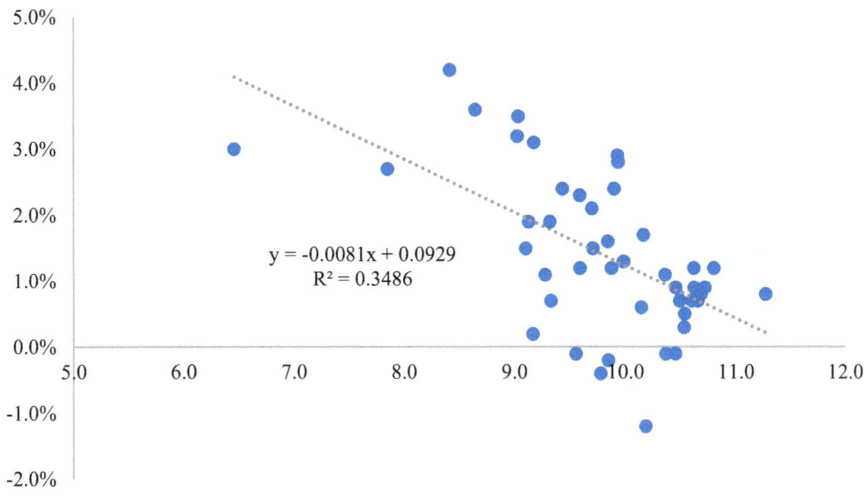

Fig. 5.8 (**a**) GDP /cap growth rate, 1700–1710, versus log GDP/cap, 1700. *Source:* Bolt and Van Zanden (2020). (**b**) GDP/Cap Growth Rate, 2010–2018, Versus Log GDP/Cap. 2010. *Source:* Bolt and Van Zanden (2020)

effect of institutions separately on this convergence.[19] In this Section, we proxy institutional environment with the duration in office of regional (or local) leaders (e.g. mayors) as they represent regional support and influence on political and economic relationships. In their capacity, mayors serve as intermediaries between central government, local interest groups, and economic agents to protect property rights and generate political stability. Local institutions, therefore, satisfactorily proxy for national institutions when looking at regions or cities that are most significant for a national economy.

To this end, Calabrese and Van Leeuwen (2024) introduce an institutional indicator based on mayors' time in office, the evolution of which between 1900 and 2010 is shown in Figs. 5.9a and b. Once a long-run perspective is taken, countries experiencing economic convergence seem to have mayors in office for a longer time. This is typically the case for countries that are below the mean income, at any level of institutional quality.[20] However, as argued by Calabrese and Van Leeuwen, shorter

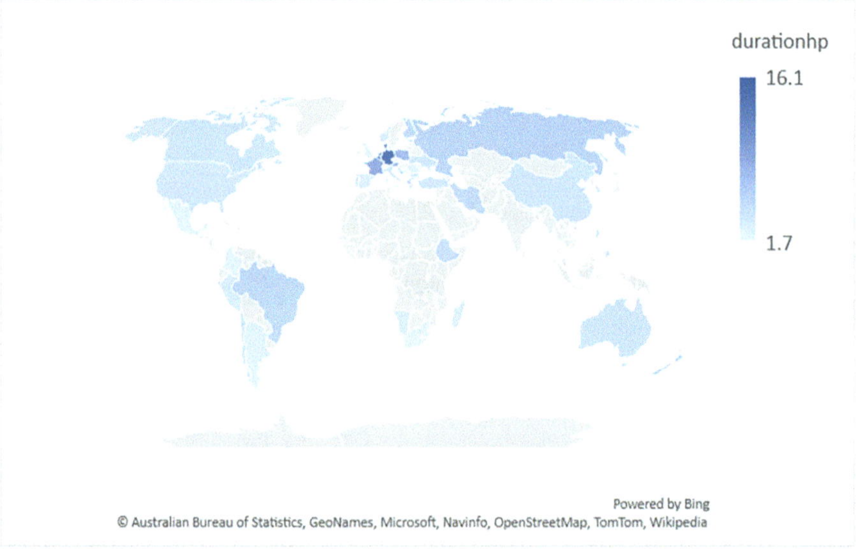

Fig. 5.9 (**a**) Mayors' time in office, 1900. *Source:* Calabrese and Van Leeuwen (2024). (**b**) Mayors' time in office, 2010. *Source:* Calabrese & Van Leeuwen (2024)

[19] Many different institutional indicators exist, yet they inevitably describe only a partial facet of institutional reality (see e.g. Calabrese & Van Leeuwen 2024). In particular, local institutional dynamics tend to be overlooked in favour of institutional indicators that are based, for example, on national political stability or democracy. As an example, see the Polity2 indicator. The Polity4 and Polity5 datasets on autocracy and democracy (Polity5 Project, 1800–2018), once combined, give with their Polity2 variable an index of autocracy–democracy ranging from total autocracy (−10) to total democracy (+10).

[20] Institutional quality is measured through other indicators, assessing for example the level of democracy of a country (e.g. the Polity Project variable).

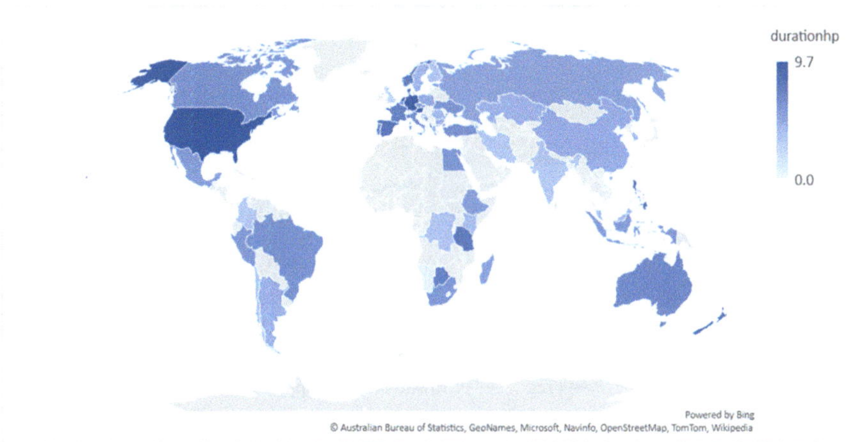

Fig. 5.9 (continued)

tenures can be associated with economic convergence only where countries have good institutional fundamentals. Countries with short mayoral tenures and bad institutional fundamentals most likely face divergence (Fig. 5.10).

In the case of Russia's institutional development, taking a Eurasian perspective, it is worth exploring the interplay of its political and economic institutions at local level by applying an institutional indicator based on mayors' time in office.

The results are shown in Fig. 5.11a and b. They show that during the imperial period,[21] the improvement of institutions was initially manifested by both series in the largest cities, Moscow and St. Petersburg.[22] But the trends were opposite in the two capital cities from 1750 to 1850. In the late nineteenth and early twentieth centuries, movement towards a better protection of property rights is more visible in the case of St. Petersburg as a political capital, but not in the case of Moscow as a commercial and industrial city. Frequent changes in local leaders in Moscow in the early twentieth century in this case can be regarded as a sign of intra-elite conflicts, a consequence of political terrorism. The trend towards improvement of institutions had an effect throughout the Soviet and post-Soviet periods in St. Petersburg and throughout the post-Second World War period in Moscow.

The proxy measure works well for the Soviet period. Specified and unspecified rights to receive benefits from economic resources were less strong in the 1930s up to the mid-1950s, when the rotation of regional leaders was high. These rights were

[21] The duration of the mayor's term in office was associated both with a person and with the position.

[22] For the Russian Empire, the mayors of Moscow and St. Petersburg were the heads of both capitals. For the Soviet Union and the Russian Federation, Moscow was and remains the only official capital city. Yet in the Soviet period, St. Petersburg was the other city whose local leadership was directly subordinate to national political power. Unofficially, it remains the second capital city of the Russian Federation.

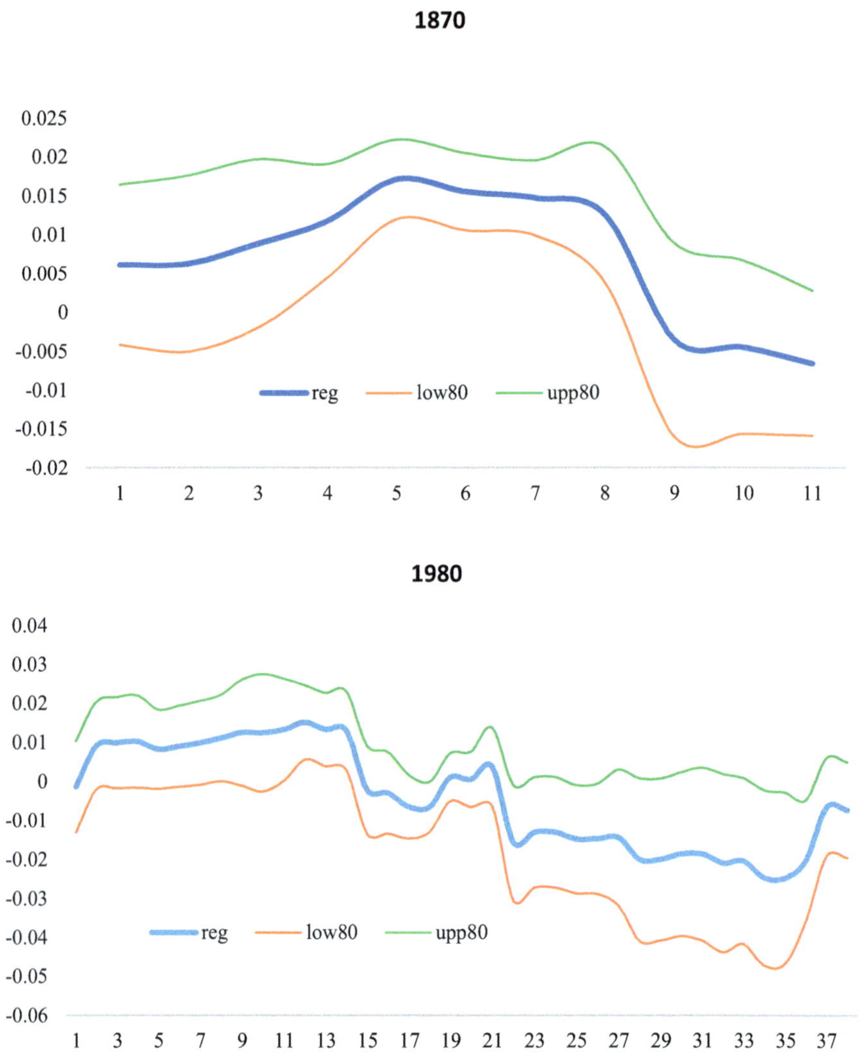

Fig. 5.10 ln (natural logarithm) of GDP/cap growth rate versus log GDP/cap by mayors' "time in office" groupings (based on years of mayors' tenures, from lower to higher), 1870 and 1980. *Source:* Calabrese & Van Leeuwen (2024).

a

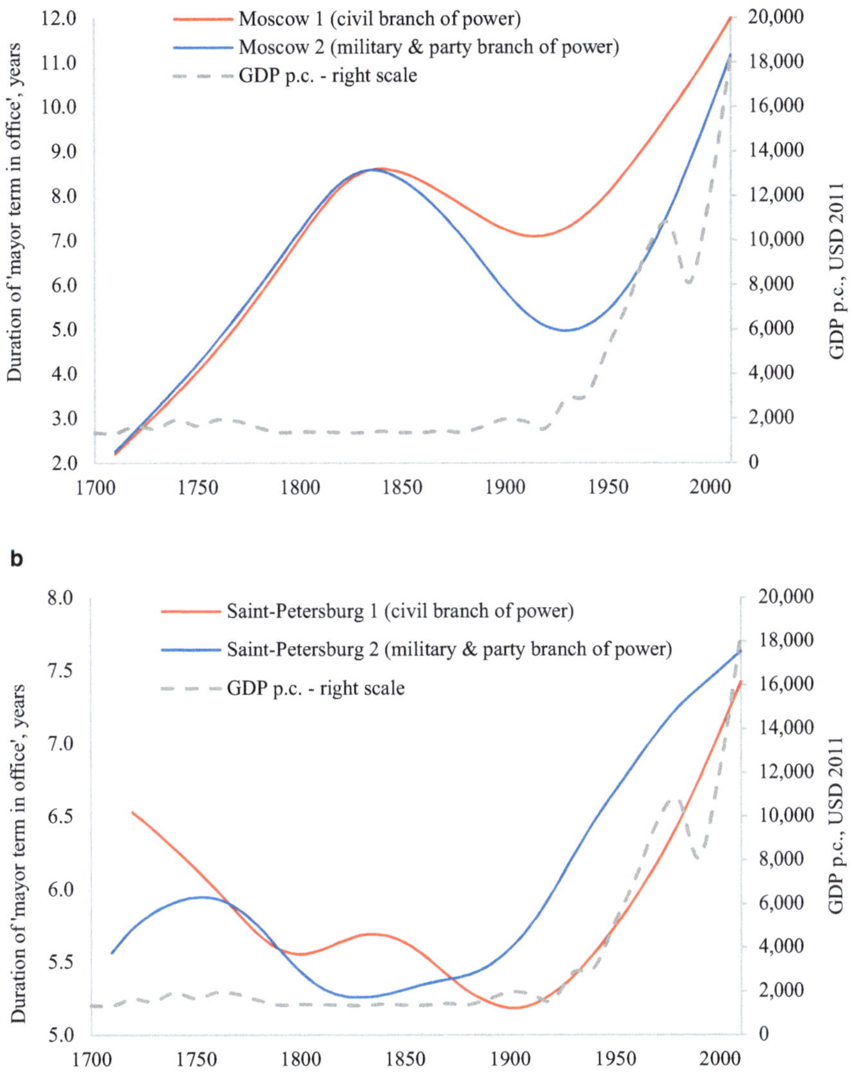

Fig. 5.11 (**a**) Dynamics of institutional development and GDP/cap in Russia (capital cities of Moscow and St. Petersburg), c. 1700–2022 (Moscow). *Source:* Broadberry and Korchmina (2024); Cheremukhin et al. (2017); Didenko et al. (2013); Bolt and Van Zanden (2020); The official portal of the Moscow Mayor and Moscow Government, https://www.mos.ru/city/about/heads/ (accessed 2022); Wikipedia, https://en.wikipedia.org/w/index.php?title=List_of_heads_of_Moscow_government, https://en.wikipedia.org/w/index.php?title=Moscow_City_Committee_of_the_Communist_Party_of_the_Soviet_Union, https://ru.wikipedia.org/wiki/Градоначальники_Москвы (accessed 2022). (**b**) Dynamics of institutional development and GDP/cap in Russia (capital cities of Moscow and St. Petersburg), c. 1700–2022 (St. Petersburg). *Source:* Broadberry and Korchmina (2024); Cheremukhin et al. (2017); Didenko et al. (2013); Bolt and Van Zanden (2020); Wikipedia, https://ru.wikipedia.org/wiki/Губернатор_Санкт-Петербурга, https://en.wikipedia.org/wiki/Governor_of_Saint_Petersburg (accessed 2022).

protected strongly in the mid-1950s–mid-1980s, when the rotation of leaders at any level slowed down.[23] We can compare this with Fig. 5.6, where our survey of the Russian population in 2022 shows a little more trust for government in Russia than in Europe, but less than in China. What is surprising is the almost equal trust of central and regional (or local) government. This is probably because central institutions of the Russian presidency, most trusted by the population, are often not associated with national government in its role as the executive branch of power and routine administration.

5.4 Geography

As indicated in Sect. 5.1, long-run growth, proxied by TFP, can also include, besides technology and institutional environment, determinants related to geography. Having dealt with the former two factors, we move on to geography.[24]

Geography has three main branches that are relevant here, namely, disease environment, natural resources, and climate. Disease environment (e.g. Sachs and Malaney, 2002) essentially claims that diseases prevalent in certain countries inhibit economic growth. For Eurasia, this effect is limited, since the difference in disease environment occurs mostly according to longitude (North–South), and it is often endogenous with economic productivity: economic growth might affect disease environment or vice versa.

The second branch is natural resources. Whereas Sachs and Warner (2001) found the tendency to confiscate natural resources in the form of wealth important, others have argued for the rise in real exchange rate. The latter implies an increased demand for non-tradable products (e.g. services or products with a low value in relation to their weight/volume), which have less of an effect on productivity growth.

Finally, there is climate. This thesis is supported by Diamond (2013), who argues that Eurasia's climate allowed for greater access to domesticated large animal species and plants. The wider usage of large domesticated animals, compared with all other areas, made Eurasians more immune to animal transmitted diseases. Because Eurasia runs from west to east rather than from north to south, animals and plants could easier spread over an area that had similar climate (Diamond 1997). This fostered, according to Diamond, faster technology adoption.

[23] The indicator (Mayors' time in office) allows for a wide range of interpretations. It can capture periods of weakening or strengthening state capacity in Russia, periods of institutional borrowing (or experimentation), and periods of stagnation. Values that are too high may indicate economic stagnation, as was the case in the countries of the former USSR in the 1970s and 1980s; while low values during the post-Soviet period can mean institutional changes.

[24] Acemoglu (2009) argues for the ultimate factors of growth being luck, geography (disease environment, natural resources, and climate), culture (beliefs, values, and economic behaviour), and institutions (rules, regulations, and policies that steer behaviour towards technology adoption and capital accumulation). However, we ignore luck (Campante et al. 2021, 99).

But why, then, did Europe eventually surpass China technologically even though both were located in Eurasia? Here Diamond (1997) claims that European geography was more heterogeneous than China's, with the latter having fewer trade-blocking mountain ranges. Consequently, China had already been "unified" since the Qin dynasty (221–206 BCE) and has stayed that way until today. In Europe, geographic division led to fragmentation of states, which led to competition and eventually to technological growth. While consistent with the theoretical framework that argues for a positive role of political fragmentation at the macro-level with regard to technology introduction (see also Sect. 2.9), a geographically based interpretation appears flawed in explaining why Chinese technology continued to grow until the Ming dynasty.[25] Hence, authors have been focusing on culture and institutions, such as the inward turn from Confucianism (Balazs 1964) and totalitarianism combined with the lack of free markets (Landes 2006) to explain China's slowing down of technology after the Ming dynasty. A similar argument is given by Van Leeuwen and Van Zanden (2019). They claim that, on the one hand, since the Qin dynasty, the infrastructure, the civil examination scheme, and the integrated tax system caused integration. Yet, on the other hand, they also claim that there was a dynastic cycle: each dynasty started powerfully but declined over time, thus leaving space for market behaviour and economic growth. The biggest problem, though, is that geography might mainly affect agricultural productivity while modern growth strongly depends on industrial (and services) wages. Obviously, as we saw in Chap. 4, agricultural productivity may also affect industrial and services productivity. Yet, as pointed out by Campante et al. (2021), the effect of geography is probably insufficient to explain the beginning of industrial growth.

The issue of the influence of natural, climatic, and geographical factors on the course of Russia's history was also highlighted in a number of works. According to Pipes (1995), natural conditions contributed to the genesis of the system of institutions of the "patrimonial state". A similar view, largely based on the ideas of Kliuchevskii (1960 [1906]) about the decisive role of geographical factors in the Russian historical process under the predominance of the agrarian economy, was presented by Milov (1998).

Turchin and Nefedov (2009, p. 6, 81) updated the concepts of "capacity of an ecological niche" and "carrying capacity of the environment", which reflect a historical level of interaction between resources and technologies. In the structural-demographic theory (Goldstone, 1991), these concepts were operationalized by such indicators as the population (and separately the elite) pressure on resources, which can be estimated by dividing actual population numbers by the maximum number that can be fed within a certain geographic region given current technology.

[25] The role of natural environment is heavily debated. For example, Confucius advocated that people should follow nature (Confucius 1999, reprint *c.* fifth century BCE, 149). But other scholars have claimed that people dominate nature, while yet others have claimed people should live in harmony with physical geography (Chiang, 2005). This view corresponds by and large with those in the West. However, it has only limited support.

Mironov (2018, vol. 1, p. 221–250) applied to a number of empirical evidence refuting hypotheses formulated on the basis of geographical determinism, which insists on the decisive role of climate in the history of Russia. His lines of argument, based on the data of the late nineteenth to early twentieth centuries, were the following:

First, interregional variations in crop yields, land productivity, heights (as a proxy for the standard of living), institutional characteristics (incidence of a redistributive commune and share of privately owned serfs) do not correlate with average temperatures and possible farmers' working hours (as a consequence of the climatic conditions of a province).

Second, disadvantages in some cases turned into advantages. A warmer and more humid climate in the European Russia spring and summer made it possible to grow annual crops much further north than in other countries. The lack of precipitation was at least partly compensated for by snow water.

Third, the geographical factor is not limited to climate; it has other important components (country location, its continentality, development of the river system, proximity of seas and oceans, fertility of soils, mineral and water resources, flora and fauna, etc. The overall interactions in the system where natural endowments were selectively used for the economic benefits, should be taken into account.

Nureev and Latov (2016) largely rested on quantitative evidence and a number of basic ideas from Pipes (1995) and Milov (1998). But the formers' conclusions about the significance of natural-geographical and institutional factors were closer to those by Mironov (2018). Nureev and Latov (2016, p. 37–46) claimed that the natural environment was a component, which significantly influenced the results of the competition of historically alternative institutions (to a greater extent in the earlier period than in the twentieth century), but hardly ever determined its outcome.

5.5 Direction of Technical Change: Land Rent to Wage Ratio

Our point is that TFP can affect productivity in the long run. This, however, does not just depend on the number of inventions or the efficiency of their use. Indeed, as pointed out in Sect. 5.3, China's speed of technological implementation slowed down, and it fell behind in terms of institutions and culturally driven growth: A lack of entrepreneurship, less competition owing to political unity, and inventions being concentrated on government and major landlords, within an underlying institutional context led by risk-averse clan-networks, were the main factors behind this. However, the direction of technological change (which idea to implement) was determined by demand (e.g. Boserup 1965).

In general, technology in China is argued to be labour using and capital/land saving while it was labour-saving in Europe. We can look at this by comparing the various phases of agriculture (from sowing to harvesting) and their geography. For example, Bray (1984, 188) suggests that Chinese ploughs were lighter than European ones, being drawn by a single ox (capital) while European ploughs required four or more animals. The more abundant number of draught animals used in England suggests their lower cost (see Table 5.6). In sowing, Europe also used capital-intensive methods for broadcasting seeds until the introduction of the seed drill. In China, broadcasting occurred in the north or where the land was dry; later the seed drill was used. Labour-intensive transplanting has a long history in rice cultivation, but mechanical harvesting appeared early on in Europe: Pliny, for example, mentions the vallum, an oxen-drawn reaping machine used in Gaul (Bray 1984, 342)—but this was forgotten until the late eighteenth century. In China, no mechanical harvesting device was introduced and the scythe remained in use even in wheat fields, where mechanization would have yielded the most profit. In addition, land was cultivated more intensively in Europe through the use of crop rotation. Although fallow was initially part of the Chinese system, it was later mostly given up. Usually, a continuous growth regime was followed (Bray 1984, 430).

Besides the China–Europe comparison, it is important to stress that the differences between northern China and southern China touched upon briefly earlier were also important for international comparisons. These regional differences were at least partly driven by geography, that is, differences in land fertility. In China, the north of the country has significant amounts of black soil; something similar occurs in southern Russia and Central Asia. Indeed, both northern China and southern Russia grow wheat-type grains such as millet, with cotton being important in Central Asia. As seen earlier, wheat demands capital, and therefore many new labour-saving technologies were introduced in the black soil areas. A similar development occurred in Russia. This can be seen in the labour structure: In the case of Russia, monetary dues prevailed in low fertile non-black earth regions from the 1850s (Moon 2001, Table 2.2) whereas labour services dominated in black earth areas and in the western borderlands (Ukraine, Belarus, Lithuania). This was because productivity was enhanced predominantly in the black earth areas, thus making labour more attractive. In less fertile non-black earth areas, however, land was much less productive than capital, thus making monetary dues more attractive. Testifying to the lower agricultural productivity, the major source of dues in the non-black earth areas of Russia was the peasants' off-farm earnings (craft production and later part-time manufacturing employment). Yet we should not overestimate the technological progress in the black earth areas. Indeed, available evidence suggests that

Table 5.6 Average value working animals/value agricultural output, c. 1200–1850

	England	China
c. 1200	30%	3–7%
c. 1400	39%	
c. 1600	24%	
c. 1850		3%

Source: Calculations based on La Feur (1927), Beveridge (1939), Liang (1980), Bai and Chen (2015), and Broadberry et al. (2015)

technologies used in fertile black earth Russian regions, where labour dues prevailed, were not always labour saving. As pointed out by Natkhov and Vasilenok (2021), not all technologies spread to black soil areas: whereas tools such as ploughs were accepted, skills such as carpentry hardly spread at all. Indeed, Liashchenko (1956, vol. 1, 494, 498, 502, 506) points out that technologies employed by both peasants and landlords were still primitive in the first half of the nineteenth century. While labour productivity appeared to be stagnant, landlords tended to increase their income by extending the cultivated lands for grain production, also including sugar beet. Milov (1998, 38, 64–65) proposes a similar view for the eighteenth century, reporting details of the three-field system and its modification to combat weeds. Ostrovskii (2013, 88–94, 159) reports that a two-field system dominated in the black-earth south until the early twentieth century, while the three-field organization using natural fertilizers was only just being introduced in the mid-nineteenth century, later than in other provinces.

Given that China also had a technologically advancing black earth area, one might expect more of a focus on labour dues compared with the south of the country. This, however, seems not to have been the case: The most frequent form of rent that peasants paid to their landlords were labour dues (rent for the land paid in kind) throughout China. Indeed, a national investigation in 1934 showed that rent paid in labour accounted for around 81.3% in Chaha'er while only 18.7% was money dues. In Suiyuan, labour dues and money dues were 68.8% and 31.2%, respectively. Ningxia and Hebei had the highest proportion of money dues (46.1% and 52.3%). In Shandong, money dues accounted for 30.4%. In southern China, such as Jiangsu and Zhejiang, money dues accounted for 27.6% and 27.2%, respectively (Central Agricultural Experimental Institute of the Kuomingtang government 1934). An explanation of this might be that, with a strongly increasing output of rice per unit of land in Tang China (owing to better irrigation systems), even surpassing land productivity in black earth northern.

China, labour-intensive rice slowly started to replace capital-intensive wheat-type grains in northern China. One can find similar patterns in Japan, where the importance of rice grown in the south started to replace northern wheat and millet around the Meiji Restoration (mid-nineteenth century).

Alongside the evidence presented here that focuses on labour-saving technology in England versus capital-saving technology in China (even though the situation varied by region), we can also apply a more formal approach to test whether China, Russia, or Europe were indeed capital-saving. If technology is land-saving (in China), a rise in technology will increase the income of landowners, first because it increases income from land rent, and second because in the long run population increases reduce wages; that is, the land rent to wage ratio increases. Since upper-class social groups increase their income this way, inequality in society increases. Hence, technological change in China is mainly driven by big landowners. Yet once human capital comes into play, and if elasticity of substitution between labour and land is bigger than 1 (wages increase faster than land rents, so the land rent to wage ratio declines), inequality declines, creating a peak in the rise and decline in the fertility transition (Madsen and Strulik 2020). In Table 5.7, we offer a rough

Table 5.7 Land rent to wage ratio in China, the Middle East and England, c. 1 CE–1600

	Land rents	Wages	Land rent to wage ratio
	Grams silver/ha	Grams silver/day	
	c. 100 BCE–200 CE		
China	1084	2.1	516
England	n.a.	n.a.	n.a.
Middle East	538.8	5.0	108
	c. 1000–1200		
China	707	3.0	236
England	25	1.4	18
Middle East	467	3.2	146
		c. 1600	
China	840	2.4	350
England	86	3.8	23
Middle East	n.a.	n.a.	n.a.

Source: Calculations based on Needham and Bray (1984); Borsch (2005, Table 5.7) Clark (1999); Scheidel (2010); Pamuk and Schatzmiller (2011); Gao (2008); Broadberry et al. (2015)

overview of this. Even though the land rent to wage ratio in China declined between about 1 CE and 1100, this should rather be interpreted as stagnation for two reasons: Human capital played a lesser role in this period, and the data are so rough that it is difficult to assume a trend.

This might be true for China, but in England, it might be mostly labour-saving technology—England's declining land rent to wage ratio (see e.g. Clark 2009). This means we witness declining income inequality both before and after the fertility transition (see also Kitsikopoulos 2000). A similar observation on declining income inequality was made by O'Rourke and Williamson (2005), who, however, attributed it to enhanced food trade.

We can make a similar argument for Russia.[26] As Domar (1989, 226) notes:

> the servitors tried to live off rents (in one form or another) to be collected from their estates. But the estates could not yield a significant amount of rent for the simple reason that land in Russia was not sufficiently scarce relative to labour, and ironically, was made even less scarce by Russian conquests. The scarce factor of production was not land but labour. Hence it was the ownership of peasants, and not of land, that could yield an income to the servitors or to any non-working landowning class thus decreasing the land rent to wage ratio.

Indeed, typically, serfs were sold with land (often wholesale by villages). To do otherwise was considered to be detrimental to the social order, and the emperors either strictly limited or even prohibited it. Therefore, it is not possible to directly differentiate between the two asset prices (land and human capital) prior to 1861.

[26] Indeed, the economic explanation of the factors behind enserfment in medieval Russia was proposed in Domar (1989, 225–234), based on the narrative scheme put forward by a prominent pre-Revolutionary Russian historian Vasily Osipovich Kliuchevskii (1960 [1906]).

The available evidence, not only including published sources of the time but also contemporary Russian fiction,[27] suggests that the size of a landholding was of less importance than the number of serfs (*dush*—literally "souls") when a noble's social status was concerned (Table 5.8). However, we may suppose that the number of serfs was strongly correlated with the total size of all estates, as land that belonged to a noble of high status was dispersed.[28]

Yet after 1861 we have some information on land to labour ratios. It looks somewhat surprisingly that these ratios increased very modestly compared to the land price movements. The real growth rate of land prices in 1885–1910 was estimated at 4.09 per annum (Leonard et al. 2021, 99), cumulatively 2.7 times over 25 years. For the longer period of 46 years (1867–1913), they skyrocketed about sixfold in real terms (Leonard 2011, 284).[29] Land productivity also increased starting from the mid-1870s and the land to wage ratio was on the rise, even with land measured by area natural units (Fig. 5.12).[30] It would rise much more if the land had been measured in monetary units according to market value (although straightforward extrapolations would be dubious in this case as only a small part of land was used in market turnover; in many cases this would hardly suffice to be representative of the total).

In Russia, the land rent to wage ratio was low, owing to the abundance of land, while in England it was owing to the scarcity of labour. In China, the land rent to wage ratio was high. This difference between China and Russia disappeared, however, in the nineteenth century when Russia land became increasingly more expensive than labour.

In China, and Russia after the mid-nineteenth century, the land rent to wage ratio thus rose. If there had been increasing education, driven by decreased fertility, this

Table 5.8 Noble Ownership of Serfs in Russia, 1719–1858

Number of serfs owned	1719–1727		1857–1858	
	% nobles	% serfs	% nobles	% serfs
501+	0.80	26.20	3.40	41.50
101–500	7.90	32.50	20.90	38.00
<100	91.30	41.30	75.70	20.50
Total	100	100	100	100

Source: Moon (2001, table 2.2)

[27] Domar (1989, 232–233) recalls just a few cases: "In Pushkin's *Dubrovskii*, the old Dubrovskii is identified as the owner of 70 souls, and Prince Vereiskii of 3000; in *The Captain's Daughter*, the commandant's wife is impressed by Grinev's father's ownership of 300 souls; in Gogol's *The Dead Souls*, Pliushkin owns more than 1000 souls; in Goncharov's *Oblomov*, the principal hero owns 350; in his *A Common Story*, a certain Anton Ivanich has 12 mortgaged over and over again…"

[28] For example, Konchakov and Korchmina (2020) explore the case of Moscow nobility in the early nineteenth century.

[29] The prices were borrowed from Koval'chenko and Milov (1974, 259–267).

[30] The size of a peasant's plot of land was used as a proxy for the land to labour ratio (Leonard 2011, 50).

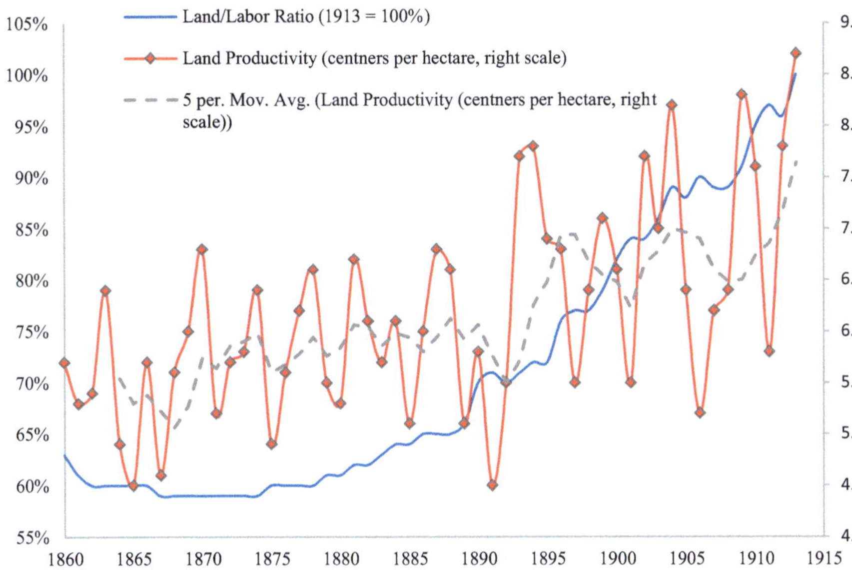

Fig. 5.12 Land to labour ratio and land productivity in agriculture in Central Eurasia, 1860–1913. *Source*: land to wage ratio: Leonard (2011, 284); land productivity: Rastyannikov and Deryugina (2009, 124–125)

human capital would have driven up wages and, hence, decreased economic inequality. This certainly happened in Russia in the nineteenth century, when the distribution of land (Table 5.9) was subject to change during early industrialization, with a tendency towards shrinking the nobility's share that was bought out by peasants (basically entrepreneurs), merchants, and industrialists. However, in China, the economic power stayed in the hands of the elite, and educational growth only began because of declining returns to education, which led to less interest in human capital (Sect. 4.3).

5.6 Conclusion: Increasing Weight of Technology

In this chapter, we have focused on the ultimate causes of economic growth. We find that the switch from Malthusian growth to modern growth occurred in around 1700 in the UK and 1900 in China. After calculating TFP as a measure of ultimate causes of growth, we witness a positive effect from the Black Death that ebbed away rapidly afterwards. Yet for England, it rebounded somewhat after about a century; for both China and Italy, it remained low until the nineteenth century. Indeed, for developed countries, in the late nineteenth century until the beginning of the twentieth century, about 84% of growth was caused by increase in physical capital

Table 5.9 Land distribution by ownership, European Russia. 1877–1905

	1877–1878			1905		
		In % of all cultivated land			In % of all cultivated land	
Categories of land	Millions of desiatina (1 desiatina = 2.7 acres = 10,926 square meters.)	Including state lands	Excluding state lands	Millions of desiatina	Including state lands	Excluding state lands
TOTAL	377.0	100		395.2	100	
State and public lands	167.9	45		154.7	39	
Total land excluding state lands	209.1	2	100	240.5		100
Peasant allotment land	116.7	31	56	133.8	33–9	56
Total owned by private persons:	92.4			108.8		
Nobles	73.1	19	35	58.2	14.7	2.4
Peasants	5.0	1	2	24.7	6.3	10
Merchants and industrialists	11.5	3	1	16.7	4.2	7
Others	2.8	1	1	7.2	1.8	3

Source: Leonard (2011, 48)

intensity (K/L) and just 16% by technology. For China, the role of technology was slightly lower.

TFP growth thus matches the switch from Malthusian to modern economic growth. This implies that the ultimate factors of growth (technology, institutional environment, and geography) at least partly explain the switch to modern economic growth. We find that, whereas for institutions and cultural factors such as entrepreneurship, lesser competition owing to political unity, and a concentration of invention with government and big landlords playing a central role, geographical endowment had only a limited effect. Two exceptions occur for geography, though. First, in the very long run, and for each macro-area such as a continent, geography has explanatory power. Second, the impact of geography can be assessed through analysis of agricultural production and of labour to capital ratios in the three areas we are comparing. The latter are affected by the demand for labour or capital-saving technology, with capital-saving technology in China mostly occurring in the geographic black soil area in the north.

Besides TFP growth (Chap. 5) and the underlying proximate factors (Chap. 4), individual sectors in which technological growth happened are important. As pointed out in Sect. 5.2, technology in Western Europe switched from service and agriculture to ndustry. As the latter had a greater impact on growth in a proto-industrial world, this gave Europe an advantage.

References

Acemoglu D (2009) Introduction to modern economic growth. Princeton University Press

Acemoglu D, Robinson J (2012) Why nations fail: origins of power, poverty, and prosperity. Crown, New York, NY

Allen RC (2003) Farm to factory: a reinterpretation of the Soviet industrial revolution. Princeton University Press, Princeton

Allen RC (2012) Technology and the great divergence: global economic development since 1820. Explor Econ Hist 49:1–16

Antras P, Voth HJ (2003) Factor prices and productivity growth during the British industrial revolution. Explor Econ Hist 40:52–77

Antonelli C, Feder Ch (2020) Total factor productivity, catch-up and technological congruence in Italy, 1861–2010. J Evol Econ 30(4):1171–1194

Arroyo Abad, L. (2006). Notes on Italy, Florence, 14th century. https://gpih.ucdavis.edu/files/Italy_Florence_14thc.xls. Accessed 19 Mar 2023

Bai S, Chen Z (eds) (2015) 中国通史 第7卷 中古时代 五代辽宋夏金时期 上(General history of China, Vol. 7). Shanghai People's Publishing House, Shanghai

Baier SL, Dwyer GP, Tamura R (2006) How important are capital and total factor productivity for economic growth? Econ Inq 44(1):23–49. https://doi.org/10.1093/ei/cbi003

Balazs E (1964) Chinese civilization and bureaucracy; variations on a theme. Yale University Press, New Haven

Bergeaud A, Cette G, Lecat R (2016) Productivity growth in advanced countries between 1890 and 2012. Rev Income Wealth 62(3):420–444. https://doi.org/10.1111/roiw.12185

Beugelsdijk S, Klasing M, Milionis P (2018) Regional economic development in Europe: the role of total factor productivity. Reg Stud 52(4):461–476

Beveridge W (1939) Prices and wages in England from the twelfth to the nineteenth century. Volume I, Price tables: Mercantile era. Longmans, Green and Company, New York

Bolt, J., & Van Zanden, J. L. (2020). Maddison style estimates of the evolution of the world economy: A new 2020 update. Maddison Project Database, versions 2018, 2020.

Borsch SJ (2005) The Black death in Egypt and England: a comparative study. University of Texas Press, Austin

Boserup E (1965) The conditions of agricultural growth: the economics of agrarian change under population pressure. G. Allen and Unwin, London

Bray F (1984) Agriculture. In: Needham J (ed) Science and civilisation in China (Vol. 6, Biology and Biological Technology, Part II). Cambridge University Press, Cambridge

Broadberry SN, Giordano C, Zollino F (2011) A sectoral analysis of Italy's development, 1861–2011. Bank of Italy economic history working paper no. 20, available at SSRN: https://ssrn.com/abstract=2239016 or https://doi.org/10.2139/ssrn.2239016. Accessed 19 Mar 2023

Broadberry, S. N . (2021). Accounting for the Great Divergence: recent findings from historical national accounting. VoxEU. Retrieved from https://voxeu.org/article/accounting-great-divergence-recent-findings-historical-national-accounting

Broadberry S, Korchmina E (2024) Catching-up and falling behind: Russian economic growth, 1960s–1880s. J Econ Hist 84(4):997–1028. https://doi.org/10.1017/s0022050724000287

Broadberry S, Campbell B, Klein A, Overton M, Van Leeuwen B (2015) British economic growth 1270–1870. Cambridge University Press, Cambridge

Broadberry S, Guan H, Li D (2018) China, Europe, and the Great Divergence: a study in historical national accounting, 980–1850. J Econ Hist 78(4):955–1000. https://doi.org/10.1017/S0022050718000403

Calabrese M, Van Leeuwen B (2024) "Time in office" of city mayors and economic convergence, c. 1870-present. J Eur Econ Hist 53(2):43–65. Associazione Bancaria Italiana

Campante F, Sturzenegger F, Velasco A (2021) Proximate and fundamental causes of growth. In: Campante IF, Sturzenegger F, Velasco A (eds) Advanced macroeconomics: an easy guide (Chap. 7). LSE Press, London. https://doi.org/10.31389/lsepress.ame.g

Central Agricultural Experimental Institute of the Kuomingtang government. (1934). 农情报告 (Agricultural Situation Report). vol 3(4).90.
Cheremukhin A, Golosov M, Guriev S, Tsyvinski A (2017) The industrialization and economic development of Russia through the lens of a neoclassical growth model. Rev Econ Stud 84(2):613–649. https://doi.org/10.1093/restud/rdw026
Chiang T-C (2005) Historical geography in China. Prog Hum Geogr 29(2):148–164. https://doi.org/10.1191/0309132505ph544oa
Clark G (1999) Too much revolution: agriculture in the industrial revolution, 1700–1860. In: Mokyr J (ed) The British industrial revolution: an economic perspective, second edn. Westview Press, Boulder, CO, pp 206–240
Clark, G. (2009). The macroeconomic aggregates for England, 1209-2008. Working Papers 295, University of California, Davis, Department of Economics.
Confucius. (1999). Lunyu (Conversations and discourses of Confucius). (Reprint with translation and notes by P. Y. Fu). Taipei: Lixu. (Original work compiled in the late fifth or early fourth century BCE).
Crafts NFR, Harley CK (1992) Output growth and the British Industrial Revolution: A restatement of the Crafts–Harley view. Econ Hist Rev 45(4):703–730. https://doi.org/10.1111/j.1468-0289.1992.tb01343.x
Crafts N, Harley CK (2000) Simulating the two views of the British Industrial revolution. J Econ Hist 60:819–842. https://doi.org/10.1017/S0022050700025760
Davies RW, Harrison M, Wheatcroft SG (1994) The economic transformation of the Soviet Union, 1913–1945. Cambridge University Press
Diamond J (1997) Guns, germs, and steel: the fates of human societies. W.W. Norton, New York, NY
Diamond J (2013) Guns, germs and steel: a short history of everybody for the last 13,000 years. Random House
Didenko D, Földvári P, Van Leeuwen B (2013) The spread of human capital in the former Soviet Union area in a comparative perspective: Exploring a new dataset. J Euras Stud 4(2):123–135. https://doi.org/10.1016/j.euras.2013.03.002. (Supplementary data retrieved from https://ars.els-cdn.com/content/image/1-s2.0-S1879366513000122-mmc1.zip, accessed via https://www.sciencedirect.com/science/article/pii/S1879366513000122)
Domar ED (1989) The causes of slavery or serfdom: a hypothesis. In: Domar ED (ed) Capitalism, socialism, and serfdom. Cambridge University Press, pp 225–238
Dugin A (2012) The fourth political theory. Arktos, Budapest
Dugin A (2021) The great awakening vs the great reset. Arktos, Budapest
Eichengreen B, Park D, Shin K (2012) When fast-growing economies slow down: International evidence and implications for China. ASEAN Econ Pap 11(1):42–87
Eicher T, Garcia-Peñalosa C, Teksoz U (2006) How do institutions lead some countries to produce so much more output per worker than others? In: Eicher T, Garcia-Peñalosa C (eds) Institutions, development, and economic growth. The MIT Press, pp 65–80
Feenstra RC, Inklaar R, Timmer MP (2015) The next generation of the Penn World Table. Am Econo Rev 105(10):3150–3182. Available for download at www.ggdc.net/pwt
Feinstein CH (1981) Capital accumulation and the industrial revolution. In: Floud R, McCloskey DN (eds) The economic history of Britain since 1700, vol 1, first edn. Cambridge University Press, Cambridge, pp 128–142
Felipe J (1999) Total factor productivity growth in East Asia: a critical survey. J Dev Stud 35(4):1–41
Gao, S.(2008). 明万历年间北京的物价和工资(Beijing price and wages in Wanli period, Ming Dynasty). 清华大学学报哲学社科版(Learned Journal of Qinghua University (Social Philosophy Science Version)), 23.
Gehringer A, Martínez-Zarzoso I, Nowak-Lehmann Danzinger F (2016) What are the drivers of total factor productivity in the European Union? Econ Innov New Technol 25(4):406–434
Goldstone JA (1991) Revolution and rebellion in the early modern world. University of California Press, Berkeley and Los Angeles

Gregory PR (2003a) An introduction to the economics of the Gulag. In: Gregory PR, Lazarev VV (eds) The economics of forced labor: the Soviet Gulag. Hoover Institution Press, Stanford, CA, pp 1–21

Gregory PR (2003b) The political economy of Stalinism: Evidence from the secret Soviet archives. Cambridge University Press, Cambridge, MT

Gumilev LN (1988) Searches for an imaginary kingdom: the legend of the kingdom of Prester John. Cambridge University Press, New York

Gumilev LN (1990) Ethnogenesis and the biosphere. Progress Publishers, Moscow

Hall RE, Jones CI (1999) Why do some countries produce so much more output than others? Q J Econ 114:83–116

Harley (1999): Harley, C. K. (1999). Reassessing the Industrial Revolution. In J. Mokyr (Ed.), The British Industrial Revolution: An Economic Perspective (2nd ed., pp. 160–205). Boulder, CO: Westview Press.

Hittle JM (1979) The service city: state and townsmen in Russia, 1600–1800. Harvard University Press, Cambridge, MA

Hulten CR (2001) Total factor productivity: a short biography. In: Hulten CR, Dean ER, Harper MJ (eds) New developments in productivity analysis, studies in income and wealth, vol 63. University of Chicago Press, pp 1–52

Kitsikopoulos H (2000) Standards of living and capital formation in pre-plague England: a peasant budget model. Econ Hist Rev 53(2):237–261. http://www.jstor.org/stable/2598697

Kliuchevskii, V.O. (1960 [1906]) A history of Russia (Vols. 1–5). Transl. by C. J. Hogarth. Russell and Russell, New York.

Konchakov RB, Korchmina ES (2020) The structure of noble property of the Moscow gentry in 1812. Istoriya 11(3). https://doi.org/10.18254/S207987840009536-8

Koval'chenko ID, Milov LV (1974) Всероссииский аграрный рынок (XVIII—начало XX вв.): опыт количественного анализа [All-Russian agrarian market in the 18th and beginning of the nineteenth century: A quantitative analysis]. Наука [The Science], Moscow

Kozlova NV (1999) Россиискиий абсолютизм и купечество в XVIII веке (20-е - начало 60-х годов) [Russian absolutism and merchants in the 18th century (20 s - early 60 s)]. Археологический центр [Archaeological Center], Moscow

Kumar R, Russell RR (2002) Technological change, technological catch-up, and capital deepening: relative contributions to growth and convergence. Am Econ Rev 92(3):527–548. https://doi.org/10.1257/00028280260136381

Landes, D. S. (2006). Why Europe and the West? Why not China? Journal of Economic Perspectives, 20(2), 3-22. https://doi.org/10.1257/jep.20.2.3

La Feur A, Foscue E (1927) Agricultural production in China. Econ Geogr 3(3):297–308. https://doi.org/10.2307/140526

Leonard CS (2011) Agrarian reform in Russia: the road from serfdom. Cambridge University Press

Leonard CS, Nazarov Z, Borodkin LI, Karpenko MA, Konchakov RB (2021) Land prices and railroad building in European Russia, 1860s to the early 1900s. Russ J Econ 7(2):93–104

Liang F (1980) Statistics on China's historical population, cultivated land and land tax. Shanghai People's Publishing House, Shanghai. (梁方仲编著. 中国历代户口、田地、田赋统计. 上海:上海人民出版社, 1980.08)

Liashchenko PN (1956) История народного хозяйства СССР [The history of the national economy of the USSR]. 3 vols, fourth edn. Institute of Economics of the Academy of Sciences of the USSR, Moscow

Lucas RE (2000) Some macroeconomics for the 21st century. J Econ Persp 14(1):159–168. https://doi.org/10.1257/jep.14.1.159

Madsen J, Strulik H (2020) Technological change and inequality in the very long run. Eur Econ Rev 129(103):532

Malanima P (2002) L'economia italiana: dalla crescita medievale alla crescita contemporanea. il Mulino, Bologna

Malanima P (2003) Measuring the Italian economy 1300–1861. Rivista di Storia Economica:265–296

Malanima, P. (2004). Labour, productivity, wages in Italy 1270–1913. Accessed from https://iisg.nl/hpw/papers/malanima.pdf

Malanima P, Zamagni V (2010) 150 years of the Italian economy, 1861–2010. J Mod It Stud 15(1):1–20

Malinowski M, Van Zanden JL (2017) Income and its distribution in preindustrial Poland. Cliometrica 11(3):375–404. https://doi.org/10.1007/s11698-016-0154-5

Mankiw NG, Romer D, Weil DN (1992) A contribution to the empirics of economic growth. Q J Econ 107(2):407–437

Mau V, Drobyshevskaya T (2013) Modernization and the Russian economy: three hundred years of catching up. In: Alexeev M, Weber S (eds) The Oxford handbook of the Russian economy. Oxford University Press, pp 29–50

Milov LV (1998) Великорусский пахарь и особенности российского исторического процесса [Great Russian ploughman and features of the Russian historical process]. Российская политическая энциклопедия (РОССПЭН) [Russian Political Encyclopedia (ROSSPEN)], Moscow

Mironov BN (2018) Российская империя: от традиции к модерну. [The Russian Empire: From Tradition to Modernity], vol 1–3), second edn. Dmitrii Bulanin, St. Petersburg

Mokyr J (1994) Cardwell's law and the political economy of technological progress. Res Pol 23(5):561–574

Moon D (2001) The abolition of serfdom in Russia, 1762–1907. Longman, New York

Moorsteen R, Powell R (1966) The Soviet Capital Stock, 1928–1962. Richard D. Irwin, Inc, Homewood, IL

Musacchio A, Werker E (2016) Mapping frontier economies: where to play and how to win. Harv Bus Rev 94:40–48

Nadiri I (1970) International studies of factor inputs and total factor productivity: a brief survey. Rev Income Wealth 18:129–148

Natkhov T, Vasilenok N (2021) Skilled immigrants and technology adoption: evidence from the Germans settlements in the Russian empire. Explor Econ Hist 81(101):399

Nureev RM, Latov YV (2010) Россия и Европа: эффект колеи (опыт институционального анализа истории экономического развития) [Russia and Europe: Effect of the Path Dependence (A study in institutional analysis of the history of economic development)]. Immanuel Kant Russian State University Publishing House, Kaliningrad

Nureev RM, Latov YV (2016) Экономическая история России (опыт институционального анализа) [Economic history of Russia (Studies in institutional analysis)]. KNORUS, Moscow

O'Rourke K, Williamson J (2005) From Malthus to Ohlin: trade, industrialization and distribution since 1500. J Econ Growth 10(1):5–34

Ofer G (1987) Soviet economic growth: 1928–1985. J Econ Lit 25(4):1767–1833

Ostrovskii AV (2013) Зерновое производство Европейской России в конце XIX– начале XX в. [Grain Production in the European Russia in the late 19th—early 20th centuries]. Poltorak Ltd., St. Petersburg

Pamuk, Ş., & Shatzmiller, M. (2011). Real wages and GDP per capita estimates for medieval Near East, 700-1500. Paper presented at the European Historical Economics Society Conference, Dublin.

Pipes R (1995) Russia under the Old Regime, second edn. Penguin Books, London

Polterovich V (2005) Institutional traps: is there a way out? Social Sciences 36:30–40

Popov V (2013) Transformational recession. In: Alexeev M, Weber S (eds) The Oxford handbook of the Russian economy. Oxford University Press, pp 102–131

Popov V (2014) Mixed fortunes: an economic History of China, Russia, and the West. Oxford University Press, New York

Prados de la Escosura LP, Rosés JR (2021) Accounting for growth: Spain, 1850–2019. J Econ Surv 35(3):804–832

Rastyannikov VG, Deryugina IV (2009) Урожайность хлебов в России, 1795–2007 [Grain crop productivity in Russia, 1795–2007]. Институт востоковедения РАН [Institute of Oriental Studies of the Russian Academy of Sciences], Moscow
Rodrik D (2008) Second-best institutions. Am Econ Rev 98(2):100–104
Sachs J, Malaney P (2002) The economic and social burden of malaria. Nature 415(6872):680–685
Sachs JD, Warner AM (2001) The curse of natural resources. Eur Econ Rev 45(4–6):827–838
Scheidel, W. (2010). Real wages in early economies: Evidence for living standards from 1800 BCE to 1300 CE. Journal of the Economic and Social History of the Orient, 53, 425-462. Data downloaded from http://www.stanford.edu/~scheidel/NumKey.htm.
Schimmelpenninck van der Oye DH (2010) Russian orientalism: Asia in the Russian mind from Peter the Great to the emigration. Yale University Press, New Haven & London
Schmelzing, P. (2019). Eight centuries of global real interest rates, R-G, and the 'suprasecular' decline, 1311–2018. Available at SSRN: https://ssrn.com/abstract=3485734 or https://doi.org/10.2139/ssrn.3485734
Sickles R, Zelenyuk V (2019) Measurement of productivity and efficiency: theory and practice. Cambridge University Press, Cambridge
Turchin P, Nefedov S (2009) Secular cycles. Princeton University Press, Princeton, NJ
Van Beveren I (2012) Total factor productivity estimation: a practical review. J Econ Surv 26(1):98–128
Van Leeuwen B, Van Zanden JL (2019) China as a nation. In: Brakman S, van Marrewijk C, Morgan PJ, Salike N (eds) China in the local and global economy: history, geography, politics and sustainability (Regions and Cities). Routledge
Van Leeuwen B, Didenko D, Földvári P (2015) Inspiration vs. perspiration in economic development of the former Soviet Union and China (ca. 1920–2010). Econ Trans 23(1):213–246
Van Leeuwen B, Li J, Foldvari P (2017) Human capital in Republican and New China: regional and long-term trends. Econ Hist Dev Reg 32(1):1–36. https://doi.org/10.1080/20780389.2016.1261629
Van Zanden JL, Van Leeuwen B (2012) Persistent but not consistent: The growth of national income in Holland 1347–1807. Explor Econ Hist 49(2):119–130
van Leeuwen B, Calabrese M, Wang M (2024) Italy's total factor productivity in a global economy: Growth and spillover effects (c. 1400–2010). Ital Econ J 10(1):43–57. https://doi.org/10.1007/s40797-023-00221-x
Vasiliev LS (1982) Феномен власти-собственности [The phenomenon of power-property]. In: Alaev LB (ed) Типы общественных отношений на Востоке в Средние века [Types of social relations in the East in the Middle Ages]. Наука [The Science], Moscow, pp 60–99
Vasiliev LS (2011) Эволюция общества: типы общества и их трансформация [Evolutione of a society: Types of society and their transformation]. KDU, Moscow
Voskoboynikov IB (2021) Accounting for growth in the USSR and Russia, 1950–2012. J Econ Surv 35(3):870–894. https://doi.org/10.1111/joes.12426
Wittfogel KA (1957) Oriental despotism: a comparative study of total power. Yale University Press, New Haven

Chapter 6
The Spread of the Industrial Revolution, *c.* 1760–Present

Abstract After the switch to modern growth, three questions remain. The first is if and how innovation and growth could spread to the rest of Europe and Asia. This mainly draws attention to which factors deviate from the long-term norm that was set by England in the late nineteenth century and at the start of the twentieth century. Besides an initially low level of capital accumulation, it was mainly a strong government that could foster (or at times hinder) growth in Asia. This could occur, for example, by building railways (as regions with high market potential held the highest shares of secondary sector employment in Asia in around 1900). The second question is how already developed countries could develop further from the First Industrial Revolution to the electric, information, and communications technology, and artificial intelligence revolutions. This depended on whether countries were inventors or accumulators. The third question is why, when in the beginning the original division was between capital-saving technologies in China and labour-saving technologies in England, over time technology also became more labour saving in China. When technologies decrease in price or demand for capital-intensive goods in developing economies increases, developed countries outsource the production of less capital-intensive goods (from a developed country's perspective; but more capital intensive from a developing country's perspective), and therefore, the whole system benefits from the introduction of new technologies. This explains why countries such as Japan and China began with capital-saving technologies but over time moved to labour-saving technologies.

This paper partly depends on:
* Van Leeuwen, B., Philips, R.C.M. & Buyst, E. (eds) (2020). *An Economic History of Regional Industrialization*. (Routledge Explorations in Economic History). Oxford and New York: Routledge.
*Van Leeuwen, B., Wang, M. & Bosma, U. (2023). "'Industrial Revolutions' in a Globalizing World, 1760–Present." In: S. Labory and P Thomlinson (eds), ***Handbook of Industrial Development***, Cheltenham: Edward Elgar, pp. 18–36.

B. Van Leeuwen et al., *Innovation and Economic Development in Eurasia, 500 BCE-Present*, Frontiers in Economic History,
https://doi.org/10.1007/978-3-031-97043-6_6

6.1 The Beginning of Industrialization

As pointed out in earlier chapters, up to about 1750 in England (and 1911 in China), agricultural technology developed faster than manufacturing technology. In addition, whereas in England, it was labour saving, in China, it was predominantly capital saving. These differences in technology development follow from various factors that can be classified as Smithian when innovation emerges in the production factors or Northian when the focus shifts on institutions. The first entails commercialization of the economy through more active entrepreneurship, borrowing foreign technological innovations, or when based on changes in the division of labour. Within the second, one can distinguish between two approaches. These are the so-called idealist approach (e.g. North and Weingast 1989; Mokyr 2016; McCloskey 2010; Acemoglu and Robinson 2012),[1] in which the arrival of culture, ideology, or social norms opens up existing potential for technological change (Chap. 5), and the so-called incentive approach,[2] in which the focus is on the material or immaterial incentives (maximands) that are necessary for technological development.[3]

Both these factors affected the First Industrial Revolution (*c.* 1760–1840) in Great Britain, with the move away from agriculture and handicraft to factory output and heavy industry. With the exception of the Spinning Jenny and steam engine, though, there were few inventions in the eighteenth century. However, the first wave of industrialization further developed into the Second Industrial Revolution (*c.* 1860–1940), which focused on innovations based on the use of power, that is, steel, electricity, the car industry. In addition, it was this Second Industrial Revolution that spread like an oil slick around Europe, North America, and Japan, and eventually many more industrializing countries. As a consequence, the factors of growth should be considered both as a local trend and as an outcome of spillover effects, resulting from synchronized global business cycles. In the context of the Second Industrial Revolution, the increasing spread of the secondary sector in occupational shares across Europe, Central Asia, and East Asia illustrates this process (Figs. 6.1 and 6.2).

[1] Based on the "old" version of institutionalism by Thorstein Veblen and German historical school of economics by Max Weber and Werner Sombart (only partially inherited by Douglass North). In this culture, ideology, or social norms affect or define rules and set a system of constraints on human interactions connected with economic activities. These rules are not necessarily a product of rational choice and competitive selection. In recent literature the importance (including the causal effects) of these aspects of a path-dependent institutional environment for economic policymaking and for long-run economic development is stressed in Tabellini (2010) and Persson and Tabellini (2021).

[2] This line is based on the "new institutionalism" described by Ronald Coase and Douglass North, which is based on neoclassical methodology; in recent literature, this is strongly voiced by Daron Acemoglu and his coauthors (Acemoglu et al. 2005; Acemoglu and Robinson 2012). The broad concept of institutions encompasses internalized norms that affect how formal rules shape behaviour.

[3] This is a mix of rewards from innovations both for the individual and for society at large (Davids 2012, 184), human capital necessary to develop new technologies (e.g. Squicciarini and Voigtländer 2015), and rising living standards and consumption levels (e.g. De Vries 2008).

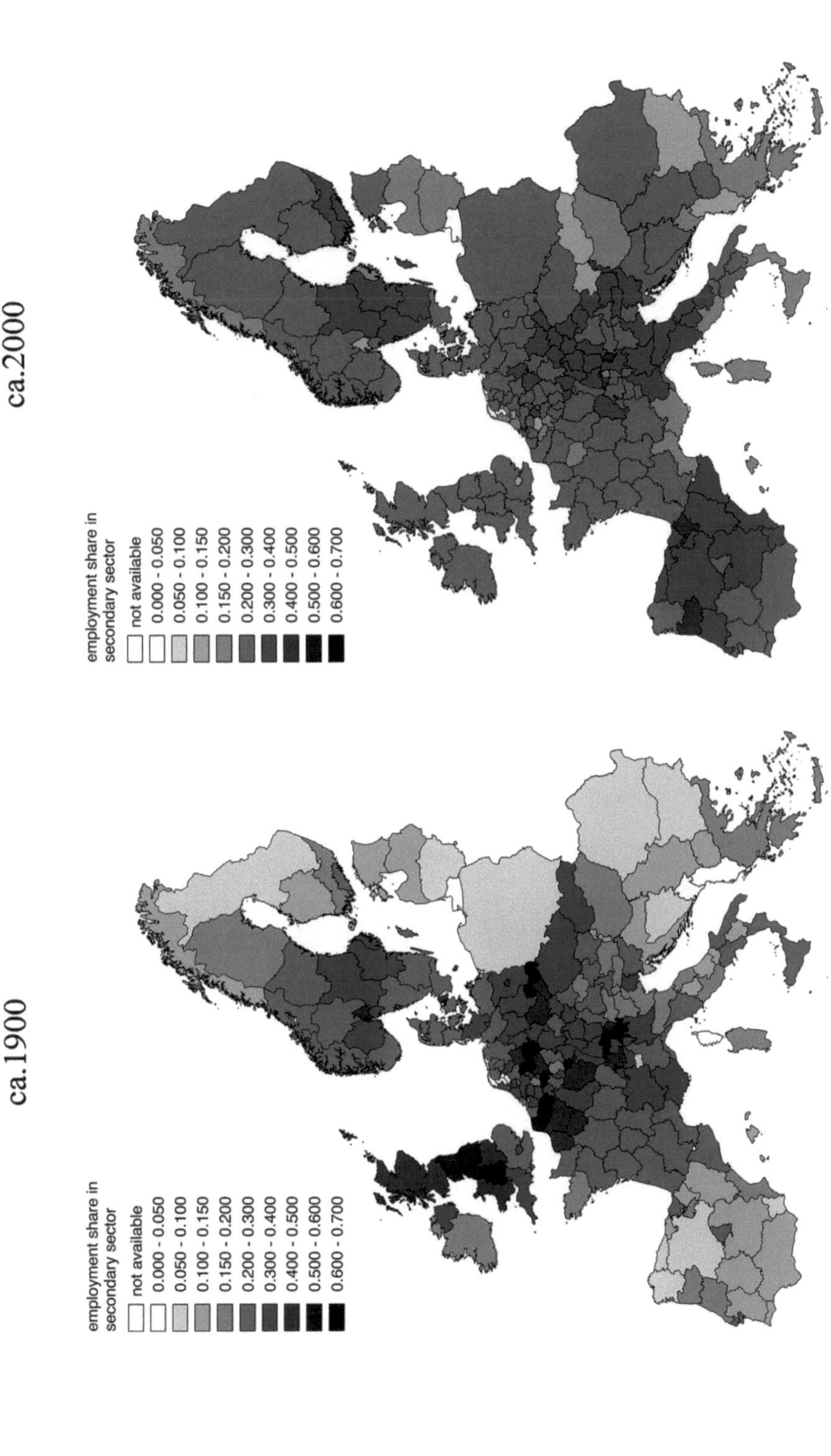

Fig. 6.1 The share of the secondary sector in the total labour force in Europe, 1900–2000. *Notes:* We define the secondary sector as all employment in the mining, manufacturing, and construction sectors. *Source:* Van Leeuwen et al. (2021)

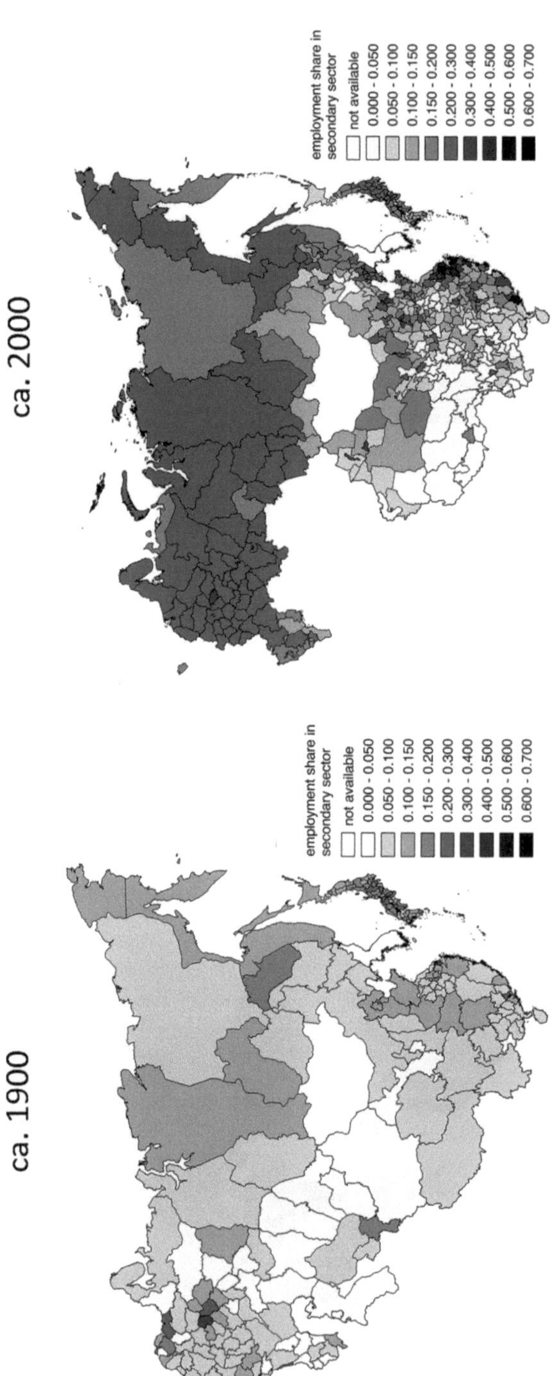

Fig. 6.2 The share of the secondary sector in the total labour force in Central Eurasia and East Asia, 1900–2000. *Notes:* We define the secondary sector as all employment in the mining, manufacturing, and construction sectors. *Source:* Van Leeuwen et al. (2021, 18–19)

We deal with the early phases of this spread in Sects. 6.2 and 6.3, while the mature phases are analysed in Sect. 6.4. We ultimately find that, for both nineteenth-century England, Europe, and mainly Asia, government intervention, though in different forms, was of primary importance. We end with a brief overview in Sect. 6.5.

6.2 From Cottage to Factory, *c*. 1760–1840

After the British First Industrial Revolution (1760–1840), new manufacturing technologies spread slowly from Britain to other parts of Europe. Yet the reception of these new technologies was highly uneven across countries and regions, something for which a wide range of explanations has been proposed.

First is the role of cottage industries, which had begun before the First Industrial Revolution. For example, as pointed out earlier, during the Chinese Song dynasty (960–1279), various industries such as silk were cottage-based owing to increased demand both from the court and from a rising population. This led to a rise in manufacturing (McDermott and Yoshinobu 2015), trade, and transport. The increased demand was mostly met by a growth in small-scale silk weaving during the Song dynasty, and later cotton-related industries and even paper-making. This typically occurred within farm households, who produced for the wider market (Bray 1994). This development was driven by a better transport network and increased income, in other words increased demand. This occurred more universally in England, where cottage and small-scale industries expanded owing to rising income and improved trade networks from the thirteenth century onwards (Van Leeuwen and Philips 2021).

Another reason for the rise, or decline, in cottage industries is the trade-off between the geopolitical goals of the state and the welfare of the elite and the whole population. This contradiction between geopolitics and welfare was particularly visible throughout Russia's path of (proto)-industrial growth over the last three centuries, and similar discussions are also relevant to China, where a modernization debate took place in the second half of the nineteenth century. For Russia, such policies can be traced back to the German economist Friedrich List, who in the 1840s advised medium-developed countries to prioritize national military growth over wealth and widespread prosperity (Ellman 2023a, b).[4]

Arguably, the best examples of an economic decrease in cottage industries in Great Britain relate to non-ferrous metals and textiles. As regards the first sector, it was usually part-time or seasonal miners/farmers in England (Burt 1991), China

[4] This is consistent with Kontorovich and Wein (2009) and Kontorovich (2015), who argued that during the Soviet period, especially during the forced industrialization drive in the 1930s–1950s, the maximand of economic policies was not material output in itself but rather actual and potential military might. The latter was the driving force that ran the economy. Much of the capacity installed was dual purpose: it produced civilian products in peacetime but could be quickly shifted to military production. Therefore, Russian industrialization could be defined as a kind of military modernization (Ellman 2023b).

(Wang and Van Leeuwen 2021), and Russia who worked in this industry. Whereas in England in the nineteenth century, bigger factories and mining operations existed, in China the old techniques and labour organization still dominated, while Russia was somewhere in between.

The origins of many of the largest industrial firms in Russia that played an important role in the industrial revolution of the late Tsarist period (1880s–1917) can be traced to 1820–1860. During this period, under serfdom, pre-industrial entrepreneurship in Russia grew primarily in rural rather than urban locations owing to the relatively lower costs in the former. It developed as a complement to, not a substitute for, agriculture, which remained the basic source of subsistence.

Why did cottage industries decline less in China and Russia than in Europe? There is a wide literature on improved trade and transport in Europe and Russia (e.g. Gatrell 1986, 145–157), while the evidence for late nineteenth-century China is far less favourable (Kingsmill 1898). In general, this was due to improved knowledge transfer in early modern Europe (Belfanti and Giusberti 2000). A second reason was the generally weak markets in eighteenth-century China and Russia. Indeed, given the weakness of markets, it was pre-industrial modernization under Peter I (1682–1725) that created conditions in Russia that facilitated the subsequent growth of markets in the eighteenth and nineteenth centuries. The result was a competitive metallurgy sector supported with strong demand from the government and large exports to Western Europe in the eighteenth century. However, this market was lost over the nineteenth century owing to technological stagnation in Russia (Crisp 1976, 25; Gatrell 1986, 145–146), while the state directly and indirectly provided a market, capital, and a labour force for the mining, metallurgical, armaments, and textile industries.

Hence, while cottage industries in England declined substantially in the nineteenth century, they still flourished in Russia prior to the Revolution of 1917. In China, the share of cottage industries in Jiangsu remained as high as 52.1% (versus 15.7% in handicraft and 32.2% in modern factories) in 1933 (Xu and Van Leeuwen 2025). But at the start of the twentieth century, China developed a more modern road network and more modern techniques in mining, thus aligning its path with that of nineteenth-century England (Fig. 6.3).

The second sector showing divergence from, and later convergence with, England (*c.* 1850–present) concerns textiles.[5] In 1851, 46% of the world production of spindles was concentrated in the Lancashire textile cluster, despite this region only being 0.002% of the world's total area (Crafts and Wolf 2014). Besides the study of

[5] A third important sector was coal. In particular, Allen's hypothesis (2011, 364) has gained popularity. This argues that Britain was the first country to experience an industrial revolution owing to a favourable ratio between high wages and low coal prices. Whereas the importance of low coal prices has been largely agreed upon in the literature (e.g. Pomeranz 2000; Wrigley 2010; Fernihough and O'Rourke 2014), the importance of high wages has been more debatable. Whereas Broadberry and Gupta (2009) and Allen (2019), for example, argue for its importance, others have doubted its relevance for the Industrial Revolution or even its very existence (e.g. Humphries and Weisdorf 2015; Stephenson 2018; Humphries and Schneider 2019).

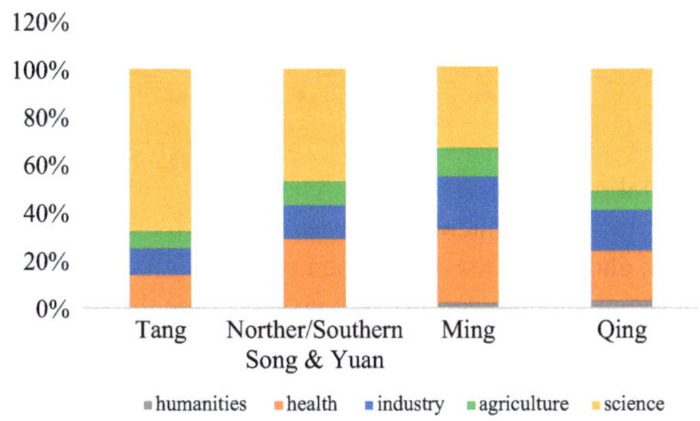

Fig. 6.3 The share of inventors by topic and time in China in the Tang to Qing dynasties. *Source:* Du (1992)

Crafts and Wolf (2014), which shows that advantages such as access to water power and coal help to explain its prominence (see also Crafts and Mulatu 2005; Fernihough and O'Rourke 2014), low wages are often argued to have encouraged industrial growth in the Midlands and North of England (e.g. Mokyr 1976; Pollard 1978; Hunt 1986). This focus on low wages is confirmed by Kelly et al. (2015), who add a large population and a productive agricultural sector to the region's advantages. There are various ways in which these initial regional advantages turned into agglomeration benefits: cheaper products owing to advantageous factor endowments (Leunig 2003), increasing returns on scale (e.g. Crafts and Wolf 2014), and lower transport costs (Bogart 2014). This occurred, for example, in Wigan, located close to Manchester, where the shift from non-ferrous metal manufacturing after about 1740 to cotton, led initially to a decline in small workshops in favour of cottage industries (Langton 1979), which were attracted by the low wages. Yet between about 1750–1850, regional advantages meant the cotton was concentrated in more modern and larger factories. This is in effect also true for India, China, and Japan, for which Clark (1987) shows that rather than factors of production and technology, it was local labour efficiency that was the main driver of growth. But no matter what factors are advocated, all studies agree that they are ultimately related to increasing technology and productivity levels (e.g. Nuvolari et al. 2011).

The second sector to provide a clear picture of cottage industries is textiles. In Russia, this was among the industries that experienced rapid growth when they were focused on the mass consumer market, even under serfdom. Alongside beet sugar, it was the manufacture of cotton cloth that predominantly used hired labour (Blackwell 1968, 39–43). By 1860, Russia ranked sixth in the world in the spinning of cotton. However, this rapid growth, as well as in some other areas of textile manufacture, was not repeated in the heavy industries, which remained either stagnant or undeveloped (Blackwell 1968, 407–409).

However, an important factor for Russia's industrial development was that since the early eighteenth century, the development of technology had become a comprehensive state policy, not only in the military, transport, mining, and manufacturing sectors, but also in the fields of education and basic scientific research (Blackwell 1968, 28–31). Even though this policy was not subsequently maintained systematically, the seeds of technological development had been sown, thus allowing for waves of technological catching up.

6.3 Factors of Production, *c.* 1760–1840

Besides the switch from cottage to factory labour, some studies stress the importance of differences in the efficiency of factor endowments when explaining the spatial pattern of the early spread of industrialization. First, Wrigley (2010) argues that on the continent, coal was relatively expensive compared with firewood and peat, and that it was only when steam engines became more efficient in the middle of the nineteenth century that coal become the more efficient choice of fuel.

Second, in this book (Chap. 4), we argue that in Western countries, the mode of labour productivity (commodified labour) increased in East and Central Asia between about 1700 and 1900. Since this improved total factor productivity (TFP) growth implies increased long-run growth, this resulted in technological advance in the First and Second Industrial Revolutions.

Third, some studies argue that British growth during the First Industrial Revolution was invention-based, while the Second Industrial Revolution in Western Europe was innovation-based (Amsden 1989). This distinction is very important since, in innovation-based development, open knowledge leading to practical innovation becomes crucial (Mokyr 2016).

Fourth, Allen (2009) argues that a high wage economy combined with low capital costs contributed to Britain's uniqueness; that is, expensive fuel and lower wages contributed to the slower growth of industries on the continent. We have to stress, though, that this point is questioned by various other scholars.

A fifth argument might be that inventions became increasingly capital intensive in developed countries. So, in less developed countries, lower capital-intensive (but still more capital intensive than previously) technologies were introduced, which were no longer suited for more capital-intensive developed countries. Hence, over time, as technologies decrease in price, the demand for these technologies increases because developed countries outsource the production of less capital-intensive goods, and other countries can gain from introducing new, and in their context labour-saving, technologies. This process of increasing capital intensification of technologies began in China after the agricultural revolution, that is, after 1911.

6.4 Institutions, *c.* 1860–Present

The previously mentioned factors caused a spread of industrialization mainly in other parts of Europe and Russia, as well as in Japan. Industrialization developed towards the Second Industrial Revolution, consistently based on the same characteristics for commodified labour and innovation instead of invention. This varied little among countries.

However, one important factor is that differences between countries still existed in terms of policy and institutions (as also seen in Chap. 5). Whereas this, in certain regions, started in the eighteenth century (Sect. 6.2), it really took off during the

Second Industrial Revolution in the late nineteenth century.[6] For example, Gerschenkron (1962) famously argues that countries away from the British industrial frontier used various measures to compensate for the lack of the previously mentioned fundamentals for growth—that is, the more "backward" a country was, the greater the emphasis on producers and capital goods and the stronger were government interventions necessary to catch up with the technological forerunner. This conception applied to Germany, Austro-Hungary, and the Russian Empire of the late nineteenth to the early twentieth centuries (Sect. 6.4). A similar point is made for Japan (Kasza 2018) at the start of the twentieth century and Soviet Russia (Allen 2003).

This catching-up implied not just more investment, but also better-quality investment. Indeed, Cheremukhin et al. (2017) argued that in the late nineteenth and early twentieth centuries, Russian industrialization and development were slowed by the lack of a competition policy. The evidence reported by Soviet-era historians suggests that the government explicitly allowed stocks of several companies engaged in the same industry to be owned by the same body,[7] and was perfectly aware that this resulted in the growth of monopolies.[8]

One of the strongest entry barriers was the concession system of incorporation: The establishment of every public joint stock company required the personal signature of the tsar or his finance minister. This resulted in much slower growth of the corporate sector, so that Russia substantially lagged behind Germany and England (Shepelev 1973, 232).

In Russia, a debate about the nineteenth century's "heavy push" has emerged in the literature. This development path began in the mid-nineteenth century. Indeed, Ellman (2023a) suggested that a policy of industrialization resulted from the need to catch up with the military powers of North-West Europe as a consequence of Russia's defeat by Great Britain and France in the Crimean War (1853–1856). This increased after 1871 when the newly created German Empire was rapidly industrializing. In much the same way, there was a modernization debate in China. However, the battle between Westernization and modernization often led to modernization in military sectors only. Similarly, for Russia, government policy in the economic sphere was rarely monolithic or consistent, not only because government did not

---

[6] Some scholars have dated the initial onset of Russia's modern industrialization to the 1840s or the Stalinist surge of the 1930s. It should be recognized, though, that in the second quarter of the nineteenth century substantive signs of modern industrial development can be observed. However, the consensus view tends to date this process to the 1880s–1890s (Markevich and Nafziger 2017, 35–37).

[7] E.g. Shepelev (1973, 233, 283–284).

[8] Aside from relatively scarce managerial skills (Crisp 1976), a key reason for the high cost of setting up a modern factory in Russia was the system of protectionism. Selectively imposed tariffs were generally a response to lobbying by relatively inefficient domestic producers (McCaffray 1996). Tariff revenues as a share of import value were 13% in 1869–1876 and then increased to 28% in 1885–1890 and further to 33% in the 1890s (Falkus 1972, 57). Such state policies not only allowed domestic producers to gain market share and increase output, but also resulted in higher retail prices for them and, therefore, stagnating real wages (Allen 2003).

speak with one voice, but also because military, political, and general financial interests took precedence over macro-economic aims (Crisp 1976, 54). Thus, during the first half of the nineteenth century, the state policy aimed at developing the industrial sector was fragmentary and experimental (Blackwell 1968, 407). Waves of economic liberalism in the 1860s–1870s were replaced by protectionist measures since the 1880s (Crisp 1976, 22–23).

Contrary to China, it was only when the Russian state stepped in during the 1890s to substitute for missing aggregate demand and to provide tariff and credit support that these "conditions of backwardness" began to disappear and industrial growth took off. Following Von Laue (1963), Markevich and Nafziger (2017) have interpreted these interventions as constituting a coherent set of industrial policies, as formulated by Sergei Witte.[9] It was a combination of various policies that were pursued with great intensity over a relatively long time. This entailed a considerable amount of government expenditure, which interacted with market forces to contribute to an industrial take-off, even though it was primarily created for the military. Indeed, militarized Listian industrialization policies, implemented by Witte in the 1890s,[10] mainly took the form of railway construction, high import tariffs (which both protected domestic industry and generated income for the state), and adoption of the gold standard, which encouraged foreign direct investment in Russia (Ellman 2023a, 6). These policies proved by and largely successful, because by the 1890s Russia already had a fair-sized market, a secure monetary system and financial institutions, a skeleton of transport and educational facilities, and a pattern of commercial and financial relations abroad (Crisp 1976, 218). But even then, when choices about the use of resources were involved, in most cases short-run fiscal interests seemed to prevail (Kahan 1989, 104).

Stressing the succession line of the old Tsarist and the new Soviet economic patterns, Cheremukhin et al. (2017) recognized that the level of institutional barriers to the inter-sectoral mobility of production factors significantly decreased in the 1930s, while the economy merely followed pre-revolutionary growth trends.

Kasza (2018) and Allen (2003) assessed the achievements of the Soviet period as relatively high, with the implementation of the "big push" (Rosenstein-Rodan 1943), "take-off" (Rostow 1960), and "great spurt" (Gerschenkron 1962) models. Yet Allen (2003) recognized that later in the 1970s the USSR authorities chose inadequate development strategies of the economy which brought its structure closer to those of "Third World" countries (see also Chap. 7). The views of Allen (2003) have not become consensus, but that work stimulated a new round of discussions in the literature on the Soviet development path.

---

[9] The Minister of Finance 1892–1903 and prime minister 1905–1906 (https://en.wikipedia.org/wiki/Sergei_Witte)

[10] He composed an essay on the ideas by F. List (Witte 1889) in his capacity as a deputy Minister of Finance..

6.5 Government, *c*. 1860–Present

The studies that followed Gerschenkron (1962) and Amsden (1989) have argued that later industrializers such as those in Asia differed in the first phase of their industrialization from early industrializers such as Europe in two ways.

First, from a Gerschenkron (1962) point of view, one would expect that later industrializers in Asia relied more upon capital and energy-intensive production than their European counterparts (see e.g. Allen 2003; Földvári et al. 2015). This view was contradicted by, for example, Sugihara (2003), who argued that Japan—and, more generally, many East Asian countries—followed, as we argue in earlier chapters, a more labour-intensive or "industrious" path of industrialization in which population growth and small increases in standards of living accommodated the adoption of labour-intensive technologies. Both views are nuanced by Vries (2019), who argued that, even though Japan during 1868–1937 was indeed characterized by low productivity levels and low wages, nevertheless labour intensity was not a sufficient condition to spur levels of modern economic growth. Rather, as pointed out earlier, increasing labour intensity may also cause rising wages while capital-using technologies may become cheaper over time, thus slowly replacing capital-saving with labour-saving technologies.

Second, we should agree that the government took a more active role in the industrialization process, in particular by supplying capital and promoting entrepreneurship. For instance, Macpherson (1995) and Vries (2019) argue that for Japan to take off in industrial terms, the state was responsible for creating the necessary physical and institutional infrastructure for modern industry, and was the most important contributor to human and physical capital formation. Likewise, whereas the nineteenth-century Chinese state is considered non-interventionist (Vries 2015), it is argued that growth in the second half of the twentieth century was largely state driven.

Nonetheless, the form government intervention took was very different in Japan than it was in China and the USSR. In Japan, government policy was mostly indirect, companies consulting with the government. In this way, the allocation of resources shifted among sectors based on long-run government development plans. On the contrary, in the USSR (from the 1920s) and China (from the 1950s), policies were directly targeted at increasing physical capital accumulation; they also led initially to high growth rates (Földvári et al. 2015; see also Chap. 7).

It is clear, therefore, that government intervention did play a role in both developed and less developed countries in the First and Second Industrial Revolutions. Indeed, government intervention in industrialization has been a widely discussed topic and still is today, with three important lines of argument continuing for the past century. First, in past economies, it was argued that the government should, above all, provide a safe place for innovation (see also e.g. Chap. 2). Second, the government was to be involved in actively encouraging industries (e.g. Chap. 7). Third, some scholars argue against the importance of government in catching up.

This controversy re-emerged in the Washington Consensus (Williamson 1989),[11] a set of prescriptions that largely entailed free markets and liberalization. This implies that any failed industrialization was due either to failed government policy or to failed markets. When this argument, which is to some extent Eurocentric, became unpopular in less developed countries, scholars began to increasingly stress that policy must be local and specific in order to be effective (e.g. Rodrik 2005), that capital-rich and militarily powerful countries had a considerable advantage (Beckert 2014), that there was a move away from the consensus towards pro-active government policies from about 1950 to 1970 (Cimoli et al. 2009), or that the West blocked the "sprouts of capitalism" that occurred in China in the nineteenth century. This development towards an increase in government, with the effect that market behaviour declined, may be noticed from 1900 onwards in the commodified labour mode of production, linked to the decline in modernization theory, which argued that more trade and investment led to increasing growth (Sect. 2.1).

These debates indicate that there is quite some disagreement, especially today, about whether government policy can be used by economically lagging countries to catch up. This disagreement can be traced back to both Gerschenkron (1962) and Amsden (1989, 2001). Gerschenkron (1962) argues that the more backward a lagging country, the more rapid its industrial development, the more capital-intensive technology is able to advance its industry (excluding light industries such as textiles), and the more ideology plays a role. Practically, this implies that in moderately backward countries, such as Germany, oligopolistic banks played an important role in industrialization while in strongly lagging countries, such as Russia or China, a strong role for the government existed in stimulating heavy industry (Kasza 2018). This means that light industries such as textiles, which played an important role in Britain, were of less importance for developing economies even though they would have had an advantage because they possessed much cheap labour and thus could function as a force towards economic equalization. Yet the focus of strongly lagging countries was on heavy, capital-intensive, industries, for which capital could only be generated by a small group of people using government mechanisms. This transition sketched by Gerschenkron is temporary, as it implies that when the share of workers in industry becomes larger, private entrepreneurship, as a basis for a civil society, takes over again.

A second disagreement about the role of government in industrialization follows from Amsden (1989, 2001). Amsden modifies the Gerschenkronian vision that capital accumulation in heavy industry is driven by the government until the catch-up is complete and (civil) institutions can take over capital accumulation from the state. Contrary to Gerschenkron, she argues that light industries could cause industrial development. Yet, because of light industries' large productivity gap with developed countries, even with low wages, it became difficult to compete with these latter economies. Likewise, with economic development, later developers received higher wages than poorer and lesser developed countries, thus leaving them their mid-tech

[11] This term was coined by Williamson (1989).

industries to nurse and protect until they caught up with developed countries (see e.g. Kasza 2018). This also implies that, contrary to Gerschenkron, such a policy could also be applied to countries that had finished their industrial revolution. Even more so, there is no evidence that post-industrial revolution countries could or could not apply the same policy. Hence, industrializing, industrialized, and follower countries might all potentially have the same policy.

It is thus clear that in the nineteenth century, high tech industries offered the best chance of catching up, while in the late twentieth century, mid-tech industries offered this possibility. However, as argued by Kasza (2018, 151), these "were the same industries – iron, steel, the metal-bending industries. But in the period Gerschenkron studied, these were high tech, whereas in the period Amsden studied, they had become mid-tech."

6.6 Transport, *c.* 1860–Present

In the Industrial Revolution, which overcame Malthusian limitations and heralded the era of modern economic growth, the transport revolution appeared to be a key element. Rapidly developing transport links were the material basis not only for global commodity circulation, but also for the population's geographical mobility.

As mentioned earlier, production factors, together with institutions and consequently the role of government, could potentially drive growth. Yet not all of these factors could be used by later developers.[12] Among studies that explain divergent growth, studies, the California School famously argues that Britain and Holland were able to overtake the Yangzi Delta in China as the wealthiest region in the world owing to colonial expansion and more accessible coal reserves (Pomeranz 2000). Since then, there have been other influential explanations, such as institutions (e.g. Acemoglu and Robinson 2012), a higher European receptiveness to technology (e.g. Mokyr 2016), and a favourable factor price combination (Allen 2011).

In addition to these factors, Fig. 6.2 (especially in comparison with the travel times represented in Fig. 4.20) reveals that it was mostly regions with high market potential (i.e. high levels of transport and high income) that held the highest shares of secondary sector employment in Asia in around 1900. From this perspective, similar to the European case, changes in transport networks and the spatial distribution of economic activity explain to a large extent the location of industry (e.g. Kingsmill 1898; Bogart 2010; Bogart and Chaudhary 2013). In particular, the port cities of Tokyo and Osaka in Japan (Bassino et al. 2020) and those of Hong Kong, Guangzhou, Shanghai, and Beijing in China (Xu et al. 2020; Zhang et al. 2020) saw notable industrial clusters arise in around 1900 owing to the benefits of having a

[12] The question of why the Industrial Revolution occurred in North-West Europe rather than in Asia sprang up in the late 1990s, in the wake of the so-called Great Divergence debate, which revolved around the question about to what degree (parts of) China remained economically on a par with Western Europe until the nineteenth century (e.g. Frank 1998).

large population, thus ensuring a domestic market, and traditional access to foreign markets. In landlocked Russia, large cities such as Moscow and St. Petersburg with extensive transport networks had notable industries, next to smaller regions with more traditional industries on its periphery, such as in parts of Ukraine and Uzbekistan.

The first improved mode of transport was the rail network. In timescale terms, Russia was not too far behind the pioneers in the railway business: its first railways were laid only 12 years later than in Great Britain (1837 versus 1825). However, they started to form some sort of a network only in the 1860s–1870s. In Russia, as in the US, railway building had an impact on urban population growth and land prices (Leonard et al. 2021).

The situation was very different in China where, even though the first railway line was built in 1865 as a showcase project that accessed the imperial court, the court found it too alien and had it dismantled. Something similar occurred in 1876 when the first commercial railroad was set up in Shanghai (the Woosung Road), only to be dismantled in 1877 (Fig. 6.4). The defeat of China in the First Sino-Japanese War (1894–1895) changed this situation, partly because the government recognized the importance of railways and also because Western countries started to build railways in their spheres of influence. This led to a Chinese railway network of about 9000 km in 1911 and about 12,000 km in 1948.

Contrary to China before 1895, railway construction in Russia appeared to be one of the key forms of militarized Listian industrialization policy, implemented by

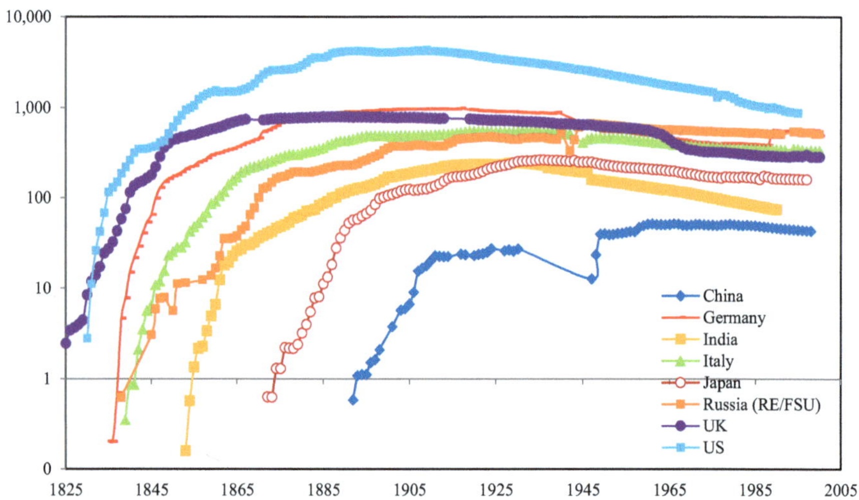

Fig. 6.4 Railway transport development in selected countries, 1825–2000s (kilometres per 1000 population). *Note:* RE—Russian Empire (prior to 1917); FSU—the countries of the former Soviet Union in actual borders (1917–2002). *Source:* Comin and Hobijn (2009) for route lengths of line open at the end of the year, Maddison Project Database (Maddison Project Database 2020) for population

S. Witte in the 1890s–early 1900s (Sect. 6.4).[13] Much of this construction, which received considerable direct financial support from the government, was implemented to allow troop movements, in case of war mobilization, rather than the economic role of freight and passenger services.

Significantly lagging behind the US, the most developed economy in terms of railway network per capita, Russia had almost caught up with the UK and Germany by the early twentieth century (Fig. 6.4).[14] This is not surprising, given Russia's vast and modestly populated areas that required rapid connections; there was not only an economic rationale but also a military one and that of a social control over the society. Even now (2024), almost half of the Russian Federation railway lines were constructed under the Russian Empire. Railroad construction continued during the Soviet period, although at a slower pace. After the Second World War, the USSR surpassed the Western economies in terms of railway lines per capita. The Russian Federation appears to be even more developed in these terms, with the shrinkage from the borders of the USSR explaining the hike since the early 1990s (Fig. 6.4). Furthermore, in the late nineteenth century the advanced economies reached a high level of railway provision, sufficient to stabilize and diffuse another transportation system, namely, aviation.

Densely populated China and India did not reach the level of railway provision typical of the advanced economies, as Russia and Japan did. In the second half of the twentieth century, they joined the general trend to stabilization or a slow decrease in the level of railroad provision. Before 1950, the majority of railways were in northern and north-east China; however, they gradually became an alternative to waterborne transportation. For instance, the Tianjin–Pukou Railway, finished in 1912, was almost parallel to the Grand Canal, so increasingly more cargo was transported via the railway instead of the canal owing to the lower costs and shorter journey times. In 1912–1927, around 4000 km of railways were built, and the total length of railways was about 13,300 km at the end of 1927. In 1932, it increased to 15,232 km. Before the foundation of New China in 1949, there were around 22,600 km of railways in use, and the railway system gradually became the main means of transporting goods and passengers. Freight volume and passengers increased from 55.89 million tons and 102.79 million persons in 1949 to 132.7 tons and 163.52 million persons in 1952.

Guangxiang (2016) also views the development of railways in Russia as an alternative to waterborne transportation (rivers and canals). It was the synergy of steamships and rail traffic that played a key role. Massive railway construction, combined with the development of steamships, contributed a lot to industrialization in Russia. A combination of railway and waterborne transportation managed effectively the problem of a logistics network deficit by intensifying the turnover of commodities,

[13] After graduating from the Imperial Novorossiysk University in Odessa, he worked as a railway specialist and manager for almost 20 years before he was appointed as responsible for the operation of the entire Russian railroad network in 1889 (https://en.wikipedia.org/wiki/Sergei_Witte)

[14] These kinds of statistical data are most reliable (compared with freight carried and number of passengers), and appear most shortly after the lines are constructed and put into operation.

facilitating the development of heavy industry (metallurgy, machinery manufacturing, mining, oil-producing industry, etc.) and innovation, promoting the development of transportation infrastructure in the cities, and by accelerating the process of an industrial revolution in general.

Indeed, in the first half of the nineteenth century, the basis of the transport system of Russia was waterways. This was determined primarily by the abundance of rivers and the cheapness of transporting freight by boat. Waterways generally met the needs of the pre-industrial economy. In the second half of the nineteenth century, the process of industrialization began in Russia, and the shortcomings of the waterways system (in particular, those associated with seasonality), which constrained the further development of industry, trade, and agriculture, were soon revealed, so railways began to play an increasingly prominent role. In the second half of the nineteenth century, the railway became the main means of transporting goods in Russia (Guangxiang 2016).

Schenk (2014) points out that globally railways were not merely a means of social mobility or economic progress but were also part of the military infrastructure and political control. Primarily through military and political arguments, the Austrian engineer and businessman Anton von Gerstner convinced Emperor Nicholas I to issue him a concession for the construction of the St. Petersburg–Tsarskoe Selo railway, which became the first in Russia (in 1837). By building railways, the Russian elite in the capital gained additional control over the vast imperial territories.

From the 1860s to the early 1890s, the construction of railways became a priority of Russian national policy, for which foreign capital was actively attracted, and as a result, it was very successful, with a whole network of railways being created in European Russia. However, there were major problems. First, private funds accounted for just a small portion of railway construction, and most of them were government-guaranteed loans that were given to companies. Taking advantage of this, some capitalists artificially inflated construction costs. By using public funds to obtain private profits, they placed a heavy burden on the Russian national budget, and this was one of the main reasons for the growth in external debt and the budget deficit (Guangxiang 2016). The system of railway concessions that took shape in Russia, with a state guarantee of return on invested capital, made it possible to attract significant volumes of private, including foreign, investment in the railways. However, abuse of the system often encouraged the construction of uneconomic routes and overvaluation of their estimated cost (Macheret et al. 2018).

During the reign of Alexander III (1881–1894), the government became disillusioned with private railway companies, and it was decided to nationalize the railways; all new lines had to be built at public expense. The government adopted a plan to buy out five railways in the south-west of the country, and subsequently the region's entire railway network was nationalized. This significantly expanded the possibilities of state regulation in the railway sector. Nationwide tariff-setting between 1887 and 1893 stimulated railway links with Siberia and the Far East. After 1894, the tariffs in Russia were among the lowest in the world. These were an important part of the policy that facilitated the movement of people and commodities (Guangxiang 2016). Low freight charges fluctuated within a narrow range both in Tsarist market and Soviet planned (command) economies during most of the period of Russian railway development (Golts 2004, 127–128).

Konchakov and Karpenko (2018, 2020) found that railways influenced urban growth. The degree of influence was higher immediately after the opening of the station and in several following decades. The influence of railways manifested itself in different ways depending on the administrative status of the city or town, leading to the most noticeable population growth in small towns (at county level). How stable the effects of a station were depended on a combination of related factors: Economic and geographical position, commercial and industrial role of the city, distance to capital city, and so on. The network topology that had developed by the second half of the nineteenth century simplified population migration to large cities, while small towns became an intermediate link between moving from a village to a larger centre.[15]

So far, we have found that the type of industry (Sect. 6.7) as well as production factor (Sect. 6.2.2) may have affected TFP growth in both Russia and China, even though production factors were mainly important before 1950. This may, however, affect certain economic sectors or, depending on labour productivity, even individual factories. Van Leeuwen et al. (2021, 255–256) tested how, besides other factors, transport affected the clustering of individual factories in the Netherlands and Hunan province (China) in about 1950–2005. Co-location of factories was overall low in the Netherlands in the second half of the twentieth century. This varied by sector: it was low in baking but high in carpets and rugs both in 1954 and 2004. More heavy industry sectors such as casting of iron and steel were heavily co-located at the start of the twentieth century in the Netherlands and dispersed in the late twentieth century. This factory co-location pattern of continued dispersion in the twentieth century for light industry, and a move from co-location to dispersion for heavy industries was similar to what happened in Hunan province.

This dispersion of heavy industry, even though partly caused by increased availability of production factors such as capital and education in both the Netherlands and Hunan, was mainly caused by a shift from water and rail transport to road transport, thus removing the necessity to cluster. Yet this observed shift in transport method in Hunan, even though contributing to industrial spread, had less of an effect since, first, high indirect transport costs and a limited number of roads made road transport less efficient, and, second, the factories in China were relatively small, making clustering more attractive. This changed in the 1950s and 1960s

[15] Leonard et al. (2021) found that the introduction of the railway can be viewed as a technological shock to the land market. As in any economic system in which market forces prevail, Russia in the late imperial era followed this trend, and a technological shock led to increased land prices (Sect. 3.4). The movements in the price of land varied in response to the extent of new railway lines in affected regions. They show the positive association between the length of the railway by region with both land prices and the land price growth rate, supporting the hypothesis that access to a railway inflated the price for tangible capital such as arable land.

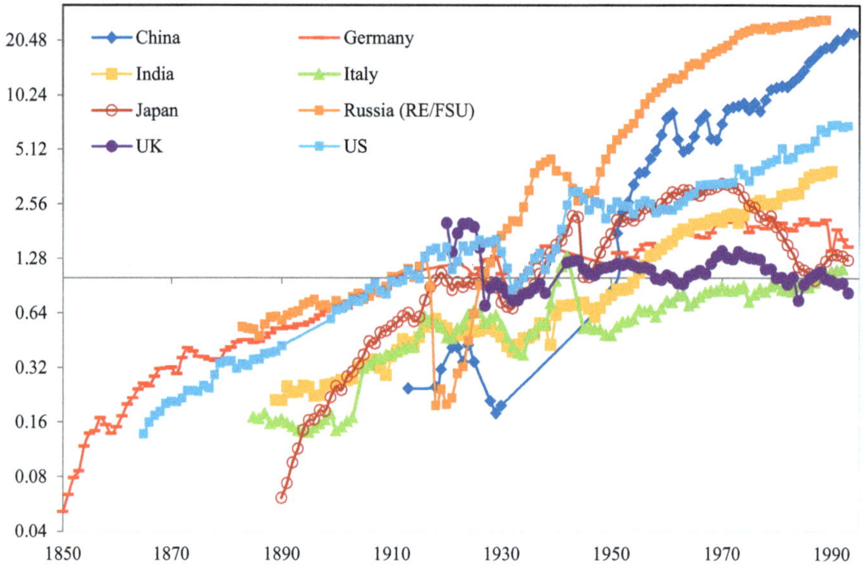

Fig. 6.5 Intensity of freight traffic on railways for selected countries (1000 million ton-kilometres/kilometres of rail length). *Note:* RE—Russian Empire (prior to 1917); FSU—the countries of the former Soviet Union in actual borders (1917–2002). *Source:* Comin and Hobijn (2009); Strumilin (1958, 640–641) for European Russia in 1883–1896

(Fig. 6.5), when railway transport rose sharply in both Russia and China while it stagnated in most Western countries.

In Russia, the average cost per kilometre was lower, as Russian railways operated rather intensively in technical terms (Figs. 6.5 and 6.6). The two relative indicators capturing both cargo (freight and passengers) and traffic distance, in relation to the existing railway length, show that Russia was basically on par with the developed economies. Moreover, as regards freight traffic, Russian railways in the Imperial period (nineteenth to early-twentieth centuries) were used as intensively as in Germany and the US, and in the Soviet period most intensively among the peer countries. The intensiveness (capacity utilization) of railway transport increased over time, most significantly in the 1930s, during the forced industrialization drive. Deceleration was associated with a slowdown in economic growth from the mid-1970s. Strong downturns occurred during the wars, the most significant of these being during the Civil War (1918–1922).

So, in the late twentieth century, the railway efficiency of both Russia and China kept growing both in terms of goods and passenger transport, yet Western Europe stagnated. However, Japan was the country in which railways were used most intensively for passenger traffic. This was also rather intensive in the two major Asian countries, China and India. China surpassed Russia and India in passenger traffic intensity when market reforms began in the 1980s. As regards freight traffic, China secured the second place after Russia from the 1950s. The US performed well as regards freight traffic although poorly as regards passengers. Development of

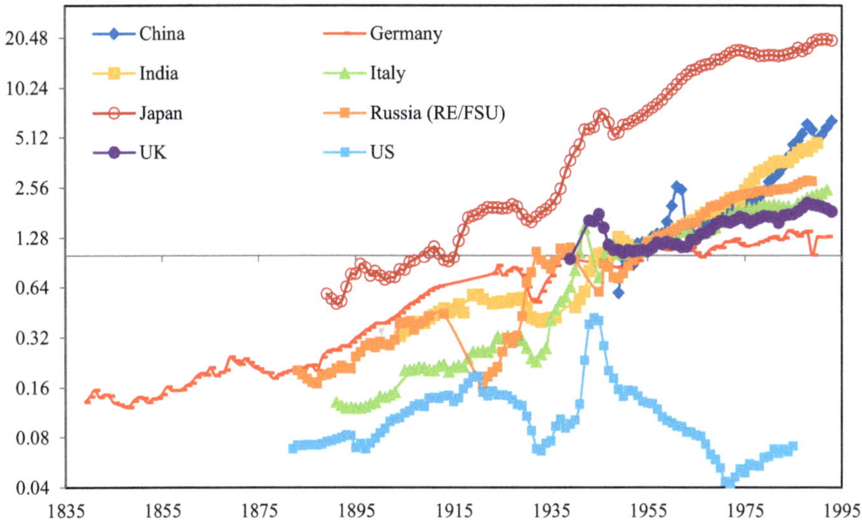

Fig. 6.6 Intensity of passenger traffic on railways (millions of passenger-kilometres/kilometres of rail length). *Note:* RE—Russian Empire (prior to 1917); FSU—the countries of the former Soviet Union in actual borders (1917–2002). *Source:* Comin and Hobijn (2009); Strumilin (1958, 640–641) for European Russia in 1883–1896

commercial aviation could partially explain this pattern. However, for all of the countries with large territories (China, India, Russia/USSR, and the US), we observe a relative shift towards more intensive use of railways for freight traffic than for passengers. This means a higher contribution to trade penetration.

This contribution appeared in line with average speeds on the railways: These roughly doubled in Russia/USSR for suburban trains and increased by more than 1.5 times for long-distance trains between 1865 and 1975 (Golts 2002, 152–153). The length of railways expanded over time in the second half of the nineteenth century and the first half of the twentieth century.

One of the factors behind the high intensity of railway operation in Russia was that they were constructed in addition to existing routes (Fig. 6.7). This is somewhat different from the situation we observed in China, where railways were constructed beside existent main roads (Fig. 4.18). It should be noted that Russian roads were unsurfaced until the 1820s, with just a few major roads begun by then. In 1850, there were only 17 routes that had a regular passenger service provided by horse-driven diligences.[16] Horse transport firmly held the first place in terms of distance and freight in the late ninteenth century (Golts 2007, 121–126). Russia had a similar level to Western Europe and the US in terms of horses per capita, but their carrying power was 1.5–2.4 times weaker owing to poor nutrition and bad care (Golts 2007, 119, 134). However, during the long period of 1865–1975, the quality of roads radically improved. The length of surfaced highways increased even faster than that of

[16] Total *c*. 10,000 km, approximately equal to the length of the railway lines in 1858–1859.

Fig. 6.7 Railway transport versus traditional routes in European Russia, early twentieth century. *Note:* Thick brown lines are railways, thinner and darker lines are routes, and blue ones are rivers and canals. *Source:* Acknowledgement to Evgenii S. Grishin (https://orcid.org/0000-0002-9521-2246)

railways from the 1920s—during the whole period of 1865–1975 by 60 as opposed to 35 times (Golts 2002, 152).

Railways played a complementary role to existing river routes and sea ports by enhancing their development. This was especially important for Russia, which was basically a continental empire, by contributing to the development of foreign trade in the late nineteenth and early twentieth centuries.

As regards shipping,[17] we can observe another pattern to railway transport. In terms of population weighted tonnage of registered ships (Fig. 6.8), such early modern "queens of the seas" as the UK and the US stagnated during the late nineteenth and late tweniteth centuries, even losing their relative positions, while the Asian

[17] This takes into account somewhat imperfect statistics; those for railways are more accurate. The criteria relating to ship registration as well as to tonnage changed over time and across countries. This means the data may not be strictly comparable.

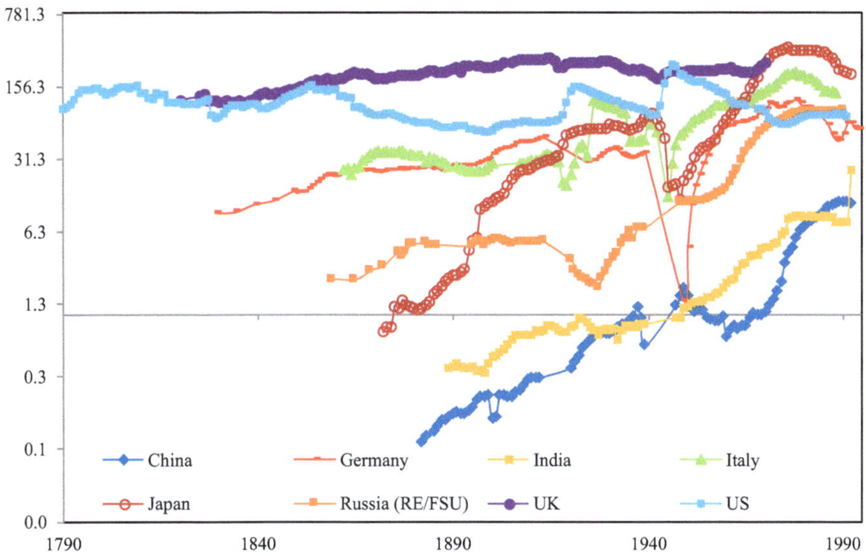

Fig. 6.8 Tonnage of registered ships for selected countries, tons per 1000 population (c. 1700–1990). *Note:* RE—Russian Empire (prior to 1917); FSU—the countries of the former Soviet Union in actual borders (1917–2002). *Source:* Comin and Hobijn (2009) for tonnage of registered ships, Maddison Project Database (Bolt and Van Zanden 2020) for population

countries (China, India, Japan) began to catch up. To some extent, European countries such as Germany and Italy did as well, and Russia/USSR appeared to be somewhere in between.

As the average tonnage of ships registered increased in all reference countries,[18] the population weighted number of ships decreased significantly in the UK and the US, and to some extent in Germany and Italy, while it held stable in Russia. In China and Japan, it increased modestly (Fig. 6.9).

Overall, transportation intensity of an economy goes up with industrial development. For Russia/USSR, this is demonstrated in Fig. 6.10 by a very high association between long-distance freight and gross domestic product (GDP) per capita over the twentieth century.

Of course, besides water and railroads, road and air freight transports also played an important role. First, the relative extent of roads (km road–100 km^2) are, just as with railways, the lowest for Russia and China (Table 6.1). Russia is even far behind China by density and quality of roads but is very close to the countries with vast but sparsely populated territory, such as Canada and Australia. Over past 150 years in the European part of Russia the progress in road density was made at a similar pace as in the US; also, the gap in quality (paved vs non-paved) narrowed (in 2024 paved roads made up 44% in the RF and 73% in the US) (Fig. 6.11).

[18] Normally 10–20 times for the century (late nineteenth–late twentieth century), with the UK (*c.* four times) and Russia (*c.* 35 times) as outliers.

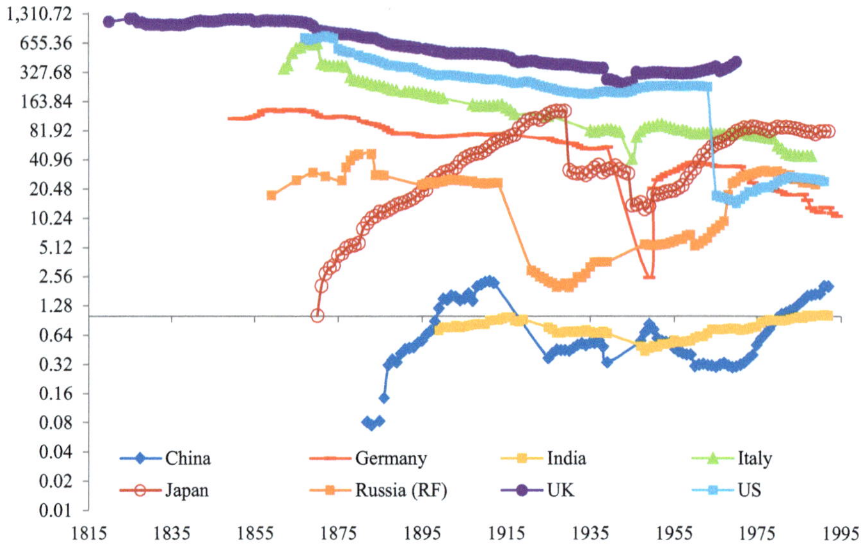

Fig. 6.9 Number of registered ships for selected countries, per 1000 population (c. 1800–1995). *Note:* RE—Russian Empire (prior to 1917); FSU—the countries of the former Soviet Union in actual borders (1917–2002). *Source:* Comin and Hobijn (2009) for number of registered ships, Maddison Project Database (Bolt and Van Zanden 2020) for population

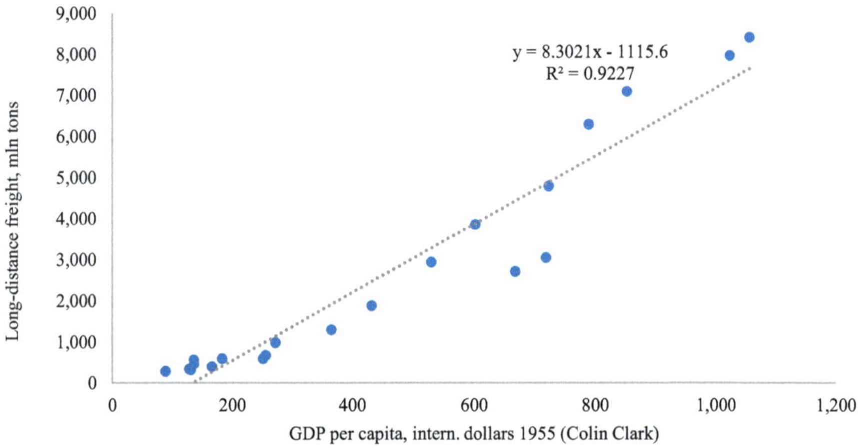

Fig. 6.10 Long-distance Freight versus GDP per capita in Russia/USSR, 1900–2000. *Source:* Golts (2004, 126)

Taking all types of transport in Russia for the period from 1865 to 1975, the speed of urban transportation increased from 9.4 to 31 km/h, suburban from 10.9 to 32.9 km/h, and long-distance from 19.2 to 87.7 km/h (Golts 2002, 153). The time needed to deliver something fell from 1.7 to 0.6 h within urban areas, from 8.8 to 0.5 h within suburban areas, and from 283.4 to 81.6 h in long-distance freight (Golts

Table 6.1 Road km per 100 km² for selected countries, c. 2024

	1865	1887	1912	1928	1950	1970	1986	2024
China								56.0
Japan				240.8	244.6	272.8	303.0	322.0
Russia	1.1	1.9	0.6	0.6	3.2	9.1	14.8	9.0
UK	66.7	60.3	81.9	118.0		132.4	144.3	175.0
Italy								162.0
USA	5.9	5.3	5.3	13.6	33.0	51.1	60.7	72.0

Note: *1865, 1887, and 2024—paved and unpaved roads; 1912–1987—only paved roads; only European part of Russia in 1865–1986; UK: England and Wales in 1865 and 1887; England, Wales, and Scotland in 1928*
Source: 1865–1987: Mironov (2018, vol. 3, p. 793); 2024: https://en.wikipedia.org/wiki/List_of_countries_by_road_network_size

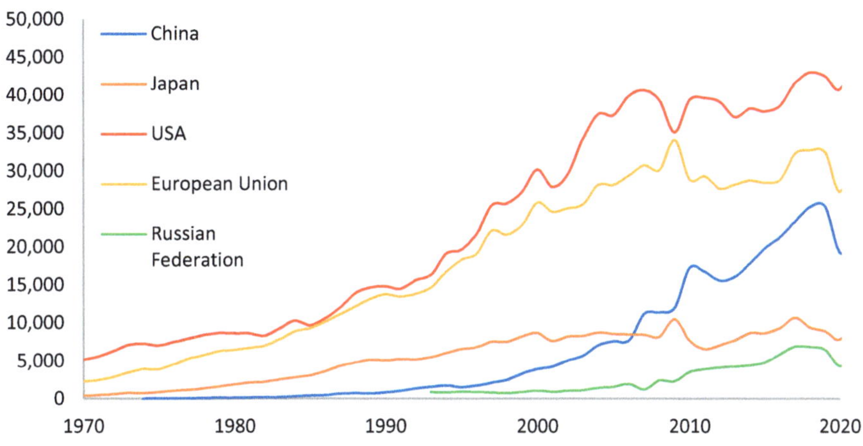

Fig. 6.11 Air freight (million tons per km) for selected countries, c. 1970–2021. *Source:* WDI updated 2024

2002, 168–170). The best improvement for long-distance transportation was of most importance, given the country's vast territories. However, it was not railway but aviation that increased its speed almost fourfold during half a century (1925–1975) and expanded its share.[19] For 110 years, passenger-active territory in Russia expanded five times faster than its population (Golts 2002, 154–156).[20] The transport mobility of population and freight increased in urban, suburban, and

[19] Aviation statistics, both freight and passengers, appear to be lacking for the USSR.

[20] Passenger-active territory is an area where the population is able to form passenger connections within daily and weekly cycles (for urban and suburban trips) and annual life cycles (for long-distance journeys) (Golts 2002, 148–149).

Table 6.2 Long-distance transport mobility in Russia, 1865–1975

	Population			Freight		
	Trips per capita	Kilometres per capita	Hours of trips per capita	Tons per capita	Kilometres per capita	Hours of delivery per capita
1865	0.44	88	5.3	0.1	47.3	
1895	0.59	172	7.2	0.4	277.6	77.3
1925	0.6	258	9.6	0.7	500.8	99.4
1955	0.91	640	17.5	6.9	5834	680.3
1975	2.48	1550	17.7	18.9	19644.4	1542.2
Change over the period, times	5.6	17.6	3.3	189.0	415.3	20.0

Note: On an annual basis; the change in hours of delivery per capita for freight is 1975–1895, all others are 1975–1865
Source: Golts (2002, 166, 171)

long-distance transportation, most impressively in the last segment.[21] Table 6.2 shows that long-distance transport mobility in Russia for a centennial period increased several times for population (passengers) and several dozen times for freight. Clearly, this is evidence that not only railways but also other types of transport contributed to trade penetration and the growth of the economy.

6.7 Conclusion: Changes During the Various Industrial Revolutions, *c.* 1760–Present

As we have seen in the previous sections, it was fundamentally cottage industries, factor of production, institutions, and government that played a role in the spread of industries. While these factors clearly differed among countries over certain time periods, the type of inventions also played a role: which country invented and which innovated.

Cottage industries in both England and China (e.g. silk, cotton, and paper) rose in the sixteenth to eighteenth centuries because of better access to the markets. This was driven by a better transport network, increased transfer of knowledge, especially within Europe, and increased income (i.e. increased demand). What is remarkable is that while in China, cottage industries remained stable (or growing) all the

[21] Transport mobility is a concept associated with passenger-active or freight-active territory. The transport mobility of a population is measured relative to the population living in passenger-active territory by three coefficients (normally on an annual basis): trips per capita, kilometres per capita, and hours for trips per capita (Golts 2002, 165–166). The transport mobility of freight is measured relative to the population living in freight-active territory by three coefficients (normally on an annual basis): Tons per capita, kilometres per capita, and hours of delivery per capita (Golts 2002, 171).

way up to 1950, in England, after an initial rise, their share started to decline in the eighteenth and nineteenth centuries. Both patterns can be observed in, for example, mining and textiles. Indeed, in nineteenth-century England, bigger mining operations started to emerge, while in China, still old techniques dominated. Likewise, cotton production in Wigan (close to Manchester) between 1700 and 1850 turned from small-scale cottage industry to larger factories.

Besides the transformation in England of the eighteenth- and nineteenth-century cottage industries, production factors also played a role in early industrialization. First, on the continent, firewood and peat were cheaper than coal. Only when steam engines became more efficient in the mid-nineteenth century did coal become the most efficient choice of fuel. Second, in Chap. 4, we argue that in Western countries, the mode of labour productivity (commodified labour) increased in relation to Asia between about 1700 and 1900. This improved TFP growth implies increased long-run growth, which led to technological advance in the First and Second Industrial Revolutions. Third, during the First Industrial Revolution, inventions dominated. This changed during the Second Industrial Revolution, which was, in Europe, innovation-based (Amsden 1989). Consequently, open access to knowledge became increasingly important over time for innovation. This was only possible because, after some time, the effect of the demographic transition on human capital formation started to depend on technology (i.e. increasing income), rather than on fertility. Fourth, according to Allen (2009), in Britain high wages existed side by side with low capital costs, thus making inventions cheaper. Likewise, expensive fuel and low wages led to a lower rise in labour-saving technology. Fifth, during shifts in inventions, the economies of leading countries may, over time, have become increasingly capital intensive. The less capital-intensive technologies then became outsourced to less developed economies.[22] Consequently, less developed economies, although still lagging in capital intensity, still became more capital intensive.

Besides, cottage industries and factors of production, government and transport also played a major role in economic development. This is essentially based on Gerschenkron, who argued that the more "backward" a country is, the bigger the emphasis on capital-intensive production and government intervention. Indeed, the role of the government is more important in East Asia than in Western Europe.

References

Acemoglu D, Robinson J (2012) Why nations fail: origins of power, poverty, and prosperity. Crown, New York, NY

Acemoglu D, Johnson S, Robinson JA (2005) Institutions as a fundamental cause of long-run growth. In: Aghion P, Durlauf SN (eds) Handbook of economic growth, vol 1A. Elsevier, Amsterdam, pp 385–472

[22] For a discussion, see also Austin (2013).

Allen RC (2003) Farm to factory: a reinterpretation of the Soviet industrial revolution. Princeton University Press, Princeton
Allen R (2009) Engels' pause: technical change, capital accumulation, and inequality in the British industrial revolution. Explor Econ Hist 46:418–435
Allen RC (2011) Why the industrial revolution was British: commerce, induced invention, and the scientific revolution. Econ Hist Rev 64(2):357–384
Allen RC (2019) Real wages once more: a response to Judy Stephenson. Econ Hist Rev 72(2):738–754
Amsden A (1989) Asia's next giant: South Korea and late industrialization. Oxford University Press, New York
Amsden AH (2001) The rise of 'The Rest': challenges to the West from late-industrializing economies. Oxford University Press, New York
Austin, G. (2013). Labour-intensive industrialization and global economic development: Reflections. In G. Austin & K. Sugihara (Eds.), Labour-Intensive Industrialization in Global History (Chapter 12). London: Routledge.
Bassino J-P, Fukao K, Settsu T (2020) Regional industrialization in Japan. In: van Leeuwen B, Phillips R, Buyst E (eds) An economic history of regional industrialization (Routledge Explorations in Economic History). Routledge, Oxon and New York, pp 180–205
Beckert S (2014) Empire of cotton: a global history. Knopf, New York
Belfanti CM, Giusberti F (2000) Institutions and technical change in early modern Europe. Hist Technol 16(3):217–222. https://doi.org/10.1080/07341510008581991
Blackwell WL (1968) The Beginnings of Russian Industrialization, 1800–1860. Princeton University Press, Princeton. NJ
Bogart D (2010) A global perspective on railway inefficiency and the rise of state ownership, 1880–1912. Explor Econ Hist 47(2):158–178. https://doi.org/10.1016/j.eeh.2009.06.001
Bogart D (2014) The transport revolution in industrializing Britain. In: Floud R, Humphries J, Johnson P (eds) The Cambridge economic history of modern Britain. Cambridge University Press, Cambridge, pp 368–391
Bogart D, Chaudhary L (2013) Engines of growth: the productivity advance of Indian Railways, 1874–1912. J Econ Hist 73(2):339–370. https://doi.org/10.1017/S0022050713000291
Bolt J, Van Zanden JL (2020) Maddison style estimates of the evolution of the world economy: a new 2020 update. Maddison Project Database, version 2020
Bray F (1994) The rice economies: technology and development in Asian societies. University of California Press, Berkeley, Los Angeles, London
Broadberry S, Gupta B (2009) Lancashire, India, and shifting competitive advantage in cotton textiles, 1700–1850: the neglected role of factor prices. Econ Hist Rev 62(2):279–305. https://doi.org/10.1111/j.1468-0289.2009.00482.x
Burt R (1991) The international diffusion of technology in the early modern period: the case of the British non-ferrous mining industry. Econ Hist Rev 44(2):249–271. https://doi.org/10.1111/j.1468-0289.1991.tb00611.x
Cheremukhin A, Golosov M, Guriev S, Tsyvinski A (2017) The industrialization and economic development of Russia through the lens of a neoclassical growth model. Rev Econ Stud 84(2):613–649. https://doi.org/10.1093/restud/rdw026
Cimoli M, Dosi G, Stiglitz JE (2009) Industrial policy and development: the political economy of capabilities accumulation. Oxford Scholarship Online, Oxford. https://doi.org/10.1093/acprof:oso/9780199235261.001.0001
Clark G (1987) Why isn't the whole world developed? Lessons from the cotton mills. J Econ Hist 47(1):141–173. https://doi.org/10.1017/S0022050700047435
Comin DA, Hobijn B (2009) The CHAT dataset. NBER Working Paper No. 15319. https://www.nber.org/papers/w15319, https://data.nber.org/data-appendix/w15319/
Crafts N, Mulatu A (2005) What explains the location of industry in Britain, 1871–1931? J Econ Geogr 5(4):499–518. https://doi.org/10.1093/jeg/lbh065

Crafts N, Wolf N (2014) The location of the UK cotton textiles industry in 1838: a quantitative analysis. J Econ Hist 74(4):1103–1139. https://doi.org/10.1017/S002205071400085X
Crisp O (1976) Studies in the Russian Economy before 1914. The Macmillan Press, London and Basingstoke
Davids K (2012) Religion, technology, and the great and little divergences: China and Europe compared, c. 700–1800. Brill, Leiden and Boston. https://doi.org/10.1163/9789004218620
De Vries J (2008) The industrious revolution: consumer behavior and the household economy, 1650 to the present. Cambridge University Press, Cambridge. https://doi.org/10.1017/CBO9780511818196
Du, S. (1992). Biography of Chinese ancient scientists (2 Volumes). Beijing: Science Press. (杜石然, 中国古代科学家传记（上下）,科学出版社1992年10月).
Ellman M (2023a) Russia as a great power: from 1815 to the present day. Part 1. J Inst Econ 19(1):1–17
Ellman M (2023b) Russia as a great power: from 1815 to the present day. Part II. J Inst Econ 19(2):159–174
Falkus ME (1972) The Industrialization of Russia, 1700–1914. The Macmillan Press, London, Basingstoke
Fernihough, A., & O'Rourke, K. (2014). Coal and the European industrial revolution. The Institute for International Integration Studies Discussion Paper Series (iiisdp439). IIIS
Földvári P, Van Leeuwen B, Didenko D (2015) Capital formation and economic growth under central planning and transition: a theoretical and empirical analysis, ca. 1920–2008. Acta Oecon 65(1):27–50
Frank AG (1998) ReORIENT: global economy in the Asian age. University of California Press, Berkeley
Gatrell P (1986) The Tsarist Economy, 1850–1917. B. T. Batsford Ltd, London
Gerschenkron A (1962) Economic backwardness in historical perspective, a book of essays. Harvard University Press, Cambridge
Golts GA (2002) Культура и экономика России за три века, XVIII-XX вв. Т. 1. Менталитет, транспорт, информация (прошлое, настоящее, будущее) [Culture and economy of Russia for three centuries, 18th–19th centuries. Vol. 1. Mentality, transport, information (past, present, future)]. Сибирский хронограф [Siberian Chronograph], Novosibirsk
Golts GA (2004) Long-term historical trends as an economic forecasting factor: transport, economy, demography. Stud Russ Econ Dev 15(2):124–131
Golts GA (2007) Гужевой транспорт и гужевые пути сообщения в России (Исторический очерк) [Horse transport and horse communication routes in Russia (An historical survey)]. Russia Contemp World 1:119–139
Guangxiang Z (2016) Transportation and economic development of Russia in 19th–beginning of 20th century. J Econ Hist Hist Econ 17(4):645–696. https://doi.org/10.17150/2308-2588.2016.17(4).645-696
Humphries J, Schneider B (2019) Spinning the industrial revolution. Econ Hist Rev 72(1):126–155. https://doi.org/10.1111/ehr.12839
Humphries J, Weisdorf J (2015) The wages of women in England, 1260–1850. J Econ Hist 75:405–447. https://doi.org/10.1017/S0022050715000662
Hunt EH (1986) Industrialization and inequality: regional wages in Britain, 1760–1914. J Econ Hist 46:935–966. https://doi.org/10.1017/S0022050700046467
Kahan A (1989) Russian economic history: the nineteenth century. Edited by R. Weiss. The University of Chicago Press, Chicago
Kasza GJ (2018) Gerschenkron, Amsden, and Japan: the state in late development. Jpn J Polit Sci 19(2):146–172. https://doi.org/10.1017/S146810991800005X
Kelly M, Mokyr J, O'Grada C (2015) Roots of the industrial revolution. UCD Centre For Economic Research Working Paper Series 2015, WP15/24. https://www.ucd.ie/economics/research/papers/2015/WP15_24.pdf
Kingsmill TW (1898) Inland communications in China. Kelley & Walsh, Shanghai

Konchakov RB, Karpenko MA (2018) The influence of railway transport on urban development in European Russia in the second half of the 19th–early 20th centuries. Inf Newslett Assoc Hist Comput 47:33–34. http://case.asu.ru/files/form_312-32961.pdf

Konchakov RB, Karpenko MA (2020) Changes in the pace of growth of the urban population of the Russian empire following the development of the railroad, 1847–1904. In: Aleshkovskii IA, Andriianov AV, Antipov EA (eds) Proceedings of the international youth academic forum "Lomonosov–2020". MAKS Press, Moscow. https://lomonosov-msu.ru/archive/Lomonosov_2020/data/18988/114179_uid348212_report.pdf

Kontorovich V (2015) The Military Origins of Soviet Industrialization. Comp Econ Stud 57(4):669–692

Kontorovich V, Wein A (2009) What did the Soviet Rulers Maximise? Eur Asia Stud 61(9):1579–1601

Langton J (1979) Geographical change and industrial revolution: coalmining in south west Lancashire 1590–1799. Cambridge University Press, Cambridge

Leonard CS, Nazarov Z, Borodkin LI, Karpenko MA, Konchakov RB (2021) Land Prices and Railroad Building in European Russia, 1860s to the early 1900s. Russ J Econ 7(2):93–104

Leunig T (2003) A British industrial success: productivity in the Lancashire and New England cotton spinning industries a century ago. Econ Hist Rev 56(1):90–117. https://doi.org/10.1111/1468-0289.00246

Macheret DA, Valeev NA, Kudryavtseva AV (2018) Formation of the railway network: diffusion of epochal innovation and economic growth. Econ Policy 13(1):252–279

Macpherson, W. J. (1995). The Economic Development of Japan 1868–1941. Cambridge: Cambridge University Press.

Markevich A, Nafziger S (2017) State and market in Russian industrialization, 1870–2010. In: O'Rourke K, Williamson J (eds) The spread of modern industry to the periphery since 1871. Palgrave Macmillan, Houndmills, pp 33–62

McCaffray S (1996) The politics of industrialization in Tsarist Russia. Northern Illinois University Press, DeKalb, IL

McCloskey D (2010) Bourgeois dignity: why economics can't explain the modern world. University of Chicago Press, Chicago

McDermott JP, Yoshinobu S (2015) Economic change in China, 960–1279. In: Chaffee JW, Twitchett D (eds) The Cambridge history of China, Part two: sung China, 960–1279, vol 5. Cambridge University Press, Cambridge, pp 321–432

Mironov BN (2018) Российская империя: от традиции к модерну. [The Russian Empire: from tradition to modernity], vol 1–3, 2nd edn. Dmitrii Bulanin, St. Petersburg

Mokyr J (1976) Growing-up and the industrial revolution in Europe. Explor Econ Hist 13(4):371–396

Mokyr J (2016) A culture of growth: the origins of the modern economy. Princeton University Press, Princeton and Oxford

North DC, Weingast BR (1989) Constitutions and commitments: the evolution of institutions governing public choice in seventeenth-century England. J Econ Hist 49(4):803–832

Nuvolari A, Verspagen B, Von Tunzelmann N (2011) The early diffusion of the steam engine in Britain, 1700–1800: a reappraisal. Cliometrica 5(3):291–321

Persson T, Tabellini G (2021) Culture, institutions and policy. In: Bisin A, Federico G (eds) The handbook of historical economics. Elsevier, Amsterdam, pp 463–490

Pollard S (1978) Labour in Great Britain. In: Mathias P, Postan MM (eds) The Cambridge economic history of Europe (Part 1), vol VII. Cambridge University Press, Cambridge, pp 97–179

Pomeranz K (2000) The great divergence: China, Europe, and the making of the modern world economy. Princeton University Press, Princeton and Oxford

Rodrik D (2005) Growth strategies. Handb Econ Growth 1:967–1014

Rosenstein-Rodan PN (1943) Problems of industrialization of Eastern and South-Eastern Europe. Econ J 53(210/211):202–211

Rostow WW (1960) Stages of economic growth: a non-communist manifesto. Cambridge University Press, London/New York

Schenk FB (2014) Russlands Fahrt in die Moderne: mobilität und sozialer Raum im Eisenbahnzeitalter (Quellen und Studien zur Geschichte des östlichen Europa, No. 82). Franz Steiner Verlag, Stuttgart. (in German; Russ. transl.: Moscow, Новое литературное обозрение [New Literary Review], 2016)

Shepelev LE (1973) Акционерные компании в России [Joint Stock Companies in Russia]. Наука [The Science], Leningrad

Squicciarini MP, Voigtländer N (2015) Human capital and industrialization: evidence from the age of enlightenment. Q J Econ 130(4):1825–1883

Stephenson JZ (2018) 'Real' wages? Contractors, workers, and pay in London building trades, 1650–1800. Econ Hist Rev 71:106–132

Strumilin SG (1958) Statistiko-ekonomicheskie ocherki [Essays on statistics and economics]. Gosstatizdat, Moscow

Sugihara, K. (2003). "The East Asian path of economic development: A long-term perspective." In Arrighi, G, Hamashita T & Selden, M (Eds), The resurgence of East Asia: 500, 150 and 50 year perspectives. Routledge, London & New York, 78–123.

Tabellini G (2010) Culture and institutions: economic development in the regions of Europe. J Eur Econ Assoc 8(4):677–716

Van Leeuwen B, Philips R (2021) Market performance in the grain market of late medieval Western Europe (ca. 1300–1650). In: Moreno Garcia JC (ed) Markets and exchanges in pre-modern and traditional societies. Oxbow Books, pp 155–169

Van Leeuwen B, Foldvari P, Philips R, Wang M (2021) Regional industrialization: evidence on industry agglomeration. In: van Leeuwen B, Philips R, Buyst E (eds) An economic history of regional industrialization. Routledge, Oxon and New York, pp 228–259

Von Laue T (1963) Sergei Witte and the industrialization of Russia. Columbia University Press, New York

Vries, P. (2015). State, economy and the Great Divergence. Great Britain and China, 1680s -1850s. Bloomsbury Publishing PLC.

Vries, P. (2019). Averting a great divergence. State and economy in Japan, 1868–1937 (Bloomsbury Academic; 1st Edition (August 8, 2019, hardback. Paperback March 2021)

Wang, M., & Van Leeuwen, B. (2021). Fenjiashu: Economic development in the Chinese countryside based on household division inventories, ca. 1750–1910. *Australian Economic History Review, 61*(3), 252–272.

Williamson J (1989) What Washington means by policy reform. In: Williamson J (ed) Latin American readjustment: how much has happened. Peterson Institute for International Economics, Washington, pp 7–20

Witte SY (1889) Национальная экономия и Фридрих Лист [A national economy and Friedrich List]. Киевское слово [The Kiev word], Kiev

Wrigley EA (2010) Energy and the English industrial revolution. Cambridge University Press, Cambridge

Xu Y, Van Leeuwen B (2025) Regional industry in China in 1933

Xu Y, Van Leeuwen B, Zhuang Z (2020) Regional industrialization in China: the Yangtze and Zhujiang regions. In: van Leeuwen B, Philips R, Buyst E (eds) An economic history of regional industrialization. Routledge, Oxon and New York, pp 159–179

Zhang Z, Van Leeuwen B, Li J (2020) Regional industrialization in China: the basic metals sector. In: van Leeuwen B, Philips R, Buyst E (eds) An economic history of regional industrialization. Routledge, Oxon and New York, pp 127–158

Chapter 7
State Intervention and Forced Industrialization in the Twentieth Century

Abstract To take the step towards invention and capital accumulation, government policies were necessary. Some countries, such as China and the USSR used a direct government-forced industrialization policy, while others, such as Japan, which also used government control to put in place all factors necessary for economic growth, applied more indirect government policies. The strategy of the USSR and China was one of catch-up: Forced industrialization, with a neglect of consumer production and wage development. This led to a rapid increase in physical capital, enabling relatively fast capital-based growth. Yet three factors contributed to stagnation and decline in gross domestic product per capita growth in this period for both China and the USSR: First, institution, second, policy, and third, resource curse.

Why did state-socialist countries focus on physical capital accumulation while they must have been aware of the negative effect of institutions, policy, and the resource curse? We show here that, from a socialist perspective, it was economically rational for these economies to maximize material output. In addition, this course of action was thought of as a means to withstand the outer capitalist world and win a war that was perceived as highly probable.

7.1 Introduction

As is pointed out in Chap. 6, catching up in terms of gross domestic product (GDP) per capita can take place by capital deepening (a shift to the right on the production frontier), a more efficient use of human and physical capital (a shift upwards towards

This chapter in part relies on: Van Leeuwen, B., Didenko, D., and Földvári, P. (2015). "Inspiration vs. Perspiration in Economic Development of the Former Soviet Union and China (ca. 1920–2010)." ***Economics of Transition*** 23(1): 213–246.

B. Van Leeuwen et al., *Innovation and Economic Development in Eurasia, 500 BCE-Present*, Frontiers in Economic History,
https://doi.org/10.1007/978-3-031-97043-6_7

the production frontier), or a rise in general technologies (a rise in the production, or technological, frontier itself, that is, in total factor productivity (TFP); see Chaps. 5 and 6). Yet to make this step, government policies were necessary. Whereas Japan used government control to put in place all the factors necessary for economic growth, this was an indirect policy. Indeed, observing that, even today, Japan has a remarkably high labour share in GDP testifies to the country's labour-saving past. One reason is that, even though labour-saving technologies have a positive effect on labour productivity, they have a negative effect on household consumption, private sector investment, net exports, and government consumption (Wolf 2014; ILO 2015; Fukao et al. 2019).

Government intervention is thus a balancing act between various positive and negative factors. This becomes increasingly difficult when more government intervention is required. For countries that have an even stronger government policy, such as China and the Former Soviet Union (FSU), the question thus becomes not just if capital deepening occurs, but also whether countries can move closer to the technological frontier, and if factors of production, physical and human capital, are used effectively in the productive process (see e.g. Krugman 1994). For both China (Chow 1993; Li et al. 1993; Wang and Yao 2003; Whalley and Zhao 2010) and, to a lesser extent, Russia and the FSU (Easterly and Fischer 1995; Meliantsev 2004), it has been argued that economic development in the period up to the 1980s was largely driven by rising capital deepening, while the economic transitions experienced by both countries resulted in enhanced growth potential based on technical developments.

Indeed, both the FSU and China recorded a remarkable growth of per capita physical and, to a lesser extent, human capital, although this growth was distributed unequally among their constituents (union republics in the USSR, provinces in China) (Van Leeuwen et al. 2015). These two countries also managed to initially converge with economically advanced countries (Western Europe and its offshoots in North America and Oceania, and, in recent decades, Japan), but fell behind again from the 1970s (see e.g. Van Leeuwen and Földvári 2008). We can also observe that the USSR outperformed China in per capita GDP growth rates between the 1930s and 1990s, despite China's lower level of economic development (and thus higher growth potential). This could likely help to explain the longevity of the central planning (also often referred to as the "command") system in the USSR, as well as the earlier start of market-oriented economic reforms in China.

Table 7.1 provides us with information on the causes of this pattern. We can see that in the FSU before the reforms (1930s–1980s), per capita physical capital growth outperformed that of human capital, which, in its turn, increased faster than GDP per capita in both the FSU and China. In the 1950s, the Chinese communist government adopted a policy of physical capital accumulation, similar to that of the FSU. However, this policy had already been changed by the 1960s–1970s, after the failure of the Great Leap Forward. Table 7.1 further shows that during the reform period, which started in the late 1970s, China's human capital rose faster than its physical capital, although its GDP/cap growth was still slower than either of these factors, implying negative TFP growth. In the FSU from the 1980s to the 2000s, while physical capital decreased dramatically (about halving), human capital

Table 7.1 Compound annual growth rates of per capita GDP, human capital, and physical capital in the FSU and China, 1930–2000

	(ex)USSR			China		
	Physical capital per capita	Human capital per capita	GDP per capita	Physical capital per capita	Human capital per capita	GDP per capita
1930–1980	6.14	4.11	3.44	2.83	9.41	1.89
1980–2000	−2.10	−0.01	0.51	9.47	12.40	6.06

Source: Van Leeuwen et al. (2015)

appeared, on average, to be slightly better (in large part because of Russia, which, owing to its large population, makes up about half of the FSU), although it did not recover in about half of the FSU countries. During this time, GDP per capita was close to recovery, although in some areas of the FSU, it was far below its pre-reform level.

Given this development, why did these countries cling to physical capital accumulation before the reforms, with all the associated positive and negative effects on technological development and growth?

In searching for an answer, we start with labour relations development under socialism. These were shaped by the challenges of a war economy, which included periods of preparation and reconstruction. This extreme institutional environment, in which the elite ideology was militantly opposed to the outside capitalist world, created and sustained expectations regarding large-scale warfare, which shaped their economic thinking. The main objective, at least an intermediate one, was the pursuit of military might (Kontorovich and Wein 2009). We can then turn to modelling based on an assumption that Marxist-influenced state-socialist regimes had a tendency to value capital goods, which are relatively more physical-capital-intensive, above consumer goods, which are more human-capital-intensive. As regards physical capital itself, we apply the idea in Popov (2007) about producers' preference for new construction instead of the renovation of obsolete equipment. These aspects of our analysis may also help us to answer the question about reasons for a focus on physical capital accumulation.

7.2 Modes of Production and Labour Relations

Since this book deals with economic history, we do not look directly at the slave–feudal–capitalist–socialist structure but rather at how it affected labour, in other words labour relations (Sect. 4.3). This implies a reciprocal (kin) mode of production, a tributary labour mode, and a commodified labour mode. Feudal labour relations (e.g. serfdom) could exist both in tributary and commodified labour modes of production. Yet in commodified labour, feudalism could only exist with a market production goal. With a non-market production goal, socialism exists, which excludes feudal labour relations. Hence, the shift from feudalism to capitalism, and eventually to socialism, can be analysed in terms of labour relations.

Marxist ideology links a move from feudalism to capitalism, and then to socialism. In Sect. 2.2 (social classes) we focus on medieval feudalism. After medieval feudalism, capitalism supposedly emerged, but quite late in China. Some scholars believe that the roots of capitalism in China could be dated back to the Tang (618–907) or Song (960–1279) dynasty or the sixteenth century. However, these roots did not grow into a big tree. Indeed, what is observable is that, according to Pomeranz (2000), China remained in its feudal stage until well after the Opium Wars (*c.* 1839–1860). Capitalist economic sectors (e.g. enterprises established by pioneers of the Westernization Movement or domestic capitalists) emerged from the late nineteenth century and they were different from the "roots." The transition towards socialism occurred in 1949, raising the question why the capitalist economic phase was so short.

First, since commodified labour-market mode is close to feudalism (even including serfs), it is easy to mistake commodified labour for feudalism, while, as mentioned before, a large part of the commodified labour market is actually capitalist. Second, much of this debate on capitalism has ended up as part of the roots of capitalism debate—that is, the idea that the (small) tendencies towards capitalism that had been present in China were either blocked or enhanced by foreign and/or Chinese factors. One example is that Western capitalism and imperialism brought capitalism to China from the Opium Wars onwards. Conversely, it is argued that the West blocked Chinese indigenous capitalist development. In addition, it is argued that a "foreign" (i.e. non-Han) dynasty blocked Chinese capitalism. These foreign and/or Chinese factors mainly include difficulties in capital accumulation, limited market scale, undeveloped modern technology, and the failure of merchants to be organized as a powerful social class owing to systematic and constitutional factors formed over a long history. Xu and Wu (2000) take a moderate position in this respect, claiming that it was primarily Chinese factors that obstructed capitalism, but these were enhanced by foreign trade and imperialism.

On foreign economies and capitalism, Xu and Wu (2000) argue that "contrasts between Qing China, Tokugawa Japan, and much of early modern Europe may have been overstated." This applies to Russia[1] too, with Moon (2001, Table 2.1) showing the dynamics of the state and private extraction over the eighteenth century. In general, estate owners increased peasants' obligations, in both quit-rent dues (basically monetary or, rarely, in kind, payments from peasants to their lord—*obrok*) and corvée labour services (cultivation of the seignior land by peasants—*barshchina*). They extracted from their estates' serfs faster than the rate of inflation, measured in grain prices, while the state increased the direct taxes it extracted from peasants, including nobles' serfs, much slower than the rate of inflation. According to Moon's estimates, throughout the eighteenth century, the average male serf's seignorial obligations in dues increased in real terms by 1.69 times and in labour by 2.5 times.

[1] Much of the evidence on Russia in this Section is from Didenko (2024).

Over the same period, the average serf's direct taxes fell in real terms by two-thirds. Thus, a growing part of the product of private serf labour was extracted by estate owners rather than the state.[2]

Several steps were undertaken by the Russian government in the first half of the nineteenth century to curtail private serfdom, thus preparing the conditions for its abolition. One major step was the state peasant reform of 1837–1841. During the first half of the nineteenth century, 10% of all serfs were emancipated from nobles' private ownership; with a comparable number of men being emancipated through military service (Mironov 2018, vol. 2, 61). As a result, the share of private serfs in the total population diminished.[3]

This aligns with a shift from a tributary/feudal to a commodified (capitalist) mode of production. This process started in Russia at least a century earlier than in China, and, in addition, was barely attributed to foreign intervention. The move to socialism followed suit at around the turn of the twentieth century. Immediately after the Bolshevik Revolution in 1917, the concept of "universal labour duty" was coined in Soviet propaganda and legislation. During 1918–1920, the first attempts at labour mobilization and labour camps were established under the policies of "war communism." These experiments were of a much smaller scale than those of the 1930s–1950s, but the ideological foundations had been laid and institutional design had been created. The dismantling of war communism in the 1920s and the subsequent construction of a mixed economy under the "new economic policy" (NEP) led to prisoners' labour shrinking in scale. As before the Revolution, wage-earners prevailed in large-scale industry and in part-time self-employment in cottage industries. The difference from pre-revolutionary practices was that the state extensively intervened in wage-setting both in the dominant state-owned enterprises and, to a lesser extent, private enterprises. Agricultural labour relations experienced much less state intervention, with the major change being confiscation of large estates that were taken over by the state in 1917–1920. Private property on land was abolished, but land could be communal or private as well as completely state owned. Therefore, the agricultural employment pattern resembled that before the revolution, when rural households as a production unit with self-employed family members prevailed. Moreover, under the NEP agriculture appeared to be even less commodified than in the years of the Stolypin reforms (from 1906). After the NEP was dismantled in the late 1920s–early 1930s, the state appeared to be the only ultimate employer of hired labour. The other forms were only collective employment and individual self-employment.

[2] These findings conform to the evidence reported in Marxist Soviet era historiography with an emphasis on private extraction, both on the part of peasants' dues and labour services. They also conform with the estimates by Mironov (2018, vol. 2, 63) that over the period 1701–1800, the amount of private income from peasants' dues increased by 62% in real terms and additionally by 70–90% over the period 1801–1860.

[3] From 51.7 in 1811 to 39.2 in 1857 (Mironov 2018, vol. 2, 61, citing Kabuzan 1971); from 50.11 in 1811 to 36.46 in 1857 (Moon 2001, Table 3.1a).

We should differentiate between everyday (civilian) labour practices and penal ones. It appears that the share of coerced labour expansion was driven by the latter, and at some point, overtook the former. Therefore, in further discussion of Soviet practices of unfree labour in the 1930s–mid-1950s, we start with the penal system, then turn to the civilian situation.

From the very beginning, the Soviet punitive system was based on the idea that criminals and offenders should be corrected and socialized through labour efforts. Therefore, its economic efficiency was of secondary priority, though not neglected. In 1929, the Soviet leadership established a system of self-supporting penal camps administered by the Main Camp Administration of the Soviet Department of the Interior,[4] which would eventually replace existing prisons around the country (Khlevniuk 2004a, 9).

In 1941, at the start of the Great Patriotic War (Second World War), the whole system of forced labour administered by separate departments of the huge Ministry of Internal Affairs (Russian acronym is *MVD – Ministerstvo vnutrennikh del*) incarcerated 5.9 million people,[5] who were distributed between labour camps (administered by the Gulag),[6] labour colonies, special settlements in exile, and local prisons, depending on the severity of punishment. Coercion to labour was most overt in the Gulag. Labour in special settlements was close to that in the civilian economy, leaving aside the fact that workers could not choose their residence or therefore, their place of employment. The share of prisoners' penal labour in GDP is estimated at 10% in Ivanova (2000, 116).[7]

The key industrial sectors of the Soviet economy, notably coal mining, metallurgy, and construction, experienced a desperate labour shortage that was filled by camp prisoners. The Gulag had almost a monopoly position in certain industrial metals and minerals. Moreover, skilled workers and specialists were concentrated in 380 special colonies that produced tanks, aircraft, armaments, and ammunition (Ivanova 2000, 69–126). The MVD also supplied a labour force (from various establishments besides the Gulags) for civilian ministries on a contractual basis, where its lack had to be covered without delay. However, the economic efficiency measured as unit cost of commodity produced and labour productivity has been assessed as 50–60% lower in the Gulag than in relevant enterprises subordinated to

---

[4] In Russian this is "Glavnoe Upravlenie Lagerei Narodnogo Komissariata Vnutrennikh Del," abbreviated as Gulag.

[5] Before the "archival revolution" of the 1990s, the share of forced labourers was estimated at 2–3% of the total labour force in 1941–1945 (Barber and Harrison 1991, 215). It follows from the revised figures in Khlevniuk (2004a, 328) that it was about 6%, if the civilian labour force is taken as estimated in Barber and Harrison (1991, 215) and about 7%, if official figures are taken (Didenko et al. 2013). The primary documents on economic aspects of the Gulag are published in Yakovlev et al. (2000) and Khlevniuk (2004b).

[6] In 1941, somewhat fewer than two million prisoners, close to 2% of the total labour force (Gregory 2003a, 19). The number of Gulag inmates rose to 2.5 million in 1950 (Sokolov 2003, 41).

[7] Even with the lower productivity of prisoners' labour compared with the relevant civilian industries, it might outperform the average for the national economy, given the much lower productivity in agriculture in which most of the population still worked. However, the figure has the potential to be revised downwards.

civilian ministries (Sokolov 2003, 39–40). Not surprisingly, Gulag workers' wages were set at 30–50% of the wages paid to the workers in corresponding civilian branches of industry, close to subsistence level. The Gulag camp administrators believed that prisoners' labour needed to be stimulated not only by overt coercion but also by positive incentives (material and non-material), and wages could be a useful instrument for managing productivity.[8] This is not surprising: Gregory (2003b, 84–98) applied the "fair wage–effort" model of Akerloff and Yellen (1990), and documents how the Stalinist leadership was searching for positive incentives for the civilian labour force, as it was believed that the people would tend to abstain from working if their wage fell below a perceived "fair" level.[9]

The substantial dismantling of the Gulag occurred quickly after Stalin's death in 1953 on the grounds of ineffectiveness, and this was accelerated by uprisings and riots in 1953 and 1954.[10] In 1959, the system was reorganized on a much smaller scale (Khlevniuk 2003, 44; Sokolov 2003, 41–42).

Despite its low economic efficiency in a conventional sense, the role of the Gulag in extensively industrializing the economy has been elaborated in the research literature. First, it provided labour resources for the development of remote regions where attracting free workers would have been prohibitively costly. Second, it supplied extremely mobile labour, which was easily transferred from project to project as the state perceived its needs. Third, inmates' labour could be exploited with far fewer restrictions than that of civilians, to the point of complete exhaustion. Fourth, the threat of falling into the Gulag's maw served to discipline "free" workers. Fifth, the existence of a substantial population of prisoners and other "special contingents" relieved pressure on the meagre consumer goods market and made it easier to solve the most serious social problems (e.g. housing). Taken as a whole, forced labour was of unique importance in the construction of the largest and most labour-intensive projects. These arguments are still being debated and need to be supported by empirical evidence that uses a broad range of sources (Khlevniuk 2003, 59–61).

As regards the civilian part of the Soviet economy in the 1930s–1950s, the most indentured section was everyday agricultural labour. From the early Soviet era, one form of agricultural employment had been state enterprise (*sovkhoz*), which used hired labour; this was closest to civilian industrial employment. As a result of the collectivization of Soviet agriculture in the late 1920s–early 1930s, another prevailing form was established: The supposedly voluntary co-operative farm organization (*kolkhoz*). This employment originated with membership in the enterprise, which unified members' lands. Remuneration was split between in kind (more) and monetary (less) shares for labour contributions measured on a daily basis (*trudodni*). This kind of enterprise was obliged to sell a fixed volume of production at fixed

[8] Borodkin and Ertz (2005) investigated the Gulag system of incentives, and found that wages had more weight over time. In the early 1950s, prisoners were being paid according to the considerable level of differentiation in the civilian economy, adjusted for the lower productivity of the former.

[9] Gregory (2003b) also documented how propaganda was employed to lower these perceptions and to shift the workers' expected rewards over time.

[10] The primary evidence is published in Kozlov et al. (2004).

prices (normally well below market prices) to the state procurement agency, and had the right to distribute the remainder (normally this was very modest) among its members, either in kind or the money raised by selling it. Up to the mid-1960s, there were no minimum wages, pensions, and social benefits from the government for *kolkhoz* employees.

Self-employment was tolerated as part-time attachment to *sovkhoz* or *kolkhoz* enterprises, but much less so as a full-time activity. This latter was heavily taxed and was just a tiny portion of total agricultural employment by the 1940s. Income from part-time farming on plots of land (*c.* 1 acre) attached to wooden homes appeared to be more dependable.

In the 1920s–1930s, urban workers could generally freely move across occupations and enterprises within cities. They opted for this on a large scale, and therefore labour mobility in the 1930s was at extremely high levels (Filtzer 1986). To address this challenge along with the problems caused by the disruption and collapse of consumer markets, enterprise managements had to develop social services, providing housing, food and clothing shops, cafeterias, healthcare, and leisure. During the early 1930s, workers relied increasingly for food and other basic necessities on the growing rationing system in their workplaces and through trade union organizations.

The mass flight of rural population to urban areas in the 1920s and early 1930s was only partly due to organized recruitment (*orgnabor*): The collectivization and famine of 1932 that ravaged the countryside intensified the flow. The government's response was the introduction of passports and an urban registration system in 1932–1933; these were aimed at making the flow more manageable (Davies and Wheatcroft 2004, 407). The government sought to restrict the movement of agricultural workers by denying them entitlement to the internal passport that was necessary to work elsewhere. They were also forbidden to travel without written permission from local authorities. It was only in 1965 that this system was abolished, with the introduction of universal passports for all citizens. In the mid-1940s–mid-1950s, one of the mass channels that allowed rural workers to migrate to urban industry was organized recruitment (Filtzer 2002, 29–34). Much of this kind of labour became indentured, formally by free choice under contract for 5 years or so, employees having no right to quit their jobs without penalty (Filtzer 2002, 28–37).

The Soviet labour legislation that was introduced between December 1938 and June 1940 imposed rigorous controls over labour mobility in the non-agricultural sector. The series of decrees that were issued introduced labour books, which contained information about workers' past employment, called for the dismissal and eviction from enterprise housing of workers who repeatedly truanted or were late to work, and criminalized these violations of labour discipline (Filtzer 1986, 236–243). During the Great Patriotic War (1941–1945), an average of 200,000 people (of a 55–75 million working population) were taken to court every year for quitting their jobs, conviction involving several months' labour in prison (Barber and Harrison 1991, 164, 215). The number of those who were subject to sanctions for labour abuses were even higher, reaching 1.5–2 million in the early 1940s (Sokolov 2003, 28). Labour turnover decreased but remained high both during and after the war, despite the continuation of penalties (Filtzer 2002, 162–164; Sokolov 2003, 28–29, 37–38).

Another aspect of Soviet labour policies during the war was the widening of skill premia. The relative wage differential between white- and blue-collar workers, adjusted per year of schooling, increased from 65 to 80%, and was at historically high levels for the whole Soviet era.[11] This required the centralized regulation of pay rates because mass mobilization to the armed forces led to the lack of less skilled relative to highly skilled labour.

Labour discipline infractions were decriminalized in 1956 after having been in abeyance for several years (Filtzer 1992, 13–34, 160–176). By the early 1950s, managers had begun to think that severe restrictions deprived their enterprises of scarce skilled labour.

The timeline for mass penal labour and strong limitations on mobility in the civilian sector indicates that these were associated with the war economy, including preparations, hostilities, and recovery. From the late 1920s, neither the Soviet leadership nor their mass media could disguise the fact that the economy was preparing for large-scale war (Kontorovich and Wein 2009; Kontorovich 2015), and this was perceived as virtually inevitable until the mid-1950s. Once the Soviet elite felt that the risks of war with the major Western powers had substantially diminished, after nuclear bombs had been tested, the scale of coercion in labour relations also lessened. Yet restrictions on labour mobility were still significant until military spending had increased even further in the late 1980s.[12]

In the 1960s–1970s, China was preparing for war as well, but relative to the USSR labour relations took a more moderate form and there was less coercion.

During 1949–1978, especially after 1956, when the Socialist Transformation was to a great extent finished, a labour relationship existing on the basis that administrative affiliation and order would adapt to the socialist planned economy system became dominant. The government adjusted the labour force flow according to its needs in different periods. The main target was to build an integrated industrial system, especially a strong heavy industry sector, and to stay safe. We cannot deny that military factors were taken into account, but they were combined with economic factors. For example, in order to avoid losses through possible wars, many enterprises were settled in remote hinterlands; consequently, many people had to relocate.

From 1949, many labourers were recruited by industrial sectors in urban areas or moved to border areas to support the national strategy; the highest priority was given to industrial development. After several years of rapid population expansion, job opportunities, urban infrastructure, and food supply became insufficient in

[11] During the First World War, without rationing, the same differential narrowed from 222% to 83% in the Russian market economy. See Sect. 10.2 on the data sources. It is assumed that the system of rationing essentially mirrored the differentials in monetary wages.

[12] We find 10–11% GDP in the mid-1950s and 15% GDP in the mid-1980s, based on Steinberg (1990), Brada and Graves (1988), and Ofer (1987), as realistic levels. There is still room for the figures to be revised upwards.

urban areas. From 1958, a household registration barrier was established between rural and urban areas, and migration permission from rural to urban areas was tightened. Furthermore, formal moves towards de-urbanization began from 1961. By the end of the 1970s, around 40 million educated urban youth, urban workers, and staff had been sent back to the countryside by the government. During this period, urban labour forces were allocated to different enterprises according to the needs of the highly planned economy. Once sent to an enterprise, a worker was deprived of the right to search for other job opportunities. In essence, labour forces were employed by the state rather than by enterprises. Administrative affiliation became the dominant relationship between employers and employees. From the late 1950s, the rural people's commune became the basic unit of China's rural society as well as a component of the socialist regime. Labour forces in each commune were collective labourers. The work point system, also called the working day system, was created as part of the rural economic system during the period of Chinese agricultural collectivization: This was a series of labour organization rules and regulations that were the basis for calculating the amount of collective labour expended and measuring the income distribution of commune members. Materials produced by these peasants were compulsorily sold to the country at a low price to support urban industry.

Along with the beginning of reform and society's opening-up, coercion in labour relations gradually faded out.

Under the Soviet "mature socialism" of the mid-1950s–1980s, labour was basically commodified. Workers could switch between enterprises. Even if all enterprises were owned by the state, which defined the rules for setting wages and salaries, managers had their own interests and flexibly used their powers to attract and stimulate the skills they perceived important so their enterprises would operate properly. The constraints entailed rights as well as obligations for labour. For example, working-age people were not allowed to live for extended periods just on their savings. Another constraint was the full employment target, which affected incentives for enterprise managers. However, firing personnel (especially managers and specialists) was possible if they did not meet all requirements. A distinctive feature of Soviet labour relations was the elevated role of enterprises in supplying housing, healthcare, and other social services for employees; this rested on long traditions of corporate paternalism.

7.3 Reasons for Focus on Capital Deepening

As pointed out earlier, capital deepening occurred both in the FSU and in China. Yet while China moved towards increased capital efficiency, this took much longer for the FSU, leading to slower growth from the 1980s (see Fig. 7.1).

There are various reasons why state socialist economies clung to physical capital, affecting patterns of convergence and divergence. Three different arguments are brought forward in the literature.

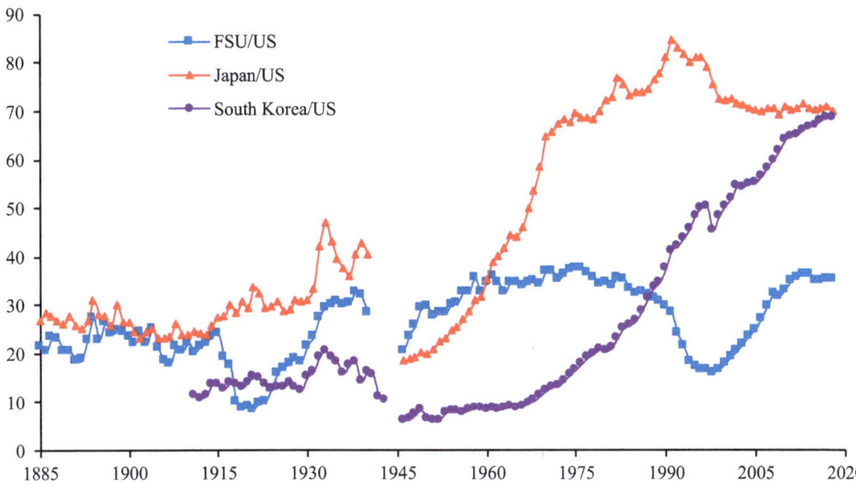

Fig. 7.1 The FSU as percentage to the US (GDP per capita, Intl'$ 2011 prices), 1885–2018. *Source:* Maddison Project Database (Bolt and Van Zanden 2020)

The first explanation for early deceleration in Soviet growth is the so-called resource curse. This means that the strategy of extracting rent through commodity exports led to many negative effects, including a decrease in the technological level of manufacturing industries and deterioration in the quality of institutions.[13] Thus, the resource curse argument is positioned as complementary to the institutional explanation.

The second argument, within the framework of the institutional approach, explains the slowdown in growth rates in the USSR, on the one hand, by the intrinsic shortcomings of the extractive institutions of state coercion. Thus, according to Acemoglu and Robinson (2012), while the extractive institutions of state coercion, central planning, and the mobilization economy were strengthened, growth rates were not sustainable, because surplus labour in the less-productive agricultural sector was exhausted, rent-seeking of the political elite was growing, and incentives to spread innovations remained weak.

The third explanation of why the Soviet economy initially outperformed those in the West in the 1930s and 1950s but started to decelerate and lag behind thereafter is offered in Popov (2007). He shows that a centrally planned economy had its own life cycle. The latter was determined by the length of the fixed assets service period (20–30 years) and by the moment when a sharp increase in the share of investment in GDP (the "big push") took place. He relies on the ideas put forward in Weitzman (1970), Desai (1976), and Easterly and Fischer (1995) on the low elasticity of production factors substitution in the centrally planned economy of the USSR.

[13] See e.g. Gaddy and Ickes (2013).

Building on the idea of a low elasticity of labour substitution by physical capital, Popov (2007) argues that this became a fatal weakness of the extensive development strategy in its later stages. The key factor in the slowdown in development rates in the 1960s–1980s was that manufacturers were not interested enough in the timely renovation of obsolete equipment. The task of renovating physical capital contradicted their short-run goal of fulfilling planned targets, and therefore, they preferred to invest in new capacity rather than upgrade older facilities. Such a policy was intended to increase output as much as possible in the short run, but in the long run, it led to declining capital productivity. As a result, the capital stock was ageing rapidly, reducing capital productivity and lowering labour productivity and TFP growth rates. Popov (2007) thus claims that it was not merely physical capital accumulation that was to blame for the slowdown but the preference for new construction over renovation. What can be added to this story is that in Soviet central planning, the principal (pursuing long-term goals) and its agents (pursuing short-term goals) had specific interests; these were often contradictory (Gregory 1990, 2003b). The planners often forced manufacturers to spend time and money to introduce innovations but required them at the same time not to let it go at the expense of output. These requirements were by nature contradictory, and consent to them depended upon the parties' bargaining trade-offs. In the 1930s, principals used much coercive power to suppress producers' opportunism. What really changed between the 1930s and the 1970s was the growing opportunism of enterprises' management and their abilities to manipulate plan indicators and planners' expectations (Gregory 2003b). Popov (2014)[14] extends his analysis of the causes of the Soviet slowdown by pointing to the deterioration in the quality of institutions that demonstrated comparative efficiency in the early stages of industrial development. So, it was economic actors' interaction that resulted in the centrally planned economy underinvesting in the replacement of fixed capital stock and overinvesting in the expansion of production capacities.

A clear demonstration of the argument in Popov (2007) is presented in Fig. 7.2. The share of accumulated depreciation in the physical capital stock (the relative difference between gross and net stock values) is a proxy for the technological quality of the stock, and is in reverse relationship to its productivity. Moreover, a relatively large share of net capital stock under this preference (investing in new capacities instead of upgrading the old ones) consisted of unfinished construction that was therefore not actually operating at all.

Popov (2007) may at first sight contradict Allen (2003, 198–201), who claims that in the 1960s, investment shifted from the construction of new manufacturing facilities to the modernization of existing ones. But they actually complement each other. Allen (2003, 201–205) documents that while reconstruction expenditure seems to be an efficient way of investing in industry, it proved highly wasteful in this case. The problem lay in faulty investment policies and management decisions that were amplified by the inflexibility of the centralized system and errors at the top of it (Allen 2003, 190, 206). The reason for this was the preferences of the planners,

[14] To be exact, Popov (2014, 36–40, 48–52, 104–115, 145–154)

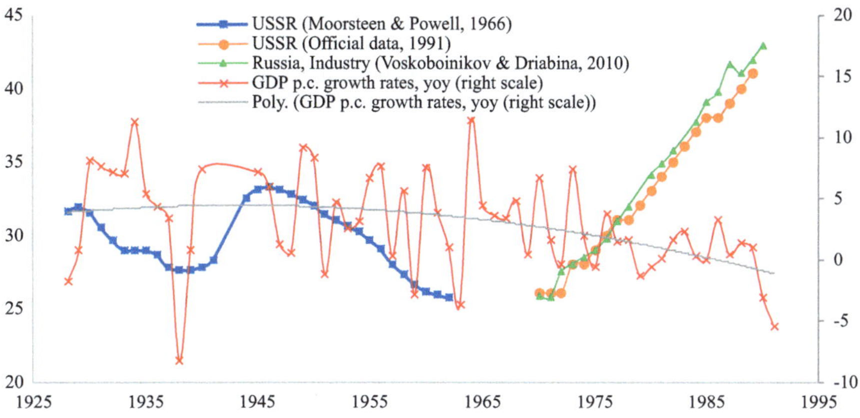

Fig. 7.2 Accumulated depreciation of fixed capital stock in the USSR and Russia (1928–1991). *Note*: 1941–1945 are omitted due to outliers caused by the Second World War. *Sources:* Accumulated depreciation: calculations based on Moorsteen and Powell (1966); Goskomstat SSSR (1991); Voskoboinikov and Driabina (2010); GDP percentage growth rates: calculations based on: Didenko et al. (2013) for 1920s–1940s; Maddison Project Database (Bolt and Van Zanden 2020) for 1950s–2010s

who tried to implement reconstruction while keeping enterprises working, although it would have been more economically efficient to shut down old enterprises and open new ones. Partial reconstruction brought about compatibility and consistency problems between the remaining old and the newly installed equipment. Furthermore, fixed-capital capacities were not matched by a sufficient and adequate labour force. The gravest problem was a poor system of incentives to economize on input costs (Allen 2003, 206–207). However, once the deficiency of capital was rectified and full employment was achieved, these institutions proved inimical to technological progress and efficiency.

To summarize, the low elasticity of capital–labour substitution is viewed in Popov (2007) as the intrinsic feature of centrally planned economies, which leads to the expansion of capital stock at the expense of the replacement or retirement. Such an investment strategy can produce good results in its first 20 or 30 years (a period equivalent to one and a half times the service life of capital stock), but later inevitably leads to a rapid decline in capital productivity. Viewed in such a way, centrally planned economies, despite all their inefficiencies and high growth costs, can show reasonable growth rates, but for just the first three decades of their existence at best. Later, they are doomed to witness a severe decline in capital productivity associated with the ageing of fixed capital stock. In this respect, Popov (2007) assesses the relatively short Chinese command economy (1949–1979) as superior to the Soviets' excessively long one (1929–1991).

To test the three factors leading to slower per capita growth (i.e. institutions, policy, and resource curse), Didenko and Grineva (2020, 2021, 2022) have created a production function that includes technology dynamics and institutions.[15] Their idea is that human and institutional capital comprise an intangible part of national wealth. It follows that institutional environment can be introduced into production function regression models (Hamilton et al. 2005, 93–98). The regression thus includes, along with stocks of physical and human capital at their replacement cost, institutional, political, and technological dynamics, and a proxy for the resource curse.[16]

The result is that selected institutional factors could play a significant role in the economic development of the late USSR (in terms of relative levels of democracy and military spending). The hypothesis about the deterioration of the institutional environment in the USSR is confirmed only partially. For example, there was an increase in the murder rate, but this was not so strong in the global context. In most of the reference countries, institutional factors played a more significant role than in the USSR. In other words, the negative contribution of institutions was not stronger and more significant than in other countries of the group sharing a deterioration of per capita income.

The effects of technological proxy indicators turn out to be more significant; they always made a negative contribution to economic growth. No reference country had such a gloomy pattern of deterioration in technological level when all the available proxy indicators contributed to negative growth.

The resource curse hypothesis, often put forward in the literature, is not confirmed: the share of natural energy resources in USSR exports turned out to be statistically insignificant, yet with a positive coefficient. Both results thus reject the resource curse argument.

In sum, in the USSR, institutions had a small effect, policy/technology had a strong effect, and resource curse had no effect. Yet once applied in an endogenous growth model, policy and institutions lost their significance, and the resource curse gained importance. The significance of each of the three factors thus depends on the growth model. During the period that was characterized by a planned economic system, China chose to initially develop an advanced capital-intensive heavy industry to catch up with the developed countries. Lin (2007) believes that this was inconsistent with China's comparative advantages determined by its endowment structure at that time. As a result, enterprises in these industries lacked viability in a free open market, and the government adopted a planned and commanding system that would

[15] Their idea was based on the works of researchers affiliated with the World Bank (Hamilton et al. 2005, 91–98; Lange et al. 2011, 96–102).

[16] The institutional environment is proxied by (alternatively) murder (homicide) rate, an indicator of the most accurately registered type of violent criminal offence, Latent Democracy Index as internationally comparable and a relative measure of political regime (from Foldvari 2014), level of military expenditure (% GDP) as the choice of political power regarding the response to external challenges, as well as by a white- versus blue-collar wage differential in industry, an indicator of trade-offs in the policies for production incentives and income distribution. The technological level of the economy was proxied by (alternatively) infant mortality, relative difference between gross and net values of physical capital stock, electrical energy produced by level of GDP, and the share of natural energy resources in commodity exports.

develop non-viable enterprises (Lin 2007). The theories explaining why forced capital accumulation eventually led to declining growth are mainly, just as in the USSR, about institutions and policies.

From the perspective of basic institutions, there are many Chinese economists who criticized the planned economic system based on Mises and Hayek's theories about the weakness of the planned economic system from the perspective of incentives, incomplete information and knowledge, a distorted price system, and the impossibility of creating the correct economic plan to realize the balance between supply and demand and reasonable resource allocation (Hui 2017).

Some core policies were also considered to be important factors that harmed economic growth. Owing to the shortage of capital and agricultural surplus, China adopted a method that reduced consumption and increased accumulation rate through government mobilization under a centralized system (Wu 2003). Labour wages and the price of agricultural products were kept quite low. Moreover, the widely existing price scissors (expensive industrial goods relative to agricultural ones), the forced government purchase of agricultural products, and the restraint of rural–urban mobility were all extractive measures that maintained a high accumulation rate and lowered the production costs of heavy industries (Lin and Yu 2009). Zhang (2021) comments that the high accumulation rate as a result of forced savings controlled by the government helped significantly to form capital, but he also emphasized the negative impacts, such as the limited living and consumption standards and consequently the low labour incentives, deteriorating cyclic economic fluctuations, and poor sectoral proportions within the whole economy. He and Wu (2007) argue that the over-development of steel-smelting caused a serious negative impact on agricultural production and the manufacturing of other consumption goods because it required too many labourers and resources. What is more, the majority of the steel products produced were of very poor quality and could not be used as industrial materials. This aggravated the state's financial difficulties and shortages in the economy (He and Wu 2007).

In sum, in both China and the USSR, it was mostly institutions and policy that suggested economic stagnation, and decline followed a period of forced capital accumulation. Yet, irrespective of which factor was the main driver of the growth slowdown, it is notable that officials continued to promote physical capital growth, even though they must have been aware of these problems. In Sect. 7.4 we return to this.

7.4 The Importance of Capital Deepening in Government-Controlled Industrialization

Based on the preceding discussion, it is clear that physical capital (capital deepening) before reforms took place cannot be disregarded as a growth factor. Its excessive accumulation eventually led to a collapse in its value in the FSU when market reforms were launched, and slower growth in China after the Great Leap Forward (1958–1961). However, one may wonder why this focus on physical capital existed if it had such adverse effects, and why these patterns eventually led to structural policy changes during the reform period.

The answer to these questions is probably best analysed based on the idea that socialist states, which follow a Marxist-influenced economic policy, have a tendency to value capital goods, which require relatively more material goods, above consumer goods, which require a different mix of material and immaterial goods. Since material goods are likely to be produced in a more physical and capital-intensive way than immaterial goods, this leads to a higher ratio of physical to human capital in the optimal growth path of the economy. This necessarily comes at the price of reduced consumption, of both tangible and intangible goods. Once a socialist regime starts to put more emphasis on the production of consumer goods relative to capital goods—likely thanks to growing social tensions arising from low consumption—its physical to human capital ratio should necessarily decrease.

These ideas were formalized in the model that was developed by Földvári et al. (2015, 39–45), based on an optimization approach taken from Barro and Sala-i-Martin (2004, chapter 5, A.3.3 and A.3.5). In this model, by setting various historical policy factors, such as the central planner's preferences and the elasticity between material and immaterial consumption, and between human and physical capital, Van Leeuwen et al. (2015, 221–224) showed that the choice of physical capital over human capital indeed led to high physical capital to human capital ratios. It was only after the reforms that this ratio declined.

It remains to be tested whether this focus on capital accumulation indeed led to higher GDP per capita for both countries (including their constituent parts). In principle, faster growth of physical capital per capita can, in one-sector growth models, lead to faster economic growth. For this reason, we expected to find that an increase in the ratio of physical to human capital (k/h ratio) led to a higher level of per capita GDP, as decreasing returns on capital should lead to zero growth in the long run (as in the case of all Solowian-type models), except when growth is driven by an exogenous process. Hence, the level of k/h affects the level of per capita income, but has only a transitory effect on growth. Since the material sector, which was stimulated during socialist planning, was also the most physical-capital intensive, it follows from this model that, during the central-planning period, the effect of the k/h ratio on aggregate income level must exceed that of market-reform periods, which were characterized by higher levels of the non-material sector (other inputs being equal). The results are reported in Table 7.2. We find that, as expected, the k/h ratio had a positive, even though insignificant, effect on per capita GDP prior to the reforms in the case of China, which was evidently at an earlier stage of industrialization than the USSR in 1950–1990. Yet after the reform period, it turned negative as expected. That is, the increase in the k/h ratio dampened economic growth, and vice versa—extending the share of human capital had a growth effect.

Furthermore, it was the case in the FSU but this effect was insignificant there during the immediate pre-reform period. This can be seen in Table 7.2, which uses panel data. However, since the data on the constituent republics are only available

Table 7.2 Fixed effect panel regressions of per capita GDP on the log of k/h ratio for the FSU area and China, 1950–2010

	(ex-)USSR		China	
	1950–1990	1990–2010	1953–1979	1980–2000
Constant	−23.1	−35.1	−65.3	−129.9
	(−3.04)	(−2.99)	(−14.0)	(−17.47)
Year	0.016	0.022	0.036	0.069
	(4.19)	(3.70)	(15.4)	(18.5)
Ln(k/h ratio)	**−0.066**	**−0.116**	**0.014**	**−0.157**
	(−0.66)	(−3.21)	(0.59)	(−3.11)
R^2	0.476	0.202	0.751	0.911
N	182	262	325	464

Note: Heteroscedasticity and serial correlation robust, standard errors in parentheses

for the period after 1970, the period is biased to the immediate pre-reform period. This period is characterized by a basically completed transition to a modern industrial society and an economic growth slowdown, while the 1950s–early 1970s appeared to be the zenith of industrialization and rapid growth in material sector supported by fixed-capital accumulation and migration from rural to urban sector. Hence, we expect that, if we were to run the same regression for the FSU area between 1950 and 1970, we would find a positive effect of the k/h ratio on per capita GDP. For the transition period (i.e. after 1990), we find, just as we did for China, that the effect of the k/h ratio on per capita GDP turns negative owing to the increased importance of human capital for economic growth.

In both the FSU and China, the increase in physical, relative to human, capital in the central planning period was based on economic models that aimed to rapidly stimulate industrialization. Based on these models alone, there is no reason to assume that this growth path could not have been sustained. However, in both countries, the system ultimately failed. One of the reasons why such kinds of growth appear to be unsustainable is the difference in the potential of physical and human capital to produce external economic and social effects. As seen in Sect. 7.2, this may include institutions, policy, and resource curse. Indeed, it is widely recognized that human capital preponderates over physical capital in this respect. Since the social returns on fixed capital are likely to be lower than those on human capital, the same amount of resources spent on increasing physical rather than human capital leads to a lower rate of economic growth.

Indeed, we find that just before the start of economic reforms in the FSU, when the physical capital to human capital ratio increased, per capita GDP growth decreased. During this period, human capital was necessary to increase GDP per capita owing to the greater importance of the non-material (human capital-intensive) consumer sector. Therefore, when human capital-intensive and physical capital-extensive sectors were on the rise, an increase in the physical to human capital ratio became negative or insignificant. In other words, the negative coefficient after the transition to a market economy can be seen as the sign of the k/h ratio converging to a lower equilibrium value, caused by increased demand for human capital-intensive consumer products. These findings are consistent with other studies on this relationship (see e.g. Erk et al. 1998; Duczynski 2002, 2003).

So far, our interpretation has focused only on production factors; that is, how human- and physical capital could have opposite effects on economic growth owing to different policy perspectives before and after reforms. Yet, as pointed out in Chap. 6, economic growth may also stem from the efficiency of both factors of production as well as from general technical growth (both captured in TFP). This is discussed in Sect. 7.5.

7.5 Long-Run Growth (TFP)

The previous section concluded on a potentially positive note: More human capital apparently increased GDP per capita after the reform period. Since human capital is assumed to also influence growth in the long run (here, TFP growth), this seems to be good news for both China and the FSU, since both countries were ultimately able to substantially increase their levels of human capital.

Both the USSR and China started with a low cost-based human-capital measure. However, while China started from almost nothing, the USSR more resembled Europe, as it already had a considerable human-capital base in the 1920s. Further, the USSR quickly caught up Europe in average years of education, but not in cost- or income-based human capital. However, in recent years, Chinese human capital has grown much faster than it ever did in the USSR, thereby suggesting that China has succeeded in narrowing the gap with more advanced economies.

The higher initial stock of human capital in the FSU in the early twentieth century may be one of the reasons why the USSR outperformed China in GDP per capita growth from the 1930s to the mid-1970s. Indeed, while both China and the FSU experienced rapid physical capital accumulation, only the FSU had relatively large stocks of human capital ready. This suggests that human capital increased the efficient use of physical capital, increasing factor efficiency and moderating TFP negative change. Table 7.3 shows that while Chinese TFP growth was positive before the socialist period, during the height of the socialist period it was −10%, much more negative than in the FSU area at about the same time.

After the reform period, however, we witness, after an initial collapse in the FSU, a rise in the growth of physical and human capital, combined with an increasingly negative TFP growth. This suggests that we have again entered a period of faster growth for factors of production, with decreasing growth rates owing to diminishing returns. However, the important difference is that human capital now plays a more important role, which might also positively influence TFP changes. Hence, it is important to analyse the effect of increases in the factors of production on both

Table 7.3 GDP per capita growth and TFP in China and the FSU, 1920–2006

	Factor share of human capital (HC)	Factor share of physical capital (FC)	Growth of GDP p.c.	Growth of HC p.c.	Growth of FC p.c.	TFP growth
	FSU					
1920–1940	40%	60%	6%	18%	8%	**−6%**
1950–1966	40%	60%	6%	4%	10%	**−2%**
1966–1977	40%	60%	3%	7%	5%	**−3%**
1978–1993	40%	60%	−1%	2%	3%	**−4%**
1994–2006	40%	60%	2%	7%	7%	**−5%**
	China					
1920–1940	53%	47%	0.1%	6%	−16%	**5%**
1950–1966	53%	47%	2%	16%	7%	**−10%**
1966–1977	44%	56%	2%	1%	5%	**−1%**
1978–1993	54%	46%	6%	12%	9%	**−5%**
1994–2006	54%	46%	8%	15%	11%	**−5%**

Note: Source factor shares for China: Chow (1993) and Li et al. (1993). Following Wang and Yao (2003), we assume the factor share of labour to be the same for both periods under the market reforms

components of TFP growth: Technical efficiency of human and physical capital,[17] and general changes in productivity.[18]

To do this, we start by using the Cobb–Douglas production function for a national economy, within the framework of the neoclassical growth model from Solow (1956, 1957).[19] Van Leeuwen et al. (2015, 229–230) showed that TFP consists of a

[17] Technical efficiency indicates how far production is from the most efficiently used set of human and physical capital among the regions within a national economy.

[18] The maximum possible output given inputs of physical and human capital.

[19]

$$Y_t = K_t^{\eta} \left(A_t L_t\right)^{1-\eta} \tag{7.1}$$

where
Y = output in monetary units (assumed to be GDP);
K = capital in monetary units (assumed by Solow to be only physical capital);
L = labour in natural units (number of workers in the labour force);
A = level of technology (assumed to be conventional TFP);
η = the elasticity of substitution (factor share) of physical capital.

Augmented with human capital accumulation (for example, Mankiw et al. 1992), this function can be modified as follows:

$$Y_t = K_t^{\eta} H_t^{\mu} \left(A_t L_t\right)^{1-\eta-\mu} \tag{7.2}$$

where (in addition, to the notation given for Eq. (7.1):
H = human capital stock in monetary units;
μ = elasticity of substitution (factor/income share) of human capital.

general production frontier and technical efficiency.[20] Therefore, we arrive at the approximate change in technical efficiency of physical and human capital in the whole country by simply subtracting that country's general technology growth from that of the TFP. It is clear that the productivity frontier moved less for the FSU than for China. Technical efficiency dynamics, though, were slightly positive in the FSU from 1978 to 1993, unlike in China (Table 7.4). This is not surprising given that China had faster growth of both human and physical capital during this period, which reduced the efficient use of these inputs. This changed in the post-1994 period, when in the FSU, human and physical capital started to grow again and their efficiency also turned negative.

Table 7.4 shows that the paths for the FSU and China diverged from the mid-1980s to the mid-1990s. However, during later periods, the difference was not in the direction of the trend of the general production frontier. This increased in both countries, but China outperformed the FSU in both magnitude and sustainability. Another difference is that upward movement of this parameter barely constituted a recovery in the FSU: By the end of the 2000s, the general production frontier for this area was not far above its pre-reform level. One plausible explanation of this pattern is that

Table 7.4 Decomposition of TFP growth in growth of technical efficiency and general productivity growth in the FSU and China, 1920–2006

	1920–1940	1950–1966	1966–1977	1978–1993	1994–2006
	FSU				
TFP growth	−6.0%	−3.6%	−2.8%	−1.6%	−4.0%
Technical efficiency			−4.0%	0.8%	−7.6%
General productivity growth			1.2%	−2.4%	3.6%
	China				
TFP growth	−4.7%	−9.8%	−1.2%	−4.6%	−5.2%
Technical efficiency		−8.6%	−0.7%	−6.6%	−8.6%
General technical growth		−1.2%	−0.5%	2.0%	3.4%

[20] The relationships among TFP growth, general technology growth, and technical efficiency of physical and human capital are as follows:

$$\frac{\dot{A}_t}{A_t} = \frac{\dot{\theta}_t}{\theta_t} + (\eta_i - \hat{\eta})\frac{\dot{k}_{it}}{k_{it}} + (\mu_i - \hat{\mu})\frac{\dot{h}_{it}}{h_{it}} \quad (7.3)$$

where (in addition, to the notation given for Eqs. (7.1) and (7.2):

θ = a time-variant general (common for all the regions of a country) productivity factor; in other words, the general technological level of a national economy. Similar to A in the standard growth accounting in Eq. (7.1), but free of the effect of technical-efficiency differences between the regions;

i = subscript denoting the province (in China) or the union republic (in the FSU);

$\hat{\eta}$ and $\hat{\mu}$ = elasticity (factor share) coefficients for the whole country;

η_i and μ_i = province- or republic-specific coefficients of elasticity between the factors of production.

increased openness in the economies of China and the FSU,[21] as well as their marked increase in the level of human capital relative to GDP, helped to extend active technological borrowing from abroad; however, China was able to benefit more owing to its better institutional environment.[22] The borrowing, however, contributed to general technical development, rather than to other components of technological level, such as the technical efficiency of factors of production.

While both regions are currently experiencing an upturn in economic development, there are two major differences. First, the FSU is generally replenishing its lost physical, and, to a lesser extent, human capital. Owing to its lower growth rates for capital stocks, this is being done with greater technical efficiency. Nevertheless, it is to be expected that diminishing returns will soon set in, along with lower growth rates, unless the FSU is able to modernize its stocks of human and physical capital in line with those of more-developed economies. In China, in contrast, a very high physical and human capital accumulation is already taking place, accompanied by increasing technical inefficiency. Growth continues because China is so far behind with regard to technology that it is easier to import, thereby increasing its productivity frontier. However, in some years China will likely face the same challenge as the FSU, with a choice between radically changing its entire field of technology or being trapped by low GDP per capita growth and diminishing return on capital. In other words, both China and the FSU have to extend their general production frontier (which is still far from a global one) and converge with advanced economies in the face of diminishing returns of physical and human capital.

7.6 Conclusion

The Former Soviet Union (FSU) and China are two countries that moved onto a path of forced modernization from a position of relative backwardness. Their strategy was one of catch-up: forced industrialization, with a neglect of consumer production and wage development. This led to a rapid increase in physical capital, enabling relatively fast, capital-based growth.

Some authors have favoured this state-socialist policy (running between 1928 and the mid-1950s in the FSU) as the best choice at the time (Allen 2003), even though it inhibited stagnation and promoted a decline in technological innovation.

[21] The source of the data (Heston et al. 2012 – PWT 7.0) defined "openness" as exports and imports as a share of GDP. During the reform period (1977–2009), it increased in China from 19.5 to 58.6% (or from 10.8 to 61.2%, according to an alternative estimation); in Russia (1990–2009), which had about half of the FSU population and GDP following reforms, it increased from 11.9 to 54.6%, most sharply at the start of that period.

[22] Although conventional measures of institutional environment (such as ease of doing business, the rule of law, government effectiveness, index of economic freedom, corruption perceptions index, and so forth) are expressed quantitatively; they are based on expert assessments and therefore are consensuses of subjective opinions that may not be directly verified.

Ellman (2004) admits that, although the Soviet breakthrough was not outstanding by international measures, it certainly stood out against the lower results of Africa, Latin America, and India between 1928 and 1989.

With the completion of the industrialization drive carried out by mobilization methods, a medium-developed industrial society was created in the USSR by the mid-1950s and in China probably closer to the end of the twentieth century. Such a society employed a principal cluster of global general-purpose technologies (albeit on a smaller scale than elsewhere). These technologies include digital information processing methods (computers), television (using space satellites) as the leading means of information transmission, obtaining energy at a nuclear level, microelectronic technology for semiconductors, artificial (chemically synthesized) materials, civil aviation, and private cars.

Why did state-socialist countries focus on physical capital accumulation when they must have been aware of the negative effect of institutions and policy? From a socialist perspective, these economies maximized material output, which was thought of as the means to withstand the outer capitalist world and win a war, which was perceived as highly probable. Applying a one-sector model to both economies, it is confirmed that policy motives were the driving force of this emphasis on physical capital accumulation. We have shown here that this strategy initially increased GDP per capita, although it eventually slowed growth rates when the focus shifted more to the production of human-capital-intensive consumer goods.

Even though decreases in growth rates were expected based on the theoretical model, there was no specific reason to assume that reforms would take place when they did, as they depended on the specific interplay of economic and social factors in both countries. There is, therefore, no direct reason why it was China that embarked earlier than the FSU on the path of increasing private consumption, which led to a decline in the physical to human capital ratio. While the FSU continued on the path of diminishing returns on physical capital, China slowly moved towards more human-capital-oriented industries, thereby avoiding the collapse experienced by the FSU and its economy in the 1990s.

After undergoing far-reaching reforms, China experienced an unprecedented rise in its human- and physical-capital stock. This initially led to decreasing technical efficiency. In the FSU, in contrast, physical capital collapsed and had not recovered by the 2010s, while human capital had a better performance. As a result of these factors, the FSU's technical efficiency growth appeared to be positive in the early 1990s, with a relatively modest decrease thereafter. Since the FSU was closer to the global production frontier, from 1970 to the present it grew little, if at all, in this dimension, while growth in China continued. However, even in China, general productivity growth was limited until market reforms were extended in the 1990s and 2000s.

After reforms in the 1980s (China) and 1990s (FSU), China was, contrary to the FSU, able to reduce the inefficiency of physical capital and safeguard physical capital against depreciation by massively investing in education; so, it was soon able to expand its production frontier, something the USSR/Russia only managed in the twenty-first century (Van Leeuwen et al. 2015). Yet the extent to which this government intervention also actively reshaped the economic geography in Asia in comparison with a less interventionist Europe remains a topic left largely unexplored (for an example of market-related government policy, see Van Leeuwen et al. 2020).

References

Acemoglu D, Robinson J (2012) Why nations fail: origins of power, poverty, and prosperity. Crown, New York, NY

Akerloff G, Yellen J (1990) The fair wage–effort hypothesis and unemployment. Q J Econ 105(2):255–283

Allen RC (2003) Farm to factory: a reinterpretation of the soviet industrial revolution. Princeton University Press, Princeton

Barber J, Harrison M (1991) The soviet home front, 1941–1945: a social and economic history of the USSR in World War II. Longman, London and New York

Barro R, Sala-i-Martin X (2004) Economic growth. MIT Press, Cambridge, MA; London, England

Bolt J, Van Zanden JL (2020) Maddison style estimates of the evolution of the world economy: a new 2020 update. Maddison Project Database, version 2020

Borodkin L, Ertz S (2005) Forced labor and the need for motivation: wages and bonuses in the Stalinist camp system. Comp Econ Stud 47(2):418–436

Brada JC, Graves RL (1988) Slowdown in Soviet defense expenditures. South Econ J 54(4):969–984

Chow G (1993) Capital formation and economic growth in China. Q J Econ 108(3):809–842. https://doi.org/10.2307/2118401

Davies RW, Wheatcroft SG (2004) The years of hunger: soviet agriculture, 1931–1933. Palgrave Macmillan

Desai P (1976) The production function and technical change in postwar soviet industry. Am Econ Rev 66(3):372–381

Didenko DV (2024) Трудовые отношения и способы производства в институциональном развитии России [Labour relations and modes of production under Russia's institutional development]. J Inst Stud 16(3):68–79. https://doi.org/10.17835/2076-6297.2024.16.3.068-079

Didenko DV, Grineva NV (2020) Анализ роли институтов и технологий в экономическом росте позднего ссср в межстрановом сопоставлении [Analysis of the role of institutions and technologies in economic growth of the late USSR in a cross-country comparison]. World New Econ 14(4):81–95. https://doi.org/10.26794/2220-6469-2020-14-4-81-95

Didenko DV, Grineva NV (2021) Soviet economic growth through the interstate prism: the role of research funding. Hist Inform 1:48–65. https://doi.org/10.7256/2585-7797.2021.1.34708

Didenko DV, Grineva NV (2022) Факторы роста экономики позднего СССР в пространственной перспективе [Factors of economic growth in the late USSR from a spatial perspective]. Econ Policy 17(2):88–119

Didenko D, Földvári P, Van Leeuwen B (2013) The spread of human capital in the former Soviet Union area in a comparative perspective: exploring a new dataset. J Eurasian Stud 4(2):123–135. https://doi.org/10.1016/j.euras.2013.03.002. (Supplementary data retrieved from https://ars.els-cdn.com/content/image/1-s2.0-S1879366513000122-mmc1.zip, accessed via https://www.sciencedirect.com/science/article/pii/S1879366513000122)

Duczynski P (2002) Adjustment costs in a two-capital growth model. J Econ Dyn Control 26(5):837–850. https://doi.org/10.1016/S0165-1889(01)00029-6

Duczynski P (2003) On the empirics of the imbalance effect. Int J Bus Econ 2(2):121–128

Easterly W, Fischer S (1995) The soviet economic decline: historical and republican data. World Bank Econ Rev 9(3):341–371. https://doi.org/10.1093/wber/9.3.341

Ellman M (2004) Soviet industrialization: a remarkable success? Slav Rev 63(4):841–849

Erk N, Altan Cabuk H, Ates S (1998) Long-run growth and physical capital-human capital concentration. Working Paper presented in International METU Conference on Economics II. http://idari.cu.edu.tr/sanli/academic.htm
Filtzer D (1986) Soviet workers and Stalinist industrialization: the formation of modern soviet production relations, 1928–1941. M. E. Sharpe, Armonk, NY
Filtzer D (1992) Soviet workers and de-Stalinization: the consolidation of the modern system of soviet production relations, 1953–1964. Cambridge University Press, Cambridge
Filtzer D (2002) Soviet workers and late Stalinism: labour and the restoration of the Stalinist system after World War II. Cambridge University Press, Cambridge
Foldvari P (2014) A latent democracy measure 1850-2000. CGEH working paper series. Working paper no. 59. www.cgeh.nl/sites/default/files/WorkingPapers/cgehwp59_foldvari.pdf
Földvári P, Van Leeuwen B, Didenko D (2015) Capital formation and economic growth under central planning and transition: a theoretical and empirical analysis, ca. 1920–2008. Acta Oecon 65(1):27–50
Fukao K, Ito K, Perugini C (2019) A microeconomic analysis of the declining labor share in Japan. ADBI working paper 925. Asian Development Bank Institute, Tokyo
Gaddy KG, Ickes BW (2013) Russia's dependence on resources. In: Alekseev M, Weber S (eds) The Oxford handbook of the Russian economy. Oxford University Press, pp 309–340
Goskomstat SSSR (1991) Сборник статистических материалов 1990 [A collection of statistical data 1990]. Финансы и статистика [Finance and Statistics], Moscow
Gregory P (1990) Restructuring the soviet economic bureaucracy. Cambridge University Press, Cambridge; New York; Port Chester, NY; Melbourne; and Sydney
Gregory PR (2003a) An introduction to the economics of the Gulag. In: Gregory PR, Lazarev VV (eds) The economics of forced labor: the Soviet Gulag. Hoover Institution Press, Stanford, CA, pp 1–21
Gregory PR (2003b) The political economy of Stalinism: evidence from the secret soviet archives. Cambridge University Press, Cambridge, MT
Hamilton K, Ruta G, Bolt K, Markandya A, Pedroso-Galinato S, Silva P, Ordoubadi MS, Lange G-M, Tajibaeva L (2005) Where is the wealth of nations?: measuring capital for the 21st century. World Bank, Washington, DC
He Y, Wu L (2007) The tide of the great leap forward. Policy Decision Inform 2007(2):53–57
Heston A, Summers R, Aten B (2012) Penn world table version 7.0—PWT 7.0. Center for International Comparisons of production, income and prices at the university of Pennsylvania. http://pwt.econ.upenn.edu/php_site/pwt_index.php. Accessed Mar 2012
Hui S (2017) Re-discussion on the controversy between planned economy and market economy. Economists 2017(09):55–57
ILO (2015) Yearbook of labour statistics. International Labour Organization, Geneva
Ivanova GM (2000) Labor camp socialism: the Gulag in the soviet totalitarian system. Edited and introduced by D. J. Raleigh, translated by C. Flath. M. E. Sharpe, Armonk, NY
Kabuzan VM (1971) Изменения в размещении населения России в XVIII—первой половине XIX в. (по материалам ревизий) [Changes in the distribution of Russia's population in the 18th—first half of the 19th century (Based on the population count records)]. Наука [The Science], Moscow
Khlevniuk OV (2003) The economy of the OGPU, NKVD, and MVD of the USSR, 1930–1953: the scale, structure, and trends of development. In: Gregory PR, Lazarev VV (eds) The economics of forced labor: the soviet Gulag. Hoover Institution Press, Stanford, CA, pp 43–66
Khlevniuk OV (2004a) History of the Gulag. Yale University Press, New Haven, CT
Khlevniuk OV (ed) (2004b) История сталинского Гулага. Конец 1920–х—первая половина 1950–х годов. Собрание документов в 7 томах [the history of Stalin's Gulag. Late 1920s–early 1950s. Collected documents in 7 volumes], vol 3, Экономика Гулага [Economics of the Gulag]. Российская политическая энциклопедия (РОССПЭН) [Russian Political Encyclopedia (ROSSPEN)], Moscow

Kontorovich V (2015) The military origins of soviet industrialization. Comp Econ Stud 57(4):669–692

Kontorovich V, Wein A (2009) What did the soviet rulers maximise? Eur Asia Stud 61(9):1579–1601

Kozlov VP, et al (eds) (2004) История сталинского Гулага. Конец 1920–х—первая половина 1950–х годов. Собрание документов в 7 томах [The history of Stalin's Gulag. Late 1920s–Early 1950s. Collected documents in 7 volumes], vol 6, Восстания, бунты и забастовки заключенных [Prison uprisings, riots and strikes]. Российская политическая энциклопедия (РОССПЭН) [Russian Political Encyclopedia (ROSSPEN)], Moscow

Krugman P (1994) The myth of Asia's miracle. Foreign Aff 73(6):62–78. https://doi.org/10.2307/20046929

Lange G-M, Hamilton K, Ruta G, Chakraborti L, Desai D, Edens B, Ferreira S, Fraumeni B, Jarvis M, Kingsmill W, Li H (2011) The changing wealth of nations: measuring sustainable development in the new millennium. World Bank, Washington, DC

Li J, Jorgenson DW, Youjing Z, Kuroda M (1993) Productivity and economic growth in China, United States and Japan. Chinese Social Science Press, Beijing

Lin Y (2007) Needham puzzle, Weber question and China's miracle: long-term performance since the song dynasty. J Peking Univ (Phil Soc Sci) 2007(4):5–22

Lin Y, Yu M (2009) The political economy of price scissors in China: theoretical model and empirical evidence. Econ Res J 2009(1):42–56

Mankiw NG, Romer D, Weil DN (1992) A contribution to the empirics of economic growth. Q J Econ 107(2):407–437

Meliantsev VA (2004) Russia's comparative economic development in the long run. Soc Evol Hist 3(1):106–136

Mironov BN (2018) Российская империя: от традиции к модерну. [The Russian Empire: from tradition to modernity], vol 1–3, 2nd edn. Dmitrii Bulanin, St. Petersburg

Moon D (2001) The abolition of serfdom in Russia, 1762–1907. Longman, New York

Moorsteen R, Powell R (1966) The soviet capital stock, 1928–1962. Richard D. Irwin, Inc., Homewood, IL

Ofer G (1987) Soviet economic growth: 1928-1985. J Econ Lit 25(4):1767–1833

Pomeranz K (2000) The great divergence: China, Europe, and the making of the modern world economy. Princeton University Press, Princeton and Oxford

Popov V (2007) Life cycle of the centrally planned economy: why soviet growth rates peaked in the 1950s. In: Estrin S, Kolodko GW, Uvalic M (eds) Transition and beyond. Studies in economic transition. Palgrave Macmillan, London, pp 35–57

Popov V (2014) Mixed fortunes: an economic history of China, Russia, and the west. Oxford University Press, New York

Sokolov AK (2003) Forced labor in society industry: the end of the 1930s to the mid-1950s (an overview). In: Gregory PR, Lazarev VV (eds) The economics of forced labor: the soviet Gulag. Hoover Institution Press, Stanford, CA, pp 23–42

Solow RM (1956) A contribution to the theory of economic growth. Q J Econ 70(1):65–94

Solow RM (1957) Technical change and the aggregate production function. Rev Econ Stat 39(3):312–320

Steinberg D (1990) The soviet economy, 1970–1990: a statistical analysis. International Trade Press, San Francisco

Van Leeuwen B, Földvári P (2008) How much human capital does Eastern Europe have? Measurement methods and results. Post-Communist Econ 20(2):189–201

Van Leeuwen B, Didenko D, Földvári P (2015) Inspiration vs. perspiration in economic development of the former Soviet Union and China (ca. 1920–2010). Econ Transit 23(1):213–246

Van Leeuwen B, Földvári P, Philips RCM, Wang M (2020) Regional industrialization: evidence on industry agglomeration. In: van Leeuwen B, Philips R, Buyst E (eds) An economic history of regional industrialization (Routledge explorations in economic history). Routledge, Oxon and New York, pp 228–259

Voskoboinikov IB, Driabina EV (2010) Историческая статистика основных фондов российской промышленности в 1970-2004 годах [Historical statistics of fixed assets of Russian industry in 1970-2004]. Issues Stat 3:28–45

Wang Y, Yao Y (2003) Sources of China's economic growth 1952-1999: incorporating human capital accumulation. China Econ Rev 14(1):32–52

Weitzman ML (1970) Soviet postwar economic growth and capital-labor substitution. Am Econ Rev 60(5):676–692

Whalley J, Zhao X (2010) The contribution of human capital to China's economic growth. NBER Working Paper No. 16592. http://www.nber.org/papers/w16592

Wolf M (2014) The shifts and the shocks: what we've learned—and have still to learn—from the financial crisis. Penguin, London

Wu L (2003) China's planned economy reconsidered and reassessed. Contemporary China Hist Stud 2003(4):37–46

Xu D, Wu C (2000) Chinese capitalism, 1522-1840 (L. Zhengde, L. Miaoru, & L. Siping, trans.; C. A. Curwen, Ed. & Abrid.). St. Martin's Press, New York

Yakovlev AN et al (eds) (2000) ГУЛАГ: Главное управление лагерей [GULAG: chief directorate of camps]. 1918–1960. MFD, Moscow

Zhang X (2021) A centennial exploration of the Communist Party of China's leading China towards prosperity and strength. Soc Sci China 2021(11):74–94

Chapter 8
The Effect of Government Expenditure and Monetary Expansion on Economic Growth

Abstract Government expenditure and monetary expansion have been key drivers of economic growth, shaping fiscal and monetary policies across historical and cultural contexts. This chapter examines how state interventions—via tax-funded projects or money supply adjustments—have stabilized economies and spurred long-term growth. Fiscal policy, channelling government spending into gross domestic product growth, has been fundamental, supporting deep monetization, infrastructure, education, and public services. Debates around its effectiveness highlight a key economic issue: balancing stability with the risks of inflation or inefficiencies from extensive spending. Monetary policy, on the other hand, affects inflation and economic cycles through adjustments in money supply and interest rates, with long-run data showing that temporary monetary boosts often yield limited long-term impact without structural changes.

Cultural attitudes towards money—as debt or commodity—significantly impact policy effectiveness. Debt-oriented economies tend to respond more dynamically to policy adjustments, while commodity-based economies (such as those anchored to the gold standard) show lower responsiveness. Regional case studies illustrate these dynamics: the USSR and China, under centralized command economies, focused on stability and growth control, whereas Western Europe relied on taxation to fund welfare and military efforts, reflecting distinct fiscal priorities and capacities.

Section 8.2 of this chapter is partly based on Van der Spek, R. J., & Van Leeuwen, B. (2018a). Money and Trust. In R. J. van der Spek, & B. van Leeuwen (Eds.), Money, Currency and Crisis: In Search of Trust, 2000 BC to AD 2000. (Routledge Explorations in Economic History). Routledge, pp. 1–12.

B. Van Leeuwen et al., *Innovation and Economic Development in Eurasia, 500 BCE-Present*, Frontiers in Economic History,
https://doi.org/10.1007/978-3-031-97043-6_8

8.1 Introduction

As discussed in previous chapters, government investment has long been a fundamental driver of economic development, with states historically investing in infrastructure such as roads, famine relief, and water management. This investment can occur through two primary channels. The first is monetary expansion, where new money is printed and introduced into circulation. The second is fiscal policy, where expenditures are funded through tax revenue. In practice, such investments can have significant impacts, as demonstrated by state-led industrialization in the latter half of the twentieth century. As we have explored, governments often leverage their spending and taxing powers to foster stable and sustainable growth.

The process towards efficient centralized taxation needs first to be tied to the levels of deep monetization of a country—the extent to which money permeates an economy, including its distribution in the form of coins and small-denomination currency for daily transactions. The path of monetization traces back centuries, with ancient economies gradually adopting coins to facilitate trade and taxation. In seventh to sixth century BCE Lydia, the abundance of electrum (a gold/silver alloy) led to the first coins, though these early forms barely functioned as currency (Kroll 2012, 38). Gold and silver coins emerged more broadly around the fifth century BCE in Greece and later in the Persian Empire. In China, precious metals were not coined, but copper and bronze coins became standard around this period, creating a foundation for monetization. By around 300 BCE, the Seleucid Empire achieved a monetization rate of roughly 60%, similar to that of China in the seventeenth century CE, suggesting that deep monetization historically required both a reliable currency and widespread use among the populace (Van Leeuwen et al. 2018).

Table 8.1 illustrates the levels of deep monetization in various countries by 1890. Western and Central European nations, particularly Portugal (17%), Spain (15%), and Italy (14%), achieved high levels of deep monetization compared with Russia (1.5%) and the United States (2.7%). This discrepancy reflects differences in fiscal policy development, monetary supply, and demand for small-denomination currency, which allowed European nations to foster a deeper penetration of currency across their economies. For example, the availability of small-denomination coins allowed people in these regions to conduct transactions, receive wages, and make daily payments, creating a consistent demand that reinforced monetization.

Table 8.2 shows long-term monetization in regions such as England, the Netherlands, Japan, and China. China achieved a high monetization level as early as 1120 owing to strong use of coinage within its extensive economy. However, by the eighteenth and nineteenth centuries, European nations began surpassing China owing to expanding fiscal policies and increasing small-denomination coin supply, which fostered broader public engagement with currency. By the late nineteenth century, these Western regions had improved their levels of deep monetization, supporting economic fluidity and stable growth as economies modernized.

Tables 8.1 and 8.2 give a first indication that the process of deep monetization is deeply entwined with fiscal policy efficiency. Fiscal policy basically uses

Table 8.1 Deep monetization for various countries, c. 1890

Country	Deep monetization
Austria Hungary	12
Belgium	10
Denmark	9
Egypt	2
France	8
Germany	10
Greece	6
Italy	14
Norway	4
Portugal	17
Russia	1.5
Serbia	11.5
Spain	15
Sweden	2.2
Switzerland	8
Turkey	4
UK	4.9
US	2.7

Source: Lucassen (2018), pp. 55–101, appendix 4.1

Table 8.2 Deep monetization for various countries, c. 1120–1885

Year	England	Netherlands	Japan	China
1120				88
1282	5			
1290	6			
1299	6			
1310	8.5			
1319	11			
1331	10.5			
1351	16			
1550		12		
1600		5		
1650		7	5.3	
1720	3	2		60
1750		11		67
1800		5		
1857	2	4.5		
1885	4.9	8	13.3	

Source: Lucassen (2018), pp. 55–101, Table 4.1, Table 4.4, Table 4.9, Table 4.10

government income in order to stabilize economic growth. According to the basic macroeconomic identity Y = C + I + G + (Export–Import), where Y = gross domestic product (GDP), C = consumption, I = investment, G = government expenditure, and fiscal expenditure (increasing G) leads to economic growth directly. Yet, the government can also affect the other factors (C, I, E, Imports) indirectly via taxation. This expenditure can have long-run effects, for example by investments in goods and services such as education; and also short run macroeconomic effects, for example temporary economic growth stabilization or enhancing of the general economy by cutting taxes.[1] Yet, even though it may have some effects, applying fiscal policy to the economy does not necessary result in dramatic changes in the general economy. Indeed, some scholars have argued that no government policy is necessary or effective. This view aligns with the laissez-faire perspective that dominated Western economic thought, particularly during the nineteenth and early twentieth centuries, when it was believed that markets, left to their own devices, would allocate resources most efficiently (e.g. Friedman 1962). Proponents of this view argue that government intervention distorts natural market equilibria and could lead to inefficiencies (Hayek 1944; Friedman and Schwartz 1963). A second brand of scholars found instead that, especially during particularly severe (economic) crises, the government could intervene with fiscal policy, as argued by the Keynesian economists. However, even Keynesians recognize that fiscal policy is not always effective under all circumstances. One significant limitation is the potential for economic "leakages", which occur when an increase in government spending does not fully stimulate domestic economic activity. This can happen if, for example, much of the government's increased spending is directed towards imports. For instance, when a country uses fiscal stimulus to boost demand, but consumers or businesses purchase foreign goods and services instead of domestic ones, the intended economic impact is diminished as money flows out of the domestic economy (Krugman 2009). As a third group, monetarist economists, such as Milton Friedman, have strongly criticized the over-reliance on fiscal policy, particularly in cases where it is poorly coordinated with monetary policy. According to Friedman, controlling the money supply and managing inflation through interest rate adjustments are more important for long-term economic stability than temporary fiscal interventions (Friedman 1968). Monetarists argue that excessive government spending, especially when not matched by sound monetary policy, can lead to inflationary pressures, currency devaluation, and other unintended economic consequences. For example, if fiscal expansion leads to rising inflation because the money cannot be productively invested, central banks might be forced to raise interest rates, ultimately countering the initial goal of the fiscal policy (Mankiw 2019).[2]

Monetary policy, therefore, basically combines decisions on economic stabilization by using inflation (i.e. comparable to fixed exchange rates) and targeted output

---

[1] Horton and El-Ganainy (n.d.).

[2] Ibidem.

levels.[3] Monetary policy can thus exert high pressure in stable inflation rates. Since most scholars argue that, owing to rising inflation, money is neutral in the long run, this implies monetary policy only results in short-run effects. Yet, not all authors agree on this perspective on short-run effects. For example, Palma (2022) finds that the exogenous shock of rising Spanish silver imports into Europe in the Early Modern Period mainly caused a rising real income and, to a lesser extent, increased inflation (the equivalent of fixed interest rates). Only later rising prices put a brake on economic growth. While both fiscal and monetary policy can thus be leveraged to stimulate or contract GDP, the key question lies in determining the appropriate timing and methods for employing these tools to achieve either short-run stabilization or sustained long-term growth. In recent economic history, however, additional factors have increasingly been mentioned that, via either fiscal or monetary policy, shaped growth outcomes, both in the short and long run. Indeed, beyond state intervention, foreign trade and financial intermediation have both become progressively influential in driving economic growth via fiscal and monetary policy, particularly as economies transition into modernity. It is no coincidence that trade and finance evolved into two fundamental sectors whose development was crucial in propelling the shift towards modern economic growth.

Financial intermediaries in particular play a pivotal role by bridging the gap between the public and private sectors. They often engage with more traditional branches of the service sector, such as public administration, which is in turn shaped by political and broader cultural influences. In some instances, these intermediaries can even emerge as alternative centres of fiscal law creation, challenging and sometimes reshaping the relationship between the state and the broader economy (see e.g. Pistor 2019; Calabrese and Majerus 2024). As such, financial intermediaries—banks and also business lawyers and notaries—are not only vital to the functioning of markets but also act as catalysts for significant structural changes within economies, often influencing the direction of fiscal and regulatory policy. In this way, financial intermediation, and other factors such as trade, have become indispensable drivers of economic transformation, shaping market dynamics as well as the regulatory frameworks that underpin them. Their growing influence underscores the complex interplay between government policy, market forces, and institutional evolution in fostering both stability and growth (Fig. 8.1).

In the following sections, we identify long-run comparative trends in the development of the monetary expansion (Sect. 8.2) and fiscal policy (Sect. 8.3) and their effect on long-run economic growth and short-run economic stabilization in the Eurasian bloc. In Sect. 8.4, we deal with a specific case: monetary command/administration economy in the USSR and China.

---

[3] Mathai (n.d.).

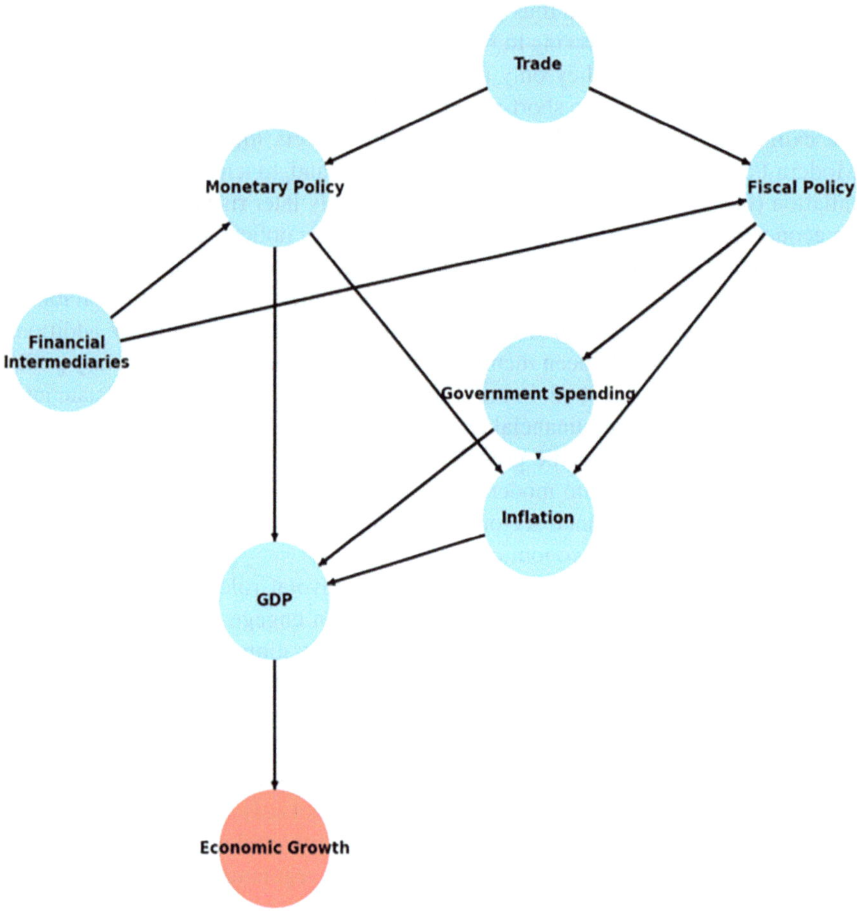

Fig. 8.1 Monetary and fiscal policy interactions within a national economic system

8.2 GDP Per Capita Growth Owing to Monetary Expansion

We start by focusing on a long-run analysis of state and private actors' financing through monetary policies. In the standard IS–LM (Investment Savings–Liquidity Preference Money Supply) model, the IS curve gives a combination of interest rate and GDP (lower interest rate gives higher GDP) and the LM curve a combination of interest rate and GDP, where increasing income implies higher interest rate—resulting from a bigger demand for money. Hence, the LM curve is upward sloping. Where the IS and LM curves intersect, the goods and money markets are in balance (Fig. 8.2).

In the IS–LM model, shifts in the IS and LM curves are driven by different factors that affect the equilibrium in the goods and money markets, respectively. The IS curve, which represents equilibrium in the goods market, shifts in response to

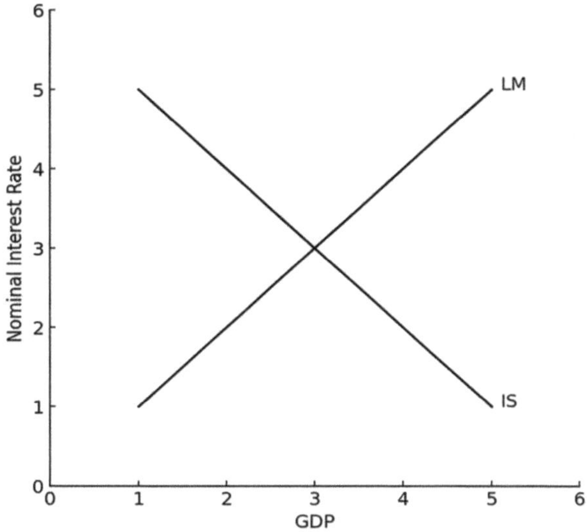

Fig. 8.2 IS (Investment–Savings)–LM (Liquidity Preference–Money Supply) model

changes in aggregate demand. Key determinants include fiscal policy actions such as changes in government spending and taxation, where increased government spending or tax cuts shift the IS curve to the right (see also Sect. 8.3), reflecting higher demand. Additionally, shifts can occur owing to changes in consumer confidence, investment demand, foreign demand for domestic goods (net exports), and household wealth. On the other hand, the LM curve, representing equilibrium in the money market, shifts primarily owing to changes in the money supply, nowadays controlled by central banks. An increase in the money supply shifts the LM curve to the right, indicating lower interest rates for a given level of income. Changes in the price level and money demand also influence the position of the LM curve, with lower price levels or decreased money demand shifting the LM curve to the right.

The slopes of these curves are determined by different factors. The slope of the IS curve is influenced by the marginal propensity to consume (MPC), the sensitivity of investment to interest rates, and the tax rate. A higher MPC or greater investment sensitivity to interest rates results in a flatter IS curve, meaning that output is more responsive to changes in interest rates. Conversely, a lower MPC, less sensitive investment, or higher tax rates makes the IS curve steeper, indicating that interest rate changes have a more muted effect on output. The LM curve's slope is determined by the sensitivity of money demand to changes in interest rates and income. If money demand is highly sensitive to interest rates, the LM curve is flatter, as even small changes in income would require significant adjustments in interest rates to maintain equilibrium. If money demand is less responsive to interest rates or highly sensitive to income, the LM curve becomes steeper, showing that changes in income lead directly to more pronounced changes in interest rates.

In the long run, both the IS and LM curves can experience changes in their slopes owing to structural shifts in the economy. For instance, financial innovations might make investment more elastic to interest rates, leading to a flatter IS curve over time.

Similarly, the LM curve may also undergo long-run changes as developments in financial markets influence how people hold and use money. For example, increased access to financial products that serve as alternatives to holding cash could make money demand more sensitive to interest rates, flattening the LM curve. Additionally, shifts in central bank policies or the structure of the banking system could alter the relationship between income, interest rates, and money demand, affecting the slope of the LM curve. Thus, while short-run shifts and slope changes reflect immediate economic policies and conditions, long-run adjustments tend to incorporate broader structural transformations in the economy.

As pointed out earlier, investments in the real economy have always been possible across different societies, but in ancient societies, the absence of a true capital market had significant implications for the IS–LM model. While loans did exist, interest rates were typically fixed by tradition and did not fluctuate in response to changes in the money supply, as they do in modern economies. As a result, investment decisions were not influenced by the lowering of saving rates or increased consumption. In these societies, when money entered the private sector, economic outcomes were largely dependent on the propensity to save, which was nevertheless likely low. In such a model, it is often argued that a rise in money stock shifts the LM curve outwards. Yet, because this causes over time lower interest rates, this will shift the curve back again, just with higher interest rates and no increase in GDP (i.e. money is neutral). The question is thus, whether the LM shifts completely back, or is there still space for economic growth by monetary expansion (see e.g. Van der Spek et al. 2018). However, if people lose trust in money, monetary spending is more quickly perceived as speculative, leading to a flatter, even horizontal, LM curve. In this scenario, monetary expansion has little to no impact on the economy, as the increase in the money supply fails to stimulate demand.

Trust in money has evolved over time and varies regionally within the Eurasian bloc. One way to understand this is by examining how different populations in different periods perceive money, whether as debt or as a commodity. In societies where money is perceived primarily as debt, there is a stronger connection to credit systems and the financial sector, with banks playing a central role in money creation. This perspective tends to produce a more elastic IS curve because investment in these societies is highly sensitive to interest rates, making it more responsive to changes in credit conditions. The LM curve in such contexts reflects the central government's control over the money supply, which directly impacts interest rates and overall economic activity.

Conversely, in societies where it is viewed more as a commodity, money is considered to have an intrinsic value, often linked to a physical substance such as gold. Here, the IS curve tends to be less elastic, as investment decisions are less influenced by interest rates and more by the availability and value of the commodity backing the money. The LM curve becomes steeper (more vertical) when the money supply is constrained by the availability of a commodity, indicating that the output (GDP) becomes less sensitive to changes in interest rates. In these societies, inflation expectations are more tied to the supply and demand of the commodity, and fiscal policy is less effective since government spending is constrained by the need to maintain the commodity reserves.

Overall, societies that view money as debt may exhibit a more dynamic and responsive IS–LM model, sensitive to monetary policy and financial market conditions, while those that view money as a commodity may display a more stable but less responsive economic environment, with slower economic growth and less impact from monetary interventions. This distinction highlights how cultural perceptions of money can shape economic behaviour and the effectiveness of policies in different contexts.

To assess whether a society was more inclined towards a debt-based or commodity-based monetary mindset, we can examine the terms used for money, particularly in ancient times (see e.g. Van der Spek and Van Leeuwen 2018). In many early cultures, the word for "money" often referred to a commodity, most notably precious metals such as silver or gold. For instance, in Sumerian logograms, "money" was written as *KÙ.BABBAR*. The sign *KÙ* (or *KU3*), which appeared in late fourth-millennium BCE documents from Uruk, southern Mesopotamia, held the dual meaning of "shining" and, as a noun, "shining metal". The accompanying word *BABBAR* means "white", referring specifically to silver. Similarly, the word for gold was written as *KÙ.GI*, meaning "yellow shining metal" (Krispijn 2016). In Akkadian—the Semitic language that developed alongside Sumerian and was spoken by the Old-Akkadian Empire, Assyrians, and Babylonians—the word for both silver and money was *kaspu*. This dual meaning extended into other Semitic languages, such as ancient and modern Hebrew, where the word *kesep* or *kesef* is used. In Hebrew, *kesef* translates as both "silver" and "money", illustrating the close association between currency and precious metals in ancient economies.

In ancient Greek, a similar pattern emerges: the word *ho argyros* (from *argos*, meaning "shining") refers to both silver and money. The Greek term *to argyrion* could mean either coin or money. Expressions such as *argyrion katharon*—literally "pure silver"—were used to signify "hard cash" (Theocritus 15.36). However, other goods also held monetary value. The term *chrēmata* refers to "things that are needed" (from *chrāsthai*, meaning "to need, to be in want of, to use"), encompassing assets, things, and money.

This duality between precious metals and other goods as money also appears in Latin, where two distinct terms exist for money: *argentum*, meaning silver, and *pecunia*, which may derive from *pecus* (genitive *pecoris*, meaning "cattle"). In early Roman society, cattle were a key indicator of wealth, and *pecunia* likely referred to property in cattle, demonstrating the importance of various commodities as forms of wealth.

This use of other commodities as money is also evident in ancient China. The Chinese word for money, *qian* (钱), originally referred to farming tools, which were used as a medium of exchange much as cattle were in early Rome. The first Chinese coins were cast in the form of these tools (Von Glahn 2018).

This contrast clearly reveals different cultural views on money. In Akkadian, for instance, there are expressions such as *ana kaspi nadānu* ("to give for silver", i.e. to sell) and *ana kaspi mahāru* ("to receive for silver", i.e. to buy). Although this partly reflects the Greek understanding, the Greeks also used an abstract term for money: *nomisma*. This term referred to coinage and was derived from *nomos*, meaning "law" or "custom". Aristotle explains it in the *Nicomachean Ethics* as follows: "Money has become by convention a sort of representative of demand; this is why it has the name 'money' [*nomisma*], because it exists not by nature but by law [*nomos*], and it is in our power to change it and make it useless" (*Nicomachean Ethics* 1133b 1). In other words, the concept of *nomisma* marked a distinction between the intrinsic value of the material and its nominal value as currency.

In contrast, the term for money in Germanic languages has a different origin. The German and Dutch word *Geld*, related to the English word "yield", literally means "recompense" and often referred to payments, particularly in the context of *wergild*—a compensation paid for injury or death. This idea of money as recompense or repayment shows that money was not just a medium of exchange or store of value, but also a means of settling debts and resolving social obligations.

In early Germanic and Norse cultures, money often existed in the form of debt payments, fines, and compensations within a broader system of social justice. The legal codes of these societies, such as the Anglo-Saxon *wergild* (man-price), required a monetary payment to compensate for wrongdoing, such as personal injury or homicide. This system reinforced the notion that money was owed as a form of restitution, emphasizing a moral and social dimension to its use. The purpose of such payments was not only economic, but also restorative, aiming to maintain social harmony by resolving disputes through financial compensation.

The Dutch word *geld* and the German word *Geld* (both derived from the Proto-Germanic root *geldam*) similarly refer to money but retain this connotation of payment and obligation. This view differs from the Greek concept of *nomisma*, which was based on the nominal value established by law or custom, and from the Akkadian *kaspu*, which associated money directly with silver.

Furthermore, in Germanic legal traditions, debts were often not only contractual, but also tied to one's honour and social standing. Failure to repay debts could result in severe penalties, including servitude or exile, further underscoring how deeply money and debt were interwoven into the social and legal fabric. This view of money as a means of fulfilling social obligations persisted well into the medieval period, especially in feudal systems where debts were owed to lords, kings, or other superiors in exchange for land, protection, or favours.

This discrepancy in the meaning of "money" can also be traced in modern languages. However, the picture becomes more complex owing to the intermingling of European languages over time, suggesting the coexistence of different mindsets within the same geographical areas. For example, while the German *Geld* and the Dutch *geld* are both derived from Germanic roots, the French word for both "money" and "silver" is *argent*. In English, both *money* and *mint* are derived from *Moneta*, the epithet of the Roman goddess Juno Moneta, in whose temple the mint was established (*monēta*). The Latin word *nummus*—used to denote "coin"—is derived from the Greek *nomos*. In Italian and Spanish, the words for money (It. *soldi*, Sp. *dinero*) have their origins in Roman coinage, from the silver *denarius* and the late Roman gold *solidus*.

When comparing past and present perspectives on money seen as debt versus money as a commodity, the key question is therefore whether the mindset surrounding money remains the same as it was approximately 2000 years ago. In Fig. 8.3, we present the results of a 2022 survey,[4] focusing on five representative countries within the Eurasian bloc: Italy, the Netherlands, Russia, China, and Japan. This survey explores cultural attitudes towards the concept of money in these nations. Participants from various demographic groups—differing in gender, education, and age—were asked the following question: "Do you think that printing money leads to more government debt?"

The figure shows responses from these countries regarding whether printing money leads to more government debt. The Netherlands has a strong majority believing it does, suggesting a debt-oriented mindset, where money is closely tied to government liabilities. This implies the potential presence of a flatter LM curve in the Netherlands, as money demand is highly sensitive to interest rate changes. In Italy, responses are more mixed, indicating a balance between debt and commodity mindsets, which could lead to a steeper LM curve with less sensitivity to interest rates. China, Russia, and Japan display similar patterns, likely resulting in steeper LM curves and less elastic IS curves, where investment and economic behaviour are less driven by interest rates and more by other factors such as government policies or the perceived intrinsic value of money. These differences highlight how cultural

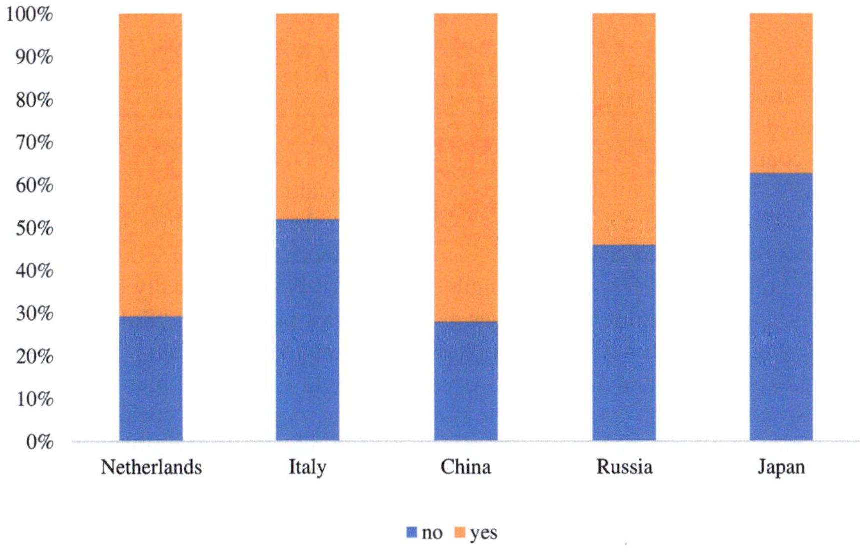

Fig. 8.3 "Do you think that printing money leads to more government debt?" Survey responses in Italy, the Netherlands, Russia, China, and Japan (2022). *Source:* This survey was conducted for this book through the service provider SurveyMonkey in 2022 (see Appendixes D and E)

[4] This survey we conducted for this book was through the service provider SurveyMonkey.

perceptions of money shape the effectiveness of monetary policy and economic behaviour across these countries.

To further investigate the presence of a cultural mindset about money, we can employ a frame-analysis methodology (see e.g. Calabrese and Van Leeuwen 2024). Using this methodology, we analyse data from the Google Ngram Viewer, a Google-provided tool that tracks the frequency of specific words or phrases in a vast corpus of books published over several centuries. By examining these trends, we can identify the prominence of certain concepts over time. For the current chapter, we selected words based on their association with either a debt or commodity mindset in particular regions and periods. This approach allows us not only to assess current cultural attitudes towards money, but also to extend our analysis over a longer historical period. By doing so, we can trace the evolution of these mindsets over the past 200 years, gaining deeper insights into how cultural attitudes within the Eurasian bloc have developed and transformed over time.

For the debt mindset, we chose keywords such as "credit", "debt", "banking", "loan", "interest rate", and "paper money". These terms are central to a financial system where lending, borrowing, and the operations of financial institutions play a pivotal role. The prevalence of these words reflects a societal focus on the extension of credit and the functioning of a debt-based economy. For instance, the term "credit" indicates a financial system heavily reliant on lending, while "debt" directly refers to obligations or liabilities, capturing the essence of borrowing and repayment in such an economy. Similarly, "banking" highlights the role of financial institutions in money creation and "interest rate" is tied to the cost of borrowing, which is a critical factor in a credit-based system. The term "paper money" suggests a shift from commodity-backed currency to a system where money's value is not intrinsic but based on trust in the government, further reinforcing a debt-oriented mindset.

In contrast, for the commodity mindset, we selected keywords such as "gold", "silver", "bullion", "gold standard", "specie", "metallic currency", and "intrinsic value". These terms are indicative of a system where the physical substance backing currency, such as gold or silver, is of paramount importance. The use of "gold" and "silver" reflects a preference for tangible assets that have historically backed currency, signalling a mindset that values money with intrinsic worth. "Bullion" refers to precious metals in bulk form, emphasizing the importance of the physical substance itself in a commodity-based system. The "gold standard" represents a monetary system in which currency value is directly tied to gold, and "specie" refers to physical coinage, particularly gold or silver, embodying the tangible aspect of money. The phrase "metallic currency" reinforces the idea of money made from or backed by metals, while "intrinsic value" reflects the belief that money should have inherent worth, not just serve as a medium of exchange.

By tracking the frequency of these keywords over time using the Google Ngram Viewer, we can identify periods where either the debt or commodity mindset was more dominant. For example, a rise in the use of terms such as "credit", "debt", and "banking" might indicate a period when the debt mindset prevailed, likely owing to the expansion of financial institutions and the growing importance of credit. Conversely, an increase in terms such as "gold", "bullion", and "gold standard" would suggest a period when the commodity mindset was more influential, reflecting a preference for money backed by physical assets with intrinsic value.

Figures 8.4 and 8.5 depict the evolution of debt and commodity mindsets in Italy from 1789 to 2022 and in the Netherlands from 1850 to 2014. Italy shows a gradual increase in the debt mindset, particularly from the mid-nineteenth century onwards, with a more pronounced rise after the Second World War. This reflects Italy's shift towards a more modern, credit-based economy where reliance on credit, loans, and paper money became central. By the late twentieth and early twenty-first centuries, the debt mindset stabilized at a relatively high level, indicating that Italy's financial system had become increasingly dependent on credit mechanisms, aligning with a debt-oriented framework. Conversely, the commodity mindset, which had dominated in the eighteenth and early nineteenth centuries, steadily declined over time. This decline mirrors the broader global trend of moving away from commodity-backed currencies, such as the gold standard, and towards fiat money. Italy's mixed responses regarding the relationship between printing money and government debt, as reflected in the graph, suggest a balance between both debt and commodity mindsets. While the debt mindset grew more prominent over time, the coexistence of both indicates a complex economic environment that retained some elements of the older commodity-based views. This shift towards a stronger debt mindset, particularly after the 1950s, supports our suggestion of a progressively flatter LM curve in Italy, implying that the economy became in the long run more sensitive to interest rate changes.

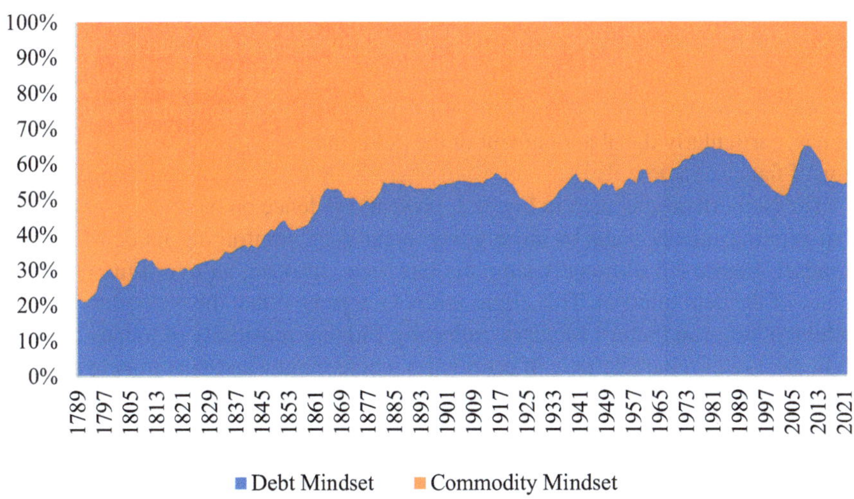

Fig. 8.4 Debt–commodity mindset for Italy (1789–2022). *Source and keywords used:* https://books.google.com/ngrams/. Words: "credito"; "debito"; "bancario"; "prestito"; "tasso di interesse"; "cartamoneta"; "oro"; "argento"; "lingotti"; "standard aureo"; "moneta metallica"; "valore intrinseco"

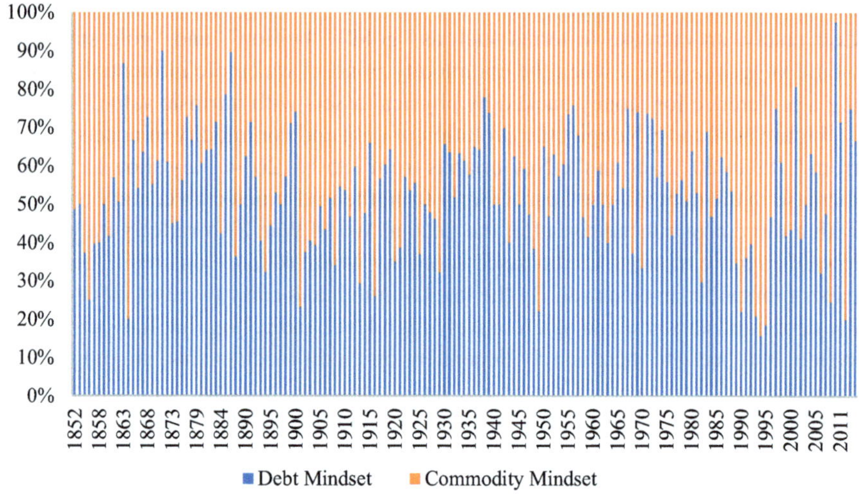

Fig. 8.5 Debt–commodity mindset for the Netherlands (1850–2014). *Source and keywords used:* https://www.dbnl.org/ngram-viewer/. Words: "krediet", "schuld", "bankwezen", "lening", "rente", "papiergeld"; "goud", "edelmetaal", "gouden standaard", and "intrinsieke waarde"

In contrast, the Netherlands exhibits a fluctuating yet generally higher trend towards a more debt-oriented mindset in the long run, with significant spikes throughout the twentieth century. By the early twenty-first century, the debt mindset had stabilized at a high level, much as in Italy, though the path to this point was marked by more volatility. This suggests that while the Netherlands moved towards a debt-oriented system, reliance on credit fluctuated at times, possibly in response to economic crises or policy shifts. The commodity mindset declined sharply in the nineteenth and twentieth centuries, and by the late twentieth century, the reliance on commodity-backed currency had nearly vanished. This is consistent with global trends, particularly the abandonment of the gold standard and the widespread adoption of fiat currencies.

The Netherlands, as seen in Fig. 8.3, presents evidence on having a strong belief that printing money leads to more government debt, reinforcing its debt-oriented mindset. Figure 8.5 ultimately supports this view, showing an over-time predominance of the debt mindset. This aligns with our argument that the Netherlands could exhibit a long-run flatter LM curve, reflecting a higher sensitivity of money demand to interest rates, characteristic of economies where money and government debt are closely linked.

Overall, both graphs highlight a historical transition from a commodity-based mindset to a debt-based one, which is in line with the broader historical narrative of modern economies increasingly relying on credit and fiat money systems. In Italy, the balance between the two mindsets suggests a more mixed approach to monetary policy, whereas the dominance of the debt mindset in the Netherlands reinforces a tighter connection between government debt and economic behaviour.

8.3 GDP Per Capita Growth and Fiscal Policy

8.3.1 *Government Taxation and the Emergence of Fiscal State: A Comparative Perspective*

We can analyse the evolution of government taxation in various countries, including the Dutch Republic, England, France, Spain, Russia, Poland-Lithuania, and China, by using tax revenue data expressed in terms of silver per capita and as a percentage of gross domestic product (GDP). Drawing from the works of Karaman and Pamuk (2010) and Ma (2011), we will explore these trends to understand the historical emergence of the fiscal state and its long-term impact on state capacity.

By the early seventeenth century, Western European states such as the Dutch Republic and England had developed robust taxation systems that far surpassed those in other parts of Europe and Asia. Figure 8.6, based on data from Karaman and Pamuk (2010), illustrates that around 1600–1650, these states extracted the highest tax revenues per capita, expressed in grams of silver. This period coincided with the rise of mercantilism and the expansion of overseas trade, both of which provided new revenue streams for these emerging fiscal states (O'Brien 1988).

The Dutch Republic, in particular, was a pioneer in fiscal innovation, introducing systems of direct taxation such as excise taxes on consumption that proved more efficient and less regressive than older forms of taxation. England followed a similar trajectory, with Parliament playing a crucial role in overseeing and legitimizing tax collection, particularly during and after the English Civil War (Tilly 1990).

In contrast, Eastern Europe (including Prussia and Poland-Lithuania) and Central Eurasia (Russia)—see also Sect. 8.3.3—lagged behind in their fiscal development. These regions, as seen in the previous chapters, were characterized by more

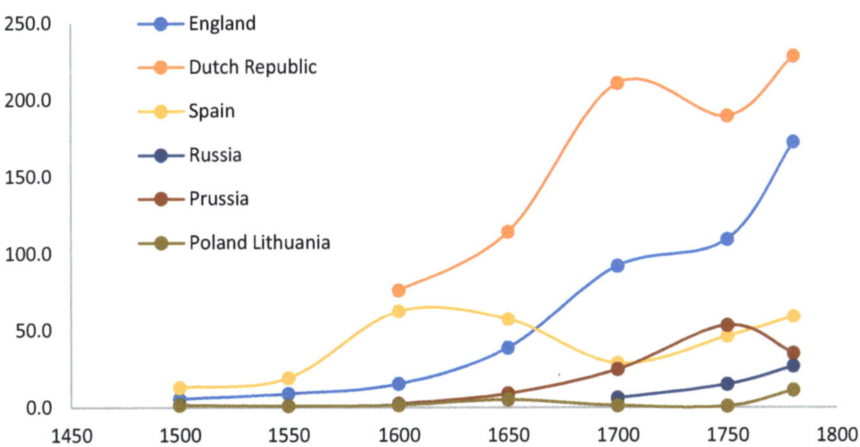

Fig. 8.6 Tax revenue per capita, annual averages in grams of silver. *Source:* Karaman and Pamuk (2010)

agrarian economies and weaker centralized states, which hindered their ability to extract revenue at the same levels as their Western counterparts. Spain, although part of Western Europe, saw its fiscal capacity weakened by its empire's over-extension and costly military ventures, particularly in the Americas (Elliott 2006). By 1700–1780, while Eastern and Southern Europe converged to some extent in terms of tax revenue per capita, the gap with Western Europe continued to widen (Karaman and Pamuk 2010).

Table 8.3, adapted from Ma (2011) and Karaman and Pamuk (2010), provides a comparative overview of per capita tax revenue expressed in days of urban unskilled wages from 1650 to 2020. These data provide valuable insights into the relative fiscal capacities of different states over time. During the second half of the seventeenth century, per capita tax revenues in Western Europe were significantly higher than in other parts of the world. For example, in the Netherlands, the tax burden was equivalent to 13.6 days of urban unskilled wages, while in England, it was 8.0 days. In contrast, in countries such as China and Turkey, the tax burden was much lighter, with China's per capita revenue equivalent to only 1.7 days of wages.

By the first half of the eighteenth century, the Netherlands further increased its tax revenue per capita, rising to 24.1 days of wages, reflecting the country's substantial commercial wealth and the fiscal demands of maintaining its naval power. England also saw an increase to 8.9 days. France, which was embroiled in a series of costly wars, saw its per capita revenue rise to 6.7 days of wages. Meanwhile, in China, this figure remained low at 2.3 days, indicative of a more agrarian economy with a lower overall tax burden—see also Sect. 8.3.2. In the second half of the

Table 8.3 Tax revenue in selected countries, c. 1650–2020

	China	Turkey	Russia	France	Spain	England/UK	Netherlands
	Per capita revenue in days of urban unskilled wages						
1650–1699		1.7		8.0	7.7	4.2	13.6
1700–1749	2.3	2.6	6.4	6.7	4.6	8.9	24.1
1750–1999	1.3	2.0	8.3	11.4	10.0	12.6	22.8
1800–1849	1.2					17.2	
1850–1899	2.0					19.4	
	Tax revenue as % of GDP						
1972	13.9	13.4		18.7	9.0	23.0	22.5
1990	11.01	11.7		18.7	15.7	24.2	23.7
2005	8.6	17.5	16.6	22.3		25.5	21.2
2020	8.1	17.7	10.8	24.8	13.5	24.3	24.3

Note: The two sets of data are not directly comparable. Yet, since urban wages are higher than agricultural ones, we may assume that the days of agricultural work thus underestimate the tax revenue as a percentage of GDP. Vice versa, GDP includes more than just wages. Hence, taking wages is likely to overestimate tax revenue as a percentage of GDP. Assuming these effects cancel each other out, we can interpret this figure as one set of estimates of tax revenue as percentage of GDP 1650–2020

Source: Per capita revenue in days of urban skilled workers taken from Ma (2011), Karaman and Pamuk (2010). Tax revenue as percentage of GDP based on World Bank (2022)

eighteenth century, the Netherlands and England continued to lead in terms of per capita tax revenue, collecting the equivalent of 22.8 and 12.6 days of wages, respectively. France, despite its fiscal struggles leading up to the Revolution, saw its per capita revenue increase to 11.4 days, reflecting the increased tax burden imposed to finance the state's military expenditures. This period marks a further divergence between Western Europe and regions such as China, Turkey, and Russia, where per capita revenues remained much lower.

The eighteenth and nineteenth centuries brought about significant changes to taxation systems across the world, driven by industrialization, state-building, and geopolitical transformations. In Western Europe, the fiscal capacity of states such as the Netherlands and England continued to grow in this period. By the first half of the nineteenth century (1800–1849), the tax burden in England had risen sharply to an equivalent of 17.2 days of unskilled wages. This increase reflected the country's growing industrial might and its need to finance the Napoleonic Wars and colonial expansion. The Netherlands, although still maintaining a relatively high tax burden, began to face challenges as it navigated the economic restructuring required by its transition from a dominant commercial power to a more diversified economy. France, emerging from the turmoil of revolution and Napoleonic rule, faced ongoing fiscal pressures as it sought to rebuild and maintain its influence in Europe. The country's tax burden during the first half of the nineteenth century remained relatively high, as state revenues were increasingly directed towards managing debt accumulated during the Napoleonic Wars and financing public infrastructure projects essential for industrial growth. In contrast, China's per capita tax revenue remained low throughout the nineteenth century, with figures from 1850 to 1899 still showing only 2 days of unskilled wages going to tax revenue. China, facing internal struggles such as the Taiping Rebellion and external pressures from Western imperial powers, lagged behind in terms of fiscal centralization and economic modernization. Similarly, Turkey and Russia maintained relatively low levels of per capita tax revenue, constrained by agrarian economies and slower state modernization.

The period from 1920 to 2020 saw significant transformations in taxation systems worldwide, influenced by major global events such as the two world wars, the Great Depression, and the subsequent decolonization and globalization of economies. The ways states extracted tax revenue evolved dramatically, as governments sought to finance warfare, reconstruction, and social welfare programmes, while also facing challenges posed by the increasingly globalized and complex nature of capital flows and multinational enterprises. The First World War placed unprecedented fiscal pressures on European countries. To finance the war, states such as the UK, France, and Germany significantly increased tax rates and expanded the scope of direct taxation. The costs of the war, combined with the subsequent economic costs of war reconstruction, forced European nations to reconfigure their fiscal policies in the post-war period. Taxation as a percentage of GDP rose significantly in countries such as the UK and France, which sought to rebuild their economies and repay war debts. Already during the war, German businesses had attempted to bypass Allied sanctions by diverting commercial flows through neutral states such as Sweden, utilizing shell corporations to conceal ownership, and employing Swiss and Dutch banks to channel capital. These strategies were designed to evade economic blockades, but in the interwar period, they were repurposed to avoid the rising taxes that many European countries imposed to finance reconstruction efforts (Calabrese and Giacomin 2025). The surge in capital flight during this time illustrated the increasing mobility of wealth, as corporations and wealthy families sought to protect their assets from heavy taxation in their home countries. This period also witnessed the emergence of small, neutral countries such as Switzerland (e.g. Farquet 2012, 2016) and Luxembourg (Calabrese and Majerus 2024) as hubs for capital attracted by lenient tax policies and favourable regulatory frameworks. These countries developed what scholars have termed "regulatory engineering" (Calabrese and Giacomin 2025)—the creation of legal and interpretational frameworks designed to provide competitive advantages to attract foreign capital.

Regulatory engineering allowed these countries to become integral players in the global tax avoidance system, enabling multinationals and wealthy families to shift their profits and capital away from higher-tax jurisdictions. The aim of these regulations was often framed in legitimate terms—such as preventing double taxation across borders—but in practice, they facilitated sophisticated tax avoidance schemes. These included the use of shell companies, transfer pricing manipulation, and the exploitation of intellectual property rights, such as fictitious patent payments, to shift profits to low-tax jurisdictions. Luxembourg, for example, became a hub for multinational corporations seeking to exploit tax treaties and loopholes, which allowed them to significantly reduce their tax liabilities across Europe (see Calabrese 2023). After the Second World War, many Western European countries expanded their tax systems to finance the development of social welfare programmes, such as universal healthcare, education, and social security. The immediate post-war decades saw significant increases in tax revenue as a percentage of GDP. By the 1970s, countries such as France and the UK were collecting between 20 and 25% of their GDP in taxes, reflecting the growing scope of the state's role in providing public services. This increase was also driven by rising economic output and more efficient tax collection systems, including income and corporate taxes. However, as these countries expanded their tax bases, multinational corporations and wealthy individuals continued to utilize the regulatory frameworks of countries like Switzerland and Luxembourg to minimize their tax obligations. These practices undermined the tax efforts of larger states and contributed to a broader trend of tax competition between nations. The development of offshore financial centres in the Caribbean and the Channel Islands further accelerated this trend, enabling capital to flow to jurisdictions where taxes were minimal or non-existent (Palan et al. 2010).

The latter part of the twentieth century saw significant transformations in tax systems across the globe, shaped by the rise of welfare states, economic globalization, and financial deregulation. By the 1970s, Western European countries such as

France, Spain, and the UK had developed comprehensive welfare systems that required higher levels of taxation to fund public services. In 1972, for instance, France collected 18.7% of GDP in taxes, while the UK collected 22.5%. Spain, still emerging from the Francoist regime, collected only 9.0% of GDP, reflecting the underdevelopment of its welfare system. In contrast, China and Russia, despite being large, populous states with centralized governments, had relatively low tax revenues as a percentage of GDP. In 1972, China collected 13.4% and Russia 18.7%, reflecting the difficulty of extracting revenue in economies dominated by state-owned enterprises and large informal sectors (Besley and Persson 2011). By the late twentieth century, the forces of globalization and financial deregulation intensified these fiscal issues. The 1990s and 2000s saw a sharp increase in cross-border capital flows, facilitated by technological advances and the liberalization of global financial markets. Countries such as Switzerland and Luxembourg as well as offshore tax havens became increasingly important players in the global economy, providing favourable regulatory environments that enabled multinational corporations to reduce their tax liabilities through profit-shifting and transfer pricing arrangements. As a result, major economies struggled to curb tax avoidance, even with efforts such as the OECD's Base Erosion and Profit Shifting initiative in the 2010s.

Despite these challenges, Western Europe maintained high levels of tax revenue relative to GDP. By 2020, France and the UK were still collecting around 24% of their GDP in taxes, highlighting their enduring fiscal strength and ability to support welfare systems. Meanwhile, Russia and China continued to experience relatively low tax revenues, with Russia collecting only 10.8% and China 8.1% of GDP in 2020. These lower tax levels reflect the persistent difficulties in enforcing tax collection in economies with large informal sectors, varying institutional capacity, and the continuing use of tax havens by corporations and wealthy individuals. In contrast, countries such as France and the UK have remained among the world's leaders in tax collection, despite the ongoing shift of profits and capital to lower-tax jurisdictions.

Governments expanded taxes during the twentieth century primarily to finance the massive costs of warfare, reconstruction, and the development of social welfare programmes. Following the world wars and the Great Depression, countries such as the UK, France, and Germany raised taxes to repay war debts, rebuild their economies, and fund essential public services, including healthcare, education, and social security. This expansion in taxation was necessary to maintain fiscal stability and support the growing role of the state in providing public goods. To avoid a leftward shift in the IS curve, which would indicate reduced private investment and economic output, governments focused on productive investments. They targeted infrastructure, technology, and education, which improved labour productivity and helped offset the slower productivity growth in the service sectors, such as healthcare and education—key areas of post-war investment.

8.3.2 The Case of China

As seen in Chap. 7, China's tax extraction capability was overtaken by Western Europe in the seventeenth century. Indeed, from the Qin dynasty (221–206 BCE), China had a central taxation system that was heavily dependent on local cooperation. This allowed new dynasties to easily take over the existing system but also created deep-seated vulnerabilities, particularly at the local level. One of the key features of China's imperial tax system was its decentralized nature in execution. Although tax policy was determined by the central government, it was left to local officials to manage the collection process. This created a paradox: while the state could exert considerable control over the general direction of fiscal policy, it was often at the mercy of local administrators for effective implementation. This reliance on local cooperation led to inefficiencies and left sufficient room for corruption, as local officials had significant discretion over how taxes were collected and spent (Zelin 1984; Wong 1997a, b). The Chinese state often lacked the administrative capacity to monitor or reform local taxation practices effectively (Von Glahn 2016). Local civil servants, burdened with quotas and performance targets that were often unrealistic, were frequently punished for financial shortfalls beyond their control. This system encouraged malfeasance as a survival strategy; officials resorted to informal or corrupt methods to meet their obligations to the central state and maintain their livelihoods. The "squeeze" on local officials, a term used by historians to describe this dynamic, created a cycle of exploitation that undermined the legitimacy and efficiency of local governance (Zelin 1984). This problem persisted across dynasties, from the Han to the Qing, and remains an issue in modern times, highlighting the deep structural roots of China's local fiscal challenges (Brandt et al. 2014). China's inability to modernize its tax system was particularly evident when contrasted with European states after the seventeenth century: Western European countries began to develop more efficient tax extraction systems that could support large-scale military campaigns and state-building efforts (Tilly 1990). This was a crucial factor in China's inability to keep up with the growing financial demands of governance in a rapidly changing world (Rosenthal and Wong 2011). China's tax system, deeply rooted in agrarian structures, could not evolve quickly enough to accommodate the changing nature of its economy and the growing complexities of governance. While Western Europe was modernizing its fiscal systems to extract revenue from diverse and increasingly urbanized economies, China's system remained largely static and focused on land taxes. This failure to adapt made it difficult for the Chinese state to fund large-scale projects or respond effectively to internal and external crises.

The nature of China's tax revenue during the Ming and Qing dynasties reflects the rigidity of its fiscal system. Table 8.4 presents the Chinese government's income by category between 1450 and 1651, showing the composition of taxation and how this evolved over the period. As the table illustrates, China relied heavily on produce taxes, with limited diversification into other forms of taxation such as textiles, copper, paper cash, and silver.

Table 8.4 Chinese government income by category (expressed in tael of silver), 1450–1651

Year	Tax in produce	Tax in textiles	Tax in copper	Tax in paper cash	Tax in silver	Total tax revenue
1450	25,880,000	255,500		4737		26,140,237
1500	30,900,000	766,000		3247	32,000	31,701,247
1552	26,590,000	386,500		2414	2,433,000	29,411,914
1602	28,370,000	345,500			4,582,000	33,297,500
1620	27,800,000	270,500		8	7,552,000	35,622,508
1651	10,482,525		2,430,722	64	23,065,302	35,978,614

Source: Xu and Van Leeuwen (2018, 34)

At the outset in 1450, the overwhelming share of government revenue came from produce taxes, which contributed 25,880,000 taels of silver out of a total revenue of 26,140,237 taels. Taxes in textiles and paper cash contributed only marginal amounts. The absence of taxation in silver or copper in 1450 reflects China's heavy reliance on agricultural production rather than more diverse or urbanized sources of income. By 1500, the share of produce taxes had risen to 30,900,000 taels, while textiles tax collections more than tripled, rising to 766,000 taels. This expansion reflects an increasing ability to capture revenues from the textile trade, an important element in China's growing economy at the time. However, the introduction of silver taxation, albeit modest at only 32,000 taels, hints at a shift towards incorporating monetary taxes in addition to agrarian revenues.

During 1552, the share of silver taxes rose dramatically to 2,433,000 taels, signalling the growing role of silver in the Chinese economy, particularly as it was becoming a central currency in international trade, especially with Spanish silver flowing into China via the Manila galleon trade routes. Despite this shift, produce taxes continued to contribute the largest share, at 26,590,000 taels, while other categories such as copper and paper cash remained relatively insignificant. The reliance on agrarian-based revenue thus persisted. By 1602, silver taxes had continued to rise to 4,582,000 taels, accounting for a larger share of total revenue, while produce taxes remained stable. Notably, by this time, copper taxes were non-existent, while paper cash taxation had vanished altogether. This shift indicates that while China was beginning to rely more on monetary taxation in silver, it had yet to fully diversify its tax base. By 1620, as fiscal pressure mounted on the state, taxation in silver reached 7,552,000 taels, representing a significant portion of total tax revenue. Despite this, produce taxes still accounted for 27,800,000 taels, reinforcing the persistent agrarian focus of the tax system. The state's inability to fully capitalize on the growing urban wealth in the form of diversified taxes is a key factor that weakened China's fiscal capacity during this period.

The most dramatic change comes by 1651, during the early Qing dynasty, when the role of silver taxation skyrocketed to 23,065,302 taels, constituting a major share of the total tax revenue of 35,978,614 taels. Meanwhile, the sharp drop in produce taxes to 10,482,525 taels suggests a significant restructuring of the fiscal system in response to the realities of a more monetized economy and increased trade with Western nations. The introduction of copper taxation, contributing 2,430,722 taels, also reflects the diversification of revenue sources during the Qing era, as the state adapted to new economic conditions.

Despite these changes, the overall system remained largely rigid, especially when compared with the dynamic tax systems developing in Western Europe. Unlike Western European states, which were implementing excise taxes, customs duties, and other forms of commercial taxation to capture revenue from urbanization and trade, China's government was slow to adapt. The state's reliance on agrarian taxes meant that significant portions of its growing urban economy remained untaxed, further weakening the state's ability to fund necessary projects and reforms.

China's booming trade during the late Ming and early Qing periods should have provided the state with a lucrative revenue base. Urban centres such as Canton (or Guangzhou) became bustling hubs of commerce, with merchants generating substantial profits from domestic and international trade, particularly with Europe. However, the Chinese state was unable to effectively tax this new wealth, as the fiscal system remained designed to capture revenue primarily from rural landowners.[5] This mismatch between economic activity and the state's capacity to extract revenue weakened China's ability to respond to the demands of a rapidly changing world (Li 2003). The failure to reform the tax system also limited China's ability to fund necessary military modernization, infrastructure projects, and public goods, especially as the state faced growing foreign incursions in the nineteenth century. As European powers began to dominate global trade routes and exert political pressure on East Asia, China struggled to finance the defence of its territory and sovereignty. For instance, during the Opium Wars (1839–1842 and 1856–1860), the Chinese state's fiscal weaknesses were laid bare. The Qing dynasty was unable to mobilize sufficient resources to fend off British forces, in part because of the inefficient tax system that could not keep pace with the financial demands of modern warfare (Fairbank 1978). Meanwhile, Britain, backed by its robust tax-extraction system, had no difficulty financing its military expeditions. In the face of internal rebellion and external pressures, the Chinese state increasingly relied on ad hoc methods of raising revenue, such as selling official ranks/titles or engaging in short-term borrowing. These methods were ultimately unsustainable and further eroded the state's fiscal foundation (Wu 2021). By contrast, European states were consolidating centralized fiscal institutions, with governments taking control of tax collection and formalizing systems of national debt (Bonney 1999).

The Chinese reliance on informal and localized tax systems, which varied widely from one region to another, compounded the problem and created inefficiencies that were difficult to correct, even as the demands on the state continued to grow. Moreover, as China attempted to modernize in the late nineteenth and early twentieth centuries, its outdated fiscal system proved to be a hindrance to broader economic reforms. Without a strong tax base to fund industrialization, public works, or

[5] For example, in 1766, the total revenue of the court was 48.54 million Liang, of which 29.91 million came from land and head tax, 5.74 million from salt tax, 5.4 million from tariffs, and the remainder from a variety of taxes and "donations". See Zhao (1977, 3703).

military upgrades, the state was left vulnerable to both internal dissent and foreign aggression. This weakening had significant effects on late nineteenth-century reformers and modernizers, who aimed to stimulate the adoption of Western techniques, particularly in the military, while avoiding the wholesale importation of Western culture (Kirby 1995). Fiscal constraints made this modernization process difficult. Factors such as the 1911 fall of the Qing dynasty and the subsequent fragmentation of power across various warlord factions further weakened the central government's position, undermining its ability to mobilize resources for development and defence (Esherick 1987). After the founding of the People's Republic of China in 1949, significant attempts were made to centralize fiscal control.

However, even during the Maoist era, the state faced challenges in balancing local governments' needs with the demands of central planning. The introduction of the "People's Communes" in the late 1950s aimed to collectivize both agricultural production and taxation, but these reforms failed to address underlying structural issues, sometimes exacerbating local financial problems (Naughton 2007). A major turning point came in 1994 when China implemented a significant tax reform aimed at increasing the central government's control over revenue. This reform was a response to the decentralization policies of the 1980s, which allowed local governments to retain a substantial portion of tax revenues, contributing to growing fiscal disparities across regions (Wong 2000). The 1994 reforms succeeded in recentralizing tax collection but left loopholes for local governments to raise funds through off-budget means, particularly through land sales and borrowing, further contributing to financial imbalances (Liu et al. 2022; Chen et al. 2022). These reforms therefore failed to completely curtail local governments' ability to raise revenues informally. Local governments often turned to land sales, borrowing, and even the exploitation of local businesses to fill financial gaps (Zhang and Barnett 2014). Despite efforts by the central government to close these loopholes, these back doors persist. As national policies (such as infrastructure investments) remain largely delegated to local governments, which often face solvency issues, evidence shows that many local governments resort to informal fundraising mechanisms (Liu et al. 2022; Chen et al. 2022).

One area that further illustrates the long-term challenges in China's fiscal system is the housing market. Since the early 2000s, local governments have increasingly relied on land sales as a critical revenue source. This has fuelled rapid urban expansion and speculation in the housing market, leading to soaring property prices, particularly in major cities such as Beijing and Shanghai (Huang and Yi 2011). However, this reliance on land sales is inherently unsustainable, as local governments face diminishing returns from land auctions while contending with growing public discontent over housing affordability (Deng et al. 2015). In the long run, the structural issues in the housing market pose a significant risk to China's economic stability. The central government has attempted to cool the housing market through regulations and restrictions on speculative purchases, but these measures have met limited success. Moreover, the debt burdens of local governments, exacerbated by reliance on land sales, create fiscal vulnerabilities that could constrain future infrastructure investments and economic growth (Wu et al. 2016). If China is to maintain its growth trajectory, reforms in both the housing market and local government financing will be essential, alongside broader efforts to address the long-term sustainability of its tax system. In conclusion, while China's taxation system has historically played a crucial role in maintaining dynastic continuity, it has struggled to adapt to the demands of modern governance. The tension between central control and local autonomy, coupled with a historical legacy of corruption and inefficiency at the local level, continues to shape China's fiscal landscape. Addressing these issues will be vital to ensuring both economic stability and the long-term sustainability of China's growth model.

8.3.3 A Case of Central Eurasia

8.3.3.1 State-Led Market Economy of the Late Russian Empire

In the early stages of fiscal state development in Central Eurasia, extraction occurred mostly not from government but from private landlords. Indeed, as Fig. 8.7 shows, the government taxation appeared to be very low even in the times of Peter I (early eighteenth century) to which the historiographical narratives ascribe very high extraction burden for the rank-and-file population. When the Russian Empire under Catherine II (1762–1796) spent much of resources for warfare with the Ottoman Empire and with Poland the government taxation really increased, yet only to the modest 5% of GDP. After some lowering of government taxation, another hike followed under Nicholas I (1825–1855, up to 8% of GDP) when the government embarked to increasing its bureaucratic apparatus to counterweight private landlords. This upward trend prolonged well into the time of the "Great Reforms" of the 1860s–1870s and the launch of modern economic growth in the late nineteenth century. The growing share of local institutions of self-government,[6] as well as increased receipts from the central government entrepreneurial activities caused some downturn in taxation in the early twentieth century. However, as Table 8.1 shows, all these levels were below the Western countries already had at the time but exceeded those in China and Turkey.

Among the significant events in the Russian financial sector during the second half of the nineteenth to the early twentieth centuries, we would like to select the transition to the treasury system of state budget execution, which was audited by the State Control Department (1860s), and the establishment of the State Bank (1860), which provided settlement services for the budget.

In Fig. 8.8, we see that in the late Russian Empire the level of penetration of the state budget system into the national economy continued its upward trend, which had been in force since the end of the seventeenth century. This trend continued during the launch of modern economic growth in the late nineteenth century. The

[6] For *zemstvos*, city and town dumas, councils, and noble assemblies we have more fragmentary fiscal statistics than for the central government. Therefore, they are not consolidated with the central government annual data.

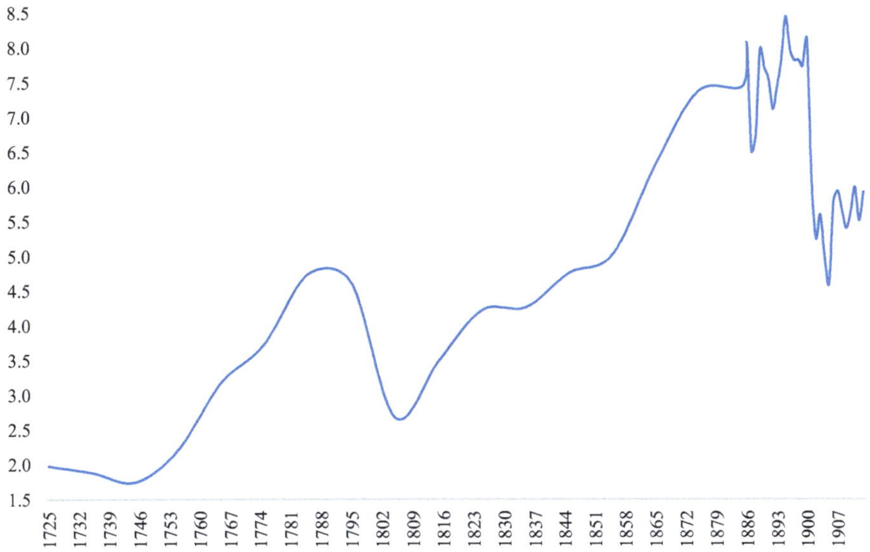

Fig. 8.7 Russia's central government taxes to GDP, 1720s–1913 (in percent). *Source:* GDP: 1690s–1880s: Broadberry and Korchmina (2024); 1885–1913: Cheremukhin et al. (2017); taxes: 1680–1710: Shumilin and Shumilina (2018, 206–207); 1724–1760: Kahan (1985, 347); 1762–1796: Chechulin (1906, 260–262); 1803–1914: Tabata and Tabata (2019)

observed decline at the beginning of the twentieth century is because we take into account central government funds only, as was the case with taxation (Fig. 8.7).

The application of fiscal incentives for national economic development was on the agenda in the late 1860s and related primarily to active participation of the government in railway construction. Expenditures on economic development (mainly railway construction,[7] and other infrastructure) in the early twentieth century reached 10–20% of the state budget expenditures,[8] or 1.5–3.6% of GDP.[9] Thus, we can talk about the emergence of the Russian "developmental state",[10] which employs basically fiscal instruments in a market economy.

From the middle of the eighteenth century, the core institutions of the Russian banking system were also established with direct state involvement. This mainstream included the establishment and operation of the Loan Bank for the Nobility

[7] From the data on government spending on railway construction in Pogrebinsky (1954, 132) and estimates of GDP in Cheremukhin et al. (2017), it follows that in the mid-1890s, they reached 7.7% of GDP.

[8] Our estimate is based on calculations in Tabata and Tabata (2019).

[9] Based on estimates of GDP in Cheremukhin et al. (2017).

[10] This term has become widely used in the literature—one of the seminal works is White and Wade (1988)—referring to the experience of industrialization in East Asian countries. To a large extent, its main characteristics (concepts) were analysed in Gerschenkron (1962) with reference to the late Russian Empire as a country of catch-up modernization.

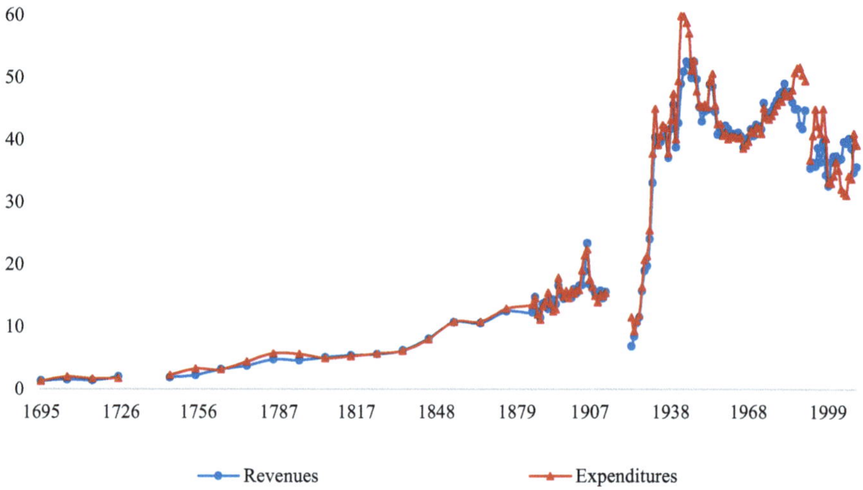

Fig. 8.8 Central government revenues and expenditures in Central Eurasia, percentage of GDP. *Source:* GDP: 1690s–1880s: Broadberry and Korchmina (2024); 1885–1913: Cheremukhin et al. (2017); revenues, expenditures: 1680–1710: Shumilin and Shumilina (2018, 206–207); 1724–1758: Troitskii (1966, 185), as revised by Kahan (1985); 1762–1796: Chechulin (1906, 256–257), as revised by Kahan (1985); 1803–2010: Tabata and Tabata (2019)

(1754–1786), the State Loan Bank (1754–1860), the State Bank of Assignats (1786–1843),[11] the State Commercial Bank (1818–1860), the State Savings Offices (since 1842), the State Bank of the Russian Empire (since 1860), the Peasant Land Bank (1882–1917), and the State Noble Land Bank (1885–1917).[12] To a large extent, their operations were aimed at serving the needs of the state budget and the ruling class (the nobility). Established a year before the abolition of serfdom, the State Bank played an important role in the redemption operation right after the Emancipation in 1861. The nobles received a ransom in bank securities and cash for allotment of land to their former private serfs, who repaid their debt with redemption payments until 1907. A significant role among the activities of the State Bank belonged to discounted purchase of promissory notes for state-owned railway companies (Petrov 2010, 26–27). The purchase of central government bonds was also practised. Given the subordination of the State Bank to the Ministry of Finance, we should consider fiscal rather than monetary stimulation of economic development. Many of the State Bank managers and the Ministry of Finance officials were of German origin, and the institutions borrowed much from German banking practices of the time.

Banking is directly related to the development of the monetary system of a national economy. In Fig. 8.9, we see that the level of monetization of the Russian economy has not increased as significantly as the fiscal penetration of the state. The

---

[11] The bank exclusively authorized to issue paper currency (*assignatsii*).

[12] More detailed account on the issue is in Bugrov (2017), Gindin (1997), and Morozan (2004).

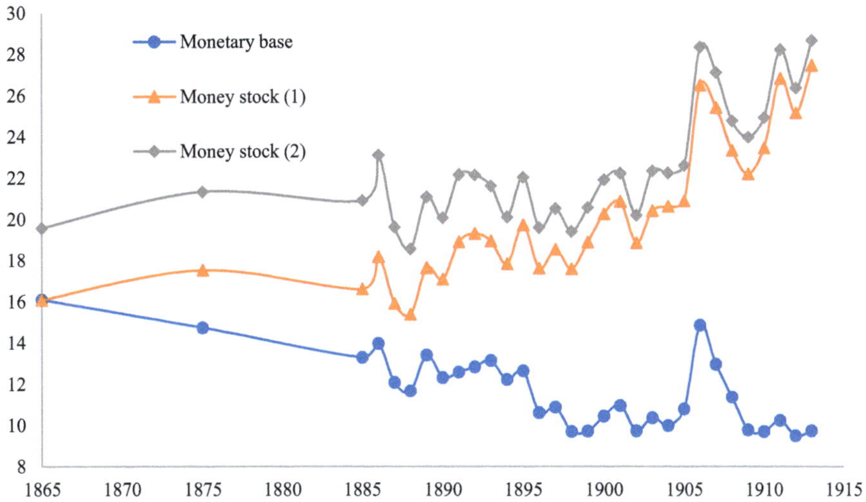

Fig. 8.9 Dynamics of the level of monetization of the economy of the late Russian Empire (monetary aggregates as percentage of GDP). *Note:* the monetary base is the most liquid part of money supply, which includes banknotes and coins in circulation; the money stock (1) includes the monetary base, transferable deposits (settlement, current and other on-demand accounts), as well as other deposits in private banks; the money stock (2) includes the money stock (1), as well as deposits with the State Bank (except for funds of the State Treasury). *Source:* monetary aggregates: Nakamura (2019, Appendix Table 7.1); GDP: 1690s–1880s: Broadberry and Korchmina (2024); 1885–1913: Cheremukhin et al. (2017)

expansion of the monetary base, consisting of cash and coins, was limited by the institutional regime of the gold standard.[13] However, other monetary aggregates had grown significantly owing to non-cash components (bank accounts). Furthermore, to a large extent, the function of money as a means of settlement was performed by promissory notes, for which circulation no reliable statistics are available. The level of monetization of the economy achieved by the late Russian Empire was historically high. Even if the composition of the monetary aggregates does not precisely correspond to modern concepts, we may argue that the level of monetization at the time exceeded that of the Russian economy in the 1990s and early 2000s.[14]

While state-owned banks continued to operate and expand their financial activities, the most important innovation of the late Russian Empire was the significant growth of private banks.[15] By 1914, the volume of joint-stock commercial banks assets was more than twice as high as the State Bank's. By the end of the nineteenth century, other types of commercial banks, such as credit unions and town public

[13] The gold standard was adopted in the mid-1890s, yet the reform was prepared a long time before.

[14] Based on data on the monetary aggregates from the Bank of Russia (downloaded at 2024, https://www.cbr.ru/Content/Document/File/76776/monetary_program_1995-2003.xls) and on the GDP in 2022 from Rosstat (downloaded at 2024, https://rosstat.gov.ru/statistics/accounts)

[15] More information is in Bovykin (2001, 160–217), Salomatina (2004).

banks, also played significant roles, as they flexibly responded to the needs for banking services at the lower levels of the business sector and among local city governments.

Table 8.5 shows the key aspects of the main types of banking institutions' penetration into the national economy. They show that both state-owned public and private banks actively contributed to economic growth by lending and investing in securities. Since the end of the 1890s, the share of state-owned banks was replaced by private ones, of which the most significant subjects were joint-stock commercial banks. In the state-controlled sector, the share of the State Bank was declining,[16] but the share of the State Savings Offices, which borrowed household funds and invested them in securities, was significantly expanding. Thus, savings were transforming into investments.

The level of penetration of retail banking services into the Russian economy is captured by the ratio of total value of retail deposits (savings of the population) to GDP (for the 1690s–1880s from Broadberry and Korchmina 2024; for 1885–1913 from Cheremukhin et al. 2017). At the provincial level, this is the ratio of total value of retail deposits (from Davydov 2016, 1031–1050) to gross regional product—GRP (from Markevich 2019). For retail depositors, their bank accounts tended to be a means of saving, as a deferred consumption, rather than business activities aimed at accumulating capital. The network of State Savings Offices was specialized in working with such depositors. Table 8.6 shows the results of our calculations, which highlight the scale and outcomes of their work with liabilities of this type, and their regional distribution.

The rate of organized household savings from 1897 to 1914 increased from 4.1 to 7.0% of GDP. In the Soviet period, this level was restored only 50 years later, in the mid-1960s (by the end of the Soviet period, it had reached 30% of GDP).[17]

In 1897, a savings rate of 7% GRP or more was typical for the central regions around Moscow. There were also several cases from the Volga region, from the North-West, and from the Baltics. Provinces with capital cities demonstrated levels higher than the national average, but far from the maximum.

Despite the fact that provision of deposits for the population remained low (fewer than 50 bank accounts per 1000 people),[18] real growth of retail deposits per capita was twice on average (compared with real growth of GDP per capita by 1.2 times). This indicates a significant increase in the penetration of financial services at the household level.

[16] Much of its assets' value originated from its operation as the authorized centre for issuing coins and banknotes.

[17] Based on estimates of the value of retail deposits in Nakamura (2019, Appendix table 7.2), Kashin and Kozlova, eds. (2012, 191), and GDP in Steinberg (1990). From the assessment of forced savings, owing to the shortage of goods in retail trade (Cottarelli and Blejer 1992, 280), it follows that their equilibrium level can be estimated at 10% of GDP, which is only about 1.5 times higher than the level of the late Russian Empire.

[18] By the end of the Soviet period, it was about 800 (Kashin and Kozlova 2012, 191).

Table 8.5 Assets, loans, and securities portfolios of major types of Russian banks, as percentage of GDP (1861–1914)

	Under central government control						Under local government control			Under private control					
Years (as of 1 January)	The State Bank			The State Savings Offices			City and town public banks			Joint-stock commercial banks			Credit unions		
	Assets	Loans	Securities	Assets	Loans	Securities	Assets	Loans	Securities	Assets	Loans	Securities	Assets	Loans	Securities
1861	**18.8**	1.1	0.0			0.0									
1862	**20.8**	1.6	0.1			0.0									
1863	**21.7**	1.1	0.2	**0.2**		0.0									
1864	**21.3**	1.0	0.3	**0.2**		0.1									
1865	**21.3**	1.0	0.1	**0.1**		0.1					0.0	0.0			
1866	**21.5**	1.5	0.3	**0.1**		0.1					0.1	0.0			
1867	**21.9**	2.4	0.6	**0.1**		0.1					0.1	0.1			
1868	**21.6**	1.6	0.2	**0.1**		0.1					0.2	0.0			
1869	**22.9**	1.5	0.2	**0.1**		0.1					0.4	0.1			
1870	**23.7**	2.3	0.2	**0.1**		0.1					0.7	0.1			
1871	**17.4**	1.6	0.2	**0.1**		0.1					1.1	0.1			
1872	**17.3**	1.3	0.2	**0.1**		0.1					1.9	0.1			
1873	**17.3**	1.5	0.2	**0.1**		0.1					2.9	0.4			
1874	**17.9**	1.7	0.1	**0.1**		0.1				**8.9**	5.8	0.3			
1875	**18.3**	2.0	0.2	**0.1**		0.1				**10.3**	6.4	0.2			
1876	**19.0**	3.0	0.2	**0.1**		0.1				**10.1**	6.4	0.3			
1877	**19.1**	3.6	0.3	**0.1**		0.1				**8.6**	5.1	0.3			
1878	**23.9**	3.2	1.2	**0.1**		0.1				**8.9**	4.2	0.5			
1879	**26.2**	3.2	0.5	**0.2**		0.1				**8.5**	4.2	0.9			
1880	**25.2**	4.6	0.5	**0.2**		0.1				**7.4**	4.3	0.5			
1885	**19.7**	3.3	0.4	**0.3**		0.3				**7.5**	4.4	0.4			

(continued)

Table 8.5 (continued)

Years (as of 1 January)	Under central government control						Under local government control			Under private control					
	The State Bank			The State Savings Offices			City and town public banks			Joint-stock commercial banks			Credit unions		
	Assets	Loans	Securities	Assets	Loans	Securities	Assets	Loans	Securities	Assets	Loans	Securities	Assets	Loans	Securities
1886	**21.1**	2.9	1.9	**0.5**		0.4				**8.5**	4.6	0.6			
1887	**18.3**	2.4	1.5	**0.6**		0.5				**7.3**	4.1	0.6			
1888	**17.7**	3.2	0.9	**0.9**		0.8				**6.7**	3.8	0.5			
1889	**20.4**	3.8	1.4	**1.3**		1.2				**8.0**	4.4	0.5			
1890	**18.5**	3.4	0.4	**1.6**		1.5				**7.6**	4.3	0.5			
1891	**19.5**	2.7	0.5	**2.1**		1.9				**9.1**	4.9	0.8			
1892	**19.1**	2.7	0.5	**2.5**		2.1				**8.5**	4.2	0.7			
1893	**18.2**	2.0	0.6	**3.0**		2.3				**8.6**	4.7	0.6			
1894	**17.5**	3.3	0.6	**3.4**		2.3				**7.9**	4.3	0.6			
1895	**19.8**	4.3	0.5	**4.2**		3.3				**10.1**	5.4	0.6	**2.0**	1.7	0.1
1896	**18.5**	4.4	0.5	**4.3**		3.5				**10.3**	5.4	0.7	**2.0**	1.6	0.1
1897	**17.4**	3.7	0.2	**4.5**		3.9				**10.8**	5.4	0.8	**2.1**	1.6	0.1
1898	**15.2**	2.5	0.2	**4.7**		3.6	**1.2**	0.9	0.1	**10.8**	5.5	0.8	**1.9**	1.5	0.1
1899	**12.0**	2.2	0.2	**5.0**		4.5	**1.1**	0.9	0.1	**11.3**	6.2	0.8	**1.9**	1.5	0.1
1900	**12.1**	3.4	0.4	**5.9**		5.1	**1.2**	1.0	0.1	**11.6**	6.2	0.9	**2.1**	1.7	0.1
1901	**11.0**	3.9	0.4	**6.2**		5.3	**1.2**	1.0	0.1	**11.3**	6.1	0.9	**2.2**	1.8	0.1
1902	**10.3**	4.1	0.3	**5.4**		4.9	**1.1**	0.9	0.1	**10.1**	5.5	0.7	**2.0**	1.7	0.1
1903	**10.6**	3.6	0.4	**6.1**		5.0	**1.2**	0.9	0.1	**11.4**	6.4	0.8	**2.2**	1.7	0.1
1904	**10.8**	3.3	0.4	**6.1**		5.6	**1.1**	0.9	0.1	**12.3**	6.8	0.8	**2.1**	1.7	0.1
1905	**10.9**	2.7	0.4	**6.3**		6.0	**1.1**	0.9	0.1	**12.5**	6.2	0.7	**2.1**	1.6	0.1
1906	**13.6**	5.4	0.6	**6.6**		6.6	**1.2**	0.9	0.1	**13.4**	6.3	0.7	**2.2**	1.7	0.1
1907	**13.0**	3.6	0.7	**7.2**		6.9	**1.1**	0.9	0.1	**12.8**	6.1	0.7	**2.2**	1.7	0.1

Years (as of 1 January)	Under central government control						Under local government control			Under private control					
	The State Bank			The State Savings Offices			City and town public banks			Joint-stock commercial banks			Credit unions		
	Assets	Loans	Securities	Assets	Loans	Securities	Assets	Loans	Securities	Assets	Loans	Securities	Assets	Loans	Securities
1908	**11.9**	3.5	0.6	**7.3**		6.9	**1.1**	0.9	0.1	**12.4**	6.0	0.7	**2.1**	1.7	0.1
1909	**11.0**	2.9	0.6	**7.1**		6.8	**1.0**	0.8	0.1	**12.9**	6.2	0.7	**2.3**	1.8	0.1
1910	**11.0**	2.5	0.4	**7.1**		6.9	**1.0**	0.8	0.1	**14.0**	6.7	0.8	**2.6**	2.0	0.1
1911	**12.2**	3.6	0.5	**7.7**	0.0	7.6	**1.1**	0.9	0.1	**20.4**	9.4	1.0	**3.6**	2.7	0.1
1912	**12.1**	4.3	0.5	**7.4**	0.0	7.2	**1.1**	0.9	0.1	**21.0**	11.3	1.1	**4.2**	3.2	0.1
1913	**12.6**	4.4	0.6	**7.6**	0.1	7.4	**1.2**	0.9	0.1	**25.0**	13.1	1.3	**4.6**	3.6	0.1

Note: Since assets of these banks were partly liabilities of the State Bank and other banks (usually as correspondent accounts and bills of exchange), we did not summarize these values

Source: Bank asset values: Salomatina (2011); GDP: Broadberry and Korchmina (2024), Cheremukhin et al. (2017)

Table 8.6 Measures of household deposits in the State Savings Offices in the provinces of the Russian Empire (1897–1914)

	Average deposit amount, rubles		Deposit amount per capita, rubles		Provision of the population with savings deposits (per 1000 people)		GRP per capita in 1897, rubles	Retail deposits/ GRP in 1897, %	Growth in provision of the population with savings deposits, times	Real increase in the value of retail deposits per capita, times
Province	1897	1914	1897	1914	1897	1914				
Russian Empire	181	180	**3.27**	**8.51**	**18.07**	**47.25**	**102.79**	**3.18**	**2.61**	**1.99**
Minimum	87	96	0.08	0.97	0.84	6.12	28.21	0.24	1.23	1.06
Maximum	286	266	14.57	41.53	98.97	231.21	303.73	12.74	7.25	9.37
Average	181	180	3.27	8.51	18.07	47.25	102.79	3.18	2.61	1.99
Median	189	180	2.65	7.17	13.97	40.44	63.46	3.77	2.66	1.95
Coefficient of variation	0.23	0.15	0.79	0.87	0.90	0.86	0.57	0.63	0.32	0.49

Notes: $N = 88$ in 1897, $N = 89$ in 1914
Source: GRP: Markevich (2019); volume of retail deposits: Davydov (2016); population: TsSK (1916)

Spatial inequality between the provinces in terms of the value of deposits per capita increased (from 0.79 to 0.87 as measured by the coefficient of variation); in terms of provision of savings deposits, it slightly decreased (from 0.90 to 0.86).

The mean value of a saving deposit was comparable to annual wages of workers in industry and agriculture (Volkov 2016; Ministry of Agriculture 1907, 1916). The mean value of deposits is moderately correlated with GRP per capita (Fig. 8.10).

As it follows from the data in (Cheremukhin et al. 2017), Russia in the late nineteenth and early twentieth centuries relied on a relatively high rate of accumulation of physical capital (on average, slightly below 20%), higher than the observed household savings rate. At the same time, no association between the savings rate and the level of GRP per capita may be found (as a proxy for material well-being) (Fig. 8.11).

In the debt securities market, which penetrated deeply into the economy, the main instruments were sovereign bonds and bonds of private (mainly railway) companies, guaranteed by the state. A rather high value of unconditional and conditional (in the form of guarantees) sovereign debt (Fig. 8.12), with positive real interest rates (about 3–4.4% per annum with an average annual inflation of about 1%),[19] was not matched by an adequate value of government revenues. But from the 1880s, there was a decrease in the level of government debt. Although this remained high

[19] Interest rates are in Flandreau and Zumer (2004), the inflation rate according to the Podtyagin wholesale price index for regional markets of Russia and the consolidated retail price index of the capital cities are in Gregory (1982).

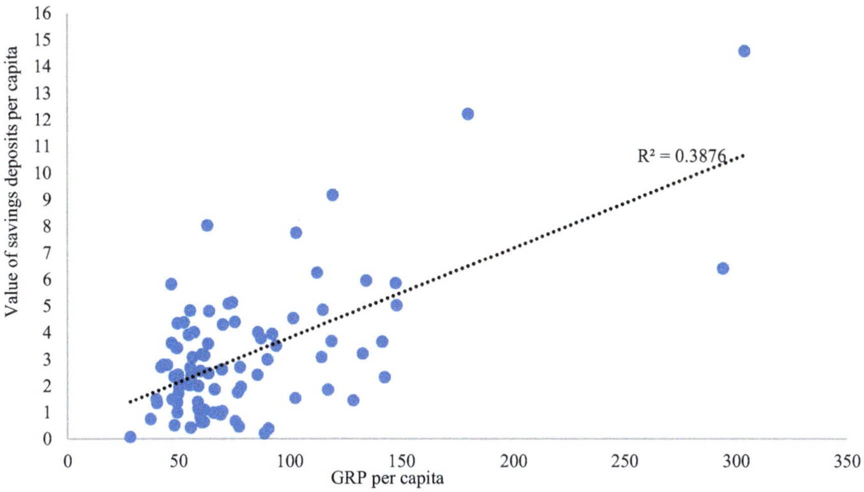

Fig. 8.10 Value of savings deposits and GRP per capita in 1897, rubles. *Source:* GRP: Markevich (2019); value of retail deposits: Davydov (2016); population: TsSK (1916)

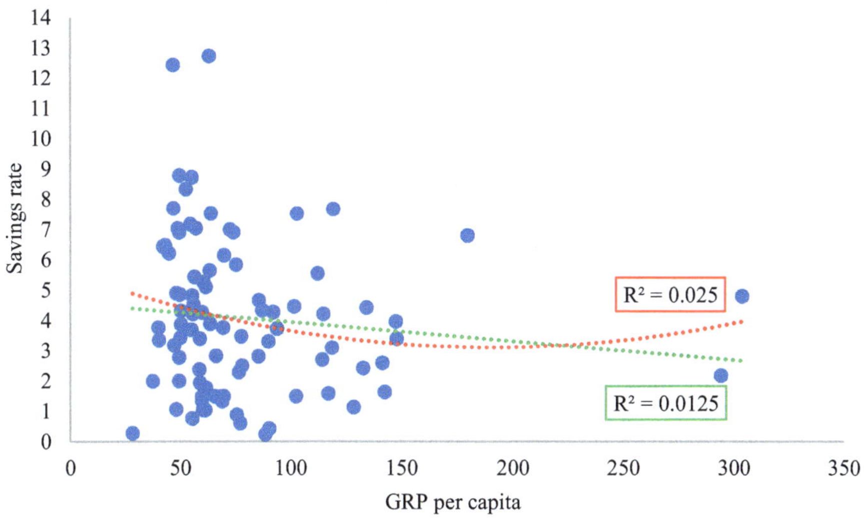

Fig. 8.11 Savings rate and GRP per capita. *Source:* GRP: Markevich (2019); volume of retail deposits: Davydov (2016)

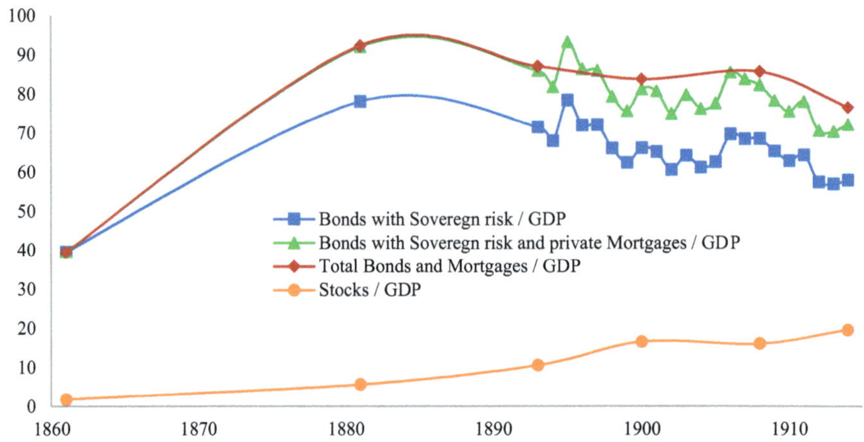

Fig. 8.12 The level of penetration of debt and equity securities market instruments into the economy, expressed as a percentage of GDP. *Source:* Volumes of issued instruments: Salomatina (2011) GDP: Broadberry and Korchmina (2024), Cheremukhin et al. (2017)

by the outbreak of the First World War, the thesis about the crisis in public finances and the growth of debt reliance is not supported by the evidence.[20] The decrease in Russia's sovereign credit risk resulted in narrowing of the yield premia to the benchmark UK bonds from 2.08–2.36 p.p. in the early 1880s to 0.93–0.94 p.p. in 1912–1913 (Flandreau and Zumer 2004, 125).

By the end of the period under review, the overwhelming majority of Russian bonds had sovereign risk (76%), with the central government either the issuer or the guarantor of payments[21]; 19% of the bonds had real estate collateral (mortgages) without additional government guarantees.

The share of equities occupied a modest place among Russian stock market assets.[22] This is characteristic for the "continental" model of the European financial market in the large countries of Central and Eastern Europe, such as Germany, Austria-Hungary, and Russia (Moshensky 2015, 139–142, 218–225, 323–325, 338–340, 367–368). At the same time, the share of equities in the value of securities increased from 4% in 1861 to 20% in 1914.[23]

The dynamics of the Russian equity market (Fig. 8.13) was characterized by an uneven pattern. A significant role was played by speculators, and appeared to be a

[20] Currently, the ratio of the similar instruments issued volume is 32% of Russia's GDP, debt obligations with sovereign risk comprise less than a half of it (based on the data on the volume of issuance from the Bank of Russia (downloaded at 2024, https://www.cbr.ru/vfs/statistics/debt_securities/66-debt_securities.xlsx, https://www.cbr.ru/vfs/statistics/credit_statistics/debt/debt_new.xlsx) and on the GDP in 2022 from Rosstat (downloaded at 2024, https://rosstat.gov.ru/statistics/accounts)

[21] In 1861, 100% of them had sovereign risk.

[22] In a broad sense (stocks and bonds).

[23] Our calculation is based on Gindin (1948), quoted by Salomatina (2011).

Fig. 8.13 Comparative dynamics of the US and Russian stock markets in the second half of the nineteenth and early twentieth centuries (January 1965 = 100). *Source:* Yale School of Management (2021)

result of various manipulative practices.[24] In the United States and Russia, with similar GDP per capita growth rates at the time,[25] the differences in the dynamics of their stock markets are striking. On the one hand, Russia, as a less developed economy, showed a twofold increase in the value of stock assets over 50 years. The surge in equity prices from 1885 to 1895, during Russia's transition to modern economic growth, largely outpaced growth of its economy. At the same time, owing to the initially overvaluation of Russian equities, the capital intensity of the Russian economy, as measured by the stock market, remained basically unchanged during the period under review (Fig. 8.14).

Thus, in the second half of the nineteenth and early twentieth centuries, Russia made a leap in the development of the financial sector of the economy. It acquired financial depth, but in some aspects ran ahead of the development needs of the real sector. This was realized in the creation of imbalances in the debt sector and an over-valuation of stock assets at an early stage of the market development. Historical data show that these problems were not fatal, the financial system remained manageable, and the imbalances gradually reduced. To a large extent, the links between the financial and real sectors of the economy were created with the direct involvement of the state. At the same time, the activities of private banks expanded at a faster pace. From this angle, it was all about state fiscal stimulation of the economy, in which monetary stimulation, limited by the institution of the gold standard, played a subordinate role at best. Nevertheless, even under these conditions, the monetary system actively developed following the banking system, and the level of monetization of the economy increased owing to non-cash components.

[24] The cases are e.g. in Borodkin and Konovalova (2010, 176–178).

[25] As it follows from Maddison Project Database (Bolt and Van Zanden 2020).

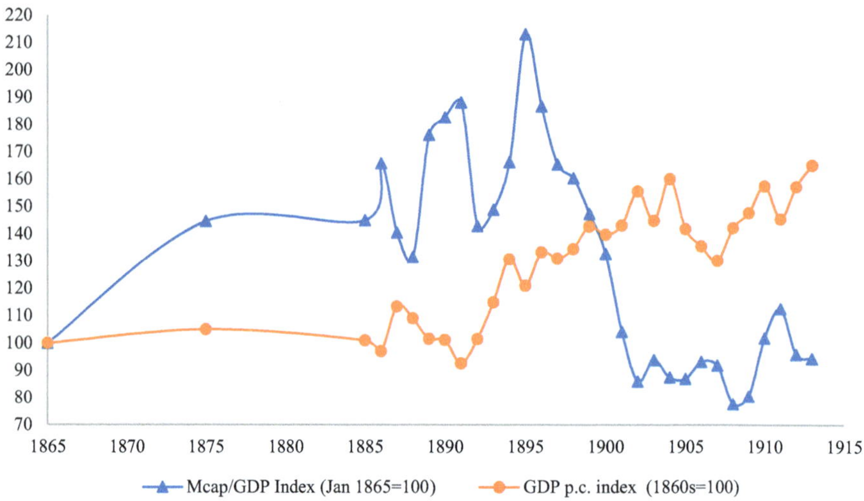

Fig. 8.14 Russian stock markets dynamics relative to the size of the economy in the second half of the nineteenth and early twentieth centuries (January 1865 = 100). *Source:* Yale School of Management (2021)

8.3.3.2 Command-Administration Economy of the USSR: Fiscal Policy: State Budget, Taxes, Forced Bonds Purchases, and Loans to the Economy

State budget funds were the main pillar of the Soviet financial management. They did not require payment of interest or repayment of principal, while financing the bulk of capital investments (Nakamura 2017, 19). This was consistent with the basic idea of the Soviet credit system, which assumed that financial needs of enterprises should be covered by funds from the state budget, the return on which should be made in the form of future tax payments to the budget; short-term credit was considered as a supplementary source of finance.

Soviet economists who specialized in finance discussed a theoretical question: whether state budgetary funds and bank loans differed in their economic nature under the Soviet economic environment. The controversy was brought about by the practical problem that one method of financing often substituted for the other: in most cases, financing from bank loans was switched to financing from the state budget.

The school of thought that dominated until the end of the 1950s, and even prevailed in the late Soviet period, argued that there was no fundamental difference between state budget funds and bank loans.

After the 1950s, another school emerged. This argued that state budgetary funds and bank loans were fundamentally different in the Soviet economy, as in market economies. This was because the 1950s were a time when monetary policy changed towards expanding financing of the economy through bank loans, with household deposits becoming the main source. According to this school, the State Bank could provide bank loans without prior accumulation of appropriate funds. It was also recognized that financing through bank loans was associated with risk and uncertainty, even in the Soviet economy.

The claims of the first school seem quite reasonable in the Soviet economic context. There was no significant reason to believe that uncertainty and risk differed between government funding and bank credit, since all of the activities in the Soviet economy were assumed to be carried out according to plans.

The main problem was whether the funds invested in the economy, through the state budget or bank credit, would bring sufficient financial return. This problem can be seen as an issue of the real sector of the economy and of the material planning: how to manage the real and financial economic resources flowing into the economy in the best possible way to obtain greater returns on them (Nakamura 2017, 35–38).

During the Soviet period, the share of state budget expenditures on economic development was very large in the early 1930s and continued to increase after its reduction in the early 1940s. Approximately 40–50% of spending on the economy was intended for industrial and the construction sector. Approximately another 20% was distributed to the agricultural sector, including costs for machine and tractor stations (Tabata and Tabata 2019, 280).

In relation to GDP, state budget expenditures on economic development increased sharply in the late 1920s and early 1930s to a historical maximum of 30% of GDP, but then adjusted below 15% of GDP (Fig. 8.15). After the Second World War, they stabilized in the range of 17.3–19.4% of GDP, and only by the end of the Soviet period reached the level of 27.5% of GDP.

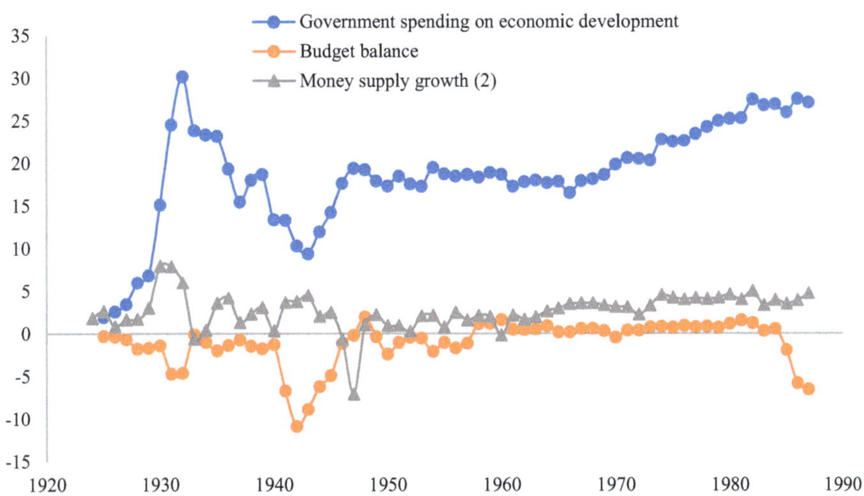

Fig. 8.15 Share of expenditures on the economy, budget balance, and growth of money supply to GDP, 1923–1990. *Source:* Government spending on economic development, budget balance (Tabata and Tabata 2019, Appendix table 8.4, 8.6); money supply growth (2): own calculation based on Nakamura (2019, Appendix table 7.2); GDP: (Didenko et al. 2013)

A significant increase in state budget expenditures and its share in GDP (Fig. 8.15) was observed in the late 1920s and early 1930s with the launch of the forced industrialization drive, as well as during the Second World War: from 40% in pre-war 1940 to 60% in the most difficult year of 1942, with a correctional decrease to 51% in 1946 (Didenko 2020).

Financing expenses for economic development and defence required an increase in the tax burden. In the USSR, the main individual direct tax was turnover tax. Its share of the state budget revenues was very high (41.6% on average in 1928–1990). During the periods of 1932–1941 and 1946–1951, it exceeded 50%, and in 1935–1937, approached 70%. Approximately 20–30% of the state budget revenues in the second half of the 1930s was provided by taxes on grain turnover. Subsequently, from the second half of the 1950s, when purchase prices for grain began gradually to increase, revenues from the grain turnover tax decreased significantly (Tabata and Tabata 2019, 283).

In the 1930s, in contrast to the late Soviet period, the share of income from state-owned enterprises was small. This was because during industrialization financed from the state budget, the enterprise sector operated as a large net borrower.

In the early Soviet period until the 1940s, the share of income from foreign trade was also small, probably because it was not active at the global level. There is a methodological problem for the analysis in that Soviet publications hid data on budget incomes from foreign economic activity for the period 1970–1984 (Birman 1981). According to the estimate in Tabata and Tabata (2019, 287), revenues from foreign economic activity amounted to 10.9% of total state budget revenues on average in the 1970s and 18.1% on average in the 1980s.

In the Soviet methodology of budget statistics, proceeds from the sale of bonds were included in the revenue side of the state budget. They provided about 5–10% of income (Nakamura 2017, 165), and in certain periods (in the early 1930s and during the Second World War) they provided more than 10% (excluding their services): 14.9% in 1931 and 14.2% in 1943 (Tabata and Tabata 2019, 278).

The forced subscription to government bonds absorbed a principal share of household savings. The limited voluntary household savings were also mobilized to finance the state budget in the period before the transfer of the thrift institutions (*sberkassy*) from the Ministry of Finance to the State Bank (1963). These funds were used to finance the economy and supported monetary management from the 1930s to the late 1950s as it was an effective tool for controlling household disposable income. This operational mechanism of Soviet monetary management resulted in a situation in which the household sector held a relatively small stock of cash and deposits and a relatively large stock of government bonds (Nakamura 2017, 161–163, 193).

Servicing government bonds was accompanied by regular defaults. Payments on them were postponed in 1938. This was motivated by the need to make preparations for a future war. In addition, the monetary reform of 1947 reduced the principal of government bonds and rescheduled their maturities. In 1957, the government postponed payments on the new bonds and extended their maturity dates by 20 years, while abandoning the previous practices of forced subscription. This decision was motivated by the fact that the Soviet government could not afford to service its debt: it was expected that if the sale and servicing of bonds proceeded according to the original schedule, their net proceeds would become negative in 1958 (Nakamura 2017, 164).

The more profound reason was low effectiveness of resources utilization, even with historically maximum economic growth rates in the 1950s (excluding periods of recovery). The Soviet understanding of money assumed that material planning guaranteed the rational behaviour of enterprises. This led to some neglect of control over "non-cash" money supply, which was considered to be a derivative of the planning of material production. Combined with other factors, the funds were used less efficiently than planned. Any estimation of macroeconomic efficiency of funds utilization in relative terms was complicated in the Soviet economy, since there was no market that generated the information necessary for such an estimation. This problem became more acute as growth rates slowed down in the 1960s–1980s.

After 1963, small-scale sales of government bonds (hybrid with lottery tickets) with a 3% coupon to households were practised. However, the government had to covertly finance the budget deficit, resorting to borrowing from the State Bank to compensate for the inefficient use of the funds. As a result, domestic government debt continued to grow, with a lack of support from the growth of the real sector of the economy.

Another acute problem of the late Soviet period was excessive savings caused by the shortage of consumer goods (see also Sect. 4.6.3). As Fig. 8.12 shows, since the mid-1960s household deposits were on an accelerated rise. The level they reached at the end of the 1980s (*c*. 30% GDP, in the State Bank assets mirrored basically as loans to the Government) was by no means high by international comparison. The risks arose from the fact that these savings, besides their inefficient use, were mostly on call, and once interest rates turned negative owing to higher inflation in the late 1980s, they exacerbated pressure on consumer markets.

8.3.3.3 Russia's Return to Financial Markets

The Soviet economy had a sizable financial sector but no financial markets. The start of market reforms in the late 1980s was associated with financial destabilization that moderated only a decade later.

At first, in 1987, a fence between cash and non-cash money circulation started to ease, with much lower transaction costs. The enterprises needed cash to run their activities and used the increased number of legal opportunities and loopholes to convert non-cash to cash. The influx of cash banknote money fuelled inflation in consumer markets; this was manifested both in hidden (deficit and quality deterioration) and open forms.

This was exacerbated with rising fiscal deficit (see Fig. 8.16, also Fig. 8.4), covered by the credit to the Soviet government from the State Bank of the USSR (later

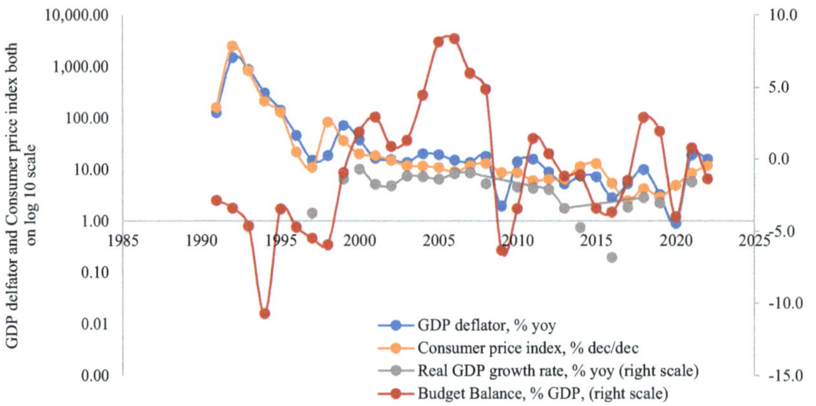

Fig. 8.16 Dynamics of the fiscal deficit, inflation, and GDP growth in the Russian Federation. *Note:* Fiscal deficit—percentage of GDP; GDP deflator—annual change, Consumer Price Index—end of year annual change. *Source:* Rosstat (downloaded at 2024, https://rosstat.gov.ru/folder/210/document/13396)

from the Bank of Russia until the mid-1990s),[26] and radical weakening of the state capacity under the proclaimed transition to democracy. The central banks of the ex-Soviet republics could give loans in rubles (i.e. to issue deposit money) to their domestic government and enterprises independently from the Bank of Russia, although they were not allowed to issue banknotes. It was impossible to control inflation under this situation. Putting aside hopes to preserve a single currency zone for the FSU, Russia issued new-face banknotes with demonetizing old-face banknotes in July 1993 (Nakamura 2019, 243–244). Then, all of the FSU countries (except Tajikistan, which did so in May 1995) introduced their national currencies. Apart from the competition between the central banks of the former Soviet republics in issuing non-cash money, there were also other reasons for the expansionary monetary policy. These included budget deficits, subsidized loans (with negative real interest rates) granted in an administrative manner in response to the pressure of agricultural and industrial lobbies, multilateral clearing of inter-enterprise debt arrears, armed conflicts, and many others (Dabrowski 2022, 98–100).

Therefore, in the 1990s, the primary issue was the restoration of financial and macroeconomic stability, rather than monetary or fiscal stimulation of the real sector. In Russia in the second half of the 1990s, money supply was depressed, especially non-cash (see Fig. 8.17). The funds from the state budget for economic development were cut substantially. Mainstream policies were corrected several times as a response to the demands from the real sector and the lobbyist activities. These corrections made the route to financial stabilization longer than in other

[26] The Central Bank of the Russian Federation (Bank of Russia) was created from the Russian Republic branch office of the Soviet State Bank in July 1990. Act on the Bank of Russia and Act on banks and banking activities in Russia were adopted in December 1990 (Doronin and Zakharov 1998, 503).

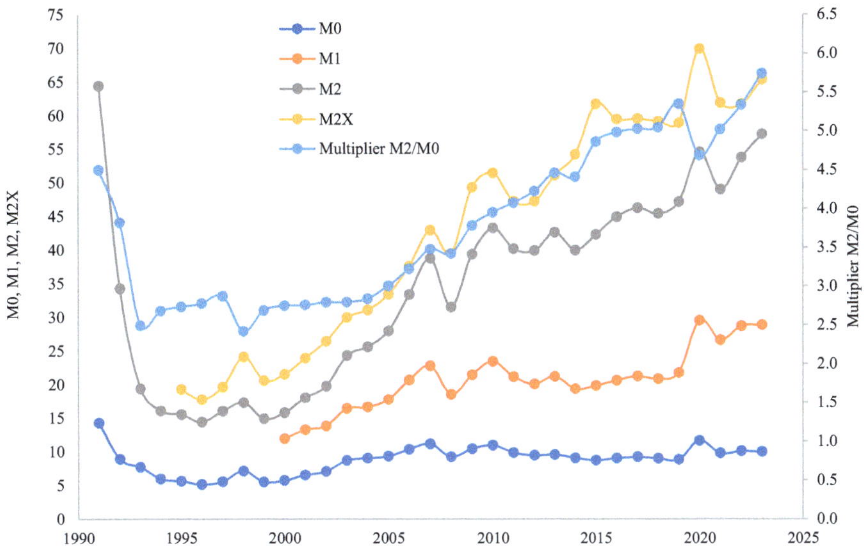

Fig. 8.17 Dynamics of the level of monetization of the economy of the Russian Federation (monetary aggregates at year end, in percentage of GDP). *Note:* M0 is the monetary base (banknotes and coins in circulation); M1 is the money supply that includes the monetary base and transferable deposits in rubles (settlement, current, and other on-demand accounts); M2 (national concept) is the money supply that includes M1 plus other deposits in rubles; M2X (Broad Money as of international concept) is M2 plus deposits in foreign currency, certificates of deposit and savings certificates issued by credit institutions (Bank of Russia 2024b). *Source:* Bank of Russia (downloaded at 2024, https://www.cbr.ru/Content/Document/File/128613/monetary_agg.xlsx; https://www.cbr.ru/vfs/statistics/credit_statistics/broadmoney_sa.xlsx), Rosstat (downloaded at 2024, https://rosstat.gov.ru/folder/210/document/13396)

former command economies. Yet, they allowed an economic collapse to be avoided, smoothed the transformation, and diminished social costs of the real sector restructuring (e.g. contributed to relatively low unemployment). Combating high inflation in a poor institutional environment produced such negative effects as barter settlements,[27] the elevated use of cash banknotes (especially foreign ones),[28] delays in wage payments, and the flourishing of multiple rent-seeking and criminal activities.

Since the late 1990s, monetization in Russia has been increasing. The monetization measures (M2 and Broad Money) demonstrated growth. At the same time, inflation was slowing down. The slowdown in Russia's GDP growth after 2009 was accompanied by a slowdown in monetization growth as measured by M1 but not Broad Money. Monetization also grew in the 2010s, owing to non-cash items. What

[27] Their share reached a maximum level of over 50% in autumn 1998, after the devaluation and sovereign selected default, but dropped soon thereafter as the economy stabilized (Sutela 2013).

[28] Half of all of the banknotes in circulation were US dollars immediately after the crisis of 1998 (Berglof and Lehmann 2009, 203).

is remarkable for Russia is the stable and even somewhat declining level of cash (M0). The money multiplier (M2/M0) also declined. Yet, the level of monetization is still lower than before the transition to a market economy. Russia's economy is monetized at a similar level to economies with a comparable level of GDP per capita, but much lower than China and lower than the advanced economies.

The strategic goal of the financial policies from the late 1980s to the 2000s was to create market institutions for the national economy while regulating foreign access to them. The banking reform of 1987 created a two-tier system when the State Bank functions became close to those of a central bank (bank for banks), while households and enterprises received limited financial services from the specialized state banks.[29] Even though this was not yet a pro-market reform proper, it marked the first departure from the mono-banking system that paved the way for subsequent chaotic creation of about 600 competing regional and inter-regional banks on the basis of their specialized predecessors. In 1988, cooperative banks established by non-state enterprises were allowed. As of the end of 1991, there were 1360 credit institutions in Russia, up from four in 1987 (Khanin 2014, 188). In addition to the privatization of special banks, over 2000 other banks were established between 1991 and 1994, many by state structures, others by private individuals and small business associations (Yudaeva and Schoors 2013, 546). By 1997, the number of banks in Russia reached its historical high of over 2600 (Doronin and Zakharov 1998, 504). Over 300 banks operated in Russia in 2024.[30]

The emerging commercial banking system was very much fragmented spatially, with low competition outside Moscow and St. Petersburg. In 1989, foreign capital was allowed to enter the capital of the Soviet banks. However, subsequently foreign participation in the Russian banking sector appeared to be rather modest relative to the countries of Eastern Europe (see below). This period of soft regulatory constraints led to much fraud, money laundering, and the collapse of trust in financial institutions by households (Yudaeva and Schoors 2013, 548–549; Khanin 2014, 196–221). The share of the state-owned Sberbank, which was a successor to the Soviet-era monopoly savings institution and had a sovereign guarantee for nominal value of households' deposits (even though this was not completely legally specified), increased from 53% in mid-1994 to over 85% at the end of 1998 (Yudaeva and Schoors 2013).

As the hyperinflation of the early 1990s wiped out households' savings, the new market banking system emerged as corporate-based and serving the demands of business groups. The further structural dynamics of key liabilities and assets reveals that the Russian banking system relied less on the government and enterprises with respect to liabilities, more on enterprises with respect to assets, and more on

[29] These banks specialized in sectors of the national economy: industry and construction, agriculture, utilities and social services, households' savings, and foreign economic relations. The details are in Simonov (2016, 27–45), Kirsanov (2011, 66–94), and Khanin (2010, 92–109).

[30] Bank of Russia (downloaded at 2024, https://cbr.ru/vfs/statistics/bank_system/inform_bs_24.xlsx)

households in both respects. Several banking crises occurred, with about half of them not spreading to the real sector.

The very high inflation of the first half of the 1990s effectively redistributed economic income in favour of the banking sector (Simonov 2016, 13). So did the high real yields on federal government bonds (GKO-OFZ) in 1995–1996 (Khanin 2014, 192–193). The main source of income for most large Russian banks was operations in the financial market (forex, government securities, and interbank loans). The high profitability of banking operations was based on a combination of working assets in rubles with interest-free liabilities in rubles (Doronin and Zakharov 1998, 521; Khanin 2014, 189–193).

The substantial changes in the balance sheet structure of the banking system occurred in the 2000s–2010s (Fig. 8.18). If in the 1990s the main assets were cash (mainly in foreign currency) and government securities, and the liabilities were interest-free accounts of enterprises and the budget, then in the 2000s the assets became loans to enterprises and households, and the liabilities became accounts of enterprises and the population. The share of loans in assets in 1998 was 27.7%, but in 2007–2015, it fluctuated between 85% and 65%. In the late 1990s, the share of long-term loans (more than a year) was insignificant, mirrored by the same deposits. As the sustainability of liabilities and the capital of the banking system increased in the 2000s, this share started to grow rapidly (Khanin 2019, 31–32).

As of the alternative estimate, the ratio of loans to GDP increased from 9.8% in 1998 to 26.9% in 2007, 40.4% in 2011, and 70.3% in 2015, reaching the level of many former socialist countries and the most advanced developing countries. Even though some of the loans were non-performing, the trend towards significant growth is evident (Khanin 2019, 31).

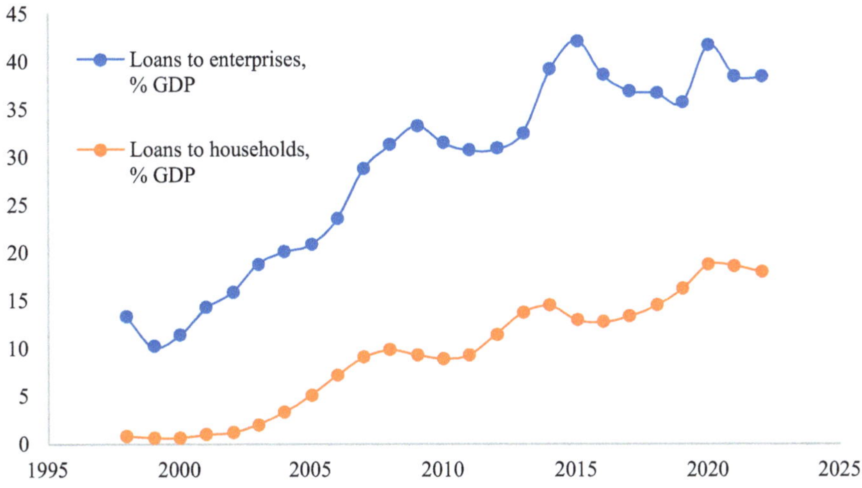

Fig. 8.18 Credit activities of the Russian banks, as percentage of GDP (1998–2023). *Source:* Rosstat (downloaded at 2024, https://rosstat.gov.ru/folder/210/document/13396), based on Bank of Russia statistics

Households' bank deposit insurance was introduced in 2004–2006 in order to increase trust and competition in the market. Concurrently, the explicit 100% state guarantee was lifted from Sberbank, thus making the rules equal for all. The share of the latter on retail deposit market fell back to about 50%. The criteria were not tight, which led to rather fast depletion of the funds and credit financing of the state insurance corporation from the Bank of Russia during the crisis of 2008–2009. In a matter of just 15 years, more than half of the insurance system members have gone out of business. The social cost of having this institution in Russia turned out to be abnormally high, while the results in terms of bank stability are questionable. Without a problem of moral hazard being addressed, the new institution was captured by interest groups and exploited for private benefit (Vernikov 2023). The growth of households' funds did not outperform those from enterprises. The share of Sberbank slid but stabilized at about 50%, as in the mid-1990s (Fig. 8.19).

In Russia, foreign capital owed about 10% of the banking system (versus 80–95% in Eastern European countries). However, foreign capital played the great role in financing the banks themselves and the real sector of the economy. By the end of 2010, the total foreign debt of Russian banks reached $142 billion, which corresponded to 25% of all bank deposits. In 2013, the share of external financing in the total volume of loans to non-financial corporate sector reached almost a half. Large businesses were financed primarily from foreign sources (Khanin 2019, 32–33).

Overall, the transition entailed the emergence of a few dominant large state and "captive" banks, which mainly provided loans to their related structures and their own companies. In the context of significant information asymmetry and the absence of legal instruments for contract enforcement, these were probably second-best

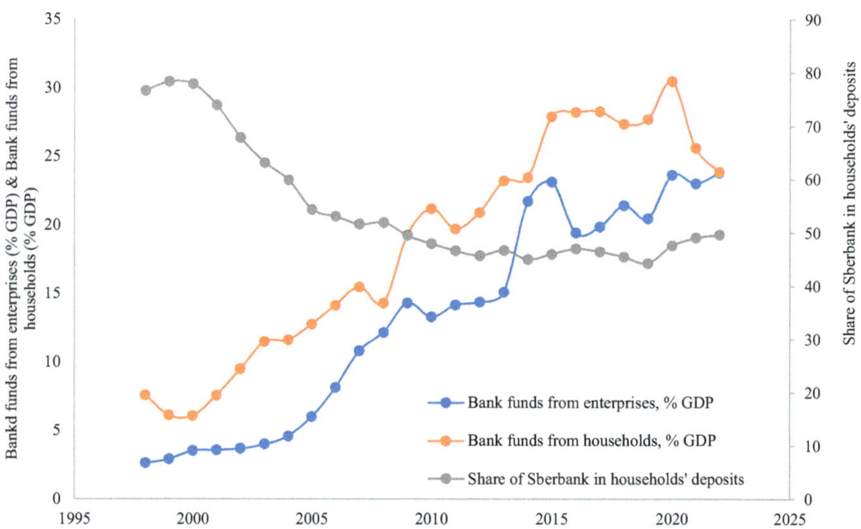

Fig. 8.19 Funding activities of the Russian banks, as percentage of GDP (1998–2023). *Source:* Rosstat (downloaded at 2024, https://rosstat.gov.ru/folder/210/document/13396) based on Bank of Russia statistics

solutions to the problems of selecting projects for financing and their control. What is specific to Russian private banks is their low efficiency compared with both state and foreign banks (Yudaeva and Schoors 2013).

The Russian financial system has been formed as bank-centred, even though strong attempts were made in the 1990s and 2000s to introduce American securities market institutions based on transparency, strong role of self-governing organizations, and regulation sharing between the government agencies.

As for macroeconomic regulation on the part of the central bank, exchange rate policy dominated over interest rate policy. Instead of multiple exchange rates in 1990–1991, since 1992 ruble became convertible for current operations with a market rate based on exchange trading. This task was exacerbated with opening up of Russia's economy, both in terms of current (with positive net exports) and capital (with net outflows) operations. When severe shocks affected both financial and real sector the Bank of Russia opted for saving the latter (in 1992 and 1998).

Like central banks in other countries, the Bank of Russia has operated since the 1990s on the state bond market (federal loan bonds—OFZ) to manage basic interest rates. Moreover, given the increased openness of the Russian economy, the Bank of Russia was accumulating large foreign currency reserves when Russia experienced an influx of foreign currency from net exports and an inflow of short-term private capital (Fig. 8.20). In the 2000s, Russia developed a complex system of banks refinancing using both market and non-market collateral. The system received an impetus for development during the financial crisis of 2004 and the economic crisis of 2008–2009. In 2005–2014, Russian capital markets were further liberalized, most

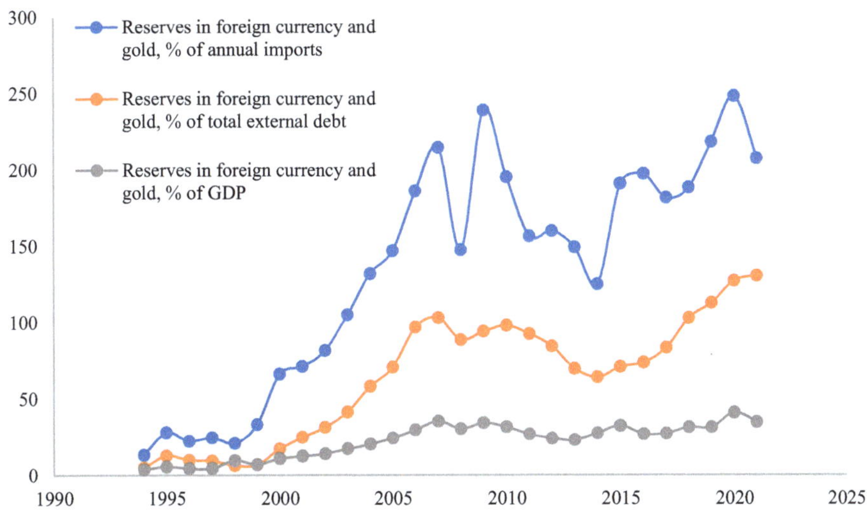

Fig. 8.20 Bank of Russia's international reserves. *Note:* About 50% of the Bank of Russia's foreign reserves were frozen in a number of foreign countries in February 2022 (Bank of Russia 2023, 121). *Source:* Rosstat (downloaded at 2024, https://rosstat.gov.ru/folder/210/document/13396) based on Bank of Russia statistics

of the capital controls being lifted in 2007. In the 2010s, there was a real shift from exchange rate targeting to inflation targeting. These policies appeared to be successful until the COVID-19 shock: inflation fluctuated within the range 2.51–5.39 (with a target of 4%) in 2016–2020. This led to extension of credit under low interest rates and longer terms.[31] These monetary policies appeared to be sustained even under economic sanctions, rising inflation, and partial restrictions of capital flows and of ruble convertibility. However, the Bank of Russia reserved the right to enter the foreign exchange market if there was a threat to the financial sector systemic stability.

During the period of economic recovery in 1999–2006, the Bank of Russia tested regimes of economic policy several times in trying not only to preserve financial destabilization, but also to support recovery growth. To sustain the competitiveness of Russian producers in the domestic market under an inflow of foreign currency (caused by higher oil prices and improvement of sentiment on the financial markets), the Bank of Russia moderated the ruble's real (accounting for the difference in inflation rates) appreciation first to the US dollar (2000–2004) and then to a currency basket (2005–2014), with an increasing share for the euro (0.55 USD and 0.45 EUR in 2007–2014). These policies appeared to be rather prudent, flexible, and effective until the economy reached its "overheating" phase.[32] The main course was the formation of expectations as regards the relative stability of the exchange rate (an implicit cap and floor within a floating regime), lower inflation, and lower interest rates. The priorities within this dual targeting and management gradually shifted to the latter. Real interest rates tended to be negative to enable the extension of credit.

During the crisis of 2008–2009, the Bank of Russia spent much of its reserves to effect smoothed devaluation of the ruble instead of a "big-bang" devaluation or leaving the forex market to its participants. Monetary stimulation was used as an anti-crisis measure, as it was by other central banks. The difference was that it was refinancing the banks to provide credit to the real sector, not so much to the government or households.

As financial stabilization was basically achieved in the 2000s, even under double-digit inflation, the state budget turned out to have a surplus. The tax reform implemented in the late 1990s and early 2000s can be assessed as the most successful of all the reforms of the period: tax rates were significantly reduced, the tax system was simplified, and the neutrality of the tax system increased, and at the same time it was possible to achieve a significant increase in tax revenues for the budget (Kadochnikov et al. 2008). The tax system had acquired a fairly consistent legislative basis. The innovations were perceived by businesses as a significant improvement, tax discipline also improved (Alexeev and Conrad 2013). The introduction of flat and relatively moderate personal income tax (13%) that succeeded for almost 20 years despite fierce criticism even from the ruling United Russia party was a

[31] See details in Bozhechkova et al. (2020).

[32] See details in Trunin (2008).

remarkable case of integrity not only of Russia's fiscal system, but also the whole economic strategy.

In the 2000s and 2010s, much Russian academic literature and mass media spoke in favour of monetary and fiscal stimulation of economic development. Many drawn from the academic community as well as politicians (even from the United Russia party in power) opposed the strategy of lasting fiscal austerity and the strategy of accumulation of foreign reserves when commodity prices went up. They backed the investment of state funds into the domestic real sector, primarily hi-tech.[33] The results appeared to be rather modest. The Bank of Russia, with presidential support, reaffirmed its reluctance to operate outside the financial sector. The Ministry of Finance succeeded in accumulation of funds mostly in foreign assets, giving some concessions to domestic ones in the late 2000s and 2010s.

The government investment policy in Russia became more active from 2005. It was mostly affected through contributions to the share capital of development institutions and enterprises (Sokolov and Kazakova 2008, 176–182). The share of government investments into the national economy in Russia is on a par with the peer countries (Germany, France, USA), although is much lower than in China. However, due to the fact that much of investments come from the Sovereign Wealth Fund as buying of shares (not changing the balance value), their size is actually more significant than reported by the national statistics and mirrored in the IMF publications (Ordynskaya et al. 2024).

The decisions to establish the Bank for Development (2007),[34] and other similar institutions, was in line with fiscal methods to stimulate the national economy. However, the funds provided for them were limited in size and within reasonable proportions in order to sustain financial stability. Even though the effects of these decisions are still being debated, the fact is that Russia has one of the lowest state debt levels; most of the debt burden is born by the corporate sector operating in a market environment. Only a tiny part of this debt is under explicit sovereign guarantee; even though a sizable part is under implicit guarantee; that is, the market perception is that the federal government would step in, as it did, for example, in the case of the Bank for Development in 2014–2016.

It should be noted that in the early 2000s the decision was made to decrease sovereign debt with the help of accumulated funds of the budgetary system, even through its redemption with some premium (London Club of commercial creditors, Paris Club of sovereign creditors, the International Monetary Fund (IMF), and the

[33] The Reserve Fund and the National Wealth Fund. At the time of the financial market turmoil in August 2008, they amounted for 8.5% and 1.9% of GDP, respectively. The Reserve Fund was depleted mainly in 2008–2010. In September 2024, the National Wealth Fund amounted to 6.7% of GDP (Ministry of Finance, downloaded at 2024, https://minfin.gov.ru/en/document?id_4=104686-volume_of_the_national_wealth_fund; https://minfin.gov.ru/en/statistics/fonds?id_57=104658-key_figures_of_reserve_fund_management)

[34] Established on the basis of the specialized Bank for Foreign Economic Activities of the USSR under Federal Law. Currently, it is the State Development Corporation VEB.RF (https://xn%2D%2D90ab5f.xn%2D%2Dp1ai/en/about-us/legal/)

World Bank).[35] The relation of government debt (with sovereign domination) to GDP decreased tenfold over several years of high prices in commodities markets against a conservative budget policy. The sovereign debt dominated in the composition of external debt in the 1990s. In the 2000s, government debt was replaced by corporate debt (the core components are shown in Fig. 8.21).

However, the lack of coordination and of mutual regard between fiscal and monetary policies in Russia militated against macroeconomic stability and complicated the economy's exit from the crises (Drobyshevsky et al. 2018).

Furthermore, the conservative fiscal policy of the Ministry of Finance tended to lower expenditures with high external effects (education, healthcare, research and development, transport infrastructure, technologically advanced sectors of the national economy) that stagnate at best (Fig. 8.22). Fiscal policy in the late 2010s increased the long-term resilience of the budget system to a possible crisis rather than stimulating economic growth (Belev et al. 2020, 219–220).

The instruments of the financial markets emerged throughout the 1990s and 2000s and developed in the 2010s. Strong corrections to this trend occurred during the crises of 1998 and 2008–2009. In the 2000s, the Russian financial market gained substantial depth. The development of financial markets and their penetration is shown in Tables 8.7, 8.8, and 8.9.

From the 1990s, regulated foreign access to Russian financial markets was employed to lower interest rates and increase valuation of equity assets. From early in that decade, foreign investors had almost unlimited access to Russian stocks

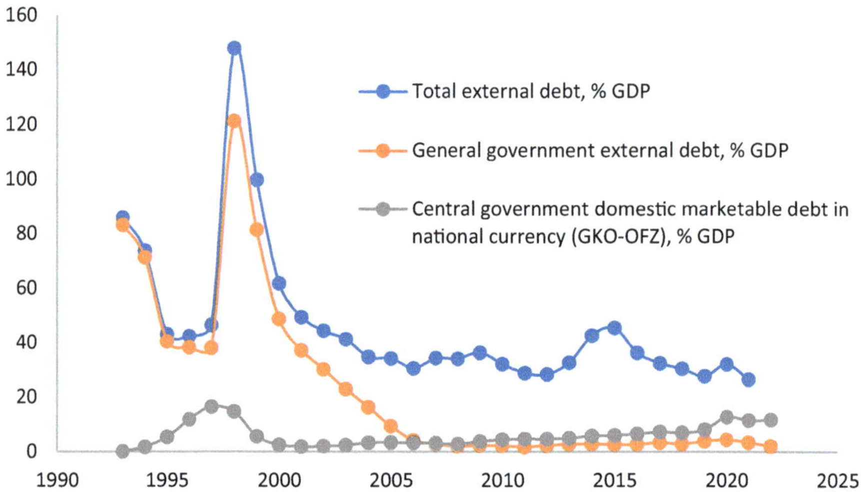

Fig. 8.21 External and domestic debt of the Russian Federation, as percentage of GDP (1993–2022). *Source:* Rosstat (downloaded at 2024, https://rosstat.gov.ru/folder/210/document/13396) based on Bank of Russia statistics

[35] For details, see Sokolov and Kazakova (2008, 158–163).

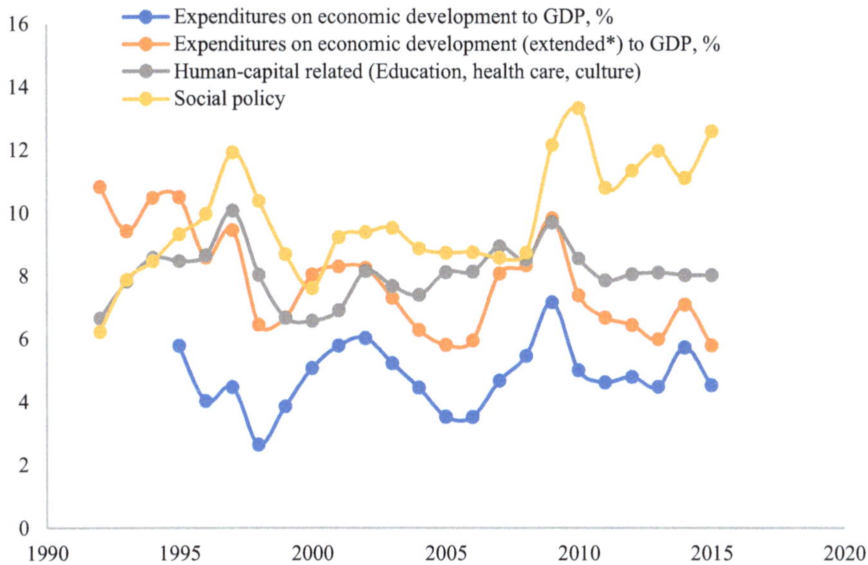

Fig. 8.22 Expenditures of the Russian consolidated budget on economic development, human capital formation, and social policy, percentage of GDP. *Note:* * Including housing and public utilities, environment, and others. *Source:* Expenditures: Tabata and Tabata (2019); GDP: Kuboniwa et al. (2019)

Table 8.7 The Russian government bond market in 1998–2016

Indicators	Unit	1998	2007	2012	2016
Liquidity	%	63.5	54.5	138.1	85.7
Duration of the market portfolio	days	150	n.d.	1553	1504.5
Market portfolio as % of GDP	%	55.1	6.4	7.1	9.9
Government to corporate debt ratio		13.3	0.35	0.4	0.65

Source: Khanin (2019, 46)

Table 8.8 The corporate bond market in 1998–2016

Indicators	Unit	1998	2007	2012	2016
Domestic corporate bond turnover ratio	%	2	2.91	1.58	0.51
Corporate bond debt to GDP ratio	%	3.4	10.6	13.9	20.4
The same for those in domestic market	%	0.01	3.81	6.6	10.9
Ratio of bond issue volume to domestic bond market	%	2.5	37.8	29.6	25.5

Source: Khanin (2019, 41–42)

(except those of enterprises involved in defence production) and federal government bonds issued in foreign currency. In 1996, they were permitted (with minor restrictions) to buy and sell ruble-denominated government bonds (GKO-OFZ) on the domestic market. Implicitly, the government targeted their level of yield in US

Table 8.9 Russian stock market in 1998–2016

Indicators	Unit	1997	1998	2001	2007	2012	2016
Market capitalization/GDP	%	16.5	4.0	22.6	98.7	40.4	71.0
Stock market concentration (share of 10% of companies in market capitalization)	%		65.8*		68.5	61.8	61.0
The same in trade turnover	%		90.4**		68.4	84.5	80.1
Free-float	%		5–6***		18.0	n.d.	32.5
Number of retail investors	Thousands of people		8****		417	800	1300
including active ones (more than one transaction per month)	Thousands of people			74.2	69	80	

Notes:
* Of the 100 largest companies by market capitalization
** October 1998
*** Beginning of the twenty-first century
**** Second quarter 1999
Source: Khanin (2019, 37–38, 53)

dollars through forward forex contracts between Russian banks and their foreign counterparts and the central bank exchange rate targeting. This scheme worked well, and the foreign participants' share reached about a third of the GKO-OFZ market—until the four-times devaluation of the ruble and partial sovereign default occurred in August–October 1998.[36]

In 1992–1998, the federal budget was chronically in deficit, which forced huge borrowings on the foreign and domestic securities markets. As a result, the government securities market was of most importance (see Table 8.7). In the 2000s, real interest rates turned out to be quite low and the duration of government borrowings became longer, approaching that in those countries with similar levels of economic development (Khanin 2019, 47).

In 2013, non-residents' access to the domestic government securities market was completely liberalized. After that, their share increased from 6.5 or more to the historical high of 34.5% in 2018 (Abramov and Chernova 2020, 321–322).

The 2000s was crucial in the development of the corporate bond market (see Table 8.8). During this period, it reached significant size in absolute terms and in relation to GDP. This was facilitated by a favourable external economic environment, a significant decrease in inflation, a noticeable improvement in the level of corporate management and accounting in companies, and more trust in them. In terms of the ratio of the market of outstanding corporate bonds to GDP and in absolute terms, this growth stopped in the 2010s. The number of bond issuers also decreased, but the number of problems increased significantly. The reduction in the number of issuers is obviously associated with stricter legal requirements. The banking sector continued to outstrip the securities market in terms of corporate debt,

[36] The details are in e.g. Khanin (2014, 204–205, 227–229) and Simonov (2016, 200–227).

but this excess was declining until 2016, when the Eurobond market contracted owing to financial sanctions (Khanin 2019, 43).

The Russian stock market was not significant in the late 1990s. In the 2000s, it became a noticeable segment of the Russian economy (see Table 8.9). By 2007, it had grown dozens of times by all measures and became comparable to those of the largest emerging markets, such as Brazil. In the 2000s, large Russian companies issued their shares through initial public offerings (IPO). In 2007, the stock market was inflated due to massive inflow of foreign short-term private capital. After the crisis of 2008–2009, some decrease in concentration (the fall in oil prices also had an effect) and especially in growth of free-float are noteworthy. The period after 2008 witnessed stagnation or even a deterioration in liquidity (one of the lowest in the world) and the number of IPOs. In 2010–2011, Russia's share in the global IPO market settled at 1.5%, in line with its share of the global stock market capitalization (Khanin 2019, 37–41, 57, 59).

Owing to the outflow of foreign investment and other factors (the abolition of mandatory pension savings, weakening competition in the domestic financial market, signs of deterioration of the investment climate) in 2007–2018, compared with the mid-2000s, the Russian stock market turned out to be a less effective mechanism for market investments in companies through public offerings of shares and bonds, as well as financing mergers and acquisitions of companies. It remains a fragmented institution focused on solving local problems of managing cash liquidity of companies and financial institutions (Abramov and Chernova 2020, 298, 335).

Stock market concentration remains high and does not seem to significantly diminish over time. State companies dominate on the stock market and state institutions dominate in the financial services. What has changed in recent years is the higher trust and radically increased participation of retail investors, meaning their relative shift from bank deposits to securities market instruments. Even combined with the other trends described earlier, this does not change the very bank-centred model of the Russian financial market, but augments it with more complex institutions founding the basis for the further development.

8.4 Monetary Command Administration Economy in the USSR Versus China

So far, we have mostly talked about private capital, or government capital used in private or profit-generating activities. Yet, the nationalization of existing financial institutions, carried out immediately after the Bolsheviks came to power in 1917, laid the foundation for overwhelming state control over the national monetary and banking system. The subsequent hyperinflation, on a comparable scale to the one in Germany in the early 1920s, accompanied with a transition to barter exchange and rationed distribution of basic consumer goods, led to the complete decay of the banking system. In January 1920, the People's Bank of the Russian Soviet Republic

(RSFSR) was liquidated and the Central Directorate of Settlement and Budgeting of the People's Commissariat for Finance of the RSFSR (the Government Financial Office) was established, taking over the powers of issue money.[37]

With the introduction of the "new economic policy" (NEP) in 1921, the State Bank was restored within the People's Commissariat for Finance.[38] In subsequent years, several state banks were re-established, as well as communal banks and credit unions in both urban and rural areas. The dominant State Bank's provision of both commercial and central banking services was a tradition inherited from the State Bank of the Russian Empire. Despite the fact that the State Bank of the USSR subsequently changed its institutional status, its activities were considered by the state as subordinate to general economic and fiscal objectives. These received the greatest priority during the period of subordination of the State Bank to the government of the USSR (1938–1946), which corresponded to the period of preparation and conduct of military operations during the Second World War. From 1954 to 1987, the State Bank again became a separate entity, in direct subordination to the USSR's government.

Monetary reform of 1922–1924, based on a quasi-gold standard, led to moderation of inflation, which in 1925 and 1926 still significantly exceeded the levels characteristic of the pre-revolutionary period, but in 1927 and 1928 even some deflation was observed.[39]

In January 1927, the rule "one enterprise–one bank branch" was introduced. This provided the State Bank with the necessary opportunities to control enterprises' operations. Additionally, the credit reform of 1930–1932 laid the foundation for the Soviet banking system, which operated until 1987. Such a mono-bank system in the USSR was characterized by the following features:

- Both short-term and long-term bank loans were allocated to enterprises in an administrative manner, similar to the allocation of material resources and state budget funds. Any type of horizontal financing between enterprises was prohibited. Under the NEP, it was possible to bypass limits on government loans through unofficial loans by means of bills of exchange that enterprise syndicates arranged (Gregory 2003, 222). Subsequently, more than 90% of short-term financing needs were met through loans from the State Bank. Financing from bank loans was of a supplementary nature, since long-term financial needs for the core economic activities of enterprises were covered by the state budget. Until the mid-1950s, there were several banks that provided long-term loans to finance investment projects in peripheral (non-priority) industries. However, the share of the State Bank was 80–90% of the total volume of loans (Nakamura 2019, 237).
- There was strict separation of circulation of cash in the narrow sense (banknotes and coins) and "non-cash" (money on bank accounts). The use of such cash for

[37] MinFin (2024).

[38] Bank of Russia (2024a).

[39] Didenko et al. (2013) based on quasi-official data of the Central Bureau of Labour Statistics.

payments between enterprises was strictly prohibited. The cash could be used to pay wages to employees, social benefits and compensations to households, and purchase office supplies. Each transaction between enterprises was carried out by transfer to a bank account; however, offsets between enterprises were tolerated.

- The State Bank for Foreign Trade of the USSR (operated since 1924, subordinate to the Foreign Trade Office, whose organizations had a monopoly on foreign trade transactions with goods) had a monopoly on transactions with foreign currency, the exchange rate to the ruble of which was strictly fixed for many years. With the reduction in the role of foreign trade in the economy from the late 1920s, the ruble exchange rate became an insignificant issue in monetary policy, although it retained some importance for fiscal policy. The problem regained more significance with the establishment of an economic integration association of the socialist countries in 1949 (the Council for Mutual Economic Assistance—known as COMECON).

The dynamics of banking activities' penetration, primarily lending, into the Soviet economy until the 1950s experienced strong fluctuations, generally showing a tendency towards expansion (Fig. 8.23).

The Soviet economy institutionally eliminated indicators such as interest rates and exchange rates for analysing the monetary situation and used them as policy instruments. In the Soviet command economy, monetary imbalances manifested themselves in a shortage of consumer goods, an increase in queues, and, in the later period, an increase in household deposits. Periods of 1928–1935, 1941–1947, and

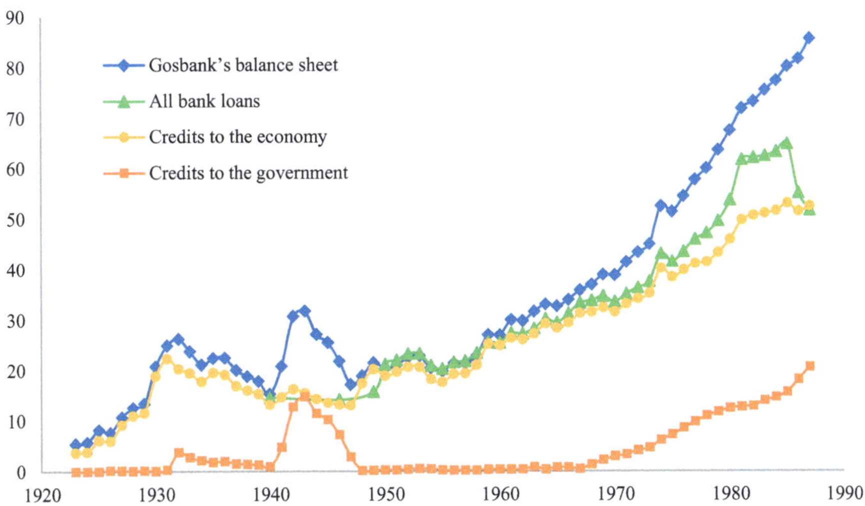

Fig. 8.23 Dynamics of the role of basic banking services in the economy, 1923–1987 (monetary aggregates as a percentage of GDP). *Source:* Estimate based on Nakamura (2019, Appendix table 7.2); GDP: Didenko et al. (2013)

1989–1991 were characterized by a rationed supply of basic consumer goods to the urban population.

With the complete destruction of the household savings system during the Russian Revolution of 1917–1922 and the loss of pre-revolutionary savings by the population, household funds could not play a significant role as a source of funds for the Soviet banking system until the 1960s. Institutionalized household savings in the 1930s–1950s basically appeared as purchases of government bonds (predominantly forced). In addition to enterprise funds, the main role in the banking resources belonged to issuance of currency (mainly "non-cash": see Fig. 8.24). In the period of establishing the mechanism for managing cash and "non-cash" money supply from 1929 to 1937, inflation remained in the elevated range of 15–21% annually, but without sharp fluctuations and without turning into hyperinflation (Didenko et al. 2013).

Much evidence suggests that the incentive system of the Soviet economy (so-called soft budget constraints) induced business managers to maximize gross output, with financial efficiency as a less significant factor. Under these soft budget constraints, the State Bank was forced to provide loans to enterprises, even if its managers did not agree (Gregory 2003, 213, 229–230). At the first stage of the credit reform of 1930/1932, the State Bank provided loans almost without limits, meeting requirements of producers to accelerate the industrialization effort. Trying

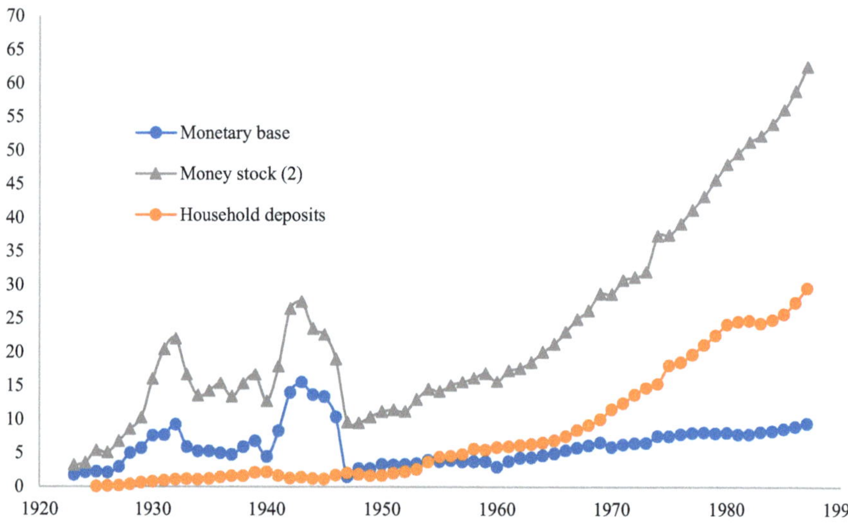

Fig. 8.24 Dynamics of the level of monetization of the economy, 1923–1987 (monetary aggregates as a percentage of GDP). *Note:* The monetary base is the most liquid part of the money supply, which includes banknotes and coins in circulation (cash in the narrow sense); Money supply (2) includes the monetary base, transferable deposits (current and other on-demand accounts of enterprises and households for payments and settlements), that is, cash and bank ("non-cash") money. *Source:* Monetary aggregates: own calculation based on Nakamura (2019, Appendix table 7.2); GDP: Didenko et al. (2013)

to combat rising inflation, the Soviet leadership then turned to the tightening of monetary policy and targeted it to maintain the rate of growth of the money supply (Gregory 2003, 224–226). Such policies could not cope with the rapid structural changes in the economy during the period of industrialization. One of the consequences was the widespread issuance and use of money surrogates, criminal penalties for which were introduced only in 1935 (Gregory 2003, 231–233).

Even though commercial credit was banned, it continued to exist as receivables and payables after the credit reform of 1930/1932 right up to the collapse of the Soviet system (Gregory 2003, 226–229). These loans between businesses amounted to 13–20% of the volume of liquid assets of the state-owned enterprises (Nakamura 2011).

Although the use of bank credit was limited, the interest rate was uniformly fixed and the terms of loans were not differentiated according to enterprise. Supply and demand for bank loans were managed administratively.

In the USSR, controlling household demand for cash appeared to be of great importance, and consequently the balance of cash income and expenses and indicators of the velocity of money circulation became the principal measures for monetary management (see Fig. 8.25). However, the separation of cash and non-cash

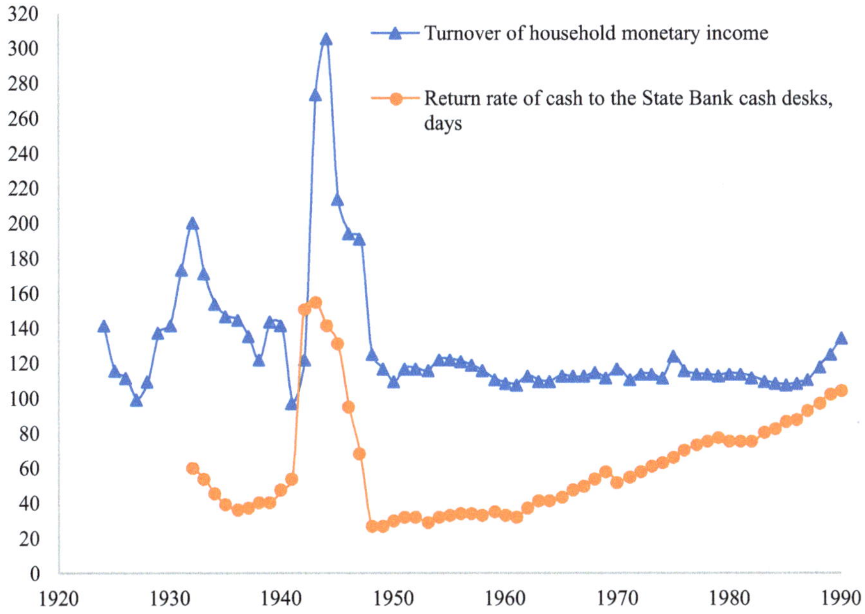

Fig. 8.25 Dynamics of indicators of the speed of money circulation, 1923–1987. *Note:* Turnover of households' monetary income is the sum of their monetary income and expenditures; cash return rate is the ratio of the average value of the monetary base and the daily receipt of money at the State Bank cash desks (actually it is the reverse measure to money velocity). *Source:* Turnover of monetary income of the population, cash return rate: Kashin and Mikov, eds. (2007, Table 1.1, 1.2.3); GDP: Didenko et al. (2013)

flows could not mean that there was no economic connection between cash and "non-cash" money. Throughout the Soviet period, producers were actually able to siphon some of their money from bank accounts into cash, which served as an unexpectedly powerful source of inflation, especially in the 1930s (Gregory 2003, 220–221). The dynamics of the monetary factors of inflation, which was relatively high in the 1930s–1940s, are shown in Fig. 8.26.

The period from 1939 to the post-war monetary reform of 1947 was a period of war economy, when issuance of currency financed the overspending of budget funds allocated primarily for military purposes. Although the issue of currency led to inflationary pressure both in the public sector and in the collective farm market, hyperinflation was avoided, contrary to the situation during the Civil War of 1918–1922.

The monetary reform of 1947, which had been planned since 1942, still under war conditions,[40] consisted of the withdrawal from households of the cash they had accumulated by making use of the difference between market and state rationed prices during the war, and the simultaneous abolition of the rationed sale of consumer goods. It included measures such as a radical slashing of cash in hand (90%), partial slashing of deposits (exceeding the threshold of 3000 rubles, which

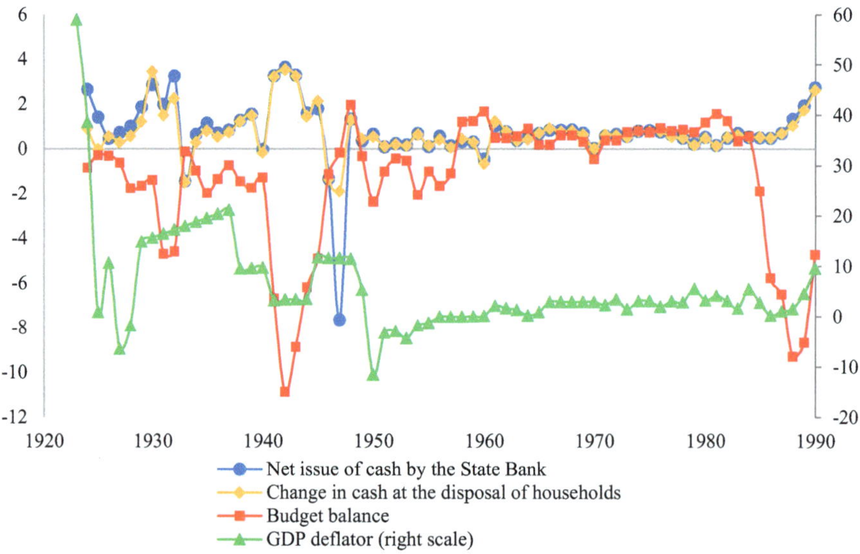

Fig. 8.26 Dynamics of monetary factors of inflation, 1923–1990 (percentage of GDP). *Note:* Net issue of cash by the State Bank is a measure of change in the monetary base over the year; budget balance is consolidated state budget revenues minus expenditures (a surplus if the sign is positive, a deficit if it is negative). *Source:* Net issue of cash, change in cash at the disposal of households: Kashin and Mikov, eds. (2007, table 1.1, 1.4); own calculation based on (Tabata and Tabata 2019, Appendix table 8.4, 8.6); GDP, GDP deflator: (Didenko et al. 2013)

[40] See: Kashin (2007).

approximately corresponded to more than 5 months' average wages in the urban sector of the economy (Didenko et al. 2013), and partial default on government bonds (mandatory conversion with a postponement of the maturity date, a reduction in the par value, and a reduction in the interest rate from 3% to 2% per annum). Deposits of state enterprises were not revalued; 20% of funds were slashed from bank accounts of collective farms and cooperatives. Nominal amounts of financial flows, including wages and pensions, remained unchanged. Thus, the monetary reform of 1947 did not provide for denomination. Nevertheless, it was successful in normalizing monetary circulation and was carried out along with abolition of the rationing system and a transition to trade with firm retail prices (Nureev and Eskindarov 2019, 273–280).

In the early 1950s, in a centrally administered economy, a policy was pursued that consisted of reducing prices in order to match them with the real incomes of the population (Nove 1992, 333–335, 354–358). The money supply, however, grew slowly and continuously between 1950 and 1960, but was kept within acceptable limits (see Fig. 8.24).

In the mid-1950s, the policy was changed to a more flexible provision of short-term loans. The use of bank loans by enterprises was expanded in anticipation of strengthening financial discipline and increasing the efficiency of use of funds. Thereafter, both short-term bank loans and household deposits increased rapidly in parallel.

In the Soviet command economy, cash money was a tool, similar to propaganda or repression, to stimulate the hard work of the labour force to achieve the goals set by the country's leadership, and "non-cash" money was a tool to help check the implementation of plans by enterprises (Ellman 2020).

The prioritized actual objective of monetary policy in the Soviet command economy was to ensure the fulfilment of enterprises' planned targets to increase output, with price stability (minimized inflation) as the balancing goal with the second priority. By the mid-1950s, the Soviet banking system had managed to achieve an optimal combination of these two parameters, resorting to confiscatory methods regarding household funds.

While the USSR embraced a command-administrative economy through the nationalization of banks and strict centralization after the Bolshevik Revolution, China's path towards monetary centralization was characterized by the coexistence of traditional monetary practices, state institutions, and the challenges posed by modern fiscal demands. China's economy during the imperial period, particularly under the Ming and Qing dynasties, was heavily reliant on agrarian structures and silver-based monetary systems, but it faced severe challenges in the twentieth century as it moved towards centralization under the People's Republic of China. Historically, China's imperial economy was predominantly agrarian, and the state's ability to control monetary policy was limited by the decentralized nature of its tax system, which depended heavily on local officials to collect produce and silver taxes. As shown in Table 8.4, the Chinese government's revenue in the early Ming period was mostly drawn from produce taxes and textile contributions, with relatively small reliance on monetary forms such as paper cash or silver. Over time, the growing importance of silver taxes reflected the increasing integration of the Chinese economy into global trade networks, particularly through silver inflows from European traders during the sixteenth and seventeenth centuries.

However, despite the monetization of the economy, China lacked a centralized banking system capable of mobilizing resources for state-driven projects. Unlike the USSR, which was able to nationalize and centralize its banking system in the twentieth century, China's reliance on local tax collection and its decentralized fiscal system meant that the state had limited control over monetary flows. This system persisted throughout the Qing dynasty, contributing to fiscal weaknesses that would become more evident in the face of internal rebellions and foreign incursions. With the establishment of the People's Republic of China in 1949, a more centralized monetary and banking system was developed under the control of the Chinese Communist Party. Like the Soviet Union, China's leadership sought to nationalize its financial institutions and place banking under direct state control. The creation of the People's Bank of China in 1948, which functioned both as a central and commercial bank, marked the first step towards centralizing the financial system.

Yet, the challenges of centralizing monetary control in such a vast and agriculturally driven economy were significant. While the USSR had already established a robust command economy during its early decades, China struggled with local autonomy and informal fiscal practices that persisted from the imperial period. This led to inefficiencies, as the central government had to manage vast rural areas with little direct control over local fiscal and monetary activities. The People's Communes, introduced during the Great Leap Forward (1958–1962), sought to collectivize agricultural production and centralize tax collection. However, these reforms failed to resolve the underlying structural issues, and China experienced economic disruptions and food shortages.

By the 1950s and 1960s, China's monetary policy began to resemble the command-administrative systems seen in other socialist states, though with notable differences:

- State control of currency: Like the Soviet Union, China monopolized the issuance of currency, with the People's Bank of China controlling the money supply. However, barter economies still persisted in many rural areas (Chang 2022). The government had strict control over foreign exchange, especially as the Chinese economy was relatively isolated from the global economy during the Maoist period.
- Restricted credit allocation: Similar to the mono-bank system in the USSR, China's banking sector allocated both short-term and long-term loans in an administrative manner. The People's Bank became the primary institution responsible for providing state-directed loans to both industrial and agricultural sectors. However, in contrast to the USSR, China's credit system was more heavily weighted towards agricultural financing, reflecting the state's reliance on the peasantry for revenue and labour.
- Separation of cash and non-cash transactions: The Chinese state, like the Soviet system, implemented a strict separation between cash used by households and

non-cash funds managed by state enterprises. Cash was primarily used to pay wages and purchase consumer goods, while non-cash payments were strictly controlled and monitored by the state to avoid financial leakage.

- Centralized planning and limited financial autonomy: By the 1950s, the Chinese banking system was fully integrated into the state's centralized planning apparatus. Enterprises could not engage in horizontal financial transactions with one another, and all transactions had to be funnelled through state-approved channels. The Chinese state exerted direct control over monetary policy, using it as a tool to achieve industrialization goals and control inflation.

Whereas the USSR largely maintained its mono-bank system until its dissolution, China began to experiment with limited market reforms in the late twentieth century. In the wake of economic failures during the Maoist period, China under Deng Xiaoping implemented gradual economic reforms beginning in the late 1970s, which included partial decentralization of fiscal policies. The 1979 banking reforms introduced dual-track pricing and allowed the creation of commercial banks, which operated alongside state banks (Wang 2019).

In the 1980s, China introduced township and village enterprises (TVEs), which operated with a degree of financial autonomy not seen under the centralized Soviet-style economy. These entities could access loans from newly established commercial banks and were allowed to retain profits, which spurred economic growth, particularly in rural areas (Xiao 2021). Despite these changes, however, the People's Bank of China remained under state control, and the government continued to set key monetary policy decisions.

While both the USSR and China implemented state-controlled banking systems, China's experience with monetary centralization was distinct in several ways:

- Decentralization versus centralization: Whereas the Soviet system was marked by strict centralization and control over monetary flows, China's experience was characterized by a persistent struggle with local autonomy and the difficulties of extending central control over a vast and agriculturally based economy.
- Gradual reforms: While the USSR maintained a rigid monetary system until its collapse in 1991, China began experimenting with market reforms and decentralized banking much earlier. The introduction of market-oriented policies in the late twentieth century allowed China to maintain a degree of economic flexibility that the USSR lacked.
- Agrarian focus: In contrast to the industrial bias of Soviet financial policy, China's monetary system remained heavily agrarian-focused until well into the twentieth century. This reliance on agricultural production limited the state's ability to finance large-scale industrial projects, which only changed with the economic reforms of the late twentieth century.

The development of China's monetary command-administrative system shared similarities with the USSR's, particularly in the centralization of monetary policy, control over credit allocation, and restriction of private financial autonomy. However, China's path was marked by greater struggles with local autonomy and a slower transition towards centralized control. As China moved into the late twentieth century, it began to diverge from the Soviet model by gradually adopting market-oriented reforms, allowing for more flexibility in its financial system and avoiding some of the rigidity that ultimately led to the collapse of the Soviet Union.

8.5 Conclusion

In Central Eurasia, fiscal policy dominated monetary strategies, with shifts between tight and loose monetary controls marking both state-led and command economies. Inflation was generally contained during monetary easing, except during the wartime periods of 1914–1922 and 1941–1945. Centralizing banking under the Soviet state allowed for efficient savings conversion into investments, supplemented by controlled currency issuance to cover savings shortfalls. A dual currency system existed in both the Russian Empire and Soviet Union: the Empire's ruble, partly backed by gold, shifted in the USSR to a split between cash and non-cash rubles, each with restricted usage. Attempts to stimulate growth included decoupling the ruble from gold and relying on fiat money, allowing a managed inflation rate lower than in many Western economies until the late Soviet period.

Western Europe's approach to fiscal and monetary policy contrasts sharply. European states, especially the Netherlands and the UK, pioneered robust fiscal systems as early as the seventeenth century, leveraging excise taxes, direct taxes, and customs duties to create efficient revenue streams. This foundation enabled European states to fund large military expenditure and infrastructure projects, fuelling early industrialization. The UK and the Netherlands became models for the fiscal state, with relatively high tax revenues supporting both warfare and economic modernization. After the Second World War, European economies such as France and the UK continued to strengthen their fiscal capacity, with tax revenue reaching as much as 20–25% of GDP to support expansive welfare programmes. Effective inflation control in these economies created stability, setting the stage for economic growth and resilience across decades of post-war recovery.

In China, the agrarian-based fiscal system faced deep structural limitations. Historically, tax collection depended on land-based produce taxes, restricting China's ability to leverage the growing wealth from urbanization and international trade. During the Ming and early Qing periods, silver became increasingly important as a source of revenue, yet the lack of administrative flexibility hindered the tax system's responsiveness. This rigidity limited the Chinese state's ability to fund necessary reforms, particularly as industrialization transformed other parts of the world. For example, as European states developed advanced fiscal systems to extract revenue from diverse economic sources, China's tax collection remained entrenched in agriculture, creating fiscal vulnerabilities as Western powers gained economic and political influence in the region.

The 1994 tax reform in China sought to recentralize revenue control after a period of decentralization in the 1980s. Although the reform improved central revenue collection, local governments continued to rely heavily on land sales to fund regional projects. This dependency contributed to an unsustainable housing market boom, with rising property prices and public discontent over affordability. Meanwhile, local fiscal imbalances grew, as the central government's control over monetary and fiscal policy struggled to adapt to regional economic needs. Despite these reforms, the constraints in China's fiscal system continued to impact economic stability, with regional governments seeking informal funding mechanisms to meet budgetary needs.

In comparing these three cases, we see distinct paths of fiscal and monetary policy evolution shaped by each region's structural and historical context. Russia's centralized banking and currency controls created unique fiscal tools, while Western Europe's adaptable tax systems became foundational to its economic growth and stability. In China, the prolonged reliance on agrarian taxes and local funding challenges underscored the difficulties of modernizing within a traditionally decentralized system. Each region's experience illustrates the critical role of flexible and responsive fiscal policies in promoting long-term economic growth and resilience.

References

Abramov AE, Chernova MI (2020) Российский финансовый рынок: уроки прошедшего десятилетия [The Russian financial market: lessons of the past decade]. In: Gurevich VS et al (eds) Экономическая политика России. Турбулентное десятилетие 2008–2018 [Economic policy in Russia. A turbulent decade of 2008–2018]. Delo RANEPA Publishing House, Moscow, pp 295–339

Alexeev M, Conrad RF (2013) The Russian tax system. In: Alexeev M, Weber S (eds) The Oxford handbook of the Russian economy. Oxford University Press, pp 246–264

Bank of Russia (2023) Annual report for 2022. Moscow. https://www.cbr.ru/Collection/Collection/File/46299/ar_2022_e.pdf

Bank of Russia (2024a) History of the Bank of Russia. https://www.cbr.ru/eng/about_br/history/

Bank of Russia (2024b) Monetary aggregates. http://www.cbr.ru/eng/statistics/macro_itm/dkfs/monetary_agg/

Belev SG, Sinelnikov-Murylev SG, Sokolov IA, Tishchenko TV (2020) Налогово-бюджетная политика в условиях внешних и внутренних вызовов [Fiscal policy in the context of external and internal challenges]. In: Gurevich VS et al (eds) Экономическая политика России. Турбулентное десятилетие 2008–2018 [Economic policy in Russia. A turbulent decade of 2008–2018]. Delo RANEPA Publishing House, Moscow, pp 218–245

Berglof E, Lehmann A (2009) Sustaining Russia's growth: the role of financial reform. J Comp Econ 37(2):198–206

Besley T, Persson T (2011) Pillars of Prosperity: The Political Economics of Development Clusters. Princeton, NJ: Princeton University Press

Birman I (1981) Secret incomes of the Soviet state budget. Martinus Nijhoff Publishers, The Hague

Bolt J, Van Zanden JL (2020) Maddison style estimates of the evolution of the world economy: a new 2020 update. Maddison Project Database, version 2020

Bonney R (1999) The rise of the fiscal state in Europe, c. 1200–1815. Oxford University Press

Borodkin LI, Konovalova AV (2010) Российский фондовый рынок в начале XX в.: факторы курсовой динамики [The Russian stock market in the beginning of the 20th century: factors of the quotes dynamics]. Алетея [Aletheia], St. Petersburg

Bovykin VI (2001) Финансовый капитал в России накануне Первой мировой войны [Financial capital in Russia on the eve of the First World War]. ROSSPEN, Moscow

Bozhechkova AV, Kiyutsevskaya AM, Sinelnikov-Murylev SG, Trunin PV (2020) Денежно-кредитная политика: стабилизация инфляции [Monetary policy: inflation has stabilized]. In: Gurevich VS et al (eds) Экономическая политика России. Турбулентное десятилетие 2008–2018 [Economic policy in Russia. A turbulent decade of 2008–2018]. Delo RANEPA Publishing House, Moscow, pp 199–217

Brandt L, Ma D, Rawski TG (2014) A new economic history of China. Cambridge University Press

Broadberry S, Korchmina E (2024) Catching-up and falling behind: Russian economic growth, 1960s-1880s. J Econ Hist 84(4):997–1028. https://doi.org/10.1017/s0022050724000287

Bugrov AV (2017) Казённые банки в России. 1754–1860 [State-owned banks in Russia. 1754–1860]. Central Bank of the Russian Federation, Moscow

Calabrese M (2023) The fund code: a history of investment funds in Luxembourg from the Holding Act to the UCITS legislation (1929–1989) [Doctoral thesis, Unilu—University of Luxembourg]. ORBilu—University of Luxembourg. https://orbilu.uni.lu/handle/10993/58853

Calabrese M, Giacomin V (2025) Business networks in small states: the emergence and evolution of Luxembourg's global mutual fund industry (1945–1988). Business Hist Rev. https://doi.org/10.1017/S0007680525000157

Calabrese M, Majerus B (2024) Archaeology of a treasure Island: actors and practices of holding companies in Luxembourg (1929–1940). Contemporary European History 33(4): 1398–1415. Cambridge University Press. https://doi.org/10.1017/S0960777323000437

Calabrese M, Van Leeuwen B (2024) Occupational titles in census data: England and Wales. J Interdiscip Hist 55(2):243–267. https://doi.org/10.1162/jinh_a_02039

Chang M (2022) Investigation of the purchase and sale of rural local specialties in the early days after the founding of New China (新中国成立初期农村土特产品购销探析). Contemp China Hist Stud 2022(3):53–67

Chechulin ND (1906) Очерки по истории русских финансов в царствование Екатерины II [Essays on the history of Russian finance in the reign of Catherine II]. Senatskaya tipografiya, St. Petersburg

Chen S, Liu X, Lu C (2022) Fiscal Decentralization, Local Government Behavior, and Macroeconomic Effects of Environmental Policy. Sustainability 14(17):11069. https://doi.org/10.3390/su141711069

Cheremukhin A, Golosov M, Guriev S, Tsyvinski A (2017) The Industrialization and Economic Development of Russia through the Lens of a Neoclassical Growth Model. Rev Econ Stud 84(2):613–649. https://doi.org/10.1093/restud/rdw026

Cottarelli C, Blejer MI (1992) Forced savings and repressed inflation in the Soviet Union: some empirical results. IMF Staff Pap 39(2):256–286. https://www.elibrary.imf.org/downloadpdf/journals/024/1992/002/article-A002-en.xml

Dabrowski M (2022) Thirty years of economic transition in the former Soviet Union: macroeconomic dimension. Russ J Econ 8:95–121. https://doi.org/10.32609/j.ruje.8.90947

Davydov MA (2016) Двадцать лет до Великой войны: российская модернизация Витте-Столыпина [Twenty years before the Great War: Russian modernization from Witte & Stolypin], 2nd edn. Алетея [Alethea], St. Petersburg

Deng L, Shen Q, Wang L (2015) Housing policy and housing markets in China. Springer

Didenko DV (2020) Trends and institutional sources of financing Russia's human capital formation (late nineteenth–early twenty-first centuries). In: Hanes C, Wolcott S (eds) Research in economic history, vol 36. Emerald Publishing Limited, pp 45–107. https://doi.org/10.1108/S0363-326820200000036002

Didenko D, Földvári P, Van Leeuwen B (2013) The spread of human capital in the former Soviet Union area in a comparative perspective: exploring a new dataset. J Eurasian Stud 4(2):123–135. https://doi.org/10.1016/j.euras.2013.03.002. (Supplementary data retrieved from https://ars.els-cdn.com/content/image/1-s2.0-S1879366513000122-mmc1.zip, accessed via https://www.sciencedirect.com/science/article/pii/S1879366513000122)

Doronin I, Zakharov A (1998) Российские банки в переходный период [Russian banks in the transition period]. In: Gaidar ET et al (eds) Экономика переходного периода: Очерки экономической политики посткоммунистической России, 1991–1997 [The economy in transition: essays on the economic policy in post-communist Russia, 1991–1997]. Institute for Economics in Transition Publishing House, Moscow, pp 503–560

Drobyshevsky S, Idrisov G, Sinelnikov-Murylev S, Trunin P (2018) Fiscal and monetary policy. In: Studin I (ed) Policy Russia: strategy, policy and administration. Palgrave Macmillan, pp 169–181

Elliott, JH (2006) Empires of the Atlantic World: Britain and Spain in America 1492–1830. Yale University Press

Ellman M (2020) Money, prices, and payments in planned economies. In: Battilossi S, Cassis Y, Yago K (eds) Handbook of the history of money and currency. Springer, Singapore, pp 473–500

Esherick JW (1987) The origins of the boxer uprising. University of California Press

Fairbank JK (1978) The great Chinese revolution: 1800–1985. Harper & Row

Farquet C (2012) Le marché de l'évasion fiscale dans l'entre-deux-guerres. L'Écon Polit 2(54):95–112

Farquet C (2016) La défense du paradis fiscal suisse avant la Seconde Guerre mondiale: une histoire internationale. Neuchâtel

Flandreau M, Zumer F (2004) The Making of Global Finance, 1880– 1913. OECD, Paris

Friedman M (1962) Capitalism and Freedom. University of Chicago Press

Friedman M (1968) The role of monetary policy. Am Econ Rev 58(1):1–17

Friedman M, Schwartz AJ (1963) A monetary history of the United States, 1867–1960. Princeton University Press

Gerschenkron A (1962) Economic backwardness in historical perspective: a book of essays. Harvard University Press, Cambridge

Gindin IF (1948) Русские коммерческие банки: Из истории финансового капитала в России [Russian commercial banks: from the history of financial capital in Russia]. Gosfinizdat, Moscow

Gindin IF (1997) Банки и экономическая политика в России: XIX–начало XX в.: Очерки истории и типологии русских банков: избранное [Banks and economic policy in Russia: 19th–early 20th centuries: essays on the history and typology of Russian banks: selected works]. Наука [The Science], Moscow

Gregory P (1982) Russian national income, 1885–1913. Cambridge University Press, London

Gregory PR (2003) The Political economy of Stalinism: evidence from the Soviet. Secret Archives. Cambridge University Press, Cambridge, UK

Hayek FA (1944) The Road to Serfdom. University of Chicago Press

Horton M, El-Ganainy A (n.d.) Fiscal policy: taking and giving away. International Monetary Fund (IMF). https://www.imf.org/en/Publications/fandd/issues/Series/Back-to-Basics/Fiscal-Policy

Huang Y, Yi C (2011) China's housing policy: challenges and prospects. Oxford University Press

Kadochnikov P, Nazarov V, Sinelnikov-Murylev S, Sokolov I, Trunin I (2008) Основное содержание и последствия налоговой реформы [Tax reform: essential features and consequences]. In: Gaidar ET et al (eds) Экономика переходного периода. Очерки экономической политики посткоммунистической России. Экономический рост 2000–2007 [The economy in transition. Essays on the economic policy in post-communist Russia. Economic growth of 2000–2007]. Delo ANE Publishing House, Moscow, pp 226–274

Kahan A (1985) The plow, the hammer and the knout: an economic history of eighteenth-century Russia. University of Chicago Press, Chicago

Karaman K, Pamuk S (2010) Ottoman state finances in European perspective (1500–1914). J Econ Hist 70(3):1–36

Kashin YI (ed) (2007) По страницам архивных фондов Центрального Банка Российской Федерации [Through the pages of the archival funds of the Central Bank of The Russian Federation]. Issue 3. Денежная реформа 1947 года в документах: подготовка, проведение и оценка результатов [Monetary reform of 1947 in documents: preparation, implementation and evaluation of results]. Bank of Russia, Moscow. http://www.cbr.ru/Content/Document/File/48231/ArchivalFonds_003.pdf

Kashin YI, Kozlova TV (eds) (2012) По страницам архивных фондов Центрального Банка Российской Федерации [Through the pages of the archival funds of the Central Bank of The Russian Federation]. Issue 13. Госбанк СССР и Минфин СССР в процессе мобилизации и использования сбережений населения (ведомственные материалы) [State Bank of the USSR and Ministry of Finance of the USSR in the process of mobilization and utilization of the household savings (departmental materials)] (1922–1990). Bank of Russia, Moscow. http://www.cbr.ru/Content/Document/File/48232/ArchivalFonds_002.pdf

Kashin YI, Mikov VV (eds) (2007) По страницам архивных фондов Центрального Банка Российской Федерации [Through the pages of the archival funds of the Central Bank of The Russian Federation]. Issue 2. Оборот наличных денег в СССР [Cash circulation in the USSR]. Bank of Russia, Moscow, pp 1922–1990. http://www.cbr.ru/Content/Document/File/48232/ArchivalFonds_002.pdf

Khanin GI (2010) Экономическая история России в новейшее время. Т. 2. Экономика СССР и РСФСР в 1988–1991 годах [Economic History of Russia in Modern Time. Vol. 2. Economics of USSR and RSFSR in 1988–1991]. Publ. House of Novosibirsk State Technical University, Novosibirsk

Khanin GI (2014) Экономическая история России в новейшее время. Т. 3. Российская экономика в 1992–1998 годы [History of the Russian Economy at the Newest Time. Vol. 3. Russian Economy (1992–1998)]. Publ. House of Novosibirsk State Technical University, Novosibirsk

Khanin GI (2019) Экономическая история России в новейшее время. Т. 4. Экономика Российской Федерации в 1999-2016 годы. [History of the Russian Economy at the Newest Time. Vol. 4. Economy of The Russian Federation in 1999-2016]. KMK Scientific Press Ltd, Moscow

Kirby WC (1995) China and the world: trade and power in the modern world. Harvard University Press

Kirsanov, R. G. (2011). Перестройка. «Новое мышление» в банковской системе СССР [Restructuring. The “New Thinking” in the USSR Banking System]. Moscow: Kashirin Publishers

Krispijn, Th. J. H. (2016). “Early silver: Thoughts about the sign KU in the earliest documents from Uruk,” in: Kleber K. and Pirngruber R. (eds), *Silver, money and credit. A tribute to Robartus J. van der Spek on Occasion of his 65th Birthday on 18th September 2014*, Leiden, the Netherlands: Nederlands Instituut voor het Nabije Oosten, 1–10.

Kroll, J.H. (2012) “The monetary background of Early coinage”, in W. E. Metcalf (ed.), *The Oxford Handbook of Greek and Roman Coinage, Oxford University Press*, 13–42.

Krugman P (2009) The return of depression economics and the crisis of 2008. W. W. Norton & Company

Kuboniwa M, Shida Y, Tabata S (2019) Gross domestic products. In: Kuboniwa M et al (eds) Russian economic development over three centuries: new data and inferences. Palgrave Macmillan, Singapore, pp 335–419

Li B (2003) The economic history of China: from antiquity to the nineteenth century. Stanford University Press

Liu AY, Oi JC, Zhang Y (2022) China’s local government debt: the grand bargain. China J 87(1):49–71

Lucassen J (2018) Deep monetization in Eurasia in the long run. In: van der Spek RJ, van Leeuwen B (eds) Money, currency and crisis: in search of trust, 2000 BC to AD 2000 (pp. 267–284), Routledge explorations in economic history. Routledge, pp 55–101

Ma D (2011) Rock, scissors, paper: the problem of incentives and information in traditional Chinese state and the origin of Great Divergence”, Economic History Working Papers 37569, London School of Economics and Political Science, Department of Economic History

Mankiw NG (2019) Principles of economics. Cengage Learning

Markevich A (2019) A regional perspective on the economic development of the late Russian Empire. SSRN. https://ssrn.com/abstract=2555273

Mathai K (n.d.) Monetary policy: stabilizing prices and output. IMF. https://www.imf.org/en/Publications/fandd/issues/Series/Back-to-Basics/Monetary-Policy

MinFin (2024) Ministry of Finance of Russia History of the Ministry. https://minfin.gov.ru/en/ministry/history/

Ministry of Agriculture (1907, 1916) Сборник статистико-экономических сведений по сельскому хозяйству России и иностранных государств [Collection of statistical and economic data on agriculture in Russia and foreign countries]. St. Petersburg/Petrograd

Morozan VV (2004) История банковского дела в России (вторая половина XVIII–первая половина XIX в.) [History of banking in Russia (the second half of the 18th–first half of the 19th centuries)]. Kriga, St. Petersburg

Moshensky SZ (2015) Между Лондоном и Парижем: Рынок ценных бумаг индустриальной эпохи [Between London and Paris: the securities market of the industrial era]. Mindstir Media, Hampton, NH

Nakamura Y (2011) Did the Soviet command economy command money? A quantitative analysis. Europe-Asia Stud 63(7):1133–1156. https://doi.org/10.1080/09668136.2011.592264

Nakamura Y (2017) Monetary policy in the Soviet Union: empirical analyses of monetary aspects of Soviet economic development. Palgrave Macmillan, New York

Nakamura Y (2019) Money and finance. In: Kuboniwa M et al (eds) Russian economic development over three centuries: new data and inferences. Palgrave Macmillan, Singapore, pp 221–249

Naughton B (2007) The Chinese economy: transitions and growth. MIT Press

Nove A (1992) An economic history of the USSR: 1917–1991, 3rd edn. Penguin Books, London/New York

Nureev RM, Eskindarov MA (eds) (2019) Денежная реформа 1947 года и ее роль в восстановлении народного хозяйства СССР [The Monetary reform of 1947 and its role in the restoration of the national economy of the USSR]. KNORUS, Moscow

O'Brien PK (1988) The political economy of British taxation, 1660–1815. Econ Hist Rev 41(1):1–32. https://doi.org/10.1111/j.1468-0289.1988.tb00453.x

Ordynskaya EV, Cherkovets MV, Savchishina KE (2024) Public investment and economic growth in different countries. Stud Russ Econ Dev 35:800–809. https://doi.org/10.1134/S1075700724700345

Palan R, Murphy R, Chavagneux C (2010) Tax havens: how globalization really works. Cornell University Press

Palma N (2022) The real effects of monetary expansions: evidence from a large-scale historical experiment. Rev Econ Stud 89(3):1593–1627. https://doi.org/10.1093/restud/rdab042

Petrov YA (2010) Коммерческие банки и экономическое развитие России в конце XIX—начале XX века [Commercial banks and economic development of Russia in the late 19th–early 20th century]. Ekonomicheskaia Istoriia [Russian Journal of Economic History] 3:25–33

Pistor K (2019) The code of capital: how the law creates wealth and inequality. Princeton University Press

Pogrebinsky AP (1954) Очерки истории финансов дореволюционной России (XIX–XX вв.). [Essays on the history of the finance in pre-revolutionary Russia (19th – 20th centuries)]. Gosfinizdat, Moscow

Rosenthal J-L, Wong RB (2011) Before and beyond divergence: the politics of economic change in China and Europe. Harvard University Press

Salomatina SA (2004) Коммерческие банки в России: динамика и структура операций. 1864–1917 гг. [Commercial banks in Russia: dynamics and structure of operations. 1864–1917]. Russian Political Encyclopedia (ROSSPEN), Moscow

Salomatina SA (2011) Финансовые рынки и институты. Проект "Динамика экономического и социального развития России в XIX–начале XX вв."/Л.И. Бородкин (руководитель) [Financial markets and institutions. Project "Dynamics of economic and social development of Russia in the 19th–early 20th centuries"] L. I. Borodkin (Principal Investigator). http://www.hist.msu.ru/Dynamics/index.html

Shumilin OV, Shumilina VO (2018) Dokhody i raskhody gosudarstvennogo biudzheta Russkogo Tsarstva i Rossiiskoi imperii za 1680-1917 gg. [Incomes and expenditures of the state budget of the Russian Tsardom and the Russian Empire, 1680-1917]. Audit Financial Analysis 5:203–209

Simonov NS (2016) Очерки истории банковской системы России. 1988–2013 гг. [Essays on the history of Russia's banking system. 1988–2013]. Dmitry Pozharsky University Publishing House, Moscow

Sokolov IA, Kazakova MV (2008) Бюджетная политика и состояние финансовой системы [Budget policy and the situation in the financial system]. In: Gaidar ET et al (eds) Экономика переходного периода. Очерки экономической политики посткоммунистической России. Экономический рост 2000–2007 [The economy in transition. Essays on the economic policy in post-communist Russia. Economic growth of 2000–2007]. Delo ANE Publishing House, Moscow, pp 143–190

Steinberg D (1990) The Soviet economy, 1970–1990: a statistical analysis. International Trade Press, San Francisco

Sutela P (2013) Financial and Credit Markets. In: Alexeev M, Weber S (eds) The Oxford Handbook of the Russian Economy. Oxford University Press, New York, pp 574–592

Tabata S, Tabata T (2019) State budget. In: Kuboniwa M et al (eds) Russian economic development over three centuries: new data and inferences. Palgrave Macmillan, Singapore, pp 251–289

Tilly C (1990) Coercion, capital, and European States, AD 990–1990. Blackwell

Troitskii SM (1966) Финансовая политика русского абсолютизма в XVIII веке [The financial policy of Russian absolutism in the 18th century]. Наука [The Science], Moscow

Trunin P (2008) Денежно-кредитная политика на различных этапах экономического роста [Monetary and credit policy at different phases of economic growth]. In: Gaidar ET et al (eds) Экономика переходного периода. Очерки экономической политики посткоммунистической России. Экономический рост 2000–2007 [The economy in transition. essays on the economic policy in post-communist Russia. Economic growth of 2000–2007]. Delo ANE Publishing House, Moscow, pp 191–225

TsSK (1916) Статистический ежегодник России. 1915 год (Год двенадцатый) [Statistical yearbook of Russia. 1915 (year twelve)]. Центральный Статистический Комитет [Central Statistical Committee], Petrograd

Van der Spek RJ, Van Leeuwen B (2018) Money and trust. In: van der Spek RJ, van Leeuwen B (eds), Money, currency and crisis: in search of trust, 2000 BC to AD 2000 (pp 1–12). (Routledge explorations in economic history). Routledge, pp 1–12

Van der Spek RJ, van Leeuwen B, van Zanden JL (eds) (2018) Money, currency and crisis: in search of trust, 2000 BC to AD 2000. Routledge, Oxon and New York

Van Leeuwen B, Iossif P, Földvári P (2018) The introduction of coinage in the Seleucid Empire and the Euro in the European Union: a comparison of stock and velocity. In: van der Spek RJ, van Leeuwen B (eds) Money, currency and crisis: in search of trust, 2000 BC to AD 2000 (pp. 149–164). (Routledge explorations in economic history). Routledge

Vernikov AV (2023) Breakdown: what went wrong with deposit insurance in Russia. Post-Communist Econ 35(1):41–58

Volkov VV (2016) "Дешево и сердито". Рынок труда в Европеиской России в конце XIX–начале XX в. [Cheaply and well done. Labour market in European Russia in the late 19th–early 20th centuries]. In 2 parts. Politekhnika-print, St. Petersburg

Von Glahn R (2016) The economic history of China: from antiquity to the nineteenth century

Von Glahn R (2018) Paper money in Song-Yuan China. In: Van der Spek RJ, van Leeuwen B, van Zanden JL (eds) Money, currency and crisis: in search of trust, 2000 BC to AD 2000. Routledge, Oxon and New York, pp 248–266

Wang G (2019) "70 years of China's Banking industry: brief history, main characteristics and historical experience" (中国银行业70年:简要历程、主要特点和历史经验). J Manag World 2019(07):15–25

White G, Wade R (1988) Developmental states and markets in East Asia: an introduction. In: White G (ed) Developmental states in East Asia. Macmillan Press, Houndmills/London, pp 1–29

Wong C (1997a) Financing local government in the People's Republic of China. Oxford Press

Wong RB (1997b) China transformed: historical change and the limits of European experience. Cornell University Press

Wong CPW (2000) Central-local relations revisited: the 1994 tax sharing reform and public expenditure management in China. China Perspect 31:52–63

World BANK (2022) World development indicators

Wu S (2021) Donations and national governance in the Qing dynasty (清代捐纳与国家治理). Social Sciences Academic Press (China), Beijing

Wu J, Gyourko J, Deng Y (2016) Evaluating conditions in major Chinese housing markets. Reg Sci Urban Econ 56:1–19

Xiao D (2021) An analysis of the history and mechanism behind the sudden emergence of township and village enterprises. CPC History Stud 2021(5):46–59

Xu Y, Van Leeuwen B (2018) Stagnation is silver, but growth is gold: China's silver period, circa 1430–1935. In: van der Spek RJ, van Leeuwen B (eds) Money, currency and crisis: in search of trust, 2000 BC to AD 2000. Routledge, pp 267–284

Yale School of Management (2021) The St. Petersburg Stock Exchange History Research Project. SPSE and NYSE Comparison. https://som.yale.edu/sites/default/files/2021-12/SPSENYSE18651917ind.xls

Yudaeva K, Schoors KV (2013) Russian banking as an active volcano. In: Alexeev M, Weber S (eds) The Oxford handbook of the Russian economy. Oxford University Press, New York, pp 544–573

Zelin M (1984) The Magistrate's Tael: rationalizing fiscal reform in eighteenth-century Ch'ing China. University of California Press

Zhang Y, Barnett S (2014) Fiscal vulnerabilities and risks from local government finance in China, vol 14. Int Monetary Fund, p 1

Zhao E (1977) History of the Qing, vol 清史稿), volume 125. Zhonghua Book Company (中华书局), Beijing

Chapter 9
Catching Up and Falling Behind: Economic Growth in the Twentieth and Twenty-First Centuries

Abstract This chapter explores the dynamics of economic growth in the twentieth and twenty-first centuries, emphasizing the interplay of modern growth theories and their applicability to varying regional contexts. It examines key growth patterns, including technological innovation, capital accumulation, and efficiency improvements, using examples from different areas within Eurasia. The chapter integrates insights ranging from growth models such as Solow-Swan, Lucasian, Romerian, and endogenous growth theories to a multivariate explanation of growth by various drivers of economic expansion, particularly highlighting human capital's dual role in enhancing efficiency and fostering innovation. These growth factors can be distinguished in long-run institutional, external, and internal and short-run factors.

Indeed, in-depth analyses of institutional frameworks and social actors, external factors such as convergence, and structural transitions illustrate their critical roles in shaping growth trajectories. First, case studies of China, Russia, and Southeast Asia reveal the importance of state-led development, institutional borrowing, and labour market dynamics in overcoming structural inefficiencies and achieving sustained growth. Second, the chapter also investigates external factors, such as global economic divergence and convergence, through the lens of World Systems Theory (WST), illustrating how international trade, technological diffusion, and geopolitical influences affect regional growth patterns. Third, internal factors such as capital investment, demographic shifts, and labour-force dynamics are scrutinized to understand their impact on economic resilience and sustainability.

The discussion includes the implications of recent technological revolutions, including the Fourth Industrial Revolution and AI, and their uneven effects on global economies. This comprehensive analysis underscores the complexity of economic growth, shaped by a confluence of long-term, external, and internal factors, and highlights the need for adaptive, context-specific policy interventions.

B. Van Leeuwen et al., *Innovation and Economic Development in Eurasia, 500 BCE-Present*, Frontiers in Economic History,
https://doi.org/10.1007/978-3-031-97043-6_9

9.1 Application of Modern Growth Theories

Invention and innovation are pivotal drivers of economic growth, yet, as explored in previous chapters, the impact of these forces depends on various key factors. Analysing growth through the production frontier approach, as discussed in Chaps. 5–7, reveals three primary growth patterns. Economic growth can result from advancements in general technology, which shift economies to a higher technology frontier, from capital deepening—marked by increased capital investment (see Fig. 6.4), or from a reduction in technical inefficiency, moving economies closer to the existing technical frontier.

The question now becomes, which model is best suited to predict growth? Using China as an example, scholars have suggested that its twentieth to twenty-first-century growth pattern aligns, to varying degrees, with several models. Some argue that China fits the Harrod-Domar, Lewis, and Solow-Swan models, in which investment plays a central role. In particular, a variant of the Solow-Swan model incorporates human capital into the production function, broadening its explanatory power. Another perspective is the Lewis model, which emphasizes productivity gains from shifting labour from low-productivity agriculture to higher-productivity industry. Additionally, endogenous growth models focus on identifying factors that drive innovation and total factor productivity (TFP), often highlighting urban agglomeration and competition as primary drivers.

Other scholars propose that China has its own unique model, shaped by a distinct blend of government influence, institutional frameworks, and market forces. This perspective challenges the Washington Consensus and is often contrasted with the Beijing Consensus, an approach rooted in state involvement and an authoritarian governance style that began with Deng Xiaoping's reforms in the late 1970s. While this "China model" has achieved notable success domestically, its international applicability remains limited. These issues therefore suggest that a combination of growth models may be the most suitable approach for understanding countries' unique and path-dependent economic trajectories, especially when considered in an international setting and in the context of the free circulation of information (in other words, in the presence of synchronized business cycles—see also Chap. 5).[1]

An example of this comprehensive approach, which integrates multiple growth models, is illustrated in Fig. 9.1. Between 1950 and 2007, economic growth in the

$$\underline{y} \approx (K/Y)^{\beta} \cdot h \cdot (R\&D\ intensity)^{\gamma} \cdot L^{\gamma}$$

	Solow	Lucas	Romer/AH/GH	J/K/S
2.0	0.0	0.4	1.2	0.4
(100%)	(0%)	(20%)	(58%)	(21%)

Fig. 9.1 Growth accounting for the United States, *c.* 1950–2007, with various growth theories. *Source:* Fernald and Jones (2014)

[1] See, for example, Economics online (2020), "Growth and development theories". Economics Online, 29 January 2020: https://www.economicsonline.co.uk/global_economics/growth_theories.html/

United States was significantly influenced by two distinct mechanisms of human capital utilization: Lucasian and Romerian growth. Lucasian growth, accounting for 20% of output growth per labour hour during this period, emphasizes the role of human capital in enhancing technical efficiency. This form of growth involves human capital being used to effectively work with existing technologies and machines, thereby reducing inefficiencies and facilitating the adoption of new inventions and innovations. On the other hand, Romerian growth played a more substantial role, contributing 58% to US economic expansion. This model focuses on specialized human capital, particularly in research and development (R&D), which drives the creation of new, often capital-intensive technologies. These innovations represent an upward shift in the technological frontier, underscoring the centrality of new inventions in sustaining long-term economic growth. Together, these mechanisms illustrate how different applications of human capital—improving efficiency versus advancing technology—shaped the trajectory of US economic development during the mid-twentieth century.

In Asia, a distinct growth trajectory emerged, contrasting with the patterns observed in the United States. Over the past century, countries such as Indonesia and India initially concentrated on building human capital to adopt and effectively utilize new, often foreign, technologies. This strategy focused on reducing technical inefficiency, aligning with the Lucasian model of growth. Japan, however, exemplified a pivotal shift in about 1950. Initially prioritizing the reduction of inefficiencies through human capital development, the country transitioned to a Romerian model of growth. This marked a move from focusing on adopting and improving existing technologies to driving innovation and creating new, often capital-intensive, inventions, thereby pushing the technological frontier forward (Van Leeuwen and Földvári 2008).

This Asian trajectory can also be compared with Robert Allen's (2012) framework for Europe, which categorizes growth into capital accumulation and technological growth. Countries such as Germany predominantly relied on capital accumulation to drive economic expansion, while nations such as the Netherlands and the UK emphasized technological growth. These categories bear a resemblance to the Lucasian and Romerian models, with the former focusing on the effective use of existing resources and technologies, and the latter on innovation and the upward shift of the technological frontier.

We can argue, therefore, that growth outcomes are heavily influenced by various underlying factors, which can be grouped into three main categories:

1. Long-term factors, which encompass elements discussed throughout the current book, spanning extended periods. Key examples include demographics, labour force dynamics, social actors, relative prices, path-dependent institutional frameworks, and similar foundational and environmental influences.
2. External factors, which involve global economic conditions, trade relationships, and other international influences.
3. Internal factors, namely shorter-term or one-time influences, including trends in the property market, national and local government policies (including, as seen

in Chap. 5, and policy outcomes of short mayoral tenures and city-specific initiatives in a context of "bad" institutions).

In the following sections, we will undertake a more in-depth analysis of these three types of factors, examining whether and how they influence current economic development.

9.2 Assessing the Role of Long-Run Factors of Growth

9.2.1 Agriculture, Economic Blockages, and Relative Prices

In analysing the role of long-run factors in predicting sustained growth, it becomes clear that elements such as human capital, state involvement, and labour force dynamics play a critical role. These factors contribute to growth by expanding the technological frontier, reducing technical inefficiencies, and enhancing capital by means of technology imports. This long-term growth potential is often conceptualized through a range of theoretical models, each describing how these forces interact, thus driving economic development. However, the practical application of these models is often constrained by realities that diverge from their foundational assumptions. Indeed, multiple realities and diverse economic conditions frequently co-exist within a single economy, each influencing growth trajectories in complex ways. For instance, in the agricultural sector, innovation-driven competition is frequently constrained by structural limitations. Even with government investment in education, farmers may struggle to develop added human capital owing to limited market opportunities and subsistence-focused production, as described by Chayanov (1925). This means that rather than prioritizing productivity and market expansion, the agricultural sector (especially when the focus of analysis goes to region or even district level) remains ultimately oriented around basic survival. In this context, while theoretical models may posit human capital as a growth driver, real-world conditions may restrict the accumulation of human capital and its impact on growth.

China's growth trajectory illustrates these complexities well, as traditional growth drivers—such as a growing labour force, rural to urban migration, high investment levels, and expanding exports—appear to have faced diminishing returns over time. This phenomenon raises questions about the long-term sustainability of growth based solely on this developmental path. Recognizing these limitations, scholars have argued that China exemplifies an East Asian government-driven model, in which the state takes an active role in fostering growth through investment in strategic industries and fundamental factors such as human capital.[2] This model aligns with the Gerschenkronian paradigm, which emphasizes the state's role in

[2] See e.g. "World Bank Group; Development Research Center of the State Council, The People's Republic of China. 2019. Innovative China: New Drivers of Growth". © Washington, DC: World Bank. http://hdl.handle.net/10986/32351

steering development, and has often been cited as a foundational element for example in Japan's post-war economic success.

However, as the history of Southeast Asia between the second half of the twentieth century and today demonstrates, this state-driven model also faces certain constraints. Issues such as market distortions arise from state-driven intervention, and these can inhibit optimal growth. To address these challenges, the World Bank has recommended that China integrate certain features of the East Asian (Tigers) model.[3] This includes three main strategies: reducing market distortions to enable a more efficient allocation of resources and foster innovation; promoting the diffusion of advanced technologies and management practices to raise productivity; and supporting an institutional environment that strengthens China's capacity for innovation and enhances its competitive advantage.[4]

Thus, in the broader context of long-run growth, policy-making must adapt to specific conditions and constraints within each economy. Long-run economic growth predictions must therefore account not only for the potential of human capital, state involvement, and labour force dynamics, but also for the structural and practical limitations that may affect how these factors influence growth.

9.2.2 *Institutions*

Institutions, which we have previously defined as the rules and norms governing economic and social interactions, play a crucial role in driving economic growth. In northern Eurasia, institutional strength was, as argued, often tied to a powerful state and collectivist structures, such as the Church in Europe. However, a fundamental distinction between China and Western Europe lies in the differing trajectories of state power. In Western Europe, the weakening influence of the state, along with a decline in collectivist institutions, enabled a more efficient use of technology. Although both regions experienced periods of strong and weakened states, China maintained a consistently stronger state presence overall. In China, this can be understood through two related concepts: disruption and adaptability (see e.g. Dijkman and Van Leeuwen 2019). Disruption refers to events such as wars, climatic crises, and famines, while adaptability encompasses the capacity to manage these disruptions. Addressing these challenges required a centralized bureaucracy capable of managing large-scale projects, the influence of legalism (the belief that strict laws are necessary to govern inherently flawed human behaviour) and Confucianism (which promotes social order, hierarchy, and traditional values), and recurring alternating cycles of market and state control dominance (Van Leeuwen and Van Zanden 2019).

[3] World Bank. *The East Asian Miracle: Economic Growth and Public Policy*. Oxford University Press, 1993.

[4] https://www.worldbank.org/en/news/press-release/2018/12/10/east-asia-needs-to-adapt-its-development-model-to-sustain-its-historic-transformation-world-bank-says

This centralized approach began with the Qin dynasty (221–206 BCE), whose state reforms, promotion of ideologies such as legalism and Confucianism, and foundational infrastructure projects such as the Great Wall created conditions in which each new invader or dynasty could establish control over all Chinese regions. According to the Dynastic Cycle Theory, when a dynasty weakened, both the bureaucracy and government influence in the economy would diminish, allowing for market forces to gain strength until a new dynasty restored state authority.[5] Although weakened during the Qing dynasty, this cyclical pattern persisted in some form until the present. The decline of the (dynastic) cycle since the Qing dynasty to the present can be attributed to three main factors: the "foreign" non-Han Qing dynasty; rising popular demands for sustainability, including concerns over environmental climate and inequality (see Sect. 9.2.3 on changing social actors); and an increased demand for the rule of law, each contributing to the gradual erosion of government influence.

In contrast, the European system evolved differently. While legalism, with its strict adherence to government rule, strengthened adaptability and sustained state control in China, the concept of liberty emerged in Europe as a counterpoint to legalism (i.e. freedom from despotic rule). Both concepts led to different state institutions and collectivist institutions. This shift led to political fragmentation, which fostered greater technological adoption and curbed collectivist institutions. Together, these factors spurred technological innovation, capital investment, and expanded labour and trade.

Beyond the institutional development in individual countries, institutional borrowing from other countries also played a pivotal role in shaping growth trajectories. As highlighted in Sect. 5.3.1, Russia began adopting Western institutions as early as 1500, incorporating ideas such as centralized bureaucratic governance, military modernization, and mercantilist economic policies. These borrowed institutions helped Russia to gradually integrate into the European framework of industrial and technological progress, albeit with significant adaptations to align with its autocratic governance structure. This partial adoption of Western institutions laid the groundwork for Russia's later industrialization efforts, particularly in the nineteenth and early twentieth centuries.

In contrast, China's development remained firmly rooted in indigenous institutions, including Confucian governance, legalist statecraft, and a deeply entrenched agrarian economy. These systems provided stability but limited the adoption of foreign ideas and technologies. It was not until the mid-twentieth century, following major political upheavals and reform efforts, that China began integrating external institutional frameworks, particularly during the post-Mao era when market-oriented reforms and international trade became central to its growth strategy.

[5] Dynastic Cycle Theory is a framework describing the rise and fall of Chinese dynasties, with economic and political implications. In a period of unrest, a new emperor, seen as strong and virtuous, takes over leading to a period of prosperity. Over time, corruption and unrest increases again, leading to a complete circle with a new emperor.

This comparison underscores how institutional borrowing, or the lack thereof, influenced the pace and nature of economic development. While Russia selectively integrated Western innovations into its governance and economic systems, China's initial reliance on indigenous frameworks delayed its engagement with global institutional trends. This divergence highlights the critical role of institutional adaptability in responding to global economic and technological changes.

9.2.3 Social Actors and Labour Relations

Social actors have been pivotal drivers of the conditions for long-term economic growth, with a history spanning from the Roman Empire in Europe and the Han Dynasty in China (*c.* 500 BCE–476 CE) to the present. Over time, three primary social groups have consistently emerged: a ruling class, such as emperors or senators; economic and political organizers; and a working class, consisting of commoners and slaves. These categories offer a useful framework, although in practice the ruling class and the economic and political organizers have often overlapped. This has been central to how social actors shape and influence the allocation of resources, labour relations, and technological progress.

In medieval Europe (476 CE–1450 CE), for example, several actors, including the Church, fulfilled the role of the ruling class, wielding both spiritual and temporal authority, while feudal lords and knights organized political and economic systems. These lords maintained local governance, enforced reciprocal labour obligations, and oversaw agricultural production, blending the roles of ruling and organizing classes. The working class, best represented by serfs bound to the land, provided the labour necessary for sustaining this predominantly agrarian economy.

The early modern period (1450–1800) brought significant shifts. Monarchs and aristocrats consolidated their position as rulers, continuing to act as economic organizers by controlling vast estates and influencing trade policies. At the same time, merchants and a rising middle class began to challenge the economic dominance of the ruling elite. This period saw the gradual emergence of commodified labour systems, as wage labour began to replace traditional reciprocal arrangements. The peasantry, while still forming the backbone of agricultural production, faced growing competition from urban labour markets. These changes later set the stage for the Industrial Revolution, during which the interactions between social actors fundamentally transformed economic growth trajectories.

The Industrial Revolution in the UK provides a compelling example of how social actors influenced economic development. A pivotal moment was the redirection of noble capital from traditional investments in agriculture to sovereign bonds, driven by the state's need for military financing (Ventura and Voth 2015). This shift in resource allocation had far-reaching consequences. As noble capital flowed into state bonds, entrepreneurs increasingly relied on reinvested profits to fund high-risk emerging industries that promised higher returns. This redirection reduced investment in agriculture, suppressing wages in rural areas and incentivizing rural to urban migration. The influx of rural workers into urban centres expanded the labour pool, providing entrepreneurs in new technology-focused industries with an affordable workforce.

By the modern era, the composition of the ruling class shifted again as nationalists and revolutionaries assumed power in many parts of the world, including Europe and China. In parallel, corporate leaders and industrialists increasingly took over economic organization, blurring the lines between political and economic power. The industrial working class became the dominant labour force during this period, driving technological and economic progress. However, as industrialization advanced, the influence of traditional labour groups began to diminish, giving way to social movements advocating for equality, sustainability, and labour rights, which have started to redefine the role of labour in shaping economic and social change.

These gradual transformations across Northern Eurasia reflect not only shifts in social classifications, but also fundamental changes in economic roles. The increasing influence of merchants and entrepreneurs, as the middle class grew, redefined economic organization. In Europe, this transition occurred earlier owing to the strong merchant class and free peasantry, which facilitated a shift to commodified labour systems. This early transition correlates with Europe's economic growth trajectory that was faster than China's, where hereditary obligations and state dominance delayed similar changes until the late twentieth century.

The overlapping roles of the ruling elite and economic organizers were particularly evident in their contributions to technological and institutional innovation. In both regions, rulers promoted practical innovations, such as papermaking and gunpowder in China and mechanical advancements in Europe. However, the overlapping responsibilities of the ruling class sometimes led to tensions between maintaining stability and fostering change. For example, traditionalist tendencies among Confucian bureaucrats often resisted disruptive technological advances, whereas Europe's fragmented political landscape allowed for more experimentation and adoption of new technologies. Scholars and literati in both regions played complex roles. While they occasionally drove intellectual and technological advancements, they also acted as barriers to change, particularly when tied to traditionalist or conservative ideologies. Similarly, skilled craftsmen in both regions contributed directly to economic progress through such innovations as the iron plough and advanced metallurgy.

Despite these shared patterns, important distinctions remain. In Europe, middle- and working-class groups generally embraced new technologies more readily, driven by the gentry's enthusiasm for innovation and market expansion. In China, by contrast, technological progress was often driven by major landowners or state initiatives, with less involvement from an independent middle class. This dynamic persisted until the economic reforms of the late twentieth century, when the state began fostering entrepreneurial activity, enabling broader participation in technological and economic advancements.

9.2.4 *Type of Inventions/Innovations/TFP*

In the general picture of evolving institutions, shifting social actors, and economic constraints, the number and additionally the type of inventions and innovations also play a crucial role in influencing long-run growth. We can summarize the concept in this way: a steam engine cannot be directly compared with today's laptops in terms of impact and application! Broadly speaking, as noted in Chap. 6, the progression of industrial revolutions has shaped distinct technological demands. The First Industrial Revolution introduced steam power, the Second (from approximately 1870 to 1960) brought electricity and industrial maturity, the Third (1960–2000) saw the rise of information technology through ICT, and the Fourth (2000–present) is characterized by advancements in robotization and artificial intelligence (AI).

In conjunction with technological innovations, the previously mentioned factors—robust institutions, active social actors, and economic constraints—are also critical in determining TFP and therefore long-term growth. In Chap. 5, we observed that, since 1700, China's TFP has generally lagged behind that of the UK, despite periods of improvement, such as during the Reform Period. Figure 9.2a highlights this trend, showing TFP gains during the reform years and a reversion to negative growth between 2015 and 2019. This aligns with our general findings for the Eurasian bloc in Chap. 7, where we observed a parallel rapid decline in TFP in Russia during the 1990s, primarily because of a shortage of human capital, contrasting with a slower decline in China.

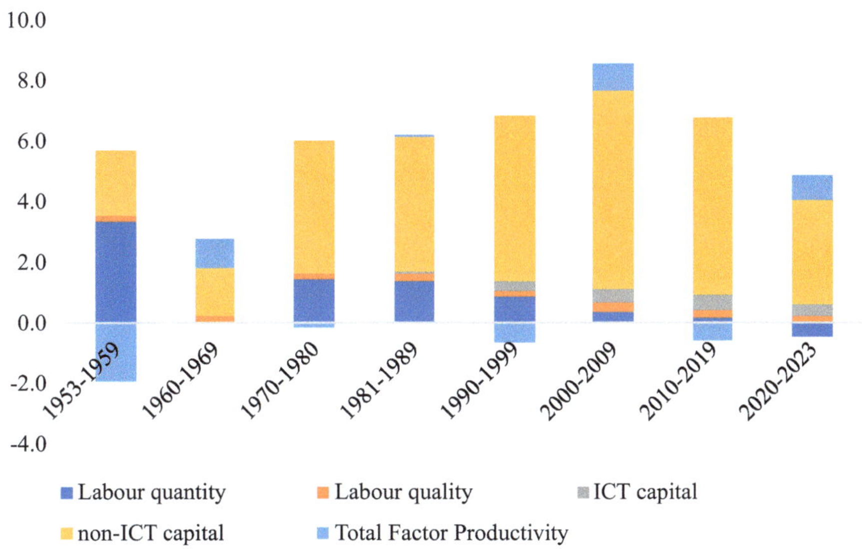

Fig. 9.2 (**a**) Contribution of TFP to GDP growth in China (modified), 1953–2023. (**b**) Contribution of TFP to GDP growth in Russia, Central Asia, and South-East Europe, 1951–2023. (**c**) Contribution of TFP to GDP growth in the UK, 1951–2023. *Source:* The conference board TED2

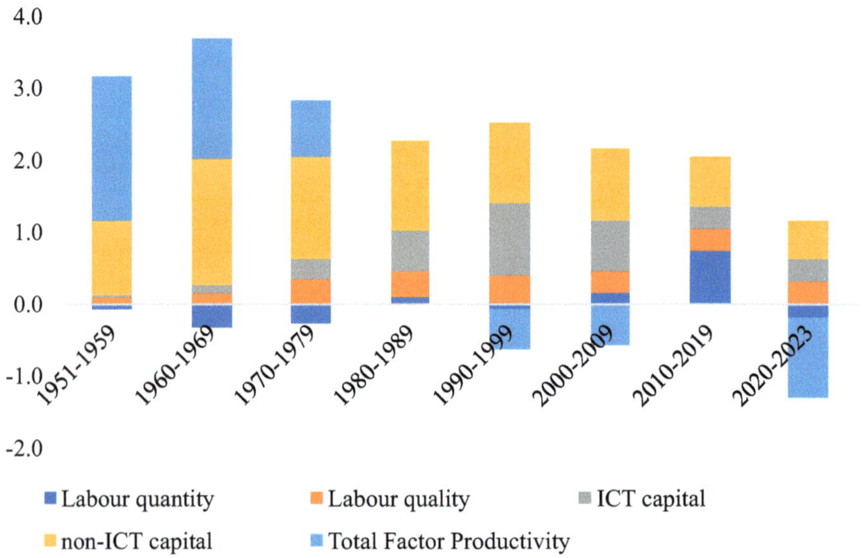

Fig. 9.2 (continued)

The argument we discuss here is that, as labour costs rise in developed countries, industries increasingly shift to countries focused on capital accumulation, providing an opportunity for these economies to grow their TFP. Moreover, as highlighted in Chap. 5, higher TFP levels in Western countries create room for TFP growth in developing countries, as they adopt and adapt foreign spillover technologies. This dynamic implies that poorer countries have the potential to achieve significant TFP growth, similar to the economic growth patterns previously discussed, but with a greater focus on increasing productivity efficiency rather than solely capital accumulation (this with a minor shift to the production frontier, besides the normal capital accumulation). This transition, however, requires that foundational elements—such as education systems, governmental support, and banking infrastructure—are all in place, as evidenced by Japan's success. When these elements align, capital accumulation (besides minimum technical efficiency) can also drive growth.

Yet, while technological advancement drives significant economic and societal shifts, its trajectory does not always seamlessly align with these changes. The Fourth Industrial Revolution, characterized by breakthroughs in robotics and AI, provides a compelling example. Initially, the widespread adoption of these technologies appears to have led to a decline in labour demand in many traditional industries, as automation replaced routine and manual tasks. However, this initial reduction in labour demand has been followed by a resurgence as new industries and job opportunities emerged. These industries—ranging from advanced robotics manufacturing to AI-driven services—require specialized skills and foster economic growth by creating roles that did not exist before (see e.g. Acemoglu and Restrepo 2019; Ghosh et al. 2024). Additionally, while new technologies are primarily developed by private companies, governments can play an indirect role by fostering an environment that supports start-up growth and innovation. In China, for example, technological advancements often occur at the lower end of the SMILE curve—a framework that illustrates the three stages of market entry for a product: R&D, fabrication, and marketing, with the "fabrication" stage contributing the least value added to the product. China's contributions typically fall within this lower-value fabrication stage, resulting in lower value added per worker. A useful distinction here is between products "Made *by* China" (produced by Chinese companies) and "Made *in* China" (produced in China for foreign enterprises), with foreign-invested firms accounting for roughly 50% of total production. These products, exported to markets such as the United States, often sell for much higher prices than Chinese producers initially receive (Su et al. 2013).

A further reason technology shifts can contribute to long-term growth is the nature and reach of innovation itself. Inventions from one industrial revolution can lay the groundwork for technological advances in later ones. The environmental impacts of coal-powered machinery, including deforestation, air pollution, and the acceleration of carbon emissions, are legacies that continue to influence the global economic and ecological landscape. These consequences have become central concerns in the Third and Fourth Industrial Revolutions, where new technologies aim to address the environmental challenges created by earlier industrial activities. The shift towards renewable energy, electric vehicles, and green technologies reflects a growing role for social movements and organizations advocating for sustainability. These modern social actors, including environmental activists, policy-makers, and green entrepreneurs, now challenge the priorities set by their predecessors, urging a re-evaluation of the economic and environmental trade-offs that characterized earlier industrial growth. Linking back to the discussion in Sect. 9.2.3, the overlapping roles of ruling elites and economic organizers are again evident in the responses to these environmental challenges. During the Third Industrial Revolution, state-led initiatives, such as subsidies for renewable energy and international agreements such as the Kyoto Protocol and the Paris Agreement, reflect the involvement of ruling elites in addressing global ecological crises. Meanwhile, corporate leaders and innovators, functioning as economic organizers, have developed technologies aimed at reducing environmental footprints, such as solar panels, wind turbines, and energy-efficient manufacturing processes. The working class, too, plays a role in this transition, as labour is reoriented towards green industries and away from traditional, fossil fuel-dependent sectors.

The Fourth Industrial Revolution amplifies these dynamics through the integration of digital technologies, artificial intelligence (AI), and advanced automation. However, these advancements are not equally transformative across all sectors or regions, creating uneven benefits and disparities in global innovation. The 2023 Global Innovation Index,[6] for example, ranks the UK and the Netherlands at fifth and seventh, respectively, while Italy is positioned at 26th, China at 12th, and the Russian Federation at 51st. This variation illustrates how innovations are not uniformly distributed across regions or economies, with some countries better positioned to capitalize on new technologies than others.

The economic impact of innovations is another important consideration. Inventions themselves are creative breakthroughs, but they often require adaptation to become economically viable. Table 9.1, for instance, highlights Great Britain's

Table 9.1 Share of inventions and innovation potential for the First to Third Industrial Revolutions

		Share no. inventions	Share innovation potential
GB	First Industrial Revolution (1760–1840)	48%	30%
	Second Industrial Revolution	26%	9%
	Third Industrial Revolution (ICT)	10%	4%
US	First Industrial Revolution (1760–1840)	10%	13%
	Second Industrial Revolution	22%	70%
	Third Industrial Revolution	56%	60%
Other	**First Industrial Revolution (1760–1840)**	**42%**	**57%**
	Second Industrial Revolution	**52%**	**21%**
	Third Industrial Revolution	**34%**	**35%**

Note: Innovation potential is total mentioned references to past invention. The innovations following from these past inventions, divided by the invention mentioned, is the innovation potential
Source: Based on Wikipedia and Google

[6] Dutta et al. (2023).

high level of invention and innovation potential during the First Industrial Revolution. Yet, by the Second Industrial Revolution, the United States had far surpassed Britain in both the number of inventions and in overall innovation potential, marking a shift in global industrial leadership.

9.3 External Factors: Divergence and Convergence

Economic divergence and convergence are shaped by a variety of external factors, with one of the most comprehensive frameworks for understanding these dynamics provided by WST. At its core, WST argues that global market exchanges are inherently unequal, systematically structured to perpetuate economic disparities between different regions of the world.[7] As a highly hierarchical system, the capitalist world economy distributes the benefits of trade unevenly—not only within individual countries but also between them. This concept evolved from Marxist thought, progressing through dependency theorists to WST. While Karl Marx identified key inequalities in trade primarily at the intra-national level, Raúl Prebisch (1950) extended this perspective internationally, introducing the concepts of "centre" and "periphery" to describe an international division of labour within a global economic system. Building on this, Immanuel Wallerstein (2011 [1974]) proposed an intermediary layer, the "semi-periphery", essential to the smooth functioning of the world economy. According to Wallerstein, unequal exchange is maintained through the enforcement of power by stronger states over weaker ones and by core states over peripheral regions. Thus, capitalism involves not only the appropriation of surplus value by capitalists from workers but also the extraction of surplus from the entire world economy by core regions.[8] Samir Amin (1976, 133–145), who identified as a Marxist, argued that global wage disparities far exceed productivity differences between regions.

From a WST perspective, growth rates in underdeveloped economies are therefore often lower than those in developed economies (as discussed in Sect. 4.6.5) and follow historically persistent economic cycles. This disparity stems from the tendency of core countries to specialize in innovation-driven production, while peripheral countries largely reproduce or copy these innovations. The mechanism works as follows: different types of goods offer different levels of added value based on their technological advancement and substitutability. Core countries focus on capital-intensive (both human and physical), highly specialized production with low substitutability, and consequently where price competition is minimal. As a result, these goods often carry a significant rent component, allowing successful innovators to capture a positive risk premium. If the innovation fails, however, the risk

[7] This presumption originates from Prebisch (1950, 8–14) who argued that from the 1870s to the 1940s, primary commodities produced in a periphery had weaker price performance relative to manufactured goods produced in industrial centres, contrary to the respective costs.

[8] See e.g. Wallerstein (2004, 28–29; 2011 [1974], 15–16).

premium is negative—a factor often overlooked. In contrast, peripheral regions, which typically pursue catch-up development, specialize in the production of easily substitutable goods whose mass production has already been optimized in core countries. This type of production is characterized by intense price competition, which suppresses prices and limits entrepreneurial income, further perpetuating global inequalities in economic development.

The unequal nature of international commodity exchange suggests that economic divergence is the prevailing trend, while convergence represents only a temporary correction.[9] Consequently, cases of economic catch-up are expected to be rare rather than frequent. World systems theorists have generally predicted global divergence with confidence, while forecasts of convergence have been more reserved. Yet, recent empirical evidence contradicts these predictions. For example, an alternative explanation within WST, presented by Grinin and Korotayev (2015), posits that the Great Divergence and the Great Convergence are actually two phases of a single process of global modernization. According to their analysis, the roots of convergence can be traced to the late nineteenth and early twentieth centuries when peripheral countries began to import capital on a larger scale. This trend gained momentum in the latter half of the twentieth century, led by transnational corporations that promoted globalization, facilitated technological transfer, and advanced infrastructure development. Scientific and technological progress, coupled with the periphery's capacity to adopt these advancements, were key drivers in the shift towards convergence. Human capital development within peripheral regions enabled more effective diffusion of capital and technology from the core countries. Western-educated intellectuals, trained abroad (notably in the West and the USSR), also played a crucial role in advocating modernization within their home countries. This occurred in many countries and time periods, ranging from Tsar Peter the Great visiting shipyards, paper-making cloth shops, and so on in around 1697, to Chinese students being send to Japan and the United States around the start of the twentieth century (Wang et al. 2020).[10]

We can ultimately argue that the shift towards convergence was not brought about by a single cause but rather by an array of interlinked factors. These included the growing need for both the West and the USSR to establish alliances with developing countries for strategic reasons; the development of policies, scientific frameworks, and programmes to mitigate challenges in these regions; structural changes within Western economies, which required shifting industrial production to developing countries; the awakening of intellectuals pushing for modernization; and the role of developing countries as suppliers of essential raw materials (particularly

[9] This is combined with the idea that technological transfer (discussed in Sects. 5.2 and 6.1–6.4) is also unequal: the periphery tends to borrow low tech to improve the production of primary goods.

[10] Additionally, some peripheral states, particularly those with abundant natural resources, leveraged collective actions—such as OPEC's oil price control—to sustain favourable economic conditions (Grinin and Korotayev 2015, 116–134). These convergence drivers, which we discussed in Chap. 5, emphasize the role of technology (see Sect. 5.2) over institutional frameworks (see Sect. 5.3), and can be seen as dynamic (see Sect. 9.1).

oil) and low-cost labour, which, through improved education, became increasingly skilled (Grinin and Korotayev 2015, 134).[11]

Taking the WST perspective, the USSR and the bloc of socialist countries, which emerged as an alternative to Western capitalism and embarked on a path of their own economic integration, actually remained a part of the capitalist world economy. This thesis was primarily based on the broad concept of capitalism. It is confirmed by the data on foreign trade in the 1920s, the first half of the 1940s, and the 1960s–1980s. In the 1920s, almost all of the trade flows (low but comparable in size with those before the First World War) were those with capitalist countries, with Germany, the United States, and the UK being the main trading partners (MVT 1967, 14). In the 1960s, when trade openness returned to the pre-Revolutionary levels of the early twentieth century, the share of the capitalist core expanded and approached 25% (MVT 1989, 645).

A schematic vision of the processes of economic convergence and catching up among core and periphery can lead to the assumption that low per capita income countries tend to grow faster than high per capita income countries, driven by cheap labour and the low cost of adopting imported technologies. However, there are several arguments that challenge this notion.

First, empirical evidence shows that faster growth is not always observed in poorer countries. As Rodrik (2013) highlights, in certain cases, richer countries exhibit higher growth rates, challenging this simplistic correlation between low income and rapid growth. As we argue throughout this book, a theory of convergence based only on labour cost and technology access overlooks a series of structural factors (e.g. the presence of inclusive institutions) that play a critical role through subsequent waves of economic development.

Second, what is important in WST's view of the Great Divergence is that it was not just a process of growing differences in the levels of development of the West and the rest, but also the process of the emergence of a new type of global economic system in which economies of various countries were incorporated into a single-world economic system (but with very different roles); this shifted to the Great Convergence that happened in recent decades (Grinin and Korotayev 2015, 7).

Third, the relationship between economic growth and technological revolutions complicates the assumption of faster growth in low-income countries. Economic development has historically been influenced by distinct technological "revolutions", such as the steam revolution (1760–1870), the electrical revolution (1870–1960), the information and communications technology (ICT) revolution (1960–2000), and the ongoing Fourth Revolution (robotization and AI). These revolutions tend to introduce capital-intensive technologies that can reduce the demand

[11] Based on what is said earlier, we can thus argue that the new wave of globalization, which started in the second half of the twentieth century, has strengthened the periphery. The demand for the main resource of poor countries, namely their workforce, increased dramatically. Development of new technologies led to a situation in which the technologies of older generations, which are subject to transfer to the periphery, became cheaper and cheaper (Grinin and Korotayev 2015, 149–158).

for labour in advanced economies. Yet, this shift does not necessarily translate into higher industrial income shares. As Van Leeuwen et al. (2023) argue, whether a technological shock leads to higher industrial income shares depends on whether the positive effects of technological advancement outweigh the negative impacts of trade dynamics. For instance, in countries with a comparative advantage in industry, such as China, both labour and income shares in industry may initially increase. However, in the context of the Fourth Revolution, characterized by robotization and AI, there is a tendency for the labour share in national income to decline as automation reduces the demand for human labour and suppressing wages. This reduction in the labour share can initially lead to a decrease in the income share of industry in gross domestic product (GDP). Over time, however, rising labour productivity driven by robotization and AI reverses this trend, resulting in an increased share of industry in GDP (Kromann et al. 2020). This nuanced relationship underscores the complexity of technological revolutions and their uneven impacts on economic structures across different countries and periods. In richer countries, capital-intensive innovations may exacerbate income inequalities and shift economic activity away from traditional industries, while in emerging economies, the same innovations might bolster industrial growth through productivity gains and competitive advantages. Obviously, this has different effects in peripheral countries. Because the focus on high capital-intensive and technological production returns in developed countries, peripheral countries might enter the market of intermediate products (e.g. robot parts) or low value-added industry. As pointed out before, the type of convergence/divergence depends on comparative advantage.

9.4 Internal Factors

9.4.1 Physical Capital

In this section, we examine internal short-run factors influencing economic growth, particularly focusing on China's policies and real estate market. One key driver of growth, especially in China, is the accumulation of physical capital (see Chaps. 5–7). Between 1960 and 2010, the compound annual growth rate (CAGR) of capital per labourer in China was approximately 7%, significantly higher than the rates observed in various Western European countries such as Britain and Italy (around 3%) and the Netherlands and the United States (around 2%). However, these figures vary depending on whether official data or corrected estimates are used, with the latter generally closer to 3%.

China's exceptionally high growth in the capital to labour ratio is partly attributable to historical events such as the Great Leap Forward (1958–1962) and the Cultural Revolution (1966–1977), as well as the subsequent economic reforms beginning in 1978. The Great Leap Forward, in particular, had a paradoxical impact. While its policies aimed to rapidly industrialize and increase physical capital, the widespread famine and social upheaval led to millions of deaths, effectively reducing the labour force. This tragic loss of life therefore contributed to a short-term increase in the capital to labour ratio, as physical capital remained in place while the labour supply contracted sharply.

The economic reforms after 1978 further intensified the focus on increasing the physical capital to human capital ratio. While this approach contributed significantly to GDP per capita growth, it did little to address technical inefficiencies. On average, countries with higher growth in physical capital also exhibited higher levels of technical inefficiency, a trend that China mirrored during this period. Nevertheless, physical capital remained a major contributor to Chinese economic growth, particularly during the reform era, when the growth rate of physical capital accounted for approximately 4% points of GDP per capita growth (see Fig. 9.2a).

However, the ongoing rise in China's capital to worker ratio is less pronounced than one might expect. Several structural factors contribute to this moderation. First, the contribution of physical capital to economic growth in China is heavily influenced by the pace of urbanization. This process is constrained by the *hukou* (household registration) system, which restricts rural–urban migration. In particular, individuals with agricultural *hukou* face significant barriers to moving to urban areas, limiting the labour mobility necessary for optimal capital allocation and urban economic development.

Second, China's capacity to further increase the capital per worker ratio is hampered by its high total debt to GDP ratio, which stood at approximately 269% in around 2020. While this is slightly below the ratios in the United States and the Eurozone, China's substantial off the books local government debt—estimated at an additional 50% of GDP—pushes the total debt ratio to roughly 330%. This elevated level of indebtedness raises concerns about the sustainability of further capital investments. The composition of this debt provides additional insights. General government debt in China, while rising, accounted for about 68% of GDP in 2020. Including the off the books local government debt, this figure increases to approximately 118% of GDP, a level comparable with that of the United States. However, research by Grennes et al. (2013) suggests that debt beyond certain thresholds significantly dampens economic growth. For developed economies, each percentage point of debt above 70% of GDP reduces real economic growth by 0.017% points. For developing economies, the effect is even more pronounced, with debt levels exceeding 64% of GDP reducing growth by 0.02% points for every additional percentage point of debt. In China's case, this implies that expanding government debt is unlikely to be a viable strategy for driving economic growth. Moreover, Grennes' framework provides a useful correction procedure for future growth predictions, particularly when factoring in the adverse effects of high debt levels. By applying Grennes' thresholds, policy-makers and economists can better estimate the growth implications of China's rising debt burden and adjust forecasts accordingly.

Besides general government debt, private debt also increased in China. This has risen strongly since 2010, and household debt made up 46% points of GDP and corporate debt 165% points by 2017. This made it one of the highest in the world. The rise in household debt follows primarily from mortgage lending and unsecured borrowings such as from credit cards. This is thanks to stimulation of the housing market and financial liberalization. Yet, just like government debt, household debt has an optimal threshold. As demonstrated by Lombardi et al. (2017), while household debt to GDP ratios generally exert negative long-term effects, these effects become significantly more pronounced once the ratio surpasses the critical threshold of 80%. As for Grennes, this model can be simultaneously applied to refine growth predictions, particularly in contexts influenced by housing market stimulation and financial liberalization (Table 9.2).

Just like household debt, corporate debt has grown fast in China in the past decades. At 139.1% of Chinese GDP, in absolute numbers Chinese corporate debt is the biggest in the world (see Fig. 9.3). This means it can have severe global effects. This is especially true given that 58% of Chinese companies are in the quartile with the highest risk, that is, mostly real estate and engineering (Standard and Poor 2021).[12]

Furthermore, we have to add that the type of investment in physical capital is important. During the Cultural Revolution, the focus was on heavy industry (see Chap. 7). This turned out to be not very efficient, thus increasing technical inefficiency. Yet, after the Reform Period this did not change much, since technical efficiency was still low in 2000. One reason, currently discussed with China's academy,[13] points out that Chinese technologies more affect "mobile-internet-enabled business models" and consumption patterns rather than new manufacturing techniques, thus not joining the real R&D. Hence, there is little evidence of rising technical efficiency of physical capital.

Table 9.2 Debt to GDP ratio in 2020 by country

		China	Russia	Italy	The Netherlands	US
General government debt		68.0%	19.3%	155.8%	52.5%	133.9%
Private debt	Corporate debt	139.1%	94.2%	76.9%	151.9%	84.7%
	Household debt	61.6%	22.1%	45.2%	104.4%	79.6%
Total debt		**268.8%**	**135.5%**	**277.9%**	**308.8%**	**298.3%**

Source: Mbaye et al. (2018). Accessed from: https://www.imf.org/external/datamapper/datasets/GDD

[12] See e.g. https://www.imf.org/external/pubs/ft/wp/2014/wp1434.pdf and https://www.stlouisfed.org/open-vault/2020/october/debt-gdp-ratio-how-high-too-high-it-depends

[13] See e.g. Zhang Jun's article in the *South China Morning Post* of 1 August 2018 (https://www.scmp.com/comment/insight-opinion/united-states/article/2157728/will-china-be-next-tech-powerhouse-maybe-next)

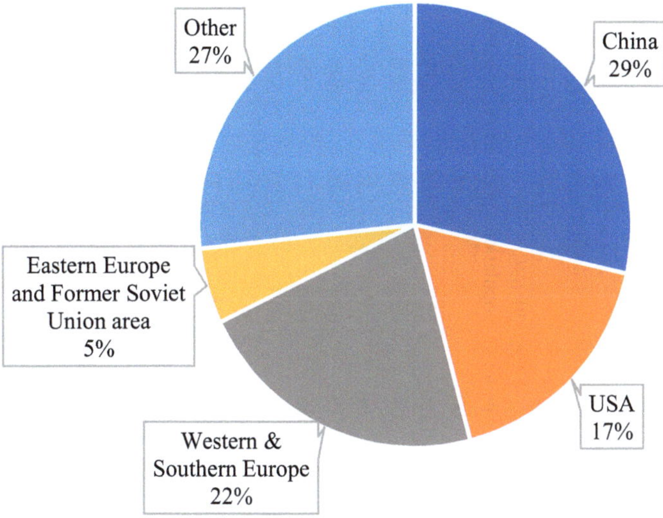

Fig. 9.3 World shares of debt to GDP ratio ca. 2020. *Source:* Corporate debt to GDP ratio from Mbaye et al. (2018). Accessed from: https://www.imf.org/external/datamapper/datasets/GDD; GDP from Maddison Project Database (Bolt and Van Zanden 2020)

9.4.2 Human Factors (Labour and Human Capital)

In addition to physical capital, human factors also play a significant role in driving economic growth. When considering the availability of labour, projections indicate that China's population will begin to decline starting in 2029. Furthermore, shifts in the age structure are expected to reduce the size of the potential labour force.

Table 9.3 clearly illustrates that population decline is projected to begin in Asia in around 2030, whereas in Europe, this trend is expected to start by 2050 or later. Coupled with a shrinking share of the potential labour force from approximately 2020 onward, this results in a rapid decrease in the total number of potential workers (Li et al. 2017). Although Europe experienced a decline in its share of potential workers about a decade earlier, the pace of this decline has been significantly slower. A comparison of trends in the potential labour force between China and the Netherlands highlights the stark difference in the rate of decline. China's potential labour force is projected to decrease much more rapidly, with a CAGR of −0.9% through 2100, compared with a much milder decline of −0.05% for the Netherlands. This stark contrast underscores the unique demographic challenges facing China relative to European countries such as the Netherlands.

One might argue that China's potential labour force (the population between 24 and 64, either employed or actively seeking employment) is too low and can hardly be expanded. Yet, from Table 9.3 it seems that in 2020, with 70% potential labour force in the population, China is higher than almost any country except South Korea. Hence, there is little possibility to increase the share of the potential labour force in

Table 9.3 Population and potential labour force for selected countries, 1990–2100

	China		Japan		South Korea		Netherlands		UK		France	
	population (1990 = 1)	20–69/ population	population	20–69/ population	population	20–69/ population	population	20–69/ population	population	20–69/ population	population	20–69/ population
1990	1.00	58%	1.00	66%	1.00	61%	1.00		1.00		1.00	63%
2000	1.10	62%	1.03	68%	1.09	66%	1.06	66%	1.03	63%	1.05	63%
2010	1.16	69%	1.03	65%	1.15	70%	1.11	66%	1.08	65%	1.11	63%
2020	1.21	70%	1.01	61%	1.20	72%	1.15	64%	1.14	63%	1.16	61%
2030	1.22	68%	0.97	60%	1.23	69%	1.19	61%	1.19	62%	1.20	59%
2040	1.20	64%	0.92	58%	1.22	63%	1.22	58%	1.36	60%	1.22	58%
2050	1.15	62%	0.86	54%	1.17	58%	1.23	59%	1.27	60%	1.23	57%
2060	1.08	57%	0.80	52%	1.10	55%	1.24	59%	1.29	59%	1.22	57%
2070	1.01	55%	0.74	52%	1.01	51%	1.25	57%	1.31	58%	1.21	57%
2080	0.93	56%	0.68	51%	0.92	51%	1.26	57%	1.33	58%	1.20	56%
2090	0.85	53%	0.63	50%	0.83	51%	1.27	56%	1.34	57%	1.18	55%
2100	0.79	52%	0.59	51%	0.76	52%	1.28	55%	1.34	56%	1.15	53%

Source: IDB (downloaded 2023) https://www.census.gov/data-tools/demo/idb/#/country?YR_ANIM=2015&FIPS_SINGLE=CH

the population. Obviously, we have to look at the share of potential labour force actually employed. This labour force participation rate, however, with about 76% in 2019 (WDI, downloaded 2022), is already on the high side globally, so there is little room for improvement either.

This does not apply to education and skills. Human capital is a fundamental part in economic growth as it not only makes it possible for labourers to use physical capital, but can also generate technology. This is made possible by the shift of human capital away from households to depending on the wider economy (see Sect. 4.4.4). As pointed out in Chap. 6, for countries below the production frontier, such as China, human capital is mostly used to apply physical capital in the productive process (a type of Lucasian growth). Yet, once the production frontier is reached, human capital is increasingly used for R&D, and can thus be qualified as Romerian.

Human capital has played a shifting yet critical role in China's economy from the late nineteenth century to the present. In the seventeenth century, human capital was primarily concentrated within households, where it served as a means of sustaining family enterprises and meeting subsistence needs. By the late nineteenth and early twentieth centuries, however, this paradigm began to change as human capital increasingly became a driver of economic growth. In China, this transition was gradual and shaped by unique sociopolitical and institutional factors that affected the accumulation and utilization of human capital in the broader economy. As discussed in Chap. 5, technical efficiency in China remained low during this period, meaning human capital was largely absorbed into the productive process rather than fostering innovation or structural transformation. The traditional examination system, abolished in the early twentieth century, had previously channelled intellectual talent towards bureaucratic functions rather than broader economic applications. Its replacement—a modern education system—was heavily influenced by political considerations, further constraining the effective deployment of human capital.

As Lee (2016) points out, human capital begins to have a significant positive impact on GDP per capita growth only when the average years of education reach six or more. During the Republican era (1912–1949), formal education levels in China remained well below this threshold, meaning that education had limited effect on economic growth. This reflects broader structural constraints during that period, including political instability and limited investment in education infrastructure, which stifled the transformative potential of human capital. Consequently, education's role in driving growth during this time was marginal. By the late twentieth century, the expansion of education in China led instead to a greater effect on economic growth. This came at the cost of reduced educational efficiency (Van Leeuwen et al. 2017). This decline reflects a broader transition: China began to shift from channelling human capital primarily into production processes to investing in R&D. However, this transition has been incomplete. For example, in 2020, China ranked 14th on the Global Innovation Index, far behind the UK and the Netherlands, ranked fourth and fifth, respectively. This ranking underscores inefficiencies in human capital utilization, as China's R&D investments have not yielded proportional increases in TFP growth.

As seen in Chap. 7, China has generated more human capital than the former Soviet Union (FSU), thereby reducing some inefficiencies. Yet, as Heckman (2003) notes, while the social returns to education in China have been substantial, private returns remain low, disincentivizing private investment in education. Combined with limited government investment, this has slowed human capital accumulation, further constraining its effective use in physical capital and economic growth. The evolution of human capital in China therefore reflects a broader tension: while its role has shifted from household sustenance to a potential engine of economic growth, inefficiencies in its accumulation and application continue to limit its transformative impact. Furthermore, China's historical lag in achieving the critical threshold of education necessary for economic growth—particularly during the Republican era—highlights how delayed investments in education can have long-term consequences for development.

Like most other transitional countries that experienced deep recession in the 1990s, Russia experienced strong deindustrialization.[14] In some of these countries (e.g. Bulgaria, Georgia, Mongolia, Uzbekistan) the share of industry significantly recovered following the steep decline (Fig. 9.4). The share of industry in Russia's

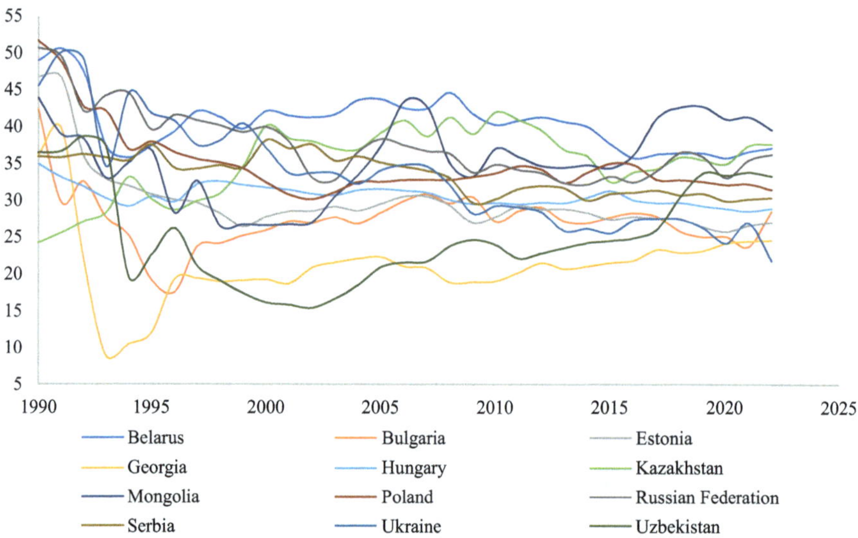

Fig. 9.4 Share of industry in a sample of former socialist countries, percentage GDP. *Source:* United Nations Statistics Division (https://unstats.un.org/unsd/snaama/Basic)

[14] This sample includes the former socialist countries of Eastern Europe, the USSR, and Mongolia (see also footnote 37). A notable exception in this group is Kazakhstan, where the share of industry increased owing to expansion of both mining and manufacturing at the expense of agriculture. Such a pattern is characteristic of China and the countries of Indochina, which underwent a transition to a market economy alongside industrialization and therefore belong to another group. The decrease of industry in Chine's GDP in recent years is associated with an increase in "other activities", which include hi-tech services.

GDP decreased from 43.7% (1989) to 28.7% (2003) and only modestly recovered up to 32.8% (2022), while the share of services increased from 28.9 (1989) to 50.4 (2022) (Kuboniwa et al. 2019). Furthermore, the share of manufacturing, a more human capital-intensive industry, decreased from 29.4% to 12.8% (2022), while mining and quarrying, a less human capital-intensive industry, increased from 3.5% (1989) to 12.7% (2022). Trade, as a less human capital-intensive service, increased from 5.5% (1989) to 11.2% (2022), with a peak of 27.7% in 1992 (Fig. 9.5). The structural dynamics are clearly not that positive if the aim is to make Russia's growth human capital based, even taking into account that the share of manufacturing has been modestly rising since 2014, and Russian trade has become much more technologically advanced than it was in the 1990s.

The basic cause of deindustrialization at the middle-income stage is the low competitiveness of the civilian manufacturing industries and rather high efficiency of mining and quarrying. As the core of the USSR, Russia heavily relied on import substitution and protectionist policies in external trade during the "big push" that forced industrialization in the 1930s–1950s. Under such policies of low external competitive environment, civilian manufacturing tended to have low technological progress. As the country started to open up in the 1990s, much production appeared to be uncompetitive. This combined with weakened state capacity, with industrial policies being difficult to implement. The very high efficiency of primary industries (rents from natural resource extraction) also hampered incentives to invest in manufacturing in the 2000s (another case of the so-called Dutch disease of the

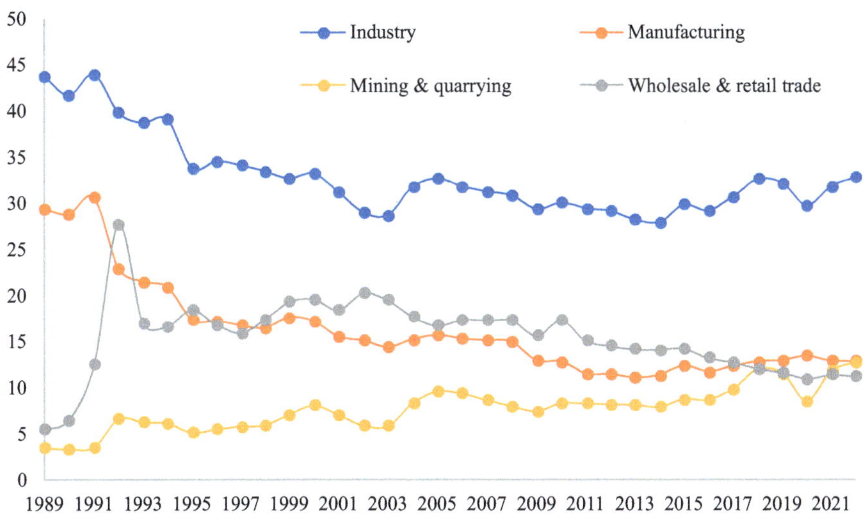

Fig. 9.5 Industry, manufacturing, and trade in Russia, percentage GDP. *Note:* Industry comprises the following economic activities: mining and quarrying; manufacturing; electricity, gas and water; construction. The share of industry is somewhat less than follows from the United Nations data because of other components of GDP that include primarily net taxes. *Source:* 1989–2010: Kuboniwa et al. (2019), 2011–2022: Rosstat (https://rosstat.gov.ru/folder/210/document/13396)

1960s–1970s), thus magnifying the negative effects of the increased openness in manufacturing.[15]

In the period of Russia's economic growth in the 2000s, the influx of private investments that came about as a result of favourable market conditions in the world markets of exportable raw material resources led to the renovation of physical capital in competitive sectors. The recovery of the state and the expansion of private expenditure on education also took place. Moreover, the level of investment (both state and non-state) in education recovered a bit more rapidly than the level of investment in physical capital. The latter did not reach the highest Soviet-era level (*c.* 20% versus 30% of GDP according to the official statistics). Throughout the 2000s, there was an accelerating rise in investment in human capital (specifically in education), which stalled in the 2010s under the influence of the financial crisis (2008–2010) and the subsequent stagnation of the Russian economy. After Russia's direct involvement in the armed conflict with Ukraine began (when the "special military operation" was launched in February 2022), the state budget expenditure for areas related to human capital had different trends. Education was basically sustained but healthcare, science, and social policy lagged behind; this poses risks for the development in these areas (Bozhechkova et al. 2023, 2024; Dezhina 2023, 2024; Zubarevich 2024).

Estimates of the contribution of human capital to economic growth, through its impact on the productivity of workers, began to diminish. During 2000–2015, the demand for educated labour in the Russian economy outpaced its supply. While the highest contribution was in the second half of the 2000s, economic and demographic factors worsened in the 2010s, and human capital accumulation slowed; by 2018–2019, its contribution to economic growth became close to zero. The subsequent decline in population health during the COVID-19 pandemic negatively affected the economic growth rates in 2020–2021 (Avdeeva 2024).

Overall, it is reasonable to say that the Russian system of education has definite potential in ensuring the country's social and economic modernization. Russia has relatively high statistical indicators and expert assessments of the educational level of the population and the country's innovative capacity (relative to its peer group of countries in terms of per capita income). Russia's place in world rankings with respect to expected and actual years of schooling (with a ranking of 49 and 34, respectively, out of 193), which are used in calculating the Human Development Index (HDI) of the United Nations Development Programme (UNDP 2024), are higher than the country's ranking in the aggregate HDI (a ranking of 56).

Over a decade (2010–2020), Russia increased its World Bank Human Capital Index (HCI) rating from 0.60 to 0.68.[16] The latter is the highest among the BRICS

[15] Thus, Russia confirmed the model by Rodrik (2016), which explained the cases of premature deindustrialization in other countries, primarily those in Latin America and Africa.

[16] The HCI ranges between 0 and 1. It is measured in terms of the productivity of the next generation of workers relative to the benchmark of complete education and full health. An economy in which a child born today can expect to achieve complete education and full health will score a value of 1 on the index. Estimates for 2020 are the most recent available.

countries, above the average for upper middle-income countries, and rather close to high income ones (World Bank 2021, 199). Its relative position also improved somewhat, even though fewer countries were estimated for 2010 than for 2020 (World Bank 2021, 40–41).

One of the most important manifestations of the post-industrial educational revolution has been a rapid rise in computer literacy, which, by the late 2000s had been acquired by the majority of the younger population of Russia. Presumably, the substantial age differences in computer literacy may account for the comparatively early upward phase and the flattened age-phase curves of earnings, the low rewards or premiums for general work experience, and the high remuneration for computer literacy in the labour market (Kapeliushnikov and Luk'ianova 2010, 30–32, 75–76).

What distinguishes Russian human capital is the age profile of earnings, not so much by the steepness of the initial rise, but by an early and rather steep decline. The peak of earnings, which is normally shifted to the end of working life, is reached on average before the age of 40, after which a decline starts. In the early 2000s, there was an expectation that such a profile was a temporary phenomenon, some kind of penalty for the Soviet legacy, and that the peak of earnings should gradually shift to older ages and the post-peak decline should decrease. However, over the period from 2005 to 2015, this pattern became even more pronounced. It is consistently reproduced with minor variations in different sources and for different years. The additional explanations are not only low incidence of vocational training and a high share of relatively primitive technology (Gimpelson 2019), but also the relatively high valuation of non-cognitive skills characteristic for young cohorts: diligence, attention to detail, perseverance, sociability, emotional stability, curiosity, creativity, friendliness, and tact (Gimpelson et al. 2020).

Accompanying the declining life cycle of economically valuable knowledge under contemporary technological progress, the accumulation of human capital becomes more accomplished not just in the standard forms of education but in lifelong education and training, and learning in the home and workplace. Therefore, in economically advanced countries, adult populations' participation in upgrading their qualifications and undergoing professional retraining is expanding over time.

However, instead of a rise in adult vocational training, there was a decline in Russia after the upsurge during the 1990s. This trend negatively distinguishes Russia from the economically advanced countries and the reference group of rapidly developing middle-income countries (Didenko and Dorofeeva 2016; Anikin 2019; Latova and Latov 2020). This may be caused by the sectoral restructuring of human capital that went on in Russia in the 1990s, which proved sufficient for the implementation of the raw materials exporting model of economic growth in a late industrial economy. Accordingly, under the conditions of the relatively weak development of innovative sectors, incentives to make additional investment in the adult population turned out not to be strong enough. The fact that being a part of "ordinary" labour (which comprises about 60% of the Russian labour force) crucially decreases the probability that workers will undertake training remains one of the main determinants of qualification improvement in Russia (Anikin 2017). The positive prediction of training is more likely to be related to post-industrial occupations (Anikin 2019).

As such, there is a predominance of quantitative rather than qualitative expansion of the educational space during the ongoing transition to universal tertiary education. However, a consensus view is that education quality worsened significantly in the 1990s–2000s (Didenko and Kliucharev 2014).

This is mirrored in another problem, which is described as "over-education" of the labour force, that is, a mismatch between educational attainment (relatively high) and skill requirements for available jobs (relatively low under the current stage of economic development) (Gimpelson and Kapeliushnikov 2019).

However, during the 2010s, traditional and innovative forms of education remained stable and relatively high in Russia. Annual returns to tertiary education reached 12–13%, with conservative estimates of 6–9% in the late 2010s. University-type tertiary education almost doubled its earnings (its premium approached to 100%), and even short-cycle tertiary education provided a premium of about 20–30% (Kapeliushnikov 2021). These average figures disguise serious variations at individual level with regard to the incomes of professionals in general and in the returns on their human capital associated with regions, industry, settlement, and other inequalities (Tikhonova and Karavai 2023, 147).

In the 2000s–2010s, Russia was characterized by relatively high levels of private return on investments in innovative forms of accumulating human capital (first and foremost, investment in life-long learning and training), especially in the case of people who had acquired a specialty that was necessary for working in sectors of the economy that were somewhat new to Russia relative to the Soviet era (office personnel, the service sector). At the same time, private returns on adult vocational training provided evidence of the weakness of the labour market, as well as the lack of adequate feedback with relation to the market for adult educational services.[17]

Besides specialty of work, the main factor in the distribution of human capital and economic benefits in modern Russia remains residence in megacities. Going to school in Moscow or St. Petersburg is significant in regression analysis for all white-collar workers (Anikin 2018; Karavai 2023).

In addition, in contrast to economically advanced countries, income premiums for adult vocational training were distributed unequally in Russia, and only to a minority. An average positive result was provided by higher premiums in terms of income for a few successful graduates from adult vocational training, while only a minority benefited. To a certain extent this can be viewed as an unmotivating factor for potential recipients of adult vocational training (Didenko and Kliucharev 2014; Didenko and Dorofeeva 2016; Anikin 2019). Extremely high wage gaps within managerial jobs can also discourage training (Anikin 2017).

Because of the unfavourable demographic cycles (population aging and reduction owing to higher mortality relative to birth rate), the Russian labour force is in a

[17] Had they been in a state of equilibrium, the influence of such factors as specialty of vocational training would be close to zero.

phase of strong contraction. Employment reduction from 2021 to 2035 is estimated at 2–5% (Uziakova and Shirov 2024) or even at 4.0–6.7% (three to five million people) (Kapeliushnikov 2023).[18] Currently, almost all potentially significant sources for replenishment of the labour force have already been exhausted. The intensification of low-skilled labour migration (mostly from Central Asia), even if it occurs,[19] is unlikely to be significant. Even an increase in the share of labour migrants in the total number employed of one or two percentage points will not be able to compensate for the losses (Kapeliushnikov 2024).

One negative consequence of rising labour migration in countries of the "semi-periphery", those countries with a highly educated population, is the net outflow of human capital, the so-called brain drain.

On the whole, over the entire post-Soviet period, Russia has been characterized by a positive balance of migration flows linked to a change in permanent residency,[20] primarily from the countries of the FSU. In the international context, the country looks more like a recipient of human capital than a donor, even though the surplus fell substantially in 2020 and 2022. At the same time, the structure of migration flows during the post-Soviet period changed as it reflected the dynamics of a higher or lower level of human capital. The average level of the human capital of people coming into Russia from other countries of the FSU has gone down noticeably since the 1990s. As regards the flows to and from economically developed OECD countries, to which people with a higher level of human capital tend to migrate, there was a period in the late 2000s–early 2010s when net outflow from Russia was close to zero, but this time was short.

It follows from an estimate based on the limited data from official Russian migration statistics and on the labour productivity data that the associated human capital losses corresponded to about 0.5% of GDP annually in 2016–2020 (Slepenkova 2022, 120).

The problem of brain drain became much more acute for Russia following the start of the military operation in Ukraine and the partial mobilization of its civilian labour force in 2022. There is no reliable data to indicate how many people left Russia since 2022, taking into account flows in both directions and the return of many migrants in 2023–2024. Guesstimates of the net external migration of Russian citizens vary from 0.5 to 1.5 million people, but this lacks sound methodological background. It is highly likely that the outflow has been quantitatively offset by

---

[18] From the official data, in the second quarter of 2024, the Russian labour force at age of 15+ was 76.124 million, of which 74.181 million were employed and 1.942 million were unemployed: (https://rosstat.gov.ru/storage/mediabank/trud_1_15-S.xlsx, https://rosstat.gov.ru/storage/mediabank/trud_2_15-s.xlsx, https://rosstat.gov.ru/storage/mediabank/trud_3_15-s.xlsx)

[19] The room for this is limited: as it follows from the most likely scenario in the coming years as that the Central Asian countries will be bridging the gap with Russia in GDP per capita.

[20] Russian official statistics take into account those whose entry or exit is linked to a change in permanent residence (not necessarily citizenship). When the cross-border trips are linked with leisure, temporary employment, and other purposes, only departures of Russian citizens are published but not their arrivals from abroad; as regards foreign citizens, both departures and arrivals are published.

inflow of refugees from Ukraine.[21] A balancing factor, reducing Russia's human capital losses, is that many high-skilled émigrés use IT-based distance employment or business management, and thus continue to operate within Russia's economy (about a quarter of them as estimated by Kartseva and Florinskaya 2025 based on their survey). However, the outflow was large by historical accounts, in terms of human capital comparable with the outflow of the late 1980s–early 1990s. It appears not to be crucial enough to undermine the economy, but is sufficient to limit the potential to grow in the years ahead.

Over the past 10 years, Russia's economy has faced three powerful negative shocks: the first sanctions crisis of 2014–2015, as the Crimea was taken over by Russia and armed conflict in the Eastern Ukraine broke out; the COVID-19 crisis of 2000–2021; and the second sanctions crisis, which began in 2022 following Russia's direct involvement in armed conflict. Even though GDP recovered in 2023, the transformation of the economy is still far from over. In manufacturing industry, the most significant growth in the second half of 2022 and 2023 has been in regions with a high share of military industrial enterprises. A strong decline may be seen in regions with an automotive industry (this mostly being owned by foreign capital). Negative dynamics have been observed in regions with a high share of export products, that is, almost a third of them (Zubarevich 2024).

The main feature of a specific Russian labour market model is that cushioning negative economic shocks and making short-term adjustments tend to mean not so much rising unemployment, but compressed working hours and reduced wages. Moreover, labour turnover tends to sharply intensify. This is fundamentally different from the standard pattern in developed economies, in which companies immediately launch large-scale reductions in their labour force when faced with a crisis (Kapeliushnikov 2001, 2023; Gimpelson and Kapeliushnikov 2019).

The reaction of the Russian labour market to the second sanctions crisis was in many ways unique, differing from previous crisis episodes. Initially, as always, wages dropped sharply and various forms of underemployment noticeably increased. But when it became clear to economic agents that the macroeconomic situation (downturn of output, hike of inflation, weakening of the ruble exchange rate, probability of being less employed, rigidity in external trade logistics) was better than expected, the labour market behaved contrary to its usual pattern: employment has grown, unemployment has significantly decreased, working hours have not changed, the hiring of labour has suddenly jumped, and, most importantly, the number of vacancies, instead of decreasing, has reached unprecedented heights. Apparently, the Russian labour market has entered a period of dramatic change, which can be described as a transition from a regime of limited demand for labour to a regime of limited supply (Kapeliushnikov 2024 who mostly draws from the official statistics, namely the Labor Force Survey by Rosstat, with some methodological adjustments).

[21] According to the estimate by the United Nations High Commissioner for Refugees, 1.227 million people migrated from Ukraine to Russia in 2022–2023 (https://data.unhcr.org/en/situations/ukraine). This inflow may be considered as basically relating to labour force, taking into account that most Ukrainians have a perfect command of the Russian language, have relatives among Russians to ensure initial support and help with getting a job, and that labour migration from Ukraine to Russia has been rather high in the years since the collapse of the Soviet Union.

The economic sanctions, exit of most of Western owners of Russian businesses, and expansion of the military sector created a need for a large-scale reallocation of labour, which could not be carried out promptly and thus has become a source of structural imbalances. These imbalances mean that in some small sectors, not covered by the official statistics in detail, the demand for workers is weak. But the whole situation is the opposite. The statistical effect is that high level of aggregation of economic activities in the Labor Force Survey can hardly capture nuances in most of them. Furthermore, the timing of the processes matters: in 2023 there was fast growth of output, with more demand for labour, compared to the downturn in spring and summer of 2022.

The key transformation process on the Russian labour market in the 2020s is the creation of a huge number of job vacancies: this is estimated at a record level of 7% and has surpassed, by a large margin, the level of overall unemployment (2.6–2.9% in 2024 as opposed to 4.4–5.5% in 2017–2019, with Rosstat applying International Labour Organization methodology).[22] The starting point of this spurt was at the peak of the COVID-19 pandemic in the second quarter of 2020. Recruitment to the armed forces, mobilization (resulting in contraction of the civilian labour force), and emigration outflow resulted in an even greater imbalance. The growth in vacancies is universal: there is no industry or occupation where it has not taken place. A sharply accelerated labour turnover, the intensity of which closely approached the record values observed back in the 1990s, was not surprising in these circumstances. Yet, the growth in real wages occurred only in 2023, reaching almost 7%. Apparently, the Russian economy will have to operate for a long time under the stressful conditions of an acute shortage of labour (Kapeliushnikov 2024).

At the same time, the restriction on the quantitative increase in employment may become an important incentive for investment in more labour-saving technologies. One of the key areas may be more efficient organization of the work of underemployed (part-time) and informally employed workers, which comprise up to 30% of the total number of employed, whose labour productivity is 22–25% lower than in the corporate sector (Uziakova and Shirov 2024). How far this process can go under sanctions remains an open question. Evidently, there is certain room for technologies to trickle through the barriers. There is an extensive R&D infrastructure that Russia has developed, even though the innovation capability is assessed as not so high.[23]

Currently, the military and civilian sectors of the Russian economy are experiencing significant divergence in institutional environment and financial conditions. The military sector is expanding, responding to the government demand, and is receiving a quite favourable operating environment. This sector clearly increases demand for the relevant human capital as it did in the Soviet period, although not on so great a

---

[22] https://rosstat.gov.ru/storage/mediabank/trud_3_15-s.xlsx

[23] Russia is assessed as 51st in the Global Innovation Index, with performance below expectation for level of development, and many polarized components: 110th in institutions versus 26th in human capital and research, even with an underestimated expenditure for education. China is assessed as 12th, with much smaller gaps between different areas: 43rd in institutions versus sixth in knowledge and technology outputs (Dutta et al. 2023, 19–20, 58).

scale. The civilian sector remains market-based and competitive, but its growth is limited by high real interest rates,[24] rising taxation, and unstable regulations.

As consensus forecasts (the median or average of individual forecasts) show (Sect. 9.5.3), fast GDP growth has not emerged as the most likely scenario for the years ahead. Moreover, while even under modest growth the military sector can grow rapidly, the civilian sector will be poised to contract. In this case, the gap between education and productivity, or between the supply of educated labour and demand for it, is likely to widen (Gimpelson and Kapeliushnikov 2019). There is a room for technological transfers from the military to the civilian sector,[25] but this seems to be quite unlikely.

A survey conducted in Russia in 2021 (before the second sanctions crisis) discovered that the gap between Russian white-collar workers (professionals) and their foreign counterparts, both in developed and in many developing countries, has tended to widen in recent years, and their ability to serve as a basis for the formation of a full-fledged class of "post-industrialists" remains limited and problematic. None of the experts involved in the survey expressed optimism about the new opportunities associated with the policy of import substitution that has been actively advocated since 2014 (Latov 2023, 417–418, 423).

In the previous sections, we have explored the contributions of physical capital, labour, human capital, and TFP to economic growth. However, any comprehensive analysis of growth must also consider the sectoral composition of a country's workforce. Shifts in labour and resources between economic sectors can significantly increase the output per worker, particularly when these transitions are from lower value-added sectors to those with higher value-added potential. Empirical data indicate that manufacturing generally exhibits the highest value added per capita, while agriculture has the lowest—although the value added in agriculture is steadily improving. Thus, transitions from agriculture to industry or services, and from services to manufacturing, can drive substantial gains in output per worker (Kuijs and Wang 2005). However, such shifts are not always straightforward, as demonstrated by China's current economic structure.

Indeed, China still maintains a substantial agricultural sector compared with advanced economies. In 2019, agriculture accounted for 25.3% of employment in China, compared with just 1% in the UK (see Figs. 9.7 and 9.8). This stark contrast highlights the untapped potential for structural transformation in China, where labour productivity in manufacturing is three to six times higher than in agriculture, compared with a more modest one to three times difference in the UK. Leveraging this disparity, China could potentially achieve annual growth of approximately

---

[24] About 10% as a difference between the key rate (established by the Bank of Russia) and consumer price index (computed by Rosstat).

[25] The first nuclear power plant in the USSR was a by-product of the research facility that was established in 1946 under the "Atomic Project", aimed at catching up with the United States (it is currently located in Obninsk, about 100 km south-west of the centre of Moscow). It was put into operation in 1954, 5 years after the nuclear bomb test (https://en.wikipedia.org/wiki/Obninsk_Nuclear_Power_Plant). However, such technological transfer, a positive external effect of defence R&D, has tended to deteriorate over time in the USSR.

0.7% between 2019 and 2060 by transitioning labour from agriculture to industry. However, this growth potential is contingent on overcoming significant hurdles. First, China's rural to urban migration has been a cornerstone of its economic transformation since the reforms initiated under Deng Xiaoping. This migration, which has involved both men and women, is essential for the shift from agriculture to industry, as urban centres are the primary hubs for industrial employment. Yet, the *hukou* system has historically posed a major barrier to mobility. Without urban *hukou* status, rural migrants face restricted access to healthcare, education, and housing, undermining the feasibility of permanent relocation. Although the gradual relaxation of *hukou* restrictions has improved mobility, these barriers remain a critical challenge to fully realizing the benefits of sectoral shifts. Migration patterns also reveal deeper socio-economic dynamics, particularly between men and women. While men have traditionally dominated migration flows owing to industrial job opportunities, female migration patterns are shaped by distinct factors, including employment and marriage. Although the total number of female migrants has increased, the sex ratio within the 19–40 age cohort remains skewed towards men, a consequence of decades of sex-selective practices exacerbated by the one child policy and earlier birth control campaigns. These practices have had lasting implications for the labour market and urban marriage patterns. In the labour market, the growing demand for female workers in urban centres continues to outstrip the supply of local urban women, creating strong incentives for rural women to migrate. Employment remains the primary driver for young women moving from rural areas to cities, supported by census data showing no significant shift in the sex composition of urban employment sectors despite persistent male unemployment.

Marriage also plays a significant role in female migration. Many rural women migrate to urban areas seeking to marry, driven by a demographic mismatch in urban populations, where men outnumber women in marriageable age groups. This trend reflects the broader societal impact of the one child policy and underscores the unique dynamics of female migration in China, which differs markedly from male migration patterns.

Second, there is the challenge of the service sector's growing prominence in the Chinese economy (see Fig. 9.6). In 2019, services accounted for 60% of China's GDP and employed 48.5% of the labour force, compared with 86% of GDP in the UK (UN 2020). While the expansion of the service sector is a hallmark of economic development,[26] it introduces complexities for labour productivity. Services generally exhibit lower value added per worker than manufacturing, which can constrain overall productivity gains. Although services have significant innovation potential, as noted by Levitt (1972), their contributions often differ from those of manufacturing and may depend on specific subsectors and technological advancements (Hipp and Grupp 2005).

The issues described for China's sectoral composition and productivity are further underscored by the data in Table 9.4. This table highlights the output per

[26] See for example Philips et al. (2022) and Calabrese et al. (2022).

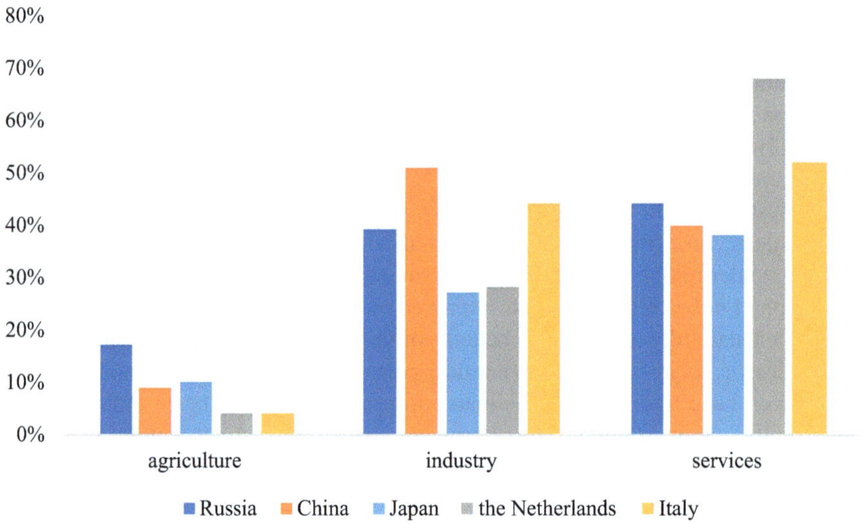

Fig. 9.6 In what sector do you think you can personally earn the highest income (2022)? *Source:* Our surveys (see Appendix D and E)

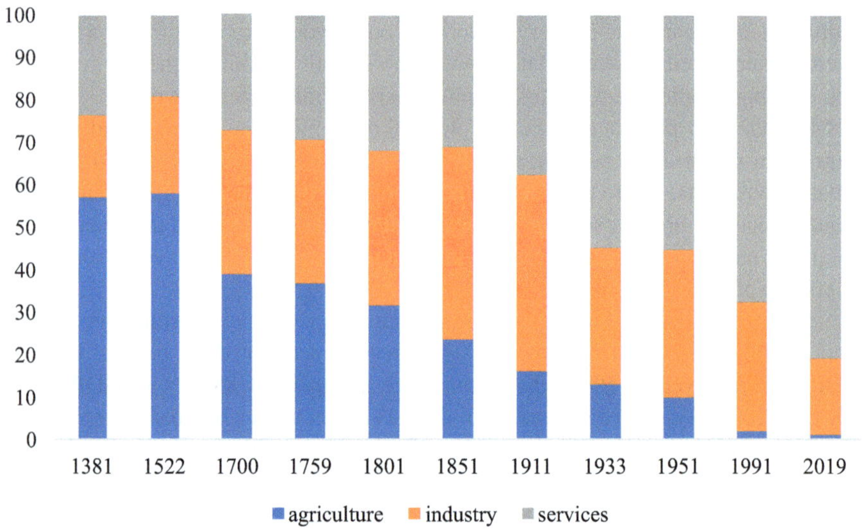

Fig. 9.7 Share of employment by sector in UK, 1381–2019. *Source:* Broadberry et al. (2013); Mitchell (1988); WDI

labourer in services as a percentage of output per labourer in industry for various countries in 2019. China ranks third lowest, with services producing only 62% of the output per labourer achieved in industry. This is only marginally higher than Indonesia (51%) and the Philippines (59%), and significantly lower than more developed economies such as Germany (88%) and the UK (95%). This relative

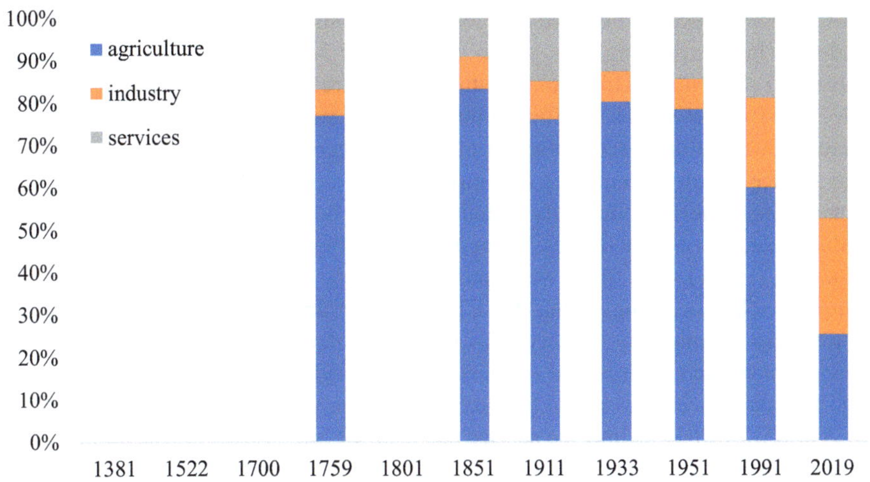

Fig. 9.8 Share of employment by sector in China, 1759–2019. *Source:* Guo et al. (2019); WDI

Table 9.4 Output per labourer in services/output per labourer in industry in 2019

	Services/industry
Indonesia	51%
Philippines	59%
China	62%
Russian Federation	70%
Netherlands	71%
Denmark	73%
Japan	81%
Bangladesh	81%
Thailand	82%
Vietnam	83%
Germany	88%
Spain	91%
UK	95%
Poland	109%
France	117%
Italy	118%
Hungary	120%
India	141%

inefficiency in China's service sector highlights the structural barriers discussed previously. While services account for 60% of China's GDP and employ nearly half of its labour force, their lower value added per labourer compared with manufacturing reveals a critical productivity gap. In contrast, countries such as Poland, France, and Italy exhibit service sectors where output per labourer surpasses that of industry, demonstrating their successful transition to high productivity service economies.

China's position in this table reflects the dual challenges it faces. First, its service sector, while expanding, has yet to achieve the levels of productivity seen in advanced economies. This could be attributed to a reliance on low-value-added service activities, as well as insufficient integration of technological and organizational innovations that drive service sector efficiency. Second, the under-performance of the service sector underscores the importance of continuing to shift labour from agriculture, where productivity remains low, to both manufacturing and higher value-added service activities. Moreover, countries such as India (141%) and Hungary (120%) show that a well-optimized service sector can outpace industry in output per labourer, suggesting that China has substantial room for improvement. Enhancing productivity in services—through technological advancements, skill development, and institutional reforms—will be critical for addressing this disparity. This dual focus is essential for sustaining China's long-term economic growth.

The shift of labour into the service sector in China has significant implications for per capita growth rates. As services exhibit lower labour productivity than manufacturing, a heavy transition into this sector reduces the overall growth potential. For instance, the previously estimated CAGR of 0.7% from 2019 to 2060, driven by a shift of labour from agriculture to manufacturing, declines to 0.42% per annum if all labour moves from agriculture to services instead. In practice, however, many workers in China transition into services rather than manufacturing. If we consider the impact of a combined shift from agriculture and manufacturing into services, the growth rate further declines to a mere 0.03% per annum. This stark reduction illustrates the challenges posed by relying heavily on the service sector for labour reallocation. It is, of course, unlikely that the entire labour force would transition into services. A more realistic scenario involves agriculture shrinking to 2% of employment, while manufacturing stabilizes at 20% of the workforce by 2060, similar to patterns observed in the UK. Under this assumption, the compound annual per capita growth rate would be approximately 0.32% per annum, reflecting a more balanced shift that still leverages the higher productivity of manufacturing while accommodating a growing service sector.

9.4.3 *Inequality*

9.4.3.1 Types of Inequality

There is a substantial literature on how various types of inequality influence growth patterns. Regarding physical capital, the wealth share of the top 10% of the wealthiest individuals serves as a useful indicator of capital inequality for the post-1900 period. As shown in Fig. 9.9, wealth distribution was highly unequal prior to approximately 1940, with the Netherlands and the UK exhibiting particularly high levels of concentration. The post-1940 period, however, saw a gradual decline in wealth inequality across most countries, reaching its lowest point in around 1990. This trough aligns with significant political and economic reforms in Russia and China, which led to sharp increases in inequality levels in these countries thereafter. By 2000, both nations had surpassed wealth inequality levels observed in Western and Southern Europe.

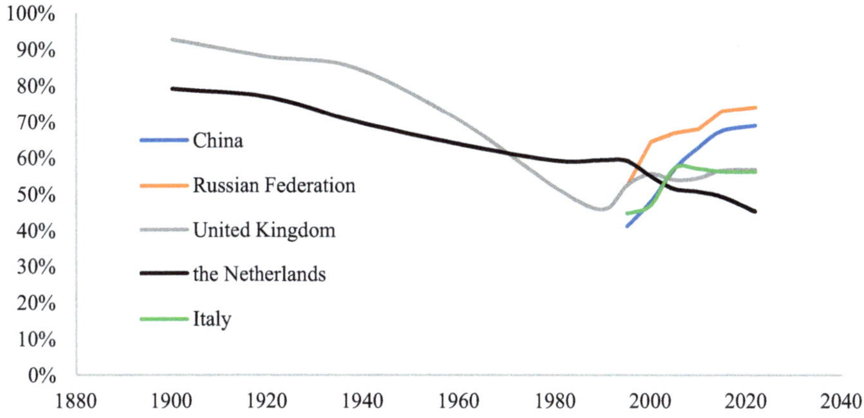

Fig. 9.9 Net wealth share of top 10% wealthiest persons. *Source:* https://wid.world/data/ downloaded 3 May 2024

For the pre-1900 period, land inequality provides a broader measure of physical capital and its transition from agriculture to industry. Around 1900, there was minimal regional variation in land ownership concentration: approximately 45% of total land was held in estates of 50 ha or more in Russia and Europe (Baten and Hippe 2018), with similar figures estimated for China at around 44% (Wang and Van Leeuwen 2021).[27]

Long-term data series on income inequality further enrich the analysis. Most studies on the pre-1900 period highlight the effects of land inequality (as a form of physical capital inequality) on human capital inequality, and ultimately on economic growth. These studies address four main debates: the impact of physical capital inequality on human capital development, the role of human capital inequality in driving economic growth, the relative importance of absolute versus relative human capital, and the direct relationship between labour inequality and GDP growth.

9.4.3.2 Physical Capital and Human Capital Inequality

We begin with how physical capital inequality, defined as the share of landholdings above 50 ha in total land, affects human capital. Galor et al. (2009) argue that inequality in land distribution (i.e. more big landowners cause higher land inequality) causes less human capital development as human capital development is less productive in agriculture than in industry.[28] This is confirmed by Baten and Hippe (2018), who use shares of landholdings of 50 ha and over. Yet, they point out that this relationship is non-linear, with it being positive in urban areas and negative in rural areas. Likewise, taking a measure of lower land inequality shares might lead to insignificant (or positive) effect on human capital. This is also found by Popov et al. (2024).

[27] Out of all farms, 2.97% was a landlord. Out of this 2.97%, 56.5% had about 30 ha and 43.5% had 50 ha or more (average 60 ha). Small farms (100%–2.97%) owned on average 0.5 ha. The share pf 50 ha and over in total agricultural land becomes 44%.

[28] See also Vanhanen (2003).

In sum, for low land thresholds (below *c.* 50 ha) and the higher (higher than 50 ha), the more positive the effect on landholding on human capital. Only around about 50 ha is it negative. The positive effect of lower landholdings on human capital is partly caused by the use of an absolute measure of landholding. If we had created a relative measure of land inequality like the Gini (or the ratio of large to small landholdings),[29] then the higher land inequality, the higher human capital. When government investment into education is low and subject to credit constraints that do not allow poor individuals to borrow to make optimal investment in their own education, rich individuals have a higher savings rate than poor, so investment into physical and human capital tends to be higher than in more egalitarian societies. However, a higher level of human capital is associated with high government education spending, which normally tends to produce equalizing effects. Therefore, a higher level of human capital is associated with lower inequality (in Gini) of human capital. We presume that the same is true for effects of physical capital inequality on human capital level and human capital inequality.

Second, some studies, for example Lopez et al. (1999), based on an educational Gini coefficient of inequality, find that lower educational inequality leads to higher per capita GDP. Yet, other scholars such as Földvári and Van Leeuwen (2011) find that, once corrected for omitted variables such as physical capital, the correlation turns insignificant. Indeed, Van Leeuwen and Li (2021, Fig. 7.3a), without correcting for omitted variables, found a stable negative and significant correlation of about −0.7 over time and among countries, and thus higher per capita GDP.

Besides the debate on physical capital and on educational inequality and omitted variables (in both cases leading to a minor increased/zero growth of per capita GDP), a third debate is whether one should use relative or absolute educational inequality. Relative inequality measures mean that, if person A has 10 years of education and person B 5 years, increasing both with 10% (i.e. 11 years and 5.5 years) results in the same level of educational inequality. Yet, absolute inequality differs from relative inequality, in that, in the previous example, the rise of 1.0 and 0.5 years of education, respectively, leads to higher inequality. The Gini is a relative measure and, for example, standard deviation is an absolute measure. Van Leeuwen and Li (2021, Fig. 7.3b) find that, using standard deviations of educational inequality, the correlation with per capita GDP runs from positive before 1950 to negative after 1950. That is, before 1950, a rise in absolute educational inequality led to rising GDP per capita, but after 1950, this increasingly led to a situation in which lower absolute educational inequality led to rising GDP per capita.

9.4.3.3 Labour Inequality

A fourth dimension of inequality relates to labour income. A closely related issue, widely debated in the literature, is income inequality—its patterns and the underlying factors. This topic becomes particularly significant during the process of

[29] E.g. ratio of the area of all land holdings over 500 *dessiatines* divided by the area of landholding of less than 10 *dessiatines* in the European part of Russia.

industrial development. In this subsection, we focus on inequality in labour incomes driven by differences in human capital, while broader factors and social dimensions of income inequality are addressed in Sect. 10.3.3.

Kuznets (1955) introduced income shares of various population groups (e.g. the top 1, 5, 10, 20, and 60%) as a measure of income inequality. He observed that income inequality tended to increase during the early stages of industrial modernization. However, as industrial development advanced and high economic growth became sustained, the trend reversed, leading to reduced inequality. Kuznets hypothesized that the trajectory of within-country income inequality could be modelled as an inverted U-shaped curve, now widely known as the Kuznets curve.

The drivers of this included growing income inequality owing to factors such as the urban–rural wage gap and skill premium, as well as spatial inter-regional inequality caused by uneven industrial concentration across sub-national regions. The rise occurs after rural labour migrates to urban areas. Inequality then declines after a certain income level is reached. That is, income inequality tended to increase during the early stages of industrialization but to moderate at an advanced stage of an industrialized society. Even though Kuznets himself was opposed to human capital theory, this theory is nonetheless often applied on human capital which means that if society is by and large equal, and a person with more human capital than the others, this will increase human capital. Each additional person with more human capital that is added increases human capital inequality. Once half of society has this additional human capital, each additional person reduces inequality.

There is evidence of long-run convergence in rural/urban labour markets in Russia for the period of 1885–1913. The first is based on aggregated all-Russian data (Borodkin and Leonard 2000). Another evidence suggests the gap narrowed from 0.55 to 0.65 (Cheremukhin et al. 2017, online appendix based on Strumilin 1966, 92; Strumilin 1982, 253, 267–268, 293), being bridged with 0.16% points annually by a linear trend.

However, the pattern was significantly different depending on the region. In the St. Petersburg province, the ratio was stable if measured as rural workers to plasterers whose wages were mostly on a par (Borodkin et al. 2008, 76, 80, 95). The ratio narrowed very modestly with the addition of skilled labourers, as skill premiums widened.

The economic history studies of the last few decades (Williamson and Lindert 1980; Williamson 1985; Van Zanden 1995; Didenko 2012) have demonstrated to us that the inverted U-shaped dynamic of income inequality was identified in leading economies that appeared to be the driving forces of world development.

The Kuznets-style dynamic of wage skill differentials in England and Wales in the nineteenth and twentieth centuries was highlighted by Williamson (1985). The skill premium tended to widen at first (until the mid-nineteenth century) before narrowing afterwards (from that point). This exposed the wage dynamics of knowledge-intensive occupations relative to other employment during the long nineteenth century. Its trend fits the inverted U-shaped curve as the Gini index dynamics does for the same period (Table 9.5). The similarity of these trends reveals that the rise and decline in income inequality was associated with the same movement in skill premiums.

The Williamson index as measured by the ratio of GDP per capita to low-skilled wages is another version of the Kuznets curve (Williamson 1997). This means that

Table 9.5 Trends in wages and inequality in England and Wales, 1797–1911

Year	All-workers to blue-collar-workers real wage indices ratio (1851 = 100%)	All-workers to blue-collar-workers real wage indices ratio (1901 = 100%)	Gini index
1797	79%		
1805	79%		
1810	79%		
1815	80%		
1819	83%		
1827	85%		29.30%
1835	94%		
1851	100%	106%	35.80%
1861		103%	
1871		103%	
1881		104%	32.80%
1891		100%	
1901		100%	33.10%
1911		93%	

Source: Williamson (1985, 17, 30, 40)

when the index goes up, the skill premium and inequality rise (because low-skilled labour wage declines vis-à-vis better paid jobs and other incomes). And vice versa: the index goes down as low-skilled wages rise, which normally means equalization.

In the case of Russia/USSR, we proxy low-skilled wages with those of agricultural workers and industrial blue-collar workers, as for these groups we have the most reliable long series.

For Russia, Fig. 9.10 shows that the modest rise of the index (i.e. skill premium) can be traced to the early phase of modern growth in Russia (late nineteenth century). After the equalization that took place in the mid-1910s–1920s that arose from the wars and egalitarian ideology of the Russian Revolution,[30] another rise belongs to the period of forced industrialization in the 1930s–mid-1950s.[31] Government policies that were aimed at stimulating the skill premium resorted to widening the urban/rural gap and increasing the skill premium in industry.[32]

For long-term trends in income inequality with underlying skill premiums in Central Eurasia, we use gross wages for blue- and white-collar workers. The figures include various types of monetary and in-kind remuneration of employees.

[30] A break in the data arises from the poor statistics during the turbulent years of the First World War, Russian Revolution, and Civil War.

[31] By the mid-1950s, the mobilization drive eased following the Soviet leader Josef Stalin's death. On the other hand, machine usage spread in agriculture, the share of agricultural workers in the labour force diminished, and industrial blue-collar workers received schooling, becoming relatively more skilled.

[32] The diminishing role of the skill premium under Soviet socialism and another wave of rising income inequality after the transition to a market economy since the late 1980s are also discussed in Sect. 10.2.

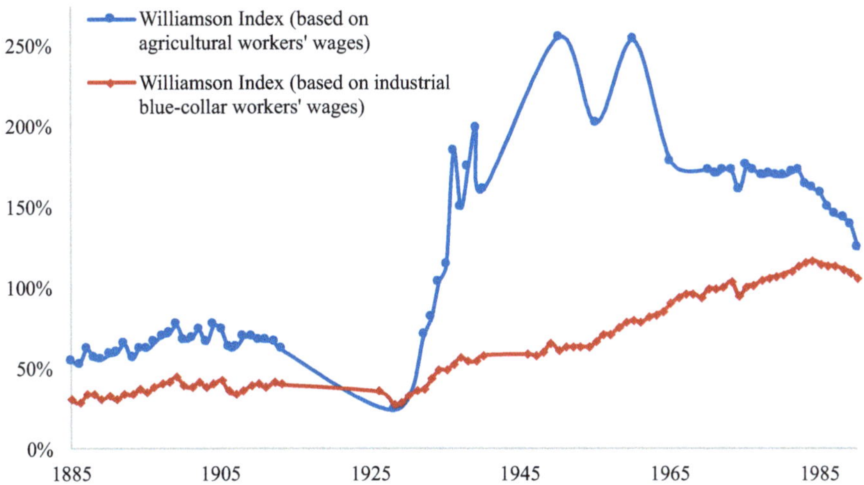

Fig. 9.10 Williamson index in European Russia/USSR, c. 1885–1955. *Source:* GDP: 1690s–1880s: Broadberry and Korchmina (2024); 1885–1913: Cheremukhin et al. (2017); 1923–1990: Didenko et al. (2013). Population: 1885–1913: Cheremukhin et al. (2017) based on Gregory (1982); 1917–1991: Didenko et al. (2013). Wages: 1885–1939: Cheremukhin et al. (2017) based on Strumilin (1966, 1982), Allen (2003); 1923–1991: Didenko et al. (2013) based on the official statistics

The Soviet ruling elite considered the industrial sector as key to the national economy. This is why the level of white- and blue-collar industrial workers' wages received good statistical coverage, and therefore left relatively reliable evidence in the official statistics that were published from 1913 onwards. The relationship between the wages of white- and blue-collar industrial workers may be considered as the core of the overall wage development and income distribution. Its relative differential (basically a skill premium) could be employed as a reliable proxy for human capital private returns, even in the Soviet quasi-market for labour.[33]

The evidence presented in Fig. 9.11 shows the cyclical pattern of the secular dynamics of income inequality. This becomes even clearer if explained from the perspective of human capital theory.[34] The private returns on human capital (that

[33] Our assumption are as follows: (1) the wage ratios are established primarily as a balance of supply and demand for certain skills (by either administration or market); (2) employees have the opportunity to choose their education and job; (3) employees' education expenditures were basically their opportunity costs (foregone earnings); (4) the ratio of visible and non-visible incomes (i.e. not reported in official data) was the same for the blue- and white-collar industrial workers in any particular year; (5) the ratio of general and specific experience of both categories remained constant over time; (6) the social transfers to both categories were proportional to their monetary wages; (7) the ratio of returns to health of both categories remains constant over time.

[34] We transform "raw" wage differential (as calculated from the figures directly drawn from the sources) into a premium for 1 year of schooling, employing our implied difference in educational level of both groups (Fig. 9.11). Reduction of the difference over decades was significant because of the spread of mass education.

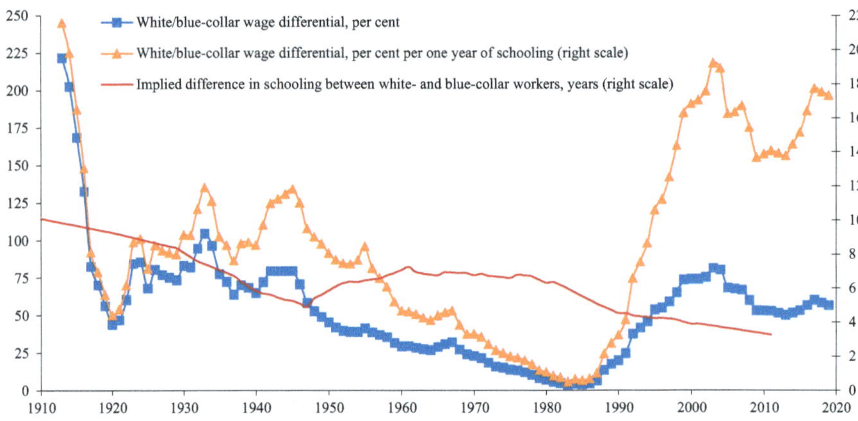

Fig. 9.11 Central Eurasia: white-collar versus blue-collar wage differential in industry, 1913–2019. *Note:* 1913–1922: European Russia; 1923–1991: USSR; 1992–2019: Russian Federation. *Source:* Didenko (2022) based on Didenko et al. (2013), Rosstat (https://rosstat.gov.ru/compendium/document/60671, https://rosstat.gov.ru/folder/210/document/12994)

underlie income inequality) tend to be higher in a market economy than in a centrally administered one. Responding to market signals, they rapidly reached the level of the early twentieth century.

The historical evidence shows (Fig. 9.11) that the Soviet period was remarkable for its relatively low premium for qualifications, although during the period of rapid industrialization (the 1930s) there was a corrective increase, in accordance with the political line of top Soviet leadership. The dynamics of the relative wage differential in industry shows that during periods when market mechanisms prevailed (in 1913 and in the 1990s–2010s), it was in the range of 10–20% for 1 year of education. This is higher than the period of centralized economy (0.5–12%), including the period of mobilization-driven industrialization (7.5–12%). It should be noted that this differential strongly varied between industries.

Skill premium and income inequality dynamics during the Soviet industrial revolution supports the hypothesis by Kuznets (1955) about the inverted U-shape form of within-country income inequality dynamics.

In the Soviet period when industrial development was catching up (the interwar period of the 1930s), the demand for a highly qualified labour force and its rare skills was growing rapidly. That is why the actual wage structure and dynamics did not fit the ideological values declared by the government, which had to adjust its Marxist-style ideology (flexibly using vocabulary and quotations from its classic authors) to contemporary social and economic challenges.[35] As a result, the rise in

[35] The turning point for the early Soviet wage policy was the speech delivered at a conference of business executives in June 1931 by the Soviet leader Josef Stalin. There he rhetorically claimed that "In a number of factories wage scales are drawn up in such a way as to practically wipe out the difference between skilled and unskilled labour, between heavy and light work. The consequence of wage equalisation is that the unskilled worker lacks the incentive to become a skilled worker and

the average nominal wage in the knowledge-producing sector outperformed that in the rest of the economy (Didenko 2012, 61).

It was acknowledged by Gregory and Stuart (1994, 182–183) that in the 1930s relative wage differentiation in the USSR was comparable with that of the United States, while the latter had a higher level of income inequality relative to other developed economies.

The first signs of a break in the trend towards increasing wage differentials appeared in 1946, and the wage structure reforms of the mid-1950s established the opposite trend towards income levelling (Nove 1982, 347, 348; Bergson 1989, 85, 87), which remained in force until the mid-1980s. In the period of steady development of the centrally planned economy, relative wages in the knowledge-producing sector declined and relative wages in other sectors increased (Didenko 2012, 62). The factors behind such a pattern seem to be both the priorities set out by the official ideology and the supply/demand structure of the quasi-labour market.[36] Such an expansion of employment in the knowledge-producing sector was largely due to the inflow of young employees who initially lacked high qualifications.

According to Bergson (1989, 66, 73, 75, 95), USSR wage differentiation in the 1970s was comparable with that in some Western European countries, especially those that adopted an economic model with a strong social policy (the Nordic countries, the UK during the Labour government).

The trend towards rising income inequality has revealed itself in Russia to a greater extent than in other transition countries.[37] The downturn in output appeared

is thus deprived of the prospect of advancement ... In order to put an end to this evil we must abolish wage equalisation and discard the old wage scales. In order to put an end to this evil we must draw up wage scales that will take into account the difference between skilled and unskilled labour, between heavy and light work ... Marx and Lenin said that the difference between skilled and unskilled labour would exist even under socialism, even after classes had been abolished; that only under communism would this difference disappear and that, consequently, even under socialism 'wages' must be paid according to work performed and not according to needs. But the equalitarians among our economic executives and trade-union officials do not agree with this and believe that under our Soviet system this difference has already disappeared. Who is right, Marx and Lenin or the equalitarians? It must be assumed that it is Marx and Lenin who are right. But it follows from this that whoever draws up wage scales on the 'principle' of wage equalisation, without taking into account the difference between skilled and unskilled labour, breaks with Marxism, breaks with Leninism" (http://www.marx2mao.com/PDFs/StWorks13.pdf, pp. 58–59).

[36] Except for certain periods of war (including preparation and reconstruction), a typical Soviet employee had substantial freedom of choice regarding his or her education and job. Yet, the Soviet labour market was strictly regulated throughout the whole period (Didenko et al. 2013, 127). Therefore, competition was even less perfect than in the Western welfare states of the 1950s–1970s that had strong labour union bargaining powers, such as France, Italy, Sweden, and the UK.

[37] The most conventional World Bank list of the countries that embarked on the path of structural transformation to change their centrally planned economies into market economies included the countries of Central and Eastern Europe (Poland, Hungary, Romania, Bulgaria, Albania, the republics of the former Czechoslovakia and Yugoslavia) and 15 newly independent republics of the FSU (https://openknowledge.worldbank.org/entities/publication/efceceb9-f9da-5ee9-bf4c-ea024d0b5c41). The IMF used a broader composition, which included the countries of East Asia (more frequently Mongolia, and occasionally Cambodia, China, Laos, Vietnam), but the list of

to be very deep and the need for industrial employment restructuring led to significant labour market shocks. Yet, the trend towards rising income inequality has reversed since the early 2000s (Fig. 9.11). This change occurred after the sharpest and most chaotic stage of the transitional process had been passed.

The trend towards moderation of income inequality was not reversed by a corrective increase in the wage differential: the last maximum level in 2017 did not exceed the peak of 2003. At the same time, there is some divergence of most of the series from our series of the wage differential, which shows that in 2009–2019, the more skilled somewhat improved their position relative to the less skilled. Moreover, the wage skill premium remains historically high, at about 17% for each additional year of schooling (Didenko 2022, 75–80).

Comparing all the above cases with the Kuznets model, it could be suggested that wage differential dynamics in twentieth-century Russia/USSR did indeed follow international trends. Both in Western-type and Soviet economies, wage differentiation patterns conformed to the Kuznets curve as regards the industrial stage of economic modernization.

9.4.3.4 Development in Inequality in a Knowledge-Based, Post-industrial Economy

In recent decades, income inequality (both in wages and non-labour incomes) has again been on the rise during the transition from an industrial to a knowledge-based post-industrial (or information) society and a globalizing economy. This trend has not been representative for all developed countries (France is the most notable exception), but for those (English-speaking above all) that have defined major trends in world economic and cultural development over the recent decades. Of these countries, the United States and the UK have major global financial centres whose role has significantly increased as financial sector expansion and globalization have taken place.

The reversal in the trend towards income levelling has been recognized in the literature and references have also been made to the new stage of technological progress, especially in information and computer technology (ICT) and the corresponding demand growth for highly skilled labour. The skill-biased technological change explanation of this new wave of upward movement in income inequality was voiced in Katz and Murphy (1992). As it is human capital that is considered to be the prime engine of postmodern economic growth, overall income

these countries underwent some changes (https://www.imf.org/en/Publications/WEO/Issues/2016/12/31/~/media/Websites/IMF/imported-flagship-issues/external/pubs/ft/weo/weo0593/pdf/_File5pdf.ashx, https://www.imf.org/external/np/exr/ib/2000/110300.htm, https://www.imf.org/~/media/Websites/IMF/imported-flagship-issues/external/pubs/ft/weo/2003/02/pdf/_appendixpdf.ashx). Since 2004, they declined to use the term in their country classification.

distribution is largely based on the difference in returns on human capital. Another idea is the race between education and technology (Goldin and Katz 2008, 89–125). When education lags behind, failing to meet growing demand for specific skills created by technological change, private returns on human capital (skill premia) tend to rise.

Globalization has also had its impact, especially on developed economies. Mobility of capital has increased the demand for skilled labour both in donor and recipient countries. Financial liberalization and deregulation of the expanding financial sector has led both to average size increase and to greater polarization of earnings, between executives and other employees primarily.

Another factor that has contributed to the rise in income inequality is that governments have preferred not to expand their reliance on redistributive tax and benefit policy, but to curtail the influence of trade unions. The latter policy line has been supported by further shifts in the employment structure in favour of knowledge sector industries and freelance and part-time labour. This has led to a weakening in the bargaining power of trade unions; this has occurred in many countries, but most notably in the United States and the UK.

Since the end of the 1980s, all transition economies have experienced the same upward trend in income inequality that previously re-emerged in developed economies from the mid-1970s (Grimalda et al. 2010).[38] In addition to the segmental formation of the information society that these countries had experienced,[39] the transition to an open market economy and pluralistic political system exacerbated many problems associated with such revolutionary changes. Dismantling of the socialist-era labour market institutions, which were heavily reliant on government regulation of earnings differentials, led to a greater role for free pricing across the entire wage scale.

In arguing the cyclical pattern of income inequality, our thesis is that the original Kuznets curve was a particular case of inverted U-shaped income inequality dynamics that both accompanied and followed the process of a historically significant systemic transformation. This transformation was based on the industrial technological revolution, with urbanization being the major social transformation. Taking into account the phenomenon of another wave of increasing within-country income inequality in the last decades, the following explanation of mechanisms that drive fluctuations of income inequality may be proposed.

The general trend is that income inequality tends to increase in the major transitional stages of social and economic development during large-scale systemic transformations and tends to decrease in periods of gradual development.

[38] See footnote 37 on the countries with transition economies.

[39] The concept was coined by the sociologists and economists of the 1980s, especially J. Masuda (1981), and focused on the social consequences of the third industrial revolution.

It appears that in periods of systemic social and economic transformations, basic (epochal) social and economic innovations usually emerge unexpectedly and lead to high demand for rare skills that were not of great value before or even did not exist at all. At the same time, rapid changes lead to a less predictable economic environment in which various risk levels tend to increase. This can be measured historically in the increasing volatility of the economic indicators in question. Another factor that exacerbates this trend is of an institutional nature. In such periods, traditional institutions that previously managed to mitigate inequality and its negative social consequences usually experience diminishing and often shattering effects.

The human capital supply and demand structure shifts more rapidly than education and labour markets (even those totally regulated by the government) are able to respond to growing imbalances and adjust to new patterns. At the same time, the supply of previously valuable skills becomes excessive and they become ordinary. In this way, a substantial proportion of the accumulated human capital appears to be historically specific and becomes functionally depreciating (or even outdated) for the new demand pattern.

However, a high degree of wage inequality provides incentives for large investments in adequate (up-to-date) human capital, and in certain circumstances this leads to future high rates of economic growth.

In periods of gradual development and relatively predictable social and economic innovations, the imbalances in labour markets tend to dampen. In market sectors that have already taken shape, price competition leads to skill premium reduction.

In a more predictable economic environment, risk levels tend to decline and economic expectations become more consensual, tending to vary from actual outcomes to a lesser extent. This leads to risk premium reduction in the overall income structure.

Summing up, we may conclude that the relationship between income inequality and the level of development appears to be a long-term cyclical process.

One part of the cycle is that income inequality tends to increase during transitional stages of economic and social system transformations such as industrial and post-industrial revolutions, innovative and catching-up modernizations, or transitions to an open market economy combined with political system change. In the second part of the cycle, during stages of development under a more or less stable social and economic system, the wage differential tends to decrease.

Inequality increases during periods of systemic transformations. Imbalances in the available supply and demand of qualifications and skills then tend to increase, while institutions that normally curtailed the level of inequality either fail or do not develop sufficient capacity. With the transition to evolutionary development, income inequality has tended to moderate. Meanwhile, the state has acquired sufficient institutional capacity not only to define its goals, to combat poverty and ease social tension, but also to effectively implement and enforce appropriate regulatory measures, primarily relating to income redistribution (Didenko 2012).

9.5 Future Growth Predictions

9.5.1 *Future Growth Predictions: Western Europe and the United States*

Regional differences in economic growth are influenced, as seen, by both the availability of foundational resources and the type of technology utilized. Fernald and Jones (2014) demonstrate that, for US GDP per capita growth over the past 50 years, human capital—primarily derived from endogenous growth theories—has been the dominant driver. Specifically, Fig. 9.1 illustrates that Lucasian and Romerian growth contributions accounted for no less than 78% of per labour hour economic growth in the Unites States after 1950. However, this pattern has not been consistent across all countries or time periods. The impact of human capital on growth is gradually diminishing, particularly in more developed economies, as its potential for income enhancement becomes increasingly exhausted. This trend is evident in Fig. 9.12, which tracks the growth of educational attainment by birth year since 1930. The data reveal a plateau in average years of education, reaching approximately 14 years in the United States and Great Britain in about 1950, in Russia in about 1970, and in China by 1990.

Despite this, human capital has historically grown at a faster rate in less developed countries than in the United States, particularly since the mid-twentieth century. This supports the validity of convergence models, which suggest that lower-income countries tend to experience higher growth rates as they catch up with more developed economies.

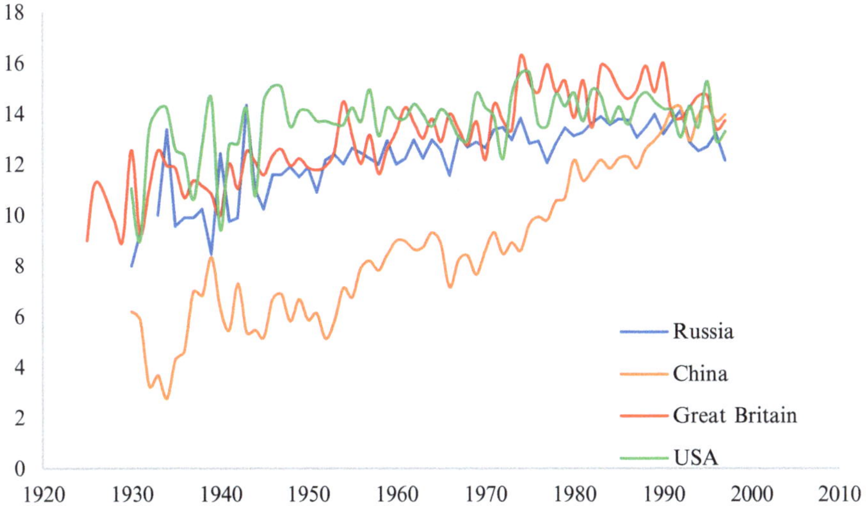

Fig. 9.12 Mean years of education by birth year, c. 1930–present for Russia, China, Great Britain, and the United States. *Source:* ISSP Research Group (2019). Downloaded from: https://www.gesis.org/en/issp/search-and-data-access

So, in developed economies, the role of human capital in driving economic growth is likely to diminish over time. Additionally, the rise of AI may further reduce the importance of labour by automating many tasks. This shift could lead to an ever-increasing capital to output ratio, marking a transition from the Solowian model of short-run growth effects to a scenario in which capital becomes a dominant long-run growth factor.

However, the prospect of indefinite growth driven by such a transition appears highly unlikely. We can identify two main categories of reasons why an infinite rise in the capital to output ratio is improbable.

That is, first, there is no complete replacement of labour by AI-related features (see *The Economist*; Goldman Sachs).[40] Indeed, some scholars even argue that this implies that only low educated jobs remain. Second, the growth of AI might initially lead to rising unemployment but ultimately increases labour demand by the rising demand of foreign countries for AI-intensive products. Hence, the researchers conclude, we "are not expecting a high probability of … AI-induced growth acceleration … on at least a 30-to-50-year time horizon".[41] This is also shown by looking at the stock markets,[42] which show some evidence in the recent fast buying of AI-related stocks but provide no evidence for a complete replacement of labour. Indeed, in Fig. 9.13, we provide stock prices from Nasdaq, with Nvidia being an AI company and Microsoft being a predominantly ICT company. They thus cover the third (ICT) and fourth (AI/robotization) industrial revolutions. Figure 9.13 shows

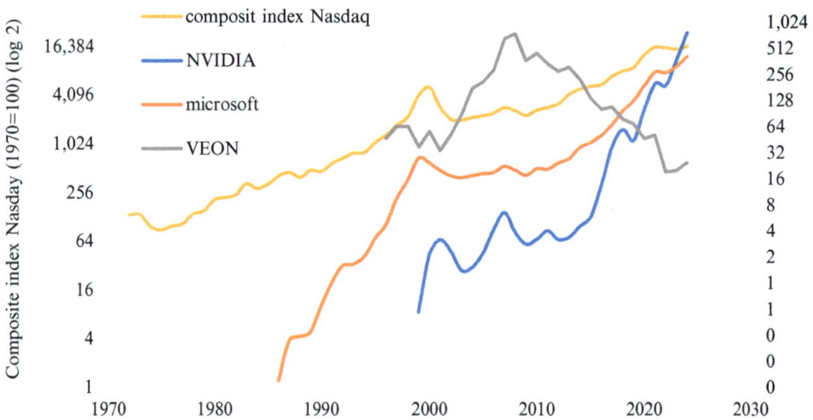

Fig. 9.13 Stock prices of Microsoft and Nvidia (and composite index) on the Nasdaq (log 2 on both vertical axes). *Source:* https://www.macrotrends.net/

[40] See: https://www.goldmansachs.com/intelligence/pages/generative-ai-could-raise-global-gdp-by-7-percent.html

[41] https://www.economist.com/finance-and-economics/2023/05/07/your-job-is-probably-safe-from-artificial-intelligence

[42] See https://basilhalperin.com/essays.html

Table 9.6 GDP per capita in 2015 PPP USD for selected countries, 2020–2060

	US	UK	Netherlands	Germany	Italy	China
2020	59,352	39,876	51,504	48,084	35,811	16,653
2023	64,881	44,678	55,866	49,809	40,880	19,567
2030	71,054	48,124	60,079	53,011	43,538	25,795
2040	79,231	56,094	67,875	60,336	49,160	33,451
2050	87,269	65,574	79,855	70,599	57,398	40,488
2060	95,839	76,072	92,099	81,411	68,263	48,584

Source: OECD (2021), "Long-term baseline projections, No. 109 (Edition 2021)", OECD Economic Outlook: Statistics and Projections (database), https://doi.org/10.1787/cbdb49e6-en (accessed on 24 April 2024)

that trust in ICT growth was strongest before about 2000, since Microsoft grew fast up to that point. For 2000–2017, Microsoft (i.e. ICT) stagnated while AI came up (Nvidia). But AI growth in this period was still limited. After 2017, we see fast growth of Nvidia (AI). Microsoft also partially grew (maybe because they went into AI too), but clearly not as fast as Nvidia (Table 9.6).

9.5.2 *Future Growth Predictions: China*

As pointed out before, various growth predictions exist mostly based on either growth accounting or convergence.

At the one extreme, Lin (2017) predicts for China 7–8% per annum until 2050 based on the growth rates of Asian miracle countries. At the other extreme, Pritchett and Summers (2014) argue for a regression to the mean with roughly 2–4% per annum growth rates. This is broadly consistent with Barro (2016a, b), who points out double 2 s—that is, each country's long-run growth rate is 2% per annum, while a country's GDP per capita tends to converge on this long-run path at 2% per annum. Indeed, as pointed out in the previous sub-section, Lee (2016) finds that a country at about half the per labourer output of a rich country grows about 1.6% points faster.

Sections 9.2–9.4 dealt with standard growth accounting factors of production driving industrialization (physical capital, labour, human capital, and TFP) and economic structure (Sect. 9.5). Yet, there is also unconditional convergence: the higher GDP per capita is, the lower the economic growth rate once corrected for other factors. This is based on the advantages of backwardness; that is, poorer countries can obtain technology cheaper and apply it with cheaper labour, thus outperforming richer countries (Gerschenkron 1962).

But this convergence is not unescapable. For example, Rodrik (2013) argues that in most times over the past centuries, it was the rich countries that grew fastest. This could be because countries might have increasing returns, or convergence only works once a country has a sufficiently high income or human capital. Sachs and Warner (1995) show that these effects only play a role in countries with relatively inefficient economic policies relating to, for example, trade and property rights

Table 9.7 Forecast GDP per capita in 2010 USD in China

	Lin (2017)	Bai and Zhang	Lee (2016)	Lowy Institute Study	OECD (2018)	Pritchett and Summers (2014)
2020	17,762	17,762	17,762	17,762	17,762	17,762
2030	42,049	29,488	28,932	26,802	26,292	23,871
2040	89,114	43,650	40,812	34,309	33,986	32,080
2050	188,857	64,612	57,569	43,918	43,931	43,113

Table 9.8 Forecast GDP per capita in 2010 USD (relative to China)

	China	UK	Netherlands	Russia
2020	1.0	2.2	2.8	1.4
2030	1.0	1.7	2.2	1.4
2040	1.0	1.6	2.0	1.1
2050	1.0	1.4	1.9	0.7

Source: OECD (2018)

while Beckley (2021) points at China's weakness in geography, institutions, and demography. Yet, as pointed out by Lee (2016), conditional convergence remains one of the main explanatory factors in long-run growth. He estimates that a country at about half the per labourer output of a rich country grows about 1.6% points faster (Table 9.7).

It is quite obvious that underlying assumptions are the major driving force of the final result. First, the shift away of human capital probably starts later in China than in, for example, the United States, so there is less slow down. Second, Bergeaud et al. (2017), based on growth accounting, found strong difference depending on whether the fourth industrial revolution (AI) is included. In addition, the capital to output ratio might first decline but later create permanent growth under AI. For that reason, we report relative numbers rather than absolute values in Table 9.8. There is clearly catch up in China per capita to the other countries, but it is limited.

Third, given the latest relatively low actual figures of growth in China (even lower than in Rajah and Lengh, technical appendix on pp. 39–40), one can expect that the deceleration has occurred that also happened in the USSR in the 1960s–1970s and in Japan in the late 1980s–1990s. The level at which the deceleration occurs in China seems to be somewhere between Japan and the USSR, that is, at about 60% of the United States in terms of per capita GDP.

Fourth, institutions and policy could shift growth rates too, with a move to a market economy. Various authors have claimed that catching up depends on implementing these structural factors (e.g., for Japan, IMF 2013) but two factors differ. On the one hand, even though all factors are significant in all countries, the effect of each factor varies from country to country. In higher developing economies, it is mostly financial sector reforms and a liberalization of product and labour markets (IMF 2013, 8) while for low developing countries, Japan's factors (banking, schools, etc.) are more important. On the other hand, the sequence of factors (Ostry et al.

2009) is important. For more developed countries, it is not just financial reforms that are important, but also trade liberalization, which is driving external capital accounts liberalization and domestic finance liberalization (Ostry et al. 2009), without being driven by factors itself. This indeed suggests that trade liberalization is more important for developed than for developing economies.

In sum, for China:

- Banking, schools, etc., were the most common factors during the early reform period. Liberalization followed later.
- Trade liberalization affects domestic finance liberalization, and external capital accounts liberalization.[43] How did China make the move from schools and so on to liberalization? Evidently, many issues are at stake here, including a failing housing market, local government debt increases, and over-education.
- Long-run institutions affect dynastic cycles. This implies that when a new dynasty arrives, it is a dictator that represses the market. Later, when the dynasty weakens, market behaviour arises (e.g. craftsman system in Ming, reform period at the end of the twentieth century). If we assume the same cycles exist today, this will lower the growth rate. This can also be applied to Republican and New China. It also affects liberalization. The old institutions in China were based on the national government gaining taxes and control via local government. Even today, local civil servants go into the countryside to sell houses because of the overburdened housing market. The historical focus on infrastructure is apparent today with, for example, the overspending on high-speed trains. Another example is that, according to Chap. 5, since 1960, countries with "bad" institutions grow faster. Why, and will this last after 2020?

Most (but not all) of these factors work via technical inefficiency (current GDP is below the GDP of the technical frontier).

9.5.3 Future Growth Predictions: Russia

As discussed above, the depressing effect of economic sanctions turned out to be much weaker than expected right after their imposition. This was primarily thanks to countermeasures in the financial sector and changes in logistics chains involved in foreign trade activities that were implemented in 2022. Even if transaction costs increased, they did not reach prohibitive levels, and losses in certain sectors were offset by gains in others.

---

[43] See
https://www.worldbank.org/en/publication/gfdr/data/global-financial-development-database
the Chinn-Ito index
https://web.pdx.edu/~ito/Chinn-Ito_website.htm.
https://ourworldindata.org/grapher/trade-openness

Another factor was state investment in infrastructure and the government support of housing construction, as opposed to the situation during previous economic crises in Russia. The increasing orientation of the Russian economy towards the domestic market was accompanied by accelerated growth in private and government consumption, and acceleration in the dynamics of gross physical capital accumulation (Izriadnova 2024, 145–146, 149, 155–156). The high-tech sector production index was 121.8% in 2023 versus 106.8% a year earlier (Izriadnova 2024, 152).

Even though the expectation of 20–40% of annual inflation (in March–April 2022) was never realized, inflation accelerated in 2023 as a result of a significant weakening of the ruble and an easing of fiscal policy in 2022, and rapid growth in aggregate demand and credit activity (Bozhechkova et al. 2024, 20).

The economy found itself in two traps: high interest rates with actively developed measures to subsidize them in priority areas, and a rapid growth of wages on the tight labour market. Both factors stimulated demand and worked as a pro-inflationary factor. Actual performance of the Russian economy and experts' sentiment on its prospects are presented as consensus forecasts (Table 9.9).

Table 9.9 Aggregated results of expert surveys on Russia's economy, August–September 2024

	Forecast period	Total GDP (%, YoY)[a]		CPI (% year-on-year, average for the year)		Real disposable income (%, YoY)
Median	2022 (actual)	−1.4		13.8		−1.0
	2023 (actual)	4.1		5.9		5,8
	2024 (actual)	4.1		8.4		8.4
	2025	1.7	1.5	9.4	4.7	3.1
	2026	1.8	1.5	5.5	3.9	2.1
	2027	2.0	1.6	4.3	3.8	1.4
	2028		1.5		4.0	1.5
	2029		1.8		4.0	1.8
	2030		2.0		4.0	1.9
	2031		1.9			1.9
	2028–2032	1.75				
Max	2025	3.3		9.9		
	2026	3.0		7.7		
	2027	3.4		6.2		
90th percentile	2025	2.4		9.8		
	2026	2.4		6.8		
	2027	2.9		5.2		
10th percentile	2025	1.1		8.3		
	2026	1.3		4.5		
	2027	1.5		4.0		
Min	2025	0.3		7.9		

(continued)

Table 9.9 (continued)

	Forecast period	Total GDP (%, YoY)[a]		CPI (% year-on-year, average for the year)		Real disposable income (%, YoY)
	2026	0.5		4.2		
	2027	0.0		4.0		
Total answers	2025	30		30		
	2026	30		30		
	2027	30		30		
Source		Bank of Russia[b]	National Research University Higher School of Economics Centre of Development Institute[c]	Bank of Russia[b]	National Research University Higher School of Economics Centre of Development Institute[c]	National Research University Higher School of Economics Centre of Development Institute[c]

[a] With decreasing population (the topic is not covered in the expert surveys) GDP per capita will tend to be somewhat higher

[b] https://www.cbr.ru/eng/statistics/ddkp/mo_br/

[c] https://dcenter.hse.ru/consensus_forecast

Estimates for military expenditures of the USSR from the 1950s to the 1980s are given in Fig. 9.14. After more than 2 years have passed since the launch of the military operation in Ukraine, the Russian economy remains much less affected by such activities than the market economy of Israel (20–30% in the 1970s versus 5.32% in 2023) or Saudi Arabia. The latter, unlike Iran, was never involved in a direct armed conflict but claims to be the major military power in the Middle East. However, the upward trend is obvious in Russia, and there is room for this expansion. Cooper (2023), affiliated with the Stockholm International Peace Research Institute (SIPRI), expected total military expenditure to rise to 7.1% in 2024, based on the analysis of the draft budget of the central government. Though it is rather high by international comparison, it is still below any reliable estimate for the USSR from the 1950s to the 1980s. In June 2024, the Russian presidency stated that actual military spending was at 6.3% of GDP and suggested that this could be a local high for the Russian economy (http://en.kremlin.ru/events/president/news/77316).

Much depends now on how much the Russian economy will be affected by military restructuring. The sanctions have had very limited effect for the biennium 2023–2024 (and less than the COVID-19 shock in 2020), given the relative self-sufficiency of the Russian economy—and they even provide some potential for import substitution. This latter is under way and makes Russia's economy less vulnerable to external risks; the problem is that it is based on much older and simpler technology in the medium term. Therefore, one can expect the under-utilization of previously accumulated knowledge and skills (Gimpelson 2022).

The model of further development in Russia is being reshaped, and there are many alternatives with significant probabilities.

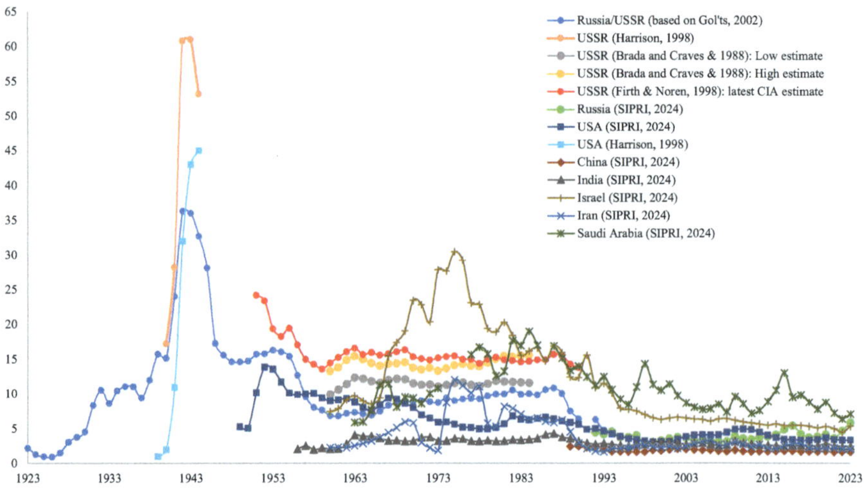

Fig. 9.14 Military expenditures of Russia/USSR and the reference countries, percentage GDP. *Notes:* (1) SIPRI (2024) estimates are based on the government budget statistics and include some points that may be omitted in the national statistics (military pensions, some kinds of troops subordinated to various government offices). They do not necessarily capture all of the military outlays, especially if they are corporate or private. The merit of the SIPRI data is application of the standard methodology that allows inter-country comparisons. As no historical estimates for the USSR are available in the SIPRI (2024) we borrow them or the input data from other literature acknowledging that they are based on a similar but not the same methodology. (2) Estimates by Harrison (1998) for the USSR during the Second World War include foreign aid (most of which was the Lend Lease from the United States, which is also included into the latter's military spending). If only domestic finance is taken into account, this reduces the level to 56% in 1942, 51% in 1943, and 43% in 1944. (3) Kontorovich (2019) claimed the above estimates for the USSR from the 1950s to 1980s, as well as some other similar, were significantly undervalued. His arguments involved distorted prices and a neglect of dual-purpose expenditures. However, he did not provide detailed accounts of his own series following conventional methodology. *Source:* Brada and Graves (1988); (Steinberg 1990); Harrison (1998), SIPRI (2024); own estimate based on Golts (2002) and the sources to Fig. 8.4

References

Acemoglu D, Restrepo P (2019) Automation and new tasks: how technology displaces and reinstates labor. J Econ Perspect 33(2):3–30

Allen RC (2003) Farm to factory: a reinterpretation of the Soviet industrial revolution. Princeton University Press, Princeton

Allen RC (2012) Technology and the great divergence: global economic development since 1820. Explor Econ Hist 49(1):1–16

Amin S (1976) Unequal development: an essay on the social formations of peripheral capitalism. Harvester Press, Hassocks, England. (Original work published 1973)

Anikin VA (2017) Occupational propensity for training in a late industrial society: evidence from Russia. Int J Train Dev 21(4):249–284

Anikin VA (2018) Человеческий капитал в пост-кризисной России: Состояние и отдача [Human capital in post-crisis Russia: State and impact]. J Instit Stud 10(2):90–117

Anikin VA (2019) The contradictory nature of lifelong learning in the post-transition Russia. J Comparat Econ Stud 14:19–50
Avdeeva DA (2024) Вклад человеческого капитала в рост российской экономики [The contribution of human capital to economic growth in Russia]. HSE Econ J 28(1):9–43
Barro RJ (2016a) China's growth prospects. VoxEU. Retrieved from https://voxeu.org/article/china-s-growth-prospects
Barro RJ (2016b) Economic growth and convergence, applied especially to China. NBER Working Paper No. 21872. https://doi.org/10.3386/w21872
Baten J, Hippe R (2018) Geography, land inequality, and regional numeracy in Europe in historical perspective. J Econ Growth 23:79–109
Beckley M (2021) Conditional convergence and the rise of China: a political economy approach to understanding global power transitions. J Glob Secur Stud 6(1):ogaa010. https://doi.org/10.1093/jogss/ogaa010
Bergson A (1989) Planning and performance in socialist economies: the USSR and Eastern Europe. Unwin Hyman, Boston
Bergeaud A, Cette G, Lecat R (2017) Future growth: secular stagnation versus technological shock scenarios. VoxEU. Retrieved from https://voxeu.org/article/secular-stagnation-versus-technological-shock-scenarios
Bolt J, Van Zanden JL (2020) Maddison style estimates of the evolution of the world economy: a new 2020 update. Maddison Project Database, version 2018, 2020
Borodkin LI, Leonard CS (2000) The rural urban wage gap in the industrialization of Russia, 1885–1913. Oxford University, Department of Economics Working Paper no. 14. https://ora.ox.ac.uk/objects/uuid:37cd0307-2972-4087-ad87-d88ca4ec9d6c
Borodkin LI, Granville B, Leonard CS (2008) The rural/urban wage gap in the industrialization of Russia, 1884–1910. Eur Rev Econ Hist 12(1):67–95
Bozhechkova AV, Knobel AY, Trunin PV (2023) Денежно-кредитная политика [Monetary and credit policy]. In: Kudrin AL, Mau VA, Radygin AD, Sinelnikov-Murylev SG (eds) Российская экономика в 2022 году. Тенденции и перспективы [Russian economy in 2022. Trends and outlooks]. Issue 44. Gaidar Institute, Moscow, pp 11–50. https://www.iep.ru/files/text/trends/2022/book.pdf
Bozhechkova AV, Knobel AY, Trunin PV (2024) Денежно-кредитная политика [Monetary and credit policy]. In: Kudrin AL, Mau VA, Radygin AD, Sinelnikov-Murylev SG (eds) Российская экономика в 2023 году. Тенденции и перспективы [Russian economy in 2023. Trends and outlooks]. Issue 45. Gaidar Institute, Moscow, pp 9–44. https://www.iep.ru/files/text/trends/2023/book.pdf
Brada JC, Graves RL (1988) Slowdown in soviet defense expenditures. South Econ J 54(4):969–984
Broadberry S, Campbell B, van Leeuwen B (2013) When did Britain industrialise? The sectoral distribution of the labour force and labour productivity in Britain, 1381-1851. Explor Econ Hist 50(1):16–27. https://doi.org/10.1016/j.eeh.2012.09.003
Broadberry S, Korchmina E (2024) Catching-up and falling behind: Russian economic growth, 1960s-1880s. J Econ Hist 84(4):997–1028. https://doi.org/10.1017/s0022050724000287
Calabrese M, Philips R, Keenan R, Leeuwen B, v. (2022) The occupational structure of England and Wales: the 1939 national register: social and economic history. Res Data J Humanit Soc Sci 7(1):1–17. https://doi.org/10.1163/24523666-bja10026
Chayanov AV (1925) Peasant Farm Organisation (originally published in Russian in 1925 as "Организация крестьянского хозяйства. Москва: Кооперативное издательство") and On the Theory of Non-Capitalist Economic Systems (originally published in Russian in 1924 as "Zur Frage einerTheorie der nichtkapitalistischen Wirtschaftssysteme. Archiv fur Sozialwissenschaft und Sozialpolitik. 51(3), 577–613) were first translated into English in 1966
Cheremukhin A, Golosov M, Guriev S, Tsyvinski A (2017) The industrialization and economic development of Russia through the lens of a neoclassical growth model. Rev Econ Stud 84(2):613–649. https://doi.org/10.1093/restud/rdw026
Cooper J (2023) Another budget for a country at war: military expenditure in Russia's federal budget for 2024 and beyond. SIPRI, Stockholm. https://doi.org/10.55163/XROI1465

Dezhina IG (2023) Состояние науки и инноваций [State of the science and innovations]. In: Kudrin AL, Mau VA, Radygin AD, Sinelnikov-Murylev SG (eds) Российская экономика в 2022 году. Тенденции и перспективы [Russian economy in 2022. Trends and outlooks]. Issue 44. Gaidar Institute, Moscow, pp 425–454. https://www.iep.ru/files/text/trends/2022/book.pdf
Dezhina IG (2024) Состояние науки и инноваций [State of the science and innovations]. In: Kudrin AL, Mau VA, Radygin AD, Sinelnikov-Murylev SG (eds) Российская экономика в 2023 году. Тенденции и перспективы [Russian economy in 2023. Trends and outlooks]. Issue 45. Gaidar Institute, Moscow, pp 349–373. https://www.iep.ru/files/text/trends/2023/book.pdf
Didenko DV (2012) Income inequality and systemic transformations: long-term trends of human capital private returns. J Comparat Econ Stud 7:53–87
Didenko DV (2022) Неравенство доходов в современной России на фоне долгосрочной исторической ретроспективы [Income inequality in contemporary Russia in the long-run historical perspective]. Terra Econ 20(2):72–85. https://doi.org/10.18522/2073-6606-2022-20-2-72-85
Didenko D, Dorofeeva Z (2016) Дополнительное профессиональное образование в России: динамика масштабов и экономической эффективности (2000–2013 gg.) [Adult education in Russia: the dynamics of scale and economic efficiency (2000–2013)]. Mir Rossii (Universe of Russia) 25(4):87–114
Didenko D, Kliucharev G (2014) On the Resources of Russian Modernization. Russ Educ Soc 56(2):3–29
Didenko D, Földvári P, Van Leeuwen B (2013) The spread of human capital in the former Soviet Union area in a comparative perspective: exploring a new dataset. J Eurasian Stud 4(2):123–135. https://doi.org/10.1016/j.euras.2013.03.002. (Supplementary data retrieved from https://ars.els-cdn.com/content/image/1-s2.0-S1879366513000122-mmc1.zip, accessed via https://www.sciencedirect.com/science/article/pii/S1879366513000122)
Dijkman J, Van Leeuwen B (eds) (2019) An economic history of famine resilience. (Routledge explorations in economic history). Routledge. https://doi.org/10.4324/9780429200632
Dutta S, Lanvin B, Rivera León L, Wunsch-Vincent S (eds) (2023) Global Innovation Index 2023: innovation in the face of uncertainty. WIPO. https://www.wipo.int/edocs/pubdocs/en/wipo-pub-2000-2023-en-main-report-global-innovation-index-2023-16th-edition.pdf
Fernald JG, Jones CI (2014) The future of US economic growth. Am Econ Rev 104(5):44–49
Földvári P, Van Leeuwen B (2011) Should less inequality in education lead to a more equal income distribution? Educ Econ 19:537
Galor O, Moav O, Vollrath D (2009) Inequality in landownership, the emergence of human-capital promoting institutions, and the great divergence. Rev Econ Stud 76:143–179
Gerschenkron A (1962) Economic backwardness in historical perspective, a book of essays. Harvard University Press, Cambridge
Ghosh D, Ghosh R, Roy Chowdhury S, Ganguly B (2024) AI-exposure and labour market: a systematic literature review on estimations, validations, and perceptions. Manag Rev Q 74(1):1–25. https://doi.org/10.1007/s11301-023-00393-x
Gimpelson V (2019) Возраст и заработная плата: стилизованные факты и российские особенности [Age and wage: stylized facts and Russian evidence]. HSE Econ J 23(2):185–237
Gimpelson VE (2022) Человеческий капитал в эпоху санкций и контрсанкций: некоторые последствия его перераспределения [Russian human capital in times of sanctions and countersanctions: some redistributive implications]. J New Econ Assoc 3(55):234–238
Gimpelson V, Kapeliushnikov R (2019) Age and education in the Russian labour market. In: Becker T, Oxenstierna S (eds) The Russian Economy under Putin. Routledge, London and New York, pp 121–148
Gimpelson VE, Zudina AA, Kapeliushnikov RI (2020) Некогнитивные компоненты человеческого капитала: что говорят российские данные [Non-cognitive components of human capital: evidence from Russian data]. Vopr Ekon 11:5–31
Goldin C, Katz LF (2008) The race between education and technology. The Belknap Press of Harvard University Press, Cambridge, MA, and London

Golts GA (2002) Культура и экономика России за три века, XVIII-XX вв. Т. 1. Менталитет, транспорт, информация (прошлое, настоящее, будущее) [Culture and economy of Russia for three centuries, 18th–19th centuries. Vol. 1. Mentality, transport, information (past, present, future)]. Сибирский хронограф [Siberian Chronograph], Novosibirsk

Gregory P (1982) Russian national income, 1885–1913. Cambridge University Press, London

Gregory P, Stuart R (1994) Soviet and post-soviet economic structure and performance, 5th edn. HarperCollins, New York

Grennes T, Caner M, Koehler-Geib F (2013) Finding the tipping point—When sovereign debt turns bad. World Bank, Policy Research Working Paper

Grimalda G, Barlow D, Meschi E (2010) Varieties of capitalisms and varieties of performances: accounting for inequality in post-Soviet Union transition economies. Int Rev Appl Econ 24(3):379–403

Grinin L, Korotayev A (2015) Great divergence and great convergence: a global perspective. Springer Cham, Heidelberg

Guo Y, Zhang Z, van Leeuwen B, Xu Y (2019) A view of the occupational structure in Imperial and Republican China (1640–1952). Aust Econ Hist Rev 59(2):134–158

Harrison M (1998) The economics of World War II: an overview. In: Harrison M (ed) The economics of World War II: six great powers in international comparison. Cambridge University Press, Cambridge, UK, pp 1–42

Heckman JJ (2003) China's investment in human capital. Econ Dev Cult Change 51(4):795–804. https://doi.org/10.1086/378050

Hipp C, Grupp H (2005) Innovation in the service sector: the demand for service-specific innovation measurement concepts and typologies. Res Policy 34:517–535

IMF (Era Dabla-Norris, Giang Ho, and Annette Kyobe) (2013) Reforms and distance to frontier. IMF. https://www.imf.org/external/pubs/ft/sdn/2013/sdn1308tn.pdf

Izriadnova OI (2024) Динамика и структура ВВП и инвестиций [Dynamics and structure of GDP and investments]. In: Kudrin AL, Mau VA, Radygin AD, Sinelnikov-Murylev SG (eds) Российская экономика в 2023 году. Тенденции и перспективы [Russian economy in 2023. Trends and outlooks]. Issue 45. Gaidar Institute, Moscow, pp 145–163. https://www.iep.ru/files/text/trends/2023/book.pdf

Kapeliushnikov RI (2001) Российский рынок труда: адаптация без реструктуризации [Russian labour market: adjustment without restructuring]. HSE Publishing House, Moscow

Kapeliushnikov RI (2021) Otdacha ot obrazovaniia v Rossii: nizhe nekuda? [Returns to education in Russia: nowhere below?]. Vopr Ekon 8:37–68

Kapeliushnikov RI (2023) The Russian labour market: long-term trends and short-term fluctuations. Russian Economic Journal 9(3):245–270

Kapeliushnikov RI (2024) Экспансия вакансий на российском рынке труда: динамика, структура, триггеры [Expansion of vacant jobs in the Russian labour market: dynamics, composition, triggers]. Vopr Ekon 7:81–111

Kapeliushnikov RI, Luk'ianova AL (2010) Transformatsiia chelovecheskogo kapitala v rossiiskom obshchestve (na baze "Rossiiskogo monitoringa ekonomicheskogo polozheniia i zdorov'ia naseleniia") [Transformation of human capital in Russian society (based on the Russian Longitudinal Monitoring Survey)]. Fond "Liberal'naia missiia", Moscow

Karavai AV (2023) Факторы качества общего человеческого капитала профессионалов: результаты регрессионного анализа [Factors of quality of general human capital of the professionals: findings based on regression analysis]. In: Tikhonova NE, Latov YV (eds) Человеческий капитал российских профессионалов: состояние, динамика, факторы [Human capital of Russian professionals: state, dynamics, factors]. Federal Centre of Theoretical and Applied Sociology, Russian Academy of Sciences, Moscow, pp 149–173. https://doi.org/10.19181/monogr.978-5-89697-420-8.2023

Kartseva MA, Florinskaya YF (2025) New Emigrants and the Russian Labor Market: An Empirical Analysis. Stud Russ Econ Dev 36(4):525–535

Katz LF, Murphy KM (1992) Changes in relative wages 1963–1987: supply and demand factors. Q J Econ 107(1):35–78

Kontorovich V (2019) Reluctant cold warriors: economists and national security. Oxford University Press, New York

Kromann L, Malchow-Møller N, Skaksen JR, Sørensen A (2020) Automation and productivity: a cross-country, cross-industry comparison. Ind Corp Chang 29(2):265–287

Kuboniwa M, Shida Y, Tabata S (2019) Gross domestic products. In: Kuboniwa M et al (eds) Russian economic development over three centuries: new data and inferences. Palgrave Macmillan, Singapore, pp 335–419

Kuijs L, Wang T (2005) China's pattern of growth: moving to sustainability and reducing inequality. World Bank Policy Research Working Paper 3767. https://doi.org/10.1596/1813-9450-3767

Kuznets S (1955) Economic growth and income inequality. Am Econ Rev 45(1):1–28

Latov YV (2023) Вектор эволюции человеческого капитала профессионалов и перспективы международной конкурентоспособности России [Vector of human capital evolution of professionals and prospects for Russia's international competitiveness]. In: Tikhonova NE, Latov YV (eds) Человеческий капитал российских профессионалов: состояние, динамика, факторы [Human capital of Russian professionals: state, dynamics, factors]. Federal Centre of Theoretical and Applied Sociology, Russian Academy of Sciences, Moscow, pp 407–439. https://doi.org/10.19181/monogr.978-5-89697-420-8.2023

Latova NV, Latov YV (2020) Опоздавшие к третьей образовательной революции (Компаративистский анализ человеческого капитала российских специалистов-профессионалов) [Latecomers to the third educational revolution (Comparative analysis of the human capital of Russian professional specialists)]. J Institut Stud 12(2):67–85

Lee J-W (2016) The Republic of Korea's economic growth and catch-up: implications for the People's Republic of China. ADBI Working Paper 571. Asian Development Bank Institute, Tokyo

Levitt T (1972) Production-line approach to service. Harv Bus Rev 50:41–52

Li H, Loyalka P, Rozelle S, Wu B (2017) Human capital and China's future growth. J Econ Perspect 31(1):25–48. http://www.jstor.org/stable/44133949

Lin JY (2017, December 1) The economics of China's new era. Project Syndicate. Retrieved from https://www.project-syndicate.org/onpoint/the-economics-of-china-s-new-era-by-justin-yifu-lin-2017-12

Lombardi M, Mohanty M, Shim I (2017) The real effects of household debt in the short and long run. BIS Working Papers No 607

Lopez R, Thomas V, Wang Y (1999) Addressing the education puzzle: the distribution of education and economic reform. The World Bank

Masuda J (1981) The information society as post-industrial society. World Future Society, Bethesda, MD

Mbaye S, Moreno-Badia M, Chae K (2018) Global debt database: methodology and sources. IMF Working Paper, International Monetary Fund, Washington, DC. https://www.imf.org/external/datamapper/datasets/GDD

Mitchell BR (1988) British historical statistics. Cambridge University Press, Cambridge

MVT (Ministry of Foreign Trade of the USSR) (1967) Внешняя торговля СССР… Статистический сборник/обзор [Foreign trade of the USSR... Statistical abstract]. Vneshtorgizdat, Moscow

MVT (Ministry of Foreign Trade of the USSR) (1989) Внешняя торговля СССР… Статистический сборник/обзор [Foreign trade of the USSR... Statistical abstract]. Vneshtorgizdat, Moscow

Nove A (1982) An economic history of the USSR. Penguin Books, Harmondsworth, NY

OECD (2018) Long-term baseline projections, No. 103. OECD Economic Outlook: Statistics and Projections (database). https://doi.org/10.1787/68465614-en

Ostry J, Prati A, Spilimbergo A (2009) Structural reforms and economic performance in advanced and developing countries. International Monetary Fund, Washington

Philips RCM, Calabrese M, Keenan R, Van Leeuwen B (2022) The regional occupational structure in interwar England and Wales. Hist Methods J Quant Interdiscip Hist 55(2):78–97. https://doi.org/10.1080/01615440.2022.2027303

Popov V, Konchakov R, Didenko DV (2024) Human capital in the regions of the russian empire and inequality in land distribution at the turn of the 20th century. SSRN, https://ssrn.com/abstract=4694578 or https://doi.org/10.2139/ssrn.4694578

Prebisch R (1950) The economic development of Latin America and its principal problems. United Nations Department for Economic Affairs, Lake Success, NY

Pritchett L, Summers LH (2014) Asiaphoria meets regression to the mean. NBER Working Paper 20573

Rodrik D (2013) The past, present, and future of economic growth. Working Paper 1. Uttar Pradesh: Global Citizens Foundation. https://drodrik.scholar.harvard.edu/files/dani-rodrik/files/gcf_rodrik-working-paper-1_-6-24-13.pdf

Rodrik D (2016) Premature Deindustrialization. J Econ Growth 21(1):1–33. https://doi.org/10.1007/s10887-015-9122-3

Sachs JD, Warner AM (1995) Economic convergence and economic policies. NBER Working Papers 5039. National Bureau of Economic Research, Inc

SIPRI (2024) Military expenditure database. Stockholm International Peace Research Institute. https://www.sipri.org/databases/milex

Slepenkova IM (2022) Loss of Human Capital Caused by Emigration. Stud Russ Econ Dev 33(4):432–439. https://doi.org/10.1134/S1075700722040104

Standard and Poor (2021) Global debt leverage: can China escape its corporate debt trap? Accessed from: https://www.spglobal.com/_assets/documents/ratings/research/100620188.pdf

Steinberg D (1990) The Soviet economy, 1970–1990: a statistical analysis. International Trade Press, San Francisco

Strumilin SG (1966) Очерки экономической истории России и СССР [Essays on economic history of Russia and the USSR]. Наука [The Science], Moscow

Strumilin SG (1982) Проблемы экономики труда [Issues of labour economics]. Наука [The Science], Moscow

Su A, Regnière M-H, Su Z (2013) "Made with the World" vs. "Made for the World": what would be the future of "Made in China" products? Transnatl Corp Rev 5(2):1–15

Tikhonova NE, Karavai AV (2023) Состояние и динамика качества человеческого капитала российских профессионалов в 2010–2020-х гг. [State and dynamics of the quality of human capital of Russian professionals in 2010–2020s]. In: Tikhonova NE, Latov YV (eds) Человеческий капитал российских профессионалов: состояние, динамика, факторы [Human capital of Russian professionals: state, dynamics, factors]. Federal Centre of Theoretical and Applied Sociology, Russian Academy of Sciences, Moscow, pp 116–148. https://doi.org/10.19181/monogr.978-5-89697-420-8.2023

UNDP (2024) United Nations Development Programme. Human development report 2023–24: breaking the gridlock: reimagining cooperation in a polarized world. Data Centre. https://hdr.undp.org/data-center

United Nations (2020) National Accounts - Analysis of Main Aggregates (AMA). https://unstats.un.org/unsd/snaama/

Uziakova ES, Shirov AA (2024) Employment and labor productivity in Russia: analysis and forecast. Stud Russ Econ Dev 35(4):467–478. https://doi.org/10.1134/S1075700724700011

Van Leeuwen B, Földvári P (2008) How much human capital does Eastern Europe have? Measurement methods and results. Postcommunist Econ 20(2):189–201

Van Leeuwen B, Li J, Foldvari P (2017) Human capital in Republican and New China: regional and long-term trends. Econ Hist Dev Reg 32(1):1–36. https://doi.org/10.1080/20780389.2016.1261629

Van Leeuwen B, Li J (2021) Inequality in educational achievement. In: How was life? Volume II: new perspectives on well-being and global inequality since 1820. OECD Publishing. https://doi.org/10.1787/d20a2c62-en

Van Leeuwen B, Van Zanden JL (2019) China as a nation. In: Brakman S, van Marrewijk C, Morgan PJ, Salike N (eds) China in the local and global economy: history, geography, politics and sustainability. Routledge

Van Leeuwen B, Bosma U, Wang M (2023) Industrial revolutions in a globalizing world, 1760–present. In: Bianchi P, Labory S, Tomlinson PR (eds) Handbook of industrial development. Edward Elgar Publishing, pp 18–36

Van Zanden JL (1995) Tracing the beginning of the Kuznets curve: Western Europe during the early modern period. Econ Hist Rev 48(4):643–664

Vanhanen T (2003) Democratization and power resources 1850–2000 [dataset], Version 1.0 (2003-03-10). Finnish Social Science Data Archive [Distributor]. https://urn.fi/urn:nbn:fi:fsd:T-FSD1216

Ventura J, Voth H-J (2015) Debt into growth: how sovereign debt accelerated the First Industrial Revolution (NBER Working Paper No. 21280). National Bureau of Economic Research. https://doi.org/10.3386/w21280

Wallerstein I (2004) World-systems analysis: an introduction. Duke University Press, Durham, NC

Wallerstein I (2011) The modern world-system. Vol. I. Capitalist agriculture and the origins of the European world-economy in the sixteenth century (Original work published 1974). University of California Press, Berkeley

Wang M, van Leeuwen B, Li J (2020) Education in China, ca. 1840–present. (The quantitative economic history of China; Vol. 17/4). Brill Academic Publishers. https://doi.org/10.1163/9789004442252

Wang M, Van Leeuwen B (2021) Fenjiashu: economic development in the Chinese countryside based on household division inventories, ca. 1750–1910. Aust Econ Hist Rev 61(3):252–272

Williamson JG (1985) Did British capitalism breed inequality? Allen & Unwin Inc, Winchester, MA

Williamson JG (1997) Globalization and Inequality, Past and Present. World Bank Res Obs 12(2):117–135

Williamson JG, Lindert PH (1980) American inequality: a macroeconomic history. Academic Press Inc, New York

World Bank (1993) The East Asian miracle: economic growth and public policy. Oxford University Press. http://documents1.worldbank.org/curated/en/975081468244550798/pdf/multi-page.pdf

World Bank (2021) The human capital index 2020 update: human capital in the time of COVID-19. https://documents1.worldbank.org/curated/en/456901600111156873/pdf/The-Human-Capital-Index-2020-Update-Human-Capital-in-the-Time-of-COVID-19.pdf

Zubarevich NV (2024) Регионы России в конце 2023 г.: удалось ли преодолеть кризисный спад? [Regions of Russia at the end of 2023: have they managed to overcome the crisis recession?]. Voprosy teoreticheskoy ekonomiki 1:34–47. https://doi.org/10.52342/2587-7666VTE_2024_1_34_47

Chapter 10
Well-Being Beyond GDP

Abstract This chapter explores the concept of well-being beyond traditional economic metrics such as gross domestic product (GDP), emphasizing the multidimensional aspects of human development, including material, immaterial, and perception-based indicators. It critically examines the evolution and application of composite indices such as the Human Development Index (HDI) and its historical variations, such as the inequality-adjusted HDI and Historical Index of Human Development (HIHD). Using long-term data from various regions, the chapter illustrates the uneven global trajectories of well-being, highlighting disparities across geographical and socio-political contexts.

Material well-being analysed, for example, through anthropometric measures and housing quality reveals the complex interplay between economic growth, inequality, and societal conditions, particularly during industrial transitions. Immaterial dimensions, such as education and health, are framed within human development theories, showcasing their role in enhancing quality of life over time. This chapter also interrogates the dynamics of income and spatial inequality, linking these to broader socio-economic transformations and policy interventions. Through innovative approaches, including the use of historical and perception-based data, the analysis expands the discourse on well-being to incorporate social factors such as corruption, urbanization, and environmental quality.

10.1 Introduction

Since the 1980s, both political discourse and academic research have increasingly recognized that traditional income indicators, such as GDP, fail to fully capture the complexities of well-being, inequality, and what might be termed the broader "human experience". Well-being encompasses far more than economic output; it

B. Van Leeuwen et al., *Innovation and Economic Development in Eurasia, 500 BCE-Present*, Frontiers in Economic History,
https://doi.org/10.1007/978-3-031-97043-6_10

reflects diverse factors such as education, health, social equity, and environmental quality.

One of the main indicators of well-being, developed in the United Nations Development Programme (UNDP), is the Human Development Index (HDI). But other indicators have also emerged, such as Bhutan's adoption of Gross Domestic Happiness in 2008–2011, with a new focus on immaterial dimensions of well-being, including education and health. This shift in approaching the idea of well-being as "beyond GDP" has been further expanded by projects such as the OECD's "How Was Life?" reports, which emphasize how various indicators—including human capital, inequality, and life expectancy—contribute to societal well-being (Rijpma 2014). These reports have highlighted the value of multidimensional frameworks in painting a more holistic picture of human progress and quality of life. However, capturing such dimensions becomes more challenging when applied to long-term historical analysis.

Therefore, for long-run studies, alternative measures have emerged that provide valuable insights. Anthropometric indicators, such as average height and health metrics, offer indirect proxies for historical well-being. Happiness indices, derived from retrospective surveys or archival materials, can also shed light on subjective well-being in past societies. Additionally, perception-based measures, such as those tracking perceived levels of corruption or pollution, serve as valuable complements. These indices not only correlate with GDP but also reflect social and environmental dynamics that are central to the lived experiences of individuals and communities. Ultimately, they highlight the need for nuanced approaches to capturing the multi-dimensional nature of human development. They underline that a society's progress cannot be fully measured by economic performance alone but must consider the broader context of human satisfaction, equality, and sustainability over time.

In this chapter, we start with composite well-being indicators, especially the Human Development Index (HDI). In Sects. 10.3 and 10.4, we deal with material and immaterial indicates of well-being, respectively. Next, we deal with perception-based indicators (such as corruption and pollution) in Sect. 10.5 and happiness in Sect. 10.6. We end with a brief conclusion.

10.2 Composite Well-Being: Human Development Index (HDI)

As pointed out in Sect. 10.1, development can be interpreted in various ways, being material, immaterial, or perception-based, for example. Rather than having to focus on one index, several indicators can be combined to create a composite indicator, the most common of which is the HDI.[1]

[1] Besides the HDI, various other composite series of well-being exist. For example, the OECD report "How Was Life", volumes I and II, find increase in well-being from about 1820 onwards,

To quantify what might otherwise seem like a highly subjective and non-standardizable concept, the capability approach (Sen 1985; Haq 1995) offers a useful framework focused on enhancement of individuals' choices to achieve a better quality of life. Within this paradigm, various economic resources are regarded as independent values for final consumption rather than merely as factors of production (like in the human capital paradigm). The resulting HDI was introduced in the late 1980s, and since 1990, has been annually published in the Human Development Reports within the framework of the UNDP.[2] It takes into account income, education (literacy rate or average years of schooling), and life expectancy (proxies for health) at birth as an average, with equal weights for all of the three components. The HDI thus captures both material and, what is more important, immaterial well-being, irrespective of its subjective perceptions. Even though the immaterial components are already a part of GDP (on the consumption side, in line with the human development concept), the idea has been to enhance their significance.

The HDI can be augmented in various ways. Van Zanden et al. (2021) combined income, longevity, and education in a version of the HDI running from about 1700 to present. They find a rise in well-being since the eighteenth century, but this was unequally distributed initially, occurring in Western Europe and its offshoots. This brings up two issues. First, Europe shows signs of growth paradox before 1900; that is, the growth per capita GDP did not necessarily lead to a growth in longevity and education. Second, the HDI rise in the Western offshoots occurred before the start of industrialization, suggesting other factors played a role too.

The picture for the developing low-income world is mixed, with rises in HDI in Latin America (especially in Argentina, Venezuela, and Cuba), but not in Asia (especially in China and India), from around 1900 causing increased regional inequality. In absolute terms, this gap continued into the twentieth century, but a relative catch-up of the periphery, mainly because of education, occurred between 1913 and 1970 (see Sect. 9.3). This leaves inequality at present even bigger than in 1900, with East Asia, Latin America, the Caribbean, Southeast Asia, and South Asia and North Africa catching up, and Central and Eastern Europe and Sub-Saharan Africa falling behind. Thus, Van Zanden et al. arrived at the historical inequality-adjusted HDI (Table 10.1). They followed the UNDP in presuming that higher inequality is considered to lower overall well-being. Inequality is calculated using the Atkinson index, in which the level of aversion to inequality is set. This can be interpreted as the percentage of well-being a person is willing to give up in order to achieve equality.

Prados de la Escosura (2015) also developed a data set with an adjustment of the HDI for the purposes of historical research running from 1870 to 2007 (HIHD). The adjustment was aimed at giving more weight to immaterial components. The non-income variables were transformed non-linearly in order to allow for two main

with the exception of sub-Saharan Africa (Rijpma 2014, 2021). Even though non-GDP aspects of well-being improved strongly, there was still considerable difference in GDP per capita around 1970. This is pretty much similar to HDI.

[2] http://hdr.undp.org/en/reports

Table 10.1 Inequality-adjusted HDI for selected countries, 1700–1930

	England	The Netherlands	Italy	Poland	Russia	China
1700	0.383	0.357	0.206	0.180		0.181
1800	0.400	0.412	0.231	0.165	0.121	0.142
1850	0.426	0.382	0.229	1.830	0.147	0.159
1900	0.579	0.561	0.396	0.320	0.171	0.195
1930	0.685	0.675	0.525	0.360	0.260	0.316

Source: Van Zanden et al. (2021)

facts: that increases of the same absolute size represent greater achievements the higher the level at which they take place, and that quality improvements are associated with increases in quantity. The HIHD relied on the UNDP methodology from 1990 to 2010; that is, the education component was based on literacy, not on average years of schooling.

As follows from the estimates in Prados de la Escosura (2015), human development in the Central Eurasia has been quite remarkable if an international perspective is taken. The late Russian Empire and the USSR more or less succeeded in catching-up with the core OECD countries.[3] Prados de la Escosura's estimates suggest there was significant catch up in human development in the period before 1900 and in the period 1913–1950, but from the 1970s, the Soviet and Russian economy started to fall behind.

Post-Soviet Russia lagged behind these OECD countries not only during the deep recession of the 1990s, associated with the systemic transformation to an open market economy, but also during the 2000s. It then succeeded only in income convergence resulting from inflows of incomes originated from natural resource extracting industries, but not from outperforming human capital development (Didenko 2020, 68–69).

As it follows from Table 10.2, the most successful periods for education were the 1880s–1890s, 1920s–1930s, and 1950s–1960s, while the most successful outcomes in healthcare were achieved in the 1910s–1920s and the 1940s.[4] In light of external challenges, the late Russian Empire and the USSR witnessed a fast growth by catching up to Europe in average years of education but probably not in cost- or income-based human capital (Didenko et al. 2013, 131). By the mid-1960s the USSR had managed to attain roughly First World level of social indicators, notably education and health (Ellman 2004, 849). However, this was followed by their relative decline, especially as regard healthcare (since the 1950s) and education (since the 1970s), in other words, long before the collapse of the Soviet Union.

[3] Australia, Austria, Belgium, Canada, Denmark, Finland, France, Germany, Greece, Ireland, Italy, Japan, Netherlands, New Zealand, Norway, Portugal, Spain, Sweden, Switzerland, UK, and US.

[4] It is somewhat surprising as these were the periods associated with severe demographic losses caused by large-scale wars within these periods, and we are uncertain as how accurately statistics were gathered to take account of the deaths caused by warfare (not only on battlefields but also from starvation and epidemic diseases) as well as deaths from natural causes.

Table 10.2 Rate of change of the alternative estimates of HDI in Russia at the start of modern growth (% average per year), 1870–1913

	HDI		Income		Education		Life expectancy	
Period	PdlE	M	PdlE	M	PdlE	M	PdlE	M
1871–1880	**0.9**	**0.7**	1.9	0.1	1.1	1.5	−0.3	2.2
1881–1890	**2.1**	**1.4**	3.7	0.7	1.2	2.5	1.3	2.8
1891–1900	**2.7**	**1.5**	4.7	0.7	1.8	2.4	2.0	2.5
1901–1913	**1.0**	**2.1**	1.9	0.9	0.6	3.1	0.7	4.5
1871–1913	**1.6**	**1.4**	2.9	0.4	1.1	2.6	0.9	3.9

Note: The education index for Russia in Prados de la Escosura (2015) was based on the literacy rate measure from Mironov (1991). The estimates of Russia's HDI by Mironov (2012) utilized the latest method adopted by the UNDP, which is based on average years of schooling
Source: *PdlE*—Prados de la Escosura (2015); M—Mironov (2012)

Regarding the periods covered both in Prados de la Escosura (2015) and Mironov (2012), we should pay attention to the fact that the estimates by the former for the 1890s are more optimistic than those by the latter. On the contrary, for the short period of 1900–1913, improvements in education, and especially in life expectancy, are estimated more significantly by Mironov than in income, while Prados de la Escosura has the opposite. For the earlier period of 1871–1880, relative life expectancy rate of change is estimated as negative by Prados de la Escosura (2015), but very positive in Mironov (2012). Our evidence (Fig. 4.8) suggests it was basically stable then in absolute terms.

10.3 Material Components of Well-Being: Standards of Living

10.3.1 Anthropometric Measures: The Importance of Being Tall

Besides composite indices, there are indices of material well-being such as anthropometric data. Indeed, indices such as stature or relative brain size have emerged as a compelling proxy for understanding nutritional and health trends, particularly in eras and regions where conventional economic metrics are unavailable or unreliable.[5] The study of human height could reveal, for example, the long-term interplay of economic growth and inequality, and eventually the state of societal, basically material, well-being.

[5] The use of height as a measure of well-being is not universally accepted among scholars and remains a subject of debate. For instance, Kron (2014) argues that the Roman world achieved a relatively high standard of well-being, with average heights not being surpassed until the eighteenth century. In contrast, others, such as Frier (2001), suggest that well-being during the Roman period was marked by already low levels, which may have further declined over time.

As seen in the previous chapters, from stagnation to systemic transformation, the historical trajectories of human development have been neither linear nor universally positive. As observed in Europe and Asia, periods of rapid industrialization often entailed physical deprivation and rising inequality, challenging the simplistic association of economic growth with societal progress. The paradox of growth without proportional gains in well-being underscores the necessity of integrating socio-economic, political, and environmental lenses into historical analysis. Key studies, including those examining Russia's industrialization and the Chinese Great Leap Forward, highlight, for example, the disjunctions between economic productivity and human welfare during systemic transitions. In the same way, historical records of people's perceptions (e.g. through the analysis of newspaper discourse) demonstrate that pollution, both visible and invisible, emerged as a significant by-product of economic transformation, with its societal impact garnering increasing attention over time. The rise of environmental awareness in the twentieth century, as reflected in policy discourse and public sentiment, marks an important shift in how societies negotiate the trade-offs of modernization.

Anthropometric indicators such as brain size and height can provide insights into the evolution of human societies and their increasingly organized structures and well-being. DeSilva et al. (2021), for example, traced the long-term trajectory of human brain size, documenting its significant expansion over millions of years, a trend largely attributed to milestones such as the emergence of hominids and advancements in tool use (see Table 10.3). However, they attribute a slight decrease in brain size over the past 3000 years to an evolutionary shift driven by increasingly complex and efficient social systems. This reduction in brain size can reflect indeed the externalization of individual cognitive tasks to collective social organization.[6] As societies developed more intricate forms of cooperation, division of labour, and knowledge sharing, the evolutionary pressure on individual brain capacity

Table 10.3 Brain size of hominids

Name	Brain size (cm^3)
Homo habilis	550–687
Homo ergaster	700–900
Homo erectus	600–1250
Homo heidelbergensis	1100–1400
Homo neanderthalensis	1200–1750
Homo sapiens (before ~3000 years ago)	~1500
Homo sapiens (after ~3000 years ago)	~1350
Homo floresiensis	417

Source: Elaboration of the authors based on data retrieved from https://en.wikipedia.org/wiki/Brain_size and DeSilva et al. (2021)

[6] However, it should be considered that there is no conclusive evidence of a causal correlation between brain size and intelligence (see Nisbett et al. 2012).

diminished. This shift aligns with broader evidence that social structures—facilitating shared problem-solving and decision-making—play a critical role in shaping human development.

For subsequent periods of human history, after brain size stabilized, alternative proxies such as height (Baten and Kopke 2005) offer valuable insights into assessing human well-being, particularly within the Eurasian bloc. In Europe, historical data reveal a prolonged period of stagnation in average height from 1 CE to 1800, followed by a marked decline that persisted until around 1900. Similarly, in China, evidence indicates a comparable pattern of stagnation or decline from 1800 to 1890, with only modest improvements emerging in the decades that followed (Baten et al. 2010).

Table 10.4 presents the development of average height in China, Russia, and the broad area that was under the Roman Empire from 100 BCE to 1900 CE, offering a glimpse into long-term trends in physical well-being. In China, the average height of men was relatively high in 0 CE, with "all China" averaging 169.5 cm and regional figures such as 165.3 cm for the Yellow River and 161 cm for the Yangtze area. Women's heights were slightly lower, with the Yellow River region showing 151 cm for women in 100 BCE and increasing to 159.2 cm in 0 CE (see Table 3.1). However, after 0 CE, there appears to be a gradual decline or stagnation in height across the regions. By 1150 CE, the "all China" average dropped to 164.5 cm for men and 156.2 cm for women, suggesting a deterioration in nutrition or living conditions during the medieval period. Modest recoveries are seen in the Yellow River region, where male heights rose to 165.3 cm in 1750 and 165.7 cm in 1800.

In contrast, data from the broader area once unified under the Roman Empire reveal differences between this macro-region and, for example, Italy. Men in the Roman Empire averaged 167 cm in 100 BCE, comparable with heights in the Yellow River region of China at that time. However, the Roman data show a decline in

Table 10.4 Male stature in selected countries, *c*. 1 ce–1940

Year	China	Russia	Italy	UK
−100	167			
0	169.5		167	
800	167			
1050				
1150	164.5			
1750		163.0	166.5	169.8
1800	165.7	159.8	164.5	169.7
1850	166.2	163.4	162.9	165.6
1900	164.0	169.2	165.6	169.4
1940	167.4	169.0	169.3	174.9

Sources: This book, Chap. 3; Baten et al. (2010), Peng (2015), Sun and Hong (2015), and Zhou (2017); https://clio-infra.eu/Indicators/Height.html; Baten and Blum (2012); Koepke and Baten (2005); https://www.quora.com/How-tall-were-ancient-Romans-on-average-How-does-this-compare-to-the-average-height-of-modern-Italians-Was-there-much-variation-in-height-between-different-regions-of-Italy-during-that-time-period-or-were-people average male height to 150 cm in Italy by 1150 CE, indicating worsening health or living conditions in the post-Roman period. By 1900, Italian male heights recovered significantly to about 169 cm, surpassing the Chinese average of 163.3 cm for "all China".

We can therefore observe several long-term trends. First, stagnation or decline in average heights aligns with periods of economic or political instability, such as during the post-Roman period and medieval China. Second, the recovery of heights in the modern era, particularly in Italy, reflects improvements in nutrition, health, and living standards following industrialization. By comparison, China's heights remained relatively stagnant through 1900, suggesting that improvements in well-being were slower to materialize.

In China, as shown in Table 10.4, the average height remained relatively stable from the eighteenth to the nineteenth century, fluctuating slightly between 164 cm and 166 cm. However, these figures were to become lower than those observed in European nations such as Italy and the Netherlands, which saw gradual increases in average height during the same period. The Netherlands demonstrated one of the most remarkable increases in height, from 169.5 cm in 1760 to 177.5 cm by 1940, highlighting advancements in agricultural productivity, dietary diversity, and public health. In contrast, Japan remained significantly shorter during the nineteenth and early twentieth centuries. For example, Japanese males averaged 157.8 cm in the late nineteenth century, a figure that only modestly improved to 162.6 cm by 1940. Interestingly, the US consistently maintained one of the highest average heights, starting at 172.1 cm in 1730 and rising to 176.1 cm by 1940. This reflects the relative abundance of food, particularly protein-rich diets, as well as the early adoption of public health measures. The UK also showed gradual gains, with heights increasing from 165.5 cm in 1730 to 174.9 cm by 1940, though it lagged slightly behind the US and the Netherlands.

Moving to Central Eurasia, Fig. 10.1 compares the dynamics of height—based on Mironov's dataset, Komlos and Cinirella (2005), and other sources from Clio Infra—with GDP per capita estimates from various sources for the available periods. Over the twentieth and early twenty-first centuries, when data reliability improves, the trends of height and GDP per capita align closely, reflecting the interconnected nature of economic growth and physical well-being.

According to the data shown in Fig. 10.1, per capita food consumption worsened during the eighteenth century, improved in the first half of the nineteenth century, decreased in the mid-nineteenth century, and grew from the late 1860s to the outbreak of the First World War in 1914.[7] The wars (including the Civil War caused by the Russian Revolution), as well as Soviet industrialization, determined the downside correction of the heights. What is surprising is that the Second World War (the disastrous Great Patriotic War for Russia/USSR) left no trace on these series tracks, especially on the heights measure that captures poor food consumption of the population more directly than GDP, which also takes into account government

[7] In Mironov (2012) there is evidence on corrections in the 1890s.

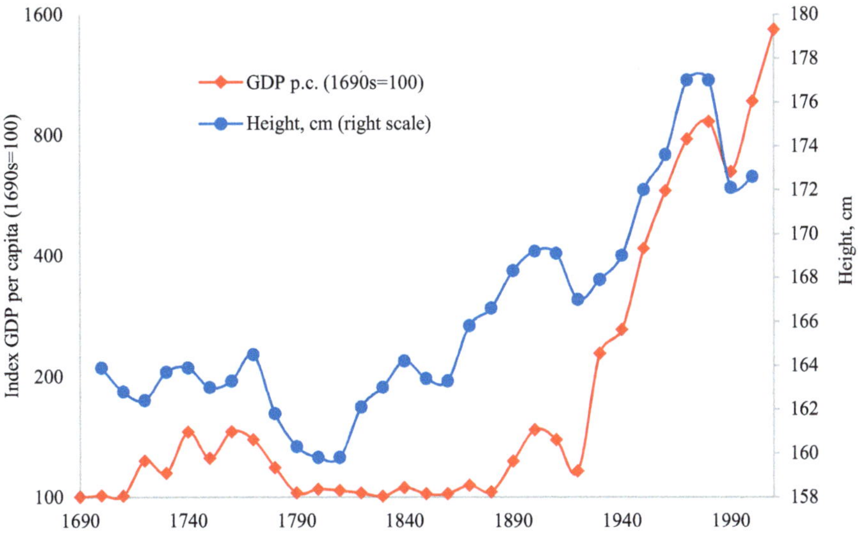

Fig. 10.1 Stature and GDP per capita in Russia/FSU, 1690–2018. *Source:* GDP p.c. index is calculated based on: 1690s–1880s: Broadberry and Korchmina (2024); 1890s–1920s: Maddison Project Database (2020); 1930s–1940s: Didenko et al. (2013); 1950s–2010s: Bolt and Van Zanden (2020); Height is borrowed from Clio Infra (Baten and Blum 2015)

consumption. Just a modest gain in height was recorded in the 1940s instead of its expected decline.[8] Furthermore, nutrition of the broad population worsened during the transitional downturn in the 1990s, leaving the evidence of depressed heights.

It is important to note that Mironov (2012) analysed anthropometric differences depending on education and qualifications, consistent with both the theory of human capital and the concept of human development. He estimated that the average height of the nobility experienced much less of a downturn over the eighteenth century than that of the peasants and lower urban estates. People with literacy skills tended to be 1.5 cm taller in 1761–1800 and 2.5 cm taller in 1901–1920. Hence, the height premium for literacy increased over time. The same is partially (because of a different time base) true for the workers (skilled versus unskilled): an increase is reported from 0.7 cm in 1801–1860 to 1.8 cm. in 1861–1900. However, the opposite is true for the difference between white-collar workers and peasants (1.7 cm in 1751–1800 and 1.0 cm in 1861–1900).[9]

---

[8] Most likely due to a sampling effect (the most suffered persons fell out of the observations), enhanced by technical factor (decadal estimation instead of annual), and basically by rapid recovery of the population's nutrition after the war in the second half of the 1940s.

[9] The most relevant criticism by B.N. Mironov of the data from other researchers who recognized the relevance of using such kind of data was directed to the timing of certain changes in well-being (anthropometric characteristics reveal information about calories received not so much in a year after a person's birth as in his or her adolescence), the reliability of the aggregated data (presented in intervals that changed over time and turned out not to be comparable), the distribution of sample

Looking at the start of the twentieth century (as later height data are no longer useful as proxy for health and stature), it is suggested that unfavourable political and socio-economic events influenced the pace of body height increase in men but did not lead to the decrease. This suggestion was drawn by Lebedeva et al. (2020) from a comparison of height changes in Russia with major Western countries (France, Germany, the Netherlands, the UK, the US), based on the evidence from the Clio Infra data set (Baten and Blum 2015).

Looking at the first industrial revolution, Komlos (1998) found that human heights decreased in times of rapid expansion of industrial output per capita in the first half of the nineteenth century in England and the US, thus suggesting physical deprivation and declining per capita income. If we follow Williamson (2000) in arguing that labour income divided by GDP per capita reflects an index of equality, a decline in heights implies a decline of this index, which, in turn, suggests rising inequality during the first industrial revolution.[10]

Similar observations are made for later industrializers. For example, Baten et al. (2010) found that in China the rising incomes in the late nineteenth century were also accompanied by declining stature. For countries that have experienced stagnation or even deindustrialization, no such rises in inequality are apparent. For example, small increases/stagnation in stature around the turn of the twentieth century were found for India (Brennan et al. 1994; Guntupali and Baten 2006), combined with declining GDP per capita (Broadberry et al. 2015), thus implying declining inequality.

Similar trends of rising inequality are also found for periods of industrialization in the twentieth and twenty-first centuries. An obvious example is forced industrialization in the 1920s–1930s in the USSR (Fig. 10.1), as well as the Chinese forced industrialization where we find, in a sample for Inner Mongolia (Jining city), declining human heights from the Great Leap Forward (1958–1962) onwards (Inner Mongolia 1977–1992).

The above-mentioned increases in inequality during the initial phases of industrialization were thus quite common. Yet this is a long historic process within which social upset may occur. Therefore, in many countries, it became common practice for the government to make significant efforts to diminish the income gap in the middle or late stage of industrialization.

data on recruited conscripts to the general population (anthropometric data on this group of population, like others, are subject to bias that lacked proper discussion), as well as the impact of other factors besides nutrition that influenced heights (Nefedov and Ellman 2016; Wheatcroft 1999). Yet, comparing Russia in Figure 10.1 and Table 10.4, the latter correcting biases by reporting adult height by year of birth and conscription bias by removing height and age truncation in military data, we find small differences.

[10] A decline in heights could thus take place both under increasing and decreasing mean per capita income. In the former case, there is evidence that income of the majority of the population decreased; that is, income inequality was on the rise.

10.3.2 Housing

Housing has long been recognized as a cornerstone of material well-being, playing a critical role in shaping individuals' quality of life and economic opportunities (see also Eichholtz et al. 2023). The OECD (2011) highlights housing as a vital component of well-being, emphasizing the detrimental effects of poor housing quality, which include risks associated with sub-standard materials, overcrowding, and limited access to basic sanitation and functional utilities. Beyond its impact on individual health and safety, housing intersects with broader socio-economic issues, such as wealth inequality, social mobility, and urban development.

In the context of contemporary debates, housing has emerged as a central focus in addressing inequalities within OECD economies. Its dual nature as both a basic human need and a wealth-generating asset has profound implications for income distribution and social equity. This dual role often results in housing being a site of tension between its social function as a place to live and its economic role as an object of speculation and investment. The housing crisis, characterized by soaring rents, limited affordable housing, and rising property values, reveals the urgency of understanding and addressing housing inequalities.

Historical and geographical variations further complicate the dynamics of housing inequality. For instance, urban areas such as today's Milan in Italy or Amsterdam in the Netherlands exemplify how housing markets can exacerbate socio-economic divides, with rising rents pricing out lower-income households and contributing to gentrification. Moreover, housing affordability is intrinsically linked to systemic issues such as intergenerational wealth transmission, access to education and employment, and demographic challenges such as declining fertility rates.

Explorations on the determinants of housing inequality should delve therefore into multifaceted dimensions, drawing on historical perspectives, socio-economic analysis, and policy evaluations. By investigating the distribution of housing resources, the relationships between outcomes of income distribution (expressed in differentiation of wages, rents, and profits), and the socio-spatial consequences of housing policies, a comprehensive understanding of how housing shapes and is shaped by broader inequalities may be provided. Additionally, innovative measures and alternative indicators, such as anthropometric and perception-based indexes, can capture the long-term and multidimensional nature of housing inequality. Through this lens, housing is situated at the heart of contemporary debates on inequality and well-being, offering insights into pathways towards more inclusive and equitable housing policies.

This complexity becomes even more apparent when examining the long-term case of Russia. One notable feature of Russian towns historically has been the predominance of wooden houses. Prior to the Bolshevik Revolution of 1917, wood was the primary building material owing to its abundance and affordability, particularly outside the southern provinces. However, the reliance on wood came at a cost, as it left urban areas highly vulnerable to frequent and devastating fires. Both the Imperial and Soviet governments sought to address this imbalance by encouraging the use of more durable materials such as stone and brick. Yet such a shift could only be achieved if living standards improved significantly, underscoring the intricate link between housing quality, material well-being, and systemic socio-economic conditions.

As shown in Fig. 10.2, throughout the nineteenth and the early twentieth centuries, the share of houses made of solid materials (stones, including bricks) increased. This indicates a rise in Russia's urban population's well-being for the period 1825–1910. This developed alongside the processes of urbanization, industrialization, and accumulation of human capital, but asynchronously and non-linearly.

The share of such structures increased from 13.65% of all urban houses in 1825 to 30.85% in 1910. The highest growth rates (almost 4% per year) were in 1904–1910. The average share of stone buildings in 1825 was 5.05% in 683 urban places and 20.53% in 1115 in 1910 (without weighting by the population). The median level increased from 1.17% in 1825 to 8.00% in 1910. The share of urban places without any stone buildings significantly reduced (from 23.32% in 1825 to 2.81% in 1910 relative to those for which data on total number of buildings are available).

The scale effect was manifested in a higher share of stone buildings in larger urban places. However, taking a long-term perspective, smaller ones experienced catch-up growth and reduced the gap. Thus, convergence was observed between Russian urban places in this measure. This is especially true for small country towns (‘*uezdnye goroda*’), which prevailed in terms of numbers and in which 40–50% of Russia's urban population lived. In the first half of the nineteenth century, these towns were distinguished by an increased share of merchants in the urban population (the share of the nobility was higher in the two capital cities and provincial

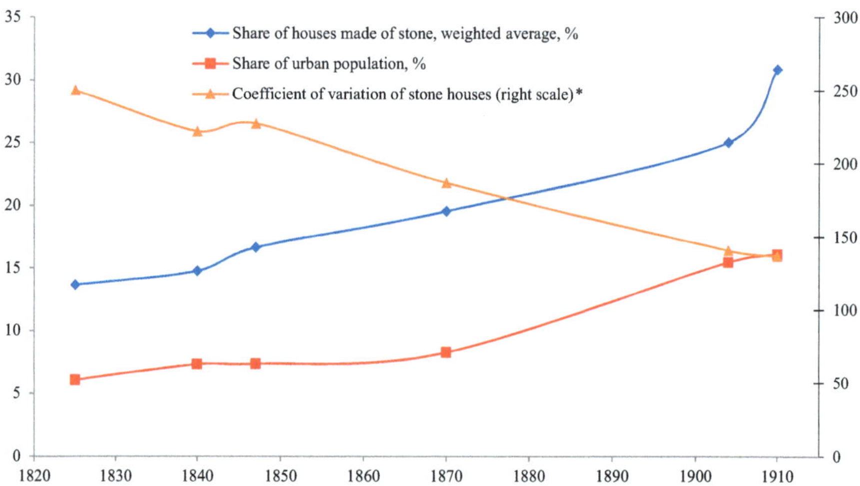

Fig. 10.2 Quality of housing for Russian urban population (1825–1910). *Note:* * Town/city is a unit of analysis. *Source:* Didenko et al. (2022); Konchakov and Didenko (2022a, b). The data were collected with qualified assistance from M. A. Karpenko

centres). They were probably the forerunners in accumulation of capital, which served the basis for Russia's transition to modern economic growth in the late nineteenth and early twentieth centuries. A town's administrative status and its provision with port infrastructure were statistically most closely associated with its population's well-being.

During the Soviet era, the most vital problems were quantity of housing space per capita and quality of access to basic facilities. The situation worsened between 1913 and 1940 (Fig. 10.3). It is highly likely this downward trend was in force from the late nineteenth century owing to the influx of workers from villages. Housing began to improve from the mid-1950s. The same is true for access to basic facilities, which improved radically in the late Soviet period (Table 10.5), but remained well below the level of advanced countries. Soviet-era statistics cover only "socialized"

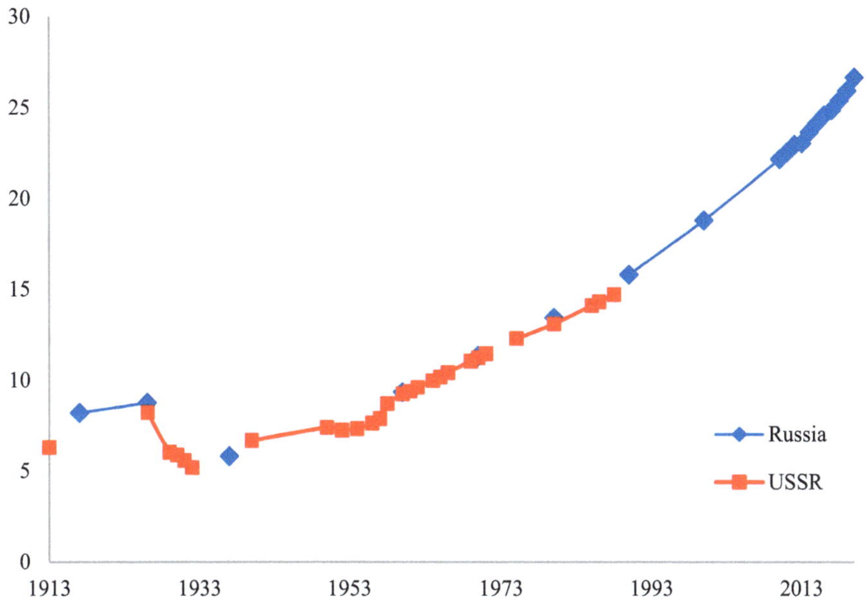

Fig. 10.3 Housing space per capita of urban population in Central Eurasia (1913–2020), square meters. *Sources:* Russia—Rosstat (https://rosstat.gov.ru/storage/mediabank/history-2021.rar); USSR—TsSU SSSR (1952, 219, https://istmat.org/node/40054/); TsSU SSSR (1955, 184, https://istmat.org/node/36699); TsUNKhU (1935); TsSU SSSR (1956–1991)

Table 10.5 Share of space in urban public houses in the USSR with access to basic facilities, percentage

	Water supply	Sewage	Air heating (central or local)	Natural gas	Heated water	Bathroom
1940	47	40	18	0.7		
1950	44	40	21	14		
1954	47	42	28	21		
1970	78.9	75.8	73.6	64.6	33.8	60.7
1980	89.8	87.8	86.5	79.4	57.1	79.9
1985	91.8	89.7	88.9	78.3	71.2	83.2
1986	92.2	90.2	89.3	78.1	72.4	84.1
1987	92.5	90.5	89.7	77.9	73.7	84.7
1988	92.7	90.8	89.9	77.3	75.3	85.4

Note: The figures include housing space in dwellings in state, corporate, and cooperative property. Predominantly, they were in multi-apartment dwellings. One-family urban houses (predominantly in individual property widespread in small towns) had much worse access to basic facilities
Sources: TsSU SSSR (1955, 185, https://istmat.org/node/36699); TsSU SSSR (1956–1991)

housing space, which could be in state, corporate,[11] or cooperative property.[12] Housing space in individual properties mostly consisted of one-family units, widespread in rural areas and in small towns.[13] Most of them, whether urban or rural, had neither water supply with sewage connection (therefore no chance of a bath or shower) nor comfortable heating.[14] Housing space was not significantly hit by the downturn,[15] and the official figures might even somewhat under-estimate actual living conditions, with the completion of single-family houses probably being under-reported to allow tax evasion. While in the 1950s–1980s, most urban housing

[11] Much Soviet housing was constructed with the funds of enterprises that normally transferred their apartments or hostel rooms into the possession of their employees for their lifetime, with the right to succession. The improvement of housing conditions was a substantial bonus in addition to wages and was one of the essential criteria for employees when deciding which government agency to work for. State and corporate apartments could not be sold but were subject to exchange, with soft restrictions.

[12] This kind of option was reserved for people of the middle-class elite groups who were considered not so valuable to be remunerated immediately with decent living conditions but earned enough money to make a down payment and pay their quasi-mortgage monthly, thus obtaining an apartment sooner than others. As of Rosstat (https://rosstat.gov.ru/storage/mediabank/history-2021.rar), at the peak of this practice (1970), 8.2% of all housing in Russia was built by such cooperatives (versus 73.6% by the state and state-owned enterprises).

[13] In addition to rights of possession, they could be bought and sold but not leased to receive fair rents.

[14] Wood-fired furnaces were frequently used for heating even in urban areas as an alternative to central or local air heating. In the 1950s, they were widespread for the collective heating of apartment blocks even in the two largest cities of Moscow and Leningrad (as St. Petersburg was known between 1924 and 1991).

[15] Even though the construction industry was in recession, as were other industries, increased mortality counterbalanced the fall in new construction.

construction was of multi-apartment dwellings, in the 1990s–2010s about half was represented by one-family units.[16] However, distribution of the new housing became less equal, as did incomes.

The low proportion of households living in separate apartments was an acute problem before the 1960s: this garnered much attention in anecdotal evidence but not so much in quantitative sources. The official statistics started to include this information only when the share of separate apartments reached about 80% in the 1980s. It cannot be denied that in the 1920s–1950s most households in large urban areas (in cities with a population of several hundred thousand people and more) inhabited communal apartments (*'kommunal'nye kvartiry'*), hostels (*'obshche-zhitiia'*), and barracks,[17] while in small towns (of several thousand or several tens of thousands) they lived in one-family houses (mostly wooden), deprived of access to basic facilities.

One might of course question if the same quality-driven prices of housing also existed in other Northern Eurasian regions. Comparing China (Raff et al. 2013) with the Netherlands (Eichholtz 1997), it may be seen that house prices from the seventeenth to the nineteenth century were pretty much stagnant. However, price differences were substantial owing to house size and access to utilities such as a well. House quality also made a significant difference with, for example, the use of clay materials reducing the house price significantly. In the twentieth century, prices in China increased somewhat, with a steep rise after 2000 (Table 10.6).

10.3.3 Income Inequality

The third indicator of well-being is inequality. It is commonly known that income inequality may be affected by factors that are unrelated to the cognitive characteristics of workers and their productivity. Such factors (e.g. race, nationality, age, gender) may be informal but relatively stable social barriers in the education and labour markets. Human development literature qualifies these as obstacles to a broader realization of individuals' and society's capabilities. It also stresses the various ways in which a high level of income inequality can affect economic development. For example, there is an increased degree of social tension and resulting negative political and economic consequences. The latter cover a wide range of phenomena,

[16] In large cities, multi-apartment dwellings prevail, while in small towns single-family units predominate.

[17] Communal apartments and hostels normally followed the principle of "one room for one family", while in barracks several families or single people could live in one large room. The latter were deprived of any basic facilities, while in communal apartments and hostels they were normally available on a shared basis.

Table 10.6 Average house price (Yuan/m^2) in China by capital city and province January 2012–2016

	2012	2013	2014	2015	2016
Beijing	25,480	32,057	37,204	35,567	39,423
Shanghai	24,654	26,686	31,487	32,183	36,661
Guangdong	15,078	17,186	19,037	19,461	20,633
Jiangsu	14,272	15,212	17,693	16,886	18,167
Zhejiang	18,020	19,289	18,631	17,907	18,026
Tianjin	13,324	13,335	14,723	14,936	15,786
Fujian	10,795	12,022	13,798	13,656	15,296
Shandong	8248	8663	9501	9864	10,242
Hubei	7710	8055	8867	9394	10,208
Henan	7150	7855	8864	9090	9550
Jiangxi	7725	8392	9146	9026	8987
Anhui	6201	6492	7281	7682	8636
Gansu	7691	7906	8585	8347	8594
Hebei	6612	7077	7937	8250	8440
Yunnan	8633	8798	8673	8157	8177
Shanxi	6538	7237	7579	7764	8079
Sichuan	8650	8749	8776	8365	7946
Hainan	7451	7145	7528	7315	7549
Heilongjiang	7590	7268	7254	7017	7410
Tibet	3457	4215	6572	7206	7314
Liaoning	7506	7710	7635	7263	7130
Guangxi	6856	6814	6843	6845	7008
Chongqing	6857	7076	7273	7113	6846
Shaanxi	7344	7194	6992	7095	6810
Xinjiang	6065	6610	7336	7099	6633
Jilin	6283	6509	6970	6793	6470
Hunan	6507	6481	6385	6317	6370
Inner Mongolia	6201	6446	6556	6345	6341
Guizhou	5588	5597	5754	5788	6177
Qinghai	4851	5304	5763	5791	5770
Ningxia	5036	5284	5288	5208	4849

Source: 全国房产市场排行榜 Chinese real estate market ranking, 转自中国房价行情网站, www.creprice.cn Transferred from the Chinese house price quotation website, www.creprice.cn, http://www.creprice.cn/rank/nationranking.html

including the costs of crime, sociopolitical conflicts, and frequent changes in legislation and law enforcement practices that are unfavourable for investment.

It is especially important to note that social and economic behaviours are determined by the subjective perceptions of income inequality. Recent empirical studies indicate that in most countries an individual's perception of his or her place within income distribution is very different from the position expressed if conventional indicators are used (Gimpelson and Treisman 2018). Tolerance to inequality is determined by the dominant ideas around fairness and justice that prevail in a society and the rules of economic and social interaction. Both extremely high and extremely low levels of income inequality are normally perceived as a result of discrimination and unfair play.[18] The former leads to growing demand for fiscal redistribution, while the latter may stimulate growth of public support for more liberal policies.

Economic inequality as a dimension of human development encompasses various measures. The first of these is wage/income inequality between individuals within a country. This comes as a result of various types of inequalities: skill premia, composition of income (share of less volatile labour income), inequality between regions, and the penetration of the redistributive system (taxes, contribution, and social transfers) into the economy. These components of income inequality create different patterns over time.

The first component is wage differentiation. Labour income normally constitutes no less than a half of net national disposable income. The major (but not the only) factor causing unequal distribution of labour income is the distribution of skills and their relative valuation. The urban/rural wage gap is a special case of the skill premium, as normally the urban economy is more complex and more productive and requires more skills than the rural economy (see Sect. 9.4.3.3).

When comparing alternative estimates of the long-term dynamics of income inequality, it is important that the periods of ascending and descending tendencies correspond to each other, and that the moments of the turning points are close in time (Fig. 10.4), which argue in favour of their relative reliability.

Commenting on our relatively high estimates of income inequality during the Soviet period, some points should be noted. As the main source for the Soviet period, Novokmet et al. (2018) used surveys of the family budgets of workers, employees, and collective farmers.[19] Owing to political sensitivity about the degree of heterogeneity in Soviet society, it was argued in the literature long before that data from these sources tended to under-estimate the actual level of inequality (Shenfield 1983; Atkinson and Micklewright 1992). At the same time, the data from these surveys can more or less reliably proxy for the prevailing trends over a period of 10–20 years, but they are less accurate and informative than official data on the distribution of wages.

The values of inequality indicators in the Soviet period are subject to upward adjustment not only because of hidden incomes but also for another reason. We should take into account unequal access to private consumption. The elite could purchase consumer goods and services at prices often several times lower than their market value. Most likely, in the late USSR, with the observed decrease in wage inequality, there was an increase in the share of income for the elite. In Morrisson

[18] Social tensions may arise when the most productive workers are underpaid, as was the case in the late USSR.

[19] In the literature, Novokmet et al. are often referred to as the "Piketty team".

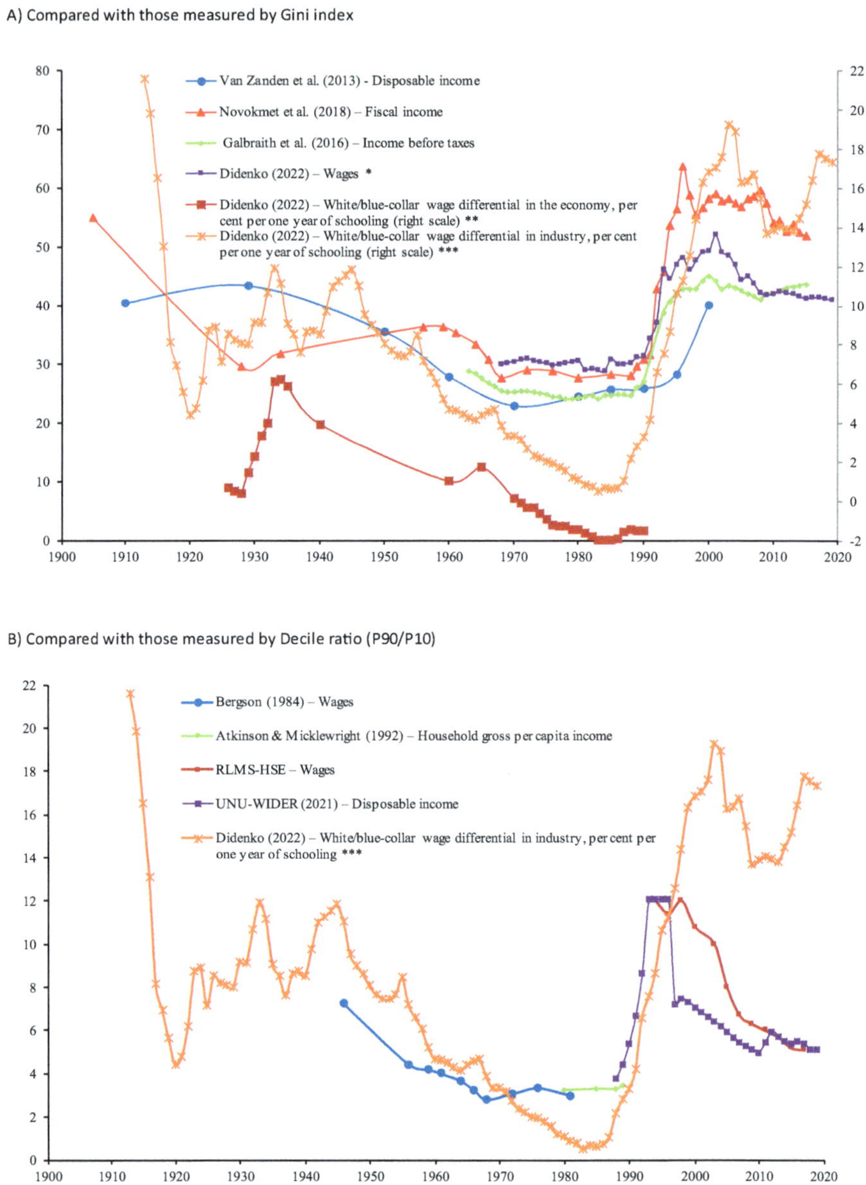

Fig. 10.4 Central Eurasia: Alternative estimates of long-term dynamics of income inequality, 1820–2019. (**a**) Compared with those measured by Gini index. (**b**) Compared with those measured by decile ratio (P90/P10). *Note:* 1820–1922: European Russia; 1923–1991: USSR; 1992–2019: Russian Federation. *Source:* RLMS HSE—as of calculations in: Kapelyuk (2019, 210). UNU-WIDER (2021)—as generated in the panel data file 'wiidglobal_0.xlsx'

* Based on: Didenko (2015, 174–176); Rosstat (https://rosstat.gov.ru/folder/210/document/13210); TransMONEE database (2011); Atkinson and Micklewright (1992, Statistical Appendix, TableUE1). In Didenko et al. (2022), the estimates for the period prior to 1991 were revised upwards by 3.9% points from Morrisson (1984)

** Based on: Didenko (2015, 297–298); Gosplan SSSR (1929, 452–455)

*** Based on: Didenko et al. (2013); Rosstat (https://rosstat.gov.ru/compendium/document/60671, https://rosstat.gov.ru/folder/210/document/12994)

(1984), the effects of the elite's non-monetary privileges in 1973 are estimated at 3.9% points by the Gini index (30.9% adjusted versus 27.0% as it follows directly from the underlying sources).

The cyclical pattern of within-country income inequality, observed in a number of large countries, was conceptualized in the "Kuznets waves".[20] They are associated with the different nature of technological progress and accompanying changes in education and financial markets; as well as with differences in technological trends, openness of national economies, and government policies (Milanovic 2016, 46–117). Thus, this conception takes into account not only wage differentiation, but broader range of the sources of income inequality and the factors affecting it.

10.3.4 The Development of Intranational Inequality

The final stage of the formation of the single labour market for Russian agricultural workers dates to the end of the nineteenth and the beginning of the twentieth century.[21] General development (national integration, responsiveness to signals from other local markets) is assessed as evidence of movement towards a single market for the European part of Russia. Its most developed labour markets appeared to be in the so-called black soil area. However, even by 1914, local markets for the rural labour force in the European part of Russia had not reached a level of integration which allowed it to be treated as a single market. In the early twentieth century, wage rates in agriculture grew at an accelerated pace. This could have led to a narrowing of the difference between wages in agriculture and manufacturing (Koval'chenko and Milov 1974, 350–351).

As well as income inequality (through the urban/rural wage gap and the skill premium), spatial inter-regional inequality (through unequal industrial concentration between sub-national regions) becomes an important issue in the process of industrial development. Theoretically, the starting point of our analysis for the long-term dynamic of spatial inequality is a bell-shaped (inverted U-shaped) curve, which was developed in Williamson (1965). The initial impetus towards "modern economic growth" first affects the main regions, and then spreads to others. This leads to a divergence between the core and the periphery, which is further exacerbated by migration of skilled labour and movement of capital from the periphery to the core, while central government policies favour investment in the core regions. At later stages of development, inter-regional connections and regional politics become increasingly important, which leads to flows of knowledge and capital from the core

[20] The Kuznets Curve is an inverted U-shaped trajectory of within (or between)-country income inequality, both over time and across countries at various stages of industrial development (see Sect. 9.4.3.3). However, later empirical evidence exposed a cyclical pattern of income inequality dynamics. This was conceptualized by B. Milanovic who coined the term "Kuznets Waves".

[21] As convincingly argued in Koval'chenko and Milov (1974, 325–351), based on the increased correlation in the dynamics of daily payments and their reduced inter-regional differentiation.

to the periphery and triggers convergence processes. This is normally paired with a decrease in intra-country income inequality (at the end of the Kuznets wave).

Thus, at the beginning and in the early stages of modern growth, both in the core and in the periphery, structural imbalances in the social, economic, and fiscal systems naturally increase. At the same time, integration efforts are undertaken politically. These include centralized budget transfers and public investment as well as moderate spatial differentiation.

In recent literature, the validity of the spatial curve (Williamson 1965) has been confirmed by the findings for such countries as the US (Kim 1998), the UK (Crafts 2005), Italy (Felice 2012), Spain (Martínez-Galarraga et al. 2015), and Switzerland (Stohr 2018), while a long-term convergence trend has been found for France (Combes et al. 2011).

For Central Eurasia, spatial inequality was an acute problem owing to the multinational and multicultural composition of the population of its territory.[22] In the late Russian Empire (1897), spatial inequality in gross regional product per capita was quite high, comparable in level with cross-country inequality at the time (Markevich 2019). A weak long-term convergence between the Russian provinces was observed between 1897 and 2014. Its pace was approximately the same as the cross-country convergence in Western Europe, but lagged behind intra-country convergence in the US and Western Europe.

As regards spatial inequality during the launch of modern growth in Russia, a convergence of industrial workers' wages between industries and provinces was noted in Kir'yanov (1979, 106, 110). This indicates the formation of a single labour market in industry.[23]

An increase in spatial differentiation between the provinces of European Russia (with institutions of local self-government—*zemstvos*) was found in education financing until the end of the 1870s (Didenko 2021). However, it started to decrease thereafter. In healthcare financing, inter-regional divergence was under way until the end of the pre-revolutionary period. These trends were associated with various central government involvement in education and health financing and its changes over time. In European Russia, the financing of education was largely carried out from central government funds. Healthcare for the most part was financed by *zemstvos*, commercial and non-profit organizations, and households; that is, from local sources.

Declining inter-regional differentiation in education was associated with the increasing share supplied by the central government and the declining share supplied by local governments (Didenko 2021).

---

[22] The Williamson (1965) curve of spatial inequality can be viewed as a dimension of the Kuznets (1955) curve of intra-country income inequality. Empirically, they mostly correlate in Russia. The underlying idea is that the spread of an industrial revolution (or post-industrial hi-tech production) tends to be uneven across a country. What is different is that intra-country spatial inequality tends to diminish over time, while there is an uncertain trend in personal income inequality.

[23] In this case, among the 20 provinces of the European part of the Russian Empire.

At the start and in the early stages of modern growth, the uneven development of the regions generated a trend towards divergence in the accumulation of human capital. This trend was clearly manifested in those segments (healthcare in European Russia) and in those periods (the end of the nineteenth century for education in European Russia, in contrast to the beginning of the twentieth century elsewhere) where and when the share of central government funding was lower. The increased participation of central government formed a trend towards divergence. The largest share of funding appeared to be in the field of education in the Far East, somewhat less in Siberia. In the field of healthcare, the share of central government participation in the eastern regions was radically higher than that in European Russia.[24]

In sum, while skill premiums tend to expose cyclical patterns, within-country spatial inequality normally tends to moderate over time (with the notable exception of Central Eurasia, where it tended to be cyclical by and large, with very weak convergence).

10.3.5 Social Spending and Social Transfers

Social transfers are a key mechanism used to reduce inequality in areas where redistribution is widely seen as socially beneficial. These transfers typically refer to social expenditures, excluding public spending on education and healthcare. While expenditures on education and healthcare are often viewed through the lens of human capital theory as productive investments within a pro-growth policy framework, social transfers primarily involve the redistribution of income derived from production activities. Social transfers do not include subsidies aimed at supporting specific industries or products (Lindert 2021a, 73–74). Instead, they encompass financial support provided by public authorities to individuals and households. Common examples include pensions, sickness-related social security allowances, affordable housing programmes, family-related benefits (often tied to the number of children), and other forms of welfare assistance. In market economies, social transfers also extend to unemployment relief, which is generally absent in command economies. These programmes are funded predominantly through general government taxation, reflecting the collective responsibility to ensure social stability and reduce economic disparities. Both in Western-type and socialist economies, the penetration of social transfers had a clear upward trend, even with strong corrections. Most of the increase in social spending and its share occurred in the twentieth century (Lindert 2021a, b).

The available fragmentary data on the share of social expenditures in GDP indicate that their relative decline in the 1990s (in Russia under economic contraction) was a correction from the trend. Post-Soviet Russia (13.09% of GDP in 2010) turns

[24] These patterns are established in Didenko (2021, 2024) with greater reliability in relation to European Russia, while with less certainty in relation to Siberia and the Far East, owing to the reduced quality of the source base, including insufficient completeness of data.

Table 10.7 China and Russia/USSR: Gross social transfers to GDP, 1870–2010

	Russia/USSR	China
1870	0.59	
1880	0.59	
1890	0.59	
1900	0.58	
1930	4.31	0.91
1940		
1950		2.94
1960	15.51	5.51
1970	16.81	
1980		7.84
1990		8.50
2000		6.77
2010	13.09	8.01

Note: Social transfers in this table include public healthcare spending, which is approximately equal to overall social spending excluding public education spending
Source: Lindert (2021b, Table 7.2)

Table 10.8 Redistributive capacity of national social systems (welfare states)

	Gini coefficient of inequality (%)			
Country	Pre-fiscal market income	Post-fiscal final income	Implied progressivity of fiscal redistribution	Public social transfers as % of GDP (%)
Argentina	50.2	29.8	20.4	19.6
Armenia	46.9	35.7	11.3	8.6
Australia	42.4	32.1	10.3	18.7
Brazil	59.3	45.2	14.1	19.9
Canada	41.1	32.5	8.6	16.8
Estonia	45.0	35.7	9.3	15.9
Finland	42.2	26.2	16.0	29.5
France	44.5	29.4	15.1	31.5
Georgia	50.7	38.3	12.4	9.3
Germany	41.9	29.9	12.1	24.8
Hungary	41.1	28.7	12.4	22.1
Iran	42.9	34.3	8.5	12.2
Israel	42.4	34.1	8.3	16.2
Italy	44.5	32.9	11.6	28.6
Japan	37.6	32.0	5.6	23.1
Korea	30.5	28.0	2.5	9.7
Mexico	50.9	42.9	8.0	7.9
Netherlands	39.6	28.4	11.2	22.9
Norway	37.7	26.2	11.5	19.4
Poland	42.3	30.4	11.9	19.0

(continued)

Table 10.8 (continued)

Country	Gini coefficient of inequality (%)			Public social transfers as % of GDP (%)
	Pre-fiscal market income	Post-fiscal final income	Implied progressivity of fiscal redistribution	
Russia	**49.1**	**32.3**	**16.8**	**17.2**
Spain	47.9	35.2	12.7	26.3
Sweden	38.3	28.1	10.2	27.4
Turkey	40.3	38.2	2.1	13.4
UK	47.1	35.3	11.8	21.9
USA	47.8	39.2	8.6	18.8

Source: Lindert (2017, 37–38)

out to be closer to the late USSR (16.81% of GDP in 1970) and quite far from both the late Russian Empire (0.59% of GDP in 1870–1890) and from the early USSR (4.31% of GDP in 1930) (Table 10.7). The redistributive effect of the tax system remained high in Russia by international comparisons (Table 10.8).

There will likely be a balance of factors driving income inequality higher and those driving it lower. Among the former, we would emphasize the AI revolution and the next round of a race between education and technology. We are sceptical as regards the prime factor put forward by Piketty (2014) that return on capital tends to be greater than economic growth rate. His thesis by and large ignores risks associated with capital accumulation that reveal themselves in defaults, bankruptcies, and rapid growth of newly created businesses and industries. From these stylized facts follow that ranks of top capital owners significantly change over time.

As regards prospects for Russia, the level of inequality will most likely remain relatively high, with a trend towards a moderate and gradual moderation. The fact is that countries with greater social, cultural, and economic heterogeneity, with a large territory and population, which is also ethnically diverse, tend to have higher levels of inequality. At present, very strong differences remain in the spatial and geographical distribution of factors of production between Russian regions with low labour mobility. Added to this is the weakness of independent trade unions given the priority of the goal of limiting unemployment over regulation of wages in state policy on the labour market during the last three decades.

The reduction of intra-country inequality in Russia can be accelerated by both institutional changes in the labour market and in the social sphere, as well as the effects of expansion of the military sector.

The first factor includes primarily the intensification of state policy in the direction of income redistribution, the likelihood of its consistent implementation being assessed as quite high. First of all, this is a soft introduction for progressive taxation of personal incomes. The first step in this direction was the adoption of the Law No. 372-FZ in November 2020.[25] The next step was amendment of the Tax Code in July

[25] http://publication.pravo.gov.ru/Document/View/0001202011230015

2024 (the Law No. 176-FZ),[26] with the introduction of a five-step scale to come into force in 2025. These steps are not so much following the recommendations of economic theory but serving as a response to social demands from society.

As for the effects of expansion of the military sector, in the twentieth century we have evidence of different scenarios for its impact on inequality in Russia. As a rule, the education and qualifications of those conscripted and mobilized into the armed forces are characterized by a downward shift in comparison with the corresponding structure of the total labour force in the national economy. This changes the structure of labour supply: all other things being equal, less skilled labour becomes scarcer than skilled labour. In an essentially market economy, this leads to a tightening in the wage differential. This effect was observed during the First World War: from 1913 to 1916, an estimated premium for 1 year of education fell by 40% (calculation based on wage differential between white- and blue-collar workers in industry, data set from Didenko 2023). In nominal terms, wages increased for blue-collar workers and decreased for white-collar workers; in real terms, it decreased for both, but for the latter it decreased more significantly. On the contrary, during the Great Patriotic War of 1941–1945, through the centralized regulation of wage rates and prices for rationed goods, it increased by 38% and was near maximum levels for the entire Soviet period.

If we assume that the Russian economy will continue to be essentially a market economy, even with strong government regulation, the expected labour market scenario is likely to be closer to the situation during the First World War: that is, towards lower inequality, despite the fact that the scale of labour participation in the armed forces is currently small compared with that period and very small compared with the situation during the Second World War. In addition, the wages of those who were either hired or mobilized into the armed forces are several times higher than they previously were in the civilian sector. This also has its effect on the reduction of income inequality.

10.4 Immaterial Components of Well-Being

10.4.1 Education and Health

Immaterial components, such as education and health, play not only a central role in well-being indexes such as the HDI (see Sect. 10.2), but also offer a deeper perspective on improvement in the quality of human life beyond material factors such as income. Taking the human capital perspective, education in particular reflects a society's long-term investment in its people. From a human development perspective, this extends the capabilities shaping not only individual opportunities but also broader economic and social outcomes. Tracing the historical dynamics of

[26] http://publication.pravo.gov.ru/Document/View/0001202407120009

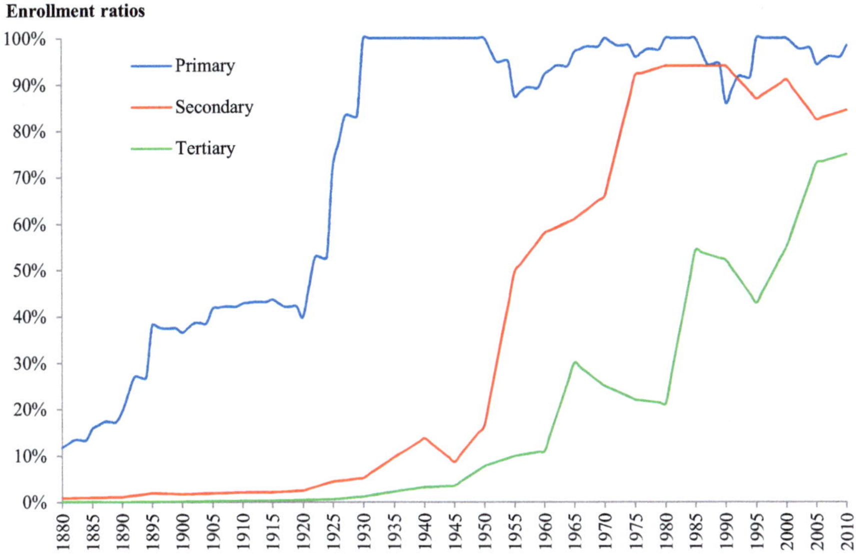

Fig. 10.5 Educational enrolment in Central Eurasia, 1880–2010. *Note:* Russian Empire prior to 1917, USSR in 1923–1991, Russian Federation since 1992. *Source:* Lee and Lee (2016, data set)

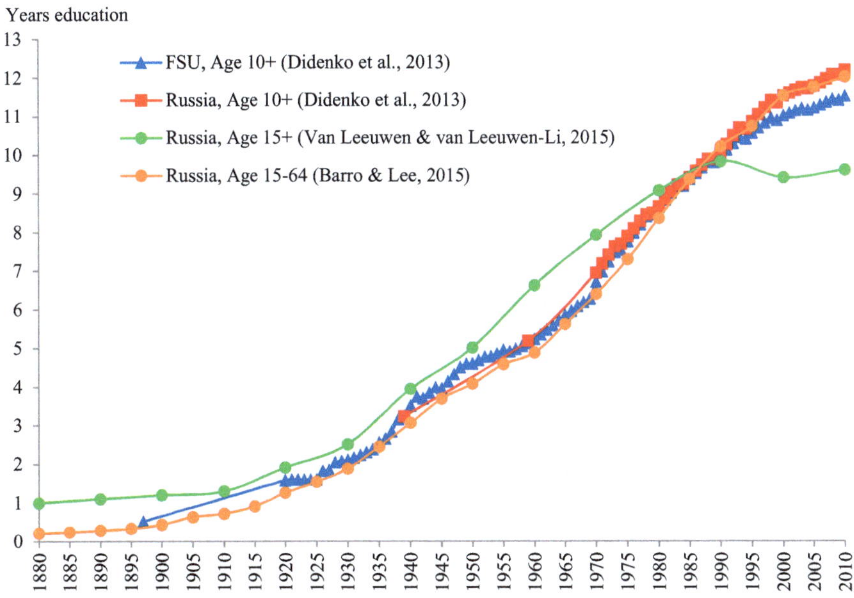

Fig. 10.6 Educational attainment in Central Eurasia, 1880–2010. *Note:* Russian Empire prior to 1917, USSR in 1923–1991, Russian Federation since 1992. *Source:* Barro and Lee (2015, data set), Didenko et al. (2013, supplementary data), Van Leeuwen and Van Leeuwen-Li (2015)

education highlights significant milestones and challenges in achieving equitable and high-quality learning opportunities for all.

Examining the long-run dynamics of HDI components, education outcomes as measured by enrolment rates (Fig. 10.5) have consistently translated into higher levels of attainment, such as years of schooling (Fig. 10.6). While estimates of schooling years vary, they all demonstrate the same upward trend. In Russia, universal primary education was achieved in the early 1930s, providing the foundation for a rapid expansion in secondary education. By 1937, junior secondary education (ISCED 2 level) became universal and compulsory in urban areas. However, owing to wartime disruptions, rural areas did not achieve the same level of access until 1956. In 1958, the duration of ISCED 2 education was extended from 7 to 8 years, marking another step in the advancement of educational opportunities. Universal secondary enrolment (ISCED 3 level) was achieved only by the mid-1970s. Tertiary education (ISCED 5 level) experienced more fluctuations during the same period. From the 1960s to the early 1980s, tertiary enrolment rates underwent a downward correction, potentially reflecting shifts in government policies or labour market demands. However, this trend reversed in the subsequent decades, with tertiary enrolment resuming its upward trajectory.

Today, Russia has approached near-universal higher education, though challenges persist in the quality of education. Short class durations and inflated official enrolment figures undermine the effectiveness of this achievement. Studies, such as those by Van Leeuwen and Van Leeuwen-Li (2015), have adjusted these figures to account for the high proportion of part-time and correspondence-based study, which may overstate true levels of educational attainment.

Gender gaps in education have also narrowed significantly over time. During the interwar period, gender disparities in enrolment steadily decreased, achieving parity by 1940 across the USSR on average (Fig. 10.7). However, male predominance persisted at postgraduate level (ISCED 6). In the Central Asian republics, gender parity in primary and secondary education (ISCED 1–3) was not reached until the 1960s. Turkmenistan, in contrast, never reported gender parity at any higher level of education, and many Central Asian republics continued to exhibit male dominance in tertiary enrolment (ISCED 5).

The vital indicators expose substantial improvement in the long run, most remarkably in the 1920s–1950s, in spite of excesses caused by famines (1921, 1933, and 1947) and the Great Patriotic War (1941–1945). They failed to improve in the period between the late 1920s and the late 1940s, but the progress in the 1920s and 1950s was great enough to overcome the negative corrections.

In the 1960s, life expectancy stopped improving and deteriorated in the 1970s and mid-1980s. The deterioration was largely brought about by an increased crude death rate,[27] while infant mortality experienced just a short correction in early 1970s before it continued to decline further. This means that the health system experienced more problems than before but not as serious as those experienced by the social

[27] Number of deaths occurring during the year, per 1000 population at midyear.

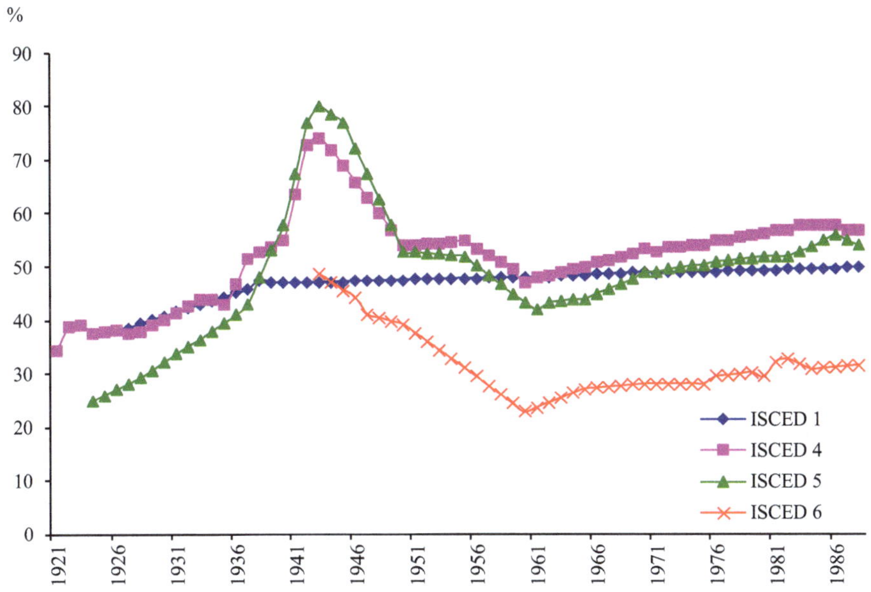

Fig. 10.7 Share of females at various levels of education in the USSR (%). *Source:* Calculations based on Didenko et al. (2013)

environment. Clearly, infant mortality is more closely associated with the performance of the healthcare system than the others, as adult mortality is affected by a number of social factors that are beyond its direct control (crime, murders, armed conflict, suicides, traffic accidents, alcohol poisoning, etc.). Even during the transitional slump in the 1990s, infant mortality experienced only a very modest increase attributable to the substantially worsened conditions of the parents—although it is also affected by socio-economic conditions in which the parents live and work.

In the 2000s, life expectancy recovered in response to better financing of healthcare and improvement in socio-economic conditions. Several large-scale public healthcare programmes have improved accessibility of medical services and drug provision for the population (Didenko 2020, 79–80).

The Soviet healthcare system was organized in the 1920s on the basis of universal access to free healthcare at outpatient points of use. It put its emphasis on prevention and primary care at local level and proved reasonably effective in the control of communicable diseases while ineffective in its treatment of non-communicable diseases and in its high reliance on in-patient care. In parallel, much of the resources were consumed by another extensive system of health services that were attached to large industrial enterprises, certain ministries, and the top of government, where specific professional needs were better treated (Popovich et al. 2011, 14–15). The late USSR appeared to become the world's leader in terms of doctors and hospital beds. Hospitals absorbed approximately 60% of state budget expenditure, while primary care provided through polyclinics and dispensaries received approximately 30% (Davis 2010, 29–30). In post-Soviet Russia, the basics of the Soviet-era system were not questioned, but some attempts were made to introduce quasi-market institutions of medical insurance. Overall, the system of compulsory health insurance has produced poor results in terms of its impact on the whole system of healthcare finance (Didenko 2020, 76).

10.4.2 Corruption

Well-being extends beyond material dimensions to encompass social factors that significantly influence quality of life. Among these, corruption, defined as the misuse of power for private gain (Svensson 2005), can represent a critical dimension of social well-being. This broad definition allows for corruption to have either a positive or negative impact on economic growth and well-being. Most scholars, however, emphasize its detrimental effects on economic performance (e.g. Shleifer and Vishny 1993; Bardhan 1997; Polterovich 2001). These adverse effects manifest in several ways. Polterovich (2001) identified that corruption distorts the distribution of resources, particularly in areas such as innovation, where government support for patents and similar mechanisms is vital. It exacerbates income disparities by disproportionately benefiting those who engage in bribery and other illicit practices (Rose-Ackerman 2008). In totalitarian systems, corruption leads to a disconnect between stated and real values, as individuals are often hired based on their alignment with the system rather than their qualifications. Furthermore, it strengthens criminal networks, further destabilizing societal structures.

However, the relationship between corruption and economic outcomes is not uni-directional. Some scholars argue that corruption can provide institutional flexibility in settings where formal institutions are under-developed or fail to meet the needs of economic actors, particularly in transforming and developing economies (e.g. Leff 1964; Huntington 1968; Lui 1985). In these contexts, corruption may act as a temporary mechanism to reduce uncertainty and ease institutional frictions. Nevertheless, the overall impact of corruption remains a subject of debate. While some studies suggest corruption has no significant effect—positive or negative—on economic growth (e.g. Mauro 1998), the prevailing consensus points to its harmful consequences (e.g. Tanzi and Davoodi 1998; Aidt 2009). Corruption is often seen as an institutional trap (Polterovich 2001, 2005). Although it may provide short-term solutions during transitional periods, it ultimately leads to a "bad equilibrium" that hampers long-term development and well-being.

Corruption can therefore be broadly understood as a social and economic phenomenon characterized by the misuse of power for personal or group benefit. It manifests in various forms, including fraud, bribery, nepotism, and cronyism.[28] This inclusive definition captures the diverse mechanisms through which corruption can influence economic growth and social well-being. To operationalize this concept,

[28] While nepotism and cronyism are closely related, they differ in scope: nepotism involves favouring family members exclusively, whereas cronyism extends these benefits to both family and close associates, such as colleagues or companions. In Dutch, *nepotisme* corresponds to nepotism, while *vriendjespolitiek* refers to cronyism, highlighting this nuanced distinction.

we can therefore consider five key terms: corruption, fraud, bribery, nepotism, and cronyism. Only a few existing measures, such as the V-Dem corruption index, provide any historical data, in some cases extending as far back as 1789. However, despite its utility, this index has limitations.[29] It does not fully align with our broader definition of corruption and exhibits minimal variation for certain periods, particularly the late twentieth century. For instance, while the V-Dem index suggests a rise in corruption in the Netherlands during the late twentieth century, it offers limited granularity. In Russia, the index similarly indicates increasing corruption in the 1990s and its modest decrease after 2000, though some scholars contest this trend.

To address these gaps, we explore alternative data sources to measure corruption. In the case of the Netherlands, mentions of corruption-related terms in books (via Google Ngram) provide a richer historical perspective. Figures 10.8 and 10.9 illustrate the temporal trends in the relative frequency of these terms, highlighting a notable rise in the use of "corruption" and "bribery" over time. This increase appears to coincide with a decline in references to "fraud".

The Google Ngram measure captures public intolerance to corruption and official media campaigns aimed at curtailing it. What it directly measures is how much

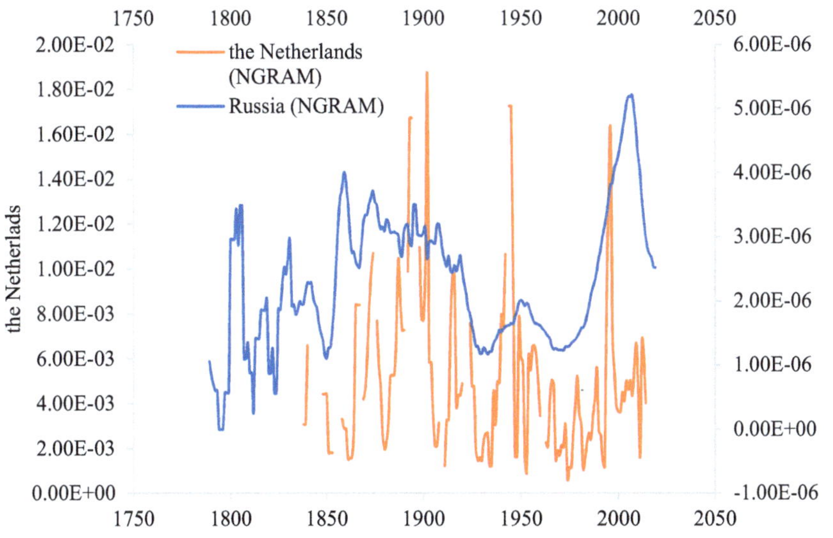

Fig. 10.8 Relative corruption mentions in Russia and the Netherlands, c. 1800–2020. *Source:* Google Ngram for Russia; and the Netherlands

[29]V-Dem has long run data too, running, in some cases, back to 1789. Yet it is rather a visualization of expert opinion than a quantitative measure. It is difficult to use without critical evaluation historically, as:

1. They are based solely on subjective perceptions of one (or a few) country expert.
2. It is unclear what measurement scale is used and whether cross-country conciliation was made.
3. It is unclear whether the experts assessed corruption using present-day criteria, rather than historically; that is, how the contemporaries thought what behaviour was corrupt and what was not.

Fig. 10.9 The last scene from The Government Inspector, depicting corrupt local administrators, 1836. *Note:* Nikolai Gogol's own sketch. *Source:* https://commons.wikimedia.org/wiki/File:Revisor_paint_by_Gogol.JPG?uselang=en

attention was devoted to corruption issues in the sample of books in Russian or Dutch.

However, even with a stricter definition of corruption, there are still ways in which corruption may affect economic growth. For example, Ugur and Dasgupta (2011) pointed out that most effects on economic growth are negative but that corruption, via factors of production such as physical capital, positively affects growth. Yet they also pointed out that this latter effect remains insignificant.

Calabrese and Van Leeuwen (2024) regressed per capita GDP growth on measures of perceived corruption, using indices derived from Google Ngram. Initial regressions without corruption measures yield an expected positive coefficient for physical capital and human capital. Incorporating a corruption proxy, however, shows no significant effect on GDP per capita growth.

Taking a non-linear equation, Calabrese and Van Leeuwen (2024) found in some cases positive, sometimes negative, and sometimes no effect on growth. This underscores the complexity of its impact. However, even with a positive effect on economic growth, it does not imply that corruption is desirable. For example, Polterovich (2001) argued that addressing corruption may sometimes be more costly than tolerating it, suggesting a balance must be struck between rooting out corruption and accepting its presence at manageable levels.

Some authors argue that corruption tends to increase during periods of modernization and economic transformation, as these phases often disrupt established norms and create new opportunities for illicit practices. Huntington (1968, 59–61) highlighted that corruption is typically more prevalent during such periods and declines both before and after. For example, during the late nineteenth and early twentieth centuries—a time of rapid industrialization and modernization in the US—corruption surged, coinciding with unprecedented economic growth and societal change. Similarly, China at the end of the twentieth century witnessed increasing corruption during its period of reform and economic growth.

According to Huntington, modernization exacerbates corruption through three interconnected mechanisms. First, it causes a shift in the fundamental values of a society, as traditional norms and practices are challenged or replaced by new ones. This normative transition can create a vacuum in which rules and expectations are unclear, enabling corrupt behaviour to thrive. Second, modernization generates new sources of wealth and power, such as industrial enterprises, financial institutions, or trade networks, which become the focus of competition and, consequently, opportunities for corruption. Third, modernization increases the demand for services and intervention by political and social groups, particularly through expanded government roles and public sector activities, which can open avenues for corrupt practices on the output side of governance. This pattern is not unique to the US, but can be observed across regions undergoing rapid growth or transformation. As societies modernize, the pressure on institutions to adapt quickly often outpaces their capacity to enforce rules and regulations, creating fertile ground for corruption. Policymakers should therefore try to anticipate corruption risks during periods of rapid change and strengthen institutional frameworks to mitigate its adverse effects while navigating modernization processes.

In sum, we can argue that while there may be instances where corruption shows a positive relationship with GDP per capita growth, particularly under specific circumstances such as minimal levels of corruption or in periods of modernization, the majority of its effects are negative. These detrimental impacts are most often channelled through education and the broader quality of institutional frameworks. Corruption undermines trust, distorts resource allocation, and weakens incentives for human capital development, which collectively hinder long-term growth and societal progress. Even in cases where corruption appears to provide short-term benefits, such as institutional flexibility during modernization, its broader and more sustained consequences tend to erode the foundation of economic and social well-being. This highlights the critical importance of strengthening institutional quality and educational systems to mitigate corruption's adverse effects and foster sustainable development.

In certain periods of Russian history, the trends and timing of the turning points of Google Ngram measurement and V-Dem visualization appear to be similar. Both find corruption higher under market economies of the late Russian Empire (prior to 1917) and the Russian Federation (since 1992) than under the Soviet state's socialism (1930s–1980s). This is probably true if just a monetary form of corruption is taken into account, putting aside exchanges of influence and reciprocity. Furthermore, direct comparisons between the late Russian Empire and Russian Federation are complicated. As corrupt practices are a way of adapting social relations to the changing social environment, their perception and classification as illegal have changed throughout Russian history (e.g. Fedotov 2024). Some corrupt practices that are prohibited in modern Russia were treated as unethical behaviour at worst in the late Russian Empire, especially in the sphere of involvement of public officials and administrators in private businesses. The rising trend in the nineteenth century, as indicated by the Google Ngram measure, can to a great extent be explained by both easing of censorship and ongoing monetary penetration of the economy, accompanied by government extraction (see Sect. 8.3.3). Rapid rise in corruption in the 1990s and its moderation in the 2010s are indicated by both sources, with a difference in magnitude. The structure of post-Soviet corruption changed towards more institutionalized forms. A strengthening of discipline in public finance probably curtailed embezzlement. Experts admit that signs of reduction in small-scale bribery were burdensome for ordinary people, while acknowledge that expansion of large-scale networked corruption was burdensome for small and medium-sized businesses (Nureev and Latov 2016, 190–198). This looks like a political achievement at the cost of slower economic growth.

Russian fiction presents more evidence of this phenomenon. One of the most famous Russian plays, *The Government Inspector* by Nikolai Gogol, which satirized corruption in local public administration, was written in 1836 (Fig. 10.10).[30] The Google Ngram measure indicates that this was the time when corruption in Russia was close to its long-term trend, while the V-Dem experts perceive that it was at its historically highest level then. The expert perception is likely to be closer to reality, taking into account that literature was then censored, as well as a substantial source of local administrators' legal income being supposed to directly originate from commissions and fees for services from households and businesses; this was

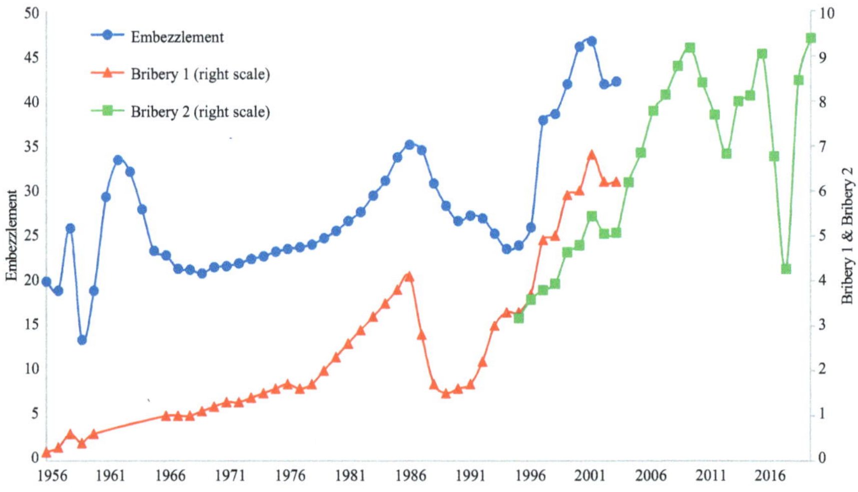

Fig. 10.10 Corruption crime rates in Central Eurasia, cases registered per 100,000 population, 1956–2019. *Note:* 1956–1990: USSR; 1991–2003: Russia. *Source:* Embezzlement, Bribery 1: Luneev (2005); Bribery 2: Rosstat (https://rosstat.gov.ru/storage/mediabank/pril-year_2023.rar)

[30] https://en.wikipedia.org/wiki/The_Government_Inspector

the state of affairs until the second half of the eighteenth century (Fedotov 2024, 131–132). Central government, being a principal, tried, if not to eradicate then, at least to curtail this among its agents. In the case of *The Government Inspector*, the censorship administrators nearly rejected it, and it was only after Emperor Nicholas's decision that it was performed on the stage of the Aleksandrinsky Theatre (which was named after the then empress). Subsequently, this classic piece was permanently present in the Russian school curricula for several generations.

The data from the criminal statistics (Fig. 10.10) provide more evidence for corruption incidence, taking into account its historical classification. The trends in the mid-1950s to the mid-1970s are the opposite to Google Ngram but in line with the V-Dem expert perception. The criminal statistics of the late Soviet and post-Soviet periods indicate that the authorities were most concerned with embezzlement: indeed, it caused direct damage to the state finances and left enough evidence to be investigated. However, these data should be interpreted with caution, taking into account the high degree of latency depending on state capacity and power struggles. When capacity weakened (second half of the 1980s to the first half of the 1990s), a

Fig. 10.11 A satirical picture portraying Soviet-era bribery, 1974. *Note:* "That is his tariff scale"—a wordplay of homonyms ("woven transparent bag" and "scale" sound the same in Russian as *setka*). Besides a bundle of large denomination banknotes, much upper-class food (champagne, cognac, caviar, poultry) is put inside the bribed low-level manager's bag. *Source: Crocodile* satirical journal (https://nzdr.ru/data/media/biblio/j/krokodil/1974/%D0%9A%D1%80%D0%BE%D0%BA%D0%BE%D0%B4%D0%B8%D0%BB,%201974%20,%20%E2%84%96%2018.pdf)

decrease in actual crime rates was hardly likely, contrary to the activities of the police and judicial powers.

Presumably, bribery was much more latent and no less widespread than embezzlement owing to the fertile ground provided by administrative management of the economy in the Soviet period (Nureev and Latov 2016, 138–139). It was not only government officials but also those employed in the state-owned service sector (especially trade) who were massively involved in corruption practices. However, monetary bribery—including in-kind form, as in Fig. 10.11—in the Soviet period was not so much spread as an exchange of influence and preferential behaviour. Therefore, it was less burdensome for ordinary people than it was for economic managers. Indeed, bribery of government employees allowed illegal private entrepreneurship to survive under state socialism.[31]

The hikes in criminal rates were also caused by campaigns that were initiated at the top in order to curtail corruption. This took place in the late 1950s and early 1960s, when ideologically motivated attacks on private activities were undertaken, and in 1982–1986, when the three Soviet leaders (L. Brezhnev, Yu. Andropov, K. Chernenko) had changed each other because of their passing away followed by M. Gorbachev's coming to power.

Overall, the hikes in corruption during the transition of the late Russian Empire to modern economic growth and the transition of post-Soviet Russia to a market economy lend support to the thesis in Huntington (1968). However, the modernization under Soviet state socialism in the 1930s–1950s does not.

10.4.3 Personal Security and Homicide

Personal security stands out as a fundamental component of social well-being, directly impacting individuals' sense of safety and societal stability. It is often evaluated through indicators such as susceptibility to criminal activities, with homicide rates emerging as a particularly robust metric. Owing to the high level of documentation and the extreme nature of the crime, homicide rates have become a widely accepted measure in historical research to assess immaterial aspects of well-being (Baten et al. 2014, 140–144). Moreover, they serve as a valuable proxy for understanding the historical institutional environment and the capacity of the state to maintain order and enforce the rule of law (Popov 2014).

First, ups and downs in homicide rates (Fig. 10.12) were caused by the underlying cycles of deterioration and recovery of institutional environment and state capacity. In Central Eurasia, two hikes in homicide rates are associated with later state failures (of the Russian Empire in 1917 and the Soviet Union in 1991). The

[31] Khlevniuk (2023) documents the cases of corruption, combined with private entrepreneurship, other economic crimes, and those embedded into everyday economic life, in the post-Second World War period (1948–1952). V-DEM visualization finds historical lows while the Google NGRAM measure indicates an upward correction.

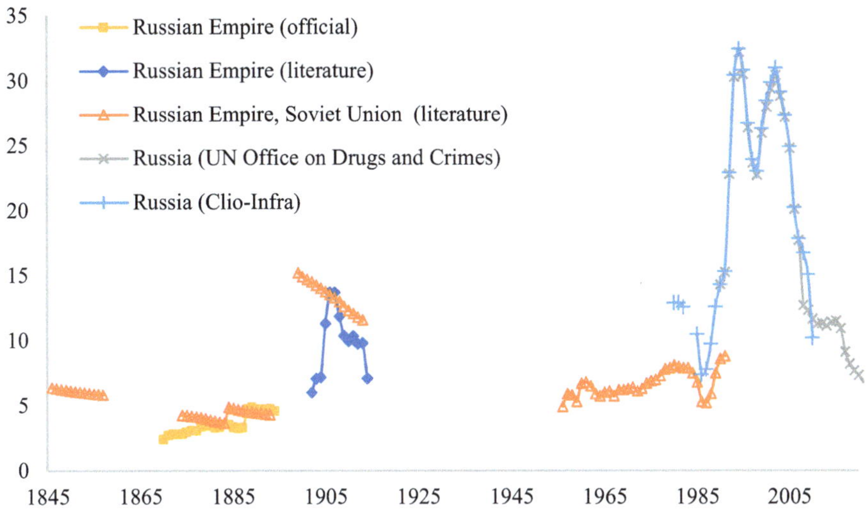

Fig. 10.12 Homicide rates in Central Eurasia, per 100,000 population (1846–2018). *Source:* Homicides: 1846–1913: Mironov (2018, v. 3), TsSk (1894, 1897), Stickley (2006); 1956–1991: Luneev (2005); Population: 1846–1914: TsSK (1918, 5), 1956–1991: Didenko et al. (2013) based on the official statistics; Homocide rates in Russia in 1980–2018: Bierman and Van Zanden (2014), UN Office on Drugs and Crimes (https://dataunodc.un.org/sites/dataunodc.un.org/files/data_cts_intentional_homicide.xlsx)

Table 10.9 Homicide rates in selected countries, per 100,000 population (1800–2010)

	China	Japan	The Netherlands	UK	US	Italy	Poland	Russia
1800				1.6		8.0		
1850			0.8	1.6		7.0		
1900		3.4	0.6	1.0	1.2	3.9		
1930		1.1	0.3	0.8	8.8	2.7	3.2	
1960		1.9	0.3	0.6	4.7	1.4	1.0	
1990		0.6	0.9	1.1	10.4	2.6	1.9	14.3
2010	1.1	0.4	0.9	1.1	4.2	2.3	1.1	10.2

Source: Jonathan Fink-Jensen (2015), http://hdl.handle.net/10622/FMI6L9, accessed via the Clio Infra website

negative trend of the 1990s in the Russian Federation was reversed after its double peak and the rate fell 4.7 times. Yet it remains above historically low levels registered both in the Russian Empire (in the early 1870s) and in the USSR (in the mid-1950s), as well as above present-day Western Europe (but not the US) and China (Table 10.9).

As it follows from Luneev (2005), the upward trends in homicide rate in the late USSR and the Russian Federation of the 1990s were associated with violent felonies, as well as with crimes against property and other economic offences, such as robbery, plunder, theft, racket, bribery, and fraud (even assuming their high degree of latency). Fluctuations in consumption of alcohol (generally strong) appeared to be an important determinant of homicide rates in Russia. The government-initiated measures to curtail its retail sales resulted in a drop in homicide rates (1985–1987 and from the mid-2000s).[32] These measures proved effective as many homicides caused by excessive alcohol consumption were associated with home criminality, frequently casual. Another cause of a hike in homicide rates was economic; that is, violent fighting for the acquisition and redistribution of control over state property subject to privatization. The growth of the government's economic activities had its positive external effect in that the grip of government agents on competing criminal gangs curtailed their violent powers (Latov 2001, 174–179).

10.5 Environment and Pollution

10.5.1 Environment and Well-Being

An exploration of well-being can also extend into the environmental domain, offering an essential complement to the social and economic dimensions discussed earlier. While personal security and corruption reflect the immediate social and institutional challenges faced by societies, the environment provides a broader, long-term context within which well-being is experienced. Environmental factors shape not only the material and economic foundations of human life, but also directly impact health, quality of life, and the sustainability of societal progress. Pollution, resource management, and ecological degradation often create ripple effects that transcend generations, illustrating the profound interplay between the environment and human development.

The environment plays a dual role in well-being: it is both a source of essential resources and a potential threat to health and stability when mismanaged. The historical development of societies demonstrates that approaches to environmental challenges, whether through policy, innovation, or cultural adaptation, have significantly influenced the trajectory of human progress. By exploring how societies have interacted with their natural surroundings, we can gain deeper insights into the multifaceted dimensions of well-being and the critical importance of sustainable environmental stewardship.

Indeed, pollution has always been a significant concern. Even 10,000 years ago, hunter-gatherer societies sought alternative methods to manage waste (Havlíček 2015). While aversion to dirt seems to be a universal human trait (Murdock 1945; Smith 2007), the ways in which societies addressed pollution varied depending on cultural and geographic contexts, as well as whether the pollution was visible or not. In Roman times, urbanization was relatively limited, organized public health systems did not exist, and visibility was confined to one's immediate surroundings. As

[32] Historically, alcohol sales appeared to be an important source of taxation and government revenues. Therefore, a drop of sales in units was accompanied by retail price hikes to increase the per unit taxation and thus partially compensate the loss in monetary terms. In the last 30 years, the role of alcohol taxation for the state budget radically diminished, which allowed the Russian government more flexibility in choosing the measures for anti-criminal and pro-health policies.

a result, pollution affecting air and fresh water received the most attention. According to Mosley (2014), Roman intellectuals expressed significant concern about urban air quality, particularly because of the burning of wood and charcoal in densely populated, poorly ventilated districts (Havlíček and Morcinek 2016). Similarly, water pollution, particularly in urban canals, was a frequent focus of government action. However, outside major cities, fresh-water contamination from human or industrial activities was not a widespread issue until the early modern period, owing to the relatively low population density. Contrary to common assumptions, medieval towns were not always the filthy, sewage-ridden spaces they are often imagined to be (Mumford 1961). As urbanization increased during the late Middle Ages, complaints about pollution began to rise, particularly about smoke from domestic heating, metal mining, and tool manufacturing. By the time of the bubonic plague in 1348, air pollution was even cited as a potential factor contributing to the spread of the disease.

Invisible pollution, although less frequently addressed in ancient times, was also a significant issue. Silver processing, involving the mining and smelting of lead-silver sulphide ores, contributed to substantial emissions of invisible pollutants. McConnell et al. (2018), using a detailed Greenland ice core lead chronology, identified peak lead emissions in Europe between 200 BCE and 200 CE. However, these emissions sharply declined during the second and third centuries, coinciding with the population loss and reduction in mining activity caused by the Antonine and Cyprian plagues. Low lead levels in Greenland ice layers persisted until approximately 700 CE. From the early medieval period onwards, lead smelting saw a significant resurgence, particularly in France and England, with the first recorded use of sea coal in England around the thirteenth century (Te Brake 1975). A subsequent reduction in lead emissions is linked to the 4-year crisis in metal production triggered by the Black Death (*c.* 1346–1353). After this period, lead levels began a steady and gradual increase, continuing until the mid-twentieth century (More et al. 2017).

Both the visible and invisible pollution increased sharply from the end of the eighteenth century. It has been argued that, pollution-wise, the first industrial revolution became visible in Europe between about 1830–1850 and in the southern hemisphere from around the twentieth century (Abram et al. 2016). However, modern pollution, combined with the rise of chemical industry, increased both visible and invisible pollution levels at the end of the nineteenth century.

10.5.2 Awareness of Pollution

During the eighteenth and nineteenth centuries, both visible pollution, such as fresh-water and air contamination, and invisible pollution such as CO_2 (carbon dioxide, see Fig. 10.13) increased significantly. Societal awareness and attitudes towards pollution varied depending on how people perceived its presence and impact. The visibility of pollution, its scale, and its interaction with other social and environmental factors played a key role in shaping public opinion and policy responses. Policy-makers approached environmental problems with differing perspectives: some framed pollution as an inevitable consequence of economic growth,

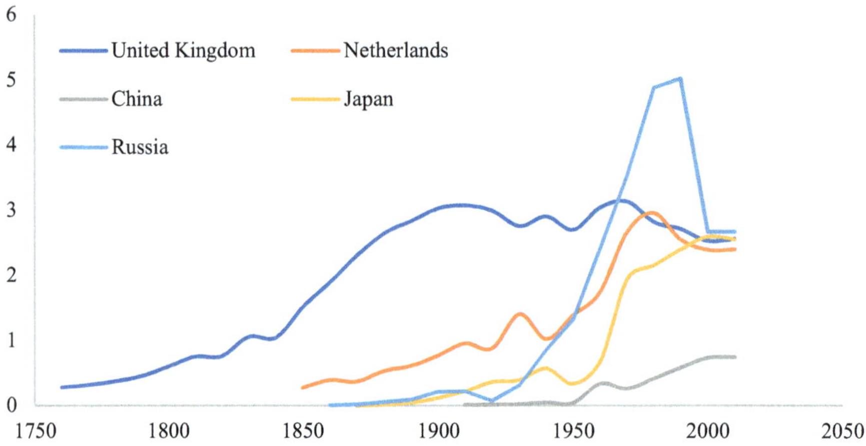

Fig. 10.13 CO_2 emissions per capita for selected countries, 1750–2000. *Source:* Klein Goldewijk (2015)

while others incorporated social considerations, and still others prioritized economic and social well-being without directly addressing productivity or environmental degradation. The press emerged as a critical force in highlighting and influencing public and political responses to pollution. The way individuals confront pollution—or fail to do so—affects their perception of its significance. Urbanization, economic growth, advancements in knowledge, and the proliferation of news media brought pollution into sharper focus, increasing awareness of its dangers. This heightened attention applied to both visible pollutants linked to public hygiene and less visible pollutants, such as CO_2, SO_2 (sulphur dioxide), and more recently, NO_2 (nitrogen dioxide) emissions (Zottola et al. 2020).

One way to trace these shifts in awareness is through the frequency of newspaper articles discussing pollution. As noted by Massard-Guilbaud and Mathis (2017), the term "pollution" originally carried a moral connotation. Its use in the modern environmental sense began in around 1860, initially referring to water pollution and later expanding to other forms of contamination. Consequently, the sharp rise in pollution-related news in the late nineteenth century reflects not only increasing environmental issues, but also a shift in the meaning of the word. For this reason, trends in pollution awareness should be analysed primarily from 1900 onwards, when the term was more consistently used in its contemporary sense.

Indeed, the low level of the number of pollution-related newspaper articles before the 1950s seems to be reflecting an actual trend caused partly by the two world wars (see Figure 10.14). A fast increase occurred in all regions in the 1960s and 1970s, only to fall in the 1980s and rise again in the 1990s and 2000s. These rises were caused mainly by a move away from fresh water, mostly sewage, to air pollution. Air pollution increased from the 1920s in England and from about 1960 in the Netherlands (Fig. 10.15). Sea pollution started a decade earlier in the Netherlands, arguably since it was more linked to sea transport than England.

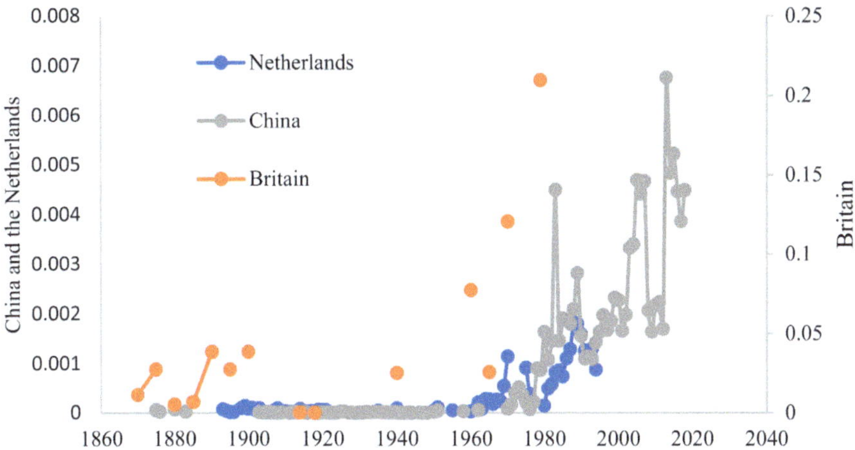

Fig. 10.14 Relative pollution in newspapers in Western Europe and China, c. 1910–present. *Source:* Koninklijke Bibliotheek, De Telegraaf: Delpher (https://www.delpher.nl/); *Newcastle Journal, Liverpool Echo., and Birmingham Daily Post*: British Newspaper Archive (https://www.britishnewspaperarchive.co.uk/); Ye et al. (2025)

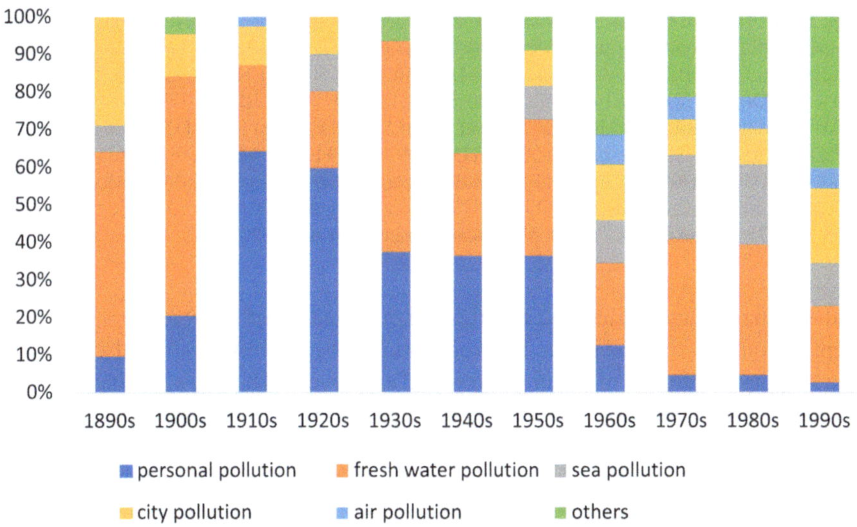

Fig. 10.15 Type of pollution reported in a newspaper in the Netherlands, 1890–1990s. *Note:* Based on De Telegraaf. *Source:* See Fig. 10.14

For Russia, we cannot replicate the same newspaper article method owing to limitations on the part of the sources (a lack of digitized mass media). However, we can track public interest in environmental issues through digitized books. In Fig. 10.16, we can see that in the Russian Empire, the USSR and the Russian Federation environmental thinking grew as the national economy was

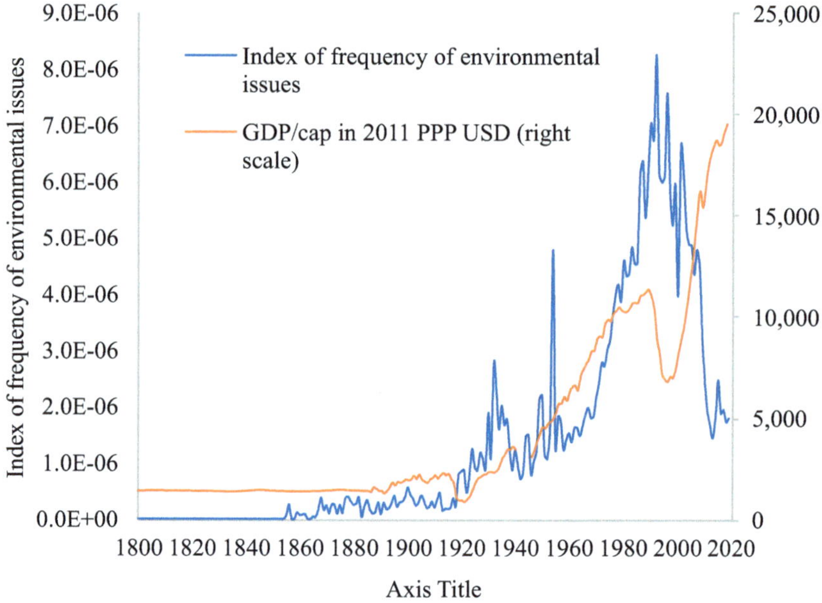

Fig. 10.16 Index of frequency of environmental issues in books published in Russian, 1800–2020. *Source:* Google Books Ngram Viewer. https://books.google.com/ngrams/graph?content=%D1%81%D0%B0%D0%BD%D0%B8%D1%82%D0%B0%D1%80%D0%BD%D0%BE%D0%B5+%D1%81%D0%BE%D1%81%D1%82%D0%BE%D1%8F%D0%BD%D0%B8%D0%B5%2B%D1%8D%D0%BA%D0%BE%D0%BB%D0%BE%D0%B3%D0%B8%D1%8F%2B%D0%BE%D0%BA%D1%80%D1%83%D0%B6%D0%B0%D1%8E%D1%89%D0%B0%D1%8F+%D1%81%D1%80%D0%B5%D0%B4%D0%B0&year_start=1800&year_end=2019&corpus=ru-2019&smoothing=0; GDP/cap in 2011 PPP USD: Broadberry and Korchmina (2024); Cheremukhin et al. (2017); Didenko et al. (2013); Maddison Project Database (2020)

industrializing, and society felt that this not only had benefits but also caused some deprivation and dissatisfaction. Environment is not just pollution, but also refers to the sanitary conditions of urban workers and employees. Therefore, we included the term that was frequently used in the Russian literature in the second half of the nineteenth and early twentieth centuries.

In Russia, environmental thinking and policies started to emerge as railways were built (Konchakov 2012). In the 1830s–1840s, nature was perceived as the main obstacle to this development. Opponents applied a sense of affection for "pure nature", for the land, as an argument for the unprofitability of this enterprise for society as a whole.

As modern economic growth was launched, the railways became the first large-scale challenge to the environment in Russia's agrarian regions. In contrast to factory enterprises, the railways to a much greater extent retained their dependence on natural resources. It was the destruction of forests where the damage to the environment caused by railway construction and operation was most pronounced. Owing to a lack of coal, wood was frequently used as a fuel. To address this problem,

"Regulations on the Preservation of Forests" (1888) was adopted. Therefore, the Ministry of Railways had to shape a policy aimed at protecting forest and water resources. This was able to be implemented as most of the forests in the Russian Empire were the government's property. In addition, the sanitary condition of stations was taken very seriously by the Ministry of Railways. In particular, a number of cholera epidemics resulted in a significant volume of circulars and decrees that regulated various sanitary standards for the maintenance of station buildings.

However, environmental thinking emerged to a great extent because of conservative writers. Those others who claimed to express progressive public opinion often did not realize the importance of environmental protection measures, and consumer attitudes towards nature in the context of industrial development dominated (Konchakov 2012).

Figure 10.16 confirms that public interest in the issue emerged somewhere around the mid-nineteenth century, as the modernizing reforms under Alexander II were launched. In the second half of the nineteenth and early twentieth centuries, public interest was focused on the improvement of environmental sanitation in urban areas. We can observe growing interest after the Russian Revolution of 1917, but this decreased during the Soviet industrialization drive of the 1930s.

Interest revived from the mid-1950s. By that time, a medium-developed industrial society had taken shape in the Soviet Union, and it had been recognized as an industrialized nation. At the same time, much of the public was concerned with environmental pollution and other negative externalities of industrial growth. As Soviet censorship on printed matter eased, compared with the extremely tough period of the 1930s to the mid-1950s, this concern was voiced by both fiction writers and scholars who became prominent public figures at the time. The problem was also heard at official level. It was addressed at the legal level in 1957–1963, when the republics of the USSR adopted their sub-national laws on nature protection (where pollution was considered among other threats to the environment). In 1982, the Russian Republic (as a constituent of the Soviet Union) adopted an additional Law on Air Pollution Prevention. This became a hot topic after the accident at the Chernobyl nuclear power station in 1986,[33] which led to the radioactive pollution of northern Ukraine, much of Belarus, and several provinces of the Russian Republic to the south-west of its capital, Moscow. The rapid easing and final abandonment of censorship under the policies of transparency (glasnost) and restructuring (perestroika) led to a jump in frequency of the topic's discussion, with the peak in 1992 (texts were mostly written a little earlier, at the turn of the 1980s and 1990s). But later on, deindustrialization in the 1990s, as a consequence of economic decline, made the pollution problem less acute than others. The downturn on the right-hand side of Fig. 10.16 reflects the change in public sentiment.

Summing up the dynamics of public interest in environmental pollution, we should conclude that in general the dynamics in lower income countries are similar

[33] https://www.iaea.org/topics/chornobyl, https://www.un.org/en/observances/chernobyl-remembrance-day/background

to those of industrialized nations, with the notable difference that despite industrial recovery during the last two decades, the pollution topic was losing its appeal and position among other public concerns.

10.5.3 Change of Pollution over Time and Region

As explored in the preceding section, public awareness of and willingness to address pollution are deeply influenced by perceptions of its seriousness and the trade-offs between environmental preservation and economic growth. These attitudes are shaped not only by cultural and institutional factors, but also by the way pollution itself is framed. Over time, this has evolved significantly, moving from tangible concerns such as dirt, smoke, and hygiene, to more specific environmental issues such as freshwater pollution and air pollution, and ultimately to broader, more abstract global challenges such as global warming and climate change. This progression mirrors changing societal priorities and reflects the interplay of scientific understanding, policy development, and public discourse in shaping how pollution is perceived and addressed (Fig. 10.17).

Concrete examples of pollution remediation often garner stronger public support owing to their tangible and immediate effects. For instance, SO_2 emissions decreased more rapidly in the late twentieth and early twenty-first centuries because SO_2 directly affects emitting regions by depositing close to the source. In contrast, CO_2 emissions, which disperse globally, offer fewer visible benefits from localized reduction efforts.

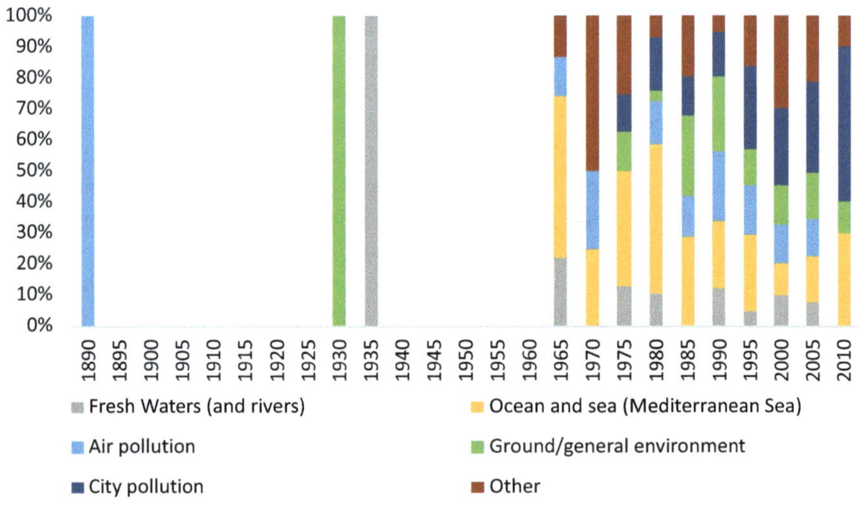

Fig. 10.17 Type of pollution reported in a newspaper in southern Italy, 1890–2010. *Source:* Gazzetta del Mezzogiorno

Abstract pollution concepts, such as air pollution and global warming, gain traction when associated with practical, observable phenomena such as smog. A 2017 study by Tvinnereim et al. illustrated this dynamic in China, where smog—a physical manifestation of air pollution—ties industrial activities to both air pollution and global warming. This connection fosters public interest in mitigating these issues. Similar patterns are observed in countries such as Norway, where public awareness extends to global warming owing to a greater familiarity with concepts such as the melting of glaciers. The perception of pollution also varies across social groups. In China, smog is predominantly identified as a problem by women, educated individuals, and younger demographics, whereas men are more likely to attribute air pollution and global warming to vehicles and factories. In Norway, however, broader environmental knowledge leads to a wider cross-section of people to recognize global warming as a critical issue.

An examination of newspaper archives further reveals how societal concerns about pollution have shifted over time (Figs. 10.18a–c). Chinese newspapers in the 1950s and 1960s predominantly framed pollution in vague and generic terms, reflecting limited public awareness and scientific understanding of distinct pollution

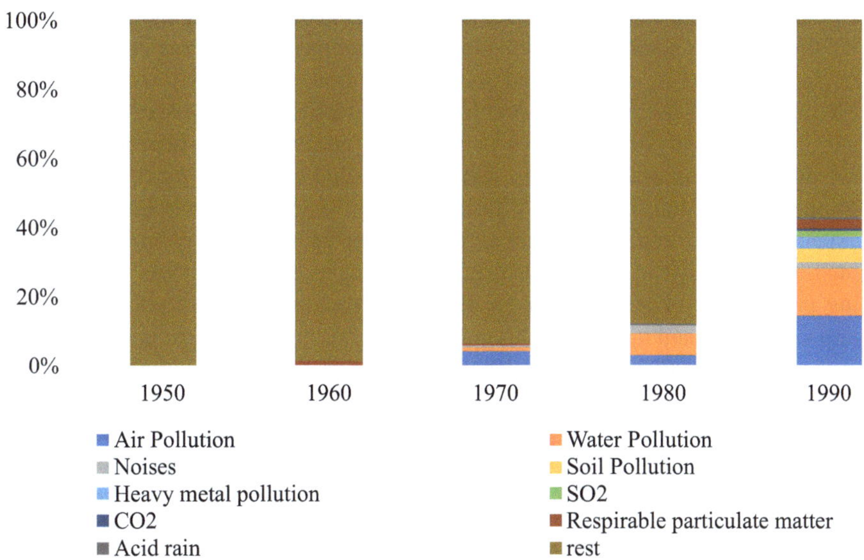

Fig. 10.18 Type of pollution reported in newspapers in China, 1950–1990. (In Chinese, the term "environment pollution" (环境污染) encompasses a broader meaning than merely referring to the natural environment. Further research is required to identify the specific keywords used in newspapers during different periods to fully understand how the concept was framed. For instance, in the 1950s, "environment pollution" (环境污染) carried a meaning distinct from its usage in the 1990s. During earlier periods, the term may have been more closely associated with localized issues, such as urban hygiene (城市卫生) or industrial smoke (工业烟尘), whereas by the 1990s, it had expanded to include broader concerns such as air pollution (空气污染), water pollution (水污染), and even global phenomena such as acid rain (酸雨) and climate change (气候变化).) *Source:* See below Fig. 10.14

types. By the 1970s, air pollution began to emerge as a specific concern, driven by the visible impacts of industrial emissions in urban centres, marking the initial shift towards more specific environmental awareness. This diversification accelerated into the 1980s and 1990s, as mentions of water pollution, soil contamination, and pollutants such as CO_2 and SO_2 became increasingly common. During this period, acid rain and particulate matter also entered public discourse, indicating a growing acknowledgement of the complex and interconnected nature of environmental challenges. In the Netherlands, reports in *De Telegraaf* between 1890 and 1990 transitioned from focusing on local hygiene and smoke to broader concerns such as air pollution and climate change. Birmingham's *Birmingham Daily Post* exhibited a similar trajectory from the 1850s to the 1970s, with initial emphasis on industrial smoke evolving into awareness of global environmental issues. Comparable trends are observed in Liverpool and Newcastle, as chronicled in the *Liverpool Echo* and *Newcastle Journal*. Italy's *Gazzetta del Mezzogiorno* also documents a striking shift from local pollution issues to discussions of national and global environmental concerns between 1890 and 2010. Early coverage, as suggested by Fig. 10.17, focused heavily on freshwater pollution, particularly in rivers, which dominated public discourse up to the 1930s. This focus reflects the essential role of clean water in sustaining agriculture and urban centres during a period of increasing industrialization. By the 1960s, a notable diversification in environmental concerns emerged, with rising attention to marine and ocean pollution, particularly regarding the Mediterranean Sea. This shift highlights the growing awareness of coastal and marine ecosystem vulnerabilities in a country geographically dependent on the Mediterranean for trade, fishing, and tourism (this being true especially for the southern part of Italy). By the 1970s and 1980s, the scope of environmental issues expanded further to include urban air pollution and general city pollution, paralleling Italy's rapid urban and industrial growth during its economic boom. The increasing prominence of air pollution in media narratives reflects not only the visible impact of smog and industrial emissions, but also the public health concerns associated with urbanization. From the 1990s onwards, the framing of pollution in Italian media became ever more comprehensive, with growing mentions of ground pollution and general environmental degradation reflecting heightened awareness of waste management and land contamination issues. Simultaneously, the "other" category of pollution began to appear more frequently in media reports, signalling an engagement with emerging global challenges such as climate change and biodiversity loss. By 2010, *Gazzetta del Mezzogiorno* had therefore transitioned from reporting primarily on local and national issues to adopting a broader, global perspective on environmental concerns, mirroring Italy's integration into international environmental policy and discourse.

Although the practical effects of air pollution can foster awareness of broader issues such as global warming, the relationship is not always linear. For example, reducing coal usage for energy simultaneously benefits public health and mitigates climate change (Haines et al. 2009). However, measures targeting air pollution can occasionally increase CO_2 emissions, as energy-intensive air-cleaning technologies in factories demonstrate (Randolph and Dolsak 1996).

10.5.4 Framing Pollution

Environmental awareness often varies depending on the type of pollution under consideration, including salt-water, fresh-water, air, and soil pollution. We can apply political or social frames relating to farming, economics, climate, scientific progress, public health, and government.

These perceptions significantly shape public attitudes towards environmental policies and their willingness to make personal sacrifices for ecological improvements. We can place this framing model (Fig. 10.19); yet these data are less evident for China. However, we might refer to Ye et al. (2025), who give an overview of how environment was reflected in the 5-year plans. The main conclusion is that the framing is the same in all countries.

But how do people respond to this framing? A survey conducted in May 2022 for this book (see Appendixes D and E) revealed notable differences in how pollution is perceived across various countries. Russian internet users expressed a higher level of concern about pollution than their Chinese counterparts, but were somewhat less alarmed than respondents in Western countries, such as the Netherlands and Italy. This trend is illustrated in Fig. 10.20, which shows public opinion on the seriousness of pollution by country. Notably, Chinese respondents, on average, regarded pollution as a less severe issue than those in other nations. Interestingly, ground pollution—despite its critical significance in modern environmental challenges—was consistently viewed as the least problematic type of pollution, a perception that perhaps reflects historical priorities and a focus on more visible or immediate environmental issues.

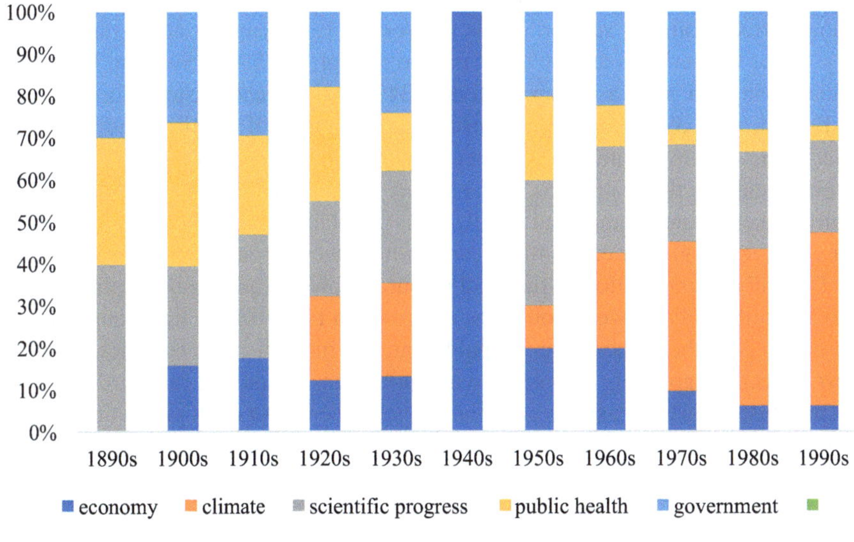

Fig. 10.19 Framing of pollution in the public debate in the Netherlands. *Source:* DELPHER. (downloaded in 2024)

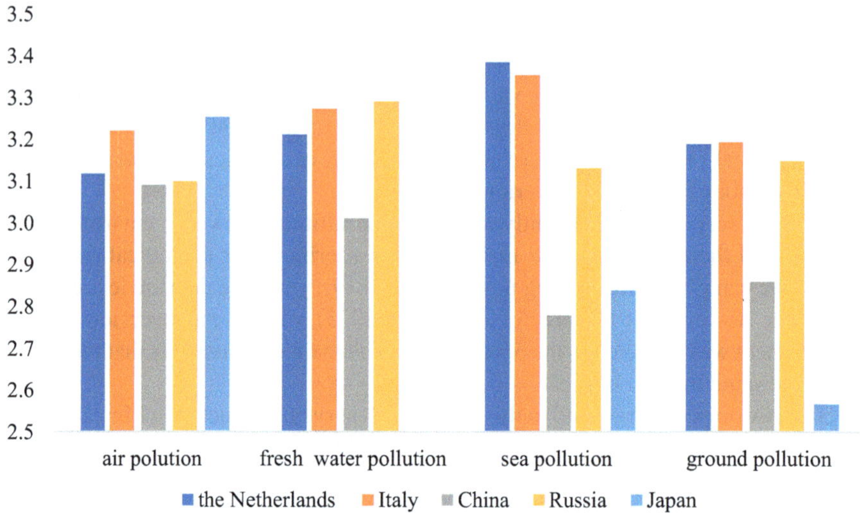

Fig. 10.20 Opinion on seriousness of pollution by country, 2022. *Note:* Higher is worse. *Source:* Our surveys (see Appendixes D and E)

These findings align with broader trends in attitudes towards the trade-off between economic growth and environmental protection. In China, for example, the share of the population supporting environmental preservation, even at the expense of slower economic growth and job loss, has grown significantly over the past decades. As shown in Table 10.10, support increased from 51.3% in 1995 to 68.2% in 2018. This upward trend in environmental prioritization likely reflects increasing public awareness of ecological issues caused by decades of rapid industrialization. Comparatively, similar support levels in Western European countries range from 50% in the Netherlands and 56% in Spain to as high as 85% in Sweden. However, countries in Asia, such as Japan, with only 34% support, and Eastern Europe, such as Poland, with 39% support demonstrate lower levels of public commitment to prioritizing the environment over economic growth. Demographic factors also play a role in shaping these attitudes, with support for environmental prioritization generally higher among women and middle-class populations, possibly reflecting stronger advocacy or greater economic security within these groups.

The willingness to allocate financial resources towards addressing pollution also varies significantly between countries, as shown in Fig. 10.21. China stands out as the nation with the highest share of public interest in eradicating pollution in 2022. This reflects a growing alignment with global environmental standards despite China's historical emphasis on economic development over ecological concerns. In Russia, however, a relatively low share of funds intended for environmental improvements suggests public distrust in government institutions or their ability to effectively manage and address ecological challenges. This discrepancy between willingness and institutional trust highlights an important barrier to collective environmental action.

Table 10.10 Share of the Chinese population who think the environment should get priority over the economy, 1995–2018

	1995	2007	2013	2018
Protecting the environment should be given priority, even if it causes slower economic growth and some loss of jobs	51.3%	53.6%	56.6%	68.2%
Economic growth and creating jobs should be the top priority, even if the environment suffers to some extent	24.4%	23.0%	28.0%	26.2%
Other answer	9.3%	4.2%	2.4%	4.7%
Don't know	15.0%	18.7%	8.4%	0.4%
No answer	0.0%	0.4%	4.6%	0.5%

Source: Inglehart et al. (2020)

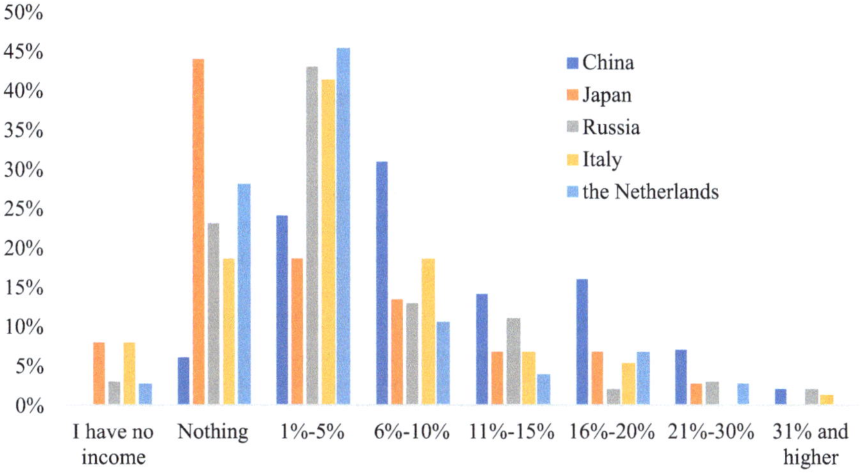

Fig. 10.21 Share among the population prepared to sacrifice a share of their income for the environment should get priority over the economy for selected countries, 1995–2018. *Source:* Our surveys (see Appendixes D and E)

Figure 10.21 and Table 10.8 ultimately give a glimpse of these global and regional disparities. The former illustrates differences in the perceived seriousness of pollution, which often guides public and governmental priorities. The latter provides a longitudinal view of the growing environmental awareness in China, emphasizing how rapid socio-economic development can influence attitudes over time. These data points reveal an ongoing shift towards greater environmental consciousness globally, albeit unevenly distributed across regions, shaped by historical, cultural, and institutional factors. Together, they paint a nuanced picture of the complex relationship between economic priorities, environmental awareness, and public action.

10.6 Measuring Happiness as a Perception-Based Indicator

As discussed earlier, anthropometric data and inequality indices provide a quantitative framework for assessing societal well-being. But can we delve even deeper to explore more intimate and subjective dimensions of well-being? Take the concept of happiness, for instance. At first glance, happiness might appear to be an abstract and unmeasurable notion—profoundly personal, culturally specific, and inherently multifaceted. How could such a subjective feeling ever be expressed in numbers?

In the last years, researchers have developed systematic methods to measure happiness, bridging the gap between subjective experiences and empirical analysis. By combining subjective assessments of well-being with broader indicators of life satisfaction, happiness can be quantified in meaningful ways. This approach captures both material and immaterial factors, offering valuable insights into quality of life and societal progress that go beyond traditional economic metrics. Through these methods, happiness changes from an elusive concept to a measurable aspect of human experience, thus opening new avenues for understanding and improving well-being.

Happiness can indeed be considered as a composite measure of both material and immaterial well-being, like HDI. But unlike HDI, it is a completely subjective concept capturing overall life satisfaction and available for both direct and indirect measurement.

In the emergence of happiness economics (Layard 2005), the discussion over the so-called Easterlin effect appeared to be an important milestone. Easterlin (1974) found that at some point in time happiness positively correlates with income, both among and within nations, but over time happiness does not trend upward as income continues to grow. However, Frey and Stutzer (2002) argued that this relationship extends only above a threshold of GDP per capita level.

Theoretical background of happiness economics has resulted in a number of reports and data sets: the World Database of Happiness, Erasmus University Rotterdam (Veenhoven 2022),[34] and the World Happiness Report, published on an annual basis starting from 2012 (since 2024 by the Oxford Well-Being Research Centre).[35]

For identification of historical patterns of happiness in certain countries, we created our Happiness indices by extracting them from the Google Books Ngram Viewer, which demonstrates frequencies of words and/or phrase usage in particular languages over a specified period of time.[36] We constructed our queries (Ngram compositions) as a ratio of sums of synonymic words for happiness and the opposite

[34] https://worlddatabaseofhappiness.eur.nl

[35] https://wellbeing.hmc.ox.ac.uk/

[36] https://books.google.com/ngrams/info. For an earlier attempt, see the work by Thomas Hills, Professor of Psychology, Warwick University; Eugenio Proto, Associate Professor, Warwick University; and Daniel Sgroi, Associate Professor of Economics, Warwick University—originally published at VoxEU.

sentiment.[37] By cross-checking with extractions from Google Books by 5-year compositions, we find that the trends are basically the same as for smoothed series extracted from the Ngram Viewer. Figure 10.22 provides a representation of the Happiness Index for the Netherlands from 1600 to 2010, alongside GDP per capita expressed in 2011 PPP USD.

The figure highlights several critical patterns and historical correlations. From 1600 to the mid-nineteenth century, the Happiness Index fluctuated within a relatively narrow range, showing stability despite changes in the broader socio-economic landscape. This period coincided with steady, albeit modest, GDP per capita growth, reflecting a pre-industrial economy with limited advancements in material wealth. A shift occurs instead during the late nineteenth and early twentieth centuries, as the Happiness Index begins to rise alongside a gradual increase in GDP per capita. This trend reflects the transformative effects of industrialization and modernization on both material well-being and societal outlooks. The post-World War II period, however, marks a particularly dramatic increase in both metrics. The GDP per capita sees exponential growth, driven by rapid economic expansion, technological advancements, and the development of a modern welfare state. Simultaneously, the Happiness Index experiences a sharp upward trajectory, suggesting a strong positive correlation between material prosperity and reported happiness. Interestingly, the graph also reveals a divergence in the late twentieth and early twenty-first centuries. While GDP per capita continues to climb steadily, the Happiness Index exhibits significant volatility, with sharp peaks and troughs. This suggests that beyond a certain threshold, economic growth may not directly translate into sustained increases in happiness. Factors such as rising inequality, environmental concerns,

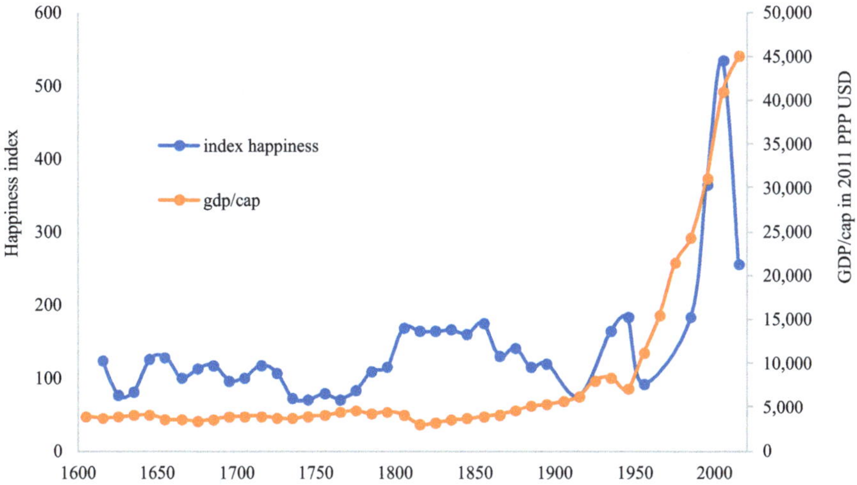

Fig. 10.22 Happiness Index as represented by Ngram for the Netherlands, 1600–2010. *Source:* *GDP: Maddison Board; Index: NGRAM Netherlands

[37] https://books.google.com/ngrams/inf

and shifts in cultural values may contribute to this decoupling of economic and emotional well-being.

When explaining the Happiness Index dynamics for Russia (Fig. 10.23), we should bear in mind the official discourse that predominated in the books published in Russian, not just in political but also in "public moral" issues.

For the late 1810s–1815, it is most likely the effect of the Napoleonic wars, which Russia eventually won with the coalition of major European powers. In the summer of 1812, the French Emperor Napoleon I invaded Russia, which participated in several campaigns against France since the late eighteenth century, although not very successfully. His army occupied Moscow, but was defeated and fled in December. That campaign (the Patriotic War in Russia) was successful in reviving the coalition against France, which led to the allies occupying Paris in 1814 and restoring the old royal regime. Unsurprisingly, the Happiness Index was low in 1808 (following the Russian army defeat together with the Prussian defeat in 1807 and the unpopular Treaty of Tilsit) and in 1812 (the invasion and occupation of Moscow), but jumped in 1813–1815 (after the French army's defeat).

The Russian government's censorship of books was not tough from the 1860s to 1905, when it was finally abolished. Yet after the Revolution of 1917, it was introduced again in a much tougher form. In the 1920s, the official discourse dominated, although alternative views were somewhat tolerated. But the 1930s to the mid-1950s were the time of total government control of publishing and proactive propaganda. We can see on Fig. 10.23 that in 1941–1945, the effects of the Great Patriotic War for the USSR (strong swings of the Happiness Index depending on losing or winning the campaigns) have not revealed themselves so strongly as was in the case of the Napoleonic wars in the 1800s–1810s. In the mid-1950s to the late 1980s, the official discourse domination somewhat eased, as its Tsarist predecessor had, despite total censorship being retained not only in political but also in cultural topics. It should not be surprising to see the Happiness Index decrease from the mid-1980s to the early 2000s if we compare it with negative GDP dynamics, even though rapid easing and abandonment of censorship occurred by the 1990s. Nor can its increase in the 2000s during economic recovery be surprising. In the 2010s, despite the intensified regulation of mass media activities, book publishing received much less of the Russian government's attention—or at least there were no significant cases of direct involvement. And the increase of the Happiness Index in the 2010s relative to the 2000s is generally supported by results of other surveys.[38]

10.7 Conclusion Beyond GDP

Up to this chapter, this book has dealt with GDP per capita as a main indicator of well-being. The analysis in this chapter shows the limitations of GDP as a comprehensive measure of well-being, emphasizing the importance of incorporating

[38] E.g. https://wciom.com/our-news/ratings/happiness-index, https://worlddatabaseofhappiness.eur.nl/wp-content/uploads/TrendsInNations_2022b.xlsx, column P "m_bw11_ru"; despite Gallup International reporting its collapse in 2019–2021 (GIA 2021, 17).

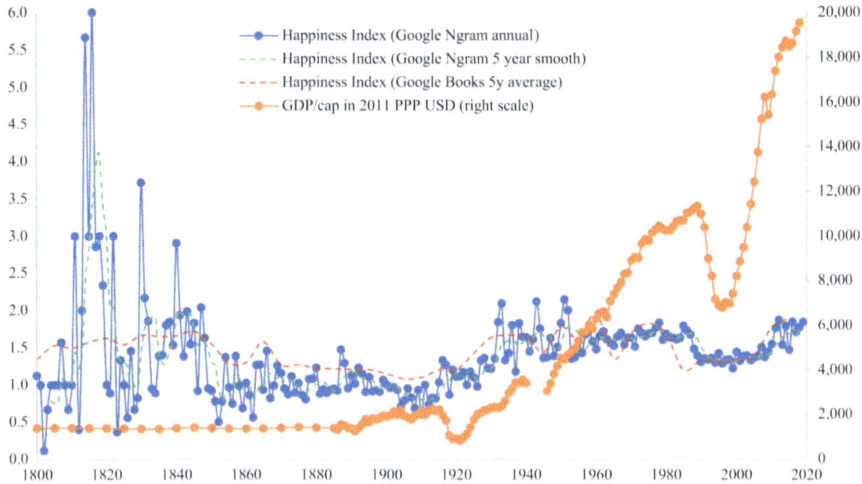

Fig. 10.23 Happiness Index as represented by books in Russian, 1800–2019. *Source:* Google Ngram annual: https://books.google.com/ngrams/graph?content=%28%D1%80%D0%B0%D0%B4%D0%BE%D1%81%D1%82%D0%BD%D1%8B%D0%B9+%2B+%D1%81%D1%87%D0%B0%D1%81%D1%82%D0%BB%D0%B8%D0%B2%D1%8B%D0%B9%29+%2F+%28%D0%B3%D1%80%D1%83%D1%81%D1%82%D0%BD%D1%8B%D0%B9+%2B+%D0%BF%D0%B5%D1%87%D0%B0%D0%BB%D1%8C%D0%BD%D1%8B%D0%B9%29&year_start=1800&year_end=2019&corpus=ru-2019&smoothing=0; Happiness Index (Google Books 5y average) obtained from: https://www.google.com/search?q=%D1%80%D0%B0%D0%B4%D0%BE%D1%81%D1%82%D0%BD%D1%8B%D0%B9+OR+%D1%81%D1%87%D0%B0%D1%81%D1%82%D0%BB%D0%B8%D0%B2%D1%8B%D0%B9&newwindow=1&tbs=bkt:b,cdr:1,cd_min:1/1/2015,cd_max:12/31/2019,bkv:a&tbm=bks&sxsrf=APwXEdcLt5oQthSG1bSLr8BEaPFdH2YjsQ:1683161175560&source=lnt&sa=X&ved=2ahUKEwjY8t__t9r-AhUMplsKHeiBAV8QpwV6BAgBEBg&biw=1536&bih=719&dpr=1.25 and https://www.google.com/search?q=%D0%B3%D1%80%D1%83%D1%81%D1%82%D0%BD%D1%8B%D0%B9+OR+%D0%BF%D0%B5%D1%87%D0%B0%D0%BB%D1%8C%D0%BD%D1%8B%D0%B9&newwindow=1&tbas=0&tbs=bkt:b,cdr:1,cd_min:1/1/2015,cd_max:12/31/2019,bkv:a&tbm=bks&sxsrf=APwXEdeAJ25uP2QiEx5mVOqqjJqFjw-icw:1683161220582&source=lnt&sa=X&ved=2ahUKEwjl25uVuNr-AhWQposKHYXuCPkQpwV6BAgBEBg&biw=1536&bih=719&dpr=1.25; GDP/cap in 2011 PPP USD: Broadberry and Korchmina (2024); Cheremukhin et al. (2017); Didenko et al. (2013); Maddison Project Database (2020)

broader metrics that account for inequality, environmental sustainability, and social dimensions of development. For example, since the 1970s in the West, and later in China, environmental history has emerged as a distinct field, initially focusing on specific environmental phenomena such as deforestation, water management, and pollution in historical contexts. More recently, efforts have been directed at integrating environmental costs into GDP calculations, reflecting the growing recognition that economic growth often comes at significant ecological and social costs. However, the challenge remains in how to adequately measure these costs, as public perceptions and political priorities vary widely across time and regions. In this regard, China, a latecomer to industrialization, saw its pollution rise sharply from the 1950s onwards, eventually becoming one of the world's largest polluters. Smog, often associated with urban air pollution, has since become a visible and politically charged issue in the country, underscoring the complex interplay between environmental degradation and societal responses.

Throughout this chapter, we have explored various individual measures of well-being, including inequality, pollution, and composite indices such as the HDI, GNH, and the OECD's "How Was Life?" series. While these frameworks provide valuable insights into different dimensions of well-being, integrating them into a single, cohesive measure remains a significant methodological challenge. Efforts to standardize such measures highlight the difficulty of balancing material prosperity with broader societal and environmental goals. Moreover, the distribution of benefits and access to resources add another layer of complexity, as economic growth and environmental impacts are often unevenly distributed both within and across nations.

The historical trends analysed in this chapter, including happiness indices derived from textual data, highlight the potential of perception-based metrics to enrich our understanding of well-being. For instance, the happiness trends in the Netherlands (Fig. 10.21) demonstrate a strong historical correlation between economic growth and happiness and also reveal growing divergence in recent decades. This suggests that beyond a certain threshold, material wealth alone does not guarantee sustained improvements in well-being, with factors such as inequality, social cohesion, and environmental degradation increasingly shaping societal satisfaction.

Further research is needed to develop robust methodologies for integrating diverse measures of well-being into cohesive indices, exploring innovative weighting systems that balance material, social, and environmental dimensions while accounting for regional and historical specificities. The role of public perceptions and cultural values in shaping environmental and social priorities warrants deeper investigation, particularly through comparative studies across different historical contexts and regions to understand how societies perceive trade-offs between economic growth and environmental sustainability. Moreover, examining the long-term consequences of environmental degradation and inequality on societal resilience and adaptability could provide valuable insights into how these factors interact over time. Finally, the effectiveness of policy interventions in mediating these relationships, such as redistributive policies, environmental regulations, and investments in public goods, could be examined to better understand pathways towards sustainable and equitable well-being. By addressing these questions, future research can contribute to the development of a more comprehensive and inclusive framework for assessing human progress, one that moves beyond GDP to better capture the multidimensional nature of well-being.

References

Abram N, McGregor H, Tierney J et al. (2016) Early onset of industrial-era warming across the oceans and continents. Nat 536:411–418. https://doi.org/10.1038/nature19082

Aidt TS (2009) Corruption, institutions, and economic development. Oxf Rev Econ Policy 25(2):271–291

Atkinson AB, Micklewright J (1992) Economic transformation in Eastern Europe and the Distribution of Income. Cambridge University Press, Cambridge

Bardhan P (1997) Corruption and development: a review of issues. J Econ Lit 35(3):1320–1346

Barro RJ, Lee J-W (2015) Education matters: global schooling gains from the 19th to the 21st century. Oxford University Press, New York. Data set: http://barrolee.com/data/oup_download_b.htm

Baten J, Blum M (2015) Height [data set]. IISH Data Collection, V1. https://hdl.handle.net/10622/IAEKLA

Baten J, Bierman W, Földvári P, Van Zanden JL (2014) Personal security since 1820. In: van Zanden JL et al (eds) How was life?: global well-being since 1820. OECD Publishing, pp 139–158. https://doi.org/10.1787/9789264214262-17-en

Baten J, Ma D, Morgan S, Wang Q (2010) Evolution of living standards and human capital in China in the 18–20th centuries: Evidences from real wages, age-heaping, and anthropometrics. Explor Econ Hist 47(3):347–359

Bierman W, Van Zanden JL (2014) Homicide rates, 1800–2010. https://clio-infra.eu/Indicators/HomicideRates.html

Bolt J, Van Zanden JL (2020) Maddison Project Database, version 2020: maddison-style estimates of the evolution of the world economy: a new 2020 update. [Database]. Maddison Project

Brennan L, McDonald J, Shlomowitz R (1994) Trends in the economic well-being of South Indians under British rule: The anthropometric evidence. Expl Econ Hist 31:225–260. https://doi.org/10.1006/exeh.1994.1011

Broadberry S, Korchmina E (2024) Catching-up and falling behind: Russian economic growth, 1960s–1880s. J Econ Hist 84(4):997–1028. https://doi.org/10.1017/s0022050724000287

Broadberry S, Custodis J, Gupta B (2015) India and the great divergence: An Anglo-Indian comparison of GDP per capita, 1600–1871. Expl Econ Hist 55:58–75. https://doi.org/10.1016/j.eeh.2014.04.003

Cheremukhin A, Golosov M, Guriev S, Tsyvinski A (2017) The industrialization and economic development of Russia through the lens of a neoclassical growth model. Rev Econ Stud 84(2):613–649. https://doi.org/10.1093/restud/rdw026

Combes P-P, Lafourcade M, Thisse J-F, Toutain J-C (2011) The rise and fall of spatial inequalities in France: a long-run perspective. Explor Econ Hist 48(2):243–271

Crafts NFR (2005) Regional GDP in Britain, 1871–1911: some estimates. Scottish J Polit Econ 52(1):54–64

Davis C (2010) Understanding the legacy: health financing systems in the USSR and central and Eastern Europe prior to transition. In: Kutzin J, Cashin C, Jakab M (eds) Implementing health financing reform: lessons from countries in transition, Observatory Studies Series No. 21. World Health Organization—European Observatory on Health Systems and Policies, Copenhagen, pp 25–63

DeSilva JM, Traniello JFA, Claxton AG, Fannin LD (2021) When and why did human brains decrease in size? A new change-point analysis and insights from brain evolution in ants. Front Ecol Evol 9:712. https://doi.org/10.3389/fevo.2021.742639

Didenko DV (2015) Интеллектуалоемкая экономика: человеческий капитал в российском и мировом социально-экономическом развитии [Knowledge-intensive economy: human capital in Russian and global socio-economic development]. Aletheia, St. Petersburg

Didenko DV (2020) Trends and institutional sources of financing Russia's human capital formation (late nineteenth–early twenty-first centuries). In: Hanes C, Wolcott S (eds) Research in economic history, vol 36. Emerald Publishing Limited, Bingley, pp 45–107. https://doi.org/10.1108/S0363-326820200000036002

Didenko DV (2021) Spatial inequality and human capital formation in the transition of European Russia to the "modern" type of economic growth (late 19th to early 20th centuries). Mir Rossii (Universe of Russia) 30(3):100–126. https://doi.org/10.17323/1811-038X-2021-30-3-100-126

Didenko DV (2023) Data set "Ряды данных о вековых тенденциях неравенства доходов в России" [Time series on secular trends of income inequality in Russia]. Registration certificate # 2023624240. https://elibrary.ru/wdhglg

Didenko DV (2024) Институциональные источники формирования человеческого капитала в регионах Европейской России, Сибири и Дальнего Востока (конец XIX–начало XX в.) [Institutional sources of human capital formation in the regions of European Russia, the Siberia, and the far east (late 19th–early 20th centuries)]. Tomsk State Univ J Hist 90:17–29

Didenko D, Földvári P, Van Leeuwen B (2013) The spread of human capital in the former soviet union Area in a comparative perspective: exploring a new dataset. J Eurasian Stud 4(2):123–135. https://doi.org/10.1016/j.euras.2013.03.002. (Supplementary data retrieved from https://ars.els-cdn.com/content/image/1-s2.0-S1879366513000122-mmc1.zip, via https://www.sciencedirect.com/science/article/pii/S1879366513000122)

Didenko DV, Konchakov RB, Karpenko MA (2022) Динамика благосостояния населения регионов России (по данным городской статистики XIX в.–начало XX в.) [Welfare Dynamics of the Russian Regions Population (Based on the Urban Statistical Data of the 19th–Early 20th Centuries)]. Information newsletter for the Association History and Computer. 47: 52–53. In: Proceedings of the international academic conference "historical informatics as historical data science" and the 18th conference of the association "history and computing": to the 30th anniversary of the AIC and the 10th Anniversary of the Journal "Historical Informatics". Moscow, 11–13 November 2022. https://aik-hisc.ru/static/pdfs/Бюллетень_АИК/Бюллетень_АИК_49/Бюллетень_АИК_49.pdf

Easterlin RA (1974) Does economic growth improve the human lot? Some empirical evidence. In: David PA, Reder MW (eds) Nations and households in economic growth: essays in honor of moses abramovitz. Academic Press, Inc., New York, pp 89–125

Eichholtz PMA (1997) A long-run house price index: the Herengracht index, 1628–1973. Real Estate Econ 25(2):175–192

Eichholtz P, Korevaar M, Lindenthal T (2023) Limited growth: 500 years of urban rents. SSRN. https://doi.org/10.2139/ssrn.3418495

Ellman M (2004) Soviet Industrialization: a Remarkable Success? Slav Rev 63(4):841–849

Fedotov DY (2024) Эволюция восприятия коррупционных практик в истории России [Evolution of the perception of corrupt practices in the history of Russia]. J Econ Hist Hist Econ 25(1):119–149

Felice E (2012) Regional convergence in Italy (1891–2001) testing human and social capital. Cliometrica 6(3):267–306

Frey BS, Stutzer A (2002) Happiness and economics: how the economy and institutions affect human well-being. Princeton University Press, Princeton, NJ

Frier B (2001) More is worse. Some observations on the population of the Roman Empire. In W Scheidel (Ed.), Debating Roman Demography (pp. 139–159). Leiden: Brill.

GIA (2021) Less hope and happiness in the world 2021. Gallup International Association. https://www.gallup-international.com/fileadmin/user_upload/surveys_and_news/2021/GIA_EoY_2021_PR1_Q1_Q2_Q3.pdf

Gimpelson VE, Treisman D (2018) Misperceiving inequality. Econ Polit 30(1):27–54

Gosplan SSSR (1929) Контрольные цифры народного хозяйства СССР на 1928/1929 г. [Control figures of the national economy of the USSR for 1928/1929]. Planovoe Khoziaistvo, Moscow

Guntupalli AM, Baten J (2006) The Development and Inequality of Heights in North, West and East India, 1915-44. Explor Econ Hist 43(4):578–608

Haines A, McMichael AJ, Smith KR, et al. (2009) Public health benefits of strategies to reduce greenhouse-gas emissions: Overview and implications for policy makers. Lancet 374:2104–2114.

Haq MU (1995) Reflections on human development. Oxford University Press, New York

Havlíček F (2015) Waste management in hunter-gatherer communities. J Landsc Ecol 8(2):47–59

Havlíček F, Morcinek M (2016) Waste and pollution in the ancient roman empire. J Landsc Ecol 9(3):33–49

Huntington SP (1968) Political order in changing societies. Yale University Press, New Haven and London

Inglehart R, Haerpfer C, Moreno A, Welzel C, Kizilova K, Diez-Medrano J, Lagos M, Norris P, Ponarin E, Puranen B (Eds.). (2020). World values survey: All rounds – Country-pooled datafile. Madrid, Spain & Vienna, Austria: JD Systems Institute & WVSA Secretariat. Retrieved from http://www.worldvaluessurvey.org/WVSDocumentationWVL.jsp

Kapelyuk SD (2019) Wage inequality: how large is the contribution of discrimination? Bull Siberian Univ Consum Cooperat 1:12–31
Khlevniuk OV (2023) Корпорация самозванцев: теневая экономика и коррупция в сталинском СССР [Corporation of impostors: shadow economy and corruption in Stalin's USSR]. NLO, Moscow
Kim S (1998) Economic integration and convergence: U.S. Regions, 1840–1987. J Econ Hist 58(3):659–683
Kir'yanov YI (1979) Жизненный уровень рабочих России (конец XIX–начало XX в.) [Living standards of Russian workers (late 19th–early 20th century)]. Nauka, Moscow
Klein Goldewijk, K. (2015a). CO2 emissions per capita. http://hdl.handle.net/10622/DG654S, accessed via the Clio Infra website.
Koepke N, Baten J (2005) The biological standard of living in Europe during the last two millennia. Eur Rev Econ Hist 9(1):61–95
Komlos J (1998) Shrinking in a growing economy? The mystery of physical stature during the industrial revolution. J Econ Hist 58(3):779–802. https://doi.org/10.1017/S0022050700021161
Komlos J, Cinnirella F (2005) European Heights in the Early 18th Century, Discussion Papers in Economics 572. University of Munich, Department of Economics.
Konchakov RB (2012) Environmental aspects of railway construction in 1860–1900s (on materials of Tambov Province). RUDN J Russian Hist 1:110–125
Konchakov RB, Didenko DV (2022a) Data set: historical statistics on human capital, economic development and urbanization for 1825, 1840, 1847 in the Russian Empire (including the number of educational institutions and the number of students for the indicated periods). Registration certificate #2022620061. https://elibrary.ru/rpilqs
Konchakov RB, Didenko DV (2022b) Data set: historical statistics on human capital, economic development and urbanization for 1904 in the Russian Empire (including the number of educational institutions and the number of students). Registration certificate #2022620024. https://elibrary.ru/lhokbe
Koval'chenko ID, Milov LV (1974) Всероссиискии аграрный рынок (XVIII–начало XX вв.): опыт количественного анализа [All-Russian agrarian market in the 18th and beginning of the 19th century: a quantitative analysis]. Наука [The Science], Moscow
Kron G (2014) Comparative evidence and the reconstruction of the ancient economy: Greco–Roman housing and the level and distribution of wealth and income. In F de Callataÿ (Ed.), Quantifying the Greco–Roman economy and beyond (pp. 123–146). Bari: Edipuglia.
Kuznets S (1955) Economic growth and income inequality. Amer Econ Rev 45(1):1–28
Latov IV (2001) Особенности национального рэкета: история и современность [Peculiarities of the national racket activities: history and present]. Mir Rossii (Universe of Russia) 10(3):153–182
Layard R (2005) Happiness: lessons from a new science. Penguin, London
Lebedeva L, Kucherova Y, Godina E (2020) Secular changes in male body height in the European part of Russia during the 20th century. Coll Antropol 44(2):63–72
Lee J-W, Lee H (2016) Human capital in the long run. J Dev Econ 122:147–169. (Data set: http://www.barrolee.com/Lee_Lee_LRdata.htm)
Leff NH (1964) Economic development through bureaucratic corruption. Am Behav Sci 8(3):8–14
Lindert PH (2017) The rise and future of progressive redistribution. CEQ Working Paper 73. https://commitmentoequity.org/wp-content/uploads/2017/11/CEQ-WP73_Lindert_RiseFutureProgressiveRedistribution_Oct17_2017.pdf
Lindert PH (2021a) Making social spending work. Cambridge University Press, Cambridge
Lindert P (2021b) Social spending and the welfare state. In: Van Zanden JL et al (eds) How was life? Volume II: new perspectives on well-being and global inequality since 1820. OECD Publishing, Paris, pp 72–102. https://doi.org/10.1787/6a204f6e-en
Lui FT (1985) An equilibrium queuing model of bribery. J Polit Econ 93(4):760–781
Luneev VV (2005) Преступность XX века: мировые, региональные и российские тенденции [Criminality of the 20th century: global, regional, and Russian trends]. Wolters Kluwer, Moscow
Markevich A (2019) A regional perspective on the economic development of the late Russian Empire. SSRN. https://doi.org/10.2139/ssrn.2555273

Massard-Guilbaud G, Mathis CF (2017) A brief introduction to the history of pollution: From local to global. In C Cravo-Laureau, C Cagnon, B Lauga, R Duran (Eds.), Microbial ecotoxicology (pp. 1–10). Springer, Cham. https://doi.org/10.1007/978-3-319-61795-4_1
Mauro P (1998) Corruption and the composition of government expenditure. J Public Econ 69(2):263–279
Martínez-Galarraga J, Rosés JR, Tirado DA (2015) The long-term patterns of regional income inequality in Spain, 1860–2000. Reg Stud 49(4):502–517
Mateu A, Domínguez M (2019) The green battle in the media: a framing analysis of environmental press coverage. Commun Soc 32(4):275–290
McConnell JR, Wilson AI, Stohl A, Arienzo MM, Chellman NJ, Eckhardt S, Thompson EM, Pollard AM, Steffensen JP (2018) Lead pollution recorded in Greenland Ice indicates European emissions tracked plagues, wars, and imperial expansion during antiquity. Proc Nat Acad Sci USA 115(22):5726–5731
Milanovic B (2016) Global inequality: a new approach for the age of globalization. Harvard University Press, Cambridge, Mass
Mironov BN (1991) The development of literacy in Russia and the USSR from the tenth to the twentieth centuries. Hist Educ Q 31(2):229–252
Mironov BN (2012) The standard of living and revolutions in Russia, 1700–1917. Routledge, Abingdon
Mironov BN (2018) Российская империя: от традиции к модерну [The Russian Empire: from tradition to modernity], vol 1–3, 2nd edn. Dmitrii Bulanin, St. Petersburg
More AF et al (2017) Next-generation ice core technology reveals true minimum natural levels of lead (Pb) in the atmosphere: insights from the black death. GeoHealth 1:211–219. https://doi.org/10.1002/2017GH000064
Morrisson C (1984) Income distribution in East European and Western Countries. J Comp Econ 8(2):121–138
Mosley S (2014) Environmental history of air pollution and protection. Wiley, Hoboken, NJ
Mumford L (1961) The city in history: Its origins, its transformations, and its prospects. Harcourt, Brace & World, New York
Murdock GP (1945) The common denominator of cultures. In: Linton R (ed) The science of man in world crisis. Columbia University Press, New York
Nefedov S, Ellman M (2016) The development of living standards in Russia before the first world war: an examination of the anthropometric data. Revolut Russ 29(2):149–168. https://doi.org/10.1080/09546545.2016.1243618
Nisbett RE, Aronson J, Blair C, Dickens W, Flynn J, Halpern DF, Turkheimer E (2012) Intelligence: new findings and theoretical developments. Am Psychol 67(2):130–159
Novokmet F, Piketty T, Zucman G (2018) From Soviets to oligarchs: inequality and property in Russia 1905–2016. J Econ Inequal 16(2):189–223. https://doi.org/10.1007/s10888-018-9383-0
Nureev RM, Latov YV (2016) Экономическая история России (опыт институционального анализа) [Economic history of Russia (studies in institutional analysis)]. KNORUS, Moscow
OECD (2011) How's Life?: Measuring well-being, OECD Publishing. http://dx.doi.org/10.1787/9789264121164-en
Peng W (2015) A textual research of the height of Chinese people in the Qin-Han period (秦汉人身高考察). J Chin Humanit 2015(6):20–44
Piketty T (2014) Capital in the twenty-first century. Harvard University Press, Cambridge, MA
Polterovich VM (2001) Corruption factors. Matekon 34(4):3–15
Polterovich VM (2005) Institutional traps: is there a way out? Soc Sci 36(1):30–40
Popovich L, Potapchik E, Shishkin S, Richardson E, Vacroux A, Mathivet B (2011) Russian Federation: health system review. Health Syst Transit 13(7):1–190
Popov V (2014) Mixed fortunes: an economic history of China, Russia, and the west. Oxford University Press, New York
Prados de la Escosura L (2015) World human development: 1870–2007. Rev Income Wealth 61(2):220–247. https://doi.org/10.1111/roiw.12104. (Supplementary data retrieved from http://espacioinvestiga.com/inicio-hihd/, via http://www.frdelpino.es/)
Raff D, Wachter S, Yan S (2013) Real estate prices in Beijing, 1644 to 1840. Explor Econ Hist 50(3):368–386

Randolph J, Dolsak N (1996) Regional versus global? Will strategies for reduction of sulfur dioxide emissions from electric utilities increase carbon dioxide emissions? SUPCON International. IL (United States): Chicago
Rijpma A (2014) A composite view of well-being since 1820. In: van Zanden JL et al (eds) How was life?: global well-being since 1820. OECD Publishing, Paris, pp 249–269. https://doi.org/10.1787/9789264214262-17-en
Rijpma A (2021) A composite view on inequality and well-being. In: van Zanden JL et al (eds) How was life? Volume II: new perspectives on well-being and global inequality since 1820. OECD Publishing, pp 241–264. https://doi.org/10.1787/2574c9e5-en
Rose–Ackerman S (2008) Corruption and government. J. Int. Peacekeep 15(3):328–343
Sen AK (1985) Commodities and capabilities. North Holland, Amsterdam
Shenfield S (1983) A note on data quality in the Soviet family budget survey. Sov Stud 35(4):561–568
Shleifer A, Vishny RW (1993) Corruption. Q J Econ 108:599–617
Smith V (2007) Clean: a history of personal hygiene and purity. Oxford University Press, Oxford
Stickley A (2006) On interpersonal violence in Russia in the present and the past: a sociological study. Ph.D. thesis, Stockholm University. https://cjrc.osu.edu/sites/cjrc.osu.edu/files/Russia-and-theEuropean-nations-of-the-formerUSSR5-2010.XLS
Stohr C (2018) Regional inequality in Switzerland. In: Hanes C, Wolcott S (eds) Research in economic history, vol 34. Emerald Publishing Limited, Bingley, pp 135–198
Sun L, Hong Z (2015) A study of human statures of skeletons found in Han, Tang and Song dynasty tombs, Zhengzhou area. Acta Anthro Sin 34(3):377–389
Svensson J (2005) Eight Questions about Corruption. J Econ Perspect 19(3):19–42
Tanzi V, Davoodi H (1998) Corruption, Public Investment, and Growth. In: Shibata H, Ihori T (eds) The Welfare State, Public Investment, and Growth, pp 41–60. Tokyo: Springer
Te Brake WH (1975) Air pollution and fuel crises in preindustrial London, 1250–1650. Technol Cult 16(3):337–359. https://doi.org/10.2307/3103030
TransMONEE Database. (2011) UNICEF Regional Office for CEECIS. Geneva. http://transmonee.org/wp-content/uploads/2016/05/Tables_TransMonee_2011.xls
TsSU SSSR (1956–1991) Центральное статистическое управление СССР [Central Statistical Board of the USSR]. Народное хозяйство СССР [National economy of the USSR]. Finansy i Statistika, Moscow
TsSK (1897) Центральный статистический комитет Министерства внутренних дел [Central Statistical Committee of the Ministry of Internal Affairs]. Умершие насильственно и внезапно в Российской империи в 1888–1893 гг. [Those who Died Violently and Suddenly in the Russian Empire in 1888–1893]. Временник Центрального статистического комитета Министерства внутренних дел [Annals of the Central Statistical Committee of the Ministry of Internal Affairs], 41. St. Petersburg
TsSK (1894) Центральный статистический комитет Министерства внутренних дел [Central Statistical Committee of the Ministry of Internal Affairs]. Умершие насильственно и внезапно в Европейской России в 1875-1887 гг. [Those who Died Violently and Suddenly in European Russia in 1875–1887]. Временник Центрального статистического комитета Министерства внутренних дел [Annals of the Central Statistical Committee of the Ministry of Internal Affairs], 35. St. Petersburg
TsSK (1918) Центральный статистический комитет [Central Statistical Committee]. Статистический ежегодник России за 1916 г. [Statistical Yearbook of Russia. 1916]. Petrograd
TsSU SSSR (1952) Статистические динамические ряды за 1913–1951 годы [Statistical Dynamic Series for 1913–1951]. Russian State Archive of the Economy (RGAE), f. 1562, op. 41, d. 64. https://istmat.org/node/40054/
TsSU SSSR (1955) Краткий статистический сборник [Concise Statistical Abstract]. Russian State Archive of the Economy (RGAE), f. 1562, op. 33, d. 2310. https://istmat.org/node/36699
TsUNKhU (1935) Центральное управление народнохозяйственного учета [Central board for national economic accounting]. In: Социалистическое строительство Союза ССР: статистический сборник [Socialist construction of the USSR: statistical abstract]. Soiuzorguchot, Moscow

Ugur M, Dasgupta N (2011) Evidence on the economic growth impacts of corruption in low-income countries and beyond. London: EPPI-Centre, Social Science Research Unit, Institute of Education, University of London

UNU-WIDER (2021) World income inequality database (WIID). Version 31, May 2021. https://www.wider.unu.edu/database/world-income-inequality-database-wiid

Van Leeuwen B, Calabrese M (2024) Corruption and economic growth: a historical analysis of The Netherlands case (ca. 1870–2010) [Unpublished working paper]

Van Leeuwen B, Van Leeuwen-Li J. (2015) Average years of education via. www.clio-imfra.eu

Van Zanden JL, Van Leeuwen B, Xu Y (2021) Consequences of growth: living standards and inequality. In: Broadberry S, Fukao K (eds) The Cambridge economic history of the modern world, volume 1 (1700–1870), The Cambridge economic history, vol 1, 1st edn. Cambridge University Press, Cambridge, pp 391–411

Veenhoven R (2022) Trends in Nations. Data file to be used for the longitudinal analysis of societal conditions for happiness. World Database of Happiness, Erasmus University Rotterdam, Netherlands. https://worlddatabaseofhappiness.eur.nl/wp-content/uploads/TrendsInNations_2022b.xlsx

Wheatcroft S (1999) The great leap upwards: anthropometric data and indicators of crises and secular change in soviet welfare levels, 1880–1960. Slav Rev 58(1):41–44

Williamson JG (1965) Regional inequality and the process of national development: a description of the patterns. Econ Dev Cult Change 13(4):1–84

Williamson JG (2000) Globalization, factor prices and living standards in Asia before 1940. In: Latham AJH, Kawakatsu H (eds) Asia Pacific dynamism 1500–2000. Routledge, London, pp 13–45

Ye M, Wang M, van Leeuwen B (2025) Macro data on wellbeing (gross domestic product, labor, climate): milestones and areas for improvement. SAGE

Zottola A, Atanasova D, Cardwell E, Forrester J, Stevens C (2020) Framing nitrogen pollution in the British Bress: 1984–2018. Discourse Commun 14(1):84–103. https://doi.org/10.1177/1750481319876772

Zhou Y (2017) Research on stature of ancient groups in Beijing district. J Tianjin Norm Univ Nat Sci Ed 2017(3):62–64

Chapter 11
Future Research: A Long-Run Overview of Human and Economic Development in Northern Eurasia

Abstract This concluding chapter synthesizes the book's key findings on long-term economic development in Northern Eurasia, emphasizing the complex interplay of technological innovation, institutions, geography, and human capital. It examines the dynamic balance between long-term structural trends and short-term economic shocks, highlighting the role of expectations, policy interventions, and technological change. A key insight emerges from the concept of regression to the mean, which suggests that economic trajectories tend to converge over time while remaining shaped by cycles of technological progress and institutional evolution. Looking ahead, future research should explore the impact of AI and automation on global labour markets and economic inequality.

11.1 Economic Volatility

This book offers an analysis of global economic growth patterns from ancient times to the present day. Long-term trends reveal remarkable stability, suggesting that ancient and medieval economies were often more prosperous than commonly believed. However, short-term shocks—such as monetary crises or population fluctuations—can significantly influence economic growth, either hindering or accelerating it. A pivotal turning point in this stability, known as the "Great Crossing", occurred between the tenth and fourteenth centuries when some urbanized regions of Italy surpassed China in per capita gross domestic product (GDP). This shift was driven by a complex interplay of factors, including Europe's technological path-dependent innovations dating back to the Palaeolithic era, the Malthusian cycle, social and class structures, agricultural practices, climate conditions, and ongoing technological development.

B. Van Leeuwen et al., *Innovation and Economic Development in Eurasia, 500 BCE-Present*, Frontiers in Economic History,
https://doi.org/10.1007/978-3-031-97043-6_11

Among these seven factors, agricultural technology was the primary driver of economic growth for the pre-Song dynasty period. For example, agricultural technological development was affected by type of land, such as the black soil regions found in China, Russia, and Ukraine. These regions benefited from the natural fertility of their soil, which reduced the need for extensive land improvement and also supported surplus production. By contrast, in non-black soil areas, such as much of Western Europe, Northern Russia, and Southern China, significant human intervention was required to sustain productivity. This led to innovations such as the creation of fertile polders in the Netherlands, a clear example of Boserupian growth in which population pressure spurred technological and agricultural advancements (Boserup 1965).

From the fourteenth century onwards, the influence of the other five factors (path-dependent Palaeolithic innovation, the Malthusian cycle, social relations, class structure, and climate) increasingly drove technological development. However, this interaction did not immediately result in sustained per capita income growth. A key divergence emerged between Western Europe and other regions, particularly China and Central Eurasia. In Western Europe, the combination of high population density, limited arable land, and non-black soil drove demand for labour-saving technologies and more intensive agricultural practices. By contrast, in China, the availability of fertile land (especially in the Yangtze River basin) allowed for extensive agriculture, which required less technological innovation but maintained high productivity. Similarly, Russia's vast black soil regions enabled large-scale grain production with relatively low population pressure, shaping its agricultural strategies differently from both Europe and China. Despite these variations, sectors such as water control, planting methods, draught animals, seed selection, and human capital development saw parallel advancements in China and England prior to 1900. Technological change alone, therefore, was not sufficient to create significant economic divergence.

Between the fourteenth and eighteenth centuries, the interplay of these seven factors gave rise to the proximate and ultimate variables influencing economic development, including demographic transition, trade and empire, urbanization, forced and free labour, government power, human capital, taxation, and colonialism. These latter factors affected growth in both positive and negative ways, depending on the region's specific economic and political structure. For example, demographic shifts in Europe, particularly during the Black Death, created labour shortages that spurred innovation, while in China, relatively stable demographics allowed for continued agrarian expansion. Meanwhile, Russia's serfdom-based labour system constrained its potential for urbanization and technological progress, despite its agricultural abundance.

In our analysis, we identify various ultimate and proximate factors that acted as key long-run drivers of economic growth. First, institutions played a critical role. These include institutions that hindered convergence—exemplified by our introduction of "time in office" for mayors as a novel indicator of how local governance impacts regional economies (ultimate factors)—and those that acted as factors of production (proximate factors). These institutions could either enhance or reduce the efficiency of newly implemented systems, shaping economic trajectories.

Second is total factor productivity (TFP), used here as a proxy for technological advancement. After the Black Death, there was a universal surge in TFP growth. However, within a century, TFP growth in regions such as China and Italy began to stagnate, while England maintained steady growth. A notable shift in the focus of European inventions occurred as well, from agriculture and services-based applications to industrial-based technologies, contributing to divergence between Western Europe and other parts of the world. In a proto-industrial context, industrial innovations had a more significant impact on economic growth, giving Europe a comparative advantage over China, where inventions often centred on service-related improvements.

Third, geography played an influential role, particularly the presence of black soil regions in northern Eurasia. These fertile areas in Russia and northern China enabled high agricultural productivity, yet their influence on technology demand diverged. In Europe, the absence of such naturally fertile soils led to labour- and capital-saving innovations, whereas in China's black soil regions, capital-saving technologies were more prevalent owing to different resource pressures and endowments.

Fourth is human capital development, which initially depended on demographic trends, such as population growth and fertility. Over time, however, human capital growth became increasingly tied to technological progress and rising incomes, rather than solely to demographic shifts.

Building on the factors listed so far, the book addresses several broader questions. How did technology spread to Asia? How did Western countries transition from the first industrial revolution to the second, based on electricity? And why did less developed countries increasingly adopt capital-intensive production methods? The spread of technology to Asia mirrors the dynamics seen in nineteenth-century Europe, with one notable difference: the presence of strong, centralized governments, particularly in countries such as China. Additionally, as technology costs fell and demand for capital-intensive goods rose in developing economies, advanced countries outsourced the production of less capital-intensive goods, creating a mutually beneficial system. This explains why countries such as Japan and China initially adopted capital-saving technologies but eventually shifted to labour-saving ones as their economies matured.

This difference between countries with labour and capital saving technologies affects long-run growth too. One can distinguish the use of technology between "innovator" nations, which pioneered new technologies, and "accumulator" nations, which adopted and refined these innovations. In the former group, countries create more inventions by placing more human capital in research and development, which is often referred to as Romerian growth. Accumulator countries, in which technologies are not home-created but rather imported, used human capital in the productive process, a Lucias growth model.

Besides these long-term trends, short-term factors also played an important role in extending economic growth. For example, monetary and fiscal policy may lead to fast growth, or, eventually, to neutrality of money if ineffectively applied by national or local governments. Moreover, the volatility of the Chinese housing market also merits consideration.

Lastly, GDP is just one factor of national well-being. Societal and environmental factors—such as happiness, equality, corruption, and pollution—are increasingly recognized as important dimensions inter-related with GDP per capita growth. While these factors gained prominence only recently, they have begun to provide a glimpse into a full understanding of the complexity of a multifaceted reality behind economic development dynamics not only in the modern era, but also in previous phases of human history.

In conclusion, the book highlights this entangled interplay of technology, institutional frameworks, geography, and human capital in shaping the global long-run history of economic growth from 500 BCE to the present. Furthermore, it argues that failure to consider the discontinuities in long-term trends and short-term cycles, as argued by Pritchett and Summers (2014), risks overlooking critical growth inflection points, indispensable when defining historical trends as well in economic forecasting.

11.2 Future Research

11.2.1 What Predicts Growth? Interaction of Cycles and Short-Run Factors

To understand long-run patterns and situate the present within broader historical trends, we can begin by analysing the relationship between past and current economic growth. A regression of the compound annual growth rate of GDP per capita from 2010 to 2020 against similar metrics from earlier decades (e.g. 1850–1860, 1860–1870) for 33 countries reveals the following patterns. Over the last 150 years, certain decades—such as the 1860s and 1890s—stand out as strong predictors of contemporary growth, whereas other periods show weaker correlations (see Fig. 11.1). Notably, the past 20–30 years emerge as relatively reliable predictors of current growth, suggesting both continuity and variability across economic cycles.

This analysis highlights the interplay between long-term cycles and short-term factors. As discussed in Sect. 11.1, long-run factors include technological innovation, demographic shifts, institutional frameworks, and political stability. These interact with short-run factors such as, for example, housing markets, government spending, and other economic shocks. Together, these elements can amplify or dampen growth, leading to periods of rapid expansion, recession, or stagnation.

Thus, how do long-run cycles and short-term factors interact? Technological innovation, a key long-term driver, often transforms the economic landscape by ushering in industrial revolutions and creating new industries or forms of industrial clustering. Similarly, demographic trends, such as ageing populations or

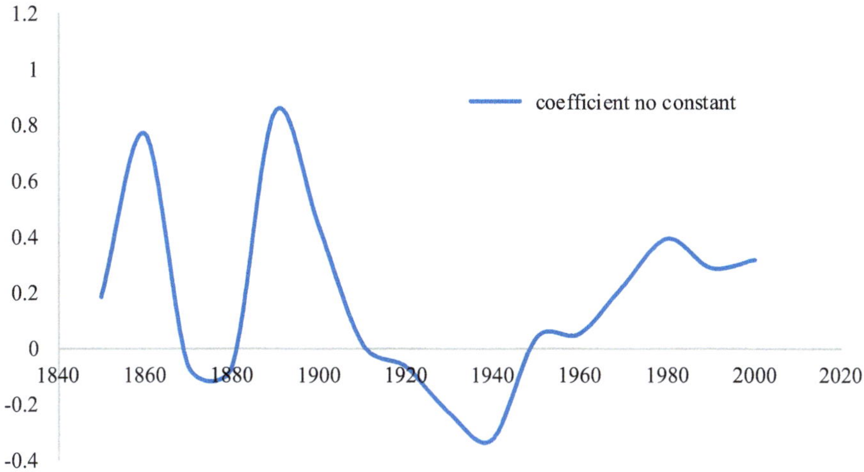

Fig. 11.1 Coefficient of regression of GDP per capita growth (2010–2020) on GDP per capita growth from previous decades. *Source:* Bolt and Van Zanden (2024)

migrations, shape labour markets and influence growth trajectories over decades. Institutions, as both enablers and constraints, can moderate the impact of these trends, while their effectiveness often hinges on the timing and design of reforms.

In the same way, short-term factors can significantly influence long-term cycles. For instance, economic shocks such as housing market crises or natural disasters may cause temporary disruptions that ripple into long-term cycles. Likewise, government policies, including monetary and fiscal measures, can stabilize or destabilize economies in the short run, with lasting consequences. For example, timely fiscal interventions during a recession can prevent prolonged stagnation, while delayed or inadequate responses might deepen long-term economic scarring. Short-term dynamics do not merely affect immediate outcomes; they can shift the trajectory of long-term cycles. A prolonged period of stagnation, for instance, might suppress technological innovation and reduce investment, ultimately lowering long-term growth potential. On the other hand, a technologically advanced economy may be better equipped to weather short-term shocks, recovering more quickly and maintaining a stable growth path.

One way to integrate an analysis of the interplay between long-term and short-term factors is to include expectations and the role of both predictors and determining factors of economic growth. Assessing expectations is indeed fundamental for policy-makers, businesses, and investors in navigating economic complexities and fostering growth. Long-term trends, such as technological progress, demographic shifts, and sectoral transitions, create the structural foundation of an economy, while short-term dynamics, such as fiscal shocks, consumer confidence, and geopolitical events, often introduce volatility that can disrupt or accelerate these broader trajectories. Expectations could play a pivotal role in this interplay, influencing investment flows, market confidence, and strategic decision-making. Figure 11.2

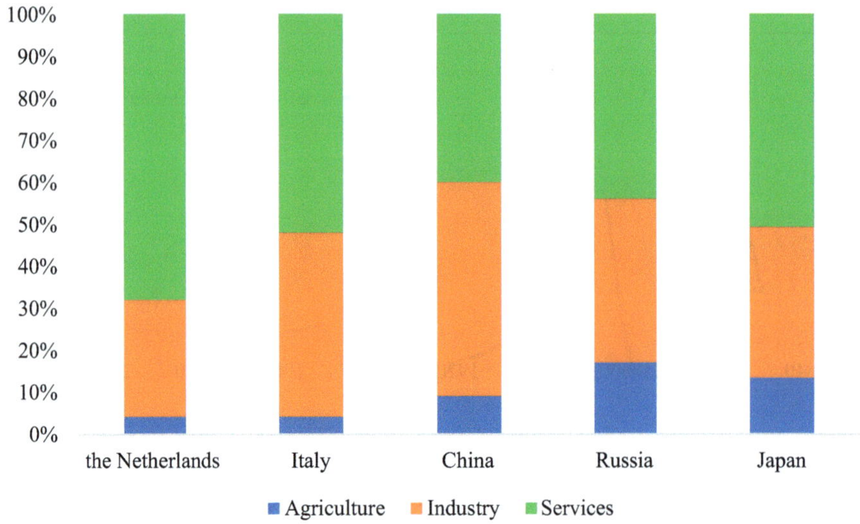

Fig. 11.2 The sector (agriculture, industry, or services) in which you think you can personally earn the highest income (population share, in %) for selected countries (2023). *Source:* Appendixes D and E

highlights the sectoral distribution of income potential—agriculture, industry, and services—based on individual perceptions. It underscores the dominance of the services sector in income generation across various economies, a trend consistent with broader global economic patterns. Countries such as the Netherlands and Japan exhibit a pronounced reliance on services, with agriculture contributing minimally to perceived income potential. On the other hand, industry continues to hold significant weight in countries such as China and Russia, reflecting a widespread belief in the manufacturing strengths of the former (see also Table 11.1) and the awareness of a growing military sector for the latter. Expectations about sectoral opportunities often shape labour market trends and investment priorities. For example, individuals perceiving higher income potential in services may drive educational and professional aspirations toward sectors such as finance, healthcare, or technology, further reinforcing the service sector's dominance. Conversely, the persistence of industry as a significant income contributor in certain economies may reflect strategic national priorities in manufacturing and overall production.

Policy-makers should consider these sectoral perceptions when designing economic strategies. By aligning educational policies, infrastructure development, and technological investments with these expectations, they can foster economic growth that meets the aspirations of the workforce. Furthermore, expectations are not static; they are shaped by immediate short-term dynamics, such as technological disruptions or policy announcements, and long-term structural shifts, such as demographic transitions and urbanization. The role of expectations becomes even more pronounced in the context of short-term shocks. For instance, a sudden fiscal policy

Table 11.1 Population share: which country do you think will be the biggest economy in Asia 30 years from now (in %) (2023)?

	China	Japan
China	92	36
India	3	27
Japan	4	28
Indonesia		5
South Korea		1
Do not know		16
Total	**100**	**100**

Source: Appendixes D and E

change or a global economic downturn can dramatically shift public confidence in specific sectors, influencing investment decisions and labour market movements. By understanding how these short-term shocks interact with long-term trends, policy-makers and stakeholders can create adaptive strategies that mitigate risks and harness opportunities.

11.2.2 Regression to the Mean

In this book, we have explored long-term trends, short-term effects, and the institutions shaping economic and social growth. While numerous factors influence long-term patterns, one particularly significant phenomenon is regression to the mean. This statistical concept describes how values significantly above or below the average tend to move closer to the mean over time. Pritchett and Summers (2014) illustrate this with several examples: "Paul Samuelson's textbook predicted in 1961 a substantial chance that the USSR would economically surpass the United States by the 1980s. Until the late 1980s, there was a widespread belief that Japan's rapid growth would lead it to outcompete the global economy. Conversely, a decade ago, there was pervasive pessimism about Africa's economic prospects, yet many African countries have since emerged as some of the fastest-growing nations in the world." These examples highlight that convergence appears to be a prevailing trend over time.

As discussed earlier, it is crucial to recognize the multitude of factors that can influence historical trends, making it challenging to isolate the specific impact of regression to the mean. Nevertheless, studies examining the determinants of economic growth frequently identify regression to the mean as one of the few consistently significant factors (e.g. Levine and Renelt 1992). This outcome often stems from an over-emphasis on short-term estimates rather than long-term historical patterns, which can obscure instances of growth discontinuities (Pritchett and Summers 2014), as highlighted in Sect. 11.2.1. The concept of regression to the mean applies broadly across various domains, including population dynamics, economic cycles, and sociopolitical fluctuations, as also noted in Sect. 11.2.1. Moreover, these cycles can differ significantly, manifesting as periods of growth or decline. For instance, rapid growth may be followed by brief but severe downturns (Jerzmanowski 2006). Modern economic growth often hinges on mitigating such abrupt declines.

Historical evidence confirms this dynamic. Between 1270 and 1500, periods of increasing growth lasted an average of 1.76 years, while declines were shorter but more intense, averaging 1.58 years (Broadberry et al. 2022). Naturally, these effects can become even more pronounced when growth slows and declines accelerate. This interplay between growth and decline underscores the importance of understanding long-term patterns to foster sustained progress.

Significant research remains to be conducted in the area of income inequality, particularly regarding intergenerational mobility. Low mobility is a critical issue, as insufficient regression to the mean implies that individuals born into poverty often remain poor. This phenomenon is evident in China, as highlighted by Hao (2021), who found low mobility in the country between 1645 and 2012. While some improvements occurred during the Republican and New China periods, mobility remained far lower than commonly assumed. Similarly, Clark and Cummins (2013) observed low mobility in medieval England, with only marginally higher levels in modern times.[1]

Non-income factors, such as education, suggest greater convergence to the mean. For instance, during China's transitional period, prioritizing education over family background led to increased mobility (Weibo and Gao 2024). This underscores the potential of non-income factors in mitigating persistent inequality. Despite China's remarkable economic development in recent decades, the persistence of "sticky" regression to the mean for income—compared with less pronounced effects in non-income factors—raises questions about the sustainability of its high growth rates. The extent and timing of any potential slowdown remain uncertain, with key determinants including government policies, technological innovation, and global economic conditions. These factors will be pivotal in shaping the trajectory of China's economic future.

11.2.3 The Impact of Technology on Human Physical and Mental Change

A further element of analysis for future research should be the relationship between technological advancement and human physical and mental states. This topic encompasses debates over whether technology's effects are predominantly beneficial or detrimental to human well-being.

One key dimension is the impact on physical health. Modern lifestyles, heavily mediated by technology, often involve sedentary behaviour such as prolonged periods of sitting—whether at desks, in cars, or using digital devices. Research has

[1] See https://milescorak.com/2014/05/22/social-mobility-fixed-forever-gregory-clarks-the-son-also-rises-is-a-book-of-scholarship-and-of-scholastic-overreach/

shown that such inactivity increases risks for conditions such as obesity, cardiovascular disease, and musculoskeletal issues (Katzmarzyk et al. 2019). Simultaneously, technology offers tools to counter these risks, such as fitness tracking apps and wearables that encourage physical activity by monitoring metrics such as step counts or heart rates (Wang et al. 2020). Future research could explore the long-term effectiveness of such interventions and their potential to mitigate the broader health impacts of sedentary lifestyles. For instance, how do cultural or socio-economic differences affect the adoption and success of health-monitoring technologies?

Another critical dimension is the effect of technology on mental health. Digital media have been associated with both positive and negative outcomes. On the one hand, social media platforms and communication technologies can foster connection, access to information, and opportunities for personal expression. On the other hand, the constant connectivity and exposure to curated, idealized representations of life can induce stress, anxiety, and feelings of inadequacy (Twenge et al. 2018). Additionally, excessive screen time has been linked to disrupted sleep patterns and reduced attention spans (Cain and Gradisar 2010). Future research might delve into the specific mechanisms by which digital media affects mental health, particularly among vulnerable populations such as adolescents and the elderly. Another promising avenue is examining how virtual reality and augmented reality technologies could be utilized therapeutically to address mental health challenges.

The emerging field of digital therapeutics suggests that technology might be harnessed to mitigate these challenges. For instance, apps designed for mindfulness or cognitive-behavioural therapy have shown promising results in improving mental well-being (Firth et al. 2017). Further research could investigate how to optimize these applications for different mental health conditions, explore barriers to access in low-income settings, and assess the ethical considerations surrounding data privacy.

11.2.4 AI, Robotization, and Labour

The rise of artificial intelligence (AI) and robotization is reshaping the global labour market, presenting both opportunities and challenges for economic and social systems. A central concern is the potential displacement of workers as machines take over tasks traditionally performed by humans. According to Acemoglu and Restrepo (2018), automation tends to reduce demand for routine, middle-skill jobs while increasing demand for high-skill and low-skill positions, leading to labour market polarization.

This shift can exacerbate economic inequality. As robots and AI take on more labour-intensive tasks, remaining workers may command higher wages, concentrating wealth among those with skills to manage or collaborate with these technologies. At the same time, though, displaced workers, often lacking the resources to upskill, may face unemployment or under-employment (Brynjolfsson and McAfee 2014). Future research could focus on policies and training programmes to support worker transitions, particularly in regions most affected by automation. What types of skills are most resilient to automation, and how can educational systems adapt to prepare future workers?

AI and robotization also influence the global distribution of labour. In theory, if labour costs decline significantly owing to automation, industries may find it less advantageous to outsource production to low-wage countries. Instead, developed countries might repatriate manufacturing tasks while exporting knowledge-intensive services. This reconfiguration could challenge the economic models of developing nations reliant on low-cost labour exports (Autor et al. 2020). Future research could explore how developing economies can diversify their growth strategies in light of these trends. Additionally, what role might international cooperation play in ensuring equitable technological diffusion across borders?

On the positive side, AI-powered robots can take on hazardous or physically demanding jobs, reducing workplace injuries and fatalities. In construction, mining, and healthcare, robots are increasingly being used to perform tasks that are dangerous or require precision, improving both safety and productivity (Chen et al. 2022). Further research might investigate the long-term economic and social benefits of deploying robots in high-risk industries, as well as the ethical implications of replacing human workers in these roles.

Additionally, by automating mundane tasks, these technologies can free workers to focus on creative, strategic, and interpersonal aspects of their roles, potentially increasing job satisfaction and innovation. A future avenue of research could examine how AI-driven job redesign affects worker productivity, mental health, and collaboration.

Key questions for future research include:

- How can policies mitigate the inequality that arises from automation?
- What strategies can help displaced workers transition into new roles or industries?
- How will labour market dynamics evolve in economies with differing levels of technological adoption?
- What ethical frameworks are needed to ensure the equitable deployment of AI and robots?

By exploring these issues, we can better understand how AI and robotization might reshape not only labour markets but also broader societal structures, offering pathways to harness their potential while minimizing their risks.

11.3 Conclusion

In this chapter, we have summed up the current book's findings while further exploring the entangled historical reality shaped by long- and short-term factors, in particular focusing on the importance of their interaction in determining long-term growth and well-being. One promising avenue for future research lies in examining how cycles and short-term effects, such as monetary policy or technological disruptions, interact with long-term structural trends. These interactions are not isolated; they are interconnected and often mutually reinforcing, highlighting their endogenous nature in economic systems.

The analysis also points to the relevance of various economic models in understanding long-term growth and patterns of convergence or divergence. For instance, the concept of regression to the mean brings up the cyclical nature of economic trajectories, where wealth disparities between either people or nations tend to balance out over time. However, it is not merely a statistical phenomenon: factors such as technological progress and growth can profoundly influence individual and societal well-being, reshaping both physical and mental capacities.

In conclusion, the transformative potential of emerging technologies, particularly AI and robotization, presents both profound opportunities and significant challenges for global socio-economic development. While these advancements promise increased efficiency, innovation, and the potential to address some of humanity's most pressing issues, they also carry the risk of deepening inequalities—both between and within societies. The deployment of AI, for example, could disproportionately benefit those with access to advanced technologies while leaving others further behind, exacerbating existing disparities.

Moreover, the growing capabilities of AI to perform complex tasks in the service sector—historically the fastest-growing sector over the last century—pose critical questions about the future of work and the economic well-being of millions who rely on service-sector employment. If managed poorly, AI could displace jobs on a massive scale, undermining livelihoods and increasing social tensions. Conversely, if managed thoughtfully, AI could enhance productivity, create new industries, and improve the quality of work by automating certain tasks and enabling people to focus on activities that each single individual could consider as more meaningful.

Given the profound implications of AI, the question of how to manage its development for the benefit of all becomes paramount. To provide further insight, we turned to ChatGPT, an advanced AI system, and asked for its perspective on the best approaches to manage AI in the present to secure a better future. Here is the response:

> Beyond economic considerations, the impact of AI on human physical and mental well-being must not be overlooked. The integration of AI into healthcare, education, and other service-oriented domains holds great promise for improving quality of life. However, the psychological effects of increasing human–AI interaction and the potential for misuse or overreach of AI technologies demand careful oversight.
>
> Given this complex interplay of factors, the development and deployment of AI must be guided by a framework of ethical principles, global cooperation, and inclusivity. Policymakers must craft regulations that promote fairness, transparency, and accountability in AI systems. Investors should prioritize technologies that align with societal well-being and sustainability goals. Researchers need to focus on advancing AI in ways that address inequality, improve access, and ensure long-term benefits for all.
>
> As we look to the decades ahead, the choices we make today will determine whether emerging technologies become tools for empowerment and equality or drivers of division and discord. By fostering collaboration among governments, businesses, academia, and civil society, we can harness the transformative power of AI and other technologies to build a more equitable, innovative, and resilient future.

References

Acemoglu D, Restrepo P (2018) Automation and new tasks: how technology displaces and reinstates labor. J Econ Perspect 33(2):3–30

Autor DH, Dorn D, Hanson GH (2020) The China shock: learning from labor market adjustment to large changes in trade. Ann Rev Econ 8:205–240

Bolt J, Van Zanden JL (2024) Maddison style estimates of the evolution of the world economy: a new 2023 update. J Econ Surv 39:1–41

Boserup E (1965) The conditions of agricultural growth: the economics of agrarian change under population pressure. G. Allen and Unwin, London

Broadberry S, Klein A, Overton M, Van Leeuwen B (2022) British business cycles, 1270–1870. CAGE Online Working Paper Series, No. 627. https://warwick.ac.uk/fac/soc/economics/research/centres/cage/manage/publications/wp627.2022.pdf

Brynjolfsson E, McAfee A (2014) The second machine age: work, progress, and prosperity in a time of brilliant technologies. W. W. Norton & Company, New York

Cain N, Gradisar M (2010) Electronic media use and sleep in school-aged children and adolescents: a review. Sleep Med 11(8):735–742

Chen Z, Sun S, Gao Y (2022) AI and robotics in occupational safety and health: applications and challenges. Saf Sci 147

Clark G, Cummins N (2013) Surnames and social mobility: England 1230–2012. London School of Economics and Political Science, Department of Economic History Working Papers, no. 181

Firth J, Torous J, Nicholas J, Carney R, Rosenbaum S, Sarris J (2017) The efficacy of smartphone-based mental health interventions for depressive symptoms: a meta-analysis of randomized controlled trials. World Psychiatry 16(3):287–298

Hao Y (2021) Social Mobility in China, 1645–2012: A Surname Study. China Econ Q Int 1(3):233–243

Jerzmanowski M (2006) Empirics of hills, plateaus, mountains and plains: a Markov-switching approach to growth. J Dev Econ 81(2):357–385

Katzmarzyk PT, Church TS, Craig CL (2019) Sitting time and mortality from all causes, cardiovascular disease, and cancer. Med Sci Sports Exerc 41(5):998–1005

Levine R, Renelt D (1992) A sensitivity analysis of cross-country growth regressions. Am Econ Rev 82(4):942–963

Pritchett L, Summers LH (2014) Asiaphoria meets regression to the mean. NBER Working Paper 20573

Twenge JM, Martin GN, Campbell WK (2018) Decreases in psychological Well-being among American adolescents after 2012 and links to screen time during the rise of smartphone technology. Emotion 18(6):765

Wang J, Xue H, Huang Y (2020) Wearable technology and physical activity in chronic disease management: systematic review. JMIR Mhealth Uhealth 8(4):e17884

Weibo Y, Gao S (2024) Family background and intergenerational mobility in a transition economy: Evidence from China. J Asian Econ 92

Appendixes

Appendix A: Chinese Imperial Dynasties and Major Polities

China is often seen as a stable set of successive dynasties. Yet, combinations of dynastic wars and local powerful warlords lead to frequent instability. We will present a simplified list below.

Qin Dynasty (221 BCE–207 BCE): Before there was no unified China. Only after 221 BCE did China unite.

Han Dynasty (202 BCE–220 CE): Rebellion of the Seven Kingdoms (154 BCE). This was a major revolt by seven vassal kingdoms against the central Han government. Another sign of instability is Wang Mang's (a Han official, usurped the throne) Interregnum (9–23 CE).

Three Kingdoms Period (220–280): Wei Ruled in the north, Shu Han: Ruled in the southwest and Wu Ruled in the southeast.

Jin Dynasty (265–420 CE): Western Jin: 265–316 CE, Eastern Jin: 317–420 CE.

Northern and Southern Dynasties (420–589 CE): In the North, 16 Kingdoms existed. This was a series of smaller, often short-lived kingdoms. In the South, while dynasties were more stable, local elites and powerful families wielded considerable influence.

Tang Dynasty (618–907): Although considered a golden age in Chinese history, it suffered from various divisions and rebellions like the An Lushan Rebellion (755–763 CE) and the rise of provincial separatism.

Five Dynasties and Ten Kingdoms (907–960): This era was defined by its fragmentation. The Ten Kingdoms were (semi-)independent kingdoms that arose in the south after the fall of the Tang Dynasty.

Southern Song Dynasty (1127–1297): The Song had lost control of northern China to the Jin Dynasty. The capital was moved south to Hangzhou.

B. Van Leeuwen et al., *Innovation and Economic Development in Eurasia, 500 BCE-Present*, Frontiers in Economic History,
https://doi.org/10.1007/978-3-031-97043-6

Yuan Dynasty (1271–1368): The Yuan faced numerous rebellions and internal strife. Very important were the, often violent, succession disputes.

Ming Dynasty (1368–1644): The Ming faced much strive and rebellion. Just one example concerns Li Zicheng whose forces captured Beijing in 1644, briefly establishing the Shun Dynasty.

Qing Dynasty (1644–1911): The Qing faced many uprisings, including the Taiping rebellion.

Republic of China (1912–1949): Beiyang government period (1912–1928), Nationalist government period (1928–1949); Period with continuous struggles for government power.

People's Republic of China (since 1949): Stability with occasional popular protest.

Appendix B: Dynasties and Major Polities Related to Russia (Central Eurasia)

Ancient (Kievan) Rus' (ca 882–1132), Rurikid dynasty.

Political fragmentation period (ca 1132–1480): North-eastern principalities of the Rurikid dynasty were forced to vassal relationships with the Mongol Empire and its successor khanates reigned by the Chinggisid dynasty (ca 1237–1480); western and southern principalities were taken over by the Grand Duchy of Lithuania reigned by the House of Mindaugas (1236–1285, with a break in 1267–1269), House of Gediminas (1285–1440), and the House of Jagiellon (1440–1569); northern Novgorod and Pskov republics retained their de-facto independence; the Principality of Moscow evolved as the centre of power (since the early fourteenth century).

Grand Principality of Moscow or Muscovite Rus' (ca 1480–1547): The final stage of the transition from political fragmentation to centralization, Rurikid dynasty.

Russian (Muscovite) Tsardom (1547–1721), Rurikid dynasty (up to 1598), Interregnum and the Time of Troubles (1598–1613), House of Romanov (since 1613).

Russian Empire (1721–1917), House of Romanov (Holstein-Gottorp-Romanov in 1762–1917).

Russian Republic (1917); Russian Soviet Republic, along with other Soviet, antagonistic Russian and secessionist national governments in the periphery during the Revolution and the Civil War (1917–1922).

Union of Soviet Socialist Republics (USSR) or the Soviet Union, under the Communist (Bolshevik) Party rule (1922–1991).

Russian Federation, one of the 15 Newly Independent States (NIS) evolved from the dismantle of the USSR (since 1991): Most of the states immediately formed the

Commonwealth of Independent States (CIS); Russia and Belarus signed a treaty on the creation of a confederate Union State (1999); 6 states, including Russia, formed the Collective Security Treaty Organization (CSTO, in 2002); 3 Baltic republics joined the European Union (2004); 5 CSTO states, including Russia, formed the Eurasian Economic Union (EAEU, in 2014–2015).

Appendix C: List of European Dynasties

Due to the many splits, mergers, and changes over time, providing a list of European dynasties is near impossible. Therefore, below we provide a mere general overview.

Antiquity (1600 BCE–1453 CE)

Ancient Greece (ca. 1600 BCE–146 BCE): Mycenaean civilization, Classical city-states (Athens, Sparta), Hellenistic kingdoms.

Roman Kingdom (753 BCE–509 BCE).

Roman Republic (509 BCE–27 BCE): Families with power but no concentration of power in the hands of a single person.
Western Roman Empire (27 BCE–476 CE): Here emperors took over power.

* Principate (27 BCE–284 CE)
* Julio-Claudian Dynasty (27 BCE–68 CE)
* Flavian Dynasty (69–96 CE)
* Nerva-Antonine Dynasty (96–192 CE)
* Severan Dynasty (193–235 CE)
* Crisis of the Third Century (235–284 CE) (various short-lasting emperors)
* Dominate (284–476 CE) (powerful emperors and split of the empire between West and East):
    * Constantinian Dynasty (306–363 CE) (moved capital to Constantinople).
    * Valentinianic Dynasty (364–392 CE).
    * Theodosian Dynasty (379–457 CE) (The last dynasty to rule the East and West Roman Empire).

Medieval Period (ca. Fifth to Thirteenth Century)

Eastern Roman Empire: Leonid Dynasty (457–518), Justinian Dynasty (518–602), Heraclian Dynasty (610–695), Isaurian (Syrian) Dynasty (717–802), Amorian Dynasty (820–867), Macedonian Dynasty (867–1056), Komnenos Dynasty (1081–1185), Palaiologos Dynasty (1259–1453): The last dynasty to rule the Byzantine Empire.
Visigothic Kingdom (418–711): Ruled Iberia after the fall of the Western Roman Empire. Frankish Kingdom (481–843): Merovingian dynasty (481–751), Carolingian Empire (751–843), Anglo-Saxon Heptarchy (ca. 500–927): Kingdoms of England (e.g. Wessex, Mercia, Northumbria).
Republic of Venice (697–1797): Governed by elected Doges.
Papal States (754–1870): Directly ruled by Renaissance popes like Alexander VI and Julius II,
Piast Dynasty (tenth to fourteenth century): Poland's first royal dynasty.
Árpád Dynasty (ninth to fourteenth century): Hungary's first royal dynasty.
Přemyslid Dynasty (tenth to fourteenth century): Czech rulers.
Nemanjić Dynasty (twelfth to fourteenth century): The most prominent Serbian dynasty.

Late Medieval Period and Renaissance (ca. Fourteenth to Sixteenth Century)

Ottoman Empire (1299–1922).
Jagiellon Dynasty (fourteenth to sixteenth century): A powerful dynasty that ruled Poland, Lithuania, Hungary, and Bohemia.
Gediminid Dynasty (thirteenth to fourteenth century): Grand Dukes of Lithuania.
Kotromanić Dynasty (thirteenth to fifteenth century): Bosnian rulers.
Holy Roman Empire (962–1806): Dominated central Europe under elected emperors. Kingdom of France (843–1792): Capetian dynasty (987–1328), Valois dynasty (1328–1589), Bourbon dynasty (1589–1792).
County of Holland (ca. 880–1299): Ruled by the House of Holland, an early precursor to modern Dutch territories; House of Avesnes (1299–1356): Controlled the County of Holland and Zeeland through inheritance; Valois-Burgundy dynasty (1384–1482): Unified much of the Low Countries under the Burgundian Netherlands; Habsburg dynasty (1482–1581): Governed the Low Countries as part of the Holy Roman Empire, later under Spanish Habsburg rule; House of Orange-Nassau (1544–present). Kingdom of England (927–1707): Wessex rul-

ers (until 1016), Danish rule (1016–1042), Norman dynasty (1066–1154), Plantagenet dynasty (1154–1399), Lancaster and York (Wars of the Roses, 1399–1485), Tudor dynasty (1485–1603), Stuart dynasty (1603–1707, with a break in 1649–1660).
Republic of Florence (1115–1532); Medici dynasty (1434–1737).

Early Modern and Modern Period (ca. Seventeenth Century to Present)

House of Savoy (1416–1860): Rulers of Piedmont-Sardinia, later instrumental in the unification of Italy.
Kingdom of Spain (1479–1716): Union of Castile and Aragon, Habsburg dynasty (1516–1700), Bourbon dynasty (1700 onward, with breaks in 1873–1874 and 1931–1975).
Habsburg Monarchy/Austrian Empire (1526–1867): Controlled Austria, Hungary, Bohemia, and later the Austro-Hungarian Empire (1867–1918).
France: First Republic (1792–1804); First Empire or Napoleonic France (1804–1814, 1815): Empire under Napoleon Bonaparte. Bourbon dynasty (1814–1830, with a short break in 1815), House of Orléans (1830–1848), Second Republic (1848–1852), Second Empire (1852–1870), Third Republic (1870–1940), French State or Vichy France (1940–1944), Fourth Republic (1946–1958), Fifth Republic (1958–present).
United Kingdom (1707–present): Great Britain formed by the union of England and Scotland (1707, House of Hanover), then by the union of Great Britain and Ireland in 1801 (House of Hanover, House of Saxe Coburg and Gotha since 1901, renamed into the House of Windsor in 1917); succeeded (1922 onward) by the United Kingdom of Great Britain and Northern Ireland, reigned by the House of Windsor.

Appendix D: Survey Questions in Italy, China, the Netherlands, Russia, and Japan in 2022

Question number	Economy and climate 2022
Q1	**Device type (Italy, China, the Netherlands, Russia, Japan)**
	iOS Phone/Tablet
	Android Phone/Tablet
	Other Phone/Tablet
	Windows Desktop/Laptop
	MacOS Desktop/Laptop
	Other
Q2	**Age (Italy, China, the Netherlands, Russia, Japan)**
	<18
	18–29
	30–44
	45–60
	>60
Q3	**Gender (Italy, China, the Netherlands, Russia, Japan)**
	Male
	Female
Q4a	**In what province do you live (Italy)**
	Campania
	Lazio
	Lombardia
	Sicilia
	Other (please specify)

Q4b	**In what province do you live (China)** Jiangsu 江苏 Zhejiang 浙江 Hebei 河北 Guangdong 广东 Other (please specify) 其他（请注明）
Q4c	**In what province do you live (the Netherlands)** Noord Holland Zuid Holland Utrecht Flevoland Other (please specify)
Q4d	**In what region do you live (Russia)** Moscow city and Moscow Region Москва и Московская область St. Petersburg city and Leningrad Region Санкт-Петербург и Ленинградская область Krasnodar Territory Краснодарский край Sveldlovsk Region Свердловская область Other (please specify)
Q4e	**In what region do you live (Japan)** Hokkaido Tohoku Kanto Chubu Kinki Chugoku Shikoku Kyushu

(continued)

Question number	Economy and climate 2022
Q5	**What is the highest level of education you have completed? (Italy, China, the Netherlands, Russia, Japan)**
	Did not attend school
	Less than primary completed
	Primary completed
	Secondary completed
	University completed
Q6a	**What is roughly your net annual income from your job(s)? (Italy)**
	I have no income
	<20.000 euro
	20.000–34.999 euro
	35.000–49.999 euro
	50.000–74.999 euro
	75.000–99.999 euro
	100.000–149.999 euro
	150.000 or more
	I prefer not to say
Q6b	**What is roughly your net annual income from your job(s)? (China)**
	I have no income
	below 60,000 yuan
	60,000–119,999 yuan
	120,000–239,999 yuan
	240,000–499,999 yuan
	499,999–999,999 yuan
	1,000,000 or more
	I prefer not to say

Q6c	**What is roughly your net annual income from your job(s)? (the Netherlands)**
	I have no income
	Below 20.000 euro
	20.000–34.999 euro
	35.000–49.999 euro
	50.000–74.999 euro
	75.000–99.999 euro
	100.000–149.999 euro
	150.000 or more
	I prefer not to say
Q6d	**What is roughly your net annual income from your job(s)? (Russia)**
	I have no income
	Below 700,000 rubles
	700,000–1,299,999 rubles
	1,300,000–2,499,999 rubles
	2,500,000–4,999,999 rubles
	5,000,000–9,999,999 rubles
	10,000,000 or more rubles
	I prefer not to say
Q6e	**What is roughly your net annual income from your job(s)? (Japan)**
	I have no income
	<499,999 yen
	500,000–999,999 yen
	1,000,000–3,999,999 yen
	4,000,000–7,999,999 yen
	8,000,000–19,999,999 yen
	20,000,000–39,999,999 yen
	40,000,000 yen or more
	I prefer not to say

(continued)

Question number	Economy and climate 2022
Q7	**In what economic sector are you employed? (Italy, China, the Netherlands, Russia, Japan)**
	Agriculture and mining
	Manufacturing
	Electricity, gas, and water
	Construction
	Wholesale and retail trade
	Transport, storage, and communication
	Financial services
	Services not mentioned above
	I am currently not employed
Q8	**Do you think that printing money leads to more government debt (there is no right or wrong answer)? (Italy, China, the Netherlands, Russia, Japan)**
	Yes
	No
Q9a	**Do you think that, if the European Central Bank prints Euro banknotes and gives everyone 10 euro, this means we all get 10 euro richer (there is no right or wrong answer)? (Italy)**
	Yes
	No
Q9b	**If the People's Bank of China prints more money and gives everyone 10 yuan, do you think that means everyone will be 10 yuan richer than before? (China)**
	Yes
	No
Q9c	**Do you think that, if the European Central Bank prints Euro banknotes and gives everyone 10 euro, this means we all get 10 euro richer (there is no right or wrong answer)? (the Netherlands)**
	Yes
	No

Q9d	**What do you think, if the Bank of Russia puts into circulation and distributes to everyone a bill of 100 rubles, will we all become richer by 100 rubles? (There is no definite right or wrong answer) (Russia)** Yes No
Q9e	**What do you think, if the Bank of Japan puts into circulation and distributes to everyone a bill of 100 yen, will we all become richer by 100 yen? (There is no definite right or wrong answer) (Japan)** Yes No
Q10	**You expect your total income next year (2023) to increase? (Italy, China, the Netherlands, Russia, Japan)** Yes No I have no income
Q11	**In what sector you think you personally can earn the highest income (there is no right or wrong answer)? (Italy, China, the Netherlands, Russia, Japan)** Agriculture Industry
Q12	Services **If you can earn similar income, would you prefer working in agriculture, industry, or services? (Italy, China, the Netherlands, Russia, Japan)** Agriculture Industry Services It makes no difference

(continued)

Question number	Economy and climate 2022
Q13	**Do you think that government-controlled companies are performing better than private companies? (Italy, China, the Netherlands, Russia, Japan)** Yes No
Q14a	**How much trust do you have in the national government? (Italy, China, the Netherlands, Russia, Japan)**

	A lot of trust	A bit of trust	No trust/no distrust	A bit of distrust	A lot of distrust
National government					

Question number	Economy and climate 2022
Q14b	**How much trust do you have in the local (municipal) government? (Italy, China, the Netherlands, Russia, Japan)**

	A lot of trust	A bit of trust	No trust/no distrust	A bit of distrust	A lot of distrust
Local government					

Question number	Economy and climate 2022
Q15a	**How bad is air pollution (very problematic to unproblematic)? (Italy, China, the Netherlands, Russia, Japan)**

	Very problematic	Problematic	A bit problematic	Unproblematic
Air pollution				

Question number	Economy and climate 2022
Q15b	**How bad is fresh water pollution (very problematic to unproblematic)? (Italy, China, the Netherlands, Russia, Japan)**

	Very problematic	Problematic	A bit problematic	Unproblematic
Fresh water pollution				

Question number	Economy and climate 2022
Q15c	**How bad is sea pollution (very problematic to unproblematic)? (Italy, China, the Netherlands, Russia, Japan)**

	Very problematic	Problematic	A bit problematic	Unproblematic
Sea pollution				

Question number	Economy and climate 2022
Q15d	**How bad is ground pollution (very problematic to unproblematic)? (Italy, China, the Netherlands, Russia, Japan)**

	Very problematic	Problematic	A bit problematic	Unproblematic
Ground pollution				

Q16	**Recently there's been speculation about mining and exploiting resources from other planets and spatial objects. Should we be setting limits on pollution also outside Earth? (Italy, China, the Netherlands, Russia, Japan)**
	Yes
	No
	Only if there are life forms
	The concept of pollution does not apply to outer space
Q17	**Which of the following alternative energy sources do you think will be MOST important in the next 10 years? (Italy, China, the Netherlands, Russia, Japan)**
	Wind
	Solar
	Nuclear
	Ethanol
	Natural gas
	Coal
	Other (please specify)
Q18	**What share of your income would you be prepared to sacrifice to completely eradicate pollution? (Italy, China, the Netherlands, Russia, Japan)**
	Nothing
	1%–5%
	6%–10%
	11%–15%
	16%–20%
	21%–25%
	26%–30%
	31% and higher
	I have no income

(continued)

Question number	Economy and climate 2022
Q19	**Looking at the current developments in your country, do you think the number of government-controlled companies is expanding? (Italy, China, the Netherlands, Russia)**
	Yes
	No
Q20	**Which country do you think will be the biggest economy in Asia 30 years from now? (China, Japan)**
	China
	India
	Japan
	Indonesia
	Other (please specify)

Appendix E: Survey Data in Japan, China, Russia, Italy, and the Netherlands in 2022

			Q1	Q2	Q3	Q4	Q5
No.	Country	Date created	Device Type (Italy, China, the Netherlands, Russia, Japan)	Age (Italy, China, the Netherlands, Russia, Japan)	Gender (Italy, China, the Netherlands, Russia, Japan)	In what province/ region do you live	What is the highest level of education you have completed? (Italy, China, the Netherlands, Russia, Japan)
1	Italy	2022-05-05 13:39:12	Windows Desktop /Laptop	45–60	Female	Liguria	Secondary completed
2	Italy	2022-05-05 13:39:12	Windows Desktop /Laptop	45–60	Female	Toscana	Secondary completed
3	Italy	2022-05-05 13:37:57	Android Phone /Tablet	30–44	Female	Calabria	Secondary completed
4	Italy	2022-05-05 13:38:08	Android Phone /Tablet	30–44	Male	Lombardia	Secondary completed
5	Italy	2022-05-05 13:37:56	Windows Desktop /Laptop	45–60	Male	Calabria	Secondary completed
6	Italy	2022-05-05 13:37:59	Android Phone /Tablet	18–29	Male	Campania	Primary completed
7	Italy	2022-05-05 13:38:50	Android Phone /Tablet	45–60	Female	Emilia Romagna	Secondary completed
8	Italy	2022-05-05 13:38:16	Android Phone /Tablet	>60	Female	Toscana	Secondary completed
9	Italy	2022-05-05 13:38:07	Android Phone/Tablet	30–44	Female	Puglia	Secondary completed
10	Italy	2022-05-05 13:38:09	Windows Desktop /Laptop	45–60	Male	Lombardia	University completed
11	Italy	2022-05-05 13:39:11	Android Phone/Tablet	45–60	Female	Puglia	Secondary completed

(continued)

			Q1	Q2	Q3	Q4	Q5
No.	Country	Date created	Device Type (Italy, China, the Netherlands, Russia, Japan)	Age (Italy, China, the Netherlands, Russia, Japan)	Gender (Italy, China, the Netherlands, Russia, Japan)	In what province/ region do you live	What is the highest level of education you have completed? (Italy, China, the Netherlands, Russia, Japan)
12	Italy	2022-05-05 13:39:20	Android Phone/Tablet	45–60	Female	Sicilia	Primary completed
13	Italy	2022-05-05 13:38:50	Android Phone/Tablet	45–60	Male	Campania	Primary completed
14	Italy	2022-05-05 13:37:41	iOS Phone/Tablet	45–60	Male	Lombardia	Secondary completed
15	Italy	2022-05-05 13:38:49	iOS Phone/Tablet	45–60	Male	Campania	Secondary completed
16	Italy	2022-05-05 13:39:27	Android Phone/Tablet	45–60	Female	Piemonte	Secondary completed
17	Italy	2022-05-05 13:38:01	Android Phone/Tablet	18–29	Female	Sicilia	Secondary completed
18	Italy	2022-05-05 13:38:24	Android Phone/Tablet	45–60	Male	Sicilia	Primary completed
19	Italy	2022-05-05 13:39:24	iOS Phone/Tablet	45–60	Female	Lombardia	Primary completed
20	Italy	2022-05-05 13:39:15	Windows Desktop/Laptop	>60	Female	Lombardia	Secondary completed
21	Italy	2022-05-05 13:39:24	Android Phone/Tablet	45–60	Female	Piemonte	Primary completed
22	Italy	2022-05-05 13:38:23	Android Phone/Tablet	18–29	Female	Calabria	Secondary completed
23	Italy	2022-05-05 13:38:30	Windows Desktop/Laptop	45–60	Male	Liguria	Secondary completed
24	Italy	2022-05-05 13:38:15	Android Phone/Tablet	30–44	Male	Emilia Romagna	Secondary completed

25	Italy	2022-05-05 13:38:59	Android Phone/Tablet	>60	Female	Piemonte	Secondary completed
26	Italy	2022-05-05 13:38:44	Android Phone/Tablet	45–60	Male	Lombardia	Primary completed
27	Italy	2022-05-05 13:38:58	Android Phone/Tablet	45–60	Male	Sicilia	Secondary completed
28	Italy	2022-05-05 13:38:16	Windows Desktop/Laptop	45–60	Male	Campania	Secondary completed
29	Italy	2022-05-05 13:39:09	iOS Phone/Tablet	45–60	Female	Toscana	Secondary completed
30	Italy	2022-05-05 13:39:31	Android Phone/Tablet	>60	Female	Lazio	Secondary completed
31	Italy	2022-05-05 13:37:51	Android Phone/Tablet	30–44	Female	Sicilia	University completed
32	Italy	2022-05-05 13:39:06	Android Phone/Tablet	>60	Male	Piemonte	Primary completed
33	Italy	2022-05-05 13:38:01	Android Phone/Tablet	30–44	Male	Lombardia	Secondary completed
34	Italy	2022-05-05 13:39:01	Android Phone/Tablet	45–60	Male	Emilia Romagna	University completed
35	Italy	2022-05-05 13:38:49	Android Phone/Tablet	45–60	Male	Liguria	Secondary completed
36	Italy	2022-05-05 13:37:59	Windows Desktop/Laptop	30–44	Female	Lombardia	Less than primary completed
37	Italy	2022-05-05 13:37:40	Windows Desktop/Laptop	>60	Female	Basilicata	University completed
38	Italy	2022-05-05 13:37:52	iOS Phone/Tablet	30–44	Male	Lombardia	Secondary completed

(continued)

			Q1	Q2	Q3	Q4	Q5
No.	Country	Date created	Device Type (Italy, China, the Netherlands, Russia, Japan)	Age (Italy, China, the Netherlands, Russia, Japan)	Gender (Italy, China, the Netherlands, Russia, Japan)	In what province/ region do you live	What is the highest level of education you have completed? (Italy, China, the Netherlands, Russia, Japan)
39	Italy	2022-05-05 13:38:16	Windows Desktop /Laptop	>60	Female	Emilia Romagna	Secondary completed
40	Italy	2022-05-05 13:38:19	Android Phone/Tablet	30–44	Female	Friuli-Venezia Giulia	Secondary completed
41	Italy	2022-05-05 13:38:05	Android Phone/Tablet	18–29	Male	Sicilia	Secondary completed
42	Italy	2022-05-05 13:38:11	Windows Desktop/Laptop	30–44	Female	Lombardia	University completed
43	Italy	2022-05-05 13:38:14	Windows Desktop/Laptop	45–60	Male	Liguria	Secondary completed
44	Italy	2022-05-05 13:37:59	Android Phone/Tablet	45–60	Male	Sicilia	Secondary completed
45	Italy	2022-05-05 13:37:49	Android Phone/Tablet	18–29	Male	Campania	Secondary completed
46	Italy	2022-05-05 13:38:37	Windows Desktop/Laptop	45–60	Male	Lombardia	University completed
47	Italy	2022-05-05 13:38:23	Android Phone/Tablet	18–29	Male	Sicilia	
48	Italy	2022-05-05 13:37:52	Android Phone/Tablet	30–44	Female	Piemonte	Secondary completed
49	Italy	2022-05-05 13:38:13	Windows Desktop/Laptop	45–60	Male	Lombardia	Secondary completed
50	Italy	2022-05-05 13:37:42	Android Phone Tablet	45–60	Female	Trentino Alto Adige	Secondary completed

51	Italy	2022-05-05 13:37:42	iOS Phone/Tablet	30–44	Female	Toscana	Secondary completed
52	Italy	2022-05-05 13:38:21	Android Phone/Tablet	18–29	Male	Toscana	Secondary completed
53	Italy	2022-05-05 13:38:21	Android Phone/Tablet	30–44	Female	Emilia Romagna	University completed
54	Italy	2022-05-05 13:38:04	Windows Desktop/Laptop	18–29	Male	Sicilia	Secondary completed
55	Italy	2022-05-05 13:38:21	Windows Desktop/Laptop	18–29	Male	Lombardia	Secondary completed
56	Italy	2022-05-05 13:37:51	iOS Phone/Tablet	30–44	Male	Piemonte	University completed
57	Italy	2022-05-05 13:38:07	Windows Desktop/Laptop	30–44	Male	Lombardia	Secondary completed
58	Italy	2022-05-05 13:37:59	iOS Phone/Tablet	45–60	Female	Emilia Romagna	Secondary completed
59	Italy	2022-05-05 13:37:38	Windows Desktop/Laptop	30–44	Male	Campania	Secondary completed
60	Italy	2022-05-05 13:37:45	Android Phone/Tablet	45–60	Female	Lombardia	Primary completed
61	Italy	2022-05-05 13:38:03	iOS Phone/Tablet	45–60	Male	Lazio	University completed
62	Italy	2022-05-05 13:37:40	Android Phone/Tablet	30–44	Female	Piemonte	University completed
63	Italy	2022-05-05 13:38:18	Windows Desktop/Laptop	30–44	Male	Lombardia	Secondary completed
64	Italy	2022-05-05 13:37:56	Android Phone/Tablet	45–60	Female	Sicilia	University completed

(continued)

			Q1	Q2	Q3	Q4	Q5
No.	Country	Date created	Device Type (Italy, China, the Netherlands, Russia, Japan)	Age (Italy, China, the Netherlands, Russia, Japan)	Gender (Italy, China, the Netherlands, Russia, Japan)	In what province/ region do you live	What is the highest level of education you have completed? (Italy, China, the Netherlands, Russia, Japan)
65	Italy	2022-05-05 13:38:05	Windows Desktop/Laptop	>60	Male	Emilia Romangna	Secondary completed
66	Italy	2022-05-05 13:38:32	Windows Desktop/Laptop	45–60	Female	Marche	Secondary completed
67	Italy	2022-05-05 13:37:52	Android Phone/Tablet	30–44	Female	Lazio	Secondary completed
68	Italy	2022-05-05 13:38:07	Android Phone/Tablet	30–44	Male	Liguria	Secondary completed
69	Italy	2022-05-05 13:37:37	Windows Desktop/Laptop	45–60	Male	Campania	Secondary completed
70	Italy	2022-05-05 13:38:12	Android Phone/Tablet	18–29	Male	Campania	Secondary completed
71	Italy	2022-05-05 13:38:16	Android Phone/Tablet	18–29	Female	Lombardia	Secondary completed
72	Italy	2022-05-05 13:38:02	Android Phone/Tablet	18–29	Female	Abruzzo	University completed
73	Italy	2022-05-05 13:37:44	Windows Desktop/Laptop	18–29	Female	Abruzzo	Secondary completed
74	Italy	2022-05-05 13:37:43	Android Phone/Tablet	30–44	Male	Piemonte	Secondary completed
75	Italy	2022-05-05 13:37:45	Android Phone/Tablet	30–44	Female	Campania	University completed
76	China	2022-04-29 14:58:26	Android Phone/Tablet	45–60	Male	Jiangsu	University completed
77	China	2022-04-29 14:52:44	Windows Desktop/Laptop	45–60	Male	Zhejiang	University completed

78	China	2022-04-29 14:48:57	Windows Desktop/Laptop	45–60	Female	Hebei	University completed
79	China	2022-04-29 14:33:12	Android Phone/Tablet	18–29	Male	Jiangsu	University completed
80	China	2022-04-29 13:53:26	iOS Phone/Tablet	45–60	Female	Jiangsu	University completed
81	China	2022-04-29 13:55:47	iOS Phone/Tablet	>60	Female	Guangdong	University completed
82	China	2022-04-29 13:54:57	Windows Desktop/Laptop	45–60	Male	Jiangsu	University completed
83	China	2022-04-29 13:54:14	iOS Phone/Tablet	45–60	Female	Jiangxi	Secondary completed
84	China	2022-04-29 13:53:30	Android Phone/Tablet	45–60	Female	Guangdong	University completed
85	China	2022-04-29 13:53:48	Windows Desktop/Laptop	45–60	Male	Jiangsu	University completed
86	China	2022-04-29 13:52:44	iOS Phone/Tablet	45–60	Female	Jiangsu	University completed
87	China	2022-04-29 13:49:01	Android Phone/Tablet	45–60	Female	Jiangsu	Secondary completed
88	China	2022-04-29 13:51:20	Android Phone/Tablet	45–60	Male	Guangdong	University completed
89	China	2022-04-29 13:50:16	Android Phone/Tablet	45–60	Female	Liaoning	University completed
90	China	2022-04-29 13:29:35	Android Phone/Tablet	30–44	Female	Beijing	University completed
91	China	2022-04-29 13:49:59	Windows Desktop/Laptop	45–60	Male	Shanghai	University completed
92	China	2022-04-29 13:47:40	Android Phone/Tablet	45–60	Male	Zhejiang	University completed

(continued)

			Q1	Q2	Q3	Q4	Q5
No.	Country	Date created	Device Type (Italy, China, the Netherlands, Russia, Japan)	Age (Italy, China, the Netherlands, Russia, Japan)	Gender (Italy, China, the Netherlands, Russia, Japan)	In what province/ region do you live	What is the highest level of education you have completed? (Italy, China, the Netherlands, Russia, Japan)
93	China	2022-04-29 13:48:31	Windows Desktop/Laptop	>60	Male	Shanghai	Secondary completed
94	China	2022-04-29 13:45:00	Windows Desktop/Laptop	45–60	Female	Beijing	University completed
95	China	2022-04-29 13:47:56	Windows Desktop/Laptop	45–60	Female	Shanghai	University completed
96	China	2022-04-29 13:48:00	Windows Desktop/Laptop	45–60	Male	Jiangsu	University completed
97	China	2022-04-29 13:46:45	Android Phone/Tablet	45–60	Male	Hebei	University completed
98	China	2022-04-29 13:44:52	Android Phone/Tablet	45–60	Male	Shaanxi	University completed
99	China	2022-04-29 13:45:36	Windows Desktop/Laptop	45–60	Male	Jiangsu	University completed
100	China	2022-04-29 13:46:00	Android Phone/Tablet	45–60	Male	Jiangsu	University completed
101	China	2022-04-29 13:44:51	Windows Desktop/Laptop	45–60	Male	Shanghai	University completed
102	China	2022-04-29 13:44:17	Windows Desktop/Laptop	45–60	Female	Shanghai	University completed
103	China	2022-04-29 13:44:55	Windows Desktop/Laptop	45–60	Female	Zhejiang	University completed
104	China	2022-04-29 13:44:04	iOS Phone/Tablet	45–60	Female	Shaanxi	Secondary completed
105	China	2022-04-29 13:45:54	Windows Desktop/Laptop	45–60	Male	Shanghai	University completed

106	China	2022-04-29 13:45:58	Windows Desktop/Laptop	45–60	Female	Hebei	University completed
107	China	2022-04-29 13:44:19	Android Phone/Tablet	45–60	Male	Guangdong	University completed
108	China	2022-04-29 13:42:33	Windows Desktop/Laptop	45–60	Male	Guangdong	University completed
109	China	2022-04-29 13:43:24	Windows Desktop/Laptop	45–60	Male	Shanxi	Secondary completed
110	China	2022-04-29 13:41:38	iOS Phone/Tablet	45–60	Male	Shanxi	University completed
111	China	2022-04-29 13:43:09	Windows Desktop/Laptop	45–60	Male	Guangdong	University completed
112	China	2022-04-29 13:41:44	Android Phone/Tablet	45–60	Male	Liaoning	University completed
113	China	2022-04-29 13:41:05	Windows Desktop/Laptop	45–60	Male	Shanxi	University completed
114	China	2022-04-29 13:39:55	Android Phone/Tablet	45–60	Male	Tianjin	Secondary completed
115	China	2022-04-29 13:36:32	Android Phone/Tablet	45–60	Female	Chongqing	University completed
116	China	2022-04-29 13:37:42	Windows Desktop/Laptop	45–60	Male	Shanghai	University completed
117	China	2022-04-29 13:40:41	Android Phone/Tablet	45–60	Male	Jiangsu	University completed
118	China	2022-04-29 13:33:41	Android Phone/Tablet	45–60	Male	Liaoning	University completed
119	China	2022-04-29 13:34:28	Android Phone/Tablet	45–60	Female	Jiangxi	Secondary completed
120	China	2022-04-29 13:36:13	Windows Desktop/Laptop	45–60	Male	Jiangsu	University completed

(continued)

			Q1	Q2	Q3	Q4	Q5
No.	Country	Date created	Device Type (Italy, China, the Netherlands, Russia, Japan)	Age (Italy, China, the Netherlands, Russia, Japan)	Gender (Italy, China, the Netherlands, Russia, Japan)	In what province/ region do you live	What is the highest level of education you have completed? (Italy, China, the Netherlands, Russia, Japan)
121	China	2022-04-29 13:35:16	Other	45–60	Male	Guangdong	University completed
122	China	2022-04-29 13:32:28	Windows Desktop/Laptop	45–60	Male	Fujian	University completed
123	China	2022-04-29 13:33:41	Windows Desktop/Laptop	45–60	Female	Tianjin	University completed
124	China	2022-04-29 13:32:16	Android Phone/Tablet	45–60	Male	Shaanxi	University completed
125	China	2022-04-29 13:28:02	Android Phone/Tablet	30–44	Male	Guangdong	University completed
126	China	2022-04-29 13:32:09	Windows Desktop/Laptop	45–60	Female	Sichuan	University completed
127	China	2022-04-29 13:33:26	Windows Desktop/Laptop	45–60	Female	Zhejiang	
128	China	2022-04-29 13:32:05	Android Phone/Tablet	30–44	Female	Guangdong	University completed
129	China	2022-04-29 13:30:03	iOS Phone/Tablet	18–29	Female	Jiangsu	University completed
130	China	2022-04-29 13:28:46	Android Phone/Tablet	18–29	Male	Guangdong	University completed
131	China	2022-04-29 13:29:46	Android Phone/Tablet	18–29	Female	Jiangsu	Secondary completed
132	China	2022-04-29 13:31:49	Windows Desktop/Laptop	45–60	Male	Zhejiang	University completed
133	China	2022-04-29 13:29:53	Android Phone/Tablet	30–44	Female	Guangdong	University completed

134	China	2022-04-29 13:29:57	iOS Phone/Tablet	30–44	Male	Guangdong	University completed
135	China	2022-04-29 13:30:20	Android Phone/Tablet	30–44	Female	Hebei	University completed
136	China	2022-04-29 13:29:28	Windows Desktop/Laptop	30–44	Female	Beijing	University completed
137	China	2022-04-29 13:30:02	Android Phone/Tablet	30–44	Male	Hebei	University completed
138	China	2022-04-29 13:29:27	Android Phone/Tablet	30–44	Male	Jiangsu	University completed
139	China	2022-04-29 13:29:30	Android Phone/Tablet	30–44	Female	Zhejiang	University completed
140	China	2022-04-29 13:30:15	Windows Desktop/Laptop	45–60	Male	Jiangsu	University completed
141	China	2022-04-29 13:30:42	iOS Phone/Tablet	30–44	Female	Beijing	University completed
142	China	2022-04-29 13:29:38	Android Phone/Tablet	30–44	Female	Guangdong	University completed
143	China	2022-04-29 13:28:50	iOS Phone/Tablet	18–29	Female	Inner Mongolia	University completed
144	China	2022-04-29 13:30:00	Android Phone/Tablet	30–44	Female	Jiangsu	University completed
145	China	2022-04-29 13:28:41	Windows Desktop/Laptop	30–44	Male	Hebei	University completed
146	China	2022-04-29 13:29:13	Android Phone/Tablet	18–29	Female	Zhejiang	University completed
147	China	2022-04-29 13:29:19	Android Phone/Tablet	30–44	Male	Shanghai	University completed

(continued)

			Q1	Q2	Q3	Q4	Q5
No.	Country	Date created	Device Type (Italy, China, the Netherlands, Russia, Japan)	Age (Italy, China, the Netherlands, Russia, Japan)	Gender (Italy, China, the Netherlands, Russia, Japan)	In what province/ region do you live	What is the highest level of education you have completed? (Italy, China, the Netherlands, Russia, Japan)
148	China	2022-04-29 13:29:44	Android Phone/Tablet	18–29	Female	Inner Mongolia	University completed
149	China	2022-04-29 13:29:06	Windows Desktop/Laptop	30–44	Male	Henan	University completed
150	China	2022-04-29 13:29:57	Android Phone/Tablet	30–44	Female	Jiangsu	University completed
151	China	2022-04-29 13:29:33	Windows Desktop/Laptop	30–44	Female	Guangdong	University completed
152	China	2022-04-29 13:29:48	Android Phone/Tablet	18–29	Female	Shanghai	University completed
153	China	2022-04-29 13:29:36	iOS Phone/Tablet	30–44	Male	Jiangsu	University completed
154	China	2022-04-29 13:30:04	Android Phone/Tablet	30–44	Male	Jiangsu	University completed
155	China	2022-04-29 13:29:18	Android Phone/Tablet	30–44	Male	Jiangsu	University completed
156	China	2022-04-29 13:29:44	Android Phone/Tablet	18–29	Female	Hubei	University completed
157	China	2022-04-29 13:28:54	Android Phone/Tablet	18–29	Male	Jiangsu	University completed
158	China	2022-04-29 13:29:33	Windows Desktop/Laptop	30–44	Female	Guangdong	University completed
159	China	2022-04-29 13:29:00	Windows Desktop/Laptop	45–60	Male	Zhejiang	University completed
160	China	2022-04-29 13:29:06	Android Phone/Tablet	30–44	Female	Hubei	University completed

161	China	2022-04-29 13:29:37	Windows Desktop/Laptop	>60	Female	Zhejiang	University completed
162	China	2022-04-29 13:29:25	Windows Desktop/Laptop	30–44	Female	Beijing	University completed
163	China	2022-04-29 13:29:03	Android Phone/Tablet	18–29	Female	Hunan	University completed
164	China	2022-04-29 13:28:45	Windows Desktop/Laptop	30–44	Female	Jiangsu	University completed
165	China	2022-04-29 13:29:20	Android Phone/Tablet	18–29	Female	Hebei	University completed
166	China	2022-04-29 13:29:20	Android Phone/Tablet	18–29	Female	Fujian	University completed
167	China	2022-04-29 13:28:49	Windows Desktop/Laptop	18–29	Male	Anhui	University completed
168	China	2022-04-29 13:28:46	Android Phone/Tablet	30–44	Male	Jiangsu	University completed
169	China	2022-04-29 13:28:49	Windows Desktop/Laptop	18–29	Female	Jiangsu	University completed
170	China	2022-04-29 13:26:47	Windows Desktop/Laptop	30–44	Male	Hebei	University completed
171	China	2022-04-29 13:27:29	Android Phone/Tablet	18–29	Male	Zhejiang	University completed
172	China	2022-04-29 13:26:51	Android Phone/Tablet	30–44	Female	Henan	University completed
173	China	2022-04-29 13:27:34	Windows Desktop/Laptop	30–44	Female	Guangdong	
174	China	2022-04-29 13:26:33	Android Phone/Tablet	30–44	Female	Guangdong	University completed

(continued)

No.	Country	Date created	Q1 Device Type (Italy, China, the Netherlands, Russia, Japan)	Q2 Age (Italy, China, the Netherlands, Russia, Japan)	Q3 Gender (Italy, China, the Netherlands, Russia, Japan)	Q4 In what province/region do you live	Q5 What is the highest level of education you have completed? (Italy, China, the Netherlands, Russia, Japan)
175	China	2022-04-29 13:25:23	Android Phone/Tablet	30–44	Male	Hebei	University completed
176	The Netherlands	2022-05-06 09:47:07	Windows Desktop/Laptop	>60	Female	N.A.	Less than primary completed
177	The Netherlands	2022-05-06 09:55:13	Windows Desktop/Laptop	>60	Male	Limburg	Secondary completed
178	The Netherlands	2022-05-06 09:46:23	Windows Desktop/Laptop	30–44	Male	Noord-Brabant	University completed
179	The Netherlands	2022-05-06 09:55:37	Windows Desktop/Laptop	>60	Male	Limburg	Primary completed
180	The Netherlands	2022-05-06 09:55:56	iOS Phone/Tablet	>60	Male	Friesland	Secondary completed
181	The Netherlands	2022-05-06 09:55:06	Android Phone/Tablet	>60	Male	Noord-Brabant	Primary completed
182	The Netherlands	2022-05-06 09:55:12	Windows Desktop/Laptop	>60	Male	Noord-Brabant	Secondary completed
183	The Netherlands	2022-05-06 09:54:50	Android Phone/Tablet	>60	Male	Zuid Holland	Secondary completed
184	The Netherlands	2022-05-06 09:54:31	Android Phone/Tablet	45–60	Male	Utrecht	University completed
185	The Netherlands	2022-05-06 09:52:38	iOS Phone/Tablet	>60	Male	Limburg	University completed
186	The Netherlands	2022-05-06 09:52:47	MacOS Desktop/Laptop	>60	Male	Overijssel	Secondary completed
187	The Netherlands	2022-05-06 09:51:55	Android Phone/Tablet	>60	Male	Overijssel	Secondary completed

188	The Netherlands	2022-05-06 09:52:13	Windows Desktop/Laptop	>60	Male	Overijsel	Secondary completed
189	The Netherlands	2022-05-06 09:52:52	MacOS Desktop/Laptop	45–60	Male	Gelderland	Secondary completed
190	The Netherlands	2022-05-06 09:51:13	Android Phone/Tablet	45–60	Female	Groningen	Primary completed
191	The Netherlands	2022-05-06 09:50:35	MacOS Desktop/Laptop	>60	Male	Limburg	Secondary completed
192	The Netherlands	2022-05-06 09:49:58	iOS Phone/Tablet	18–29	Male	Zuid Holland	Secondary completed
193	The Netherlands	2022-05-06 09:51:38	Android Phone/Tablet	30–44	Female	Utrecht	University completed
194	The Netherlands	2022-05-06 09:51:16	Android Phone/Tablet	>60	Female	Friesland	Secondary completed
195	The Netherlands	2022-05-06 09:51:40	Android Phone/Tablet	18–29	Female	Flevoland	Secondary completed
196	The Netherlands	2022-05-06 09:49:10	iOS Phone/Tablet	18–29	Female	Utrecht	University completed
197	The Netherlands	2022-05-06 09:51:35	iOS Phone/Tablet	30–44	Female	Gelderland	Secondary completed
198	The Netherlands	2022-05-06 09:50:46	Android Phone/Tablet	18–29	Female	Zuid Holland	Secondary completed
199	The Netherlands	2022-05-06 09:51:04	Android Phone/Tablet	30–44	Female	Overijssel	Secondary completed
200	The Netherlands	2022-05-06 09:49:55	iOS Phone/Tablet	18–29	Female	Zuid Holland	Secondary completed
201	The Netherlands	2022-05-06 09:50:27	Android Phone/Tablet	18–29	Male	Zuid Holland	Secondary completed
202	The Netherlands	2022-05-06 09:51:11	iOS Phone/Tablet	30–44	Male	Zuid Holland	Secondary completed

(continued)

			Q1	Q2	Q3	Q4	Q5
No.	Country	Date created	Device Type (Italy, China, the Netherlands, Russia, Japan)	Age (Italy, China, the Netherlands, Russia, Japan)	Gender (Italy, China, the Netherlands, Russia, Japan)	In what province/ region do you live	What is the highest level of education you have completed? (Italy, China, the Netherlands, Russia, Japan)
203	The Netherlands	2022-05-06 09:51:40	MacOS Desktop/Laptop	45–60	Female	Utrecht	Less than primary completed
204	The Netherlands	2022-05-06 09:50:59	Android Phone/Tablet	18–29	Female	N.A.	Secondary completed
205	The Netherlands	2022-05-06 09:51:57	iOS Phone/Tablet	45–60	Male	Utrecht	Secondary completed
206	The Netherlands	2022-05-06 09:51:34	iOS Phone/Tablet	18–29	Male	Gelderland	Secondary completed
207	The Netherlands	2022-05-06 09:48:08	Android Phone/Tablet	45–60	Female	Zuid Holland	Secondary completed
208	The Netherlands	2022-05-06 09:51:40	iOS Phone/Tablet	18–29	Female	Noord Holland	University completed
209	The Netherlands	2022-05-06 09:50:38	iOS Phone/Tablet	18–29	Female	Zuid Holland	Secondary completed
210	The Netherlands	2022-05-06 09:50:52	iOS Phone/Tablet	45–60	Female	Noord-Brabant	Secondary completed
211	The Netherlands	2022-05-06 09:49:50	iOS Phone/Tablet	18–29	Female	Utrecht	Secondary completed
212	The Netherlands	2022-05-06 09:51:26	Android Phone/Tablet	45–60	Male	Zuid Holland	University completed
213	The Netherlands	2022-05-06 09:50:52	Windows Desktop/Laptop	30–44	Male	Friesland	University completed
214	The Netherlands	2022-05-06 09:49:41	Windows Desktop/Laptop	>60	Male	Zuid Holland	Secondary completed
215	The Netherlands	2022-05-06 09:50:32	Windows Desktop/Laptop	>60	Female	Noord Holland	Secondary completed

216	The Netherlands	2022-05-06 09:50:20	Other	45–60	Male	Utrecht	Secondary completed
217	The Netherlands	2022-05-06 09:49:36	Android Phone/Tablet	45–60	Male	Utrecht	Secondary completed
218	The Netherlands	2022-05-06 09:49:47	iOS Phone/Tablet	18–29	Female	Limburg	Secondary completed
219	The Netherlands	2022-05-06 09:50:48	iOS Phone/Tablet	30–44	Male	Noord Holland	University completed
220	The Netherlands	2022-05-06 09:49:33	Android Phone/Tablet	45–60	Female	Noord Holland	Secondary completed
221	The Netherlands	2022-05-06 09:48:19	Android Phone/Tablet	30–44	Female	Zuid Holland	University completed
222	The Netherlands	2022-05-06 09:50:38	iOS Phone/Tablet	18–29	Female	Noord Holland	University completed
223	The Netherlands	2022-05-06 09:48:39	Android Phone/Tablet	45–60	Female	Noord Brabant	Secondary completed
224	The Netherlands	2022-05-06 09:49:37	Android Phone/Tablet	45–60	Male	Zuid Holland	Secondary completed
225	The Netherlands	2022-05-06 09:47:51	Windows Desktop/Laptop	45–60	Male	Groningen	Less than primary completed
226	The Netherlands	2022-05-06 09:50:25	iOS Phone/Tablet	18–29	Female	Friesland	Secondary completed
227	The Netherlands	2022-05-06 09:47:41	iOS Phone/Tablet	45–60	Female	Overijssel	Primary completed
228	The Netherlands	2022-05-06 09:49:17	Android Phone/Tablet	30–44	Male	Noord-Brabant	University completed
229	The Netherlands	2022-05-06 09:48:24	Android Phone/Tablet	>60	Female	Zuid Holland	Secondary completed
230	The Netherlands	2022-05-06 09:48:01	Windows Desktop/Laptop	>60	Female	Noord-Brabant	Secondary completed

(continued)

			Q1	Q2	Q3	Q4	Q5
No.	Country	Date created	Device Type (Italy, China, the Netherlands, Russia, Japan)	Age (Italy, China, the Netherlands, Russia, Japan)	Gender (Italy, China, the Netherlands, Russia, Japan)	In what province/ region do you live	What is the highest level of education you have completed? (Italy, China, the Netherlands, Russia, Japan)
231	The Netherlands	2022-05-06 09:48:45	iOS Phone/Tablet	18–29	Male	Noord Holland	Secondary completed
232	The Netherlands	2022-05-06 09:47:55	Windows Desktop/Laptop	18–29	Male	Friesland	Secondary completed
233	The Netherlands	2022-05-06 09:46:38	Windows Desktop/Laptop	45–60	Female	Noord Holland	Secondary completed
234	The Netherlands	2022-05-06 09:47:14	Android Phone/Tablet	45–60	Male	Noord Holland	Secondary completed
235	The Netherlands	2022-05-06 09:48:00	iOS Phone/Tablet	18–29	Female	Overijssel	Secondary completed
236	The Netherlands	2022-05-06 09:47:19	iOS Phone/Tablet	30–44	Female	Limburg	Secondary completed
237	The Netherlands	2022-05-06 09:47:34	Android Phone/Tablet	18–29	Male	Limburg	Secondary completed
238	The Netherlands	2022-05-06 09:48:07	Windows Desktop/Laptop	45–60	Male	Noord Holland	
239	The Netherlands	2022-05-06 09:47:27	iOS Phone/Tablet	18–29	Female	Utrecht	Secondary completed
240	The Netherlands	2022-05-06 09:46:48	Android Phone/Tablet	45–60	Male	Gelderland	Secondary completed
241	The Netherlands	2022-05-06 09:47:15	Android Phone/Tablet	30–44	Female	Zuid Holland	University completed
242	The Netherlands	2022-05-06 09:47:01	Windows Desktop/Laptop	18–29	Female	Overijssel	
243	The Netherlands	2022-05-06 09:46:06	Android Phone/Tablet	30–44	Female	Noord Holland	Secondary completed

244	The Netherlands	2022-05-06 09:46:57	Windows Desktop/Laptop	45–60	Male	Zuid Holland	Secondary completed
245	The Netherlands	2022-05-06 09:46:50	Android Phone/Tablet	45–60	Female	Limburg	Secondary completed
246	The Netherlands	2022-05-06 09:47:24	Windows Desktop/Laptop	18–29	Male	Limburg	University completed
247	The Netherlands	2022-05-06 09:46:21	Android Phone/Tablet	>60	Female	Zuid Holland	Secondary completed
248	The Netherlands	2022-05-06 09:45:58	Windows Desktop/Laptop	45–60	Male	Zuid Holland	Secondary completed
249	The Netherlands	2022-05-06 09:46:28	iOS Phone/Tablet	30–44	Female	Utrecht	Secondary completed
250	The Netherlands	2022-05-06 09:46:08	Windows Desktop/Laptop	30–44	Male	Noord Holland	University completed
251	Russia	2022-05-05 12:40:07	Windows Desktop/Laptop	18–29	Male	Moscow city and Moscow Region	University completed
252	Russia	2022-05-05 12:46:45	Android Phone/Tablet	45–60	Female	Moscow city and Moscow Region	Secondary completed
253	Russia	2022-05-05 12:45:39	Windows Desktop/Laptop	18–29	Female	Moscow city and Moscow Region	Secondary completed
254	Russia	2022-05-05 12:40:04	Android Phone/Tablet	18–29	Male	Moscow city and Moscow Region	HePrimary completed
255	Russia	2022-05-05 11:40:00	Windows Desktop/Laptop	30–44	Female	Krasnodar Territory	University completed
256	Russia	2022-05-05 11:58:19	Windows Desktop/Laptop	45–60	Male	Novosibirsk Region	Secondary completed

(continued)

			Q1	Q2	Q3	Q4	Q5
No.	Country	Date created	Device Type (Italy, China, the Netherlands, Russia, Japan)	Age (Italy, China, the Netherlands, Russia, Japan)	Gender (Italy, China, the Netherlands, Russia, Japan)	In what province/ region do you live	What is the highest level of education you have completed? (Italy, China, the Netherlands, Russia, Japan)
257	Russia	2022-05-05 11:38:26	Windows Desktop/Laptop	45–60	Male	Rostov Region	University completed
258	Russia	2022-05-05 11:42:41	Windows Desktop/Laptop	>60	Female	Moscow city and Moscow Region	University completed
259	Russia	2022-05-05 11:41:29	Windows Desktop/Laptop	45–60	Female	Saratov Region	University completed
260	Russia	2022-05-05 11:43:42	Windows Desktop/Laptop	45–60	Female	Irkutsk Region	Secondary completed
261	Russia	2022-05-05 11:41:02	Windows Desktop/Laptop	45–60	Female	Astrakhan Region	Secondary completed
262	Russia	2022-05-05 11:41:07	Windows Desktop/Laptop	45–60	Female	Perm Territory	University completed
263	Russia	2022-05-05 11:44:05	Windows Desktop/Laptop	45–60	Female	Sveldlovsk Region	
264	Russia	2022-05-05 11:44:16	Windows Desktop/Laptop	>60	Female	Samara Region	University completed
265	Russia	2022-05-05 11:44:51	Windows Desktop/Laptop	45–60	Female	Kaluga Region	University completed
266	Russia	2022-05-05 11:43:17	Windows Desktop/Laptop	45–60	Female	Rostov Region	Secondary completed
267	Russia	2022-05-05 11:43:35	Windows Desktop/Laptop	>60	Female	Yaroslavl Region	University completed
268	Russia	2022-05-05 11:42:21	Windows Desktop/Laptop	45–60	Female	Chelyabinsk Region	Secondary completed

269	Russia	2022-05-05 11:43:10	Windows Desktop/Laptop	45–60	Female	Stavropol Region	Secondary completed
270	Russia	2022-05-05 11:44:28	Android Phone/Tablet	45–60	Female	Rostov Region	University completed
271	Russia	2022-05-05 11:43:36	Windows Desktop/Laptop	45–60	Female	Kirov Region	University completed
272	Russia	2022-05-05 11:44:25	Android Phone/Tablet	45–60	Female	Moscow city and Moscow Region	University completed
273	Russia	2022-05-05 11:36:16	Other	45–60	Male	Penza Region	University completed
274	Russia	2022-05-05 11:42:05	Windows Desktop/Laptop	45–60	Female	Perm Territory	University completed
275	Russia	2022-05-05 11:41:58	Windows Desktop/Laptop	45–60	Female	Arkhangelsk Region	Secondary completed
276	Russia	2022-05-05 11:41:14	Windows Desktop/Laptop	45–60	Female	Krasnodar Territory	Secondary completed
277	Russia	2022-05-05 11:39:16	Windows Desktop/Laptop	30–44	Female	Kaluga Region	Secondary completed
278	Russia	2022-05-05 11:38:00	Android Phone/Tablet	30–44	Female	Moscow city and Moscow Region	Secondary completed
279	Russia	2022-05-05 11:39:57	Other	18–29	Female	Moscow city and Moscow Region	Secondary completed
280	Russia	2022-05-05 11:41:46	Windows Desktop/Laptop	45–60	Female	Samara Region	University completed
281	Russia	2022-05-05 11:36:38	Windows Desktop/Laptop	45–60	Female	Yaroslalvl Region	University completed

(continued)

			Q1	Q2	Q3	Q4	Q5
No.	Country	Date created	Device Type (Italy, China, the Netherlands, Russia, Japan)	Age (Italy, China, the Netherlands, Russia, Japan)	Gender (Italy, China, the Netherlands, Russia, Japan)	In what province/ region do you live	What is the highest level of education you have completed? (Italy, China, the Netherlands, Russia, Japan)
282	Russia	2022-05-05 11:38:47	Windows Desktop/Laptop	45–60	Male	Moscow city and Moscow Region	Secondary completed
283	Russia	2022-05-05 11:38:04	Android Phone/Tablet	45–60	Female	Khabarovsk Territory	University completed
284	Russia	2022-05-05 11:41:17	Windows Desktop/Laptop	45–60	Female	St. Petersburg city and Leningrad Region	University completed
285	Russia	2022-05-05 11:36:39	Windows Desktop/Laptop	45–60	Male	St. Petersburg city and Leningrad Region	University completed
286	Russia	2022-05-05 11:36:22	Android Phone/Tablet	30–44	Female	Kirov Region	Secondary completed
287	Russia	2022-05-05 11:39:18	Windows Desktop/Laptop	45–60	Female	Arkhangelsk	Secondary completed
288	Russia	2022-05-05 11:38:43	Windows Desktop/Laptop	45–60	Male	Perm Territory	University completed
289	Russia	2022-05-05 11:41:03	Windows Desktop/Laptop	45–60	Female	Novosibirsk Region	University completed
290	Russia	2022-05-05 11:40:40	Windows Desktop/Laptop	>60	Female	Moscow city and Moscow Region	University completed

291	Russia	2022-05-05 11:36:01	Windows Desktop/Laptop	30–44	Male	Moscow city and Moscow Region	HePrimary completed
292	Russia	2022-05-05 11:38:44	Windows Desktop/Laptop	18–29	Male	Moscow city and Moscow Region	Secondary completed
293	Russia	2022-05-05 11:37:18	Android Phone/Tablet	30–44	Male	Nizhny Novgorod Region	University completed
294	Russia	2022-05-05 11:38:35	Windows Desktop/Laptop	45–60	Male	Arkhangelsk Region	Secondary completed
295	Russia	2022-05-05 11:38:59	Windows Desktop/Laptop	30–44	Female	Sveldlovsk Region	University completed
296	Russia	2022-05-05 11:39:47	Other	18–29	Female	Krasnodar Territory	University completed
297	Russia	2022-05-05 11:37:57	Windows Desktop/Laptop	30–44	Female	Khabarovsk Territory	Secondary completed
298	Russia	2022-05-05 11:36:11	Windows Desktop/Laptop	45–60	Male	St. Petersburg city and Leningrad Region	Secondary completed
299	Russia	2022-05-05 11:37:42	Android Phone/Tablet	45–60	Male	Kostroma Region	University completed
300	Russia	2022-05-05 11:38:55	Android Phone/Tablet	30–44	Male	Omsk Region	University completed
301	Russia	2022-05-05 11:37:35	Windows Desktop/Laptop	18–29	Female	Volga Federal District	Secondary completed

(continued)

			Q1	Q2	Q3	Q4	Q5
No.	Country	Date created	Device Type (Italy, China, the Netherlands, Russia, Japan)	Age (Italy, China, the Netherlands, Russia, Japan)	Gender (Italy, China, the Netherlands, Russia, Japan)	In what province/ region do you live	What is the highest level of education you have completed? (Italy, China, the Netherlands, Russia, Japan)
302	Russia	2022-05-05 11:38:56	Windows Desktop/Laptop	45–60	Female	Moscow city and Moscow Region	Secondary completed
303	Russia	2022-05-05 11:36:17	Android Phone/Tablet	>60	Female	Moscow city and Moscow Region	Secondary completed
304	Russia	2022-05-05 11:36:34	Windows Desktop/Laptop	30–44	Male	St. Petersburg city and Leningrad Region	Secondary completed
305	Russia	2022-05-05 11:36:14	Android Phone/Tablet	30–44	Male	Kemerovo Region	Secondary completed
306	Russia	2022-05-05 11:38:55	Windows Desktop/Laptop	30–44	Male	St. Petersburg city and Leningrad Region	University completed
307	Russia	2022-05-05 11:36:33	Windows Desktop/Laptop	30–44	Female	Volgograd Region	University completed
308	Russia	2022-05-05 11:38:51	Windows Desktop/Laptop	30–44	Female	Kirov Region	University completed
309	Russia	2022-05-05 11:38:46	Windows Desktop/Laptop	>60	Male	Sveldlovsk Region	University completed
310	Russia	2022-05-05 11:36:51	Android Phone/Tablet	45–60	Male	Moscow city and Moscow Region	Secondary completed

311	Russia	2022-05-05 11:36:02	Android Phone/Tablet	30–44	Female	Republic of Daghestan	Secondary completed
312	Russia	2022-05-05 11:38:15	Android Phone/Tablet	45–60	Male	St. Petersburg city and Leningrad Region	University completed
313	Russia	2022-05-05 11:38:45	Windows Desktop/Laptop	30–44	Female	Moscow city and Moscow Region	Secondary completed
314	Russia	2022-05-05 11:35:34	Android Phone/Tablet	18–29	Male	St. Petersburg city and Leningrad Region	Secondary completed
315	Russia	2022-05-05 11:36:04	Windows Desktop/Laptop	45–60	Female	Other (please specify)	Secondary completed
316	Russia	2022-05-05 11:39:30	Android Phone/Tablet	18–29	Female	St. Petersburg city and Leningrad Region	University completed
317	Russia	2022-05-05 11:36:03	Windows Desktop/Laptop	>60	Male	Sveldlovsk Region	University completed
318	Russia	2022-05-05 11:38:59	Windows Desktop/Laptop	30–44	Female	Moscow city and Moscow Region	University completed
319	Russia	2022-05-05 11:36:47	Windows Desktop/Laptop	45–60	Male	Vladimir Region	University completed

(continued)

			Q1	Q2	Q3	Q4	Q5
No.	Country	Date created	Device Type (Italy, China, the Netherlands, Russia, Japan)	Age (Italy, China, the Netherlands, Russia, Japan)	Gender (Italy, China, the Netherlands, Russia, Japan)	In what province/region do you live	What is the highest level of education you have completed? (Italy, China, the Netherlands, Russia, Japan)
320	Russia	2022-05-05 11:36:36	Android Phone/Tablet	30–44	Female	Orenburg Region	University completed
321	Russia	2022-05-05 11:36:36	Android Phone/Tablet	45–60	Male	Volgograd Region	Secondary completed
322	Russia	2022-05-05 11:37:17	iOS Phone/Tablet	18–29	Female	Rostov Region	Secondary completed
323	Russia	2022-05-05 11:36:26	Windows Desktop/Laptop	18–29	Male	Volgograd Region	University completed
324	Russia	2022-05-05 11:36:41	Windows Desktop/Laptop	18–29	Male	Orenburg Region	University completed
325	Russia	2022-05-05 11:38:34	Windows Desktop/Laptop	30–44	Male	Moscow city and Moscow Region	University completed
326	Russia	2022-05-05 11:36:48	Windows Desktop/Laptop	30–44	Male	Moscow city and Moscow Region	Secondary completed
327	Russia	2022-05-05 11:36:24	Windows Desktop/Laptop	30–44	Male	Moscow city and Moscow Region	University completed
328	Russia	2022-05-05 11:36:15	Windows Desktop/Laptop	30–44	Male	Moscow city and Moscow Region	University completed
329	Russia	2022-05-05 11:36:25	Windows Desktop/Laptop	30–44	Male	Tula Region	University completed
330	Russia	2022-05-05 11:36:23	Windows Desktop/Laptop	45–60	Male	Murmansk Region	University completed

331	Russia	2022-05-05 11:36:29	Windows Desktop/Laptop	45–60	Male	Moscow city and Moscow Region	University completed
332	Russia	2022-05-05 11:35:51	Windows Desktop/Laptop	30–44	Male	Sveldlovsk Region	University completed
333	Russia	2022-05-05 11:35:53	Windows Desktop/Laptop	45–60	Female	Voronezh Region	University completed
334	Russia	2022-05-05 11:37:11	Windows Desktop/Laptop	18–29	Male	St. Petersburg city and Leningrad Region	University completed
335	Russia	2022-05-05 11:35:48	Windows Desktop/Laptop	45–60	Male	Republic of Mordovia	Secondary completed
336	Russia	2022-05-05 11:36:51	Windows Desktop/Laptop	30–44	Male	Moscow city and Moscow Region	University completed
337	Russia	2022-05-05 11:36:16	iOS Phone/Tablet	45–60	Male	Moscow city and Moscow Region	University completed
338	Russia	2022-05-05 11:35:57	Android Phone/Tablet	30–44	Male	Samara Region	University completed
339	Russia	2022-05-05 11:36:13	Windows Desktop/Laptop	30–44	Male	Moscow city and Moscow Region	University completed
340	Russia	2022-05-05 11:35:44	Windows Desktop/Laptop	>60	Male	Murmansk Region	Secondary completed
341	Russia	2022-05-05 11:36:21	Windows Desktop/Laptop	45–60	Male	Volgograd Region	University completed

(continued)

			Q1	Q2	Q3	Q4	Q5
No.	Country	Date created	Device Type (Italy, China, the Netherlands, Russia, Japan)	Age (Italy, China, the Netherlands, Russia, Japan)	Gender (Italy, China, the Netherlands, Russia, Japan)	In what province/ region do you live	What is the highest level of education you have completed? (Italy, China, the Netherlands, Russia, Japan)
342	Russia	2022-05-05 11:35:59	Windows Desktop/Laptop	18–29	Male	Siberian Federal District	Secondary completed
343	Russia	2022-05-05 11:35:54	Windows Desktop/Laptop	30–44	Male	Krasnodar Territory	University completed
344	Russia	2022-05-05 11:35:55	Android Phone/Tablet	30–44	Male	St. Petersburg city and Leningrad Region	University completed
345	Russia	2022-05-05 11:36:26	Windows Desktop/Laptop	30–44	Female	Saratov Region	University completed
346	Russia	2022-05-05 11:36:03	Windows Desktop/Laptop	30–44	Male	Sveldlovsk Region	Secondary completed
347	Russia	2022-05-05 11:36:07	Windows Desktop/Laptop	30–44	Male	Sveldlovsk Region	Secondary completed
348	Russia	2022-05-05 11:36:02	Windows Desktop/Laptop	45–60	Male	Moscow city and Moscow Region	University completed
349	Russia	2022-05-05 11:35:54	Windows Desktop/Laptop	>60	Male	Moscow city and Moscow Region	University completed
350	Russia	2022-05-05 11:36:03	Windows Desktop/Laptop	18–29	Male	Moscow city and Moscow Region	University completed

351	Japan	2022-10-14 13:05:16	Windows Desktop/Laptop	30–44	Female	Kinki	University completed
352	Japan	2022-10-14 13:03:21	Windows Desktop/Laptop	45–60	Female	Kanto	Secondary completed
353	Japan	2022-10-14 12:29:11	iOS Phone/Tablet	18–29	Female	Shikoku	University completed
354	Japan	2022-10-14 12:02:31	iOS Phone/Tablet	30–44	Female	Kinki	Secondary completed
355	Japan	2022-10-14 12:01:30	Windows Desktop/Laptop	30–44	Female	Chubu	Primary completed
356	Japan	2022-10-14 12:01:03	iOS Phone/Tablet	30–44	Male	Chugoku	University completed
357	Japan	2022-10-14 12:01:26	Windows Desktop/Laptop	30–44	Male	Chubu	University completed
358	Japan	2022-10-14 12:00:26	iOS Phone/Tablet	45–60	Male	Tohoku	University completed
359	Japan	2022-10-14 11:59:06	iOS Phone/Tablet	45–60	Male	Shikoku	Secondary completed
360	Japan	2022-10-14 12:00:21	iOS Phone/Tablet	>60	Male	Chubu	Secondary completed
361	Japan	2022-10-14 12:01:10	iOS Phone/Tablet	45–60	Female	Shikoku	Secondary completed
362	Japan	2022-10-14 12:01:29	Android Phone/Tablet	45–60	Male	Shikoku	University completed
363	Japan	2022-10-14 12:01:41	iOS Phone/Tablet	45–60	Female	Chubu	Secondary completed
364	Japan	2022-10-14 12:01:12	Android Phone/Tablet	45–60	Male	Hokkaido	University completed

(continued)

			Q1	Q2	Q3	Q4	Q5
No.	Country	Date created	Device Type (Italy, China, the Netherlands, Russia, Japan)	Age (Italy, China, the Netherlands, Russia, Japan)	Gender (Italy, China, the Netherlands, Russia, Japan)	In what province/region do you live	What is the highest level of education you have completed? (Italy, China, the Netherlands, Russia, Japan)
365	Japan	2022-10-14 12:01:27	Android Phone/Tablet	45–60	Male	Kanto	Secondary completed
366	Japan	2022-10-14 12:01:01	Other	45–60	Male	Chubu	University completed
367	Japan	2022-10-14 12:00:53	Android Phone/Tablet	>60	Female	Shikoku	Secondary completed
368	Japan	2022-10-14 12:01:06	iOS Phone/Tablet	45–60	Male	Kinki	University completed
369	Japan	2022-10-14 12:01:25	Windows Desktop/Laptop	30–44	Male	Kanto	Secondary completed
370	Japan	2022-10-14 12:01:01	Android Phone/Tablet	45–60	Male	Kanto	Secondary completed
371	Japan	2022-10-14 12:01:46	Android Phone/Tablet	30–44	Male	Hokkaido	University completed
372	Japan	2022-10-14 12:01:43	iOS Phone/Tablet	45–60	Female	Chugoku	Secondary completed
373	Japan	2022-10-14 12:01:34	iOS Phone/Tablet	45–60	Female	Kinki	University completed
374	Japan	2022-10-14 12:01:29	Windows Desktop/Laptop	45–60	Male	Kinki	Secondary completed
375	Japan	2022-10-14 12:01:50	Windows Desktop/Laptop	30–44	Female	Kanto	Secondary completed
376	Japan	2022-10-14 12:02:05	Windows Desktop/Laptop	30–44	Female	Kanto	Secondary completed
377	Japan	2022-10-14 12:01:16	iOS Phone/Tablet	30–44	Female	Chubu	University completed

378	Japan	2022-10-14 12:01:20	Windows Desktop/Laptop	30–44	Female	Kanto	Secondary completed
379	Japan	2022-10-14 12:01:28	Windows Desktop/Laptop	45–60	Male	Kanto	University completed
380	Japan	2022-10-14 12:01:29	Android Phone/Tablet	45–60	Male	Kanto	University completed
381	Japan	2022-10-14 12:01:07	Windows Desktop/Laptop	45–60	Female	Chubu	University completed
382	Japan	2022-10-14 12:01:15	Windows Desktop/Laptop	45–60	Male	Hokkaido	Secondary completed
383	Japan	2022-10-14 12:02:41	iOS Phone/Tablet	30–44	Male	Kanto	Secondary completed
384	Japan	2022-10-14 12:01:35	MacOS Desktop/Laptop	45–60	Male	Kanto	University completed
385	Japan	2022-10-14 12:01:09	Windows Desktop/Laptop	45–60	Male	Kanto	Secondary completed
386	Japan	2022-10-14 12:00:20	Android Phone/Tablet	45–60	Female	Hokkaido	University completed
387	Japan	2022-10-14 12:02:09	Android Phone/Tablet	30–44	Female	Tohoku	Secondary completed
388	Japan	2022-10-14 12:01:51	Windows Desktop/Laptop	18–29	Male	Chubu	University completed
389	Japan	2022-10-14 12:01:18	Android Phone/Tablet	18–29	Male	Kinki	University completed
390	Japan	2022-10-14 12:00:47	Android Phone/Tablet	45–60	Female	Kanto	Secondary completed
391	Japan	2022-10-14 12:00:36	iOS Phone/Tablet	30–44	Female	Kanto	University completed
392	Japan	2022-10-14 12:00:27	Android Phone/Tablet	30–44	Female	Kinki	University completed

(continued)

			Q1	Q2	Q3	Q4	Q5
No.	Country	Date created	Device Type (Italy, China, the Netherlands, Russia, Japan)	Age (Italy, China, the Netherlands, Russia, Japan)	Gender (Italy, China, the Netherlands, Russia, Japan)	In what province/ region do you live	What is the highest level of education you have completed? (Italy, China, the Netherlands, Russia, Japan)
393	Japan	2022-10-14 12:00:58	iOS Phone/Tablet	30–44	Female	Kanto	University completed
394	Japan	2022-10-14 12:01:28	iOS Phone/Tablet	45–60	Male	Kinki	University completed
395	Japan	2022-10-14 12:01:10	iOS Phone/Tablet	45–60	Male	Hokkaido	University completed
396	Japan	2022-10-14 12:00:54	iOS Phone/Tablet	45–60	Male	Kinki	University completed
397	Japan	2022-10-14 12:01:42	Android Phone/Tablet	30–44	Female	Shikoku	Secondary completed
398	Japan	2022-10-14 12:00:53	iOS Phone/Tablet	45–60	Female	Kinki	University completed
399	Japan	2022-10-14 12:01:11	Android Phone/Tablet	45–60	Female	Chugoku	Secondary completed
400	Japan	2022-10-14 12:02:03	iOS Phone/Tablet	18–29	Female	Kinki	University completed
401	Japan	2022-10-14 12:00:20	Windows Desktop/Laptop	45–60	Male	Kanto	University completed
402	Japan	2022-10-14 12:00:36	Android Phone/Tablet	30–44	Male	Chubu	Secondary completed
403	Japan	2022-10-14 12:00:54	Windows Desktop/Laptop	45–60	Male	Kanto	University completed
404	Japan	2022-10-14 12:00:58	iOS Phone/Tablet	45–60	Female	Kinki	University completed
405	Japan	2022-10-14 12:00:36	iOS Phone/Tablet	45–60	Female	Kinki	Secondary completed

406	Japan	2022-10-14 12:00:34	Android Phone/Tablet	45–60	Male	Kinki	Secondary completed
407	Japan	2022-10-14 12:01:09	iOS Phone/Tablet	18–29	Female	Kinki	University completed
408	Japan	2022-10-14 12:00:46	Windows Desktop/Laptop	45–60	Male	Hokkaido	Secondary completed
409	Japan	2022-10-14 12:00:41	iOS Phone/Tablet	30–44	Male	Chubu	Secondary completed
410	Japan	2022-10-14 12:00:51	Android Phone/Tablet	30–44	Female	Hokkaido	University completed
411	Japan	2022-10-14 12:00:26	Windows Desktop/Laptop	>60	Male	Chubu	University completed
412	Japan	2022-10-14 12:01:22	Android Phone/Tablet	18–29	Female	Kanto	University completed
413	Japan	2022-10-14 12:01:25	iOS Phone/Tablet	30–44	Male	Shikoku	University completed
414	Japan	2022-10-14 11:59:40	Android Phone/Tablet	45–60	Male	Hokkaido	Secondary completed
415	Japan	2022-10-14 12:00:17	iOS Phone/Tablet	45–60	Male	Chugoku	University completed
416	Japan	2022-10-14 12:00:54	Windows Desktop/Laptop	30–44	Male	Chubu	University completed
417	Japan	2022-10-14 12:00:34	Windows Desktop/Laptop	45–60	Female	Kanto	Secondary completed
418	Japan	2022-10-14 12:01:14	Android Phone/Tablet	30–44	Female	Chugoku	University completed
419	Japan	2022-10-14 12:00:44	iOS Phone/Tablet	45–60	Female	Shikoku	University completed
420	Japan	2022-10-14 12:00:37	iOS Phone/Tablet	30–44	Female	Kanto	University completed

(continued)

			Q1	Q2	Q3	Q4	Q5
No.	Country	Date created	Device Type (Italy, China, the Netherlands, Russia, Japan)	Age (Italy, China, the Netherlands, Russia, Japan)	Gender (Italy, China, the Netherlands, Russia, Japan)	In what province/ region do you live	What is the highest level of education you have completed? (Italy, China, the Netherlands, Russia, Japan)
421	Japan	2022-10-14 12:00:19	MacOS Desktop/Laptop	30–44	Female	Chubu	Secondary completed
422	Japan	2022-10-14 11:59:32	Android Phone/Tablet	30–44	Male	Kanto	University completed
423	Japan	2022-10-14 11:58:47	iOS Phone/Tablet	30–44	Male	Kanto	Secondary completed
424	Japan	2022-10-14 12:00:22	Android Phone/Tablet	30–44	Female	Chubu	University completed
425	Japan	2022-10-14 11:59:14	Android Phone/Tablet	30–44	Female	Kanto	University completed

Q6	Q7	Q8	Q9a	Q9b	Q9c	Q9d	Q9e
What is roughly your net annual income from your job(s)? (in Chian Yuan, in Japan Yen, in Russia rubles, in the Netherlands Euro, in Italy Euro)	In what economic sector are you employed? (Italy, China, the Netherlands, Russia, Japan)	Do you think that printing money leads to more government debt (there is no right or wrong answer)? (Italy, China, the Netherlands, Russia, Japan)	Do you think that, if the European Central Bank prints Euro banknotes and gives everyone 10 euro, this means we all get 10 euro richer (there is no right or wrong answer) (Italy)?	If the People's Bank of China prints more money and gives everyone 10 yuan, do you think that means everyone will be 10 yuan richer than before? (China)	Do you think that, if the European Central Bank prints Euro banknotes and gives everyone 10 euro, this means we all get 10 euro richer (there is no right or wrong answer) (Netherlands)?	Do you think that, if the Bank of Russia prints banknotes and gives everyone 10 rubles, this means we all get 10 rubles richer (there is no right or wrong answer) (Russia)?	Do you think that, if the Japanese Central Bank prints banknotes and gives everyone 100 yen, this means we all get 100 yen richer (there is no right or wrong answer) (Japan)?
I have no income	I am currently not employed	Yes	No				
<20,000 Euro	Services not mentioned above	No	Yes				
50,000–74,999 Euro	Wholesale and retail trade	No	No				
<20,000 Euro	Services not mentioned above	No	Yes				
50,000–74,999 Euro	Electricity, gas, and water	No	Yes				
20,000–34,999 Euro	Services not mentioned above	No	No				
20,000–34,999 Euro	Services not mentioned above	No	No				
<20,000 Euro	I am currently not employed	Yes	No				

(continued)

Q6	Q7	Q8	Q9a	Q9b	Q9c	Q9d	Q9e
What is roughly your net annual income from your job(s)? (in Chian Yuan, in Japan Yen, in Russia rubles, in the Netherlands Euro, in Italy Euro)	In what economic sector are you employed? (Italy, China, the Netherlands, Russia, Japan)	Do you think that printing money leads to more government debt (there is no right or wrong answer)? (Italy, China, the Netherlands, Russia, Japan)	Do you think that, if the European Central Bank prints Euro banknotes and gives everyone 10 euro, this means we all get 10 euro richer (there is no right or wrong answer) (Italy)?	If the People's Bank of China prints more money and gives everyone 10 yuan, do you think that means everyone will be 10 yuan richer than before? (China)	Do you think that, if the European Central Bank prints Euro banknotes and gives everyone 10 euro, this means we all get 10 euro richer (there is no right or wrong answer) (Netherlands)?	Do you think that, if the Bank of Russia prints banknotes and gives everyone 10 rubles, this means we all get 10 rubles richer (there is no right or wrong answer) (Russia)?	Do you think that, if the Japanese Central Bank prints banknotes and gives everyone 100 yen, this means we all get 100 yen richer (there is no right or wrong answer) (Japan)?
<20,000 Euro	I am currently not employed	No	Yes				
35,000–49,999 Euro	Services not mentioned above	Yes	No				
20,000–34,999 Euro	I am currently not employed	No	No				
<20,000 Euro	I am currently not employed	No	Yes				
I have no income	I am currently not employed	No	Yes				
35,000–49,999 Euro	Manufacturing	No	Yes				
<20,000 Euro	Services not mentioned above	No	Yes				
20,000–34,999 Euro	Services not mentioned above	No	No				
I prefer not to say	Wholesale and retail trade	No	No				

<20,000 Euro	Agriculture and mining	Yes	Yes				
I have no income	I am currently not employed	Yes	No				
35,000–49,999 Euro	Services not mentioned above	Yes	No				
20,000–34,999 Euro	I am currently not employed	No	No				
I prefer not to say	Services not mentioned above	No	Yes				
20,000–34,999 Euro	Wholesale and retail trade	Yes	No				
35,000–49,999 Euro	Manufacturing	Yes	No				
20,000–34,999 Euro	I am currently not employed	No	No				
<20,000 Euro	Services not mentioned above	No	No				
35,000–49,999 Euro	Transport, storage and communication	Yes	Yes				
20,000–34,999 Euro	Services not mentioned above	Yes	No				
20,000–34,999 Euro	Services not mentioned above	No	No				
<20,000 Euro	Services not mentioned above	Yes	No				
I prefer not to say	Services not mentioned above	No	No				
20,000–34,999 Euro	Wholesale and retail trade	Yes	Yes				

(continued)

Q6	Q7	Q8	Q9a	Q9b	Q9c	Q9d	Q9e
What is roughly your net annual income from your job(s)? (in Chian Yuan, in Japan Yen, in Russia rubles, in the Netherlands Euro, in Italy Euro)	In what economic sector are you employed? (Italy, China, the Netherlands, Russia, Japan)	Do you think that printing money leads to more government debt (there is no right or wrong answer)? (Italy, China, the Netherlands, Russia, Japan)	Do you think that, if the European Central Bank prints Euro banknotes and gives everyone 10 euro, this means we all get 10 euro richer (there is no right or wrong answer) (Italy)?	If the People's Bank of China prints more money and gives everyone 10 yuan, do you think that means everyone will be 10 yuan richer than before? (China)	Do you think that, if the European Central Bank prints Euro banknotes and gives everyone 10 euro, this means we all get 10 euro richer (there is no right or wrong answer) (Netherlands)?	Do you think that, if the Bank of Russia prints banknotes and gives everyone 10 rubles, this means we all get 10 rubles richer (there is no right or wrong answer) (Russia)?	Do you think that, if the Japanese Central Bank prints banknotes and gives everyone 100 yen, this means we all get 100 yen richer (there is no right or wrong answer) (Japan)?
I have no income	I am currently not employed	No	Yes				
I have no income	I am currently not employed	Yes	No				
35,000–49,999 Euro	Services not mentioned above	No	Yes				
I have no income	Agriculture and mining	No	No				
50,000–74,999 Euro	Services not mentioned above	Yes	No				
20,000–34,999 Euro	Manufacturing	Yes	Yes				
I prefer not to say	Services not mentioned above	No	Yes				
35,000–49,999 Euro	Services not mentioned above	No	Yes				
20,000–34,999 Euro	I am currently not employed	Yes	No				

35,000–49,999 Euro	Services not mentioned above	Yes	No				
20,000–34,999 Euro	Finnacial services	Yes	No				
20,000–34,999 Euro	Services not mentioned above	Yes	Yes				
I have no income	I am currently not employed	Yes	No				
<20,000 Euro	I am currently not employed	No	No				
I prefer not to say	I am currently not employed	Yes	No				
<20,000 Euro	I am currently not employed	No	Yes				
<20,000 Euro	I am currently not employed	Yes	No				
I have no income	I am currently not employed	No	Yes				
<20,000 Euro	I am currently not employed	Yes	Yes				
<20,000 Euro	I am currently not employed	Yes	No				
20,000–34,999 Euro	Manufacturing	No	Yes				
<20,000 Euro	I am currently not employed	No	No				
I prefer not to say	I am currently not employed	Yes	No				
35,000–49,999 Euro	Wholesale and retail trade	No	Yes				
20,000–34,999 Euro	Wholesale and retail trade	No	Yes				

(continued)

Q6	Q7	Q8	Q9a	Q9b	Q9c	Q9d	Q9e
What is roughly your net annual income from your job(s)? (in Chian Yuan, in Japan Yen, in Russia rubles, in the Netherlands Euro, in Italy Euro)	In what economic sector are you employed? (Italy, China, the Netherlands, Russia, Japan)	Do you think that printing money leads to more government debt (there is no right or wrong answer)? (Italy, China, the Netherlands, Russia, Japan)	Do you think that, if the European Central Bank prints Euro banknotes and gives everyone 10 euro, this means we all get 10 euro richer (there is no right or wrong answer) (Italy)?	If the People's Bank of China prints more money and gives everyone 10 yuan, do you think that means everyone will be 10 yuan richer than before? (China)	Do you think that, if the European Central Bank prints Euro banknotes and gives everyone 10 euro, this means we all get 10 euro richer (there is no right or wrong answer) (Netherlands)?	Do you think that, if the Bank of Russia prints banknotes and gives everyone 10 rubles, this means we all get 10 rubles richer (there is no right or wrong answer) (Russia)?	Do you think that, if the Japanese Central Bank prints banknotes and gives everyone 100 yen, this means we all get 100 yen richer (there is no right or wrong answer) (Japan)?
20,000–34,999 Euro	Wholesale and retail trade	Yes	Yes				
<20,000 Euro	I am currently not employed	No	No				
<20,000 Euro	Services not mentioned above	No	No				
20,000–34,999 Euro	Services not mentioned above	Yes	No				
<20,000 Euro	I am currently not employed	No	Yes				
75,000–99,999 Euro	Manufacturing	Yes	No				
I prefer not to say	Services not mentioned above	Yes	No				
20,000–34,999 Euro	I am currently not employed	Yes	Yes				
20,000–34,999 Euro	Manufacturing	No	No				

I have no income	I am currently not employed	Yes	Yes				
20,000–34,999 Euro	Services not mentioned above	Yes	No				
20,000–34,999 Euro	Services not mentioned above	Yes	No				
20,000–34,999 Euro	Electricity, gas, and water	Yes	Yes				
<20,000 Euro	I am currently not employed	Yes	Yes				
I prefer not to say	I am currently not employed	No	Yes				
75,000–99,999 Euro	I am currently not employed	Yes	No				
20,000–34,999 Euro	Wholesale and retail trade	No	Yes				
20,000–34,999 Euro	Construction	No	Yes				
Below 60,000 Yuan	Wholesale and retail trade	Yes		Yes			
500,000–999,999 Yuan	Manufacturing	Yes		Yes			
120,000–239,999 Yuan	Manufacturing	Yes		No			
240,000–499,999 Yuan	Construction	Yes		No			
500,000–999,999 Yuan	Services not mentioned above	No		No			
60,000–119,999 Yuan	Manufacturing	Yes		No			
120,000–239,999 Yuan	Construction	Yes		No			
Below 60,000 Yuan	I am currently not employed	Yes		No			
240,000–499,999 Yuan	Construction	Yes		No			

(continued)

Q6	Q7	Q8	Q9a	Q9b	Q9c	Q9d	Q9e
What is roughly your net annual income from your job(s)? (in Chian Yuan, in Japan Yen, in Russia rubles, in the Netherlands Euro, in Italy Euro)	In what economic sector are you employed? (Italy, China, the Netherlands, Russia, Japan)	Do you think that printing money leads to more government debt (there is no right or wrong answer)? (Italy, China, the Netherlands, Russia, Japan)	Do you think that, if the European Central Bank prints Euro banknotes and gives everyone 10 euro, this means we all get 10 euro richer (there is no right or wrong answer) (Italy)?	If the People's Bank of China prints more money and gives everyone 10 yuan, do you think that means everyone will be 10 yuan richer than before? (China)	Do you think that, if the European Central Bank prints Euro banknotes and gives everyone 10 euro, this means we all get 10 euro richer (there is no right or wrong answer) (Netherlands)?	Do you think that, if the Bank of Russia prints banknotes and gives everyone 10 rubles, this means we all get 10 rubles richer (there is no right or wrong answer) (Russia)?	Do you think that, if the Japanese Central Bank prints banknotes and gives everyone 100 yen, this means we all get 100 yen richer (there is no right or wrong answer) (Japan)?
240,000–499,999 Yuan	Manufacturing	Yes		No			
240,000–499,999 Yuan	Construction	Yes		No			
Below 60,000 Yuan	Manufacturing	Yes		No			
240,000–499,999 Yuan	Wholesale and retail trade	Yes		No			
Below 60,000 Yuan	Services not mentioned above	Yes		No			
500,000–999,999 Yuan	Financial services	Yes		No			
120,000–239,999 Yuan	Services not mentioned above	No		No			
Below 60,000 Yuan	Wholesale and retail trade	Yes		No			
60,000–119,999 Yuan	I am currently not employed	No		No			
120,000–239,999 Yuan	Services not mentioned above	No		No			

60,000–119,999 Yuan	Manufacturing	Yes		No			
120,000–239,999 Yuan	Manufacturing	Yes		No			
60,000–119,999 Yuan	Electricity, gas, and water	Yes		No			
60,000–119,999 Yuan	I am currently not employed	Yes		No			
120,000–239,999 Yuan	Wholesale and retail trade	Yes		No			
60,000–119,999 Yuan	Manufacturing	Yes		No			
120,000–239,999 Yuan	Services not mentioned above	Yes		No			
500,000–999,999 Yuan	Manufacturing	Yes		No			
60,000–119,999 Yuan	Manufacturing	Yes		Yes			
Below 60,000 Yuan	Wholesale and retail trade	Yes		No			
1,000,000 Yuan or more	Services not mentioned above	Yes		No			
240,000–499,999 Yuan	Manufacturing	Yes		Yes			
240,000–499,999 Yuan	Manufacturing	No		No			
60,000–119,999 Yuan	Services not mentioned above	No		No			
60,000–119,999 Yuan	Services not mentioned above	Yes		No			
Below 60,000 Yuan	Services not mentioned above	Yes		No			
240,000–499,999 Yuan	Financial services	Yes		Yes			
120,000–239,999 Yuan	Services not mentioned above	Yes		No			

(continued)

Q6	Q7	Q8	Q9a	Q9b	Q9c	Q9d	Q9e
What is roughly your net annual income from your job(s)? (in Chian Yuan, in Japan Yen, in Russia rubles, in the Netherlands Euro, in Italy Euro)	In what economic sector are you employed? (Italy, China, the Netherlands, Russia, Japan)	Do you think that printing money leads to more government debt (there is no right or wrong answer)? (Italy, China, the Netherlands, Russia, Japan)	Do you think that, if the European Central Bank prints Euro banknotes and gives everyone 10 euro, this means we all get 10 euro richer (there is no right or wrong answer) (Italy)?	If the People's Bank of China prints more money and gives everyone 10 yuan, do you think that means everyone will be 10 yuan richer than before? (China)	Do you think that, if the European Central Bank prints Euro banknotes and gives everyone 10 euro, this means we all get 10 euro richer (there is no right or wrong answer) (Netherlands)?	Do you think that, if the Bank of Russia prints banknotes and gives everyone 10 rubles, this means we all get 10 rubles richer (there is no right or wrong answer) (Russia)?	Do you think that, if the Japanese Central Bank prints banknotes and gives everyone 100 yen, this means we all get 100 yen richer (there is no right or wrong answer) (Japan)?
60,000–119,999 Yuan	Services not mentioned above	No		No			
120,000–239,999 Yuan	Transport, storage and communication	Yes		Yes			
120,000–239,999 Yuan	Electricity, gas, and water	No		Yes			
240,000–499,999 Yuan	I am currently not employed	Yes		No			
120,000–239,999 Yuan	Financial services	Yes		No			
60,000–119,999 Yuan	Manufacturing	Yes		No			
60,000–119,999 Yuan	Manufacturing	Yes		No			
240,000–499,999 Yuan	Manufacturing	Yes		No			
120,000–239,999 Yuan	Services not mentioned above	No		No			
60,000–119,999 Yuan	Manufacturing	Yes		No			
120,000–239,999 Yuan	Construction	Yes		No			

60,000–119,999 Yuan	Services not mentioned above	Yes		No			
60,000–119,999 Yuan	Construction	No		No			
Below 60,000 Yuan	Services not mentioned above	Yes		No			
240,000–499,999 Yuan	Construction	Yes		No			
240,000–499,999 Yuan	Services not mentioned above	No		Yes			
120,000–239,999 Yuan	Services not mentioned above	No		No			
120,000–239,999 Yuan	Agriculture and mining	Yes		No			
Below 60,000 Yuan	Services not mentioned above	Yes		Yes			
120,000–239,999 Yuan	I am currently not employed	Yes		No			
500,000–999,999 Yuan	Manufacturing	Yes		No			
500,000–999,999 Yuan	Services not mentioned above	Yes		Yes			
240,000–499,999 Yuan	Financial services	No		No			
500,000–999,999 Yuan	Services not mentioned above	No		Yes			
1,000,000 Yuan or more	Services not mentioned above	Yes		No			
120,000–239,999 Yuan	Services not mentioned above	Yes		No			
120,000–239,999 Yuan	Services not mentioned above	Yes		No			
120,000–239,999 Yuan	Manufacturing	Yes		No			

(continued)

Q6	Q7	Q8	Q9a	Q9b	Q9c	Q9d	Q9e
What is roughly your net annual income from your job(s)? (in Chian Yuan, in Japan Yen, in Russia rubles, in the Netherlands Euro, in Italy Euro)	In what economic sector are you employed? (Italy, China, the Netherlands, Russia, Japan)	Do you think that printing money leads to more government debt (there is no right or wrong answer)? (Italy, China, the Netherlands, Russia, Japan)	Do you think that, if the European Central Bank prints Euro banknotes and gives everyone 10 euro, this means we all get 10 euro richer (there is no right or wrong answer) (Italy)?	If the People's Bank of China prints more money and gives everyone 10 yuan, do you think that means everyone will be 10 yuan richer than before? (China)	Do you think that, if the European Central Bank prints Euro banknotes and gives everyone 10 euro, this means we all get 10 euro richer (there is no right or wrong answer) (Netherlands)?	Do you think that, if the Bank of Russia prints banknotes and gives everyone 10 rubles, this means we all get 10 rubles richer (there is no right or wrong answer) (Russia)?	Do you think that, if the Japanese Central Bank prints banknotes and gives everyone 100 yen, this means we all get 100 yen richer (there is no right or wrong answer) (Japan)?
500,000–999,999 Yuan	Manufacturing	Yes		Yes			
120,000–239,999 Yuan	Construction	Yes		No			
Below 60,000 Yuan	Services not mentioned above	No		No			
240,000–499,999 Yuan	Manufacturing	No		Yes			
120,000–239,999 Yuan	Manufacturing	No		No			
60,000–119,999 Yuan	Wholesale and retail trade	No		Yes			
1,000,000 Yuan or more	Services not mentioned above	No		Yes			
Below 60,000 Yuan	Agriculture and mining	No		No			
60,000–119,999 Yuan	Services not mentioned above	No		No			
240,000–499,999 Yuan	Financial services	Yes		No			
240,000–499,999 Yuan	Services not mentioned above	Yes		No			
120,000–239,999 Yuan	Financial services	No		No			

240,000–499,999 Yuan	Manufacturing	Yes		No			
120,000–239,999 Yuan	Manufacturing	Yes		No			
120,000–239,999 Yuan	Transport, storage and communication	Yes		No			
Below 60,000 Yuan	I am currently not employed	Yes		No			
120,000–239,999 Yuan	Transport, storage and communication	Yes		No			
240,000–499,999 Yuan	Manufacturing	Yes		No			
120,000–239,999 Yuan	Manufacturing	No		No			
1,000,000 Yuan or more	Manufacturing	Yes		No			
120,000–239,999 Yuan	Financial services	No		No			
500,000–999,999 Yuan	Electricity, gas, and water	Yes		No			
Below 60,000 Yuan	I am currently not employed	Yes		No			
120,000–239,999 Yuan	Financial services	Yes		No			
500,000–999,999 Yuan	Financial services	Yes		Yes			
Below 60,000 Yuan	I am currently not employed	Yes		No			
Below 60,000 Yuan	Manufacturing	No		No			
500,000–999,999 Yuan	Manufacturing	Yes		No			
60,000–119,999 Yuan	Services not mentioned above	No		Yes			
120,000–239,999 Yuan	Manufacturing	Yes		No			
I have no income	I am currently not employed	No		No			

(continued)

Q6	Q7	Q8	Q9a	Q9b	Q9c	Q9d	Q9e
What is roughly your net annual income from your job(s)? (in Chian Yuan, in Japan Yen, in Russia rubles, in the Netherlands Euro, in Italy Euro)	In what economic sector are you employed? (Italy, China, the Netherlands, Russia, Japan)	Do you think that printing money leads to more government debt (there is no right or wrong answer)? (Italy, China, the Netherlands, Russia, Japan)	Do you think that, if the European Central Bank prints Euro banknotes and gives everyone 10 euro, this means we all get 10 euro richer (there is no right or wrong answer) (Italy)?	If the People's Bank of China prints more money and gives everyone 10 yuan, do you think that means everyone will be 10 yuan richer than before? (China)	Do you think that, if the European Central Bank prints Euro banknotes and gives everyone 10 euro, this means we all get 10 euro richer (there is no right or wrong answer) (Netherlands)?	Do you think that, if the Bank of Russia prints banknotes and gives everyone 10 rubles, this means we all get 10 rubles richer (there is no right or wrong answer) (Russia)?	Do you think that, if the Japanese Central Bank prints banknotes and gives everyone 100 yen, this means we all get 100 yen richer (there is no right or wrong answer) (Japan)?
240,000–499,999 Yuan	I am currently not employed	No		No			
240,000–499,999 Yuan	Manufacturing	Yes		No			
240,000–499,999 Yuan	Manufacturing	Yes		Yes			
120,000–239,999 Yuan	Financial services	Yes		No			
I prefer not to say	I am currently not employed	No			Yes		
20,000–34,999 Euro	I am currently not employed	Yes			No		
100,000–149,999 Euro	Services not mentioned above	Yes			Yes		
I prefer not to say	Construction	Yes			No		
50,000–74,999 Euro	Services not mentioned above	Yes			No		
<20,000 Euro	I am currently not employed	Yes			Yes		
20,000–34,999 Euro	Services not mentioned above	Yes			No		

50,000–74,999 Euro	Services not mentioned above	Yes			No		
20,000–34,999 Euro	Services not mentioned above	Yes			No		
20,000–34,999 Euro	I am currently not employed	Yes			No		
20,000–34,999 Euro	Services not mentioned above	No			Yes		
<20,000 Euro	I am currently not employed	No			No		
35,000–49,999 Euro	I am currently not employed	Yes			Yes		
I prefer not to say	Wholesale and retail trade	Yes			No		
<20,000 Euro	Services not mentioned above	No			Yes		
20,000–34,999 Euro	I am currently not employed	No			Yes		
150,000 Euro or More	LandConstruction en mijnConstruction	Yes			No		
20,000–34,999 Euro	Finnacial services	Yes			No		
I prefer not to say	I am currently not employed	Yes			Yes		
20,000–34,999 Euro	Services not mentioned above	No			Yes		
75,000–99,999 Euro	Finnacial services	Yes			Yes		
35,000–49,999 Euro	Services not mentioned above	No			No		

(continued)

Q6	Q7	Q8	Q9a	Q9b	Q9c	Q9d	Q9e
What is roughly your net annual income from your job(s)? (in Chian Yuan, in Japan Yen, in Russia rubles, in the Netherlands Euro, in Italy Euro)	In what economic sector are you employed? (Italy, China, the Netherlands, Russia, Japan)	Do you think that printing money leads to more government debt (there is no right or wrong answer)? (Italy, China, the Netherlands, Russia, Japan)	Do you think that, if the European Central Bank prints Euro banknotes and gives everyone 10 euro, this means we all get 10 euro richer (there is no right or wrong answer) (Italy)?	If the People's Bank of China prints more money and gives everyone 10 yuan, do you think that means everyone will be 10 yuan richer than before? (China)	Do you think that, if the European Central Bank prints Euro banknotes and gives everyone 10 euro, this means we all get 10 euro richer (there is no right or wrong answer) (Netherlands)?	Do you think that, if the Bank of Russia prints banknotes and gives everyone 10 rubles, this means we all get 10 rubles richer (there is no right or wrong answer) (Russia)?	Do you think that, if the Japanese Central Bank prints banknotes and gives everyone 100 yen, this means we all get 100 yen richer (there is no right or wrong answer) (Japan)?
<20,000 Euro	I am currently not employed	No			No		
50,000–74,999 Euro	Services not mentioned above	Yes			No		
<20,000 Euro	Services not mentioned above	No			Yes		
20,000–34,999 Euro	Services not mentioned above	Yes			No		
35,000–49,999 Euro	Services not mentioned above	Yes			No		
I have no income	Manufacturing	Yes			Yes		
20,000–34,999 Euro	Services not mentioned above	No			Yes		
75,000–99,999 Euro	Finnacial services	Yes			No		
<20,000 Euro	Wholesale and retail trade	Yes			Yes		
20,000–34,999 Euro	I am currently not employed	Yes			No		

75,000–99,999 Euro	Finnacial services	Yes			Yes		
<20,000 Euro	Services not mentioned above	No			Yes		
I prefer not to say	I am currently not employed	No			Yes		
<20,000 Euro	I am currently not employed	Yes			Yes		
20,000–34,999 Euro	Wholesale and retail trade	Yes			Yes		
35,000–49,999 Euro	Services not mentioned above	Yes			Yes		
50,000–74,999 Euro	I am currently not employed	Yes			No		
20,000–34,999 Euro	Services not mentioned above	No			No		
20,000–34,999 Euro	Finnacial services	Yes			No		
20,000–34,999 Euro	I am currently not employed	Yes			No		
<20,000 Euro	I am currently not employed	Yes			Yes		
75,000–99,999 Euro	Finnacial services	Yes			No		
20,000–34,999 Euro	I am currently not employed	Yes			No		
50,000–74,999 Euro	Services not mentioned above	No			No		
<20,000 Euro	Finnacial services	Yes			Yes		
<20,000 Euro	Services not mentioned above	Yes			Yes		
I prefer not to say	Services not mentioned above	No			No		

(continued)

Q6	Q7	Q8	Q9a	Q9b	Q9c	Q9d	Q9e
What is roughly your net annual income from your job(s)? (in Chian Yuan, in Japan Yen, in Russia rubles, in the Netherlands Euro, in Italy Euro)	In what economic sector are you employed? (Italy, China, the Netherlands, Russia, Japan)	Do you think that printing money leads to more government debt (there is no right or wrong answer)? (Italy, China, the Netherlands, Russia, Japan)	Do you think that, if the European Central Bank prints Euro banknotes and gives everyone 10 euro, this means we all get 10 euro richer (there is no right or wrong answer) (Italy)?	If the People's Bank of China prints more money and gives everyone 10 yuan, do you think that means everyone will be 10 yuan richer than before? (China)	Do you think that, if the European Central Bank prints Euro banknotes and gives everyone 10 euro, this means we all get 10 euro richer (there is no right or wrong answer) (Netherlands)?	Do you think that, if the Bank of Russia prints banknotes and gives everyone 10 rubles, this means we all get 10 rubles richer (there is no right or wrong answer) (Russia)?	Do you think that, if the Japanese Central Bank prints banknotes and gives everyone 100 yen, this means we all get 100 yen richer (there is no right or wrong answer) (Japan)?
<20,000 Euro	I am currently not employed	Yes			Yes		
35,000–49,999 Euro	Electricity, gas, and water	Yes			No		
<20,000 Euro	I am currently not employed	Yes			Yes		
75,000–99,999 Euro	Transport, storage and communication	No			No		
I have no income	I am currently not employed	Yes			Yes		
I prefer not to say	Services not mentioned above	Yes			No		
50,000–74,999 Euro	Services not mentioned above	No			Yes		
<20,000 Euro	Services not mentioned above	Yes			No		
I prefer not to say	I am currently not employed	Yes			Yes		

20,000–34,999 Euro	I am currently not employed	Yes			No		
35,000–49,999 Euro	Services not mentioned above	No			No		
20,000–34,999 Euro	Services not mentioned above	No			No		
35,000–49,999 Euro	Wholesale and retail trade	Yes			Yes		
<20,000 Euro	Manufacturing	Yes			Yes		
50,000–74,999 Euro	Services not mentioned above	No			No		
<20,000 Euro	Transport, storage and communication	Yes			Yes		
20,000–34,999 Euro	Finnacial services	Yes			Yes		
I prefer not to say	Services not mentioned above	Yes			No		
20,000–34,999 Euro	I am currently not employed	Yes			No		
35,000–49,999 Euro	Services not mentioned above	Yes			No		
35,000–49,999 Euro	Services not mentioned above	No			No		
20,000–34,999 Euro	Services not mentioned above	Yes			Yes		
50,000–74,999 Euro	Services not mentioned above	Yes			No		
75,000–99,999 Euro	Services not mentioned above	No			No		

(continued)

Q6	Q7	Q8	Q9a	Q9b	Q9c	Q9d	Q9e
What is roughly your net annual income from your job(s)? (in Chian Yuan, in Japan Yen, in Russia rubles, in the Netherlands Euro, in Italy Euro)	In what economic sector are you employed? (Italy, China, the Netherlands, Russia, Japan)	Do you think that printing money leads to more government debt (there is no right or wrong answer)? (Italy, China, the Netherlands, Russia, Japan)	Do you think that, if the European Central Bank prints Euro banknotes and gives everyone 10 euro, this means we all get 10 euro richer (there is no right or wrong answer) (Italy)?	If the People's Bank of China prints more money and gives everyone 10 yuan, do you think that means everyone will be 10 yuan richer than before? (China)	Do you think that, if the European Central Bank prints Euro banknotes and gives everyone 10 euro, this means we all get 10 euro richer (there is no right or wrong answer) (Netherlands)?	Do you think that, if the Bank of Russia prints banknotes and gives everyone 10 rubles, this means we all get 10 rubles richer (there is no right or wrong answer) (Russia)?	Do you think that, if the Japanese Central Bank prints banknotes and gives everyone 100 yen, this means we all get 100 yen richer (there is no right or wrong answer) (Japan)?
20,000–34,999 Euro	Services not mentioned above	Yes			Yes		
50,000–74,999 Euro	Services not mentioned above	Yes			No		
Below 700,000 rubles	Services not mentioned above	No				No	
700,000–1,299,999 rubles	Services not mentioned above	Yes				No	
Below 700,000 rubles	I am currently not employed	Yes				Yes	
Below 700,000 rubles	Transport, storage and communication	No				No	
Below 700,000 rubles	Transport, storage and communication	No				Yes	
700,000–1,299,999 rubles	Services not mentioned above	No				No	

Below 700,000 rubles	Wholesale and retail trade	No				No	
I prefer not to say	I am currently not employed	Yes				Yes	
Below 700,000 rubles	Transport, storage and communication	Yes				No	
Below 700,000 rubles	I am currently not employed	Yes				No	
I have no income	I am currently not employed	Yes				No	
2,500,000–4,999,999 rubles	Agriculture and mining	Yes				No	
Below 700,000 rubles	Construction	Yes				No	
700,000–1,299,999 rubles	I am currently not employed	Yes				No	
Below 700,000 rubles	Services not mentioned above	Yes				No	
Below 700,000 rubles	Construction	Yes				No	
Below 700,000 rubles	I am currently not employed	No				No	
Below 700,000 rubles	I am currently not employed	Yes				No	
Below 700,000 rubles	I am currently not employed	No				No	
700,000–1,299,999 rubles	Services not mentioned above	No				Yes	
Below 700,000 rubles	Services not mentioned above	No				No	

(continued)

Q6	Q7	Q8	Q9a	Q9b	Q9c	Q9d	Q9e
What is roughly your net annual income from your job(s)? (in Chian Yuan, in Japan Yen, in Russia rubles, in the Netherlands Euro, in Italy Euro)	In what economic sector are you employed? (Italy, China, the Netherlands, Russia, Japan)	Do you think that printing money leads to more government debt (there is no right or wrong answer)? (Italy, China, the Netherlands, Russia, Japan)	Do you think that, if the European Central Bank prints Euro banknotes and gives everyone 10 euro, this means we all get 10 euro richer (there is no right or wrong answer) (Italy)?	If the People's Bank of China prints more money and gives everyone 10 yuan, do you think that means everyone will be 10 yuan richer than before? (China)	Do you think that, if the European Central Bank prints Euro banknotes and gives everyone 10 euro, this means we all get 10 euro richer (there is no right or wrong answer) (Netherlands)?	Do you think that, if the Bank of Russia prints banknotes and gives everyone 10 rubles, this means we all get 10 rubles richer (there is no right or wrong answer) (Russia)?	Do you think that, if the Japanese Central Bank prints banknotes and gives everyone 100 yen, this means we all get 100 yen richer (there is no right or wrong answer) (Japan)?
Below 700,000 rubles	Services not mentioned above	Yes				No	
700,000–1,299,999 rubles	Services not mentioned above	No				No	
1,300,000–2,499,999 rubles	Financial services	Yes				No	
Below 700,000 rubles	Services not mentioned above	No				No	
I have no income	I am currently not employed	No				No	
700,000–1,299,999 rubles	Wholesale and retail trade	No				No	
I prefer not to say	Construction	Yes				No	
I have no income	Transport, storage and communication	No				Yes	
1,300,000–2,499,999 rubles	Electricity, gas, and water	Yes				No	

Below 700,000 rubles	I am currently not employed	Yes				No	
Below 700,000 rubles	I am currently not employed	Yes				No	
Below 700,000 rubles	Wholesale and retail trade	No				Yes	
700,000–1,299,999 rubles	Services not mentioned above	Yes				No	
2,500,000–4,999,999 rubles	Electricity, gas, and water	Yes				No	
I prefer not to say	Services not mentioned above	No				Yes	
700,000–1,299,999 rubles	Wholesale and retail trade	No				Yes	
700,000–1,299,999 rubles	Construction	Yes				No	
1,300,000–2,499,999 rubles	Wholesale and retail trade	Yes				Yes	
700,000–1,299,999 rubles	Wholesale and retail trade	Yes				No	
I have no income	I am currently not employed	No				Yes	
700,000–1,299,999 rubles	Financial services	Yes				No	
Below 700,000 rubles	Transport, storage and communication	No				No	
Below 700,000 rubles	Services not mentioned above	Yes				No	

(continued)

Q6	Q7	Q8	Q9a	Q9b	Q9c	Q9d	Q9e
What is roughly your net annual income from your job(s)? (in Chian Yuan, in Japan Yen, in Russia rubles, in the Netherlands Euro, in Italy Euro)	In what economic sector are you employed? (Italy, China, the Netherlands, Russia, Japan)	Do you think that printing money leads to more government debt (there is no right or wrong answer)? (Italy, China, the Netherlands, Russia, Japan)	Do you think that, if the European Central Bank prints Euro banknotes and gives everyone 10 euro, this means we all get 10 euro richer (there is no right or wrong answer) (Italy)?	If the People's Bank of China prints more money and gives everyone 10 yuan, do you think that means everyone will be 10 yuan richer than before? (China)	Do you think that, if the European Central Bank prints Euro banknotes and gives everyone 10 euro, this means we all get 10 euro richer (there is no right or wrong answer) (Netherlands)?	Do you think that, if the Bank of Russia prints banknotes and gives everyone 10 rubles, this means we all get 10 rubles richer (there is no right or wrong answer) (Russia)?	Do you think that, if the Japanese Central Bank prints banknotes and gives everyone 100 yen, this means we all get 100 yen richer (there is no right or wrong answer) (Japan)?
700,000–1,299,999 rubles	Financial services	Yes				No	
Below 700,000 rubles	Services not mentioned above	No				No	
Below 700,000 rubles	Services not mentioned above	No				No	
Below 700,000 rubles	Wholesale and retail trade	Yes				No	
700,000–1,299,999 rubles	Construction	No				Yes	
700,000–1,299,999 rubles	Construction	Yes				No	
700,000–1,299,999 rubles	Services not mentioned above	No				No	
Below 700,000 rubles	Services not mentioned above	Yes				No	
Below 700,000 rubles	I am currently not employed	Yes				No	

Below 700,000 rubles	Services not mentioned above	Yes				No	
Below 700,000 rubles	Wholesale and retail trade	Yes				Yes	
1,300,000–2,499,999 rubles	Financial services	No				No	
Below 700,000 rubles	Services not mentioned above	No				No	
1,300,000–2,499,999 rubles	Services not mentioned above	No				No	
2,500,000–4,999,999 rubles	Wholesale and retail trade	No				No	
Below 700,000 rubles	Services not mentioned above	Yes				Yes	
I have no income	I am currently not employed	No				No	
700,000–1,299,999 rubles	Agriculture and mining	No				No	
Below 700,000 rubles	Services not mentioned above	Yes				Yes	
Below 700,000 rubles	Transport, storage and communication	Yes				No	
700,000–1,299,999 rubles	Construction	No				No	
I prefer not to say	Agriculture and mining	Yes				Yes	
Below 700,000 rubles	I am currently not employed	No				No	

(continued)

Q6	Q7	Q8	Q9a	Q9b	Q9c	Q9d	Q9e
What is roughly your net annual income from your job(s)? (in Chian Yuan, in Japan Yen, in Russia rubles, in the Netherlands Euro, in Italy Euro)	In what economic sector are you employed? (Italy, China, the Netherlands, Russia, Japan)	Do you think that printing money leads to more government debt (there is no right or wrong answer)? (Italy, China, the Netherlands, Russia, Japan)	Do you think that, if the European Central Bank prints Euro banknotes and gives everyone 10 euro, this means we all get 10 euro richer (there is no right or wrong answer) (Italy)?	If the People's Bank of China prints more money and gives everyone 10 yuan, do you think that means everyone will be 10 yuan richer than before? (China)	Do you think that, if the European Central Bank prints Euro banknotes and gives everyone 10 euro, this means we all get 10 euro richer (there is no right or wrong answer) (Netherlands)?	Do you think that, if the Bank of Russia prints banknotes and gives everyone 10 rubles, this means we all get 10 rubles richer (there is no right or wrong answer) (Russia)?	Do you think that, if the Japanese Central Bank prints banknotes and gives everyone 100 yen, this means we all get 100 yen richer (there is no right or wrong answer) (Japan)?
1,300,000–2,499,999 rubles	Construction	No				Yes	
Below 700,000 rubles	Services not mentioned above	No				No	
Below 700,000 rubles	Transport, storage and communication	Yes				No	
Below 700,000 rubles	Construction	No				No	
Below 700,000 rubles	I am currently not employed	No				No	
Below 700,000 rubles	Services not mentioned above	No				No	
Below 700,000 rubles	Agriculture and mining	No				No	
1,300,000–2,499,999 rubles	Electricity, gas, and water	Yes				Yes	
700,000–1,299,999 rubles	Manufacturing	Yes				No	

5,000,000–9,999,999 rubles	Services not mentioned above	Yes				No	
Below 700,000 rubles	I am currently not employed	Yes				No	
700,000–1,299,999 rubles	Services not mentioned above	Yes				No	
700,000–1,299,999 rubles	Services not mentioned above	Yes				Yes	
700,000–1,299,999 rubles	Wholesale and retail trade	No				Yes	
700,000–1,299,999 rubles	Wholesale and retail trade	Yes				No	
1,300,000–2,499,999 rubles	Services not mentioned above	No				No	
Below 700,000 rubles	Financial services	Yes				No	
1,300,000–2,499,999 rubles	Construction	No				Yes	
Below 700,000 rubles	Transport, storage and communication	Yes				Yes	
1,300,000–2,499,999 rubles	Wholesale and retail trade	Yes				No	
Below 700,000 rubles	Transport, storage and communication	No				Yes	
700,000–1,299,999 rubles	Manufacturing	No				No	
700,000–1,299,999 rubles	Manufacturing	Yes				No	

(continued)

Q6	Q7	Q8	Q9a	Q9b	Q9c	Q9d	Q9e
What is roughly your net annual income from your job(s)? (in Chian Yuan, in Japan Yen, in Russia rubles, in the Netherlands Euro, in Italy Euro)	In what economic sector are you employed? (Italy, China, the Netherlands, Russia, Japan)	Do you think that printing money leads to more government debt (there is no right or wrong answer)? (Italy, China, the Netherlands, Russia, Japan)	Do you think that, if the European Central Bank prints Euro banknotes and gives everyone 10 euro, this means we all get 10 euro richer (there is no right or wrong answer) (Italy)?	If the People's Bank of China prints more money and gives everyone 10 yuan, do you think that means everyone will be 10 yuan richer than before? (China)	Do you think that, if the European Central Bank prints Euro banknotes and gives everyone 10 euro, this means we all get 10 euro richer (there is no right or wrong answer) (Netherlands)?	Do you think that, if the Bank of Russia prints banknotes and gives everyone 10 rubles, this means we all get 10 rubles richer (there is no right or wrong answer) (Russia)?	Do you think that, if the Japanese Central Bank prints banknotes and gives everyone 100 yen, this means we all get 100 yen richer (there is no right or wrong answer) (Japan)?
700,000–1,299,999 rubles	Financial services	Yes				No	
Below 700,000 rubles	Services not mentioned above	No				No	
Below 700,000 rubles	Financial services	No				Yes	
700,000–1,299,999 rubles	Construction	Yes				No	
700,000–1,299,999 rubles	Transport, storage and communication	No				No	
Below 700,000 rubles	Electricity, gas, and water	Yes				No	
Below 700,000 rubles	Electricity, gas, and water	Yes				No	
1,300,000–2,499,999 rubles	Wholesale and retail trade	No				Yes	
Below 700,000 rubles	I am currently not employed	Yes				No	

2,500,000–4,999,999 rubles	Construction	Yes				No	
20,000,000–39,999,999 yen	Services not mentioned above	No					No
<499,999 yen	Services not mentioned above	No					No
4,000,000–7,999,999 yen	Services not mentioned above	Yes					Yes
500,000–999,999 yen	Services not mentioned above	Yes					Yes
1,000,000–3,999,999 yen	Manufacturing	Yes					No
1,000,000–3,999,999 yen	Services not mentioned above	Yes					No
4,000,000–7,999,999 yen	Manufacturing	No					Yes
4,000,000–7,999,999 yen	Services not mentioned above	No					No
I prefer not to say	Construction	Yes					No
1,000,000–3,999,999 yen	I am currently not employed	Yes					No
4,000,000–7,999,999 yen	Services not mentioned above	No					No
1,000,000–3,999,999 yen	Services not mentioned above	Yes					No
I have no income	I am currently not employed	Yes					No
4,000,000–7,999,999 yen	I am currently not employed	Yes					No

(continued)

Q6	Q7	Q8	Q9a	Q9b	Q9c	Q9d	Q9e
What is roughly your net annual income from your job(s)? (in Chian Yuan, in Japan Yen, in Russia rubles, in the Netherlands Euro, in Italy Euro)	In what economic sector are you employed? (Italy, China, the Netherlands, Russia, Japan)	Do you think that printing money leads to more government debt (there is no right or wrong answer)? (Italy, China, the Netherlands, Russia, Japan)	Do you think that, if the European Central Bank prints Euro banknotes and gives everyone 10 euro, this means we all get 10 euro richer (there is no right or wrong answer) (Italy)?	If the People's Bank of China prints more money and gives everyone 10 yuan, do you think that means everyone will be 10 yuan richer than before? (China)	Do you think that, if the European Central Bank prints Euro banknotes and gives everyone 10 euro, this means we all get 10 euro richer (there is no right or wrong answer) (Netherlands)?	Do you think that, if the Bank of Russia prints banknotes and gives everyone 10 rubles, this means we all get 10 rubles richer (there is no right or wrong answer) (Russia)?	Do you think that, if the Japanese Central Bank prints banknotes and gives everyone 100 yen, this means we all get 100 yen richer (there is no right or wrong answer) (Japan)?
1,000,000–3,999,999 yen	I am currently not employed	Yes					Yes
500,000–999,999 yen	Manufacturing	No					No
I prefer not to say	I am currently not employed	Yes					No
4,000,000–7,999,999 yen	Services not mentioned above	Yes					No
I prefer not to say	I am currently not employed	Yes					No
<499,999 Yen	Services not mentioned above	No					No
4,000,000–7,999,999 yen	Agriculture and mining	Yes					No
1,000,000–3,999,999 yen	Manufacturing	Yes					Yes
I prefer not to say	Manufacturing	Yes					No
I have no income	I am currently not employed	No					Yes

<499,999 Yen	I am currently not employed	No					No
I have no income	I am currently not employed	No					No
1,000,000–3,999,999 yen	Manufacturing	Yes					No
<499,999 Yen	Manufacturing	No					Yes
4,000,000–7,999,999 yen	Transport, storage and communication	No					No
4,000,000–7,999,999 yen	Financial services	No					No
I have no income	I am currently not employed	No					No
4,000,000–7,999,999 yen	Construction	No					No
500,000–999,999 yen	Construction	No					No
8,000,000–19,999,999 yen	Manufacturing	No					No
8,000,000–19,999,999 yen	Services not mentioned above	No					No
1,000,000–3,999,999 yen	Services not mentioned above	Yes					No
I have no income	Manufacturing	No					No
1,000,000–3,999,999 yen	Services not mentioned above	No					No
4,000,000–7,999,999 yen	Services not mentioned above	No					Yes
1,000,000–3,999,999 yen	Wholesale and retail trade	No					No

(continued)

Q6	Q7	Q8	Q9a	Q9b	Q9c	Q9d	Q9e
What is roughly your net annual income from your job(s)? (in Chian Yuan, in Japan Yen, in Russia rubles, in the Netherlands Euro, in Italy Euro)	In what economic sector are you employed? (Italy, China, the Netherlands, Russia, Japan)	Do you think that printing money leads to more government debt (there is no right or wrong answer)? (Italy, China, the Netherlands, Russia, Japan)	Do you think that, if the European Central Bank prints Euro banknotes and gives everyone 10 euro, this means we all get 10 euro richer (there is no right or wrong answer) (Italy)?	If the People's Bank of China prints more money and gives everyone 10 yuan, do you think that means everyone will be 10 yuan richer than before? (China)	Do you think that, if the European Central Bank prints Euro banknotes and gives everyone 10 euro, this means we all get 10 euro richer (there is no right or wrong answer) (Netherlands)?	Do you think that, if the Bank of Russia prints banknotes and gives everyone 10 rubles, this means we all get 10 rubles richer (there is no right or wrong answer) (Russia)?	Do you think that, if the Japanese Central Bank prints banknotes and gives everyone 100 yen, this means we all get 100 yen richer (there is no right or wrong answer) (Japan)?
I have no income	I am currently not employed	Yes					No
<499,999 Yen	Manufacturing	No					Yes
1,000,000–3,999,999 yen	Financial services	No					Yes
8,000,000–19,999,999 yen	Manufacturing	Yes					Yes
4,000,000–7,999,999 yen	Services not mentioned above	Yes					Yes
8,000,000–19,999,999 yen	Financial services	No					Yes
I prefer not to say	I am currently not employed	No					No
500,000–999,999 yen	Services not mentioned above	Yes					No
<499,999 Yen	Services not mentioned above	No					No
4,000,000–7,999,999 yen	Services not mentioned above	No					No

8,000,000–19,999,999 yen	Manufacturing	No					No
500,000–999,999 yen	I am currently not employed	No					Yes
40,000,000 yen以上	Manufacturing	No					No
I have no income	I am currently not employed	No					No
500,000–999,999 yen	Services not mentioned above	Yes					No
<499,999 Yen	Construction	No					No
1,000,000–3,999,999 yen	Construction	No					No
500,000–999,999 yen	Construction	No					No
1,000,000–3,999,999 yen	Services not mentioned above	No					Yes
I have no income	I am currently not employed	No					No
1,000,000–3,999,999 yen	Services not mentioned above	No					No
<499,999 Yen	Services not mentioned above	No					Yes
I prefer not to say	I am currently not employed	No					No
1,000,000–3,999,999 yen	Services not mentioned above	No					No
I prefer not to say	Transport, storage and communication	Yes					No
I prefer not to say	Services not mentioned above	No					No

(continued)

Q6	Q7	Q8	Q9a	Q9b	Q9c	Q9d	Q9e
What is roughly your net annual income from your job(s)? (in Chian Yuan, in Japan Yen, in Russia rubles, in the Netherlands Euro, in Italy Euro)	In what economic sector are you employed? (Italy, China, the Netherlands, Russia, Japan)	Do you think that printing money leads to more government debt (there is no right or wrong answer)? (Italy, China, the Netherlands, Russia, Japan)	Do you think that, if the European Central Bank prints Euro banknotes and gives everyone 10 euro, this means we all get 10 euro richer (there is no right or wrong answer) (Italy)?	If the People's Bank of China prints more money and gives everyone 10 yuan, do you think that means everyone will be 10 yuan richer than before? (China)	Do you think that, if the European Central Bank prints Euro banknotes and gives everyone 10 euro, this means we all get 10 euro richer (there is no right or wrong answer) (Netherlands)?	Do you think that, if the Bank of Russia prints banknotes and gives everyone 10 rubles, this means we all get 10 rubles richer (there is no right or wrong answer) (Russia)?	Do you think that, if the Japanese Central Bank prints banknotes and gives everyone 100 yen, this means we all get 100 yen richer (there is no right or wrong answer) (Japan)?
<499,999 Yen	Services not mentioned above	Yes					Yes
1,000,000–3,999,999 yen	Electricity, gas, and water	Yes					No
I prefer not to say	Services not mentioned above	No					No
8,000,000–19,999,999 yen	Manufacturing	Yes					Yes
4,000,000–7,999,999 yen	Manufacturing	Yes					Yes
8,000,000–19,999,999 yen	Services not mentioned above	No					No
8,000,000–19,999,999 yen	Manufacturing	No					Yes
<499,999 Yen	Services not mentioned above	No					No
I have no income	I am currently not employed	No					No

Q10	Q11	Q12	Q13	Q14a	Q14b	Q15a	Q15b
You expect your total income next year (2023) to increase? (Italy, China, the Netherlands, Russia, Japan)	In what sector (agriculture, industry, or services) you think you personally can earn the highest income (there is no right or wrong answer)? (Italy, China, the Netherlands, Russia, Japan)	If you can earn similar income, would you prefer working in agriculture, industry or services? (Italy, China, the Netherlands, Russia, Japan)	Do you think that government-controlled companies are performing better than private companies? (Italy, China, the Netherlands, Russia, Japan)	How much trust do you have in the national government? (Italy, China, the Netherlands, Russia, Japan)	How much trust do you have in the local (municipal) government? (Italy, China, the Netherlands, Russia, Japan)	How bad is air pollution (very problematic to unproblematic)? (Italy, China, the Netherlands, Russia, Japan)	How bad is fresh water pollution (very problematic to unproblematic)? (Italy, China, the Netherlands, Russia, Japan)
I have no income	Services	Agriculture	No	A bit of trust	A bit of trust	Problematic	Problematic
No	Services	Agriculture	No	A bit of trust	A bit of distrust	Problematic	A bit problematic
No	Services	Agriculture	No	A bit of distrust	A bit of distrust	Problematic	Problematic
No	Industry	Agriculture	No	A bit of distrust	No trust/No distrust	Problematic	Very problematic
No	Services	Agriculture	No		A bit of distrust		
Yes	Services	Agriculture	No	A bit of distrust	No trust/No distrust	Very problematic	Problematic
No	Industry	Agriculture	No	A bit of distrust	A bit of distrust	A bit problematic	Problematic
No	Services	Agriculture	Yes	A lot of distrust	A bit of distrust	Very problematic	Very problematic
Yes	Agriculture	Agriculture	No	A bit of distrust	A bit of distrust	Problematic	Very problematic
No	Services	Industry	No	A bit of trust	A bit of distrust	Problematic	Very problematic
No	Industry	Industry	No	A lot of distrust	A bit of distrust	Very problematic	Very problematic
No	Industry	Industry	Yes	A bit of trust	No trust/No distrust	Problematic	Problematic
I have no income	Services	Industry	No	No trust/No distrust	No trust/No distrust	Very problematic	Very problematic
Yes	Industry	Industry	No	A bit of distrust	A lot of distrust	Problematic	A bit problematic

(continued)

Q10	Q11	Q12	Q13	Q14a	Q14b	Q15a	Q15b
You expect your total income next year (2023) to increase? (Italy, China, the Netherlands, Russia, Japan)	In what sector (agriculture, industry, or services) you think you personally can earn the highest income (there is no right or wrong answer)? (Italy, China, the Netherlands, Russia, Japan)	If you can earn similar income, would you prefer working in agriculture, industry or services? (Italy, China, the Netherlands, Russia, Japan)	Do you think that government-controlled companies are performing better than private companies? (Italy, China, the Netherlands, Russia, Japan)	How much trust do you have in the national government? (Italy, China, the Netherlands, Russia, Japan)	How much trust do you have in the local (municipal) government? (Italy, China, the Netherlands, Russia, Japan)	How bad is air pollution (very problematic to unproblematic)? (Italy, China, the Netherlands, Russia, Japan)	How bad is fresh water pollution (very problematic to unproblematic)? (Italy, China, the Netherlands, Russia, Japan)
Yes	Industry	Industry	No	A lot of distrust	A lot of distrust	Very problematic	Problematic
No	Industry	Industry	Yes	A bit of distrust	A bit of distrust	Problematic	A bit problematic
Yes	Industry	Industry	No	A bit of distrust	No trust/No distrust	Problematic	Problematic
No	Agriculture	Industry	Yes	No trust/No distrust	A lot of distrust	Very problematic	Very problematic
I have no income	Services	Industry	No	A bit of distrust	A bit of distrust	Problematic	Problematic
No	Services	Industry	No	A bit of distrust	A lot of distrust	Problematic	Problematic
No	Services	Industry	No	A bit of trust	A bit of trust	Very problematic	Very problematic
No	Services	Industry	Yes	A bit of distrust	No trust/No distrust	A bit problematic	Problematic
Yes	Services	It makes no difference	Yes	A lot of distrust	A lot of distrust	Problematic	Problematic
Yes	Services	It makes no difference	Yes	A bit of distrust	A bit of trust	Very problematic	Very problematic
No	Industry	It makes no difference	No	A lot of distrust	A lot of distrust	Very problematic	Very problematic
No	Industry	It makes no difference	Yes	A lot of distrust	A lot of trust	Very problematic	Very problematic

Yes	Industry	It makes no difference	No	A bit of distrust	A bit of distrust	Problematic	Problematic
No	Industry	It makes no difference	No	A bit of distrust	A bit of distrust	Very problematic	Very problematic
No	Industry	It makes no difference	No	A bit of distrust	A bit of distrust	Problematic	Problematic
No	Services	It makes no difference	Yes	A bit of distrust	No trust/No distrust	Very problematic	Very problematic
No	Services	It makes no difference	No	A lot of distrust	A lot of distrust	Very problematic	Very problematic
Yes	Services	It makes no difference	No	A lot of trust	A bit of trust	A bit problematic	Very problematic
I have no income	Services	It makes no difference	No	A lot of distrust	A bit of distrust	Very problematic	Very problematic
No	Services	It makes no difference	No	A bit of distrust	A bit of distrust	Problematic	Problematic
No	Services	It makes no difference	No	A lot of trust	A bit of distrust	Very problematic	Very problematic
No	Services	It makes no difference	No	A bit of trust	A bit of trust	A bit problematic	A bit problematic
No	Services	It makes no difference	No	A bit of trust	No trust/No distrust	Very problematic	Very problematic
No	Services	It makes no difference	No	A bit of trust	A bit of trust	Problematic	Problematic
No	Industry	Services	Yes	A bit of distrust	A bit of distrust	Problematic	Very problematic
No	Industry	Services	Yes	A bit of trust	A bit of trust	Very problematic	Very problematic
No	Services	Services	No	A bit of distrust	A bit of distrust	A bit problematic	A bit problematic
No	Services	Services	No	No trust/No distrust	No trust/No distrust	Problematic	Problematic

(continued)

Q10	Q11	Q12	Q13	Q14a	Q14b	Q15a	Q15b
You expect your total income next year (2023) to increase? (Italy, China, the Netherlands, Russia, Japan)	In what sector (agriculture, industry, or services) you think you personally can earn the highest income (there is no right or wrong answer)? (Italy, China, the Netherlands, Russia, Japan)	If you can earn similar income, would you prefer working in agriculture, industry or services? (Italy, China, the Netherlands, Russia, Japan)	Do you think that government-controlled companies are performing better than private companies? (Italy, China, the Netherlands, Russia, Japan)	How much trust do you have in the national government? (Italy, China, the Netherlands, Russia, Japan)	How much trust do you have in the local (municipal) government? (Italy, China, the Netherlands, Russia, Japan)	How bad is air pollution (very problematic to unproblematic)? (Italy, China, the Netherlands, Russia, Japan)	How bad is fresh water pollution (very problematic to unproblematic)? (Italy, China, the Netherlands, Russia, Japan)
No	Services	Services	No	A bit of distrust	No trust/No distrust	Problematic	Problematic
Yes	Industry	Services	No	A bit of trust	A bit of trust	Problematic	Very problematic
I have no income	Services	Services	Yes	A bit of trust	A bit of trust	Very problematic	Problematic
Yes	Industry	Services	Yes	A bit of distrust	A bit of trust	Very problematic	Very problematic
Yes	Industry	Services	No				
No	Industry	Services	No	A bit of distrust	A bit of trust	A bit problematic	A bit problematic
No	Services	Services	No	A bit of distrust	A bit of distrust	A bit problematic	A bit problematic
I have no income	Industry	Services	No	A lot of distrust	A bit of trust	A bit problematic	A bit problematic
No	Industry	Services	No	A lot of distrust	A bit of trust	Problematic	Problematic
Yes	Services	Services	No	No trust/No distrust	A bit of trust	Unproblematic	A bit problematic
No	Services	Services	No	A bit of distrust	A lot of distrust	A bit problematic	Problematic
I have no income	Industry	Services	No	A bit of distrust	A bit of distrust	Very problematic	Very problematic
Yes	Industry	Services	Yes	A bit of trust	A bit of trust	Problematic	Problematic
Yes	Industry	Services	Yes	No trust/No distrust	No trust/No distrust	Problematic	Problematic
No	Industry	Services	No	A bit of distrust	No trust/No distrust	Very problematic	Very problematic

No	Industry	Services	Yes	No trust/No distrust	A bit of distrust	Problematic	Problematic
No	Industry	Services	No	A lot of distrust	A lot of distrust	Problematic	Very problematic
No	Services	Services	No	A bit of distrust	A bit of distrust	Problematic	Problematic
No	Services	Services	No	No trust/No distrust	No trust/No distrust	Very problematic	Very problematic
Yes	Industry	Services	No	A bit of distrust	A bit of trust	A bit problematic	Problematic
Yes	Industry	Services	No	A bit of trust	A bit of trust	Very problematic	Very problematic
No	Industry	Services	No	A bit of trust	A bit of distrust	Very problematic	Very problematic
No	Services	Services	No	A bit of trust	A bit of trust	Problematic	Problematic
No	Services	Services	No	A lot of distrust	A lot of distrust	Very problematic	Very problematic
Yes	Services	Services	No	No trust/No distrust	No trust/No distrust	A bit problematic	Problematic
Yes	Services	Services	No	A bit of trust	A bit of trust	Very problematic	Very problematic
No	Services	Services	Yes	A bit of trust	A bit of distrust	Very problematic	Very problematic
Yes	Agriculture	Services	Yes	A lot of trust	A bit of distrust	Very problematic	A bit problematic
No	Services	Services	No	A bit of distrust	No trust/No distrust	A bit problematic	Problematic
No	Industry	Services	No	No trust/No distrust	A bit of distrust	Very problematic	A bit problematic
No	Services	Services	No	A bit of distrust	A bit of distrust	Very problematic	Very problematic
No	Industry	Services	Yes	A lot of distrust	A lot of distrust	A bit problematic	Problematic
Yes	Industry	Services	Yes	No trust/No distrust	No trust/No distrust	Very problematic	A bit problematic
Yes	Services	Services	Yes	A lot of trust	No trust/No distrust	Problematic	Very problematic
Yes	Industry	Industry	Yes	A lot of trust	A bit of trust	Problematic	Very problematic
Yes	Services	Services	No	A lot of trust	A lot of trust	Problematic	Problematic

(continued)

Q10	Q11	Q12	Q13	Q14a	Q14b	Q15a	Q15b
You expect your total income next year (2023) to increase? (Italy, China, the Netherlands, Russia, Japan)	In what sector (agriculture, industry, or services) you think you personally can earn the highest income (there is no right or wrong answer)? (Italy, China, the Netherlands, Russia, Japan)	If you can earn similar income, would you prefer working in agriculture, industry or services? (Italy, China, the Netherlands, Russia, Japan)	Do you think that government-controlled companies are performing better than private companies? (Italy, China, the Netherlands, Russia, Japan)	How much trust do you have in the national government? (Italy, China, the Netherlands, Russia, Japan)	How much trust do you have in the local (municipal) government? (Italy, China, the Netherlands, Russia, Japan)	How bad is air pollution (very problematic to unproblematic)? (Italy, China, the Netherlands, Russia, Japan)	How bad is fresh water pollution (very problematic to unproblematic)? (Italy, China, the Netherlands, Russia, Japan)
Yes	Services	Services	Yes	A lot of trust	A bit of trust	Problematic	Problematic
Yes	Services	Services	No	A bit of trust	A bit of trust	Problematic	Problematic
No	Services	Services	No	A bit of trust	A bit of trust	Problematic	A bit problematic
No	Agriculture	Agriculture	Yes	A lot of trust	A lot of trust	A bit problematic	A bit problematic
Yes	Industry	Industry	No	A bit of trust	A bit of trust	Very problematic	Very problematic
Yes	Industry	It makes no difference	No	A lot of trust	A lot of trust	Very problematic	Very problematic
No	Services	Services	No	A bit of trust	A bit of distrust	Very problematic	A bit problematic
No	Industry	Agriculture	No	No trust/No distrust	No trust/No distrust	Problematic	Problematic
Yes	Services	Industry	No	A bit of trust	A bit of trust	Problematic	Very problematic
Yes	Industry	It makes no difference	No	A lot of trust	A lot of trust	A bit problematic	A bit problematic
Yes	Services	Services	No	A lot of trust	A lot of trust	Problematic	A bit problematic
Yes	Services	Industry	No	A bit of trust	A bit of trust	Problematic	A bit problematic
Yes	Agriculture	Agriculture	Yes	A lot of trust	A lot of trust	Problematic	Very problematic
No	Industry	Services	No	A bit of trust	No trust/No distrust	Problematic	Problematic
Yes	Services	Industry	Yes	A lot of trust	No trust/No distrust	Problematic	Very problematic

Yes	Services	Services	No	A bit of trust	A bit of distrust	Problematic	Very problematic
No	Industry	Industry	No	A bit of trust	No trust/No distrust	A bit problematic	Problematic
Yes	Industry	Industry	Yes	A lot of trust	A bit of trust	A bit problematic	Problematic
Yes	Industry	Agriculture	Yes	A lot of trust	A bit of trust	Very problematic	Very problematic
No	Services	Services	No	A bit of trust	No trust/No distrust	Very problematic	Very problematic
No	Agriculture	Agriculture	Yes	A lot of trust	A lot of trust	Very problematic	Very problematic
Yes	Industry	Industry	No	A lot of trust	A bit of trust	Problematic	A bit problematic
Yes	Services	Industry	No	A bit of trust	A bit of trust	A bit problematic	A bit problematic
Yes	Industry	Industry	No	A lot of trust	A bit of trust	Very problematic	Problematic
Yes	Industry	Industry	Yes	A lot of trust	A bit of trust	A bit problematic	A bit problematic
No	Industry	Industry	No	A lot of trust	A bit of trust	Problematic	Problematic
Yes	Industry	Industry	Yes	A lot of trust	A lot of trust	Problematic	A bit problematic
Yes	Industry	Services	No	A bit of distrust	A lot of distrust	Very problematic	Very problematic
No	Industry	Agriculture	No	A bit of trust	No trust/No distrust	Problematic	Problematic
Yes	Services	It makes no difference	Yes	A lot of trust	A lot of trust	A bit problematic	A bit problematic
Yes	Services	Services	No	A lot of trust	A bit of trust	Problematic	A bit problematic
No	Services	Services	No	A lot of trust	A bit of trust	A bit problematic	A bit problematic
Yes	Industry	Industry	Yes	A bit of trust	A bit of trust	Very problematic	Problematic
Yes	Services	It makes no difference	No	A lot of trust	A lot of trust	A bit problematic	A bit problematic
No	Services	Services	No	A lot of distrust	A bit of distrust	Very problematic	Very problematic
Yes	Industry	Industry	Yes	A lot of trust	A bit of trust	A bit problematic	A bit problematic
Yes	Industry	Agriculture	Yes	A bit of trust	No trust/No distrust	Very problematic	Very problematic

(continued)

Q10	Q11	Q12	Q13	Q14a	Q14b	Q15a	Q15b
You expect your total income next year (2023) to increase? (Italy, China, the Netherlands, Russia, Japan)	In what sector (agriculture, industry, or services) you think you personally can earn the highest income (there is no right or wrong answer)? (Italy, China, the Netherlands, Russia, Japan)	If you can earn similar income, would you prefer working in agriculture, industry or services? (Italy, China, the Netherlands, Russia, Japan)	Do you think that government-controlled companies are performing better than private companies? (Italy, China, the Netherlands, Russia, Japan)	How much trust do you have in the national government? (Italy, China, the Netherlands, Russia, Japan)	How much trust do you have in the local (municipal) government? (Italy, China, the Netherlands, Russia, Japan)	How bad is air pollution (very problematic to unproblematic)? (Italy, China, the Netherlands, Russia, Japan)	How bad is fresh water pollution (very problematic to unproblematic)? (Italy, China, the Netherlands, Russia, Japan)
No	Services	Services	No	A lot of trust	A lot of trust	Very problematic	Very problematic
Yes	Services	Services	Yes	A lot of trust	A bit of trust	Very problematic	Very problematic
Yes	Industry	Industry	Yes	A lot of trust	A bit of trust	Very problematic	Problematic
Yes	Industry	It makes no difference	No	A bit of trust	A bit of trust	A bit problematic	A bit problematic
No	Services	Services	Yes	A bit of trust	A bit of trust	A bit problematic	A bit problematic
Yes	Services	Services	Yes	A lot of trust	A lot of trust	Problematic	Problematic
Yes	Industry	Industry	Yes	A bit of trust	A bit of trust	A bit problematic	A bit problematic
No	Industry	Industry	Yes	A lot of trust	A bit of trust	Very problematic	Very problematic
Yes	Industry	Industry	Yes	A lot of trust	A bit of trust	Problematic	Problematic
Yes	Industry	Industry	No	A bit of trust		A bit problematic	Very problematic
No	Industry	Industry	Yes	A bit of trust	A bit of trust	Problematic	Problematic
Yes	Industry	Industry	No	No trust/No distrust	A bit of distrust	Very problematic	Problematic
No	Services	It makes no difference	No	A bit of trust	A bit of trust	Unproblematic	Unproblematic
Yes	Services	Services	Yes	A lot of trust	A bit of trust	Very problematic	Very problematic
Yes	Services	Agriculture	No	A lot of trust	A lot of trust	Problematic	Very problematic
Yes	Agriculture	Industry	No	A bit of trust	A bit of trust	Problematic	Problematic

No	Services	Services	Yes	A bit of trust	A bit of trust	Problematic	Problematic
Yes	Services	Services	No	A lot of trust	A lot of trust	Problematic	Problematic
Yes	Services	Services	Yes	A lot of trust	A bit of trust	Very problematic	Problematic
Yes	Services	Services	No	A bit of trust	A bit of trust	Very problematic	Very problematic
Yes	Industry	Industry	Yes	A lot of trust	A lot of trust	Very problematic	Very problematic
Yes	Industry	Industry	Yes	A bit of trust	A bit of trust	Problematic	Problematic
Yes	Services	Services	Yes	A lot of trust	A lot of trust	Problematic	Very problematic
No	Services	It makes no difference	Yes	No trust/No distrust	No trust/No distrust	Problematic	Problematic
No	Industry	Industry	No	A lot of trust	A lot of trust	Very problematic	Problematic
Yes	Industry	Industry	Yes	A lot of trust	A bit of trust	Problematic	Problematic
Yes	Agriculture	Agriculture	Yes	A lot of trust	A lot of trust	Very problematic	Very problematic
Yes	Industry	Industry	No	A lot of trust	A lot of trust	Very problematic	Problematic
Yes	Industry	Industry	Yes	No trust/No distrust	No trust/No distrust	A bit problematic	A bit problematic
Yes	Industry	Services	Yes	A bit of trust	No trust/No distrust	Very problematic	Problematic
Yes	Services	Services	Yes	A lot of trust	A bit of trust	Very problematic	Very problematic
Yes	Services	Services	Yes	A lot of trust	A bit of trust	Very problematic	Problematic
Yes	Agriculture	Agriculture	Yes	A lot of trust	A lot of trust	A bit problematic	A bit problematic
Yes	Services	Services	No	A lot of trust	A lot of trust	Very problematic	Very problematic
Yes	Services	It makes no difference	Yes	A lot of trust	A bit of trust	Very problematic	Very problematic
Yes	Services	Services	No	A lot of trust	A lot of trust	Very problematic	Problematic
Yes	Agriculture	Services	Yes	A lot of trust	A bit of trust	Problematic	A bit problematic
Yes	Industry	Industry	No	No trust/No distrust	A bit of trust	Very problematic	Problematic
Yes	Industry	Industry	Yes	A bit of trust	A lot of trust	Problematic	Problematic

(continued)

Q10	Q11	Q12	Q13	Q14a	Q14b	Q15a	Q15b
You expect your total income next year (2023) to increase? (Italy, China, the Netherlands, Russia, Japan)	In what sector (agriculture, industry, or services) you think you personally can earn the highest income (there is no right or wrong answer)? (Italy, China, the Netherlands, Russia, Japan)	If you can earn similar income, would you prefer working in agriculture, industry or services? (Italy, China, the Netherlands, Russia, Japan)	Do you think that government-controlled companies are performing better than private companies? (Italy, China, the Netherlands, Russia, Japan)	How much trust do you have in the national government? (Italy, China, the Netherlands, Russia, Japan)	How much trust do you have in the local (municipal) government? (Italy, China, the Netherlands, Russia, Japan)	How bad is air pollution (very problematic to unproblematic)? (Italy, China, the Netherlands, Russia, Japan)	How bad is fresh water pollution (very problematic to unproblematic)? (Italy, China, the Netherlands, Russia, Japan)
Yes	Industry	Industry	No	A bit of trust	A bit of trust	Problematic	Very problematic
Yes	Industry	It makes no difference	Yes	A lot of trust	A bit of trust	Problematic	A bit problematic
Yes	Industry	Industry	Yes	A lot of trust	A bit of trust	Very problematic	Very problematic
Yes	Industry	Industry	Yes	A bit of trust	A bit of trust	Problematic	Very problematic
No	Industry	It makes no difference	No	A bit of trust	No trust/No distrust	Very problematic	Problematic
Yes	Industry	Industry	Yes	A lot of trust	A lot of trust	A bit problematic	A bit problematic
Yes	Industry	Industry	Yes	No trust/No distrust	No trust/No distrust	A bit problematic	A bit problematic
Yes	Industry	Industry	No	A lot of trust	A lot of trust	A bit problematic	A bit problematic
Yes	Industry	It makes no difference	No	A lot of trust	A bit of trust	Problematic	Problematic
No	Industry	Services	No	A lot of trust	A bit of trust	A bit problematic	A bit problematic
Yes	Agriculture	Services	Yes	A lot of trust	A lot of trust	A bit problematic	A bit problematic
No	Services	Services	Yes	A lot of trust	A lot of trust	Problematic	Problematic
Yes	Industry	It makes no difference	Yes	A lot of trust	A lot of trust	A bit problematic	A bit problematic
Yes	Agriculture	Industry	Yes	A lot of trust	A bit of trust	Problematic	Problematic

Yes	Industry	Industry	Yes	A bit of trust	No trust/No distrust	Problematic	Problematic
Yes	Services	It makes no difference	Yes	A lot of trust	No trust/No distrust	Very problematic	Problematic
Yes	Services	Services	No	A lot of trust	A lot of trust	A bit problematic	A bit problematic
Yes	Industry	Industry	Yes	A lot of trust	A bit of trust	Problematic	Problematic
Yes	Industry	It makes no difference	Yes	A bit of trust	A bit of trust	Very problematic	Problematic
Yes	Industry	Industry	Yes	A bit of trust	A bit of trust	Problematic	Very problematic
Yes	Services	Services	No	A lot of trust	A bit of trust	Problematic	Very problematic
I have no income	Services	Services	No	A lot of trust	A lot of trust	Problematic	Problematic
No	Services	Services	Yes	No trust/No distrust	No trust/No distrust	A bit problematic	A bit problematic
Yes	Services	Industrie	No	A lot of trust	A bit of trust	Problematic	Problematic
Yes	Services	Services	Yes	A lot of distrust	A bit of distrust	A bit problematic	A bit problematic
Yes	Services	Services	No	A lot of trust	A lot of trust	Problematic	Problematic
No	Services	Services	No	A lot of distrust	No trust/No distrust	Very problematic	Very problematic
No	Industry	Services	No	A bit of trust	A bit of trust	Problematic	Very problematic
Yes	Industry	Services	No	A bit of trust	No trust/No distrust	Problematic	Problematic
Yes	Services	Services	No	A bit of distrust	A bit of distrust	Very problematic	Very problematic
No	Industry	It makes no difference	No	No trust/No distrust		Problematic	Problematic
Yes	Industry	Services	No	A bit of trust	A bit of trust	Very problematic	Very problematic
No	Industry	It makes no difference	No	A lot of distrust	A bit of distrust	A bit problematic	Problematic
No	Services	It makes no difference	No	A lot of trust	A lot of trust	Very problematic	Very problematic

(continued)

Q10	Q11	Q12	Q13	Q14a	Q14b	Q15a	Q15b
You expect your total income next year (2023) to increase? (Italy, China, the Netherlands, Russia, Japan)	In what sector (agriculture, industry, or services) you think you personally can earn the highest income (there is no right or wrong answer)? (Italy, China, the Netherlands, Russia, Japan)	If you can earn similar income, would you prefer working in agriculture, industry or services? (Italy, China, the Netherlands, Russia, Japan)	Do you think that government-controlled companies are performing better than private companies? (Italy, China, the Netherlands, Russia, Japan)	How much trust do you have in the national government? (Italy, China, the Netherlands, Russia, Japan)	How much trust do you have in the local (municipal) government? (Italy, China, the Netherlands, Russia, Japan)	How bad is air pollution (very problematic to unproblematic)? (Italy, China, the Netherlands, Russia, Japan)	How bad is fresh water pollution (very problematic to unproblematic)? (Italy, China, the Netherlands, Russia, Japan)
No	Services	Services	No	A bit of trust	A bit of trust	Problematic	Problematic
No	Services	Services	Yes	A lot of trust	A lot of trust	Very problematic	Very problematic
No	Services	It makes no difference	No	A lot of distrust	A bit of distrust	Very problematic	Very problematic
Yes	Agriculture	Agriculture	Yes	A bit of trust	A bit of trust	Problematic	Problematic
No	Services	Services	Yes	A lot of trust	A bit of trust	Problematic	Problematic
No	Services	It makes no difference	Yes	No trust/No distrust	No trust/No distrust	Problematic	Problematic
Yes	Industry	Industrie	No	No trust/No distrust	No trust/No distrust	Problematic	Very problematic
Yes	Services	Services	No	A bit of trust	A bit of trust	Problematic	Problematic
Yes	Industry	Services	No	No trust/No distrust	No trust/No distrust	Problematic	A bit problematic
No	Services	Services	No	A bit of distrust	A bit of distrust	Very problematic	Very problematic
I have no income	Industry	Industrie	Yes	A lot of distrust	A bit of distrust	Problematic	Very problematic
Yes	Services	It makes no difference	Yes	No trust/No distrust	No trust/No distrust	Problematic	Problematic
No	Industry	Industrie	No	A bit of distrust		Problematic	Problematic

No	Services	Services	Yes	A bit of distrust	No trust/No distrust	A bit problematic	A bit problematic
Yes	Industry	It makes no difference	No	A lot of trust	No trust/No distrust	Problematic	Very problematic
Yes	Services	Services	Yes	A bit of distrust	A bit of distrust	Problematic	Problematic
Yes	Industry	Agriculture	No	No trust/No distrust	No trust/No distrust	Very problematic	A bit problematic
Yes	Services	Services	No	A bit of trust	A bit of trust	Very problematic	Very problematic
No	Services	It makes no difference	Yes	A lot of distrust	A lot of distrust	Problematic	Problematic
Yes	Services	Services	Yes	A lot of trust	A lot of trust	Very problematic	Very problematic
Yes	Industry	Services	Yes	No trust/No distrust	No trust/No distrust	Problematic	Problematic
No	Services	Services	No	No trust/No distrust	No trust/No distrust	Problematic	Problematic
No	Agriculture	Industrie	Yes	A lot of trust	No trust/No distrust	Very problematic	Very problematic
Yes	Industry	Industrie	Yes	A bit of trust	A bit of trust	Problematic	A bit problematic
Yes	Services	Services	No	A bit of trust	A bit of trust	Problematic	Problematic
Yes	Services	It makes no difference	No	A bit of trust	A bit of trust	Very problematic	Very problematic
No	Services	It makes no difference	No	A bit of distrust	A bit of distrust	Problematic	Problematic
No	Services	It makes no difference	No	A bit of trust	A bit of trust	Very problematic	Very problematic
No	Services	Services	No		A bit of distrust	Very problematic	Very problematic
No	Services	It makes no difference	Yes	A lot of distrust	A lot of distrust	Problematic	Problematic
Yes	Services	Industrie	Yes	A lot of trust	A bit of trust	A bit problematic	Problematic

(continued)

Q10	Q11	Q12	Q13	Q14a	Q14b	Q15a	Q15b
You expect your total income next year (2023) to increase? (Italy, China, the Netherlands, Russia, Japan)	In what sector (agriculture, industry, or services) you think you personally can earn the highest income (there is no right or wrong answer)? (Italy, China, the Netherlands, Russia, Japan)	If you can earn similar income, would you prefer working in agriculture, industry or services? (Italy, China, the Netherlands, Russia, Japan)	Do you think that government-controlled companies are performing better than private companies? (Italy, China, the Netherlands, Russia, Japan)	How much trust do you have in the national government? (Italy, China, the Netherlands, Russia, Japan)	How much trust do you have in the local (municipal) government? (Italy, China, the Netherlands, Russia, Japan)	How bad is air pollution (very problematic to unproblematic)? (Italy, China, the Netherlands, Russia, Japan)	How bad is fresh water pollution (very problematic to unproblematic)? (Italy, China, the Netherlands, Russia, Japan)
Yes	Industry	It makes no difference	Yes	No trust/No distrust	A bit of distrust	A bit problematic	A bit problematic
No	Services	Services	Yes	A lot of trust		Problematic	Very problematic
No	Services	It makes no difference	No	A lot of trust	A bit of trust	Problematic	Problematic
No	Services	Services	No	No trust/No distrust	No trust/No distrust	Problematic	Problematic
No	Industry	It makes no difference	No	No trust/No distrust	No trust/No distrust	Problematic	Very problematic
No	Industry	Industrie	Yes	No trust/No distrust	A bit of distrust	A bit problematic	A bit problematic
No	Services	It makes no difference	Yes	No trust/No distrust	No trust/No distrust	Problematic	A bit problematic
No	Services	Agriculture	No	A bit of trust	A bit of trust	Problematic	Very problematic
Yes	Services	It makes no difference	No	No trust/No distrust	No trust/No distrust	Problematic	Problematic
I have no income	Services	Services	No	No trust/No distrust	No trust/No distrust	A bit problematic	A bit problematic
No	Services	It makes no difference	No	No trust/No distrust	No trust/No distrust	Problematic	Problematic

Yes	Industry	It makes no difference	Yes	A bit of trust	A lot of trust	Problematic	Very problematic
Yes	Industry	Services	No	A bit of distrust	A bit of trust	Problematic	Problematic
I have no income	Services	Services	No	A bit of trust	A bit of trust	Very problematic	Very problematic
No	Services	Agriculture	No	A bit of trust	A bit of trust	Problematic	Problematic
Yes	Industry	Services	No	A bit of trust	A bit of trust	A bit problematic	Problematic
Yes	Services	Services	No	No trust/No distrust	No trust/No distrust	Problematic	Problematic
No	Services	Services	No	A bit of distrust	A bit of distrust	A bit problematic	A bit problematic
Yes	Agriculture	Agriculture	Yes	No trust/No distrust	No trust/No distrust	Problematic	Problematic
No	Services	Services	No	A bit of distrust	A bit of distrust	Very problematic	Very problematic
No	Services	It makes no difference	No	A bit of distrust	A lot of distrust	Very problematic	Very problematic
No	Industry	Agriculture	Yes	A lot of trust	A lot of trust	Very problematic	Very problematic
No	Services	Services	No	No trust/No distrust	No trust/No distrust	Very problematic	Very problematic
No	Services	It makes no difference	No	No trust/No distrust	No trust/No distrust	A bit problematic	Problematic
No	Services	Services	No	No trust/No distrust	No trust/No distrust	Problematic	Problematic
No	Services	It makes no difference	No	A lot of distrust	A lot of distrust	Very problematic	Very problematic
Yes	Services	It makes no difference	Yes	A bit of trust	No trust/No distrust	Problematic	A bit problematic
No	Services	Services	No	No trust/No distrust	No trust/No distrust	Not Problematic	A bit problematic
Yes	Services	Services	No	A lot of distrust	A lot of distrust	Problematic	Very problematic

(continued)

Q10	Q11	Q12	Q13	Q14a	Q14b	Q15a	Q15b
You expect your total income next year (2023) to increase? (Italy, China, the Netherlands, Russia, Japan)	In what sector (agriculture, industry, or services) you think you personally can earn the highest income (there is no right or wrong answer)? (Italy, China, the Netherlands, Russia, Japan)	If you can earn similar income, would you prefer working in agriculture, industry or services? (Italy, China, the Netherlands, Russia, Japan)	Do you think that government-controlled companies are performing better than private companies? (Italy, China, the Netherlands, Russia, Japan)	How much trust do you have in the national government? (Italy, China, the Netherlands, Russia, Japan)	How much trust do you have in the local (municipal) government? (Italy, China, the Netherlands, Russia, Japan)	How bad is air pollution (very problematic to unproblematic)? (Italy, China, the Netherlands, Russia, Japan)	How bad is fresh water pollution (very problematic to unproblematic)? (Italy, China, the Netherlands, Russia, Japan)
Yes	Industry	Industrie	No	A bit of trust	No trust/No distrust	Very problematic	Problematic
Yes	Services	It makes no difference	No	A bit of trust	A bit of trust	Very problematic	Very problematic
No	Services	Industry	No	A lot of distrust	A lot of distrust	Very problematic	Very problematic
No	Industry	Industry	No	A lot of distrust	A lot of distrust	Problematic	Problematic
Yes	Industry	Services	No	A lot of trust	No trust/No distrust	A bit problematic	A bit problematic
Yes	Agriculture	It makes no difference	No	No trust/No distrust	No trust/No distrust	Problematic	Problematic
No	Services	Services	Yes	A bit of distrust	No trust/No distrust	Very problematic	Very problematic
Yes	Industry	It makes no difference	Yes	A lot of trust	A lot of trust	Very problematic	Very problematic
Yes	Agriculture	Services	No	A bit of trust	A bit of trust	Problematic	Problematic
Yes	Services	Services	Yes	A lot of trust		Problematic	Problematic
Yes	Services	Services	Yes	A lot of trust	A lot of trust	Very problematic	Very problematic
Yes	Services	Services	Yes	A lot of trust	A bit of trust	Very problematic	Very problematic
I have no income	Industry	Industry	No	A lot of distrust	A lot of distrust	Very problematic	Very problematic

Yes	Industry	It makes no difference	Yes	A lot of trust	A lot of trust	Problematic	Problematic
Yes	Services	It makes no difference	Yes	No trust/No distrust	No trust/No distrust	Very problematic	Very problematic
Yes	Services	Services	No	A lot of trust	A lot of trust	Problematic	Problematic
No	Services	Industry	No	A bit of trust	A bit of distrust	A bit problematic	A bit problematic
No	Industry	Industry	No	A bit of distrust	A bit of distrust	Very problematic	Very problematic
No	Services	Services	No	A lot of distrust	A bit of distrust	Problematic	Problematic
No	Services	Services	No	A bit of trust	A bit of trust	Very problematic	Very problematic
Yes	Agriculture	Agriculture	Yes	A bit of trust	A bit of trust	Very problematic	Very problematic
Yes	Services	It makes no difference	No	A bit of trust	A bit of trust	Problematic	Problematic
Yes	Industry	Industry	Yes	A lot of trust	A lot of trust	A bit problematic	A bit problematic
No	Services	Services	Yes	A bit of trust	A bit of trust	Problematic	Problematic
No	Industry	Industry	No	A lot of distrust	A lot of distrust	Problematic	Very problematic
Yes	Services	Services	No	A bit of trust	A bit of distrust	Problematic	Problematic
No	Services	It makes no difference	Yes	A lot of trust	A bit of trust	Very problematic	Very problematic
I have no income	Services	It makes no difference	No	A bit of trust	A bit of trust	Very problematic	Very problematic
Yes	Industry	Industry	No	A bit of trust	A bit of trust	A bit problematic	A bit problematic
Yes	Industry	Industry	No	A bit of trust	A bit of trust	A bit problematic	Very problematic
Yes	Services	Services	No	A bit of trust	A bit of trust	Very problematic	Very problematic
Yes	Industry	Industry	Yes	A lot of trust	A lot of trust	Very problematic	Very problematic
Yes	Agriculture	Agriculture	No	A bit of trust	A bit of trust	Problematic	Problematic
No	Agriculture	Agriculture	No	A bit of distrust	No trust/No distrust	A bit problematic	Problematic
No	Industry	Services	No	A bit of distrust	A bit of distrust	Very problematic	Very problematic

(continued)

Q10	Q11	Q12	Q13	Q14a	Q14b	Q15a	Q15b
You expect your total income next year (2023) to increase? (Italy, China, the Netherlands, Russia, Japan)	In what sector (agriculture, industry, or services) you think you personally can earn the highest income (there is no right or wrong answer)? (Italy, China, the Netherlands, Russia, Japan)	If you can earn similar income, would you prefer working in agriculture, industry or services? (Italy, China, the Netherlands, Russia, Japan)	Do you think that government-controlled companies are performing better than private companies? (Italy, China, the Netherlands, Russia, Japan)	How much trust do you have in the national government? (Italy, China, the Netherlands, Russia, Japan)	How much trust do you have in the local (municipal) government? (Italy, China, the Netherlands, Russia, Japan)	How bad is air pollution (very problematic to unproblematic)? (Italy, China, the Netherlands, Russia, Japan)	How bad is fresh water pollution (very problematic to unproblematic)? (Italy, China, the Netherlands, Russia, Japan)
Yes	Industry	Services	No	A bit of trust	A bit of trust	Problematic	Problematic
No	Industry	Industry	No	A lot of distrust	A lot of distrust	Very problematic	Very problematic
Yes	Services	Services	Yes	A bit of trust	A bit of trust	A bit problematic	A bit problematic
Yes	Agriculture	Agriculture	No	A bit of trust	A bit of trust	Very problematic	Very problematic
Yes	Industry	Industry	No	A lot of distrust		Very problematic	Very problematic
Yes	Industry	Services	No	A lot of trust	A lot of distrust	Very problematic	Very problematic
No	Industry	Industry	No	A lot of distrust	A lot of distrust	Very problematic	Very problematic
Yes	Agriculture	Agriculture	Yes	A bit of distrust	A lot of distrust	A bit problematic	A bit problematic
Yes	Industry	Industry	Yes	A lot of trust	A bit of trust	Very problematic	Very problematic
Yes	Services	It makes no difference	Yes	A lot of trust	A lot of trust	A bit problematic	A bit problematic
No	Industry	Industry	No	A bit of distrust	A lot of distrust	Problematic	A bit problematic
No	Services	Services	No	A bit of trust	No trust/No distrust	A bit problematic	Problematic
Yes	Services	Services	No	A lot of trust	A lot of trust	Very problematic	Very problematic
Yes	Industry	Industry	No	A bit of distrust	A bit of distrust	A bit problematic	A bit problematic
Yes	Services	Services	No	A lot of trust	A bit of trust	Problematic	Problematic
No	Industry	Industry	Yes	A lot of distrust	No trust/No distrust	Problematic	Problematic

Yes	Industry	Industry	No	No trust/No distrust	No trust/No distrust	Problematic	Problematic
No	Services	Services	Yes	A bit of distrust	No trust/No distrust	A bit problematic	A bit problematic
No	Services	Agriculture	No	A bit of trust	A bit of distrust	Very problematic	Very problematic
Yes	Agriculture	Agriculture	No	A bit of trust	A lot of trust	Problematic	Problematic
No	Industry	Industry	No	A bit of distrust	A bit of distrust	Problematic	Problematic
Yes	Agriculture	Agriculture	Yes	A bit of trust	A bit of trust	Very problematic	Problematic
Yes	Services	Agriculture	No	A lot of trust	A lot of trust	Problematic	Problematic
Yes	Agriculture	Agriculture	Yes	A bit of trust	A bit of trust	Very problematic	Very problematic
Yes	Services	Services	No	A bit of trust	A bit of trust	Very problematic	Very problematic
No	Agriculture	Agriculture	No	A bit of distrust	No trust/No distrust	Very problematic	Very problematic
Yes	Agriculture	Agriculture	Yes	A bit of trust	A bit of trust	Very problematic	Very problematic
Yes	Services	Services	Yes	A bit of trust	A bit of trust	Very problematic	Very problematic
Yes	Industry	It makes no difference	Yes	A bit of trust	A bit of trust	A bit problematic	Problematic
No	Services	Services	No	A lot of distrust	A lot of distrust	Very problematic	Very problematic
Yes	Agriculture	It makes no difference	No	No trust/No distrust	No trust/No distrust	Very problematic	Problematic
Yes	Services	It makes no difference	No	A bit of trust	A bit of trust	Problematic	Problematic
I have no income	Services	Industry	Yes	A lot of trust	A bit of trust	Very problematic	Problematic
No	Industry	Industry	No	A bit of trust	A bit of trust	Problematic	A bit problematic
Yes	Agriculture	Agriculture	No	A lot of trust	A bit of trust	Very problematic	Very problematic
No	Industry	Industry	No	A bit of trust	A bit of trust	Problematic	Problematic
No	Services	It makes no difference	No	A lot of trust	A bit of trust	Very problematic	Problematic

(continued)

Q10	Q11	Q12	Q13	Q14a	Q14b	Q15a	Q15b
You expect your total income next year (2023) to increase? (Italy, China, the Netherlands, Russia, Japan)	In what sector (agriculture, industry, or services) you think you personally can earn the highest income (there is no right or wrong answer)? (Italy, China, the Netherlands, Russia, Japan)	If you can earn similar income, would you prefer working in agriculture, industry or services? (Italy, China, the Netherlands, Russia, Japan)	Do you think that government-controlled companies are performing better than private companies? (Italy, China, the Netherlands, Russia, Japan)	How much trust do you have in the national government? (Italy, China, the Netherlands, Russia, Japan)	How much trust do you have in the local (municipal) government? (Italy, China, the Netherlands, Russia, Japan)	How bad is air pollution (very problematic to unproblematic)? (Italy, China, the Netherlands, Russia, Japan)	How bad is fresh water pollution (very problematic to unproblematic)? (Italy, China, the Netherlands, Russia, Japan)
Yes	Industry	Industry	Yes	A lot of trust	A bit of trust	A bit problematic	A bit problematic
Yes	Services	It makes no difference	No	A bit of trust	A bit of trust	A bit problematic	Problematic
Yes	Services	Services	No	A bit of distrust	No trust/No distrust	Very problematic	Very problematic
Yes	Agriculture	Agriculture	Yes	A lot of trust	A bit of trust	Very problematic	Very problematic
Yes	Services	Services	Yes	A lot of trust	A lot of trust	Very problematic	Very problematic
No	Industry	Industry	Yes	A bit of trust	No trust/No distrust	Very problematic	Problematic
No	Industry	Agriculture	No	A bit of distrust	A bit of distrust	A bit problematic	Problematic
No	Industry	Industry	Yes	A lot of trust	A bit of trust	Unproblematic	Problematic
Yes	Services	Services	Yes	A lot of trust	A lot of trust	Very problematic	Very problematic
No	Services	Agriculture	No	A bit of trust	A bit of distrust	A bit problematic	Very problematic
No	Services	Services	No	A bit of trust	A bit of trust	Problematic	A bit problematic
No	Services	Services	No	A bit of trust	No trust/No distrust	A bit problematic	Problematic
No	Industry	Services	Yes	A lot of trust	A bit of trust	Problematic	Problematic
Yes	Services	It makes no difference	No	No trust/No distrust	A bit of trust	Problematic	Very problematic

No	Industry	Industry	No	A bit of trust	A bit of distrust	Problematic	Problematic
Yes	Industry	Industry	Yes	A lot of trust	A bit of distrust	Problematic	Very problematic
Yes	Services	Services	Yes	A bit of trust	A bit of trust	Very problematic	Very problematic
No	Agriculture	Agriculture	No	A bit of trust	No trust/No distrust	Problematic	Problematic
No	Industry	It makes no difference	No	A lot of distrust	A bit of distrust	Very problematic	Very problematic
No	Services	Services	No	A bit of distrust	A bit of distrust	Very problematic	Very problematic
Yes	Services	Services	No	A lot of trust	A bit of trust	A bit problematic	A bit problematic
Yes	Services	Services	No	A lot of trust	A bit of trust	Very problematic	Problematic
Yes	Services	Services	Yes	A lot of trust	A lot of trust	Problematic	Problematic
Yes	Industry	Services	No	A lot of trust	A lot of trust	Problematic	Problematic
No	Agriculture	It makes no difference	No	A lot of distrust	A lot of distrust	Problematic	Very problematic
No	Industry	Industry	No	A bit of trust	A bit of trust	Very problematic	Very problematic
Yes	Industry	Industry	Yes	A lot of trust	A bit of trust	Very problematic	Very problematic
No	Industry	Industry	No	No trust/No distrust	No trust/No distrust	A bit problematic	A bit problematic
No	Services	It makes no difference	No	No trust/No distrust	No trust/No distrust	Problematic	Problematic
Yes	Industry	Industry	No	A bit of trust	A lot of trust	Problematic	A bit problematic
No	Services	It makes no difference	No	No trust/No distrust	No trust/No distrust	Problematic	Problematic
Yes	Services	Services	Yes	No trust/No distrust	No trust/No distrust	Problematic	Problematic
No	Services	Services	No	No trust/No distrust	No trust/No distrust	A bit problematic	A bit problematic
No	Industry	It makes no difference	No	A bit of trust	A bit of trust	Problematic	Problematic

(continued)

Q10	Q11	Q12	Q13	Q14a	Q14b	Q15a	Q15b
You expect your total income next year (2023) to increase? (Italy, China, the Netherlands, Russia, Japan)	In what sector (agriculture, industry, or services) you think you personally can earn the highest income (there is no right or wrong answer)? (Italy, China, the Netherlands, Russia, Japan)	If you can earn similar income, would you prefer working in agriculture, industry or services? (Italy, China, the Netherlands, Russia, Japan)	Do you think that government-controlled companies are performing better than private companies? (Italy, China, the Netherlands, Russia, Japan)	How much trust do you have in the national government? (Italy, China, the Netherlands, Russia, Japan)	How much trust do you have in the local (municipal) government? (Italy, China, the Netherlands, Russia, Japan)	How bad is air pollution (very problematic to unproblematic)? (Italy, China, the Netherlands, Russia, Japan)	How bad is fresh water pollution (very problematic to unproblematic)? (Italy, China, the Netherlands, Russia, Japan)
No	Services	Agriculture	No			Very problematic	A bit problematic
Yes	Services	It makes no difference	Yes	A bit of trust	A bit of trust	Problematic	A bit problematic
No	Services	Industry	No	A bit of trust	A bit of trust	A bit problematic	Unproblematic
No	Industry	It makes no difference	No	A bit of distrust	A bit of distrust	Unproblematic	Unproblematic
No	Agriculture	Services	No	A bit of distrust	A bit of distrust	A bit problematic	A bit problematic
No	Industry	Industry	No	A lot of distrust	A bit of distrust	Unproblematic	A bit problematic
No	Industry	Industry	No	A bit of distrust	No trust/No distrust	A bit problematic	A bit problematic
No	Services	Services	No	A bit of trust	A bit of trust	A bit problematic	A bit problematic
I have no income	Industry	Services	No	A lot of distrust	A bit of distrust	Problematic	Problematic
Yes	Services	Services	No	A lot of distrust	A lot of distrust	Unproblematic	Unproblematic
No	Industry	It makes no difference	No	A lot of distrust	A lot of distrust	Very problematic	Very problematic
No	Services	It makes no difference	Yes	No trust/No distrust	A bit of trust	A bit problematic	A bit problematic
No	Industry	Services	Yes	A bit of distrust	No trust/No distrust	Problematic	Problematic

No	Agriculture	Services	Yes	A lot of distrust	A lot of distrust	Problematic	Problematic
I have no income	Services	Industry	Yes	A bit of trust	A bit of trust	A bit problematic	A bit problematic
No	Services	Services	No	No trust/No distrust	No trust/No distrust	Very problematic	Very problematic
No	Agriculture	Agriculture	No	A bit of distrust	A bit of distrust	A bit problematic	A bit problematic
Yes	Agriculture	Agriculture	Yes	A bit of trust	A bit of trust	Very problematic	Very problematic
No	Industry	Services	No	A bit of distrust	A bit of trust	Very problematic	Very problematic
I have no income	Industry	It makes no difference	Yes	No trust/No distrust	No trust/No distrust	A bit problematic	Problematic
No	Industry	It makes no difference	No	A bit of trust	A bit of trust	Problematic	Problematic
I have no income	Agriculture	It makes no difference	No	A lot of distrust	A bit of distrust	A bit problematic	A bit problematic
No	Industry	Industry	Yes	A lot of distrust	A bit of trust	Problematic	Problematic
No	Services	It makes no difference	Yes	A lot of distrust	A bit of distrust	Problematic	Problematic
Yes	Industry	It makes no difference	No	A lot of distrust	No trust/No distrust	Problematic	Problematic
No	Services	Services	No	A lot of trust	A lot of trust	A bit problematic	Unproblematic
No	Industry	Industry	Yes	A bit of trust	A bit of trust	Problematic	Problematic
No	Agriculture	It makes no difference	No	A lot of distrust	A bit of distrust	Problematic	Problematic
No	Services	Services	No	A bit of distrust	A lot of distrust	Problematic	Problematic
No	Services	Services	No	No trust/No distrust	No trust/No distrust	A bit problematic	A bit problematic
No	Services	Services	Yes	A lot of distrust	A bit of distrust	Very problematic	Problematic
No	Industry	It makes no difference	Yes	A bit of distrust	A bit of distrust	Unproblematic	Unproblematic
No	Agriculture	Agriculture	No	A lot of distrust	A lot of distrust	Unproblematic	Unproblematic

(continued)

Q10	Q11	Q12	Q13	Q14a	Q14b	Q15a	Q15b
You expect your total income next year (2023) to increase? (Italy, China, the Netherlands, Russia, Japan)	In what sector (agriculture, industry, or services) you think you personally can earn the highest income (there is no right or wrong answer)? (Italy, China, the Netherlands, Russia, Japan)	If you can earn similar income, would you prefer working in agriculture, industry or services? (Italy, China, the Netherlands, Russia, Japan)	Do you think that government-controlled companies are performing better than private companies? (Italy, China, the Netherlands, Russia, Japan)	How much trust do you have in the national government? (Italy, China, the Netherlands, Russia, Japan)	How much trust do you have in the local (municipal) government? (Italy, China, the Netherlands, Russia, Japan)	How bad is air pollution (very problematic to unproblematic)? (Italy, China, the Netherlands, Russia, Japan)	How bad is fresh water pollution (very problematic to unproblematic)? (Italy, China, the Netherlands, Russia, Japan)
No	Services	Services	No	No trust/No distrust	No trust/No distrust	Unproblematic	Unproblematic
Yes	Industry	It makes no difference	No	A lot of distrust	No trust/No distrust	Unproblematic	Unproblematic
No	Services	Services	No	A bit of trust	A bit of trust	A bit problematic	A bit problematic
I have no income	Industry	It makes no difference	Yes	A bit of distrust	A bit of trust	Problematic	Problematic
No	Services	It makes no difference	No	A lot of distrust	A lot of distrust	Problematic	Problematic
No	Industry	Industry	Yes	A lot of distrust	A lot of distrust	Very problematic	Very problematic
No	Industry	Industry	No	A bit of trust	A bit of trust	Unproblematic	Unproblematic
No	Agriculture	Agriculture	Yes	A lot of trust	A lot of trust	Unproblematic	Unproblematic
No	Services	Services	Yes	A bit of trust	A bit of trust	A bit problematic	A bit problematic
No	Services	It makes no difference	No	No trust/No distrust	No trust/No distrust	A bit problematic	A bit problematic
No	Agriculture	Agriculture	Yes	A bit of distrust	A bit of distrust	Very problematic	Very problematic
No	Services	Services	No	No trust/No distrust	No trust/No distrust	A bit problematic	Unproblematic
Yes	Industry	Services	Yes	A bit of distrust	A bit of distrust	Very problematic	Very problematic

No	Services	It makes no difference	Yes	No trust/No distrust	No trust/No distrust	A bit problematic	Problematic
No	Services	It makes no difference	No	A bit of trust	A bit of trust	Unproblematic	Unproblematic
No	Industry	Agriculture	No	A bit of trust	A bit of trust	A bit problematic	A bit problematic
I have no income	Services	Services	No	A bit of distrust	A bit of distrust	A bit problematic	A bit problematic
No	Services	It makes no difference	Yes	A lot of distrust	A bit of distrust	Very problematic	Very problematic
No	Industry	Industry	Yes	No trust/No distrust	No trust/No distrust	A bit problematic	Problematic
Yes	Services	Industry	No	A lot of distrust	A lot of distrust	Problematic	Problematic
No	Services	It makes no difference	No	A bit of trust	A bit of trust	Problematic	Problematic
No	Services	Services	Yes	No trust/No distrust	No trust/No distrust	A bit problematic	A bit problematic
I have no income	Services	It makes no difference	Yes	No trust/No distrust	No trust/No distrust	Very problematic	Very problematic
No	Industry	Industry	No	No trust/No distrust	A lot of trust	Unproblematic	Unproblematic
No	Services	It makes no difference	No	A bit of distrust	A bit of distrust	A bit problematic	A bit problematic
I have no income	Services	It makes no difference	No		A lot of distrust		Unproblematic
No	Industry	Services	No	A lot of distrust	A lot of distrust	A bit problematic	A bit problematic
No	Services	Industry	No	No trust/No distrust	No trust/No distrust	A bit problematic	Problematic
No	Services	It makes no difference	No	A bit of trust	A bit of trust	Problematic	Problematic

(continued)

Q10	Q11	Q12	Q13	Q14a	Q14b	Q15a	Q15b
You expect your total income next year (2023) to increase? (Italy, China, the Netherlands, Russia, Japan)	In what sector (agriculture, industry, or services) you think you personally can earn the highest income (there is no right or wrong answer)? (Italy, China, the Netherlands, Russia, Japan)	If you can earn similar income, would you prefer working in agriculture, industry or services? (Italy, China, the Netherlands, Russia, Japan)	Do you think that government-controlled companies are performing better than private companies? (Italy, China, the Netherlands, Russia, Japan)	How much trust do you have in the national government? (Italy, China, the Netherlands, Russia, Japan)	How much trust do you have in the local (municipal) government? (Italy, China, the Netherlands, Russia, Japan)	How bad is air pollution (very problematic to unproblematic)? (Italy, China, the Netherlands, Russia, Japan)	How bad is fresh water pollution (very problematic to unproblematic)? (Italy, China, the Netherlands, Russia, Japan)
No	Services	It makes no difference	Yes	A bit of trust	A bit of trust	Problematic	Problematic
No	Industry	Industry	No	A bit of distrust	A bit of distrust	Problematic	Very problematic
No	Services	It makes no difference	No	A lot of distrust	A lot of distrust	Very problematic	Very problematic
No	Agriculture	Industry	Yes	No trust/No distrust	No trust/No distrust	A bit problematic	A bit problematic
Yes	Industry	Industry	No	No trust/No distrust	A bit of trust	Very problematic	Problematic
Yes	Services	Services	Yes	A lot of trust	A lot of trust	A bit problematic	Problematic
No	Industry	Industry	No	A lot of distrust	A bit of trust	Problematic	Problematic
Yes	Industry	Industry	Yes	A bit of trust	No trust/No distrust	A bit problematic	Problematic
I have no income	Services	It makes no difference	No	A lot of distrust	A lot of distrust	Unproblematic	Unproblematic

Q15c	Q15d	Q16	Q17	Q18	Q19	Q20
How bad is sea pollution (very problematic to unproblematic)? (Italy, China, the Netherlands, Russia, Japan)	How bad is ground pollution (very problematic to unproblematic)? (Italy, China, the Netherlands, Russia, Japan)	Recently there's been speculation about mining and exploiting resources from other planets and spatial objects. Should we be setting limits on pollution also outside Earth? (Italy, China, the Netherlands, Russia, Japan)	Which of the following alternative energy sources do you think will be MOST important in the next 10 years? (Italy, China, the Netherlands, Russia, Japan)	What share of your income would you be prepared to sacrifice to completely eradicate pollution? (Italy, China, the Netherlands, Russia, Japan)	Looking at the current developments in your country, do you think the number of government-controlled companies is expanding? (Italy, China, the Netherlands, Russia)	Which country do you think will be the biggest economy in Asia 30 years from now? (China, Japan)
Problematic	Problematic	Only if there are life forms	Wind	I have no income	No	
A bit problematic	Problematic	Only if there are life forms	Solar	6–10%	Yes	
Problematic	Problematic	The concept of pollution does not apply to outer space	Solar	6–10%	No	
Problematic	Problematic	Yes	Solar	1–5%	Yes	
		Only if there are life forms	Wind	1–5%	No	
Problematic	Problematic	Yes	Natural gas	Nothing	Yes	
Very problematic	Problematic	No	Solar	1–5%	No	
Very problematic	Very problematic	Yes	Natural gas	1–5%	No	
Problematic	Problematic	Yes	Wind	6–10%	Yes	
Very problematic	Problematic	Yes	Solar	6–10%	No	
Very problematic	Very problematic	Yes	Wind	1–5%	Yes	

(continued)

Q15c	Q15d	Q16	Q17	Q18	Q19	Q20
How bad is sea pollution (very problematic to unproblematic)? (Italy, China, the Netherlands, Russia, Japan)	How bad is ground pollution (very problematic to unproblematic)? (Italy, China, the Netherlands, Russia, Japan)	Recently there's been speculation about mining and exploiting resources from other planets and spatial objects. Should we be setting limits on pollution also outside Earth? (Italy, China, the Netherlands, Russia, Japan)	Which of the following alternative energy sources do you think will be MOST important in the next 10 years? (Italy, China, the Netherlands, Russia, Japan)	What share of your income would you be prepared to sacrifice to completely eradicate pollution? (Italy, China, the Netherlands, Russia, Japan)	Looking at the current developments in your country, do you think the number of government-controlled companies is expanding? (Italy, China, the Netherlands, Russia)	Which country do you think will be the biggest economy in Asia 30 years from now? (China, Japan)
Problematic	Problematic	Yes		6–10%	Yes	
Very problematic		Yes	Wind	I have no income	Yes	
Problematic	A bit problematic	No	Nuclear	Nothing	No	
Very problematic	Very problematic	Yes	Solar	1–5%	Yes	
Problematic	Problematic	No	Natural gas	16–20%	No	
Very problematic	Very problematic	No	Nuclear	31% and higher	Yes	
Very problematic	Very problematic	Yes	Solar	6–10%	Yes	
Problematic	Problematic	Yes	Solar	I have no income	Yes	
Problematic	Problematic	The concept of pollution does not apply to outer space	Nuclear	Nothing	Yes	
Very problematic	Very problematic	Yes	Solar	1–5%	No	
Problematic	Problematic	Yes	Nuclear	Nothing	No	
Problematic	Problematic	Yes	Solar	16–20%	Yes	
Problematic	Problematic	The concept of pollution does not apply to outer space	Natural gas	Nothing	Yes	

Very problematic	Very problematic	The concept of pollution does not apply to outer space	Wind	1–5%	No	
Very problematic	Very problematic	Yes	Solar	1–5%	Yes	
Problematic	Problematic	Only if there are life forms	Nuclear	6–10%	No	
Very problematic	Very problematic	Only if there are life forms	Nuclear	1–5%	No	
Problematic	Problematic	No	Solar	Nothing	No	
Very problematic	Very problematic	The concept of pollution does not apply to outer space	Nuclear	Nothing	No	
Very problematic	Very problematic	Yes	Solar	11–15%	No	
Very problematic	Problematic	Yes	Ethanol	1–5%	Yes	
Very problematic	Very problematic	Yes	Wind	I have no income	No	
Problematic	Problematic	Yes	Solar	I have no income	No	
Very problematic	Problematic	Yes	Solar	6–10%	No	
A bit problematic	Problematic	Only if there are life forms	Solar	16–20%	Yes	
Very problematic	Very problematic	Yes	Solar	1–5%	No	
Problematic	Problematic	Yes	Nuclear	6–10%	No	
Very problematic	Problematic	Yes	Solar	6–10%	No	
Very problematic	Very problematic	Yes	Solar	16–20%	No	
Problematic	Problematic	Yes	Solar	1–5%	Yes	
Problematic	Problematic	Yes	Nuclear	1–5%	No	
Problematic	A bit problematic	Only if there are life forms	Solar	1–5%	No	
Very problematic	Problematic	Only if there are life forms	Solar	1–5%	Yes	

(continued)

Q15c	Q15d	Q16	Q17	Q18	Q19	Q20
How bad is sea pollution (very problematic to unproblematic)? (Italy, China, the Netherlands, Russia, Japan)	How bad is ground pollution (very problematic to unproblematic)? (Italy, China, the Netherlands, Russia, Japan)	Recently there's been speculation about mining and exploiting resources from other planets and spatial objects. Should we be setting limits on pollution also outside Earth? (Italy, China, the Netherlands, Russia, Japan)	Which of the following alternative energy sources do you think will be MOST important in the next 10 years? (Italy, China, the Netherlands, Russia, Japan)	What share of your income would you be prepared to sacrifice to completely eradicate pollution? (Italy, China, the Netherlands, Russia, Japan)	Looking at the current developments in your country, do you think the number of government-controlled companies is expanding? (Italy, China, the Netherlands, Russia)	Which country do you think will be the biggest economy in Asia 30 years from now? (China, Japan)
Problematic	Problematic	Yes	Solar	I have no income	Yes	
Problematic	Problematic	Yes	Solar	1–5%	Yes	
				1–5%	No	
A bit problematic	A bit problematic	Only if there are life forms	Natural gas	1–5%	Yes	
A bit problematic	A bit problematic	The concept of pollution does not apply to outer space	Solar	Nothing	No	
Problematic	A bit problematic	The concept of pollution does not apply to outer space	Solar	Nothing	No	
Problematic	Problematic	Yes	Solar	1–5%	No	
A bit problematic	Problematic	Only if there are life forms	Solar	Nothing	Yes	
Problematic	A bit problematic	No	Nuclear	1–5%	No	
Very problematic	A bit problematic	Yes	Solar	Nothing	Yes	

Problematic	Problematic	Only if there are life forms	Solar	1–5%	No	
Very problematic	Very problematic	Yes	Solar	6–10%	Yes	
Very problematic	Very problematic	The concept of pollution does not apply to outer space	Solar	Nothing	No	
Problematic	Problematic	Yes	Nuclear	11–15%	Yes	
Very problematic	Very problematic	Yes	Solar	1–5%	No	
Problematic	Problematic	Only if there are life forms	Solar	1–5%	Yes	
Very problematic	Problematic	Yes	Solar	1–5%	No	
Problematic	A bit problematic	No	Solar	6–10%	No	
Very problematic	Very problematic	No	Natural gas	1–5%	Yes	
Very problematic	Very problematic	Yes	Solar	1–5%	No	
Problematic	Problematic	No	Nuclear	11–15%	Yes	
Very problematic	Very problematic	No	Nuclear	Nothing	No	
Very problematic	Problematic	Yes	Solar	1–5%	Yes	
Very problematic	Very problematic	Only if there are life forms	Solar	1–5%	No	
Very problematic	Very problematic	Yes	Wind	1–5%	No	
A bit problematic	Problematic	Yes	Nuclear	6–10%	No	
A bit problematic	A bit problematic	Only if there are life forms	Solar	6–10%	No	
A bit problematic	Problematic	No	Nuclear	11–15%	Yes	
Very problematic	Very problematic	The concept of pollution does not apply to outer space	Solar	1–5%	No	
Problematic	Problematic	The concept of pollution does not apply to outer space	Wind	Nothing	No	

(continued)

Q15c	Q15d	Q16	Q17	Q18	Q19	Q20
How bad is sea pollution (very problematic to unproblematic)? (Italy, China, the Netherlands, Russia, Japan)	How bad is ground pollution (very problematic to unproblematic)? (Italy, China, the Netherlands, Russia, Japan)	Recently there's been speculation about mining and exploiting resources from other planets and spatial objects. Should we be setting limits on pollution also outside Earth? (Italy, China, the Netherlands, Russia, Japan)	Which of the following alternative energy sources do you think will be MOST important in the next 10 years? (Italy, China, the Netherlands, Russia, Japan)	What share of your income would you be prepared to sacrifice to completely eradicate pollution? (Italy, China, the Netherlands, Russia, Japan)	Looking at the current developments in your country, do you think the number of government-controlled companies is expanding? (Italy, China, the Netherlands, Russia)	Which country do you think will be the biggest economy in Asia 30 years from now? (China, Japan)
Very problematic	Problematic	Yes	Ethanol	11–15%	Yes	
Very problematic	Very problematic	Yes	Solar	6–10%	Yes	China
Problematic	Problematic	Yes	Natural gas	21–30%	Yes	China
Problematic	Problematic	Yes	Nuclear	11–15%	No	China
A bit problematic	A bit problematic	Yes	Solar	1–5%	No	China
Problematic	Problematic	Yes	Nuclear	1–5%	No	China
Very problematic	Problematic	Only if there are life forms	Solar	6–10%	Yes	China
Problematic	Problematic	Yes	Solar	1–5%	Yes	China
Very problematic	Very problematic	Only if there are life forms	Nuclear	6–10%	No	China
Very problematic	Very problematic	Yes	Solar	16–20%	No	China
Problematic	Problematic	Yes	Solar	16–20%	Yes	India
Problematic	Very problematic	Yes	Solar	6–10%	Yes	China
Problematic	Problematic	Yes	Solar	11–15%	No	China
Problematic	A bit problematic	Yes	Solar	1–5%	No	China

Problematic	A bit problematic	Yes	Solar	Nothing	No	China
A bit problematic	A bit problematic	Yes	Solar	6–10%	No	China
Problematic	Problematic	Yes	Nuclear	21–30%	Yes	China
Problematic	A bit problematic	Only if there are life forms	Solar	1–5%	No	China
A bit problematic	Problematic	The concept of pollution does not apply to outer space	Nuclear	6–10%	No	China
Very problematic	Very problematic	Only if there are life forms	Nuclear	6–10%	Yes	Japan
Very problematic	Very problematic	Yes	Natural gas	16–20%	No	China
Very problematic	Problematic	Only if there are life forms	Natural gas	21–30%	Yes	China
Very problematic	Very problematic	Yes	Nuclear	6–10%	Yes	China
Problematic	Very problematic	Yes	Nuclear	1–5%	No	India
Very problematic	Problematic	Yes	Solar	11–15%	No	China
Problematic	A bit problematic	Yes	Natural gas	1–5%	No	China
Problematic	A bit problematic	Yes	Solar	1–5%	Yes	China
Problematic	Problematic	Yes	Wind	6–10%	No	China
A bit problematic	A bit problematic	Yes	Solar	1–5%	Yes	China
A bit problematic	Problematic	Only if there are life forms	Solar	16–20%	No	China
A bit problematic	A bit problematic	Yes	Nuclear	16–20%	Yes	China
Problematic	Problematic	No	Solar	11–15%	No	Japan
Problematic	Very problematic	Only if there are life forms	Solar	Nothing	No	China
A bit problematic	A bit problematic	Yes	Natural gas	1–5%	No	China
Problematic	A bit problematic	Yes	Natural gas	1–5%	No	China

(continued)

Q15c	Q15d	Q16	Q17	Q18	Q19	Q20
How bad is sea pollution (very problematic to unproblematic)? (Italy, China, the Netherlands, Russia, Japan)	How bad is ground pollution (very problematic to unproblematic)? (Italy, China, the Netherlands, Russia, Japan)	Recently there's been speculation about mining and exploiting resources from other planets and spatial objects. Should we be setting limits on pollution also outside Earth? (Italy, China, the Netherlands, Russia, Japan)	Which of the following alternative energy sources do you think will be MOST important in the next 10 years? (Italy, China, the Netherlands, Russia, Japan)	What share of your income would you be prepared to sacrifice to completely eradicate pollution? (Italy, China, the Netherlands, Russia, Japan)	Looking at the current developments in your country, do you think the number of government-controlled companies is expanding? (Italy, China, the Netherlands, Russia)	Which country do you think will be the biggest economy in Asia 30 years from now? (China, Japan)
A bit problematic	A bit problematic	Only if there are life forms	Solar	1–5%	Yes	China
Problematic	Very problematic	Yes	Nuclear	16–20%	Yes	China
Problematic	Problematic	Only if there are life forms	Nuclear	16–20%	No	China
Very problematic	Very problematic	Yes	Solar	11–15%	Yes	India
A bit problematic	A bit problematic	Yes	Solar	6–10%	No	China
Problematic	Very problematic	Yes	Wind	6–10%	Yes	China
Very problematic	Very problematic	Yes	Nuclear	Nothing	No	China
Problematic	Problematic	Yes	Wind	16–20%	Yes	China
Very problematic	Problematic	Only if there are life forms	Nuclear	1–5%	No	China
A bit problematic	A bit problematic	Yes	Solar	1–5%	No	China
Problematic	A bit problematic	No	Solar	1–5%	Yes	China
Very problematic	A bit problematic	Yes	Solar	1–5%	Yes	China
A bit problematic	A bit problematic	Only if there are life forms	Solar	6–10%	No	China

Problematic	Very problematic	Only if there are life forms	Solar	6–10%	No	Japan
Problematic	A bit problematic	Yes	Solar	1–5%	Yes	China
Very problematic	Problematic	Only if there are life forms	Wind	1–5%	Yes	China
A bit problematic	Problematic	Yes	Natural gas	6–10%	No	China
Problematic	Very problematic	Yes	Solar	11–15%	Yes	Japan
Unproblematic	A bit problematic	The concept of pollution does not apply to outer space	Solar	16–20%	No	China
Very problematic	Very problematic	Yes	Solar	1–5%	Yes	China
Very problematic	Problematic	Yes	Solar	16–20%	No	China
Problematic	Problematic	Only if there are life forms	Solar	6–10%	No	China
Problematic	Problematic	No	Solar	Nothing	No	China
Problematic	Problematic	Yes	Natural gas	21–30%	No	China
Problematic	A bit problematic	Yes	Solar	16–20%	Yes	China
Very problematic	Very problematic	Yes	Nuclear	16–20%	No	China
Very problematic	Very problematic	Yes	Solar	31% and higher	Yes	China
Problematic	Problematic	Yes	Solar	21–30%	No	China
Problematic	Problematic	Yes	Nuclear	16–20%	No	China
Very problematic	Very problematic	Yes	Solar	Nothing	No	China
Problematic	A bit problematic	Yes	Solar	1–5%	No	China
Problematic	Problematic	Yes	Wind	21–30%	Yes	China
Problematic	Very problematic	Yes	Wind	11–15%	Yes	China
Problematic	Problematic	Yes	Solar	31% and higher	Yes	China
A bit problematic	A bit problematic	Yes	Nuclear	11–15%	Yes	China
Problematic	A bit problematic	Yes	Natural gas	16–20%	Yes	China

(continued)

Q15c	Q15d	Q16	Q17	Q18	Q19	Q20
How bad is sea pollution (very problematic to unproblematic)? (Italy, China, the Netherlands, Russia, Japan)	How bad is ground pollution (very problematic to unproblematic)? (Italy, China, the Netherlands, Russia, Japan)	Recently there's been speculation about mining and exploiting resources from other planets and spatial objects. Should we be setting limits on pollution also outside Earth? (Italy, China, the Netherlands, Russia, Japan)	Which of the following alternative energy sources do you think will be MOST important in the next 10 years? (Italy, China, the Netherlands, Russia, Japan)	What share of your income would you be prepared to sacrifice to completely eradicate pollution? (Italy, China, the Netherlands, Russia, Japan)	Looking at the current developments in your country, do you think the number of government-controlled companies is expanding? (Italy, China, the Netherlands, Russia)	Which country do you think will be the biggest economy in Asia 30 years from now? (China, Japan)
Very problematic	Very problematic	Only if there are life forms	Solar	1–5%	Yes	China
Problematic	Problematic	Yes	Solar	11–15%	Yes	China
Problematic	Unproblematic	Yes	Solar	6–10%	Yes	China
Very problematic	Very problematic	Yes	Natural gas	1–5%	No	China
Very problematic	Problematic	Yes	Solar	11–15%	Yes	China
Problematic	Problematic	Yes	Solar	6–10%	No	China
A bit problematic	A bit problematic	Only if there are life forms	Nuclear	6–10%	Yes	China
Very problematic	A bit problematic	Yes	Solar	11–15%	No	China
Very problematic	Very problematic	Yes	Solar	6–10%	Yes	China
Problematic	Very problematic	Yes	Natural gas	11–15%	Yes	China
Problematic	Problematic	Yes	Natural gas	16–20%	Yes	China
Very problematic	Problematic	Yes	Solar	11–15%	Yes	China
Very problematic	Very problematic	Yes	Solar	6–10%	No	China
Very problematic	Problematic	Yes	Solar	6–10%	No	China

Unproblematic	Unproblematic	Yes	Solar	6–10%	No	China
A bit problematic	A bit problematic	Only if there are life forms	Natural gas	1–5%	Yes	China
A bit problematic	A bit problematic	Yes	Solar	21–30%	No	China
Problematic	Very problematic	Yes	Solar	11–15%	No	China
Problematic	Problematic	Yes	Solar	6–10%	Yes	China
Problematic	A bit problematic	Yes	Solar	16–20%	Yes	China
Problematic	A bit problematic	Yes	Solar	Nothing	No	China
A bit problematic	A bit problematic	Yes	Nuclear	6–10%	Yes	China
Very problematic	Very problematic	Yes	Solar	6–10%	Yes	China
Very problematic	Problematic	Only if there are life forms	Wind	6–10%	Yes	China
Very problematic	Very problematic	Yes	Solar	1–5%	No	China
A bit problematic	A bit problematic	Yes	Solar	6–10%	Yes	China
Problematic	Problematic	Yes	Wind	6–10%	No	China
Very problematic	Problematic	Only if there are life forms	Solar	6–10%	No	China
Problematic	Problematic	Yes	Solar	6–10%	No	China
Problematic	Problematic	Yes	Solar	6–10%	No	China
Problematic	Problematic	Yes	Other	I have no income	No	
A bit problematic	A bit problematic	Yes	Solar	Nothing	Yes	
Problematic	Problematic	Yes	Solar	1–5%	No	
Problematic	A bit problematic	Yes	Nuclear	1–5%	Yes	
Very problematic	Problematic	Yes	Solar	6–10%	No	
Very problematic	Very problematic	Yes	Solar	Nothing	No	
Very problematic	Very problematic	Yes	Nuclear	1–5%	No	
Problematic	Problematic	Yes	Nuclear	1–5%	Yes	
Very problematic	Very problematic	Yes	Solar	1–5%	No	

(continued)

Q15c	Q15d	Q16	Q17	Q18	Q19	Q20
How bad is sea pollution (very problematic to unproblematic)? (Italy, China, the Netherlands, Russia, Japan)	How bad is ground pollution (very problematic to unproblematic)? (Italy, China, the Netherlands, Russia, Japan)	Recently there's been speculation about mining and exploiting resources from other planets and spatial objects. Should we be setting limits on pollution also outside Earth? (Italy, China, the Netherlands, Russia, Japan)	Which of the following alternative energy sources do you think will be MOST important in the next 10 years? (Italy, China, the Netherlands, Russia, Japan)	What share of your income would you be prepared to sacrifice to completely eradicate pollution? (Italy, China, the Netherlands, Russia, Japan)	Looking at the current developments in your country, do you think the number of government-controlled companies is expanding? (Italy, China, the Netherlands, Russia)	Which country do you think will be the biggest economy in Asia 30 years from now? (China, Japan)
Problematic	A bit problematic	The concept of pollution does not apply to outer space	Nuclear	16–20%	Yes	
Very problematic	Very problematic	Yes	Solar	1–5%	No	
Very problematic	Very problematic	Yes	Other	Nothing	No	
Very problematic	Very problematic	Yes	Solar	Nothing	No	
Problematic	Problematic	Yes	Nuclear	Nothing	No	
Very problematic	Very problematic	Yes	Solar	1–5%	No	
Very problematic	Very problematic	Yes	Wind	1–5%	No	
Very problematic	Problematic	Yes	Solar	6–10%	Yes	
Problematic	Problematic	The concept of pollution does not apply to outer space	Solar	1–5%	No	
Problematic	Problematic	The concept of pollution does not apply to outer space	Solar	Nothing	No	
Very problematic	Very problematic	Yes	Solar	1–5%	No	

Very problematic	Problematic	Only if there are life forms	Solar	16–20%	No	
Problematic	A bit problematic	Only if there are life forms	Solar	1–5%	Yes	
Very problematic	Very problematic	Yes	Solar	Nothing	Yes	
Very problematic	Very problematic	Yes	Solar	1–5%	Yes	
Problematic	Problematic	Yes	Natural gas	1–5%	Yes	
Problematic	Problematic	Yes	Solar	1–5%	Yes	
A bit problematic	A bit problematic	Yes	Solar	Nothing	No	
Very problematic	A bit problematic	Yes	Coal	1–5%	Yes	
Problematic	Problematic		Solar	1–5%	Yes	
Very problematic	Problematic	Yes	Solar	6–10%	Yes	
Very problematic	Very problematic	Yes	Natural gas	16–20%	Yes	
Problematic	Problematic	The concept of pollution does not apply to outer space	Solar	1–5%	Yes	
Very problematic	Very problematic	Yes	Wind	21–30%	Yes	
Problematic	Problematic	Yes	Natural gas	1–5%	Yes	
Problematic	Problematic	Only if there are life forms	Nuclear	Nothing	Yes	
Very problematic	Very problematic	No	Coal	16–20%	Yes	
A bit problematic	Problematic	Yes	Wind	6–10%	Yes	
Problematic	Problematic	Only if there are life forms	Wind	1–5%	No	
Very problematic	Very problematic	Only if there are life forms	hydrogen	1–5%	No	
Problematic	Problematic	Yes	Solar	Nothing	No	
Very problematic	Very problematic	Yes	Nuclear	6–10%	No	

(continued)

Q15c	Q15d	Q16	Q17	Q18	Q19	Q20
How bad is sea pollution (very problematic to unproblematic)? (Italy, China, the Netherlands, Russia, Japan)	How bad is ground pollution (very problematic to unproblematic)? (Italy, China, the Netherlands, Russia, Japan)	Recently there's been speculation about mining and exploiting resources from other planets and spatial objects. Should we be setting limits on pollution also outside Earth? (Italy, China, the Netherlands, Russia, Japan)	Which of the following alternative energy sources do you think will be MOST important in the next 10 years? (Italy, China, the Netherlands, Russia, Japan)	What share of your income would you be prepared to sacrifice to completely eradicate pollution? (Italy, China, the Netherlands, Russia, Japan)	Looking at the current developments in your country, do you think the number of government-controlled companies is expanding? (Italy, China, the Netherlands, Russia)	Which country do you think will be the biggest economy in Asia 30 years from now? (China, Japan)
Very problematic	Very problematic	Yes	Nuclear	1–5%	No	
Very problematic	Problematic	Yes	Solar	1–5%	Yes	
Very problematic	Problematic	No	Nuclear	16–20%	No	
A bit problematic	A bit problematic	Yes	Wind	Nothing	No	
Problematic	Problematic	Yes	Wind	1–5%	No	
Very problematic	Problematic	No	Ethanol	Nothing	Yes	
A bit problematic	A bit problematic	Only if there are life forms	Solar	Nothing	No	
Very problematic	Very problematic	Yes	Wind	Nothing	No	
Problematic	A bit problematic	Yes	Solar	Nothing	No	
Very problematic	Problematic	Only if there are life forms	Nuclear	6–10%	No	
Very problematic	Very problematic	Yes	Wind	1–5%	No	
Problematic	Problematic	Only if there are life forms	Nuclear	1–5%	No	
A bit problematic	A bit problematic	Only if there are life forms	Wind	Nothing	Yes	

Problematic	Problematic	Yes	Solar	1–5%	No	
Problematic	Problematic	Yes	Wind	1–5%	Yes	
Very problematic	Problematic	Yes	Nuclear	1–5%	Yes	
Very problematic	Very problematic	Yes	Other	I have no income	No	
Very problematic	Problematic	Yes	Solar	1–5%	No	
Problematic	A bit problematic	The concept of pollution does not apply to outer space	Wind	Nothing	Yes	
Problematic	Problematic	Yes	Coal	Nothing	No	
A bit problematic	A bit problematic	Only if there are life forms	Solar	Nothing	No	
Problematic	Problematic	Yes	Solar	1–5%	Yes	
Very problematic	Very problematic	Yes	Natural gas	1–5%	No	
Very problematic	Very problematic	Yes	Wind	21–30%	No	
Very problematic	Very problematic	No	Solar	11–15%	Yes	
Very problematic	Very problematic	Yes	Other	Nothing	No	
Problematic	Problematic	No	Wind	1–5%	Yes	
Problematic	Very problematic	Yes	Nuclear	1–5%	No	
Very problematic		Yes	Wind	6–10%	Yes	
A bit problematic	Problematic	No	Solar	11–15%	Yes	
A bit problematic	A bit problematic	Yes	hydrogen	1–5%	No	
Problematic	Problematic	Yes	hydrogen	Nothing	No	
Very problematic	Very problematic	No	Wind	6–10%	Yes	
Very problematic	Very problematic	Yes	Solar	11–15%	No	
Very problematic	Very problematic		Nuclear	Nothing	Yes	
Problematic	Problematic	Yes	I don't know	1–5%	Yes	
A bit problematic	A bit problematic	Yes	Wind	16–20%	Yes	
Problematic	Problematic	Yes	Natural gas	31% and higher	Yes	

(continued)

Q15c	Q15d	Q16	Q17	Q18	Q19	Q20
How bad is sea pollution (very problematic to unproblematic)? (Italy, China, the Netherlands, Russia, Japan)	How bad is ground pollution (very problematic to unproblematic)? (Italy, China, the Netherlands, Russia, Japan)	Recently there's been speculation about mining and exploiting resources from other planets and spatial objects. Should we be setting limits on pollution also outside Earth? (Italy, China, the Netherlands, Russia, Japan)	Which of the following alternative energy sources do you think will be MOST important in the next 10 years? (Italy, China, the Netherlands, Russia, Japan)	What share of your income would you be prepared to sacrifice to completely eradicate pollution? (Italy, China, the Netherlands, Russia, Japan)	Looking at the current developments in your country, do you think the number of government-controlled companies is expanding? (Italy, China, the Netherlands, Russia)	Which country do you think will be the biggest economy in Asia 30 years from now? (China, Japan)
Very problematic	Very problematic	Only if there are life forms	Natural gas	6–10%	No	
Very problematic	Very problematic	No	Solar	1–5%	Yes	
Problematic	Problematic	Yes	Nuclear	6–10%	No	
Problematic	Problematic	Yes	Natural gas	1–5%	No	
Very problematic	Very problematic	Yes	Solar	6–10%	No	
Very problematic	Very problematic	Only if there are life forms	Nuclear	1–5%	Yes	
Very problematic	Very problematic	No	Wind	Nothing	No	
Problematic	Problematic	Only if there are life forms	Natural gas	1–5%	Yes	
Problematic	Very problematic	Yes	Solar	6–10%	No	
Problematic	Problematic	Only if there are life forms	Solar	1–5%	No	
A bit problematic	A bit problematic	No	Nuclear	Nothing	No	
Very problematic	Very problematic	Yes	Nuclear	1–5%	No	

Problematic	Problematic	Yes	Wind	Nothing	No	
Very problematic	Very problematic	Yes	Nuclear	1–5%	Yes	
Problematic	Very problematic	Only if there are life forms	Wind	Nothing	No	
Problematic	Problematic	Only if there are life forms	Wind	1–5%	Yes	
A bit problematic	A bit problematic	The concept of pollution does not apply to outer space	Natural gas	Nothing	Yes	
Problematic	Problematic	Yes	Nuclear	1–5%	Yes	
Very problematic	Problematic	Yes	Nuclear	Nothing	No	
Problematic	Problematic	Yes	Nuclear	11–15%	No	
Very problematic	Very problematic	No	Solar	Nothing	No	
Very problematic	Very problematic	Only if there are life forms	Natural gas	I have no income	No	
A bit problematic	A bit problematic	The concept of pollution does not apply to outer space	Solar	11–15%	Yes	
Problematic	Very problematic	The concept of pollution does not apply to outer space	Natural gas	6–10%	No	
A bit problematic	Very problematic	No	Solar	1–5%	Yes	
Problematic	Problematic	Yes	Natural gas	1–5%	No	
Problematic	Problematic	Yes	Natural gas	1–5%	No	
A bit problematic	A bit problematic	Yes	Coal	11–15%	No	
Very problematic	Very problematic	Yes	Nuclear	1–5%	Yes	
A bit problematic	Problematic	Only if there are life forms	Solar	6–10%	No	
Very problematic	Problematic	Yes	Natural gas	21–30%	Yes	

(continued)

Q15c	Q15d	Q16	Q17	Q18	Q19	Q20
How bad is sea pollution (very problematic to unproblematic)? (Italy, China, the Netherlands, Russia, Japan)	How bad is ground pollution (very problematic to unproblematic)? (Italy, China, the Netherlands, Russia, Japan)	Recently there's been speculation about mining and exploiting resources from other planets and spatial objects. Should we be setting limits on pollution also outside Earth? (Italy, China, the Netherlands, Russia, Japan)	Which of the following alternative energy sources do you think will be MOST important in the next 10 years? (Italy, China, the Netherlands, Russia, Japan)	What share of your income would you be prepared to sacrifice to completely eradicate pollution? (Italy, China, the Netherlands, Russia, Japan)	Looking at the current developments in your country, do you think the number of government-controlled companies is expanding? (Italy, China, the Netherlands, Russia)	Which country do you think will be the biggest economy in Asia 30 years from now? (China, Japan)
A bit problematic	A bit problematic	The concept of pollution does not apply to outer space	Solar	11–15%	Yes	
Very problematic	Very problematic	The concept of pollution does not apply to outer space	Natural gas	31% and higher	No	
Problematic	Problematic	Yes	Nuclear	1–5%	Yes	
Very problematic	Very problematic	Yes	Nuclear	Nothing	No	
Very problematic	Very problematic	Yes	Natural gas	Nothing	No	
Problematic	A bit problematic	Yes	Solar	Nothing	No	
Very problematic	Very problematic	No	Oxygene	11–15%	Yes	
A bit problematic	A bit problematic	No	Natural gas	1–5%	No	
A bit problematic	A bit problematic	No	Natural gas	Nothing	No	
Problematic	Very problematic	Only if there are life forms	Natural gas	1–5%	Yes	
Very problematic	Very problematic	Yes	Wind	6–10%	Yes	

A bit problematic	A bit problematic	Yes	Natural gas	1–5%	No	
Problematic	Problematic	The concept of pollution does not apply to outer space	Solar	1–5%	Yes	
A bit problematic	Problematic	The concept of pollution does not apply to outer space	Natural gas	Nothing	No	
A bit problematic	A bit problematic	Only if there are life forms	Nuclear	1–5%	Yes	
A bit problematic	A bit problematic	Only if there are life forms	Solar	1–5%	No	
Very problematic	Very problematic	Yes	Solar	1–5%	No	
Very problematic	Problematic	The concept of pollution does not apply to outer space	Wind	1–5%	No	
Problematic	Problematic	The concept of pollution does not apply to outer space	Solar	1–5%	No	
Very problematic	Problematic	No	Plasma	11–15%	Yes	
Problematic	Problematic	Only if there are life forms	Solar	1–5%	No	
Very problematic	Very problematic	Yes	Solar	1–5%	No	
Very problematic	Very problematic	Yes	Solar	1–5%	No	
Very problematic	Very problematic	The concept of pollution does not apply to outer space	Nuclear	1–5%	Yes	
Very problematic	Very problematic	Yes	Solar	6–10%	Yes	
Very problematic	Problematic	Yes	Solar	1–5%	No	
A bit problematic	Problematic	Yes	Wind	Nothing	No	

(continued)

Q15c	Q15d	Q16	Q17	Q18	Q19	Q20
How bad is sea pollution (very problematic to unproblematic)? (Italy, China, the Netherlands, Russia, Japan)	How bad is ground pollution (very problematic to unproblematic)? (Italy, China, the Netherlands, Russia, Japan)	Recently there's been speculation about mining and exploiting resources from other planets and spatial objects. Should we be setting limits on pollution also outside Earth? (Italy, China, the Netherlands, Russia, Japan)	Which of the following alternative energy sources do you think will be MOST important in the next 10 years? (Italy, China, the Netherlands, Russia, Japan)	What share of your income would you be prepared to sacrifice to completely eradicate pollution? (Italy, China, the Netherlands, Russia, Japan)	Looking at the current developments in your country, do you think the number of government-controlled companies is expanding? (Italy, China, the Netherlands, Russia)	Which country do you think will be the biggest economy in Asia 30 years from now? (China, Japan)
Very problematic	Very problematic	Yes	Solar	21–30%	No	
Very problematic	Problematic	No	Solar	11–15%	No	
A bit problematic	Problematic	No	Solar	1–5%	Yes	
Very problematic	Problematic	No	Solar	21–30%	Yes	
A bit problematic	Problematic	Yes	Nuclear	1–5%	No	
Very problematic	Very problematic	Yes	Solar	11–15%	No	
A bit problematic	A bit problematic	Yes	Nuclear	1–5%	No	
Problematic	Problematic	No	Wind	6–10%	No	
A bit problematic	A bit problematic	No	Natural gas	11–15%	Yes	
A bit problematic	Problematic	No	Coal	I have no income	No	
Very problematic	Problematic	Only if there are life forms	Natural gas	6–10%	Yes	
Very problematic	Very problematic	Only if there are life forms	Solar	1–5%	Yes	
Very problematic	Very problematic	Yes	Solar	16–20%	Yes	

Problematic	Problematic	Only if there are life forms	Solar	1–5%	Yes	
Very problematic	Very problematic	Only if there are life forms	Nuclear	1–5%	Yes	
A bit problematic	Problematic	No	Nuclear	Nothing	Yes	
Problematic	Problematic	Yes	Solar	11–15%	No	
Problematic	A bit problematic	Yes	Nuclear	Nothing	No	
Problematic	Problematic	Yes	Natural gas	Nothing	No	
A bit problematic	A bit problematic	No	Nuclear	Nothing	No	
Very problematic	Problematic	No	Nuclear	1–5%	Yes	
Problematic	Problematic	Yes	Solar	1–5%	Yes	
A bit problematic	A bit problematic	Yes	Natural gas	1–5%	Yes	
Very problematic	Problematic	Only if there are life forms	Wind	Nothing	Yes	
Very problematic	Very problematic	Yes	Natural gas	1–5%	Yes	
Problematic	Problematic	Only if there are life forms	Natural gas	1–5%	No	
Problematic	Problematic	Yes	Nuclear	Nothing	No	
Very problematic	Problematic	Yes	Nuclear	1–5%	No	
A bit problematic	A bit problematic	Only if there are life forms	Wind	Nothing	Yes	
A bit problematic	Problematic	The concept of pollution does not apply to outer space	Nuclear	Nothing	Yes	
Problematic	Problematic	Yes	Nuclear	1–5%	Yes	
Problematic	Problematic	Yes	Wind	6–10%	No	
Very problematic	Problematic	Yes	Nuclear	1–5%	No	
Problematic	Very problematic	Yes	Natural gas	6–10%	No	

(continued)

Q15c	Q15d	Q16	Q17	Q18	Q19	Q20
How bad is sea pollution (very problematic to unproblematic)? (Italy, China, the Netherlands, Russia, Japan)	How bad is ground pollution (very problematic to unproblematic)? (Italy, China, the Netherlands, Russia, Japan)	Recently there's been speculation about mining and exploiting resources from other planets and spatial objects. Should we be setting limits on pollution also outside Earth? (Italy, China, the Netherlands, Russia, Japan)	Which of the following alternative energy sources do you think will be MOST important in the next 10 years? (Italy, China, the Netherlands, Russia, Japan)	What share of your income would you be prepared to sacrifice to completely eradicate pollution? (Italy, China, the Netherlands, Russia, Japan)	Looking at the current developments in your country, do you think the number of government-controlled companies is expanding? (Italy, China, the Netherlands, Russia)	Which country do you think will be the biggest economy in Asia 30 years from now? (China, Japan)
Very problematic	Very problematic	Yes	Solar	6–10%	Yes	
A bit problematic	A bit problematic	Yes	Nuclear	Nothing	Yes	
Problematic	Problematic	Yes	Nuclear	I have no income	Yes	
A bit problematic	Problematic	Yes	Coal	11–15%	No	
Problematic	Problematic	Yes	Solar	21–25%		Japan
Problematic	Problematic	Yes	Solar	6–10%		India
A bit problematic	Problematic	Only if there are life forms	Solar	1–5%		South Korea
Problematic	Problematic	Yes	Nuclear	6–10%		Japan
Very problematic	Problematic	Yes	Solar	1–5%		Japan
Problematic	Problematic	No	Solar	1–5%		Japan
A bit problematic	Unproblematic	Yes	Ethanol	6–10%		India
Unproblematic	Unproblematic	No	Hydrogen	Nothing		India
A bit problematic	A bit problematic	Yes	Solar	1–5%		India
A bit problematic	Unproblematic	Yes	Wind	Nothing		India
A bit problematic	A bit problematic	No	Solar	Nothing		I do not know

Problematic	A bit problematic	Yes	Nuclear	Nothing		India
Problematic	Problematic	Yes	Nuclear	I have no income		India
Unproblematic	Unproblematic	Yes	Solar	Nothing		China
Very problematic	Very problematic	The concept of pollution does not apply to outer space	Hydrogen	Nothing		India
A bit problematic	A bit problematic	Only if there are life forms	Nuclear	Nothing		India
Very problematic	Problematic	Only if there are life forms	Wind	1–5%		China
Problematic	Problematic	Yes	Natural gas	6–10%		India
	A bit problematic	Yes	Solar	6–10%		India
Very problematic	Very problematic	No	Wind	Nothing		China
A bit problematic	A bit problematic	Only if there are life forms	Solar	1–5%		China
Very problematic	Very problematic	Yes	Solar	Nothing		Japan
Very problematic	Very problematic	Yes	Wind	Nothing		India
Problematic	Problematic	Only if there are life forms	Ethanol	Nothing		India
Problematic	Problematic	Yes	Nuclear	1–5%		India
Problematic	Problematic	The concept of pollution does not apply to outer space	Nuclear	Nothing		China
Problematic	Problematic	Only if there are life forms	Solar	Nothing		China
Problematic	Problematic	Yes	Nuclear	Nothing		China
Problematic	Problematic	Yes	Nuclear	Nothing		China

(continued)

Q15c	Q15d	Q16	Q17	Q18	Q19	Q20
How bad is sea pollution (very problematic to unproblematic)? (Italy, China, the Netherlands, Russia, Japan)	How bad is ground pollution (very problematic to unproblematic)? (Italy, China, the Netherlands, Russia, Japan)	Recently there's been speculation about mining and exploiting resources from other planets and spatial objects. Should we be setting limits on pollution also outside Earth? (Italy, China, the Netherlands, Russia, Japan)	Which of the following alternative energy sources do you think will be MOST important in the next 10 years? (Italy, China, the Netherlands, Russia, Japan)	What share of your income would you be prepared to sacrifice to completely eradicate pollution? (Italy, China, the Netherlands, Russia, Japan)	Looking at the current developments in your country, do you think the number of government-controlled companies is expanding? (Italy, China, the Netherlands, Russia)	Which country do you think will be the biggest economy in Asia 30 years from now? (China, Japan)
A bit problematic	A bit problematic	The concept of pollution does not apply to outer space	Nuclear	1–5%		India
Problematic	Problematic	Only if there are life forms	Solar	I have no income		India
Problematic	Problematic	Only if there are life forms	Solar	16–20%		Indonesia
Unproblematic	Unproblematic	No	Ethanol	16–20%		Japan
A bit problematic	A bit problematic	Yes	Nuclear	1–5%		Japan
Very problematic	Problematic	Yes	Solar	16–20%		India
A bit problematic	A bit problematic	Only if there are life forms	Natural gas	Nothing		China
Unproblematic	Unproblematic	The concept of pollution does not apply to outer space	Natural gas	Nothing		Japan
Unproblematic	Unproblematic	No	Natural gas	I have no income		Japan

Unproblematic	Unproblematic	No	Natural gas	Nothing		China
Problematic	Problematic	Yes	Wind	1–5%		India
Problematic	A bit problematic	Yes	Solar	I have no income		China
Problematic	Problematic	Yes	Nuclear	Nothing		China
Very problematic	Very problematic	Yes	Solar	Nothing		Indonesia
A bit problematic	A bit problematic	Yes	Solar	1–5%		China
Unproblematic	Unproblematic	The concept of pollution does not apply to outer space	Nuclear	1–5%		China
Problematic	Problematic	Yes	Solar	Nothing		Japan
A bit problematic	A bit problematic	The concept of pollution does not apply to outer space	Solar	Nothing		China
Very problematic	Problematic	Yes	Solar	16–20%		China
A bit problematic	A bit problematic	Only if there are life forms	Nuclear	Nothing		China
Very problematic	Very problematic	No	Ethanol	6–10%		Japan
Problematic	Problematic	Yes	Hydrogen	6–10%		I do not know
Unproblematic	Unproblematic	Only if there are life forms	Solar	Nothing		Japan
Very problematic	A bit problematic	The concept of pollution does not apply to outer space	Nuclear	11–15%		China
A bit problematic	Problematic	No	Solar	Nothing		China
Very problematic	Very problematic	Yes	Solar	1–5%		China
Problematic	Problematic	Only if there are life forms	Ethanol	11–15%		China
Problematic	Problematic	Yes	Solar	Nothing		China

(continued)

Q15c	Q15d	Q16	Q17	Q18	Q19	Q20
How bad is sea pollution (very problematic to unproblematic)? (Italy, China, the Netherlands, Russia, Japan)	How bad is ground pollution (very problematic to unproblematic)? (Italy, China, the Netherlands, Russia, Japan)	Recently there's been speculation about mining and exploiting resources from other planets and spatial objects. Should we be setting limits on pollution also outside Earth? (Italy, China, the Netherlands, Russia, Japan)	Which of the following alternative energy sources do you think will be MOST important in the next 10 years? (Italy, China, the Netherlands, Russia, Japan)	What share of your income would you be prepared to sacrifice to completely eradicate pollution? (Italy, China, the Netherlands, Russia, Japan)	Looking at the current developments in your country, do you think the number of government-controlled companies is expanding? (Italy, China, the Netherlands, Russia)	Which country do you think will be the biggest economy in Asia 30 years from now? (China, Japan)
Problematic	Problematic	Only if there are life forms	Solar	6–10%		China
A bit problematic	A bit problematic	No	Nuclear	Nothing		Japan
Very problematic	Very problematic	Yes	Solar	Nothing		Japan
Unproblematic	Unproblematic	Yes	Natural gas	Nothing		China
Problematic	A bit problematic	No	Nuclear	Nothing		Japan
Unproblematic	Unproblematic	The concept of pollution does not apply to outer space	Coal	I have no income		Indonesia
A bit problematic	A bit problematic	Yes	Nuclear	Nothing		India

Problematic	Problematic	No	Ethanol	21–25%		Japan
Problematic	Problematic	No	Natural gas	I have no income		China
Problematic	Problematic	Yes	Solar	1–5%		China
Problematic	Very problematic	No	Ethanol	6–10%		Japan
Very problematic	Very problematic	The concept of pollution does not apply to outer space	Other	Nothing		China
Problematic	A bit problematic	Yes	Solar	11–15%		Japan
A bit problematic	Problematic	No	Solar	11–15%		Japan
Problematic	Problematic	Only if there are life forms	Nuclear	16–20%		Japan
Problematic	Problematic	Only if there are life forms	Solar	6–10%		Indonesia
Problematic	Problematic	Only if there are life forms	Nuclear	11–15%		India
A bit problematic	A bit problematic	No	Coal	Nothing		Japan

MIX
Papier aus verantwortungsvollen Quellen
Paper from responsible sources
FSC® C105338

If you have any concerns about our products,
you can contact us on
ProductSafety@springernature.com

In case Publisher is established outside the EU,
the EU authorized representative is:
Springer Nature Customer Service Center GmbH
Europaplatz 3, 69115 Heidelberg, Germany

Printed by Libri Plureos GmbH
in Hamburg, Germany